2026
중등영어 교사임용

권영주

전공영어 2차
수업실연 and
면접

METHODS of
ENGLISH TEACHING

PREFACE

영어선생님이 되기 위한 임용시험에서 1차 필기시험을 통과하는 것은 시작의 반을 이룬 매우 훌륭한 일입니다. 하지만 그 후에 기다리고 있는 2차 시험인 수업실연과 심층면접은 최종 합격까지 가기 위한 더 어려운 과정일 수 있습니다. 복잡한 현대 사회의 변화와 함께 선생님들에게 확고한 인성이 요구되면서 최근 2차 실기시험을 더 강조하여 평가하는 모습을 다음과 같이 알 수 있습니다.

첫째, 교원임용시험에서는 1차 합격자의 약 67%만이 최종합격자가 될 수 있습니다. 또한 2017년 임용시험에서부터 개인 간 변별도의 간격을 100점 만점의 최저 80점에서 60점으로 확대시키면서 더 상세하고 정확한 평가로 2차 시험의 비중이 강화되었습니다.

둘째, 심층면접에서 교육과정 평가원과 각 지역 교육청 개별 문제들이 개별적으로 출제되면서 일반적이고 이론적인 내용뿐만이 아니라, 각 지역에서 요구되는 특수하고 구체적인 내용을 평가 하고자 합니다. 선생님들이 근무하게 될 학교에서 해내어야 할 교사의 미래핵심역량을 평가한다고 할 수 있습니다.

셋째, 경기도에서는 2026년 임용시험부터 수업실연과 면접에 더하여, "수업설계역량"을 추가 평가함으로서 미래 선생님들이 갖추어야 할 능력과 인성을 동시에 평가하고자 합니다. 그에 맞추어 기계적인 연습보다는 각 활동마다의 목적과 신념을 이해하고 연습하여야 하겠습니다.

이와 같은 변화에 맞추어 수업 실연과 심층면접을 위하여 우리 선생님들이 갖추어야 할 핵심역량을 살펴보기로 하겠습니다.

첫째, 자신감과 겸손함을 동시에 갖추도록 합니다. 자신감 없는 태도는 어떠한 수업이나 면접에서도 좋은 인상을 주기 어렵습니다. 눈을 마주치지도 못하고 손을 만지작거리고 목소리에 힘이 없다면 선생님에 대한 신뢰감이 떨어질 수 있습니다. 선생님의 자신감이 학생에게는 동기부여로 전환되어 학습의 효과성을 올려줄 수 있습니다. 하지만 과한 자신감은 교만함으로 비추어 질 수 있으므로 학생과 함께 배워간다는 겸손한 태도를 발전시키도록 하는 것이 중요합니다.

둘째, 기본적으로 영어실력이 있으면 좋습니다. 영어실력은 여러 가지 면에서 돋보일 수 있습니다. 수업 실연을 할 때 학생들에게 풍부한 예시와 정확한 영어 구사로 이해도를 높이고 다양한 입력을 줄 수가 있습니다. 심층면접에서는 설득력 있는 언어를 구사하여 표현하려는 내용이 논리적으로 보일 수 있게 만들 수도 있습니다. 하지만, 영어발음이나 유창성이 부족하다면 내용을 충실하게 하고 설명을 더 명확하게 하거나, 학생과의 협동수업을 통해 충분히 보충할 수 있는 기회가 있습니다.

셋째, 그 무엇보다 가장 중요한 것은 태도입니다. 태도는 모든 것을 대변합니다. 수업실연과 심층면접 동안에 여러분의 태도는 여과 없이 드러날 것이며, 긴장된 상태에서 무의식적으로 나오는 태도는 여러분들의 인성, 가치관, 그리고 교육관 등 모든 것을 놀라울 정도로 보여줄 것임을 꼭 기억하여야 하겠습니다.

지금부터 '나는 선생님이다'라는 생각이 여러분을 준비된 선생님으로 만들어 줄 것입니다.

CONTENTS

PART I 영어교사임용 2차 시험 분석 _ 7

CHAPTER 01 영어임용 2차 시험 내용 분석 ·· 8
- 01 영어임용 2차 지역별 시험 항목 ··· 8
- 02 영어임용 2차 시험 과목 ·· 9
- 03 평가 기준표 ··· 11
- 04 수업지도안 예시 ·· 15
- 05 합격자 후기와 예시 ··· 20
- 06 교실영어 스크립트 ·· 26
- 07 수업실연 개정안과 지역별 교육청 정책 ······························ 35

CHAPTER 02 영어과 수업실연 기출문제 모음 ····································· 49

CHAPTER 03 교실 영어 표현 ·· 86
- 01 Teaching Vocabulary (Middle school) ······························ 86
- 02 Teaching Listening Skills (Middle School Level) ············ 90
- 03 Teaching Speaking Skills (Middle School Level) ··········· 92
- 04 Teaching Reading Skills ·· 95
- 05 Teaching Writing Skills (Elementary level) ······················ 97
- 06 Classroom expressions for all purposes ························· 100

PART II 교사용 지도서 _ 105

CHAPTER 01 영어과 교수·학습 운영 계획 ·· 106

CHAPTER 02 고교 (진로 영어) ··· 114
- 01 Help! I'm Worried about My Career! ······························· 114
- 02 교육과정 성취기준·평가기준 가이드 ································· 116
- 03 영역별 성취수준 (단원 단위) ··· 120
- 04 수업 지도안 ··· 122

CHAPTER 03	고교 영어 1	131
	01 Give the Earth a Hand!	131
	02 수업 계획서와 교실 활동	133

CHAPTER 04	중학 영어 2	154
	01 Your Life is a Gift!	154
	02 수업계획서와 교실활동	156

CHAPTER 05	중학 영어 3	165
	01 Change Your Life, Change the World	165
	02 수업계획서와 활동	167

CHAPTER 06	고교 (문화 영어)	177
	01 Korean Wave Around the World	177
	02 수업 계획서와 교실 활동	178
	03 4기능을 위한 수업 실연 활동	197

PART III 수업실연 모의문제 _ 205

PART IV 심층면접 _ 241

CHAPTER 01	심층면접 기출 문제 (한국어 + 영어)	242
CHAPTER 02	심층 면접 핵심 개념 정리 (한국어 + 영어)	308
CHAPTER 03	한국어 면접 핵심문제와 답안	344
CHAPTER 04	영어 면접 핵심문제와 답안	368
CHAPTER 05	임용 면접 모의문제와 답안 (한국어 + 영어)	395

memo

PART I

영어교사임용 2차 시험 분석

CHAPTER 01 영어임용 2차 시험 내용 분석

01 영어임용 2차 지역별 시험 항목

지역	심층면접 (영어 & 한국어)	지도안 (한국어)	수업실연 (영어)
서울	구상 15분 (평가 15분)	60분	수업구상(20분)+수업실연(20분)
경기	구상 15분 (평가 15분)	X	수업구상(20분)+수업설계역량(5분)+ 수업실연(15분)
경기지제			
인천	구상 20분 (평가 20분)	X	수업구상(20분)+수업실연(20분)
인천지제			
세종	구상 10분 (평가 10분)	60분	수업구상(20분)+수업실연(20분)
대전	구상 10분 (평가 10분)	60분	수업구상(20분)+수업실연(20분)
대구	구상 25분 (평가 25분)	X	수업구상(25분)+수업실연(25분)
광주	구상 10분 (평가 10분)	X	수업구상(20분)+수업실연(20분)
울산	구상 10분 (평가 10분)	60분	수업구상(20분)+수업실연(20분)
부산	구상 10분 (평가 10분)	60분	수업구상(20분)+수업실연(20분)
충북	구상 10분 (평가 10분)	X	수업구상(20분)+수업실연(20분)
충남	구상 10분 (평가 10분)	60분	수업구상(20분)+수업실연(20분)
충남지제			
전북	구상 20분 (평가 20분)	X	수업구상(20분)+수업실연(20분)
전남	구상 10분 (평가 10분)	X	수업구상(20분)+수업실연(20분)
전남지제			
경북	구상 10분 (평가 10분+즉답 5분)	60분	수업구상(20분)+수업실연(20분)
경남	구상 10분 (평가 10분)	60분	수업구상(20분)+수업실연(20분)
제주	구상 10분 (평가 10분)	60분	수업구상(20분)+수업실연(20분)
제주지제			
강원	구상 10분 (평가 10분)	X	수업구상(20분)+수업실연(20분)

02 영어임용 2차 시험 과목

1 수업실연과 교수 학습 지도안

(1) 수업 실연
- 교사로서의 학습지도 능력과 의사소통 능력을 평가한다.
- 20분 안에 지시문에 나오는 수업 활동을 실제와 같이 구현할 수 있도록 한다.
- 학생들과의 실제와 같은 상호작용과 rapport형성이 핵심이 된다.
- 점수 폭이 큰 항목이고 시간 안배가 중요하다.

(2) 교수 학습 지도안
- 교과 과정의 일정 주제에 대한 교수 학습 지도안을 한글로 작성한다.
- 주어진 주제에 대한 일관성 있는 지도안 작성이 중요하다.
- 세부요소나 구체적인 조건이 실현될 수 있도록 작성한다.
- 수업실연과 연결하여 실시할 수 있는 내용을 작성한다.
- 오류가 없도록 검토하고 제출한다.

2 심층 면접
- 교사로서의 적성, 교직관, 인격 및 소양을 보여줄 수 있도록 한다.
- 평가 항목에 대하여 구체적으로 설명할 수 있는 문제 해결능력이 중요하다.
- 시간 배분을 잘하고 즉답형이나 추가 문제가 있을 때 즉각적으로 대답할 수 있도록 한다.

3 경기 추가 시험

시험 항목	출제 범위	점수
수업설계	"수업설계역량"은 교사가 효과적인 수업을 체계적으로 기획하고 실행할 수 있는 종합적인 능력을 의미한다. 수업실연 전에 5분 발표 형식으로 평가된다.	30점

보충자료

수업설계역량 (경기)

"수업설계역량"은 교사가 효과적인 수업을 체계적으로 기획하고 실행할 수 있는 종합적인 능력을 의미합니다. 수업실연과의 차이점은, 수업설계역량은 "기획 과정"을 평가하는 반면, 실연은 "실제 교수 실행력"을 보는 점입니다. 설계 발표에서는 교사로서의 사고과정과 교육철학이 잘 드러나도록 준비하는 것이 중요합니다.

(1) 수업 설계의 체계성
- 목표 명확성: 학습목표를 교육과정과 연계해 구체적으로 제시하는가?
- 단계적 흐름: 도입–전개–정리 단계의 논리적 연결성, 학생 참여 유도를 위한 활동 설계.
- 시간 관리: 5분 발표 내에서 핵심 내용을 압축해 전달하는 효율성.

(2) 교육과정 이해도
- 표준교육과정 반영: 해당 학년/과목의 성취기준을 정확히 해석했는가?
- 맞춤형 설계: 학생 수준(예: 학습 격차)을 고려한 차별화된 접근.

(3) 창의성과 실제 적용력
- 창의적 방법: 기존 방식과 차별화된 교수법(예: 문제기반학습, 역설계 모델).
- 자료 활용: 교구/ICT(디지털 도구)를 활용한 구체적 예시 제시.

(4) 평가 연계성
- 형성평가 설계: 수업 중 피드백 방안(예: 빠른 질문, 관찰 기록).
- 성취도 검증: 학습목표 달성을 확인할 간단한 도구(예: exit ticket) 제안.

(5) 발표 전달력
- 구조적 설명: "왜 이 활동을 선택했는가?" 등 설계 근거를 논리적으로 설명.
- 청중 집중: 시각 자료(간단한 PPT 또는 실제 교구)를 활용한 효과적 전달.

> ★ 실제 시험 대비 팁
> - 템플릿 준비: 5분 분량에 맞춘 발표 구조(예: 1분–목표, 3분–활동 설계, 1분–평가)를 연습.
> - 구체성 강조: 이론보다는 실제 수업장면을 상상케 하는 생생한 예시 (예: "학생 A가 어려워할 부분은 ~으로 지원한다").
> - 최신 교육 트렌드 반영: 학생 주도성(메타인지), 인공지능 도구 활용 등 현장 감각 있는 접근

03 평가 기준표

1 수업 실연

평가 영역		평가 요소	점수				
			5	4	3	2	1
수업 능력 평가	학생과의 의사소통 능력	• 학생들의 눈높이에 맞추어 학생들과 효과적으로 의사소통을 할 수 있으며 학생들의 학습동기를 유발한다. • 적절한 질문과 연습기회, 피드백 이용, 교실에서의 움직임					
	교수 내용에 대한 지식	• 교수하는 내용에 대한 깊은 관련 분야의 지식을 가지고 있어서 학생들에게 효율적으로 내용을 설명한다. • 교과서 분석능력, 레벨에 맞는 어휘, 문법내용에 대한 지식					
	교육관 및 인성	• 영어교사로서 확고한 교육관을 가지고 있으며 학생들의 문제점을 이해하려는 자세가 되어 있으며 이에 대한 대비가 충분히 갖춰져 있다. • 학습자를 이해하는 정서적 태도가 보인다.					
	수업 준비 및 교재, 교구 활용	• 교재에서 다루지 못한 심층적인 부분과 학생들의 학습동기를 부여할 수 있는 내용을 철저히 준비하여 학생들이 효율적으로 학습을 진행하고 학습에서 즐거움을 느낄 수 있도록 한다. • 다양하면서도 상황에 맞게 이용될 수 있는 교구 사용이 가능하다.					
	교수 방법의 효율성	• 학습하는 내용에 적합한 교수방법을 선택하여 교수하고 있으며 교수하는 과정에서 외국어 교수 및 학습에 관한 전문적 지식이 잘 갖춰져 있는 것이 분명하게 드러남					
	영어 의사 소통 능력	• 원어민과 유사한 정도 혹은 훌륭한 언어모델이 될 수 있는 정도의 영어 의사소통 능력이 있다. • 명확한 발음, 다양한 억양과 body language 이용을 한다.					

총점 _____ / 60

2 교수 학습 지도안

항목	평가내용	점수	
창의성 (5점)	교사 자신만의 창의적이고 독창적인 요소를 잘 반영하고 있는가? 학생의 생활경험과 관련된 동기 유발을 통해 학습 흥미를 유발하고 있는가?	창의성을 적극적으로 장려한다.	(5점)
		창의성에 도움이 된다.	(4점)
		창의성을 이루기 어렵다.	(3점)
목적성 (5점)	수업지도안에 주어진 수업목표에 따른 활동을 잘 제시하고 있는가? 목표의 수업내용이 활동에 잘 포함되어 있는가?	목표와 활동이 잘 일치한다.	(5점)
		목표에 활동이 약간 빗나간다.	(4점)
		목표와 전혀 다른 활동을 한다.	(3점)
통합성 (5점)	수업지도안의 전개가 차시 특성에 따라 전개 흐름을 잘 갖추고 있는가? 이전 과업을 연결하여 통합적 수업이 되도록 잘 연결하고 있는가?	내용의 통합이 잘 이루어진다.	(5점)
		이전 내용과 통합하기 어렵다.	(4점)
		내용들이 분리되어 설명된다.	(3점)

총점 _____ / 15점

3 심층 면접 (예시)

문항	평가항목	평가 척도	배점
1.	문제해결능력	학급 따돌림에 제시된 원인이 타당하고 3개의 해결방안이 구체적이다.	10
		학급 따돌림에 제시된 원인이 타당하고 3개의 해결방안이 대체로 이해가능하다.	8
		학급 따돌림에 제시된 원인이 추상적이고 2개의 해결방안이 실현하기 어려워 보인다.	6
		학급 따돌림에 제시된 원인과 해결방안이 문제와 관련이 없고 이해가 어려워 보인다.	1-4
2.	교사 인성	교사의 역할을 잘 이해하고 최선을 다하는 모습이 나타난다.	10
		교사의 역할을 잘 이해하고 주어진 업무에만 충실하려고 한다.	8
		교사의 역할을 이해하나 주어진 업무와 스스로 하려는 책임감이 약해 보인다.	6
		교사의 역할을 정확히 이해하지 못하여 학교의 업무에 어려움을 겪는 것으로 보인다.	1-4
3.	교직관	교육과정 운영 전반에 걸쳐 협력학습 모형을 구체적으로 제시하고 학생들에게 공동체 인식 함양을 해주고 있다.	10
		교육과정 운영 전반에 걸쳐 협력학습 모형을 이론적으로 제시하고 학생들에게 공동체 인식 함양을 설명한다.	8
		교육과정 운영과 관련하여 협력학습 모형을 제시하나 학생들에게 적용해주지 못하고 있다.	6
		교육과정 운영 전반을 이해하지 못하고 학습 모형을 제시하지 못하여 학생들과 통합교육이 이루어지지 못하고 있다.	1-4
4.	고교 학점제	학생들의 과목선택에 대한 어려움을 이해하고 내실있는 진로교육을 통한 학생관리를 실시한다.	10
		학생들의 과목선택에 대한 어려움을 이해하나 진로교육이 구체적이지 못하여 학생들에 적용이 어렵다.	8
		학생들의 과목선택에 대한 어느 정도 어려움을 이해하나 진로교육의 방향이 잘 못되어 학생관리가 어렵다.	6
		학생들의 과목선택에 대한 어려움을 이해하지 못하여 교사가 해줄 수 있는 진로교육에 어려움을 겪는다.	1-4
	의사 소통 능력	• 말할 때의 자세를 바르게 하고 긍정과 열정적인 태도를 보여주도록 한다. • 자신의 생각을 명확하고 논리적으로 표현하는 것이 중요하다. • 길게 설명하기보다는 핵심을 간결하게 전달하고, 필요시 예시를 들어 이해하기 쉽게 답변하는 것이 필요하다. • 질문의 의도와 맥락에 맞게 답변을 구성하는 것이 중요하다.	

4 경기도 수업설계역량

(평가영역 1) 수업 설계의 체계성	
목표 명확성	학습목표를 교육과정과 연계해 구체적으로 제시하는가?
단계적 흐름	도입-전개-정리 단계의 논리적 연결성, 학생 참여 유도를 위한 활동 설계.
시간 관리	5분 발표 내에서 핵심 내용을 압축해 전달하는 효율성.
(평가영역 2) 교육과정 이해도	
교육과정	해당 학년/과목의 성취기준을 정확히 해석했는가?
맞춤형 설계	학생 수준(예: 학습 격차)을 고려한 차별화된 접근.
(평가영역 3) 창의성과 실제 적용력	
창의적 방법	기존 방식과 차별화된 교수법 (예: Problem-based learning, Project-based learning).
자료 활용	교구/ICT(디지털 도구)를 활용한 구체적 예시 제시.
(평가영역 4) 평가 연계성	
형성평가 설계	수업 중 피드백 방안(예: 빠른 질문, 관찰 기록).
성취도 검증	학습목표 달성을 확인할 간단한 도구(예: exit ticket) 제안.
(평가영역 5) 발표 전달력	
구조적 설명	"왜 이 활동을 선택했는가?" 등 설계 근거를 논리적으로 설명.
청중 집중	청중에게 잘 이해될 수 있도록 하는 효과적 전달.

04 수업지도안 예시

1 한글 수업 지도안 예시

단계	교수와 학습 활동
	교사-학생
수험생 답안 1	〈준비활동〉 교사는 학생들에게 주어진 미켈란제로의 명언에 근거하여 'Beyond your comfort zone'을 추론하게 한다. 학생들은 자신들의 다양한 생각을 토론, 발표하고 표현한다: 자신들의 꿈, 목표, 미래등의 핵심어 등을 통해 그동안 생각해 보지 못했던 영역을 시도해 보는 구체적인 목표를 세우는 시간을 가진다. 교사는 자신이 어떻게 '안전망을 넘어서서' 성공했는지 경험담을 이야기한다. 교사의 경험담을 통해 학생들은 우리가 왜 이러한 안전망을 넘어서 시도해 볼 필요가 있었는지 토론한다: "Venturing outside your comfort zone might feel a bit awkward, but it's a valuable way to learn and expand your horizons."
수험생 답안 2	〈어휘 활동〉 교사는 학생들에게 제시문을 빠르게 읽게 하고 모르는 단어를 찾아 동그라미를 하게 한다: confidence, at ease, proud of myself 학생들은 교사의 예시문을 통해 의미를 추론한다. (eg) I am an extreme I type, introverted. So when I am in a new situation, I often lose confidence. 〈읽기 전 활동〉 교사는 각 zone이 의미하는 것을 설명하고, 학생들은 글을 읽으면서 자신의 경험과 각 zone이 연결되는 것이 있다면 적용해 보도록 한다. 학생들은 도표에 나타난 감정 단어를 이용하여 빈 칸을 채워 넣는다.
수험생 답안 3	〈쓰기 활동〉 교사는 예시문을 제시하고 학생들은 짝활동으로 표를 완성한다. 학생들은 단어, 숙어, 문장에 상관없이 쓸 수 있는 내용을 작성한다. 서로의 글을 읽고 궁금하거나 이해가 안되는 내용을 보충하여 작성한다. 교사는 학생의 언어적 오류에 피드백을 제공한다. (eg) I feel comfortable when I walked around my neighborhood. (verb tense) (eg) My new goal is to go oversea to be a famous designer. (lexical error)

2. 학생활동중심 교수·학습 과정안 예시 (서울 교육청 2024년)

단원	Lesson5. Follow Your Dreams	차시
학습 주제	• Bookcreator를 활용하여 문법 신문 만들기 • ChatGPT를 활용하여 문법을 포함한 대화문을 만들어 역할극하기	6/12
학습 목표	• Bookcreator를 활용하여 배운 문법을 적용할 수 있다: 학생이 어려워하고 지루해하는 영문법을 Bookcreator라는 흥미롭고 창의적인 에듀테크 도구를 통해 서로 창의적인 생각을 공유하고, 배운 문법을 자기의 지식으로 만드는 시간을 만들어 주려고 한다. • ChatGPT를 활용하여 문법이 포함된 대화문 만들고, 역할극을 할 수 있나: 문법요소를 흥미진진하게 학습하도록 speaking과 접목하고, 학생이 직접 performance까지 하도록 하여 영어의 여러 기능을 동시에 익힐 수 있도록 한다.	수업모형
성취 기준	[9영04-03] 일상생활에 관한 그림, 사진 또는 도표 등을 설명하는 문장을 쓸 수 있다. [9영02-06] 주변의 사람, 사물에 대해 묻거나 답할 수 있다.	에듀테크 활용수업, 모둠협력 수업
탐구 질문	• 비교급과 최상급의 차이를 설명할 수 있는가? • 생활 속에서 비교급과 최상급을 만들 수 있는 대상은 무엇인가?	

단계	학습 과정	교수·학습 활동	학습자료/ 평가/ 유의사항
배움 열기 (5)	전시학습 확인& 동기 유발& 학습목표 제시	• 전 차시에서 배운 비교급, 최상급, 접속사 'that'의 쓰임을 복습한다. • 요즘 수업에 많이 사용하고 있는 Bookcreator와 ChatGPT를 어떻게 활용할 것인지 대략적으로 설명한다. • 북크리에이터로 교사가 만든 책자 안에 있는 문법신문을 학생이 완성할 수 있다. • ChatGPT와 대화하여 수업에서 배운 문법이 들어가는 대화문을 생성하고, 짝과 역할극을 할 수 있다.	PPT 학습목표 구체적 제시
배움 활동 (30)	활동1	[Bookceator Activity] • 교사가 만든 책자 안에 있는 English Garmmar Newspaper(영어문법신문)를 앱안에서 공유하여 개별적으로 작성하는 방법을 설명한다. • 처음에는 교사가 만든 문제를 수동적으로 해결하지만, 이후에는 학생이 직접 문제를 만들고 그것을 해결함으로써 문제해결능력을 키울 수 있다. • Bookcreator를 통해 학급의 학생들은 창의적인 문법신문을 완성할 수 있다. • 본인의 책자를 다른 학생들과 같이 열어보고 공유함으로써 문법을 다양하게 적용한 사례를 함께 익힐 수 있다.	tablet work- sheet
	활동2	[Speaking Activity using ChatGPT] • ChatGPT를 활용하여 자신이 얻고 싶은 답을 도출해내는 방법을 예시를 통해 소개한다. 　- 답을 필요로 하는 이유와 상황 밝히기 　- 구체적인 요구사항 쓰기(문장의 종류, 문장의 개수 등) • 학생이 직접 ChatGPT와 대화하여 배운 문법을 포함하는 7개 정도의 문장으로 된 대화문을 도출하도록 지도한다. • 도출한 대화문을 짝과 훑어보면서 수정 및 보안 작업을 거친다. • 대화문의 역할을 나누어 Role Play를 한다.	
배움 정리 (5)	정리& 차시 예고	• 다른 사람이 만든 문법 신문을 토대로 자신이 만든 문법 신문에 대해 평가한다. • 생활 속에서 비교급과 최상급을 만들 수 있는 대상에 대해 말해본다. • 다음 차시를 미리 예습하고 준비할 수 있도록 안내한다.	

3 서울 합격자 수업지도안 예시(I)

Vocabulary & Reading	– 교사는 학생들에게 글을 빠르게 읽고 어려운 어휘에 동그라미 하게 한다. – 학생들이 단어들을 부른다. – 교사는 학생들에게 의미를 추측하도록 예시를 든다. – 교사는 학생들에게 글을 다시 읽고 '걱정'의 요소를 찾게 한다. – 교사는 학생들과 함께 답을 확인한다. – 교사는 학생들에게 짝과 함께 빈칸을 채우게 한다. – 교사는 학생들의 적극적인 참여로 답을 함께 확인한다.
Grammar	– 교사는 학생들에게 밑줄 친 구의 의미를 추측하게 한다. – 교사는 밑줄 친 구가 포함된 예시의 문장을 제시한다. – 교사는 학생들과 함께 이해도를 확인한다. – 교사는 학생들이 개별적으로 글의 요약본을 쓰게 한다. – 교사는 학생들 중 자신의 요약본을 자원해서 발표하게 한다.
Writing	– 교사는 빈칸의 내용을 채워넣는 쓰기 활동을 학생들에게 설명한다. – 교사는 학생들과 함께 글의 이해도를 확인한다. – 교사는 교실을 돌아다니며 학생들의 활동을 모니터하고 필요한 도움을 제공한다. 1. 조를 형성하고 각 역할을 분담한다. | Leader | Writer | | Uploader | Grammar checker | | Time keeper || 2. 빈칸의 내용에 대한 예상한 내용을 이야기 한다. 3. 교사의 모델 글을 제시한다. 4. 학생들이 글을 쓴다.
Speaking	– 교사는 말하기 활동을 설명한다. 1. 조를 형성한다. 2. 조원들과 함께 주어진 주제에 대하여 토론하고 이야기의 결론을 예상한다. 3. 교사는 연습지를 제공한다. (교사는 각 조의 결론을 만들어 빈칸을 채우도록 한다.) – 교사는 전체 학생들과 함께 이해도를 확인한다.
Feedback	– 교사는 형성평가지를 나누어주고 글의 전체적인 이해도를 평가한다. – 교사는 학생들의 연습지에 나타난 문법/ 어휘 오류를 확인해서 분석 연습한다.

4 서울 합격자 수업지도안 예시(II)

수업 목표

학생들은 다음의 활동을 수행할 수 있다.
- 상황안에서 새로운 단어의 의미를 알아낸다.
- 짝과 함께 글의 특정한 정보를 이용하여 테이블을 완성한다.
- 친구를 좋은 사람으로 소개하는 그들의 글을 조별로 제시한다.

수업 과정

- 교사와 학생들은 인사를 나누고 출결을 확인한다.
- 교사는 지난시간의 내용을 확인한다.
- 교사는 오늘의 수업목표를 제시한다.

전개

1. 읽기 전 활동

〈어휘〉
- 교사는 학생들에게 글에서 모르는 어휘를 찾아 밑줄을 긋고 소리내어 읽어보게 한다.
- 교사는 화면에 그림과 예시문장을 제시하면서 모르는 단어들을 학생들에게 추측하게 한다.
- 교사는 학생들과 함께 어휘의 의미를 확인한다.

〈읽기〉
- 교사는 학생들과 제목을 읽어보면서 오늘 읽을 글의 주제가 무엇인지 추측해 보도록 한다.
- 교사는 학생들에게 글을 상세하게 읽도록 한다.
- 교사는 연습지를 나누어 주고 학생들이 짝을 이루어 활동하도록 한다.
- 교사는 연습지의 표에 있는 빈칸을 어떻게 채우는지 설명한다.
- 학생들의 활동을 마친 후에 교사는 표의 답안을 학생들과 함께 확인한다.

2. 읽기와 쓰기 활동

〈쓰기〉
- 교사는 학생들이 4명씩 8그룹을 만들도록 하고 각각의 역할을 정하도록 한다. (역할: Word master, Presenter, Writer, Grammar checker)
- 교사는 쓰기의 주제를 소개한다.
- 교사는 화면에 모델쓰기를 제시하여 글의 시작을 어떻게 해야 하는지 보여준다.
- 학생들은 화면에 나타난 모델을 참조하여 조별 쓰기를 시작한다.
- 교사는 학생들에게 자신이 쓴 글을 다시 한번 읽고 오류가 있다면 오류를 수정하게 한다.
- 학생들은 자신들의 조별 쓰기를 읽고 오류를 수정한다.

5 경북 합격자 수업지도안 예시

〈어휘 지도〉 IW
- 학생들이 글을 읽고 확실치 않은 어휘들을 선택한다: supplement, strength, posture
- 교사는 그림과 예시문장들을 제시한다.
- 학생들은 뜻을 추론하고 교사는 의미를 정리한다: supplement (vitamin, protein power), strength (example sentence), posture (context with students)

〈Table 완성〉 IW
- 워크시트를 나누어준다.
- 학생들이 글을 상세하게 읽고 테이블을 완성한다.
- 교사는 학생들의 이해도를 체크한다.
- 교사는 테이블에 근거하여 어떻게 요약하는지를 보여준다.
- 학생들은 글을 요약한다.

〈의식 올리기 활동〉 PW
- 교사는 학생들이 짝을 구성하도록 한다.
- 교사는 화면에 목표 구조가 포함된 문장을 제시하고 학생들은 강조된 표현을 자세히 보도록 한다.
- 교사는 학생들이 의논하여 짝과 함께 자신들의 규칙을 끌어내도록 한다.
- 대표 몇 명이 자신의 결과물을 발표한다.
- 목표형태의 의미와 용례를 이해하도록 교사는 정리한다.

〈토론 & 쓰기 활동〉 GW
- 5명씩 6개의 조를 만든다.
- material 2의 워크시트를 배포한다.
- 교사는 활동에서 무엇을 할지, 어떻게 할지 설명한다.
- 학생들이 자신의 걱정을 워크시트에 개별적으로 작성한다.
- 조의 친구들과 자신이 작성한 워크시트를 교환한다.
- 학생들은 서로에게 주는 조언을 작성한다.

〈역할극〉 PW
- 교사는 활동에서 무엇을 할지 어떻게 할지 설명한다.
- 각 짝에게 역할 카드를 나누어 준다.
- 학생들은 역할극을 위한 스크립트를 작성한다.
- 교사는 연습시간을 주고 자신의 역할을 위한 역할극을 연습하게 한다.
- 몇 명의 지원자들이 나와 역할극을 공연한다.

〈형성평가〉
- 교사는 형성평가 시험지를 배포한다: According to the speech bubble in cartoons, give 3 advices by using "If I were you, I would ...."
- 학생들은 문제의 답을 쓰고 교사는 답을 확인한다.

Note: IW=individual work, GW=group work, PW=pair work

05 합격자 후기와 예시

1 서울 합격자의 심층 면접 합격 TIP

- "즉답형이나 추가문제에서는 순발력이 필요하다." 구상형은 복합적인 상황을 분석해야 답할 수 있는 내용으로 여러 영역을 포괄하고 있는 질문이지만 즉답형도 단순히 해결방안을 제시하라는 것만이 아니라 문제점을 제시하고 해결방안을 제시하라는 질문이었다. 그래서 즉석에서 바로 답안을 만들어내는 연습이 없었다면 대답하기가 정말 어려웠을 것이다.
- "구상형에서 묻고 있는 논점을 파악하는 게 중요하다." 구상형 문제의 지문은 용지 한 장을 가득 채운 경우가 많아서 짧은 시간에 요구사항을 파악하고 지문을 분석하는 데 많은 애를 먹었다. 구상하는 내용을 메모를 할 수 있기는 하나 공간도 적고 시간도 짧아서 실제로 시험장에 가서 새로운 내용을 만들어 낸다는 것은 거의 불가능해 보였다. 난이도는 꽤 높았고 구상형 문제는 긴 지문을 면밀히 분석해서 문제점을 찾아내고 지도방안을 말해야 되는 경우가 많았기 때문에 교직논술 논제파악보다 훨씬 어렵다.
- "구상형 답변에서 시간을 조정하여 답을 해야한다." 구상형 문제를 답변하는 시간은 보통 9분 정도 제공되었다. 그런데 시간배분을 잘못해서 문제의 답변을 모두 말하지 못했다. 심지어는 면접실에 있는 디지털시계가 남은 시간을 가리키는 것이었는데 그것을 착각하여 반대로 생각해서 정신이 없었다.
- "현재 중요한 교육 문제를 알고 있어야 한다." 쟁점이 되고 있는 교육현안 중에서는 수업시간 중 휴대폰 사용에 대한 학생지도, 학생들의 미래직업과 부모의 희망직업과의 차이, 바람직한 교사상등의 문제 등이 출제되었다. 그 외에 일반 시사에 관련된 문제는 출제되지 않았다.

2 서울 합격자의 심층면접을 위한 정리 NOTE

인성교육	<ul><li>교사는 학생의 모범</li><li>창의적 체험활동: 봉사, 동아리 → 책임감 증진</li><li>1인1체육, 1인1음악: 전인적 성장</li><li>수업: 협동학습, 역할놀이, 토론</li><li>가정연계</li><li>학교: 캠페인 → 민주시민의식 향상</li><li>학급 자치 활동: 학급회의 (기본생활규칙 협의/ get along programs)</li></ul>	
상벌제	문제점	해결방안
	불명확한 기준	교사, 학생, 학부모, 지역사회구성원으로 이뤄진 위원회에서 기준설정.
	행동의 반성기회 없음	반성기회제공: 반성문, 봉사, 사과
	제도에 대해 잘 모름	정보공시: 가정통신문 & 학교 홈페이지

	문제점	해결방안
수행평가	실용도 (시간, 돈, 노력: 비효과적)	1) 교원업무 축소 2) 수업연구 전념 여건 조성
	신뢰도	1) 기준공동설정 2) 공동채점 3) 성적확인 후 논의 기회 제공
	타당도 (측정하고자 하는 능력 측정)	1) 이원분류표 (중요하고 배운 내용-내에서 출제) 2) 익숙한 과제에서 출제

교사의 전문성 신장방안	• 자기장학. 동료장학. 컨설팅장학 • 선배교사의 도움 (멘토링 장학) • 자기 연찬: 대학원, 학회, 세미나, 전문서적 탐독 • 학생과 학부모의 의견 수렴 + 교원평가결과 활용
수업의 질 향상 방안	1. 수업준비차원: 수요조사 & 진단평가 2. 수업전략: 목표 명확히 & 형성평가 3. 자료: ICT + 판서 4. 수업활동(학생참여): 모둠활동, 프로젝트활동, 토론등 실제적이고 관련있는 과제 (relevant & realistic) *모둠활동의 장점: 협력기술습득 (또래교수, 도움교환, pleasure discussing & share work) 리더십함양 (개별역할+분담+통솔) → 미래에 도움, Enliven the content 5. 수준별 수업 (level-differentiated/ tailored instruction): 기초학력 책임지도제, 이동수업 6. 자기 주도 학습! 7. 장기적으로는 적성중심 교육관 함양: 사교육 경감, 창의성 증가
교사인성	소통　　　공감　　　이해 협업　　　인내　　　긍정적기대 (낙인× 자성예언효과) 책임감　　노력
교사의 자질	• professionalism: expertise & develop teaching skills • respect students- rapport - consult & understand • collaborative attitude toward co-teachers • morally a role model to students • self supervision
교직관과 행복한 교실 비전	• 지성: 수준별. 프로젝트 등 → 학력신장. 학습 부진아 없음 • 인성: 체험, 학생중심 • 꿈 & 끼 발휘하는 글로벌 인재: 창의적체험활동
학급운영	• 1인 1기여 프로젝트: 역할. 흥미. 책임감. 자기주도성 • 조회, 종례시간 활용: 조회에서 소소한 일상 공유, 종례에서 서로 하루 일과 답변 • 새해첫날: 학급 운영규칙회의 + 왕따 청정구역 등 소통방안 만들기 • 비전 찾기 강조

초임교사가 겪는 문제	• skillfully 수업 못함→ T training, skill in classroom management높이기 • no balance between teaching & administrative work→ checklist, priority • strive to win Ss' favor→ make rules about the reward & keep dignity
떠드는 학생	1. 개별상담: 공감, 원인(학습동기, 지루, 관심끌기) + 해결책 (eg) 상담순서: 공감적이해 - 긍정적측면 - 문제상황객관적진술 - 교사감정진술 (i-message: 선생님이 속상하고 아쉽다) - 학생문제의 이유 (~라는건 생각해봤니?) - 대안제시/ 자발적 해결유도 (선택권 부여하기! 지금처럼 하면 친구랑 선생님이 실망하고, 개선하면 뿌듯해하고 친구들도 잘 따를꺼야. 어떻게 하겠니?) - 긍정직예언! 꼭하기 2. 상반행동강화 + 소거 3. 수업을 흥미있게 하고 참여기회 높이고 역할제공 4. 지속적 관리
진로	진로계발 역량 키우기! 1. 교과통합진로교육: 학생흥미 & 적성에 맞는 교과찾기 2. 창의적 체험활동: 자동봉진 (각 활동 연계!) (eg) 봉사: 견학. 인터뷰. ICT활용. 지역 사회 연계 3. 자유학기제 활용/ 진로의날 4. 조별토론 & 발표 5. 적성검사실시 6. 비전선언문 쓰기, 미래명함 만들기
창의력	Broaden their perspectives! 독서(문학)　　　　브레인 스토밍법　　　프로젝트법　　　　문제중심학습 개방형질문　　　　토론, 역할놀이　　　평가 (포트폴리오, 형성평가)
자기주도 학습	학습목표 명확히 제시　　　학습전략 알려주기　　　학습일지 사이버 가정학습　　　　　형성평가　　　　　　　　가정연계지도 체크리스트 (자기주도플래너) + 자기평가
학교폭력, 왕따, 담배 등	**피해자 (왕따)** • 개별상담 (따뜻한 상담): 공감, 원인, 해결책 • 또래 짝 도우미 • 학급 자치활동→ 협력 & 유대감 • 학부모, 전문상담가 (특히 우울증), 대학생 멘토 **가해자** • 개별상담: 들어보고 원인파악(일회성? 가정/ 교우관계/ 성격장애등 구조적 원인?) 역지사지 깨닫도록 (i-message사용/ 비디오 활용/ 행동 계약/ 교사기대/ 선택권 부여) • 진심으로 사과 • 학부모 연계 지도 • 실천/체험중심 인성교육: 봉사활동, 운동팀 구성, 사제동행 • 학교폭력을 주제로 연극준비: 친밀감 형성 & 폭력에 대한 인식상승 & 반성

★ 1. 대응	
	• 현장조치 (아이들 떼놓기) + 다친 학생 응급조치
	• 학교폭력전담위원회: 담임. 교장. 교감
	• 학부모 연락
	• 피해자. 가해자 상담
	• 자료수집: 목격자 & 현장 상황
	2. 예방책
	• 학급자치활동: 학급회의 (규칙제정 & 예방), 반노래 부르기 (공동체 의식 상승/ 친밀도 향상)
	• 학교캠페인 (학생주도): raise collaborative spirit! 학교폭력 신고하자는 구호 만들기 (멈춰), 포스터, 예방도우미, 익명신고방
	• build network: 지역사회. 학부모 (지킴이. 캠페인. 학교수호천사)
	(eg) 학교수호천사는 전학 후 부적응 겪는 친구에게도 도움 됨 (역할까지 부여하기)
	• 협동학습
	• 반 대항전→ 협동 정신 높아짐
	• 체험중심인성교육: 봉사
	• systematic counseling
특수 & 장애	• 배려일지: 배려의 중요성강조. 일지작성. 서로칭찬
	• 또래도우미
	• 역할극
다문화	• 반친구와 관계 개선-수호천사활동, 문화소개, 공동체교육, 배려일지
	• 학습문제: 다문화 예시, 모둠활동(협력), 연극
	• 정체성 교육 - festival
학원에서 배웠다	• 학급에 나쁜 영향
	• 도전적 과제 제공하기
	• 동료교수의 기회주기
	• 협동학습 + 팀점수 + 팀보상 - 참여도 증진
학부모 상담	• 공감적 이해 + 학생 긍정적인 측면 + 현재 상황 (supporting documentation) + 개선방안
	• 가정연계지도 방법 + 부탁 + 기대
	• 평소관찰일지 작성
	• 정기적 소통의장 마련
	• 학부모가 비협조적이면 녹음하기/ "자주인"임을 명시/ 학생 인격 비난 NO. 행동비난!
교사 이기주의	• 동료교사와의 협동: 조직화된 무질서 조직→ 목표달성 방법 불확실→ 업무 분배 필요
	• 교사로서의 사명감
	• 교사는 모델링의 대상!
	• 이기적인 태도로는 리더십 못 지님
교육 정책	• 획일성 (X) 다양성 있는 교육(O)
	• Number One 아니고 Only One이라는 생각으로 대한다.

3 서울 합격자의 수업실연시 유의사항

- 지시사항 제발제발 다 지키자: topic & goals & 지시문 (level-differentiated)
- 지도안에 써놓고 빼먹은거 많음. 암기하기 (단어등 내 수업구조 암기하기)
- 이름 암기하기; ABCDEFGHIJK등... 써놓기
- 쉬운 mindmap으로 시작하되, 지우지 말기: 이후에 vocabulary와 topic을 왜 배우는지 계속 설명해 주면 좋음
- 칭찬은 다양하게 해주기: 너무 오버해서 똑같은 말 하지 않기
    - "Great job on that exercise!"
    - "You're really improving in your English skills."
    - "Excellent effort in today's class."
    - "I'm impressed by your pronunciation!"
    - "Well done! Your speaking is getting much clearer."
    - "You're doing a fantastic job with your vocabulary."
    - "Keep up the good work!"
    - "I love how you're participating in discussions."
    - "Your writing is showing real progress."
    - "You're making great strides in understanding grammar."
- 침착함 + 활발함의 균형을 맞추는게 필요
- 판서시 일정한 곳에 써주기: 판서 줄이고 깔끔하게 연습!
- Feedback 줄때 구체적으로 말하기: slight mistake라고 하기 보다는, ★Let's focus on the details. We can make it better!
- 욕심을 버리고, natural하게 침착할 수 있는, 평상시대로 하기!
- 수업지도안에 (학생들이 동기부여가 되어 학습한다)처럼 반응적인 내용보다는 실제 학생의 행동을 쓴다. ★(교사는 학생들이 실제로 어려운 일이 있었을 때 어떻게 대처했는지 토론하게 한다)
- 단어를 내가 선택해야한다면, 중요한 것이되, 최대한 간결하고 이해하기 쉽게 설명한다.
- 연계 연계 연계! 앞으로 가르쳐야하는 linking words가 있다면, vocab때 그것을 활용해주는 것도 아주 좋음. 앞의 활동에 연결되어 다음 활동 나올 수 있도록 한다.
- 지시사항에서 알려주라는 것 이외의 것은 알려주지 말자! 부가적으로 더 알려주면 혼란스러우니까, 1개를 제대로 하자.
- Don't worry about grammar는 위험! 그보다는 ★Don't worry about grammar right now, because we will review common grammatical mistakes later, at the end of the class.라고 해결책과 함께 편안한 수업을 만들 수 있도록 한다.
- 영어가 너무 informal해지지 않도록 guys & gonna라고 하지않고 "Alright, team", "Listen up, everyone", "Attention, class", "Let's focus, everybody", "Can I have your attention, please?", "Settle down, friends" 등으로 표현할 수 있다.
- 더 중요한 내용은 중요하다고 별표 쳐주기

4 서울 합격자의 수업실연을 위한 만능틀 만들기

1) schema activation
- 교사는 학생들 책상위에 영어이름표가 있는지 확인한다.
- 교사는 학생들에게 스크린에 있는 매핑과 사진을 보고 의미를 유추하게 한다.
- 교사는 오늘의 수업 주제를 소개한다.

2) Vocabulary
- 교사는 학생들에게 글을 빠르게 읽고 모르는 어휘에 동그라미 하게 한다.
- 교사는 새로운 어휘를 맥락안에서 설명하고 학생들에게 의미를 추론하게 한다.
- 교사는 학생들에게 어휘를 이용하여 문장을 생성하도록 한다.

3) Reading
- 교사는 학생들에게 짝 활동을 통해 읽기 활동을 하게 한다. (Direction: 짝을 지어서 글을 빠르게 읽고, graphic organizer를 이용하여 상세 내용을 이해한다.)
- 교사는 학생들에게 글의 주제문을 찾아 발표하게 하고 확인해 준다.
- 교사는 학생들에게 상세 내용을 이해하기 위해 graphic organizer을 어떻게 이용하는지 설명한다.
- 교사는 학생들이 짝을 이루고 graphic organizer을 채우게 한다.
- 교사는 지원 학생이 답을 발표하게 하고 확인해 준다.

4) Writing
- 교사는 4명의 학생들이 6개의 조를 만들고 각 역할을 가지고 자신의 역할을 명확하게 이해하게 한다. (monitor, writer, word master, grammar checker…)
- 교사는 쓰기 활동을 설명한다. (모델 글을 제시하고 목표언어를 활용하여 글을 작성한다.)
- 교사는 스크린위에 모델 글을 제시한다.
- 교사는 각 조에서 5개의 문장이 포함된 하나의 단락을 작성한다.
- 교사는 confident한 조가 있다면 2개의 문장을 추가할 수 있다고 설명한다.
- 교사는 교실을 돌아다니며 학생들의 어려워 하는 점을 도와주고 격려한다.

5) Presentation
- 교사는 대표학생이 발표할 때 다른 학생들이 지켜야 할 수칙을 이야기하고 동료평가를 진행할 수 있게 한다.
- 학생들은 각자 그룹의 글 혹은 표를 제출하고 그에 따라 서로 최고의 작품에 투표한다.

6) Feedback
- 교사는 학생들의 글이나 발표에서 두 가지 언어에 대한 피드백을 제공한다. (eg) 어휘, 문법

06 교실영어 스크립트

수업과정		교수 학습 활동		자료와 시간
		교사 발화	목표	
도입	인사와 소개	Hello! Everyone! Is everyone here? Okay. Good to see you all today. As we do all the time, today you have to do your best. Got it? Let's start today's lesson.	• 인사하기	(1′)
	복습	Before we start today's lesson, let's have a short review of what we learned last class. You are going to watch a short movie that has the new words from this lesson. If you can guess what that is, please say the word out loud.	• 영화보는 동안 지난 시간에 배운 어휘 말해보기	computer, electronic board, a movie (3′)
	수업목표 소개와 동기부여	Now, let's take a look at a music video. It will show you the things we will learn today. If you can guess today's topic or objectives, please raise your hand. If you get the answer I will give you a point. These are what we will do today. First, After you learn shopping expressions, you will be able to properly answer or question in any given shopping situation. Second, you will be able to make the shopping script using learned expressions and act out your own dialogue. Now tell me the reason why we have to learn them. Right. We buy things in our every day lives. So, these expressions are important. Are you ready to learn how to buy or sell things? Ok! Let's start.	• 영화를 보면서 오늘 주제나 목표를 추론하기 • 다함께 오늘의 수업목표를 읽어보기 • 학생들은 교사의 질문에 답하기	computer electronic board, music video, ppt

전개	쇼핑표현에 대한 의미 추론	Before we learn the expressions, you will have the chance to guess what these expressions mean by yourselves. Then, figure out who may say this sentence between a shopper and a clerk. Finally stick each sentence on your worksheet according to role. You have 2 mins. Go!	• 팀에서 쇼핑표현의 의미를 나누고 워크시트에서 쇼핑표현 배우기	worksheet (that has several shopping expressions), glue, ppt (3′)
	쇼핑표현 학습1	You might have figured out the brief meaning of each expression. Now, you will learn what exact meaning they have and in which situation they can be used. You can see this game board. Each cell has a short conversation between a shopper and a clerk in a different shopping situation. One of the lines is deleted.	• 게임에서 선택한 대화 완성하기	computer, electronic board, ppt, a cup of chopsticks (15′)
	쇼핑표현 학습2	I'm going to choose you with the chopsticks. The person stand up and complete the shopping dialogue with appropriate expressions. If your answer is right, your points will show up later. Are you ready? Let's start.	• 선택한 대화 완성하기	computer, electronic board, ppt, a cup of chopsticks (15′)
	쇼핑대화 연습	Now, you practice the shopping dialogue with your group for 2 min. Two of you will be shoppers and rest of you will be clerks. When you are done, please change your roles. While you are practicing, try to memorize them.	• 역할 바꾸어 쇼핑대화 연습하기	worksheet (3′)
	암기 게임하기	We are going to play a game with the expressions you learned. You will keep passing this parcel to the next person in your group while listening to the song. When the music stops, the person who has the parcel rips off the top layer and write down an answer on the white board within 5 seconds. If your answer is right, your team will get a point and you will get a prize. You will keep doing this until the last parcel is ripped off. Of course, the last parcel has the biggest gift. Good luck!	• 음악 들으면서 다음 사람에게 소포를 패스하고 질문에 답하기	game parcels, pop-song, computer, ppt (3′) miniwhite board, markers

	스크립트 작성하기	From now on, you will be actual shoppers or clerks. Each sheet has a different shopping situation. According to the situation, make a script on your worksheet with your team until a song ends, using the expressions you learned today. When you are done with it, give it to me. If you do a good job, I'll give you a point.	• 워크시트의 상황에 근거하여 자신의 대화 만들기	worksheet (5′)
	역할극하기	Today I will have a couple of groups come up here and act out the script they wrote. Please, act out like a shopper or clerk.	• 역할극하고 다른팀 평가하기	electronic board (3′)
정 리	정리 & 복습	We are done with what we have to learn today. It's time to review. While filling in this review worksheet, you will check yourself on how much you could understand today's lesson. Please teach yourself the expressions you won't be able to fill in. I will collect your worksheet. And next class I will have you stand up and explain the expressions you don't know well today.	• ppt보면서 워크시트 완성하기	computer, electronic board, worksheet, ppt (3′)
	보상 & 과제	Thank you for your energy and participation. Today's winning team is team ____. I will give you a coupon as a prize. Good job! Which is the bottom team? Team ___ will have to memorize the 25 words in *Erin's Words List*. I will check it next time.	• 점수로 보상 주기	Elecrtronic board, Computer, ppt (2′)
	다음수업 안내	We will keep evaluating the remaining teams that couldn't show their acting in the next class. And we will also learn the grammar point 'it is … that …' structure.	• 다음수업 안내하기	Elecrtronic board, Computer, ppt (1′)

9 합격생 수업실연 후기

- Lesson title: What Should I do?
- 고1, 30명, 3차시
- Reading text: Title/Topic Worries and Advice

(1) 지도안 지시문

[읽기 전 활동]

1. Material 1 활용해서 리딩 지도, 단어도 가르쳐라.
2. 테이블을 완성해라. (commentary: 수업목표와 디렉션의 지시사항이 다르게 나와서, summary에 대한 구체적 지시가 없이, 구상실에서 혼동이 오는 활동이었다.)

[읽기 중 활동]

3. 언어의 구조를 가르치는 활동을 설계해라. (If I were you ~)
4. Material 2로 그룹 활동을 설계해라.

[읽기 후 활동]

5. 말하기 활동을 설계해라. (commentary: 짝활동이 적절한 post활동으로 보여 짝활동을 선택했다)

[마침]

6. formative 평가를 설계해라.

(2) 수업실연 후기

지도안 작성

지도안 내기 전에 학습목표 다시 한 번 기억하고 활동 순서대로 암기하려고 노력하면서 시간 딱 맞춰서 냈습니다. 마지막에 formative assessment 예시 문제 3개 만들려고 했는데 3 questions 해놓고 예시 그리는데 시간이 딱 맞거나 아슬아슬 할 것 같아서 3 자에 두 줄 긋고 그냥 questions 해놓고 1. 2.까지만 하고 3.적어놓은 데도 두줄 그었음. 그리고 관리번호 1번 뽑아서 관리번호 순서대로 자리 재배치하고 중얼중얼 거리면서 수업 어떻게 할지 한번 처음부터 끝까지 멘트랑 순서랑 속으로 중얼중얼 거리면서 맨 앞에 앉았다보니 허공을 보면서 입으로 손짓으로 시뮬레이션. 한번 하는데 30분 걸리고, 그 이후부터 점심이랑 간식 먹으면서 계속 연습. 하지만 엄청 추운 날이라서 히터 틀어주었고 따뜻했습니다. 다시 머릿속으로 연습.

구상실

12시에 구상실 들어가서 순서대로 번호 매겨서 메모하고, 학생이름과 표 채우거나 판서할 내용, 학생 반응 메모, 활동 시간, 디렉션 및 워크시트 나눠주는 순서 등 메모. development 만 하는데 내가 작성한 것만 하라고 한 것 봄. 그래서 formative는 빼먹자고 생각함. 그래도 시간이 남으면 내가 표현하려고 했던 시험지를 설명하자라고 생각함. 근데 앞에 activation 이랑 기타 오늘 활동 순서에서는 인생이 등산과 같다고 생각하는 인성이 드러날 거고, topic guessing 시켜서 title이랑 확인하는 거는 내 무기라고 생각했고, 채점관 선생님께서 디렉션을 따라서 하는 것을 중요하게 볼 수도 있지만, 사실 그런 기준표보다 내 자연스러운 모습, 교사로서의 자질 느낌을 보고 5분 내에 판단 난다는 현직 선생님 말씀. 색분필을 5분 이내에 사용하고 첫인상을 좋게 하자는 말씀에 자연스럽게 인사부터는 아니라도 development 부터 하기로 결론.

수업실연

문 열고 들어가서 닫고 인사. 걸어가서 중앙에서 인사 안녕하십니까. 영어과 관리번호 1번입니다. 수업 실연 프레젠테이션 시작하겠습니다. 눈빛교환 시작. 분필체크 했는데, 빨강, 흰, 파랑 밖에 없었음....... 파랑은 쓰면 안되고 노란색이 없어서.. 당황 중요한걸 다 빨강으로 해야겠다고 속으로 생각. 시간 스타트. Okay class. So far we have seen today's objectives. Are you confident in completing all of these? Yes??!!! Wow I love your loud voice. (미소로 시작, 교사 멘트때는 손 모으고 동작 큰 편, 스크린에 띄워서 같이 봤다고 가정하고 손으로 위아래 쓸며) Let's start today's class with my episode. Look at my face~ Can you see these? Yes pimples! I am so worried about my pimples. It makes me ugly. Oh. 소영, you have same problem? skin troubles! (실제로 본인의 얼굴에 여드름 나서 그것을 가리키며 힘들었던 경험을 이야기한다. 왼쪽 4분단) Wow 희선, I envy your skin. WHAT SHOULD I DO to have skin like you? You don't have any trouble at all! Wash off my face often? It's a good advice! Yes, over there? Do not eat chocolate. Maybe that's why I got these. I love ice cream. This conversation was related to today's topic. Can you guess the topic for today? Any ideas would be welcomed. (중앙에서 멘트 정리하면서 칠판 좌측으로 가서 판서) Bad habits. It could be~ I will write anything you say, Skin Care? Anymore? Concerns~ Wow how did you know this word! It's quite difficult one. Then lets' see who made correct guess later. (세 개 써놓고)

판서

Everyone as I always say, I believe that learning or life is like climbing up the mountain. So hills 그림. 세 언덕을 넘으면 산을 오르는 모양 (계단에서 변형..아까 topic guess 아래 부분 판서를 4등분 해서 가장 왼쪽 채움) So, today we are going to hike up reading hill, writing hill, speaking hill. At the end, we would achieve success. Are you confident in reaching at the peak? yes!!! I love your energy. I will write the lesson title first. 칠판 중앙 위에 Lesson 3. What Should I Do? 판서. 대문자 지킴. Now Take out your textbook. And Open your book to page 100. 100. (칠판 최우측에 위에 판서 p.100) I'll write page number here. Are we in same page? What can you see? There is a reading text. Let's read the title together WORRIES AND (everyone read it aloud together~) ADVICE Wow. He got a correct answer. 하면서 concerns에 빨간색으로 동그라미.

VOCABULARY

This time I want you to read the text very quickly, as fast as you can. and pick out the words you don't know. Okay? I'll give you 30 seconds. Ready! Go! (오른쪽으로 좀 걸어나가는 척 하다가 바로) OK time is up. Please call out the words you are not familiar with. 칠판에 Worries and Advice 빨간색으로 쓰고 (2/4 부분) ① supplement: I heard someone says supplement. ②strength: As I expected, I heard strength. ③posture: good point. No more? I think these are enough. Let's start with supplement. 중앙으로 걸어 나오면서 Look at the screen. I prepared pictures. What can you see? Yes 김종국! He is muscle man. right? What does he eat? yes pills and yes! protein power. These things are supplements. Can you guess the meaning of the supplement? Oh, Thank you, 수현. Something that fills up, if they are lack of. Good. I will write the simple definition here '= the thing that make up, lack→fill. Good. Then, lets move on the next word. I'll give you example sentence here. As you know, I think things in positive ways. Positive thinking skill is my strength. Like this, can you guess the meaning of the word, strength? Yes. good point!! Thank you 은혜. It means strong points, advantages, It comes from 'strong'이라고 하면서 streng_부분에 빨간색으로 밑줄 So this time I'll write the opposite word here '↔ weakness /disadvantage' And last word. This time, Lets talk about our friends. Everyone, look at 경은. (경은이랑 지원이 2분단 중앙, 앞으로 나가서 채점관 앞을 가리키며 보게 함.) Does she have good posture or bad posture. She always straighten her back. Yes good posture. What about 지원. He always leaning against his arms. And bending over his back. Bent over, crooked. Right? Yes. He has bad posture. (몸으로 허리피고 팔에 턱 괴고, 허리 굽히고 연기… 다시 칠판으로 돌아와서) Can you guess the meaning of the word posture? Yes, it's the way you stand or sit. So now we are ready to read the text. 정의부분은 빨간색으로 판서

수업운영

(관리번호 1번이라서 시험실 세팅이 아직 어수선하고, 판서실수가 나와서 지우개로 지우려는데 지우개에 물기가 하나도 없는 겁니다. 그래서 칠판옆에 가서 지우개 다시 가져와서 할까 하는데 그러면 쉬지않고 말을 해야하고 말을 하지 않으면 버퍼링이 3~5초는 되서 채점관들 집중력 흐려질 것 같고 내가 분필이나 뭐 떨어뜨리면 oops sorry 라고 원래 영어가 튀어나오는 사람이라는 느낌을 주려고는 생각했었지만, 영어로 이렇게 문법에 맞게 잘 할 수 있을까..웃음을 이끌어낼 수 있을까 어떻게 할까 하다가, No one plays their roles in class management. I have to make eraser myself. 라고 학생들 꾸짖는 멘트를 하면서 오타 지우고 다시 판서 했습니다.)

TABLE 작성

I prepare a worksheet for you. Have one and pass them around. Have one and pass it to the back. 1,2,3 분단 나눠줌. 순서대로 오른쪽부터 왼쪽까지. 그리고~ Did you get it? Show it to me~ Ok. Look at the worksheet. What can you see? Yes, there is a table. Read the text carefully in detail and complete the table. Okay? I'll give you 3 minutes. Ready Set begin! 순회지도 3분단. Yes 은혜. Oh, you don't know the meaning of 'decent'? Oh, It seems 동현 knows the meaning of that word. 동현. would you help 은혜? Good~ Okay time is up. Let's check your answers together. (학생들과 표 채우는 것 같이 채우는 것처럼 하는 모습을 보여주면 좋았을 것이라 생각된다.) You didn't finish it? It's okay. Let's check the answer with me. What is the answer for the first part. Andy's worry 라고 하면서 표를 크직하게 그림. 3/4 부분에 표 그림. Anyone~ 하고, Yes 소정. Yes~~ tall~ He is worried about his height. Why don't you read the sentence? 'want to grow taller 인지 can't grow taller'인지 표에 적음. And Another? Why is he worried? Yes parents are not tall and 이유 두개라고 하나 더 있었는데 까먹었지만 두 가지 이야기 하면서. And what was Ken's advice? Focus on your strength. 표에 판서함. What was his evidence? Yes, thank you (이름 생각 안나서 그냥 얼굴 보면서 누구 말 들은 것처럼) ex. his brother. 라고 씀. Next, What was Julie's advice? Anyone? Yes, 영진 improve my posture. Oh, this word 'posture' we learned before. right? Good job. You comprehend the reading text very well.

발표

Everyone, look at the table. When we use the table, we can summarize the text easily. Just add some introduction, like this. 빨간 분필로 표 밑에 summary를 씀

Andy is worried about _____.
So, Ken give advice by saying _____.
Also, Julie " _____.

(여기서 또 판서가 잘못되어 지워야하는데 잘 안 지워져서 쎄개 문지르면서 I am not that strong woman. 하면서 힘들게 지우고 다시 판서) You can summarize like this. Just put the phrases in the blank. I will give you 2 minutes. There are empty space underneath the table, right? Right your summary. 시간 주고 you are doing very good 이런 말 하면서 순회지도 대충 넘어감. 시계 보니까 10분도 안남았는데 아직 문법, 라이팅, 스피킹까지 갈길이 멀다는 생각에 여유롭게 차분하게 잘해왔는데 급한 느낌을 받기 시작. 그래서 꼭 수업목표를 활동 끝에 말해줄려고 했는데, 까먹음. Now you can write a summary after reading the text 라고 하고 싶었는데 까먹고 못함. 발표를 시켰는지 안 시켰는지 모르겠음.

GRAMMAR

One more thing to do. We are going to learn today's target structure. I prepared some example sentences. Look at the screen. Can you notice today's target phrase? Yes, If I (everyone together) were you. Yes, I highlighted the words Right? Oh, 형식. Why did you raise your hand? Oh, you saw this on the reading text? Yes. I love your sense. It was written twice. Great. From now on, you are going to make a rule. draw your own rule out of these. Ok? It is a pair work. So left side and right side. You are a pair. Say hello to your partners. I'll give you 2 minutes. Yes 철수 you need more explanation? Make your own rules, Compare it with your partner. OK GO!

발표

Time is up. Who is going to share your rules? Oh, 인영 and 종신. 인영, Oh you think it is wrong. 마지막 4/4 에 <target structure> 쓰고 If I were you, i would 는 빨간색. were 동그라미 하고 you think it should be changed into was? Good point. Uhm. In this situation, When you describe unreal thing, It is exceptional, special case. So, we need to use, 밑에 If + S + V + O, 라고 쓰면서 If plus subject~ plus verb~ 하면서 V 밑에 past verb 라고 씀. However, if the subject is I, you have to use were. It is exceptional, special use. Okay? Thank you for sharing your rule. (급하고, 생각보다 문법 설명을 내가 하게 되가지고 인영이랑 종신이가 말해준 것처럼 말한척 하고 넘어감.)

그룹 활동

This time, we will do group work. / Why don't we do group work? 인지 모르겠고 암튼 말함. I want you to make 6 groups of 5. 1,2,3,4,5 group 1, 2, 3 and 4, 5and 6. Did you meet your group members? I will assign the student number. 1,2,3,4,5. Please remember your number. 저는 발표도 시킬 생각이었기 때문에 중간에 뻥 비면 이상할 것 같아서 formative 안한다고 생각하고 수업을 쭉 할 거라서 we'll choose today's presenter in random order 한다고 말하고 And one more~ Worksheet. Have one Have one~ (role play를 스피킹에 남겨뒀기 때문에 이때부터 한 6분 남아서 랩을 하기 시작. 말이 빨라짐 급해짐) Look at the worksheet. The worksheet says I need your help!!! So, You will write your worry first for

2 minutes. And You will exchange, switch your writing, worry to friends. Like this. 1조에 가서 보여줌. 1 to 2, 2 to 3, 3 to 4, 4 to 5, 5 to 1. (원래, 1조 학생 이름 다 불러서 해줄려고 했는데 숫자로하면서 손으로 보여줌 어떻게 돌려가는지.) And you are going to give advice in writing for 4 minutes. Ready. Get Begin! (원래 2분 주고 순회지도 하고 따로 4분주고 순회지도 하고 할려고 했는데 시간이 없어서 한번에 하게됨) 그리고는 순회지도, 은혜~ You can think of your worry. Then, start with the simple one. bad habits? 칠판에 와서 You need to use the words we have learned and use 'If i were you~'. 4분단 쪽 가서 Oh OO, you are using the words we learned. Ok everyone time is up.

PRESENTATION

구상실에서 읽은 바로는 내가 적은 전개부분만 하는 거니까 발표 안 해도 되는거지만 안해야하는 거지만 이상할 것 같아서 대신 아주 간단하게 보여주고 넘어가기로 했습니다. 체크는 하는게 맞는 것 같아서. Let's share our outcome I will choose today's presenter 라고 하면서 페이지 적어뒀던 제일 오른쪽 칠판에 가서 좌석을 그립니다. 표로 5칸. 그리고 12345 쓰고. please하고는 today's presenters would be!!!! student number 2! Number 2 raise your hands. Yes I can see 6 presenters. From group 1, Ok 경희 stand up, please share your worry first. Oh, you are biting your nails when you feel nervous. Then, tell me the most impressive, creative, interesting advice you got. Oh, 재욱 said, if I were you, I would post the idol stars paper on the wall in my room? Wow it makes sense! 재욱, I love your idea. Then, you can have someone who observe you and you can change your behavior, 경희. Ok we have listened all the group presentation. Give big hands to everyone. (1조 듣고 전체 들은 척 그러고 보니 3분 가량 남았음.)

ROLE PLAY

Now this is our last activity. We will practice speaking. We'll do role play. Now I will rearrange you into pairs. 빠르게 말함. I prepares 4 role cards. 하면서 들고 있는 척 보여주고 나눠줌. Have one in each pair. Let me explain how to do the activity. There are 4 kinds of role cards. 칠판에 role card 그림. 네모 네 개 해서 teacher student like you and me. police and thief. Mom and Son. And it can be you and your friend. You can talk about your worry and advice. In pairs, You are going to write a brief script for 2 minutes. And perform in front of the class later. Ok 형식. Why don't you explain what we should do one more time to the class? (급한 와중에 이해 체크...) First, write a brief script. Second, practice speaking. Okay? I'll give you 2 minutes. Ready, Go! 순회지도 하는 중. It looks interesting. Oh you are using the words we learned. Ok. Did you finish writing the script. Then, this time i will give you rehearsal time. Be actor and actress. Start! OK. time is up. Now let's watch some pairs performance. 철수 and 기영, would you come to the front and show us your performance? 라고 중앙에서서 이야기 하는데 시간종료!

(role card에서 demonstration도 보여주고, 학생과 교사의 예시로 복도에서 뛰어서 다칠까봐 고민이야. 라던가 아니면 엄마와 아들에서 우리애가 밤에 게임만 해서 걱정이야. If I were you, I would kick off my son naked without any clothes. 이런거 준비했었는데 시간이 없어서 그냥 빠르게 시켰습니다. 그래도 덕분에 발표만 하면 speaking 활동 끝이니까 시간이 아슬아슬하게 맞춰 끝났습니다.)

10 경기 합격자 수업실연 합격 TIP

　　Reading 활동에서는 읽기를 통해 주어진 표를 완성하는 활동에서 gist reading을 먼저 진행한 뒤 reading for details로 나아가려 하였으나 시간관계 상 다하지 못할 것 같아 바로 reading for details를 하였습니다. careful reading에 대한 팁을 설명하고 고민을 적는 칸을 교사와 함께 해본 뒤 나머지 조언에 해당하는 칸을 짝 활동으로 함께 완성해 보도록 하였습니다. 이 때 교실 가운데로 나가 학생들에게 조언이 무엇인지 물어보고 어떻게 그러한 결과를 얻게 되었는지 물어본 뒤 읽기 방법에 대한 전략을 수정해주고 학생이 그를 통해 적절히 답을 이끌어내는 상호작용활동을 보여주었습니다. 읽기 후 전체학생 답을 확인 단계에서는 답이 상이한 학생들에게 정답을 찾은 학생들이 자신들의 답을 어떻게 찾았는지 해당 학생들에게 다가가 대화해주는 모습을 보여주고 상호이해를 확인하였습니다.

　　제 경우에는 판서가 많은 편이라 상대적으로 오류 수정활동에서 오늘 배웠던 표현과 단어의 활동이 고스란히 남아있었기 때문에 학생들이 판서를 통해서도 배운 것을 상기시키고 그에 따라 오류를 수정해 나갈 수 있었다는 모습을 보여주었습니다. 총 두 가지 오류를 고안하였지만 하나의 오류에 대해 다루고 나니 시간이 종료되었습니다.

　　기본적으로 학생들에게 많은 질문을 던지고 학생들의 답변을 재진술 하였으며 생각 되돌리기, 연결하기 식 대화를 진행하였습니다. 대화에 항상 칭찬과 피드백을 제공하였구요. 시간 관계로 인하여 교탁 앞으로 나가 학생들의 상호작용을 도와주고 함께 참여하는 모습은 한번만 보여주었습니다. 수업시연에서 가장 논쟁이 되는 부분은 시간 내에 모든 지시사항을 다 완수하는 것이 중요한가 또는 완수하지 못하여도 이미 앞서 한 시연의 모습이 활발한 의사소통과 유의미한 활동, 교사의 유창한 대화와 진행으로 인상적인 학생중심의 배움을 보여주면 되는 것인가의 문제입니다. 어느 하나 소홀히 할 수 없는 부분이지만 우선을 따지자면 지시사항을 모두 지키는 것이 가장 중요합니다. 수업 나눔의 3번 문제에서 절반정도 분량을 답변하지 못하고 끝난 것이 0.17이 감점된 결과이지 않았나 싶습니다. 이 역시 앞서 답변한 것에 대한 인상점수가 반영된 것으로 보입니다. 경기지역 수업 나눔의 경우 한 문제당 3분 분량의 답변을 해야 해서 많은 양의 내용을 풀어서 설명했습니다. 수업에서 했던 내용과 연결하여 구체적으로 설명하려고 노력하였습니다.

07 수업실연 개정안과 지역별 교육청 정책

2016년도부터 중등교원임용을 위한 2차 시험에 심층면접과 함께 수업실연의 내용과 평가에 변화가 생겼다. 가장 큰 변화는 2차 평가의 최저 점수를 80점에서 60점으로 낮추면서 전체적인 변별력을 높여 인원을 선발하고 있다. 경기와 강원지역에서는 각 지역 고유의 개정안을 제시하고 있으며 교육청에서는 지역 고유의 심층면접을 이용하여 교원의 지역 준비성을 평가하고자 노력하고 있다. 경기에서는 수업실연을 마친 후 수업 나눔 시간을 따로 마련하여 평가자가 수험자에게 수업실연에 대하여 질의 응답할 수 있도록 계획하고 있다. 우리가 하는 수업실연의 기본에는 수업하는 교사가 자신이 하는 수업에 대하여 정확히 이해하고 그 목적을 가지고 수업할 수 있도록 해야 한다는데 있다. 우리나라에서 추구하고 있는 교수학습계획의 방향을 살펴보면 다음과 같다.

① 교육과정을 기반으로 학습 목표와 내용에 맞도록 교수·학습 계획을 수립한다.
② 영어 학습에 대한 학생들의 동기를 유발하고, 흥미와 자신감을 유지할 수 있도록 교수학습 계획을 수립한다.
③ 학생들의 영어 사용 능력 및 인지적, 정의적 특성에 있어서의 개인차를 함께 고려한 교수·학습 계획을 수립한다.
④ 학생 중심의 과업 및 체험 학습을 통해 자기 주도적 학습이 이루어지도록 교수·학습 계획을 수립한다.
⑤ 의사소통능력 신장, 창의성 계발 및 인성 교육이 함께 이루어지도록 교수·학습계획을 수립한다.

이러한 전체적인 교수학습계획을 이해하면 수업과정에서 어디에 중점을 두고 무엇을 목적을 하여 가르쳐야 할지 방향을 잡을 수 있게 된다. 그리고 교수·학습 계획의 단계는 다음과 같이 이루어 질 수 있다.

① 교육과정에 제시된 교육목표와 성취 기준을 검토하고, 수업시간에 학습할 구체적인 학습 목표를 설정한다.
② 학습 내용(언어적 요소, 의사소통적 요소, 문화적 요소 등)을 분석하고 학생의 특성에 맞게 교재를 재구성할 수 있도록 교수·학습 계획을 수립한다.
③ 학습자 요인과 학습 환경 요인 (학생 수, 교실의 크기, 교실 구조, 교수·학습 기자재, 교수·학습 자료 등)을 파악한다.
④ 출발점 행동, 학습 활동 수행과정, 학습 목표 달성 여부 등을 진단하거나 점검하기 위한 평가 방법을 결정한다.
⑤ 교수·학습을 효과적이고 일관성 있게 수행하기 위하여 교수·학습 과정안을 작성한다.
   - 교수·학습의 대상과 시기
   - 교수·학습의 목표
   - 교수·학습 내용: 언어 기능, 의사소통 활동, 언어 형식, 소재(필요시 문화도 포함)
   - 교수·학습 자료: 교과용도서, 수준별 교수·학습자료, 시청각 자료 등
   - 교수·학습 활동 및 절차: 교수·학습 목표와 학습 내용에 적합한 구체적 학습절차 및 학습 활동, 활동별 시간 배분

⑥ 평가 방법 및 지도상의 유의점
- 지도안이 있는 지역의 경우, 지도안의 내용에서 벗어나는 수업 실연은 감점 혹은 정도가 심한 경우 불합격처리 될 수도 있다.
- 수업실연에 필요한 교재 및 교구는 수험자가 가상으로 시연한다.
- 다양한 교재 및 교구를 사용하는 모습을 보인다. 적절한 멀티미디어를 사용한다.
- 수업 실연시에 실제 교실상황이 최대한 반영될 수 있도록 노력한다.
- pair나 group work를 한다. 실제처럼 교실 안을 다니며 학생들에게 피드백을 제공한다.
- 평가자와 수험자와의 의사소봉은 철저하게 영어로만 진행한다.
- 용모, 복장, 구두나 악세사리등은 교사의 품위에 맞게 착용한다.
- 평가위원의 구성
  - 평가 위원 영어 교육 전문가 2인, 1급 정교사 자격증을 소지한 교육 경력 5년 이상의 현직 교사 2인, 각 시도 교육청 영어교과 담당 장학사 1인
- 채점 기준: 불합격 기준
  - 채점 기준표에서 원점수가 3점 미만을 얻는 경우
  - 60점 만점에서 총점이 36점을 넘지 않는 경우 (60%)

경기도 교육청
기본인성과 기초역량을 갖춘 미래 인재 양성

1. **교육과정 내용과 운영의 다양성을 강화합니다.**
   - 학생들이 자신의 삶과 연계한 다양한 체험을 하고, 자신에게 맞는 배움의 경로를 통해 고유한 빛깔을 가진 시민으로 성장할 수 있도록 학생이 주도하는 다양한 교육과정을 만들어가겠습니다.
   - 역량기반 교육과정, 배움중심수업, 성장중심평가, 프로젝트 학습 활성화를 통해 학생주도 학습을 강화하겠습니다.
   - 고교학점제 안착, 학생의 학습선택권 확대, 학교별 특색있는 교육활동, 삶을 설계하는 진로·직업교육으로 교육과정을 다양화하겠습니다.
   - 삶 속에서의 민주시민교육 내실화, 평화·통일교육 확산, 기후위기 대응 생태·환경교육으로 시민교육을 강화하겠습니다.

2. **학생의 배움을 학교에서 마을로, 미래로 확장합니다.**
   - 학생이 공동체 속에서 자신의 가치를 발견하고 키울 수 있도록 교육공동체가 함께 결정하고, 책임지며, 성장하는 학교자치를 통해 학교의 울타리를 넘어 시간의 한계를 넘어 학생의 배움을 마을로, 미래로 확장해 나가겠습니다.
   - 학생자치 활성화, 학부모 학교 참여 확대, 교직원 성장 지원으로 민주적 학교자치를 이루어 가겠습니다.
   - 혁신학교의 새로운 도약, 마을교육공동체 활성화로 마을과 함께 하는 혁신교육을 실천하겠습니다.
   - 디지털 교육환경 기반 조성, 미래형 학교공간 재구조화, 다양한 미래학교 설립 및 운영으로 미래교육 기반을 조성하겠습니다.

3. **현장과 적극적으로 소통하는 교육행정을 구현합니다.**
   - 교육환경의 변화에 맞는 행정체계의 조직화를 통해 교육행정을 혁신하고 행정의 중심을 현장에 두어 적극적으로 소통하며 교육 공공성을 강화해나가겠습니다.
   - 스마트워크 기반 업무효율화, 역량중심의 인사혁신, 교육지원청의 역할 변화로 교육행정을 혁신하겠습니다.
   - 유아교육 및 사학의 공공성 강화, 고교평준화 확대, 청렴 문화 정착으로 교육 공공성을 강화하겠습니다.

강원도 교육청

미래를 여는 학교

1. 수업성장 – 수업으로 성장하는 학교
- 학생 개별화 맞춤형 교육 강화
- 상시 연수를 통한 교원 전문성 향상
- 온·오프라인 연계 미래형 수업 활성화
- 온·오프라인 연계 수업 자료 개발 및 연수 운영
- 학생중심 온·오프라인 연계 대체학습자료 개발 및 보급
- 온·오프라인 연계 수업 유튜브연수 운영〈학기당 2회〉
- 교육지원청별 온·오프라인 연계 미래형 수업 연수 추진

2. 학교자치 – 시민을 키우는 학교
- 교육공동체의 학교 운영 참여 활성화
- 자유롭고 평등한 학교 문화 조성
- 교육과정에서 실천하는 민주시민교육
- 민주시민교육 핵심가치 주제 프로젝트 학습·동아리 활동 지원
- 읽고 만드는 미디어로 성장하는 시민교육
- 협력기관 연계 미디어교육 배움터 운영 확대

3. 평화·생태 – 더불어 실천하는 학교
- 체험·교류·교육의 장을 통한 평화 교육
- 지금·바로, 아이들을 위한 생태환경 교육
- 생태환경 교육과정 운영 활성화
- 교육과정 연계·융합 생태환경교육 운영 지원
- 교육공동체의 생태환경 역량 성장 및 실천 문화 확산 지원
- 생태환경교육 지역사회 연대와 협력체제 강화

4. 안전·건강 – 행복을 가꾸는 학교
- 감성미래학교 조성
- 교육공동체가 함께 하는 사회안전망 확대
- 교육정책 및 주요 시책사업 홍보 강화로 교육공동체 참여 활성화
- 적극적인 언론 소통으로 도민들의 강원교육 신뢰도 향상
- SNS 등 다양한 매체를 활용한 도민 소통으로 정책 공감대 확산

서울시 교육청
다양성이 꽃피는 공존의 혁신미래 교육

1. 교육비전
　　창의적 민주시민을 기르는 혁신미래교육: 교육의 중요한 기능인 지식의 축척·구성 및 학습의 지향을 "창의"에 담고, 시대정신과 추구하는 인간상을 고려하여 "민주시민" 육성의 목표를 명확히 하였으며, 교육의 혁신을 통해 희망의 미래를 열어가는 "혁신미래교육"을 제시합니다. 이는 "혁신미래교육"을 통해 자율과 창의성을 기르는 민주주의 교육이 단단히 뿌리내릴 수 있도록 우리 아이들에게 균등하고 질 높은 교육의 기회가 제공되어야 함을 의미합니다.

2. 교육지표
　　질문이 있는 교실, 우정이 있는 학교, 삶을 가꾸는 교육: '질문이 있는 교실, 우정이 있는 학교'는 우리 학생들이 공부하고 생활하는 가장 기본적인 공간인 교실의 이상적인 모습과 배려와 따뜻한 어울림이 넘치는 학교의 모습을 그리고 있습니다. '삶을 가꾸는 교육'은 삶의 참된 가치를 일깨워주는 '살림의 교육'으로서 우리 아이들에게 스스로 살아갈 수 있는 역량뿐 아니라 더불어 함께 살아가는 지혜를 키워주는 교육을 의미합니다.

- 학생 진로 맞춤형 교육과정 운영으로 학생의 학습 선택권 확대
- 많이 가르치는 교육 → 행복교육으로 교육 패러다임 변화
- 미래 사회가 요구하는 핵심역량을 위한 교육과정 및 교실 수업 개선
- 수능 중심 교육과정(문·이과 구분)에 따른 지식 편중 현상 개선
- 문·이과 통합형 교육과정 실현을 위한 종합적인 제도 개선 필요

3. 서울 교육 방향과 의미
- 서울 교육 방향: 다양성이 꽃피는 공존의 혁신미래 교육
- 생각이 자라는 교실, 함께 성장하는 학교, 미래를 여는 교육

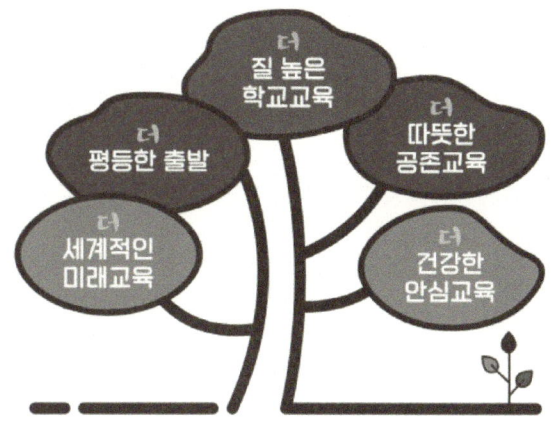

인천 교육청

학생 성공 시대를 여는 인천교육

1. **꿈을 실현하는 혁신미래교육**
   - 배움과 성장을 돕는 미래교육
   - 평화·공존을 위한 동아시아시민교육
   - 기초학력보장 사업 강화, 일반고 역량 강화 및 진로·직업 교육 확대
   - '책 읽는 도시, 인천' 만들기

2. **신뢰받는 안심교육**
   - 안전하고 건강한 학교환경 조성
   - '폭력 없는 인천, 생명존중 인천' 시민운동 확대
   - 공감·감성을 내면화하는 예술·체육교육

3. **자치와 협력의 소통교육**
   - 학교와 마을이 협력하는 마을교육공동체 활성화
   - 학교자치 시대를 열어가는 기반 지원
   - 발로 뛰고 귀를 여는 현장 중심의 정책수립

4. **모두를 책임지는 교육복지**
   - 더불어 행복한 교육복지
   - 무상·평등교육 지속 추진

5. **현장 중심의 교육행정**
   - 건강하고 행복한 조직 문화 조성
   - 현장 중심의 공정하고 청렴한 인천교육

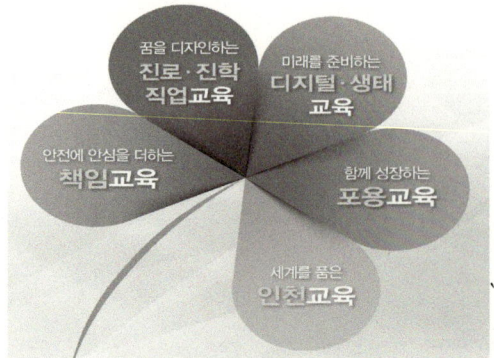

부산 교육청

맞춤 · 안심 · 공감 교육

1. **창의성과 감성을 키우는 미래교육 (학생성장 중심의 수업혁신)**
   - 미래지향적 학교교육과정 운영
   - 삶의 기본을 익히는 초등 교육과정, 꿈을 키우는 부산 자유학년제 운영
   - 꿈에 날개를 다는 고교학점제 기반 조성
   - 체험 중심의 맞춤형 진로교육
   - 배움이 즐거운 학생참여 중심 수업, 배움과 성장을 지원하는 학생평가
   - 자율적 학교 성장을 지원하는 동행장학
   - 교원 역량 강화 체계 구축, 안전하고 믿을 수 있는 책임교육

2. **핵심역량을 키우는 창의융합교육 (탐구 중심의 창의적 인재교육)**
   - 생각하는 힘을 키우는 재미있는 수학교육
   - 핵심역량을 키우는 통합적 독서교육
   - 미래핵심역량 강화를 위한 SW교육, 클라우드 시스템 기반 수업혁신 지원
   - 인공지능 및 에듀테크 활용 수업혁신, 영어교육 및 국제이해교육
   - 대입 변화에 대응하는 맞춤형 진학지도
   - 내일이 행복한 전문기술인재 양성

3. **소통과 협력의 참여교육 (존중과 배려의 인성교육)**
   - 존중과 배려 중심의 학생 생활교육
   - 존중 · 자율 · 연대 중심의 학교 민주시민교육
   - 역사의식 기반의 평화통일교육
   - 공감 · 감성 플러스 학교예술교육
   - 신나는 체육수업, 청렴한 학교운동부, 함께 뛰고 즐기는 학교스포츠클럽

제주 교육청
올바른 인성, 생각하는 힘을 키우는 미래교육

1. 모든 아이를 위한 학습회복
- 학습부진 원인의 통합적·전문적 진단 및 지원
- 기초 학력 향상 지원체제 강화, 교과 방과후 활동(학습역량 도움 프로그램) 운영
- 교육과정 연계 독서교육
- 학생 참여·활동 중심 교수·학습 전개, 과밀학급 해소

2. 건강하고 안전한 학교
- 코로나19 대응 학교 감염병 예방 관리 강화
- 건강하고 안전한 학교 급식 운영, 학생 비만 예방
- 맞춤형 체육교육 및 학교스포츠클럽 활성화
- 안전한 교육환경 조성, 학교폭력 예방교육(회복적 생활교육) 활성화

3. 학생 맞춤형 통합 지원
- 학교·교육청 혼디거념팀 운영
- 정서위기 학생 유형별 맞춤형 지원, 다문화·탈북학생 지원 강화
- 장애학생, 난독학생 유형별 맞춤 교육, 학생 중독 예방, 학업중단 위기학생 통합지원

4. 역량을 키우는 교육과정 운영
- 유아·놀이 중심 유치원 교육과정 운영, 기본에 충실한 초등 교육과정 운영
- 학생 성장을 지원하는 중학교 "제주 꿈끼이음123 교육과정" 운영
- 학습 선택권을 확대하는 고교학점제 기반 조성, 특성화고 학생 역량 강화

5. 4차 산업혁명 시대 미래교육
- 미래교육을 위한 스마트 학습 환경 구축
- 원격수업 콘텐츠 개발 및 우수 콘텐츠 공유 활성화
- 그린스마트 미래학교 조성 지원, 학생활동 중심 창의융합 프로그램 운영
- 창의융합교육 실현 위한 미래체험 공간 구축
- 4차 산업혁명 시대 맞춤형 미래진로교육 강화

6. 기후위기 대응 지구생태시민교육
- 환경학습권 보장을 위한 교육환경 조성, 학생실천중심 탄소중립 생태환경교육 활성화
- 교육과정연계 多가치 주제통합 수업운영
- 건강생태학교 운영, 학교 숲 조성

대전 교육청
미래를 선도하는 창의융합 교육

1. 문·예·체 체험 중심의 인성교육
- 지역사회 연계 효교육 운영
- 나라사랑교육 내실화
- 학교도서관 연계 독서교육 활성화
- 대전시민과 함께하는 대한민국 어린이 놀이 한마당 개최
- 예드림(藝-Dream)홀 구축
- 예술교실 환경개선
- 학교스포츠클럽 활성화 지원 확대

2. 창의성을 키우는 융합교육
- 노벨과학 꿈키움 프로젝트 강화
- 지역 연계 AI 융합 체험 교육 운영
- AI·SW 교육과정 지원 강화
- 체험중심 수학교육 내실화
- 메이커교육 운영

3. 대전형 그린스마트 미래학교 조성
- 학교 안 생태전환교육 체험장 구축
- 에듀테크 기반 미래교실 구축
- 사용자와 함께하는 학교공간혁신사업 확대

충북 교육청
지속 가능한 공감 동행 교육

충북 미래교육의 핵심은 사람이다. 모든 아이들이 삶의 주도성을 확립하고, 학교, 지역, 국가가 지원하는 체제를 확립한다. 학생들의 주도성을 역량으로 길러내는 역량중심 교육과정으로 전환하고, 디지털과 친환경을 기반으로 언제 어디서든 온·오프라인 융합교육이 가능한 미래교육환경을 구축한다. 사람 중심의 가치를 바탕으로 학교 구성원 모두가 주체가 되어 시민성을 실천하고, 학교교육과정의 자율성을 확보하며, 학교·대학·마을·지역사회가 지역교육생태계를 조성하여 모두의 성장을 지원한다.

1. 교과교실제 운영
각 교과마다 특성화된 전용교실을 갖추고 학생들이 수업시간 마다 교과의 특성에 적합하게 구축된 교과교실로 이동하며 수업을 듣는 학교 운영 방식이다. 최근에는 교과교실제가 전용교실의 구축과 학생 이동에 국한되지 않고 초점을 맞추었지만, 최근에는 '학생 맞춤형 교육'과 '학생 참여형 활동수업의 활성화' 등 수업 혁신에 초점을 두고 운영됨

2. 정책방향
중학교 자유학기제, 자유학년제 실시/ 고등학교 고교학점제 도입에 따라 이를 뒷받침하는 학생 맞춤형 교육, 학생참여형 활동수업을 활성화하는 교과교실제 추진

3. 운영내용
- 학교의 여건 및 특색을 반영한 다양한 교육과정 운영, 교과교실 활용 학생참여형 수업, 블록 타임제 운영 등 교과교실제 운영 세부계획을 수립하여 추진함
- 교과교실을 정규 수업뿐만 아니라 선택형 방과후 학교와 연계하여 활용하여 시설의 활용도를 높이고, 교과 특성을 살린 방과후 수업 실시로 방과후 학교에 대한 학생 만족도 상승
- 교육과정–수업–평가–기록의 일체화를 위해 학생 참여형 수업 운영
- 시간제근무 기간제 교사 활용한 확대학급(주로 영어, 수학) 운영
- 교과교실, 교과존, 홈베이스 등을 활용한 학습결과물 및 우수작품 상설 전시를 통해 학습활동에 대한 정보와 우수사례 공유
- 학교 여건을 반영한 블록타임수업 주간 운영으로 수업과 평가(수행평가) 실질적으로 연계되는 교육과정 운영

핵심가치	주도형	미래형	참여형	협력형
혁신 과제	주도성 성장 교육과정	학생 배움중심 교육공간	디지털 시민성	공동체 기반 지역교육 생태계

전북 교육청
실력과 바른 인성을 키우는 전북교육

1. 교과 교육과정

현재의 교육	• 과다한 학습량으로 진도 맞추기 수업 • 어려운 시험 문제로 수포자 양산, 높은 학업 성취도에 비해 학습 흥미도 저하 • 지식 암기식 수업으로 추격형 모방 경제에 적합한 인간
미래의 교육	• 핵심 개념 중심의 학습 내용 구성 • 진도에 급급하지 않고 학생 참여 중심 수업을 통한 학습 흥미도 제고 • 창의적 사고 과정을 통한 선도형 창조 경제를 이끌 창의융합형 인재 양성 • (학습량 적정화) 단편적인 지식이 아니라 다양하게 전이 · 확장이 가능한 교과별 핵심개념 및 원리 중심으로 학습량 적정화 • 대부분 선진국의 교과 교육과정은 "넓고 얕게" 학습하기 보다는 "적은 양을 깊이 있게 (less is more)" 가르쳐 학습의 전이를 높이고 심층적인 학습을 통해 사고력을 신장하고 학습의 질을 높이는 것을 중시하고 있음

2. 우리가 추구하는 교육과정

- 미래 사회에는 지식을 많이 습득하는 것 보다 학습한 내용을 바탕으로 새로운 환경과 상황 속에서 선택, 조정, 통합하여 문제를 해결하고 새로운 가치를 생성할 수 있는 창의융합형 인재가 필요합니다.
- 지금 우리 교육은 성취도는 높지만 학생들의 흥미와 학습 동기를 효과적으로 이끌어 내지 못하고 있습니다.
- 우리 교육과정은 문 · 이과 칸막이 없는 인문 · 사회 · 과학기술에 관한 기본 소양을 토대로 미래 사회가 요구하는 인문학적 상상력과 과학기술 창조력을 두루 갖춘 창의융합형 인재를 양성하는 교육과정입니다.
- 미래 사회 역량을 갖춘 능동적이고 창조적인 인재 육성, 그 안에 우리의 미래가 있습니다.
- 학생의 참여 수업을 통해 학습의 흥미와 동기를 높여, 배움의 즐거움을 경험하게 함으로써 행복교육을 구현하는 것이 우리 교육과정의 핵심입니다.
- (교실 수업 개선) 토론·협력학습, 탐구학습 등 교수·학습 방법 및 평가 방법 개선을 통해 핵심 역량 함양 및 행복한 교실 구현

교육지표

배움이 즐거운 교실

함께 성장하는 교육

꿈을 키우는 학교

전남 교육청
미래를 가꾸는 창의적이고 포용적인 사람

(1) 공부하는 학교를 만듭니다.
- 성장단계별 평가 및 학습이력관리시스템 운영
- AI튜터와 함께하는 맞춤형 책임교육강화
- 전남형 온라인 학습 J-MOOC 실현
- 모든학교에 원어민 보조 교(강)사 지원
- 자유학기제와 고교학점제 연계활동 확대
- 교직원 역량강화 연수 활성화
- 학습권과 교권이 조화로운 학교문화 조성

(2) 모든 학생의 꿈을 소중하게 키웁니다.
- 진로, 진학, 직업교육 통합 지원체제 구축
- 다양하고 내실있는 학교예술교육 활성화
- 다문화 강점 강화교육을 통한 글로벌 인재 육성
- 특수학교(급) 진로교육 지원 강화
- 지역 사범대학 교육감 추천 전형 및 임용제도 도입
- 지방공무원 지역인재 채용 확대

(3) 마을과 함께 사람을 키웁니다.
- 학생 1인당 전남교육 기본소득 지급
- 민관산학 통합 교육발전협의 체제 구축
- 가정-학교-지역사회와 함께하는 인성교육
- 학교시설 개방 확대 및 주민복합시설 확충
- 지역업체 제품 구매 활성화
- ESG 전남교육지원센터 운영

(4) 따뜻하고 안전한 교육환경을 만듭니다.
- 무상 교복·체육복 및 수학여행비 지원 확대
- 학생 등·하교 0원 버스 실현
- ADHD 진단 및 치료비 무상 지원
- 아침을 여는 건강한 간편식 제공
- 선제적으로 대응하는 안전한 학교 환경 구축
- 대규모 개발지구 고등학교 설립 추진

(5) 신뢰받는 행정으로 교육가족의 긍지를 높입니다.
- 열심히 일하는 교직원이 대우받는 공정한 인사
- 학교기본운영비(학급운영비 포함) 지원 확대
- 교육공무직 직종 간 차별 해소 및 근무여건 개선
- 물품 계약 및 시설공사 투명성 강화
- 교원능력개발평가와 성과상여금 폐지 추진

경남 교육청
배움이 즐거운 학교 함께 배우는 경남 교육

1. 함께 배우며 미래를 열어가는 민주시민 육성
(1) 배움중심의 새로운 교육
(2) 더불어 행복한 교육복지
(3) 안전하고 건강한 교육환경
(4) 소통과 공감의 교육공동체
(5) 깨끗하고 공정한 지원행정

2. 정책 방향
(1) 학생의 개별성을 삶의 힘으로 만드는 교육
(2) 모두의 가능성을 실현하는 미래역량 중심 교육
(3) 모든 곳이 학교, 모든 이가 선생님이 되는 교육

3. 학교급별 학생 공약 지도
(1) 미래역량 중심 학생 개별 맞춤교육
- 미래역량 중심 학생 개별 맞춤 교육을 강화
- 빅데이터-AI 활용 교육과정 운영 권역별 기초학력지원센터 운영
- 체계적인 학습종합클리닉센터 운영(진단-코칭-치료집중지원)
- 도농간 교육격차해소를 위한 아이톡톡 국영수 심화과정 개설 학교폭력 조기 감지 온라인 시스템 도입

(2) 지역 맞춤형 진로·진학 지원을 강화
- 빅데이터-AI 활용 교육과정 운영 고교학점제 지원을 위한 온라인교실 운영
- 대입정보센터 신설
- 다양성교육지원센터 운영
- 과밀학급 해소를 위한 학교 신설

광주 교육청

단 한명의 아이도 포기하지 않는 광주 교육

미래를 함께 여는 혁신적 포용 교육

(1) 교육상: 미래를 함께 여는 혁신적 포용교육
- '미래를 함께 여는'은 다양한 교육 구성원과 더불어 소통하고 협력하여 미래사회 변화를 준비하고 열어가자는 의미
- '혁신적 포용교육'은 다양성, 책임, 공정, 미래, 상생의 5대 가치를 중심으로 학생이 꿈꾸는 미래를 실현하기 위한 인간중심 교육을 의미

(2) 교육지표: 창의성을 갖춘 가슴 따뜻한 세계민주시민
- '창의성을 갖춘'은 광주학생이 미래사회를 주도하기 위해 반드시 필요한 창의성과 인지적 능력을 쌓는 것을 의미
- '가슴 따뜻한 세계민주시민'은 따뜻한 정의적 품성과 예술적 감수성을 함양하고, 기후위기와 생태환경 등에 관심을 갖는 세계민주시민으로 성장하는 것을 의미

(3) 슬로건: 단 한 명의 아이도 포기하지 않는 광주교육
- 학생이 처한 환경과 상황에 따라 차별받지 않고 교육적 혜택을 통해 자신이 원하는 미래를 실현할 수 있도록 지원하는 공정과 책임 교육을 의미
- 교육구성원의 다양한 상황을 인정하고 누구나 원하는 교육을 받을 수 있도록 지원하는 다양성 교육을 의미

(4) 실천 공약
- 다양성을 담은 실력광주로 아이들이 꿈을 실현: 공부를 원하는 학생에게는 더 깊은 공부를, 취업을 원하는 학생에게는 미래기술을 반영한 직업교육을, 새로운 교육을 원하는 학생에게는 새 교육을 받게 하여 아이들 각자가 바라는 미래의 삶이 현실이 되도록 다양한 실력을 갖추도록 한다.
- 미래사회 변화에 대비한 미래교육을 추진: AI를 비롯한 4차 산업혁명 기술을 학교교육에 도입해 미래교육을 활성화하고, AI 중점도시 광주에 걸맞게 지역 인재와 지역 자원을 활용한 미래교육을 추진한다.
- 보편적 교육복지를 완성: 모든 아이들이 차별 없이 공평하게 교육받으며 자신의 꿈을 키우고 실현할 수 있도록 보편적 교육복지를 완성해 갈 것이며, 단 한 명의 아이도 소외받지 않고 교육적 혜택을 누리며 자신이 꿈꾸는 미래를 실현할 수 있도록 지원한다.

CHAPTER 02 영어과 수업실연 기출문제 모음

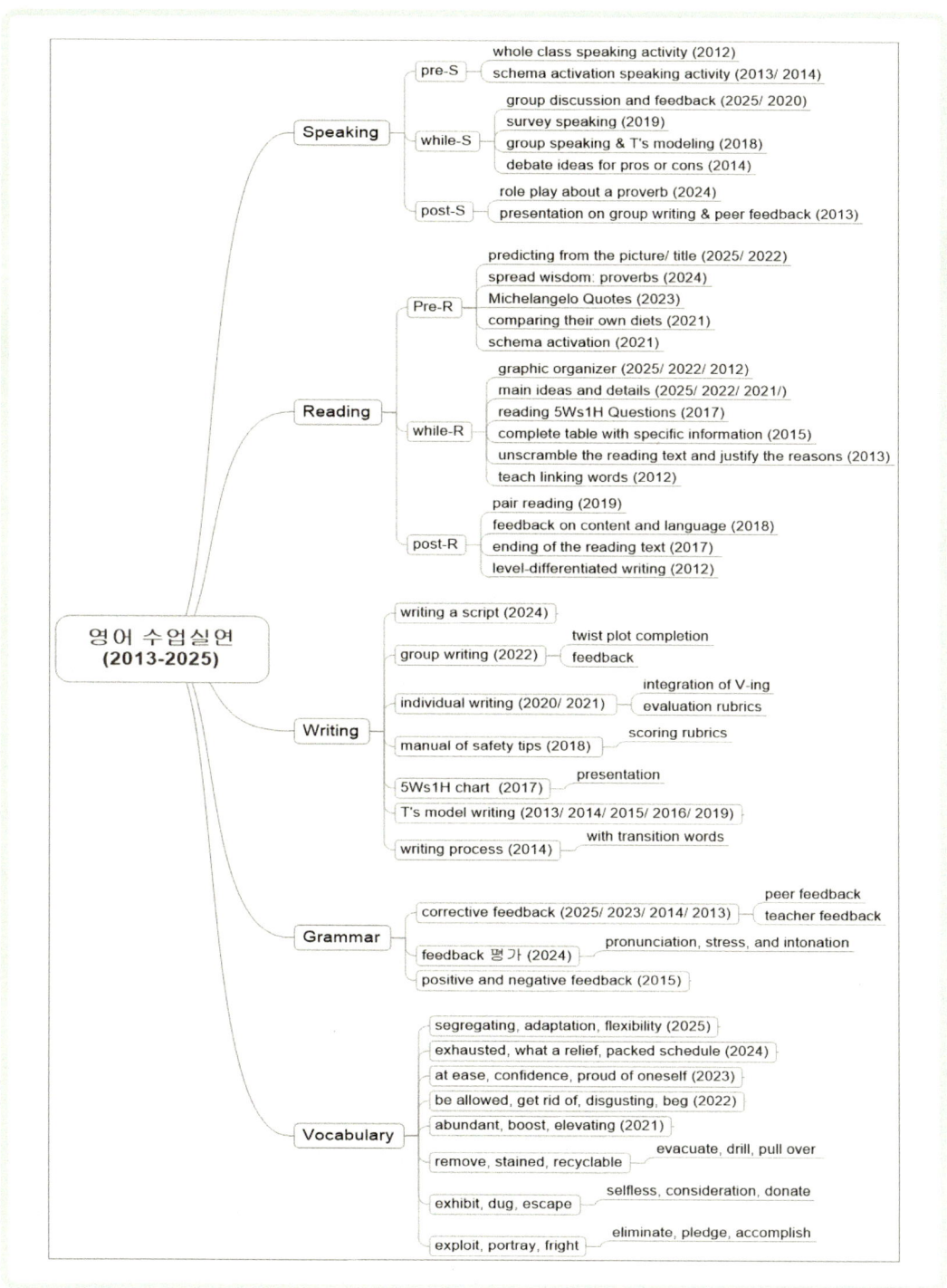

2025학년도 중등학교 교사 임용후보자 선정경쟁시험 2차 수업실연
(영어 version)

이름		수험번호		관리번호		감독확인	

1. Class information

Grade	Students	Work	Aids	Time	Feedback
High school 1	24	GW, PW, IW	Tablet, Beam projector, Online dictionary	100mins. (block time)	peer/ teacher

2. Directions

- Answer Examinee's Answer 1-4.
- Use the board properly.
- Present the lesson based on your lesson planning.

3. Unit Title: Designing Inclusive Environment

Examinee's Answer 1.	⟨Implement Pre-reading with Material 1.⟩ A. T lets Ss guess the topic using the picture image (children, elderly, persons with wheelchair....). B. In pairs, T lets Ss guess the features of Universal Design using the picture image. C. T explains ONE of the three underlined vocabulary and lets Ss guess the meaning.
Examinee's Answer 2.	⟨Implement Reading with Material 2.⟩ A. T lets Ss to complete the graphic organizer in ⟨material 2⟩. B. T asks Ss to complete the features and examples in the organizer.
Examinee's Answer 3.	⟨Implement Pre-writing with Material 3.⟩ A. As a group activity, T lets Ss to discuss and analyze "how Universal Design is used in our school." B. T asks Ss to complete the group organizer with problem, solution, and expectations.
Examinee's Answer 4.	⟨Implement Writing with Material 4⟩ A. As a group activity, T lets Ss to write a 'Suggestion writing for our school' in ⟨material 4⟩. B. T lets Ss to exchange ⟨peer feedback⟩ to each other for Creativity, Organization, and Language Use. C. T provides corrective feedback on the Ss' language errors.

Note: T=teacher, Ss=students

4. Lesson Procedure

Class	Skills	Objectives
1-2	Listening, Vocabulary	
3	Speaking	
4-5	Reading	
6-7	Listening, Reading, Writing, Role-play (지도안 작성)	Students will be able to: • read and understand the meaning of Universal Design. • read and understand the details of the text. • write their problem and solution to make school environment better.
8		

2025학년도 중등학교 교사 임용후보자 선정경쟁시험 2차 수업실연

(한국어 version)

이름		수험번호		관리번호		감독확인	

1. 학급 정보

학년	학생수	활동조	수업자료	시간	평가
고등학교 1	24명	개별/전체/ 모둠	태블릿, 빔프로젝터, 보드, 온라인 사전	100분 (연속차시)	교사/자기 평가

2. 지시문

- 1번부터 4번까지 답하시오.
- 판서를 적절히 활용하시오.
- 수업 계획에 따라 수업을 순차적으로 진행하시오.

3. 제목: Designing Inclusive Environment

수험생 작성부분 1	자료1을 이용하여 다음 사항들에 대한 읽기 전 활동을 진행하시오. A. 그림의 이미지(children, elderly, persons with wheelchair....)를 이용하여 주제를 추측하기 B. Universal Design의 특성을 추측하기 위하여 짝 말하기 활동 진행 C. 세 단어에서 *segregating, adaptation, flexibility* 하나의 의미를 설명하고 학생들에게 추론할 기회 제공
수험생 작성부분 2	자료2을 이용하여 다음 사항들에 대한 읽기 중 활동을 진행하시오. A. 글을 읽고 〈자료 2〉를 활용한 글의 세부사항을 위한 읽기 활동하기 B. 〈자료2〉의 특성과 예시를 이용하여 표를 완성하기
수험생 작성부분 3	자료3을 이용하여 다음 사항들에 대한 쓰기 전 활동을 진행하시오. A. "Universal Design이 우리학교에서 어떻게 시행"되는지 토론하고 분석하는 조 활동 진행하기 B. 문제, 해결책과 전망에 대하여 도표 완성하기
수험생 작성부분 4	자료4을 이용하여 다음 사항들에 대한 쓰기활동을 진행하시오. A. 자료4에 우리 학교환경을 개선하기 위한 글 쓰기를 조 활동으로 진행 B. Creativity, Organization, Language Use에 대하여 〈동료피드백〉 교환하기 C. 언어적 오류에 대하여 교사의 피드백 제공

4. 수업 절차

차시	언어능력	목표
1-2	듣기와 어휘	
3	말하기	
4-5	읽기	
6-7	듣기, 읽기, 쓰기와 역할극 (지도안 작성)	학생들은 다음의 수업목표를 성취할 수 있다: - Universal Design의 의미를 읽고 이해할 수 있다. - 글의 상세내용을 읽고 이해할 수 있다. - 학교 환경을 개선하기 위한 글을 쓸 수 있다.
8		

⟨Material 1⟩

Designing Inclusive Environment

Universal Design refers to the idea of creating environments, products, and learning experiences that are accessible and usable by all people, regardless of their age, ability, disability, or background—without the need for adaptation or specialized design. A fundamental principle of Universal Design is <u>flexibility</u>, which ensures that spaces and products can be used in multiple ways to meet different needs.

A classroom might provide lecture transcripts for deaf or hard-of-hearing students, audio descriptions for visually impaired learners, and interactive hands-on activities for kinesthetic learners, ensuring that no one is excluded. Adjustable-height desks allow both wheelchair users and standing individuals to use the same workspace comfortably. Traditional accessibility solutions often result in <u>segregating</u> users—such as separate entrances for wheelchair users or isolated assistive technology labs.

Universal Design, however, promotes integration by creating spaces that everyone can use together. Ramps and stairs can be designed as a single entrance, eliminating the stigma of a "special" access route. Another feature is minimizing the need for <u>adaptation</u>. Many environments require costly and inefficient last-minute adaptations. Universal Design anticipates diverse needs from the beginning, such as smart home technology that allows voice, touch, or app-based controls to accommodate different mobility and sensory needs.

⟨Material 2⟩

Universal Design	
Definition	
Feature 1	Feature 2
Examples • •	Examples • •

⟨Material 3⟩

Group name		Members	
Problem	Solution	Expectations	
• •	• •	• •	

⟨Material 4⟩

Suggestion Writing for Our School

Problem:
_____

Solution:
_____

Expectation:
_____

⟨Peer Feedback⟩

Content	Descriptions	Evaluation		
		1	2	3
Creativity	Does the writing offer fresh ideas, unique perspectives, or imaginative solutions?			
Organization	Does the text use paragraphs, headings, or transitions effectively to guide the reader?			
Language Use	Are sentences grammatically correct with proper punctuation, spelling, and syntax?			

2024학년도 중등학교 교사 임용후보자 선정경쟁시험 2차 수업실연

이름		수험번호		관리번호		감독확인	

1. 학급 정보

학년	학생수	활동조	수업자료	시간	평가
고등학교 1	24명	개별/전체/ 모둠	태블릿, 빔프로젝터, 보드, 온라인 사전	100분 (연속차시)	관찰/자기 평가

2. Directions

- 1번부터 3번까지 답하시오.
- 판서를 적절히 활용하시오.
- 수업 계획에 따라 수업을 순차적으로 진행하시오.

3. UNIT TITLE: SPREAD WISDOM

Examinee's Response 1.	⟨Pre-writing (Reading)⟩ A. T lets Ss guess one of the underlined words/grammar (exhausted/ what a relief/ packed schedule) in contexts. B. T makes Ss choose a proverb in ⟨Material 1⟩ related to a situation given by the T. C. T makes Ss find out the theme for the play in ⟨Material 2⟩ based on the title proverbs in ⟨Material 1⟩.
Examinee's Response 2.	⟨Writing⟩ A. T has Ss as a group choose one proverb and set background. B. T lets Ss write a script for a play based on ⟨Material 3⟩. C. T provides guidelines on how to write using ⟨Material 4⟩.
Examinee's Response 3.	⟨Post-Writing (Speaking)⟩ A. T has Ss practice their role in role play and present their script. B. T provides Ss with feedback on pronunciation, stress, and intonation.

Note: T=teacher, Ss=students

4. Lesson Procedure

Class	Skills	Objectives
1–2	Listening, Vocabulary	
3	Speaking	
4–5	Reading	
6–7	Listening, Reading, Writing, Role-play (지도안 작성)	1. Students will be able to understand the main ideas after they read wisdoms and listen to the related themes. 2. Students will be able to understand themes of role play and write a script for a role play. 3. Students will be able to perform the role play in groups.
8		

〈Material 1〉 Reading Passage

Proverbs around the World

- A smooth sea never makes a skilled sailor. (English proverb)
- Experience is the best teacher, but <u>tuition</u> is high. (Norwegian proverb)
- Fear makes a wolf bigger than he is. (German proverb)
- Great oaks grow from little acorns. (English proverb)
- Still waters run deep. (African proverb)
- A tree is known by its fruit. (Jewish proverb)

〈Material 2〉 Reading Passage (Genre: skit) (*exhausted, what a relief, packed schedule*)

- Title (Proverb): A smooth sea never makes a skilled sailor.
- Setting: At a high school during a challenging week of quizzes and projects
- Character (description): Alex (high school grade 1), Jessica (friend), Paul (friend)

Scene #1 〈Script (lines)〉 During a challenging schedule

Paul:	We have a <u>packed schedule</u> with a lot of quizzes, projects, and assignments.
Alex:	Right. It has been a tough week.
Paul:	(Looking <u>exhausted</u>) I stayed up late last night for preparing math quiz!
Alex:	Math quiz is not so easy to get high scores.
Jessica:	I agree with you. I'm also having a hard time.
Paul:	How can we improve it?
Alex:	I can help you if you want.
Jessica:	<u>What a relief</u>!

Scene #2 〈Script (lines)〉 After a challenging schedule

Paul:	The exam is over.
Alex:	We learned a lot after all.
Jessica:	Storm makes us stronger.
Paul:	(Bouncing ball) This reminds me of the proverb, "A smooth sea never makes a skilled sailor." Let's go and play basketball.

〈Material 3〉 (Skit worksheet)

Group Name: _____   Members: _____

Title (Proverb):
Setting:
Characters (description): (more than 3 is OK)

Scene #1
Character 1:
Character 2:

〈Material 4〉

<u>Self-Assessment Criteria</u>

Criteria	Scale		
Does the writing contain all the requirements?	1	2	3
Is the script well organized?	1	2	3
Is the language clear and accurate?	1	2	3

2023학년도 중등학교 교사 임용후보자 선정경쟁시험 2차 수업실연

이름		수험번호		관리번호		감독확인	

1. Class Information
- Middle school 3rd grade, 26 students
- Unit: Beyond Your Comfort Zone!
- Evaluation: Observation, Peer-feedback
- Group work(GW), Pair work(PW), Individual work(IW)
- Aids: Beam projector, Online dictionary

2. Directions
- Answer Examinee's Answer 1-3.
- Use the board properly.
- Present the lesson based on your lesson planning.

Examinee's Answer 1. (20mins)	⟨Warmup⟩ A. T lets Ss infer the meaning of 'Beyond Your Comfort Zone!' based on the quote in ⟨Material 1⟩. B. T describes her experiences how to 'Beyond her Comfort Zone!' C. T lets Ss discuss and acknowledge the reason why they need to go 'Beyond Your Comfort Zone!'.
Examinee's Answer 2. (20mins)	⟨Pre-Reading⟩ A. T explains the characteristics of each zone in ⟨Material 1⟩ and let Ss read and apply their own experiences to the zones in ⟨Material 2⟩. B. T explains underlined THREE vocabulary words using the example sentences. C. T lets Ss fill in the blanks using the emotion words.
Examinee's Answer 3. (35mins)	⟨Writing⟩ A. T provides her example writing and let Ss complete the chart in ⟨Material 3⟩ with pair work. (Words, phrases are possible not only with sentences.) B. T provides corrective feedback on the Ss' errors on their language use or vocabulary use.

Note: T=teacher, Ss=students

3. Lesson Procedure

Class	Skills	Objectives
6-7	Speaking, Reading and Writing (지도안 작성)	Students will be able to: - discuss the reasons they need 'Beyond Your Comfort Zone!' - write about themselves or their daily lives. - give peer-feedback to each other.

⟨Material 1⟩

⟨Michelangelo Quotes⟩
The greater danger for most of us lies not in setting our aim too high and falling short; but in setting our aim too low, and achieving our mark.

There are FOUR psychological zones that individuals may experience when they are faced with challenges, change, or personal development. The comfort zone is a psychological state where a person feels at ease, experiences low anxiety, and operates within familiar routines and boundaries. The fear zone is a mental space characterized by discomfort and anxiety, often experiencing fear of the unknown or failure. The learning zone is a state of active engagement and cognitive growth, where individuals willingly embrace new experiences, acquire knowledge and skills, and seek personal development. The growth zone represents self-improvement and continuous personal and professional development beyond their previous capabilities.

My experience taught me that growth comes from embracing challenges, out of comfort zone. Initially, singing in a choir seemed daunting; my voice lacked melody. Despite this, I decided to join, craving a challenge. Among the choir members, I felt <u>at ease</u>, which boosted my <u>confidence</u>. With their support, my voice steadily improved. As the performance approached, I pushed beyond my comfort zone and practiced relentlessly. When the day arrived, I sang confidently, hitting every note. Afterward, I was <u>proud of myself</u>. From a hesitant singer, I had become a confident choir member, thanks to stepping out of my comfort zone.

⟨Material 2⟩

Choose the appropriate word(s) for each blank box in the diagram from the ⟨Word Box⟩. Note that some words can be used more than ONCE.

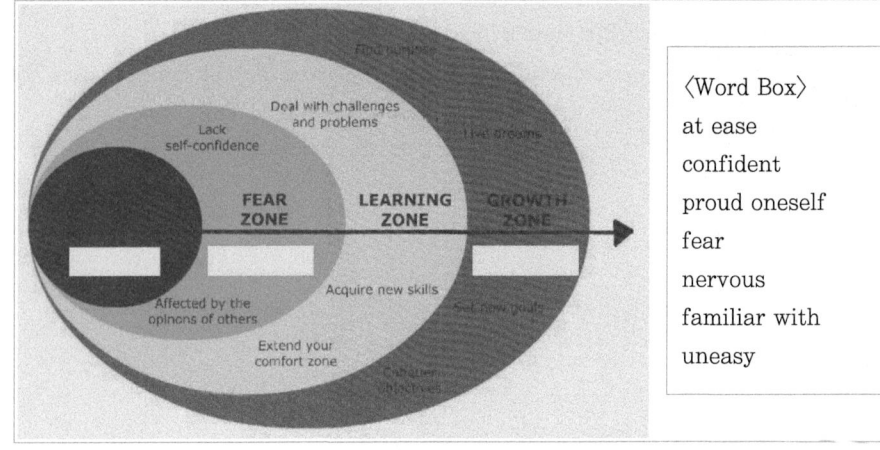

⟨Word Box⟩
at ease
confident
proud oneself
fear
nervous
familiar with
uneasy

⟨Material 3⟩

My Comfort Zone: _____
New Goal: _____
Reasons for New Goal: _____
Difficulties expected: _____
Plans of Action: _____

⟨My Text⟩
I feel comfortable when _____.
My new goal is to _____.
The reasons are _____.

2022학년도 중등학교 교사 임용후보자 선정경쟁시험 2차 수업실연

이름		수험번호		관리번호		감독확인	

1. Class Information
- Middle school 3rd grade, 26 students
- Block time (90 minutes)
- Unit: How to Make Friends!

2. Directions
- 답안 1부터 4까지 시연하시오.
- 자신이 쓴 지도안에 맞게 시연하시오.

Examinee's Answer 1.	⟨Pre-reading⟩ A. Let Ss predict the content of the story on the topic. B. Let Ss share their experiences about the topic in pair work. C. Teach ONE of four underlined words (be allowed, get rid of, disgusting, beg).
Examinee's Answer 2.	⟨Reading⟩ A. Let Ss look for gist of the text. B. Use a graphic organizer T developed to check the Ss' reading comprehension.
Examinee's Answer 3.	⟨Writing⟩ A. Make a group and assign each group role to Ss. B. Let Ss complete the missing parts of the story including twist plot. C. Check Ss' group work and provide feedback.
Examinee's Answer 4.	⟨Speaking⟩ A. Engage Ss in a group presentation. B. Give scoring rubric for evaluation for peer assessment. C. Let Ss in pairs, discuss how to resolve the conflict. D. Provide T's feedback to group presentation.

Note: T=teacher, Ss=students

3. Lesson Procedure

Class	Skills	Objectives
6-7	Speaking, Reading and Writing (지도안 작성)	Students will be able to: - read the text to predict the main ideas from the title. - read the text to find out the details for comprehension. - fill the twist plot to lead to the unexpected result. - give peer-feedback to each other.

⟨Material 1⟩

Enemy Pie

It was all good until Jeremy Ross moved into the neighborhood, right next door to my best friend Stanley. I did not like Jeremy Ross. He laughed at me when he struck me out in a baseball game. He had a party on his trampoline, and I wasn't even invited. But my best friend Stanley was. Jeremy Ross was the one and only person on my enemy list. I never even had an enemy list until he moved into the neighborhood. But as soon as he came along, I needed one. I hung it up in my tree house, where Jeremy Ross was not allowed to go.

Dad understood stuff like enemies. He told me that when he was my age, he had enemies, too. But he knew of a way to get rid of them. I asked him to tell me how. "Tell you how? I'll show you how!" he said. He pulled a really old recipe book off the kitchen shelf. Inside, there was a worn-out scrap of paper with faded writing. Dad held it up and squinted at it. "Enemy Pie." he said, satisfied. You may be wondering what exactly is in Enemy Pie. I was wondering, too. But Dad said the recipe was so secret, he couldn't even tell me. I decided it must be magic. I begged him to tell me something—anything. Now, of course, this got my mind working. What kinds of things — disgusting things — would I put into a pie for an enemy?

I brought Dad some weeds from the garden, but he just shook his head. I brought him earthworms and rocks, but he didn't think he'd need those. I gave him the gum I'd been chewing on all morning. He gave it right back to me. I went out to play, alone. I shot baskets until the ball got stuck on the roof. I threw a boomerang that never came back to me. And all the while, I listened to the sounds of my dad chopping and stirring and blending the ingredients of Enemy Pie. This could be a great summer after all.

....

Enemy Pie was delicious! After dessert, Jeremy rode his bike home but not before inviting me over to play on his trampoline in the morning. He said he'd teach me how to flip. As for Enemy Pie, I still don't know how to make it. I still wonder if enemies really do hate it or if their hair falls out or their breath turns bad. But I don't know if I'll ever get an answer, because I just lost my best enemy.

> * Plot twists: a sudden unexpected variation or reversal that is often associated with a joke in a novel, short story, movie, or TV series and colloquially used in reference to an act of intentionally or unintentionally swapping two objects

〈Material 2〉 Teacher's material for reference only

> The story is narrated by a young boy. He was looking forward to a really great summer. That was until Jeremy Ross moved into the neighborhood! After laughing at him when he struck him out at baseball and not inviting him to his trampoline party, Jeremy Ross became the first person on the boy's enemy list. He talked to his dad about his problem. His dad said he has a sure fire but secret way of getting rid of enemies. Enemy Pie! The boy is excited by the prospect of his enemy's hair falling out or his breath turning bad but there's more to the secret plan than just pie! His dad says the key to the plan is that he had to spend the entire day playing with Jeremy if he wanted to get him off his enemy list!
>
> After a pretty fun day hanging out with Jeremy, the boys go inside to have dinner. As dad serves up the much-anticipated enemy pie his son starts to panic. He has to stop him from eating the pie and being poisoned or something because Jeremy's actually not that bad after all! After dinner, Jeremy invites his new friend to his house to play on his trampoline the next morning and the boy realizes that he's just lost his best enemy! The enemy pie turned enemy into friends.

〈Material 3〉 Completion of Plot Twist

I brought Dad some weeds from the garden, but he just shook his head. I brought him earthworms and rocks, but he didn't think he'd need those. I gave him the gum I'd been chewing on all morning. He gave it right back to me.

....
....
....

But, Enemy Pie was delicious! As for Enemy Pie, I still don't know how to make it.

2021학년도 중등학교 교사 임용후보자 선정경쟁시험 2차 수업실연

이름		수험번호		관리번호		감독확인	

1. Class Information
- High school 2nd grade, 30 students
- Block time (100 minutes)
- Unit: Healthy Food, Healthy Life

2. Directions
- 답안 1부터 4까지 시연하시오.
- 자신이 쓴 지도안에 맞게 시연하시오.

Examinee's Answer 1.	⟨Using Material 1, include the following tasks.⟩ A. Stimulating students' schema about their favorite dishes B. Engaging students in pairs to compare theirs from the menu in diagram
Examinee's Answer 2.	⟨Using Material 2, include the following tasks.⟩ A. Asking students to read the text and find the main idea B. Checking students' understanding of the details of the text C. Teaching one of the three underlined words in the text (abundant, boost, elevating)
Examinee's Answer 3.	⟨Using Material 3, include the following tasks.⟩ A. Engaging students in a group writing activity using ⟨Material 3⟩ B. Facilitating students' participation C. Giving feedback on the outcomes
Examinee's Answer 4.	⟨Using Material 4, include the following tasks.⟩ A. Engaging students in an individual writing activity using ⟨Materal 4⟩ B. Giving scoring rubric for evaluation with each specific criteria C. Students' peer review on their writing

Note: T=teacher, Ss=students

3. Lesson Procedure

Class	Skills	Objectives
6-7	Speaking, Reading and Writing (지도안 작성)	Students will be able to: - read the text to find out the main ideas. - read the text to find out the details for comprehension. - express their opinions about the ideal menu for healthy diet. - write a suggestion of a new dish for the school lunch menu.

〈Material 1〉

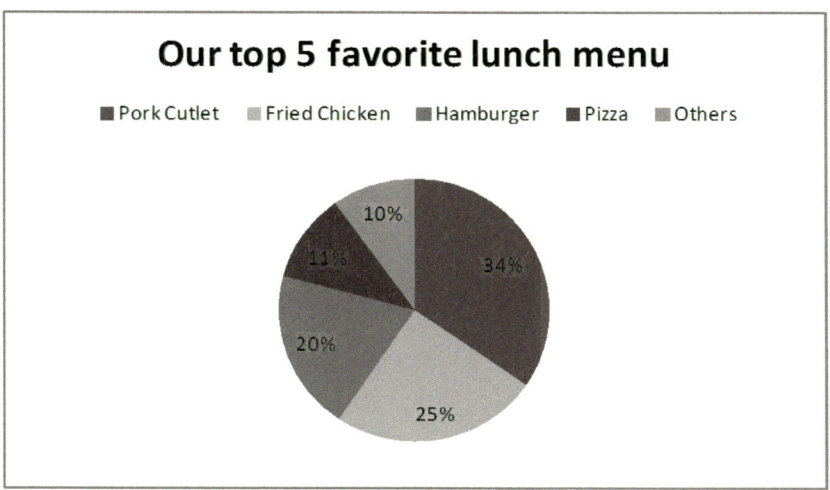

〈Material 2〉

The teenage years are a time of rapid growth and development, so a healthy balanced diet is particularly important. Healthy, active young people can have large appetites. If you're a teenager, it's important to eat well-balanced meals, rather than too many snacks that are high in fat, sugar or salt. The diet can have a significant impact on the brain's function. A brain-healthy diet that is abundant in salmon, eggs, nuts, and pumpkin seeds can boost your brain power, memory. Eating more nuts and seeds may be good for functioning the brain and for increasing the bone density and elevating your moods.

〈Material 3〉 Our group's New Dish for the School Lunch Menu

Dish Name	Ingredient	Reasons

〈Material 4〉

Suggestion Letter for New Lunch Menu

....
....
....
....
....

2020학년도 중등학교 교사 임용후보자 선정경쟁시험 2차 수업실연

이름		수험번호		관리번호		감독확인	

1. Class Information
- High school 1st grade, 30 students
- Block time (100 minutes)
- Unit: Your Future Jobs

2. Directions
- 답안 2부터 4까지 시연하시오.
- 자신이 쓴 지도안에 맞게 시연하시오.

Examinee's Answer 1.	⟨Using Material 1, motivate students by asking questions about the topic.⟩ A. Ask questions related to Material 1. B. Complete the chart on the promising jobs in the future in pairs. C. Utilize multimedia as a whole class.
Examinee's Answer 2.	⟨Using Material 2, design a reading activity.⟩ A. Ask students to read and find the main ideas of Material 2. B. Ask students to read and check the understanding of the details of Material 2. C. Teach the underlined the target form, be + -ing, after reading of the text.
Examinee's Answer 3.	⟨Using Material 3, encourage students in a speaking activity⟩ A. Form a group and design a speaking activity using Material 3. B. Ask students to discuss to complete the job descriptions and required skills. C. Act as a facilitator while speaking activity. D. After the speaking activity, give feedback on the students' presentation.
Examinee's Answer 4.	⟨Using Material 4, engage students in writing.⟩ A. Design a writing activity using Material 4. B. Integrate with the target form, 'V-ing'. C. Provide the teacher's evaluation rubric including detailed criteria.

3. Lesson Procedure

Class	Skills	Objectives
6-7	Reading and Writing (지도안 작성)	Students will be able to: - read the text about general topic and find out the main ideas. - read the text to find out the details. - discuss and share their opinions about general topic. - write about their future jobs.

〈Material 1〉

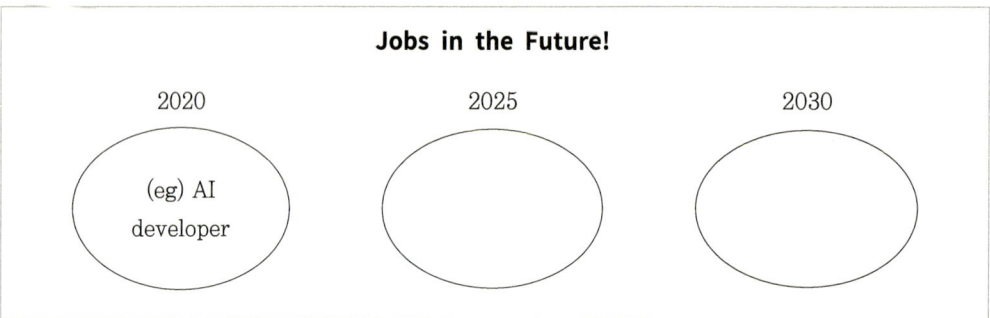

〈Material 2〉

Many <u>will be doing</u>... and a lot of them haven't even been invented yet. Many of tomorrow's jobs will likely result from today's scientific and technological advances. But most jobs of the future probably don't exist yet, and a lot of them haven't even been imagined. According to one estimate, almost two thirds of kindergarten students will have occupations that don't currently exist. Of course, many of today's occupations will continue to be part of the future, but they'll undergo changes just like everything else. Many of tomorrow's jobs will likely result from today's scientific and technological advances, especially artificial intelligence. Many <u>will be pursuing</u>... in the near future. Drone traffic monitors..., and self-driving mechanic, who repairs a self-driving car. There are many other jobs like these.

〈Material 3〉

1. Discuss descriptions and skills for the future jobs
    - Drone traffic monitor
    - Self-driving car mechanic
    - Weather modification police
    - (your group's own idea)

2. Complete the following:

   Career Guide for Future Jobs

   (1) Drone traffic monitor
       - Description: Drone traffic monitor can detect passing vehicles and recognize their classes on the traffic. It helps to reduce travel time, congestion, and emissions.
       - Skills: good computing skills, eyes for details, driving license

   (2) Self-driving car mechanic   (3) Weather modification police   (4) ☐
       - Description: - Description: - Description:
       - Skills: - Skills: - Skills:

〈Material 4〉

Write a paragraph about a future job for yourself and follow the instructions:

〈Instructions〉
- Your future job and reason(s)
- Description and required skills
- Use will be V-ing
- Write 5 sentences or more.

A Future Job for Me

_____
_____
_____
_____

2019학년도 중등학교 교사 임용후보자 선정경쟁시험 2차 수업실연

이름		수험번호		관리번호		감독확인	

1. Class Information
- Middle school 3rd grade, 24 students
- High and Low intermediate level mixed
- Block time (90 minutes)
- Unit: Small Activity for the Earth

2. Directions
- 답안 1부터 4까지 다 시연하시오.
- 자신이 쓴 지도안에 맞게 시연하시오.

Examinee's Response 1.	〈Using Material 1, design a pre-reading activity〉 A. Encourage students to activate their background knowledge related to Material 1. B. Encourage students to read for the main idea of the text. C. Teach One of the three underlined words. (**remove**, **stained**, **recyclable**) in the text.
Examinee's Response 2.	〈Using Material 1 and 2, design a post-reading activity〉 A. Ask students to do pair reading and find details using Material 1 and Material 2. B. Encourage students to do pair work while circulating the class. C. Confirm with students for their comprehension after reading of the text.
Examinee's Response 3.	〈Using Material 3, encourage students in a speaking activity〉 A. Design a survey speaking activity using Material 3. B. Act as a facilitator while speaking activity. C. After the speaking activity, give feedback on either content or language use.
Examinee's Response 4.	〈Using Material 4, engage students in writing.〉 A. Design a group writing activity using Material 4. B. Provide the teacher's modeling before students' writing.

3. Lesson Procedure

Class	Skills	Objectives
6-7	Reading and Writing (지도안 작성)	Students will be able to: - read the text and comprehend the detailed information. - speak about experiences related to their own or others' daily lives. - write their suggestion for recyling.

⟨Material 1⟩

Let's Recycle Properly!

First, non-recyclables like plastic bags or broken glass are in the recyling bin together. Different types of recycling such as paper, plastic and glass are mixed together. We should place items individually in the correct bins.

Second, recyclables are not prepared properly, such as not rinsing containers. Don't forget to rinse them off before putting in the recycling bin.

Third, a pizza box that is <u>stained</u> with grease or food is not <u>recyclable</u>. We should not forget that there are also two sides to a pizza box. If there's a side that's not oily, tear that off and recycle it. Unless you have a clean cardboard pizza box, please do not put cheesy, oily pizza boxes in your recycling bin. Throw out all food and food-<u>stained</u> paper when possible.

Fourth, you often put the bottle with label in the bin. If you have time, please <u>remove</u> all tape and all plastic wrap that might be attached to the bottle. The bottle recycling processors will greatly appreciate it, if you remove all plastic materials from the bottle.

⟨Material 2⟩

Problems	Suggestions

⟨Material 3⟩

	never	seldom	often	always
Do you rinse recyclable items off before recycling?				
Do you put recyclable items in a recycling bin?				
Do you remove the label from the plastics before recycling?				
(Make your own question) _____?				

⟨Material 4⟩

Our Suggestions for Better Recycling

The most serious problem of recycling habits in our class is that _____
_____.

We should _____
_____.

2018학년도 중등학교 교사 임용후보자 선정경쟁시험 2차 수업실연

이름		수험번호		관리번호		감독확인	

1. Class Information
- High school 1st grade, 30 students
- High and Low intermediate level mixed
- Block time (100 minutes)

2. Directions

Examinee's Response 1.	⟨Using material 1, design a while-reading activity⟩ A. Encourage students to think about the content and organization of the text. B. Teach three underlined words for both high and lower level students. (*evacuate, drill, pull over*) C. Check students' understanding of the key vocabulary in the text.
Examinee's Response 2.	⟨Using material 1, design a post-reading activity⟩ A. Check comprehension of students after reading the text. B. Give feedback on students' comprehension. C. Encourage students to think why specific behaviors are necessary in earthquake safety.
Examinee's Response 3.	⟨Using material 2, encourage students in a speaking activity⟩ A. Design a group speaking activity with the picture cards showing the safety tips for an earthquake in school. B. Provide the teacher's modeling. C. Give feedback on both content and language use.
Examinee's Response 4.	⟨Using material 3, engage students in writing their own safety manual.⟩ A. Design a group writing activity for a manual of safety tips that can occur in school. B. Present specific scoring criteria for evaluating students' writing work. (peer evaluation) C. Facilitate and observe the group activity.

3. Lesson Procedure

Class	Skills	Objectives
6-7	**Reading and Writing** (지도안 작성)	Students will be able to: - read the text and comprehend the detailed information. - speak about earthquake safety tips with their group members. - write a school manual of six earthquake safety tips with their group members.

⟨Material 1⟩

Earthquake Safety Tips!

All natural disasters are frightening, but what makes earthquakes unique is that they give no warning. Therefore it is important to know how to prepare for an earthquake, what to do during an earthquake, and what to do after an earthquake hits. Here are some earthquake safety tips for before, during, and after an earthquake.

Safety Tips for Before an Earthquake
1. Choose earthquake safe locations in every room of your house, office, school, or any place that you <u>evacuate</u> on a regular basis.
2. Be sure you know how to turn off the water, gas, and electricity in your home. A multi-function tool may be needed.
3. Secure heavy items, such as shelves, bookcases, mirrors, and light fixtures to the wall. Anything that could fall over during an earthquake and land on a person is a hazard. Do not leave any heavy items on shelves, because they will fall off the shelves during an earthquake.
4. Make sure you have a fire extinguisher in your home, and that you know where it is stored and how to use it.
5. Conduct school earthquake <u>drills</u> regularly and prepare a school earthquake evacuation plan.

What to Do During an Earthquake

1. Drop down to your knees. This way the earthquake cannot knock you over.
2. Take cover. This is one of the most important safety measures to be taken during an earthquake. Cover your head and neck with your arms or an object so that you are protected from any debris or furniture falling during the earthquake. For example, if you are in a bed, protect your head with a pillow.
3. Hold on. If you have anything sturdy near your safe spot, hold on to it tight until the shaking stops.
4. If you are outside, get away from anything that could fall on you, such as trees, power lines, buildings, and houses.
5. If you are in a car, pull over to a spot that is away from trees, power lines, and buildings. Wait in the car until the shaking stops.

〈Material 2〉 6 Tips for Safety in School

(teacher's direction)

⟨Material 3⟩ Safety Manual

Six Tips for Safety in Our School

Direction: Write down six tips for safety in school. Add pictures for the tips.

2017학년도 중등학교 교사 임용후보자 선정경쟁시험 2차 수업실연

이름		수험번호		관리번호		감독확인	

1. Class Information
- Middle school 3rd grade, 30 students
- Low intermediate level
- Block time (90 minutes)
- Reading & Writing

2. Directions

Examinee's Response 1. (수업실연 X)	⟨Using material 1, teach a vocabulary activity⟩ A. Teach the underlined words (escape, exhibit, dug) and check Ss' understanding of the key vocabulary. B. Let Ss read for details using 5Ws1H Questions.
Examinee's Response 2.	⟨Using material 1, design a post-reading activity⟩ A. Check comprehension of students after reading the text. B. Let Ss make an ending of the reading text. C. Give feedback on students' content and language use of writing. D. Give helps to groups as needed.
Examinee's Response 3.	⟨Using material 2, encourage students in a writing activity⟩ A. Design a group writing activity showing the picture card. B. Let Ss complete 5Ws1H Chart. C. Provide T's modeling of story writing. D. Give feedback on both content and language use.
Examinee's Response 4.	⟨Using material 3, engage students in writing of 5Ws1H Chart.⟩ A. Design a group writing activity of writing a story with the picture. B. Present specific scoring criteria for evaluating students' writing work. (peer-feedback) C. Facilitate and observe the group activity. D. Make sure that Ss not concentrate on language use.

Note: Ss=students, T=teacher

3. Lesson Procedure

Class	Skills	Objectives
6-7	Reading and Writing (지도안 작성)	Students will be able to - read the text and comprehend the detailed information. - make an ending of the story. - write a story with the picture for 5Ws1H Chart with their group members.

〈Material 1〉

Stories Behind Pictures

It was a hot summer day in Chicago. The Kemper family decided it was a good day to go to the Brookfield Zoo. Janet and Kevin Kemper had two children: Thomas, 3, and Sally, 6 months. Thomas loved going to the zoo. He liked watching all the animals, but he especially loved the gorillas.

The Kempers went straight to the gorilla <u>exhibit</u>. There were six adult gorillas and a three-month-old baby gorilla. In the Brookfield Zoo, the animals are not in cages. They are in large areas <u>dug</u> out of the ground. These areas have fences around them so the animals cannot <u>escape</u> and people cannot fall in.

But, three-year-old boys are good climbers. While the Kempers were watching the gorillas, little Sally started to cry. Kevin took her from Janet, and Janet looked in her bag for a bottle of juice. In those few seconds, Thomas climbed up the fence.

(결말) ....
....
....
....

〈Material 2〉 5Ws1H Chart

	5Ws1H Chart
who	
where	
why	
when	
what	
how	

⟨Material 3⟩

Direction: Write down your story for the picture. Complete the chart of 5Ws1H.

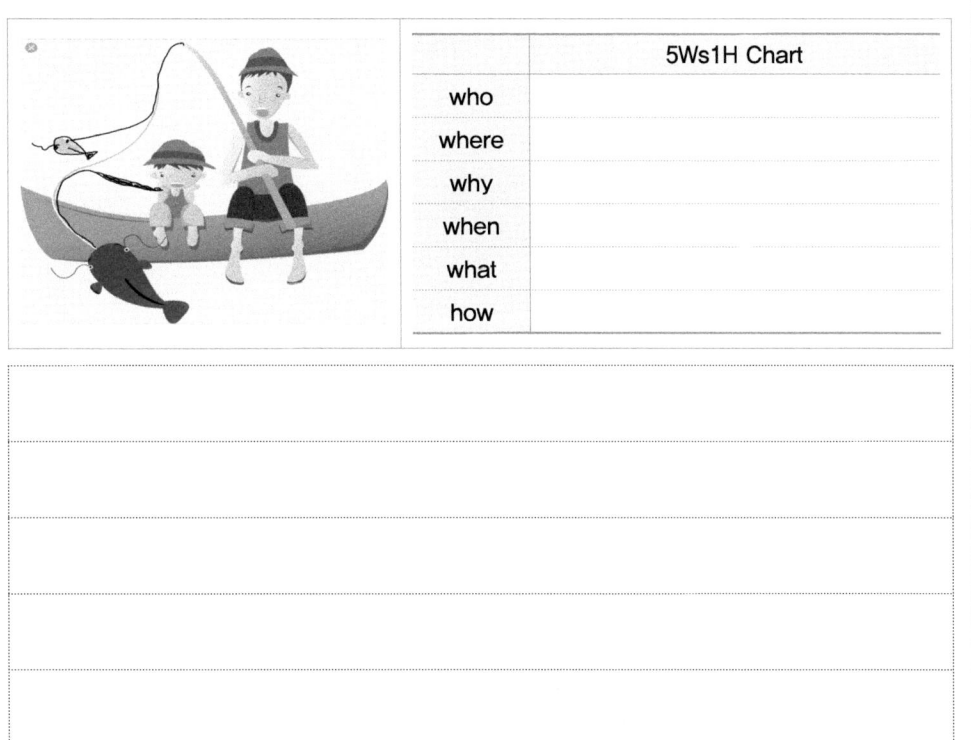

	5Ws1H Chart
who	
where	
why	
when	
what	
how	

[실제 신문기사 참고자료 'Thomas and Gorillas']

A woman saw him and shouted, "Stop him!" A tall man reached up to get him, but it was too late. Thomas fell down the other side of the fence. He fell eighteen feet onto the hard concrete floor. He lay very still, with blood on his head. Janet and Kevin shouted for help. People crowded around the fence, and someone ran to get a zoo worker. But before the zoo worker arrived, a gorilla went over to Thomas. It was Binti Jua, an eight-year-old mother gorilla. She had her baby gorilla on her back. With one arm she picked up the little boy. She carried him carefully over to a door, walking on three legs. There she put Thomas down so a zoo worker could get him. Janet and Kevin ran to the door, too. Thomas was badly hurt and had to go to the hospital, but after a few days he was better. The story was on the evening news in Chicago. Some people cheered and others cried when they heard it. But many of them thought about that mother gorilla and asked themselves, "What is she doing in a zoo? What is the difference between a gorilla and me?"

2016학년도 중등학교 교사 임용후보자 선정경쟁시험 2차 수업실연

이름		수험번호		관리번호		감독확인	

1. Class Information
- Middle school 3rd grade, 30 students
- Low intermediate level
- 45 minutes
- Reading & Writing

2. Directions

Examinee's Response 1.	⟨Using material 1, teach a vocabulary activity⟩ A. Teach three words and fill in the chart of reading of ⟨table 1⟩. B. Check students' understanding of the key vocabulary.
Examinee's Response 2.	⟨Using material 1, design a post-reading activity⟩ A. Let students use the underlined phrase (if I were you). B. Make a summary of the reading text.
Examinee's Response 3.	⟨Using material 2, encourage students in a writing activity⟩ A. Design a group writing activity showing the picture card. B. Provide the teacher's modeling of story writing. C. Let students write about students' own worries and advice using the target phrase D. Give feedback on both content and language use.
Examinee's Response 4.	⟨Using material 2, engage students in speaking activity⟩ A. Make a group. B. Plan a speaking activity that students will promote students' participation. C. Let students talk about their own worries and advice using the target phrase. D. Make sure that students not concentrate on language use.
Examinee's Response 5.	⟨closing activity⟩ A. Provide formative assessment that checks if students have achieved the objectives of using the target phrase.

3. Lesson Procedure

Class	Skills	Objectives
6-7	Speaking, Reading and Writing (지도안 작성)	Students will be able to - summarize the reading and fill in the chart. - write about students' own worries and advice using the target phrase. - talk about their own worries and advice using the target phrase.

⟨Material 1⟩

Worry: (Name 1)
I have one serious problem. I am 152 cm now. But I'm worried that I wouldn't grow any taller. You know my parents are not very tall. So, I take some supplements and herb medicine. Do you think it will work?

Advice: (Name 2)
Don't worry about it too much. You will grow in no time. And think about all the good points about yourself. My brother is also about your height but he's very popular in his school. He has a good personality. Focus more on your strengths.

Advice: (Name 3)
Do you take supplements and herb medicine? I don't think it will be good for your health. And if you use the smartphone too much, you can lean forward, which leads to poor posture. So, if you reduce the time, you will look at least 3 cm taller.

⟨Table 1⟩

Worry	Advice
(Name 1)	(Name 2) : (Name 3) :

⟨Material 2⟩ Writing

Name :

My worry is that _____.

Advice : If I were you,
I would _____.
I would _____.
I would _____.

2015학년도 중등학교 교사 임용후보자 선정경쟁시험 2차 수업실연

이름		수험번호		관리번호		감독확인	

- Title: Unit 5. Good People Around Us.
- Period: 8차시 중 4차시
- Reading & Writing Integrated Lesson

1. Class Information

- Middle school 3rd grade, 30 students
- Low intermediate level

2. Directions

Examinee's Response 1.	⟨Using material 1, teach a vocabulary activity⟩ A. Teach three words using guessing strategy, selfless, consideration, donate B. Check students' understanding of the key vocabulary.
Examinee's Response 2.	⟨Using material 1, design while Reading & Writing Activities⟩ A. Give questions to students to check their understanding of the reading text in Material 1. B. Have students find out specific information in pairs to complete Table1 in Material 1.
Examinee's Response 3.	⟨Using material 2, engage students in Writing activity⟩ A. Make a group. B. Present a model writing to help them to write with. C. Have students write in groups about a good friend in our school using Material 2 in a process-based writing. D. Make sure that students not concentrate on language use.
Examinee's Response 4.	⟨Using material 2, encourage students in an Evaluation activity⟩ A. Have students present their writing, and provide a scoring rubric with 3 criteria for peer evaluation of each group's presentation. B. Give 2 feedbacks after the presentation. One should be a positive feedback and the other should be a negative feedback.

3. Lesson Procedure

Class	Skills	Objectives
4-5	Reading and Writing (지도안 작성)	Students will be able to - figure out the meaning of new words in the context. - complete the table using the specific information of the reading text in pairs. - present their writings in groups to introduce a friend as a good person.

⟨Material 1⟩

Look For Good People Around Us

In this world, there are good people around us and you can find some in your neighborhood. Yujin is the most selfless classmates. I believe that **selflessness** should be the basis of every relationship. If a person truly cares about you, they'll get more pleasure from the way they make you feel, rather than the way you make them feel. The good news is that charitable giving is contagious. For example, she tidies the classroom every morning even it isn't the day of her turn to clean the classroom. She also carries her disabled friend's bag to the class every day. It's so refreshing to see someone in my age to show such **consideration** for others. Mr. Kahn is a good person. He came to Korea 10 years ago. His business has thrived and he tries to reward his success to his neighborhood. He offers free meals to homeless people. He also **donates** money to an organization for muti-cultural families. Most people support charities in one way or another, but often we struggle to make donations as often as we think we should. Although many people would like to leave a gift to charity in their will, they forget about it when the time comes.

⟨Table 1⟩

Yujin	Mr. Kahn
Why is she a good person? - She cleans the classroom every day. -	Why is he a good person? - -

⟨Material 2⟩

Good People in our school

Group _____

I would like to introduce _____ as a good person.
I think _____ is a good person, _____.
1) because (he/she) is _____.
2) because (he/she) is _____.
3) because (he/she) is _____.

CHAPTER 03 교실 영어 표현

01 Teaching Vocabulary (Middle school)

Basic Expressions for Vocabulary

What's in here?
Take some.
Can you say it?
That is something different.
Can you guess the meaning in the passage?
Repeat after me.
Who knows what 'keep fit' means?
Something to do with ~
Possibly.
Who knows what jogging is?
Who can write it on the board for me?

T: We are going to have a discussion today, but first I want you to read a short passage about an American businessman. He's a businessman, with an office job, and he wants to keep fit. Who knows what 'keep fit' means? Keep fit?
S: This jacket fits me.
T: Well, that was a good sentence, but 'keeping fit' has a different meaning. Anyone? No?
S: Er, sport? Something to do with sport?
T: Possibly, yes. Some people do exercises every morning, like this (mimes) to keep fit, to keep healthy, to keep your muscles in trim. If you are fit, you can run a long way. OK?
S: Yes.

T: Do you do exercises sometimes?
S: Yes, I do.
T: Why? …to…?
S: To? …er… to keep fit.
T: Good! He wants to keep fit. Now, some people in the USA go jogging every day. Jogging; who knows what jogging is?
S: (Students mime)
T: Yes. Everybody knows what jogging is. It is running. Running slowly to keep fit. Who can write it on the board for me? You? Thank you. j..o..g..g..ing. Excellent. Now, open your book to page 27.

Tip

수업의 마지막 부분에서는 간단한 게임을 이용하여 그 날 배운 어휘를 복습할 수 있다. 교사는 간단하게 그 날 배운 어휘를 카드에 적어서 두 명씩 짝을 지은 학생들에게 나누어준다. 학생들은 단어가 적힌 카드의 면을 바닥에 대고 교대로 카드를 집어서 상대방이 카드에 쓰여 있는 단어를 알아맞힐 수 있도록 영어로 설명을 한다.

예 A: If you travel somewhere you need this.
  B: A ticket.
  A: No, it's something you carry, big.
  B: A Bag.
  A: Yeah, nearly. Where do you put your clothes?
  B: A suitcase.
  A: That's right. (A then gives the card to B)

	suitcase		T.V.
	in a hurry		dig
		exhausted	

Key Expressions

1. 단어 소개의 말

• First, • Before we begin,	I want to	• check that • make sure	you know	• the meaning of a few words. • what these words mean.

• I want • I'm going	to teach you	• a few new • some useful	words that we shall need	• later on today. • for a dialogue. • for some role play.

2. 학생들에게 어휘의 의미를 추측하게 할 때

• Who knows • Does anyone know • Can anyone tell me	• what this word means? • when you would use the word, _____? • where you would see(hear) the word, _____?

• I'll give you	• a clue. • some help.	• It's something to do with _____. • You might hear a ___ saying it.	
• Let's see if you can guess.		• I'll give you	• a context: _____. • an example: _____.

• Not really. • Nearly right! • Almost right! • Not quite! • Wait!	• Listen to me and I'll • Watch me and I'll	• explain. • give you (another) example. • show you. • draw one. • act it.

3. 문맥상에서 어휘 보기

Now look at the	picture opposite.		
	sentence	• before. • carefully. • after _____ • beginning ___	What	• does that tell you? • does the word ___ tell you? • is the author talking about?
So what could this word		• be about? • refer to? • mean?	

4. 어휘 설명의 예

Look. The word	ends in	• 'tion' • 'ness'	so it must be a noun.
	begins with 'un' so it means 'not' something.		

5. 시각 자료 이용하여 어휘 설명하기

• Who knows • Does anyone know	what	• this is, • we call this, • this person is doing, • we say when _____,	in English?
		this	• does, • shows,	

02 Teaching Listening Skills (Middle School Level)

Basic Expressions for Listening

Can you answer questions?
Fill in the blanks on the handout.
You check the answers after solving the problems.
We'll go over a section of (a part of)~
Listen to it and summarize (sum up).
Are you ready to~?
Pick out a word (phrase)
After listening, refer to~
While listening, think about~

T: Today, we'll be listening to a section of a story about American Thanksgiving. While listening to the story, please pay attention to the key points. You don't really have to understand every single word. I'm going to ask you some questions after listening. So, it might be a good idea to take some notes while listening. Are you ready? (After listening) Did you all find the main ideas from the story?

S: (A moment of silence) Can we listen one more time?

T: Well, that's it. We'll listen to it again later. Could anyone tell us briefly what this was about?

S: (A student briefly summarizes the story.)

T: Very good. Now, I'm going to pass out these worksheets to you. Please complete the worksheet while listening or after listening. We're going to go over that together. OK, are you all ready to listen carefully and answer these questions?

Tip

듣기를 할 때 아무 목적 없이 듣는 것보다는 듣기 본문 중 주요한 내용을 질문으로 만들어 제시함으로써 학생들로 하여금 특정한 목적과 방향을 갖고 보게 하는 것이 바람직하다. 질문은 일반적인 이해 수준을 평가하는 비교적 쉬운 문제, 본문의 주요한 내용에 대해 집중적으로 묻는 문제, 상위권 학생들이 도전할 만한 문제 등 다양한 난이도를 갖은 문제를 고르게 배합하여 준비하는 것이 효과적이다.

Key Expressions

1. 배울 내용 소개하기

Listen carefully, and then	• complete the worksheet.
While listening,	• answer some question on the sheet.
After listening,	• fill in the blanks.

Who	• can tell us • knows	about this topic?
What	do you know	

2. 듣기 준비하기

• You're going • You're about	to listen and	• answer these questions. • fill in the blanks. • solve the problems.	I'll	• start the audio clip. • play the audio. • begin my talk. • begin reading.

3. 집중적 듣기 연습

Listen again and	• notice how • tell me why	• his/her • my	voice	• rises. • changes. • falls.
• Study • Read • Think about	• the questions • the problems • the points	• on the worksheet • on the handout • on the transparency	and	listen carefully.

4. 듣기 후

That's it.	• We'll hear • We'll listen to	it again later.

Could	• anyone tell me • you in pairs tell each other • you summarize • you sum up	• quickly • briefly	what	• this was about? • might be said next?

• Would • Could	• someone • you	write answers	on the board?
		• give • tell	us the answers?

Let's	• go over the worksheet. • check the answers.

03 Teaching Speaking Skills (Middle School Level)

> **Basic Expressions for Speaking**
>
> Let's talk about ~
> We're going to do some role play now (in groups).
> We're going to have a short conversation about ~ (in twos)
> Is there any volunteer that would like to go first?
> Now that you've had time for your conversation,
> I will ask you to report to me what you heard.
> First of all, I want you to think of ~
> Can you ask A about B?
> Thanks for sharing.
> That's interesting.
> That sounds like fun.
> Any other ideas?

T: Good morning, class. Today we are going to talk about past events, what people used to be like when they were young. I want you to think about when you were a child. Think about what you used to do for fun, how you used to spend your time. For example, what was your favorite toy when you were young? Who was your close friend? What made you feel excited? Are there any volunteers to begin the conversation? Okay, Bomi. Can you tell me what you used to do for fun as a child?

S: I always used to meet my elementary school friends at the park close to my house. We would meet on Saturday afternoons to read comic books together.

T: That sounds like fun! What else did you use to do with your friends?

S: We used to climb the mountain behind our apartment building.

T: Okay, Bomi. Thanks for sharing. Now, let's ask Youngbai. What did you use to do as a child?

S: I used to play war games with all my friends after school.

T: War games? Did you want to be a soldier?

S: Yes. I used to think it was great to grow up and be a soldier. Now, I don't want to be a soldier. I want to be a public official instead.

T: Well, I hope you can reach your dream. Now, class, you've heard two examples of conversations with Bomi and Youngbai. I want you to have your own conversation with a partner about the same topic. Get together in pairs and ask your partner about their childhood. After a few minutes, I will ask you to report to me what you heard. (A few minutes later) Now that you've had time for your conversation, I want to ask a few questions. Let's see… Minkyoung, what memories did you hear from Jiyon?

S: Jiyon always used to watch TV after school, even when her mother would yell at her to do her homework!

T: Oh! What were her favorite TV shows?

S: Jiyon's favorite shows were cartoons.

T: Good. Now, Jiyon, can you tell us what Minkyoung used to be like as a child?

S: Minkyoung used to stop on the way home from school to buy snacks all the time. Her hobby used to be eating!

Key Expressions

1. 설명·묘사하기

In	• pairs • groups	• I want you to • could you • can you	give someone	• directions from the building to your school. • a description of your family. • instruction to use a computer.		
			how to	• cook pasta. • operate the computer. • drive a car.		
			explain to someone what	• it • the graph • the picture • the map • the diagram	• shows. • indicates.	

2. 연습하기

Let's	have practice all together, so that you know	• what to do. • how to play.
	go over some	• words • phrases	that might be useful.

3. Information Gap Activity 활용하기

You work in twos, with similar pictures, but	• don't let the other person see yours. • don't show yours to the other person.
Ask each other questions to	• find out what is different. • find the differences between the two.
When you have found out,	• write down the differences. • then pass the two pictures on to another pair.

4. 토론하기

You're going to Can you	• discuss • talk about	the problems of	• pollution. • traffic jam. • drug addiction. • juvenile crimes.
		• your future goals. • your hobbies. • your best friend.	
Can you discuss in	• pairs • twos • groups	• what would you do about the problem(s)? • how the problem(s) might influence you?	

04 Teaching Reading Skills

Basic Expressions for Reading

Read the passage silently.
Read the text to yourselves.
Study the chapter on your own.
Prepare the next three paragraphs.
Have a look at the next section.
Check the new vocabulary from the list at the back.
If there are any words you don't know, please ask.
Read what it says at the top of the page first.
Let's read the text aloud.
I'll read it to you first.
Read the first ten lines.
Read as far as/down to the end of the chapter.
Three sentences for each of you.
Let's take turns reading.

T: We are on page 45. Now, read the text by yourselves. You can check the new vocabulary from the list below, and if there are any words you still don't know, please ask.

S: Do you want us to read it all?

T: Oh... Let's see. Maybe it is too long. OK, read the first fifteen lines then.

Tip

Dialogue 1의 첫 번째 대화를 보면 "You can check the new vocabulary from the list below"라는 표현이 나오는데, 'check'라는 동사와 관련된 숙어의 예를 잠깐 살펴보기로 하자.

(1) check through: Let's check through the answers. (정답을 점검할 때)
(2) check up: I'll check this up in a dictionary.
(3) check on: Could you check on the spelling of it? Could you check for spelling mistakes?
(4) check off: Check off the answers on your list.

> T: Let's read the text on page 45. We are going to read it by taking turns, OK? Three sentences for each of you. Let's start with Sunhee.
> S: (Students read the sentences taking turns. And it is Midal's turn, and she is hesitant.)
> T: Midal, go on from where Giwon left off. Let's see, start reading from line 10.
> M: Yes, Miss Kim.

> **Tip**
>
> Dialogue에서 "Midal, go on from where Giwon left off."의 뜻은 Giwon이 멈춘 곳에서 읽기 시작하라는 뜻이다. 또한 "각각의 사람들이 세 문장씩 읽는다"라는 것을 표현할 때에는 위의 대화에서 보는 것처럼 "Three sentences for each of you"로 할 수도 있고 "Read three sentences each" "Each one of you will read three sentences" 등과 같이 말할 수도 있다.

05. Teaching Writing Skills (Elementary level)

Basic Expressions for Writing

We need to start organizing ideas.
After you look at list of brainstorming,
You need to start organizing the similar ideas together.
Put the similar words together.
I want you to tell me what it is.
I want you to write some sentences about each word.
What are some sentences that you could write?
Those are all sentences about ~.
That is a good guess!
That's correct!
Exactly!
Try again!
Let's try again!

T: Today, we're going to spend some time writing in English. Before you write, you must first think of the English vocabulary words. I'm going to show you a picture. I want you to tell me what the picture is and then write down the vocabulary word. Are you ready?

S: Yes!

T: Here is the first picture.

S: Apple! (The students write down the word 'apple.')

T: Let's check the spelling. How do you spell "apple?"

S: A-p-p-l-e.

T: That's correct. Here is the next picture.

S: Boat! (The students write down the word 'boat.')

T: Good! Now, how do you spell "boat?"
S: B-o-u-t?
T: That is a good guess! But, that is not the correct spelling of "boat." Let's try again. Does anyone else know how to spell "boat?"
S: B-o-a-t?
T: Yes! That is correct! (After showing 5 pictures) Now, I want you to write some sentences about each word. For the first picture, apple, what are some sentences that you could write?
S: I like apples!
S: Apples are red.
S: My mother gave me an apple.
T: Good! Those are all sentences about apples. For each picture, I want you to write three sentences. I am going to walk around the room and check your writing. Please ask questions if you don't understand.

(Intermediate level)

T: Good morning, class. We are going to continue learning about writing skills today. Yesterday we talked about brainstorming. To review, can anyone tell the class what brainstorming is?
S: Brainstorming is collecting many ideas before you begin writing.
T: Exactly! What is a very important point to remember about brainstorming?
S: When you brainstorm, you shouldn't ignore any idea. You should write down every idea that comes to your mind.
T: Good. Today we are going to look at the next step after brainstorming. This step is the organization of ideas. ……

Key Expressions

1. 소재 구상하기

Tell me	what you're	going to write.	

Get together in groups and	discuss your	• plans. • ideas. • topics.

2. 다른 글 연구하기

• Read • Study	it and	• see how ideas are organized. • find the main ideas. Write them down.		
		• underline • highlight	the	• phrases which introduce new ideas. • link words. • topic sentences.

3. 쓰기 활동

How can you	• join • link	these two sentences to make	it sound better?	

• Now that you've got • Based on	• all the key points • the ideas you have	• start • write • develop • expand • organize	your paper.

4. 교정 활동

• After • Upon	• writing • finishing your paper	• edit • look for • correct	• misspelled words. • some grammatical mistakes. • errors.
• After • When	• you finish your paper • you are done with your writing	I'd like you to	• read it carefully and edit mistakes. • proofread it. • revise it.

06 Classroom expressions for all purposes

인사	• I hope you are all okay today. • I hope you've recovered from your cold. How are you feeling now? • My name is John Smith and I'm your new English teacher. • Let me introduce myself. I am Lee Jinho. Nice to meet you.
과제 검사	• I want to see what you have done. • If the deadline is too soon, I'll give you an extension. This class next week. Is that all right with you? • Yunhe, please collect all the homework and bring it to me after this class. • Let me check your homework now. • Tomorrow, you should bring it to my desk.
본수업 시작	• Let's do it once more. • Stop talking now so that we can start. • Now you are ready to do today's work. • I want these handouts back at the end of the class. • Class, will you please be quiet? • It's about time to start the lesson. Are you ready for today's lesson?
발음지도	• How do you pronoune this word? • Which one is pronounced differently? • Choose the same sound as the examples. • Choose the word that has letters which are silent. • Let's pronounce the words more slowly and clearly. • Choose the one word that is different from the others. • Read the dialog and correct the errors. • Please fill in the blanks with the proper articles. • Do you know the different usages of 'a' and 'the'? • If you don't need an article, please put an 'x' in the blank. • Read the sentences and fill in the blanks with the correct article, 'a(n)' or 'the'. • Write the simple past tense of the verb. • Fill in the blank with 'do', 'does', or 'did'. • Fill in the blank with the correct preposition from the list above. • Write the correct adjectives in the blanks. Use each adjective once. • Make comparisons between each pair of words. Don't use the superlative. • 'Which' and 'who' in the sentences are used as relative pronouns.

대화 설명	• What is the first dialog about? • Read over the first dialog and think about what is being said • There are two dialogs on this page. They are not difficult to understand.
문장연결하기	• Make a sentence using 'if' or 'whether'. • Combine the following two sentences. • Combine the following two sentences as shown in the example. • Combine the two sentences using relative pronouns. • Combine the two sentences using the words in parentheses. Just follow the example.
선택하기	• Choose the right(correct) one. • Choose the best answer among the four choices. • Choose the word that fits each sentence. • Choose the word or phrase which is the closest in meaning. • Choose the word that has the opposite meaning of the underlined word. • Choose the suitable words for the blanks. You can use the same word twice. • There are two words in the parenthesis. They are 'study' and 'to study'. Choose the right words to make the sentence perfect.
수정하기	• Correct the underlined part. • Give the proper form of the word in parenthesis. • Write the proper form of the given word. • Change the verb in the parenthesis to its proper form for the sentence. • Point out the grammatical mistakes in the sentences below and correct them.
다시쓰기	• Change the underlined part into one word. • Rewrite the following as shown in the example. • Rewrite the underlined parts using the pronoun 'one'. • Rewrite the following beginning part with the given words. • Rewrite the following using the phrase or word in each parenthesis. • Rewrite the following by putting the given words in the beginning.
배열하기	• Put the following words in the correct order. • Arrange the words in the parenthesis to complete the sentence. • Rearrange the words in parentheses as shown in the example. • Put the words in the parenthesis in the correct order to make the sentence understandable.

빈칸채우기	• Fill in the blanks as shown. • Fill in the blank with a word from the list below. • Put 'is' or 'are' in the following blanks. • Choose the most suitable word for the blank. • Fill in the blanks with the words given above. • Fill in the blank with a word(phrase) given below. • Fill in each blank with a suitable preposition. • Fill in each blank with a suitable form of the given word in each parenthesis. • Fill in each blank with a suitable form of the underlined word. • Fill in each blank so that both sentences have the same meanings. • Fill in the blanks to make each pair of sentences mean the same things.
문장완성하기	• Complete the sentences. • Complete the following in English. • Complete the sentence as shown in the example. • Complete the following sentences with your own words. • Fill in each blank with the word that has the same sound and the same spelling but a different meaning. • Can you fill out the blank by figuring out the relation between A and B? • There are two sentences below. Each of the sentences has a blank in it. Fill in each blank with the same word to make both sentences perfect.
참거짓 파악하기	• Choose the true statements. • Choose one incorrect expression. • Cross out the wrong statements. • Mark T or F according to the text. • Mark T or F in the blank at the end of each sentence. • Mark T if the following statements are true, and F if false. • Say "yes" if you think it is true and say "no" if you think it's wrong. • Mark T if the statement (a) is similar in meaning to statement (b), and mark F if you think it is not.
문장변환 연습하기	• Change the sentence by using 'which'. • Make each pair same in meaning. • Fill in the blank without changing the meaning of the sentence. • Change the sentence pattern by using a relative pronoun.

이해도 확인	- No question? - Any questions on page 11? - Do you have any questions about the text? - Are there any points you are not sure of? - If you don't understand, raise your hands. - Are there any words you are not familiar with? **(상세설명이 필요할 때)** - Would you like anything explained? - Let's look at the passage in more detail. - Let's have a look at some of the difficult points. - I'd like to point out some difficult constructions. - There are one or two difficult points we should look at. - The meaning of the sentence is something like 'he didn't understand'.
수업 종료	**(수업내용 평가 및 반성)** - Is everyone finished? - You've all done quite well. - Well done. - I hope you do better next time. - Most of you have done that very nicely. - It seems that you need to practice more. - Some of you have prepared for the class, but other of you haven't. When you come back to this class next time, please be well prepared. - How much of today's lesson did you grasp? Was it hard or just so-so? **(차시예고)** - Next time, we're going to continue to write a paragraph about hobbies. - Please don't forget to bring some pictures for next class. - Today, we studied the meaning of 'tense'. Next class, we will study more, so if you aren't prepared, you will be totally lost.

memo

PART II

교사용 지도서

CHAPTER 01 영어과 교수·학습 운영 계획

1 단원명: Lesson 1. A Life Full of Experiences (New words, Listen & Talk)

교육과정 성취기준:

[9영01-01] 어구나 문장을 듣고, 연음, 축약된 소리를 식별할 수 있다.
[9영01-02] 일상생활 관련 대상이나 친숙한 일반적 주제에 관한 말이나 대화를 듣고 세부 정보를 파악할 수 있다.
[9영02-03] 일상생활에 관한 그림, 사진, 또는 도표에 대해 설명할 수 있다.
[9영02-08] 개인 생활에 관한 경험이나 계획에 대해 묻거나 답할 수 있다.

평가요소	수업방법	수업·평가 연계의 주안점
– 바람에 대해 묻고 답하기 – 만족이나 불만족에 대해 묻기 – 의미 있었던 경험 발표하기	– 묻고 답하기 – 발표하기 – 협력 학습	⇒ (자기성찰) 　– 바람에 대해 묻고 답할 수 있는지 점검 　– 만족이나 불만족에 대해 물을 수 있는지 점검 ⇒ (동료 피드백) 의미 있었던 경험 발표 시 의미가 잘 전달되었는지 피드백 ⇒ (교사관찰 및 피드백) 　– 듣기 활동 시 세부 정보 파악의 정확성 점검 　– 발표 시 모둠의 의미 있었던 경험에 대한 내용 충실도, 전달 태도(눈맞춤) 등 피드백 제공 ⇒ (형성평가) 어휘, 듣기, 말하기

2 단원명: Lesson 1. A Life Full of Experiences
(Grammar & Read on & Comprehension)

교육과정 성취기준:

[9영04-04] 개인 생활의 경험이나 계획에 대해 문장을 쓸 수 있다.

[9영03-03] 일상생활이나 친숙한 일반적 주제의 그림, 사진, 또는 도표에 관한 글을 읽고 세부 정보를 파악할 수 있다.

[9영03-08] 일상생활이나 친숙한 일반적 주제의 글을 읽고 일이나 사건의 원인과 결과를 추론할 수 있다.

[9영03-04] 일상생활이나 친숙한 일반적 주제의 글을 읽고 줄거리, 주제, 요지를 파악할 수 있다.

[9영03-02] 일상생활이나 친숙한 일반적 대상이나 주제에 관한 글을 읽고 세부 정보를 파악할 수 있다.

평가요소	수업방법	수업·평가 연계의 주안점
- 자신과 단짝 친구에 대한 문장 완성하기 - 방과후 활동에 대한 문장 완성하기 - 자신이 좋아하는 것과 좋아하지 않는 것 소개하기 - 소개되는 인물에 대한 세부 내용 파악하기 - 인물의 세부 정보를 모아 도표로 정리하여 비교하기 - 줄거리, 요지 파악	- information gap - 상호 협력 읽기 (jigsaw) - 추론하기 - 소규모(짝) 토론 학습 - Guided Writing - 에듀테크 활용 학습	⇒ (동료 피드백) 소개되는 인물에 대한 구체적 정보 공유 및 확인 ⇒ (교사관찰 및 피드백) 　- 주어와 문장의 의미에 일치되는 동사의 형태 활용 　- 소개되는 인물과 주인공의 정보 연결에 대한 추론 능력 　- Guided writing으로 온라인 친구 요청 메시지 작성의 정확성 및 유창성 ⇒ (형성평가) be 동사, 일반 동사의 활용, 긍정문, 부정문의 활용, 본문이해 　- AI 코스웨어 활용 과제 학습

3 단원명: Lesson 2. Discover Your Culture
   (New Words, Listen & Talk)

교육과정 성취기준:

[9영01-03] 일상생활이나 친숙한 일반적 주제에 관한 그림, 사진, 또는 도표에 관한 말이나 대화를 듣고 세부 정보를 파악할 수 있다.

[9영01-06] 일상생활이나 친숙한 일반적 주제에 관한 말이나 대화를 듣고 화자의 의도나 목적을 추론할 수 있다.

[9영02-07] 주변의 위치나 장소에 대해 묻거나 답할 수 있다.

[9영02-08] 개인 생활에 관한 경험이나 계획에 대해 묻거나 답할 수 있다.

평가요소	수업방법	수업·평가 연계의 주안점
- 계획 묻고 답하기 - 장소 설명하기 - 그림에 대한 대화 듣고 답하기 - 여행 일정 소개하기	- 묻고 답하기 - 묘사하기 - 자료 조사하기 - 발표하기	⇒ (자기성찰) 무엇을 할 계획인지 묻고 답할 수 있는지 점검 ⇒ (동료 피드백) 여행 일정을 구체적으로 발표하였는지 피드백 전달 ⇒ (교사관찰 및 피드백) 세부 정보 파악에 대한 정확성과 자신의 계획 표현 능력 ⇒ (형성평가) 어휘, 듣기

4 단원명: Lesson 2. Discover Your Culture
(Grammar & Read on & Comprehension)

교육과정 성취기준:

[9영04-01] 일상생활에 관한 주변의 대상이나 상황을 묘사하는 문장을 쓸 수 있다.

[9영04-03] 일상생활에 관한 그림, 사진, 또는 도표 등을 설명하는 문장을 쓸 수 있다.

[9영03-02] 일상생활이나 친숙한 일반적 대상이나 주제에 관한 글을 읽고 세부 정보를 파악할 수 있다.

[9영03-05] 일상생활이나 친숙한 일반적 주제의 글을 읽고 필자의 심정이나 태도를 추론할 수 있다.

[9영03-09] 일상생활이나 친숙한 일반적 주제의 글을 읽고 문맥을 통해 낱말, 어구 또는 문장의 함축적 의미를 추론할 수 있다.

평가요소	수업방법	수업·평가 연계의 주안점

- 각 인물의 행동 묘사하는 문장 완성하기
- 그림과 사진을 설명하는 간단한 문장 쓰기
- 한국 문화 소개 글의 세부 정보 파악하기
- 타문화를 수용하는 글쓴이의 심정이나 태도 파악하기
- 다의어 의미 파악하기
- 한국문화를 소개할 선물을 설명하는 글쓰기
	- Scanning
	- Skimming
	- 강의식
	- 에듀테크 활용학습
		⇒ (동료 피드백) 현재진행형을 정확히 활용하여 그림 묘사하기
		  - 조동사 can, will 정확히 활용하여 짝과 자신에 대해 설명하기
		⇒ (교사관찰 및 피드백) 다양한 의미를 가진 단어를 문장 내에서 정확히 이해하는지 확인
		  - 그림이나 사진 자료를 활용하여 우리 문화 간단히 소개하는 표현 능력 확인
		  - 단/복수에 따른 동사 활용 능력 확인
		⇒ (형성평가) there is/are~, be going to ~, 현재진행형, 조동사 can, will 구문의 활용, 본문 이해
		  - AI 코스웨어 활용 과제 학습

5 단원명: Lesson 2. Discover Your Culture
         (Think & Write)

교육과정 성취기준:

[9영04-01]   일상생활에 관한 주변의 대상이나 상황을 묘사하는 문장을 쓸 수 있다.
[9영04-03]   일상생활에 관한 그림, 사진, 또는 도표 등을 설명하는 문장을 쓸 수 있다.
[9영04-06]   간단한 초대, 감사, 축하, 위로, 일기, 편지 등의 글을 쓸 수 있다.

평가요소	수업방법	수업·평가 연계의 주안점
− 우리나라의 세계유산을 묘사하는 글쓰기 − 그림/사진/도표를 설명하는 간단한 문장 쓰기 − 편지글의 형식에 맞춰 글쓰기	− Descriptive Writing − Process-oriented Writing − 에듀테크 활용 학습	⇒ (동료 피드백) 소개하는 장소에 대한 설명이 구체적인지 확인 ⇒ (교사관찰 및 피드백) 편지글의 형식에 맞게 글을 작성하였는지 점검 ⇒ (자기성찰) 우리 문화와 다른 나라의 문화에 대한 소개와 이해 과정을 통한 공감, 배려, 존중의 태도 갖추기 ⇒ (형성평가) 단원 내용 이해 ⇒ 수행평가: 우리나라의 세계유산 소개하는 글 쓰고 발표하기

6 단원명: Lesson 3. Spend Smart, Save Smart
         (New Words, Listen & Talk)

교육과정 성취기준:

[9영01-01]   어구나 문장을 듣고, 연음, 축약된 소리를 식별할 수 있다.
[9영01-07]   일상생활이나 친숙한 일반적 주제에 관한 말이나 대화를 듣고 일이나 사건의 순서, 전후 관계를 추론할 수 있다.
[9영02-03]   일상생활에 관한 그림, 사진, 또는 도표에 대해 설명할 수 있다.
[9영02-04]   일상생활에 관한 방법과 절차에 대해 설명할 수 있다.

평가요소	수업방법	수업·평가 연계의 주안점

– 조언하기
– 허락 요청하고 답하기
– 연음, 억양에 유의하여 말하기
– 사건의 순서, 전후 관계 추론하기
– 대화를 듣고 도표 완성하기
– 구매 목록 작성하기
– 역할극하기
– 시각 자료 구성하여 발표하기
	– 묻고 답하기
	– Role Play
	– 문제 해결 학습
	– 시각 자료와 함께 발표하기
		⇒ (자기성찰) 상대방에게 허락을 요청할 수 있는 말을 할 수 있는지 점검
		⇒ (동료 피드백) 모둠원의 소비 습관에 대해 조사한 후 자료를 종합하여 발표하였는지 점검
		⇒ (교사관찰 및 피드백)
		  – 소비 습관을 나타내는 표현의 정확성
		  – 일상생활의 맥락에서 자주 사용되는 표현의 유창성
		  – 자신의 소비 습관에 대한 성찰을 바탕으로 조언 구하는 표현력
		  – 상점에서 물건을 사기 위해 요청하는 표현의 정확성/ 유창성
		  – 사건의 전후 관계 파악하기 능력
		⇒ (형성평가) 듣기, 말하기

7　단원명: Lesson 3. Spend Smart, Save Smart
(Grammar & Read on & Comprehension)

교육과정 성취기준:

[9영04-04]　개인 생활의 경험이나 계획에 대해 문장을 쓸 수 있다.

[9영03-01]　문장을 의미 단위로 끊어 읽으면서 의미를 파악할 수 있다.

[9영03-03]　일상생활이나 친숙한 일반적 주제의 그림, 사진, 또는 도표에 관한 글을 읽고 세부 정보를 파악할 수 있다.

[9영03-04]　일상생활이나 친숙한 일반적 주제의 글을 읽고 줄거리, 주제, 요지를 파악할 수 있다.

[9영03-08]　일상생활이나 친숙한 일반적 주제의 글을 읽고 일이나 사건의 원인과 결과를 추론할 수 있다.

평가요소	수업방법	수업·평가 연계의 주안점
- 지난주에 한 일과 앞으로의 각오에 대한 문장 쓰기 - 문장의 의미 파악하기 - 팔고 싶은 물건에 대한 세부 정보 파악하기 - 벼룩시장에서 발생한 에피소드에 대한 원인과 결과 추론하기 - 다의어의 문맥상 의미 파악하기	- Jigsaw Reading - Scanning - Skimming - 에듀테크 활용학습	⇒ (동료 피드백) 자신이 좋아하는 것과 싫어하는 것을 동명사를 활용하여 정확하게 표현 ⇒ (교사관찰 및 피드백) 　- 자원의 재활용과 나눔에 대한 성찰 　- 읽기 전략 활용 능력 확인 　- 과거 동사의 규칙성과 불규칙성에 대한 정확한 활용 　- 글의 표현 방법(일기: 대화문)에 따른 이해의 정확성 ⇒ (자기성찰) 소규모 경제 활동을 위한 준비, 실행, 결과에 대한 현명한 소비 습관 형성 ⇒ (형성평가) 과거 동사의 활용, 동명사를 목적어로 취하는 동사, 본문 이해 　- AI 코스웨어 활용 과제 학습

8 단원명: Lesson 3. Spend Smart, Save Smart
(Think & Write)

교육과정 성취기준:

[9영04-03] 일상생활에 관한 그림, 사진, 또는 도표 등을 설명하는 문장을 쓸 수 있다.

[9영04-04] 개인 생활의 경험이나 계획에 대해 문장을 쓸 수 있다.

평가요소	수업방법	수업·평가 연계의 주안점
- 자신이 팔고 싶은 물건 설명하는 문장 쓰기 - 자신의 경험이나 계획 쓰기	- mindmapping - Process-oriented writing - Guided wirting	⇒ (동료 피드백) 팔고 싶은 물건의 특징 표현하기 ⇒ (교사관찰) 문장 표현의 정확성 & 내용 충실도 ⇒ (형성평가) 단원 내용 이해 ⇒ 수행평가: 팔고 싶은 물건 홍보하는 글 쓰기 & 시제 활용의 적절성

CHAPTER 02 고교 (진로 영어)

01 Help! I'm Worried about My Career!

[Worry 1]

Dohun: I'm worried about my career in the future. Parents, friends and teachers are all pressuring me to choose a dream and prepare for that career during high school. How on earth do I know what I want? I don't know what I like and I don't know what to do. What should I do?

[Response 1]

Minhui: I know how you feel. I was in the same situation a long time ago. When I think about it now, I remember I couldn't figure out what I wanted to do or what I liked. I still have regrets about that time. First, you must be willing to face your fears and take on difficult challenges. When you do that, you will find your answers.

[Response 2]

Minsu: I had bad scores and didn't know what I could do well. I shared my troubles with my friends and they gave me heartwarming advice like "Your dream is already inside your mind. Think deeply and you'll figure it out." It is important to try hard to find a dream and to figure out what you truly want. Being resilient and determined is truly more important than making up your mind quickly. So, with that spirit of toughness and bravery, look inside your mind for your dream.

[Response 3]

Sejin: The word "career" means "road you will take in the future." I understand that your career is a very important thing and that you will want to very quickly decide on and plan for your career. However, right now I recommend that you focus more on knowing yourself rather than clinging to the search for a career. Find the activities you like and the things you value. You can't do this quickly. I think you will find your career, your road to the future, after many attempts and many failures. That's natural and good.

[Worry 2]

Suhyeon: I'm a 17 year-old high school student. I really like drawing and illustrating, so I want to be an illustrator or animator. However, my parents are really opposed to me pursuing my dream. More importantly, I doubt I could be successful with this job. I guess I might have some regrets later if I become an illustrator and I am not sure if that's what I really want. I feel like I'm losing confidence. What should I do?

[Response]

Counselor: I see lots of cases where parents don't like their child's dream. This is because parents are thinking about the future economic competitiveness and stability of their children. At its base, parents love their children deeply. So if you are sure about how much you want to follow your dream and if you explain it to your parents, I think your parents will support you and you will feel much better. But here, what is most important is that you need to have self-confidence about yourself and your future. Just like any other type of job, you can't succeed unless you try your best. So, if you want to be an illustrator you need to try your best for your dream and make sure that you are dedicated to seeing it through.

Here are some steps you can take to build your confidence and bring your self-esteem up.
1. Positive self-talk: The way you think about yourself has a huge influence on your self-esteem. If you keep telling yourself that you're no good, you might just start to believe it even though it's not true. If you notice that you practice negative self-talk often, try to find some ways you can get rid of your negative thinking.
2. Don't compare yourself with others: It can be really tempting to measure our own worth against other people. So what if your friend is awesome at table tennis and gets great marks? You just need to figure out what your niche is. Everyone is great at something —what are your strengths?
3. Exercise: Exercise helps to improve your mood.
4. Don't beat yourself up when you make a mistake: Everyone on the planet makes mistakes. Why should you be any different? When you fail, don't stress out, just learn from it and move on.
5. Focus on the things you can change: There is no use wasting all your energy thinking about things that you can't change. Why don't you think about some of the things that you can control?
6. Celebrate the small stuff: Start small and work your way up — you can't expect huge progress to be made overnight.
7. Be helpful and considerate: Not only is helping people a great way to boost the moods of others, but you might find that you feel better about yourself after doing something particularly excellent.
8. Surround yourself with supportive people: Don't hang around people who bring you down. Find a group of people who make you feel good about yourself.

02 교육과정 성취기준·평가기준 가이드

1 듣기영역

교육과정 성취기준		평가기준
다양한 직업 및 진로에 관한 말이나 대화를 듣고 세부 정보를 파악할 수 있다.	상	다양한 직업 및 진로에 관한 말이나 대화를 듣고 세부 정보를 정확하게 파악할 수 있다.
	중	다양한 직업 및 진로에 관한 말이나 대화를 듣고 세부 정보를 대략적으로 파악할 수 있다.
	하	다양한 직업 및 진로에 관한 말이나 대화를 듣고 세부 정보를 부분적으로 파악할 수 있다.
다양한 직업 및 진로에 관한 말이나 대화를 듣고 주제 및 요지를 파악할 수 있다.	상	다양한 직업 및 진로에 관한 말이나 대화를 듣고 주제 및 요지를 정확하게 파악할 수 있다.
	중	다양한 직업 및 진로에 관한 말이나 대화를 듣고 주제 및 요지를 대략적으로 파악할 수 있다.
	하	다양한 직업 및 진로에 관한 말이나 대화를 듣고 주제 및 요지를 부분적으로 파악할 수 있다.
다양한 직업 분야에서 수행하는 업무에 관한 말이나 대화를 듣고 내용의 논리적 관계를 파악할 수 있다.	상	다양한 직업 분야에서 수행하는 업무에 관한 말이나 대화를 듣고 내용의 논리적 관계를 정확하게 파악할 수 있다.
	중	다양한 직업 분야에서 수행하는 업무에 관한 말이나 대화를 듣고 내용의 논리적 관계를 대략적으로 파악할 수 있다.
	하	다양한 직업 분야에서 수행하는 업무에 관한 말이나 대화를 듣고 내용의 논리적 관계를 부분적으로 파악할 수 있다.
다양한 직업 분야에서 수행하는 업무에 관한 말이나 대화를 듣고 화자의 의도나 말의 목적을 파악할 수 있다.	상	다양한 직업 분야에서 수행하는 업무에 관한 말이나 대화를 듣고 화자의 의도나 말의 목적을 정확하게 파악할 수 있다.
	중	다양한 직업 분야에서 수행하는 업무에 관한 말이나 대화를 듣고 화자의 의도나 말의 목적을 대략적으로 파악할 수 있다.
	하	다양한 직업 분야에서 수행하는 업무에 관한 말이나 대화를 듣고 화자의 의도나 말의 목적을 부분적으로 파악할 수 있다.
다양한 직업 및 진로에 관한 말이나 대화를 듣고 화자의 심정이나 태도를 추론할 수 있다.	상	다양한 직업 및 진로에 관한 말이나 대화를 듣고 화자의 심정이나 태도를 정확하게 추론할 수 있다.
	중	다양한 직업 및 진로에 관한 말이나 대화를 듣고 화자의 심정이나 태도를 대략적으로 추론할 수 있다.
	하	다양한 직업 및 진로에 관한 말이나 대화를 듣고 화자의 심정이나 태도를 부분적으로 추론할 수 있다.

2 말하기영역

교육과정 성취기준		평가기준
다양한 직업 및 진로에 관하여 듣거나 읽고 세부 정보를 설명할 수 있다.	상	다양한 직업 및 진로에 관하여 듣거나 읽고 세부 정보를 정확하게 설명할 수 있다.
	중	다양한 직업 및 진로에 관하여 듣거나 읽고 세부 정보를 대략적으로 설명할 수 있다.
	하	다양한 직업 및 진로에 관하여 듣거나 읽고 세부 정보를 부분적으로 설명할 수 있다.
다양한 직업 및 진로에 관하여 듣거나 읽고 중심 내용을 말할 수 있다.	상	다양한 직업 및 진로에 관하여 듣거나 읽고 중심 내용을 정확하게 말할 수 있다.
	중	다양한 직업 및 진로에 관하여 듣거나 읽고 중심 내용을 대략적으로 말할 수 있다.
	하	다양한 직업 및 진로에 관하여 듣거나 읽고 중심 내용을 부분적으로 말할 수 있다.
다양한 직업 및 진로에 관해 자신의 의견이나 감정을 표현할 수 있다.	상	다양한 직업 및 진로에 관해 자신의 의견이나 감정을 정확하게 표현할 수 있다.
	중	다양한 직업 및 진로에 관해 자신의 의견이나 감정을 대략적으로 표현할 수 있다.
	하	다양한 직업 및 진로에 관해 자신의 의견이나 감정을 부분적으로 표현할 수 있다.
다양한 직업 및 진로에 관한 정보를 묻고 답할 수 있다.	상	다양한 직업 및 진로에 관한 정보를 정확하게 묻고 답할 수 있다.
	중	다양한 직업 및 진로에 관한 정보를 대략적으로 묻고 답할 수 있다.
	하	다양한 직업 및 진로에 관한 정보를 부분적으로 묻고 답할 수 있다.
그림, 표, 서식 등을 활용하여 프레젠테이션을 할 수 있다.	상	그림, 표, 서식 등을 활용하여 프레젠테이션을 정확하게 할 수 있다.
	중	그림, 표, 서식 등을 활용하여 프레젠테이션을 대략적으로 할 수 있다.
	하	그림, 표, 서식 등을 활용하여 프레젠테이션을 부분적으로 할 수 있다.
다양한 직업 및 진로에 필요한 인터뷰를 적절하게 수행할 수 있다.	상	다양한 직업 및 진로에 필요한 인터뷰를 정확하게 수행할 수 있다.
	중	다양한 직업 및 진로에 필요한 인터뷰를 대략적으로 수행할 수 있다.
	하	다양한 직업 및 진로에 필요한 인터뷰를 부분적으로 수행할 수 있다.

3 읽기영역

교육과정 성취기준		평가기준
다양한 직업 및 진로에 관한 글을 읽고 세부 정보를 파악할 수 있다.	상	다양한 직업 및 진로에 관한 글을 읽고 세부 정보를 정확하게 파악할 수 있다.
	중	다양한 직업 및 진로에 관한 글을 읽고 세부 정보를 대략적으로 파악할 수 있다.
	하	다양한 직업 및 진로에 관한 글을 읽고 세부 정보를 부분적으로 파악할 수 있다.
다양한 직업 및 진로에 관한 글을 읽고 주제 및 요지를 파악할 수 있다.	상	다양한 직업 및 진로에 관한 글을 읽고 주제 및 요지를 정확하게 파악할 수 있다.
	중	다양한 직업 및 진로에 관한 글을 읽고 주제 및 요지를 대략적으로 파악할 수 있다.
	하	다양한 직업 및 진로에 관한 글을 읽고 주제 및 요지를 부분적으로 파악할 수 있다.
다양한 직업 및 진로에 관한 글을 읽고 논리적 관계를 파악할 수 있다.	상	다양한 직업 및 진로에 관한 글을 읽고 논리적 관계를 정확하게 파악할 수 있다.
	중	다양한 직업 및 진로에 관한 글을 읽고 논리적 관계를 대략적으로 파악할 수 있다.
	하	다양한 직업 및 진로에 관한 글을 읽고 논리적 관계를 부분적으로 파악할 수 있다.
다양한 직업 및 진로에 관한 글을 읽고 필자의 의도나 글의 목적을 파악할 수 있다.	상	다양한 직업 및 진로에 관한 글을 읽고 필자의 의도나 글의 목적을 정확하게 파악할 수 있다.
	중	다양한 직업 및 진로에 관한 글을 읽고 필자의 의도나 글의 목적을 대략적으로 파악할 수 있다.
	하	다양한 직업 및 진로에 관한 글을 읽고 필자의 의도나 글의 목적을 부분적으로 파악할 수 있다.

4 쓰기영역

교육과정 성취기준		평가기준
다양한 직업 및 진로에 관하여 듣거나 읽고 세부 정보를 기록할 수 있다.	상	다양한 직업 및 진로에 관하여 듣거나 읽고 세부 정보를 정확하게 기록할 수 있다.
	중	다양한 직업 및 진로에 관하여 듣거나 읽고 세부 정보를 대략적으로 기록할 수 있다.
	하	다양한 직업 및 진로에 관하여 듣거나 읽고 세부 정보를 부분적으로 기록할 수 있다.
다양한 직업 및 진로에 관하여 듣거나 읽고 간단하게 요약할 수 있다.	상	다양한 직업 및 진로에 관하여 듣거나 읽고 간단한 요약을 정확하게 할 수 있다.
	중	다양한 직업 및 진로에 관하여 듣거나 읽고 간단한 요약을 대략적으로 할 수 있다.
	하	다양한 직업 및 진로에 관하여 듣거나 읽고 간단한 요약을 부분적으로 할 수 있다.
다양한 직업 및 진로에 관해 의견이나 감정을 쓸 수 있다.	상	다양한 직업 및 진로에 관해 의견이나 감정을 정확하게 쓸 수 있다.
	중	다양한 직업 및 진로에 관해 의견이나 감정을 대략적으로 쓸 수 있다.
	하	다양한 직업 및 진로에 관해 의견이나 감정을 부분적으로 쓸 수 있다.
사람, 사물, 사건에 대하여 상세하게 묘사하는 글을 쓸 수 있다.	상	사람, 사물, 사건에 대하여 상세하게 묘사하는 글을 정확하게 쓸 수 있다.
	중	사람, 사물, 사건에 대하여 상세하게 묘사하는 글을 대략적으로 쓸 수 있다.
	하	사람, 사물, 사건에 대하여 상세하게 묘사하는 글을 부분적으로 쓸 수 있다.
자기소개서, 서식, 이메일 등을 상황과 목적에 맞게 작성할 수 있다.	상	자기소개서, 서식, 이메일 등을 상황과 목적에 맞추어 정확하게 작성할 수 있다.
	중	자기소개서, 서식, 이메일 등을 상황과 목적에 맞추어 대략적으로 작성할 수 있다.
	하	자기소개서, 서식, 이메일 등을 상황과 목적에 맞추어 부분적으로 작성할 수 있다.
자신의 직업 및 진로에 대한 계획서를 쓸 수 있다.	상	자신의 직업 및 진로에 대한 계획서를 정확하게 쓸 수 있다.
	중	자신의 직업 및 진로에 대한 계획서를 대략적으로 쓸 수 있다.
	하	자신의 직업 및 진로에 대한 계획서를 부분적으로 쓸 수 있다.

03 영역별 성취수준 (단원 단위)

1 듣기영역

성취수준	일반적 특성
A	다양한 직업 및 진로에 관한 말이나 대화를 듣고 세부 정보를 정확하게 파악할 수 있다. 다양한 직업 및 진로에 관한 말이나 대화를 듣고 주제 및 요지를 정확하게 파악할 수 있다.
B	다양한 직업 및 진로에 관한 말이나 대화를 듣고 세부 정보를 정확하게 파악할 수 있다. 다양한 직업 및 진로에 관한 말이나 대화를 듣고 주제 및 요지를 대략적으로 파악할 수 있다.
C	다양한 직업 및 진로에 관한 말이나 대화를 듣고 세부 정보를 대략적으로 파악할 수 있다. 다양한 직업 및 진로에 관한 말이나 대화를 듣고 주제 및 요지를 대략적으로 파악할 수 있다.
D	다양한 직업 및 진로에 관한 말이나 대화를 듣고 세부 정보를 대략적으로 파악할 수 있다. 다양한 직업 및 진로에 관한 말이나 대화를 듣고 주제 및 요지를 부분적으로 파악할 수 있다.
E	다양한 직업 및 진로에 관한 말이나 대화를 듣고 세부 정보를 부분적으로 파악할 수 있다. 다양한 직업 및 진로에 관한 말이나 대화를 듣고 주제 및 요지를 부분적으로 파악할 수 있다.

2 말하기영역

성취수준	일반적 특성
A	다양한 직업 및 진로에 관해 자신의 의견이나 감정을 정확하게 표현할 수 있다. 다양한 직업 및 진로에 관한 정보를 정확하게 묻고 답할 수 있다.
B	다양한 직업 및 진로에 관해 자신의 의견이나 감정을 정확하게 표현할 수 있다. 다양한 직업 및 진로에 관한 정보를 대략적으로 묻고 답할 수 있다.
C	다양한 직업 및 진로에 관해 자신의 의견이나 감정을 대략적으로 표현할 수 있다. 다양한 직업 및 진로에 관한 정보를 대략적으로 묻고 답할 수 있다.
D	다양한 직업 및 진로에 관해 자신의 의견이나 감정을 대략적으로 표현할 수 있다. 다양한 직업 및 진로에 관한 정보를 부분적으로 묻고 답할 수 있다.
E	다양한 직업 및 진로에 관해 자신의 의견이나 감정을 부분적으로 표현할 수 있다. 다양한 직업 및 진로에 관한 정보를 부분적으로 묻고 답할 수 있다.

3 읽기영역

성취수준	일반적 특성
A	다양한 직업 및 진로에 관한 글을 읽고 세부 정보를 정확하게 파악할 수 있다. 다양한 직업 및 진로에 관한 글을 읽고 주제 및 요지를 정확하게 파악할 수 있다.
B	다양한 직업 및 진로에 관한 글을 읽고 세부 정보를 정확하게 파악할 수 있다. 다양한 직업 및 진로에 관한 글을 읽고 주제 및 요지를 대략적으로 파악할 수 있다.
C	다양한 직업 및 진로에 관한 글을 읽고 세부 정보를 대략적으로 파악할 수 있다. 다양한 직업 및 진로에 관한 글을 읽고 주제 및 요지를 대략적으로 파악할 수 있다.
D	다양한 직업 및 진로에 관한 글을 읽고 세부 정보를 대략적으로 파악할 수 있다. 다양한 직업 및 진로에 관한 글을 읽고 주제 및 요지를 부분적으로 파악할 수 있다.
E	다양한 직업 및 진로에 관한 글을 읽고 세부 정보를 부분적으로 파악할 수 있다. 다양한 직업 및 진로에 관한 글을 읽고 주제 및 요지를 부분적으로 파악할 수 있다.

4 쓰기영역

성취수준	일반적 특성
A	사람, 사물, 사건에 대하여 상세하게 묘사하는 글을 정확하게 쓸 수 있다.
B	사람, 사물, 사건에 대하여 상세하게 묘사하는 글을 대략적으로 쓸 수 있다.
C	사람, 사물, 사건에 대하여 상세하게 묘사하는 글을 부분적으로 쓸 수 있다.

04 수업 지도안

1 Master Plan

(1) Text
Career English

(2) Lesson
Help! I'm Worried About My Career!

(3) General Aims

① **Main Aims**
- Students will be able to listen to a talk, an announcement, and a dialogue, and answer questions.
- Students will be able to think about common career concerns that teens have and their own worries.
- Students will be able to read a text about career worries that teens have and their solutions.
- Students will be able to discover their career type and think about what kind of jobs will be appropriate for them.

② **Communicative Functions**
- To express how much you are sure about something
- To express that you are worried/scared about something

③ **Language Forms**
- To make sentences using unless instead of 「if ~ not」 clause
- To make sentences using 「expect + object + to infinitive」

(4) Teaching Aids
textbook, computer, teacher's guide, worksheets

(5) **Time Allotment** : 7 periods, 50 minutes each

Contents	Period	Min	Teaching and Learning Aims
Lesson Map	1/7	10	to preview the topics and learning points in Lesson 1
Listen Up		40	to understand a talk about a career assessment test to understand an announcement about counseling camp jobs for teenagers to understand a dialogue about a career counseling application
Speak Out / Ready to Read	2/7	50	to talk with a partner about their career worries to make predictions about the main text after guessing the meaning of the given words
Read 1	3/7	50	to read the text and understand common worries teens have about their future careers and their solutions to discover good solutions to their worries from others' advice
Read 2	4/7	50	to read the text and understand what steps they can take to build their confidence and bring their self-esteem up to think about what steps they need to take and apply them to their everyday lives
After You Read/ Think & Write	5/7	50	to summarize the main text and identify detailed information to learn the structure of logical writing to write about their strengths and weaknesses
Language Focus / Review	6/7	50	to know how to make sentences using unless instead of 「if ~ not」 clause to learn the verbs which take to-infinitive as their object complement to review what was learned in this lesson
Mission Task/ Culture	7/7	50	to measure their self-esteem by taking the Rosenberg Self-Esteem Scale Test to discover their career type by answering the questions

2 Sub Plan

(1) Period: 1 of 7

- **Section:** Lesson Map & Listen Up (pp. 8–11)
- **Time:** 50 minutes
- **Objectives:**
  1. Students will be able to preview the topics and learning points.
  2. Students will be able to listen to and understand dialogues where expressions for expressing how much they are sure about something and how much they are worried/scared about something are used.
- **Teaching Aids:** textbook, dictation worksheet
- **Procedure:**

Step	Contents	Activities
Introduction	Greeting	• Exchange greetings. • Check attendance.
	Reviewing	• Check assignments. • Review the last lesson.
	Presenting Objectives	• State the aims of this period.
Development	Lesson Map	• Students read the title of Lesson 1. • Students look at the pictures on page 8, read the topics for each section, and preview Lesson 1.
	Listen Up A, B, C	• (A) Students read the question, look at the pictures before listening to the talk, and guess what the talk will be about. • Students listen to the talk and answer the question. • (B) Students read the question before listening to the announcement. • Students listen to the announcement and answer the question. • (C) Students read the two questions before listening to the dialogue. • Students listen to the dialogue and answer the questions.
	Listen Up D	• Students read the questions and look at the pictures before listening to the dialogue. • Students listen to the dialogue and answer the question. • Students listen to the dialogue again and fill in the blanks with the proper words. • Students talk with a partner about what kind of person they want as their mentor and what help they need from their mentor. • Students share their ideas with the class.
Consolidation	Wrap-Up	• Students check the expressions for expressing how much they are sure about something and how much they are worried/ scared about something. • Students listen to the talk, the announcement, and the dialogue again to complete the worksheet.
	Assignment	• Give the assignment and preview the next class with students.

(2) **Period**: 2 of 7

- **Section**: Speak Out, Ready to Read (pp. 12-14)
- **Time**: 50 minutes
- **Objectives**:
    1. Students will be able to think about common career concerns that teens have and share their career worries with a partner.
    2. Students will be able to use the expressions for expressing how much they are sure about something and how much they are worried/scared about something in a conversation with a partner.
- **Teaching Aids**: textbook
- **Procedure**:

Step	Contents	Activities
Introduction	Greeting	• Exchange greetings. • Check attendance.
	Reviewing	• Check assignments. • Review the last lesson.
	Presenting Objectives	• Stating the aims of this period.
Development	Speak Out A, B	• (A) Students choose an expression that has the same meaning as the underlined phrases. • Students practice the dialogue with a partner using the other expressions and then switch roles. • (B) Students think about common career concerns that teens have and share their own answers with a partner.
	Speak Out C, D	• (C) Students read the given dialogue and guess what will be appropriate for the blank. • Students complete the dialogue with the phrases and practice it with a partner. • Students write down their opinions for the blank, and practice the dialogue with a partner using their opinions. • (D) Students make groups of four and each student gets a piece of paper. • Students write down their problem on the piece of paper. • Students collect all the pieces of paper and choose one by one. • Students talk about the problems and possible solutions.
	Ready to Read	• (A) Students guess the meaning of the given words looking at the pictures. • Students fill in the blanks with the proper words using context clues. • (B) Students read the example career worries and check if it is the same as their worry. • Students write down what other worries they have and share them with the class.
Consolidation	Wrap-Up	• Students check the expressions that are used for expressing how much they are sure about something and how much they are worried/scared about something.
	Assignment	• Give the assignment and preview the next class with students.

(3) **Period:** 3 of 7

- **Section:** Read 1 (pp. 15–17)
- **Time:** 50 minutes
- **Objectives:**
  1. Students will be able to read the text and understand common worries that teens have about their careers and their solutions.
  2. Students will be able to discover good solutions to their worries from the given responses.
- **Teaching Aids:** textbook, word list worksheet
- **Procedure:**

Step	Contents	Activities
Introduction	Greeting	• Exchange greetings. • Check attendance.
	Reviewing	• Check assignments. • Review the last lesson.
	Presenting Objectives	• State the aims of this period.
Development	Read (pp. 15–17) Step 1	• Students learn the meaning of words from the text using the word list worksheet. • Students read the title and look at the pictures to predict the content of the text. • Students skim through the text to figure out what the main idea is.
	Read (pp. 15–17) Step 2	• Students read the text again to understand the specifics. • Students write down the answers of the questions on page 15, 16, and 17 to check their understanding. • Students talk about their career worries and compare them with the given two worries.
	Read (pp. 15–17) Step 3	• Students learn the grammatical structures of the sentences that are helpful for understanding the text. • Students fill in the blanks of "Scan and search for the missing word" on page 15, 16, and 17 to complete the sentences.
Consolidation	Wrap-Up	• Ask students to think about which response helps the most and why they think so. • Ask students to share their opinions with the class.
	Assignment	• Give the assignment and preview the next class with students.

(4) **Period: 4 of 7**
- **Section:** Read 2 (pp. 18–19)
- **Time:** 50 minutes
- **Objectives:**
  1. Students will be able to read the text and understand what steps they can take to build their confidence and bring their self-esteem up.
  2. Students will be able to think about what steps they need and apply them to their everyday lives.
- **Teaching Aids:** textbook, word list worksheet, vocabulary worksheet
- **Procedure:**

Step	Contents	Activities
Introduction	Greeting	• Exchange greetings. • Check attendance.
	Reviewing	• Check assignments. • Review the last lesson.
	Presenting Objectives	• State the aims of this period.
Development	Read (pp. 18–19) Step 1	• Students learn the meaning of words from the text using the word list worksheet. • Students look at the pictures and guess what the text will be about. • Students skim through the text to figure out what the main idea is.
	Read (pp. 18–19) Step 2	• Students read the text again to understand the specifics. • Students write down the answers to the questions on page 18 and 19 to check their understanding.
	Read (pp. 18–19) Step 3	• Students learn the grammatical structures of the sentences to help improve their reading comprehension skills. • Students fill in the blanks of "Scan and search for the missing word" on page 18 and 19 to complete the sentences. • Students review the words from the text using the vocabulary worksheet.
Consolidation	Wrap-Up	• Ask students to tell the class how they felt and what they learned from the main text. • Ask students to think about what steps they want to take to build their confidence and bring their self-esteem up.
	Assignment	• Give the assignment and preview the next class with students.

(5) Period: 5 of 7

- **Section:** After You Read, Think & Write (pp. 20–23)
- **Time:** 50 minutes
- **Objectives:**
  1. Students will be able to summarize the main text by filling in the blanks using the given words.
  2. Students will be able to write about their strengths and weaknesses based on the structure of logical writing.
- **Teaching Aids:** textbook
- **Procedure:**

Step	Contents	Activities
Introduction	Greeting	• Exchange greetings. • Check attendance.
	Reviewing	• Check assignments. • Review the last lesson.
	Presenting Objectives	• State the aims of this period.
Development	After You Read A, B	• (A) Students use the words from the word bank to fill in the blanks and complete the summary. • (B) Students read examples of how to build self-esteem and then match each example with the appropriate sentence.
	After You Read C, D	• (C) Students make detailed plans based on the given strategies to boost their self-esteem. • Students share their plans with the class. • (D) Students make groups of four and then write some good things about themselves. • Students take turns sharing their good points in front of other members. • Students give the presenter a big hand when he/she finishes talking. • Students share good things about their group members with the class.
	Think & Write Sample, Step 1	• Students read the writing sample and learn the structure of logical writing. • Students read the examples of strengths and weaknesses and check their strengths and weaknesses.
	Think & Write Step 2–4	• Students make groups of three and then write down their friends' strengths using expressions from Step 1. • Students think about and write down their weaknesses and how to overcome them in the blank. • Students write about their strengths and weaknesses based on Step 1 to Step 3 referring to the logical structure of the writing sample.
Consolidation	Wrap-Up	• Give each student some short feedback on their work. • Ask students to tell the class how they felt or what they learned from writing about their strengths and weaknesses.
	Assignment	• Give the assignment and preview the next class with students.

(6) **Period**: 6 of 7

- **Section**: Language Focus, Review (pp. 24–27)
- **Time**: 50 minutes
- **Objectives**:
  1. Students will be able to understand the word partners of the two verbs bring and get.
  2. Students will be able to make sentences using unless instead of 「if ~ not」 clause.
  3. Students will be able to learn the verbs which take to-infinitive as their object complement.
  4. Students will be able to answer the review questions.
- **Teaching Aids**: textbook
- **Procedure**:

Step	Contents	Activities
Introduction	Greeting	• Exchange greetings. • Check attendance.
	Reviewing	• Check assignments. • Review the last lesson.
	Presenting Objectives	• State the aims of this period.
Development	Language Focus A, B	• (A) Students read the given sentences out loud. • (B) Students read the example sentences and learn the adverbs or prepositions that go with bring and get. • Students choose the correct words to complete the sentences using context clues.
	Language Focus C, D	• (C) Students complete the sentences by filling in the blanks with the appropriate words. • (D) Students read the three example sentences and identify the target grammar points. • Students learn how to make sentences using unless instead of 「if ~ not」 clause. • Students learn how to make sentences using 「expect + object + to-infinitive」. • Students learn the verbs which take to-infinitive as their object complement. • Students complete the sentences based on the grammar points they learned.
	Review 1–4	• Students listen to the dialogues and the monologue and answer the questions. • Students complete the sentences by filling in the blanks with the appropriate words.
	Review 5–7	• Students read the passage and answer the questions. • Students read an article about a favorite subject and complete it with a concluding sentence.
Consolidation	Wrap-Up	• Students share their answers with the class.
	Assignment	• Give the assignment and preview the next class with students.

(7) Period: 7 of 7

- **Section:** Mission Task, Culture (pp. 28-29)
- **Time:** 50 minutes
- **Objectives:**
  1. Students will be able to measure their self-esteem by taking the Rosenberg Self-Esteem Scale Test.
  2. Students will be able to discover their career type and think about what kind of jobs will be appropriate for them.
- **Teaching Aids:** textbook, computer
- **Procedures:**

Step	Contents	Activities
Introduction	Greeting	• Exchange greetings. • Check attendance.
	Reviewing	• Check assignments. • Review the last lesson.
	Presenting Objectives	• State the aims of this period.
Development	Mission Task	• Students look at the picture and think about what self-esteem is. • Students read the 10 statements of the Rosenberg Self-Esteem Scale Test and answer each statement by agreeing with one of the four possibilities. • Students check the score for each statement and calculate the total score of the test. • Students share how they feel about the result and what they think of themselves. • Students talk with a partner about how to bring their self-esteem up and share their ideas with the class.
	Culture	• Students read the title, look at the pictures, and guess what the text will be about. • Students use the chart to find their career type and answer the questions. • Students discover their career type among the six different types. • Students search online for other jobs related to their career type and think about what kind of jobs will be appropriate for them.
Consolidation	Wrap-Up	• Ask students to tell the class how they felt or what they learned from the mission task.
	Assignment	• Ask students to review Lesson 1.

CHAPTER 03 고교 영어 1

01 Give the Earth a Hand!

Like many other people, you probably have a lot of questions about environmental protection but haven't been able to find the answers easily. Here are answers to some of the things you may be curious about.

Q1: What should I do with my old cell phone when I buy a new one?
A: People usually just throw their old cell phones in the trash. In fact, according to the Ministry of the Environment of Korea, more than 18 million used cell phones were thrown away in 2010 in Korea alone. In the United States, more than 130 million cell phones are thrown away every year. Cell phones contain hazardous materials that damage the environment such as lead, mercury and arsenic. They also contain valuable metals such as gold, silver and copper. This makes it all the more important to recycle old cell phones. Manufacturers can repair them for resale or reuse some materials and parts.

Q2: Why aren't clam shells, chicken bones or fish bones considered food waste?
A: Only waste that can be processed into food for animals is regarded as food waste. Hard things like clam shells, nut shells, bones and certain seeds are not edible so they make animals sick and can also disrupt the processing of food. Even onion and garlic peels are harmful to livestock and should be thrown away as garbage.

Q3: I recently saw a T-shirt that was said to be "upcycled." What is upcycling?
A: In upcycling, materials are not simply reused just as they are. Instead, waste materials are converted into new products that are of better quality and that are less harmful to the environment. Many upcycled products also have creative designs. For example, a famous sports brand makes upcycled shoes using old magazines. Although upcycling is not as popular in Korea yet as it is in North America and Europe, more and more Koreans are becoming interested in it.

Q4: Is the exhaust of cars and buses that burn compressed natural gas(CNG) free of pollutants?
A: Although the exhaust from burning CNG is not completely free of pollutants, CNG produces only one third of the pollution caused by other fuels. It's also a lot safer, because it's lighter than air, so if there's a leak, it quickly disperses.

Q5: Is email more eco-friendly than regular paper mail?

A: Sending one message of average length by email produces only one sixtieth of the carbon dioxide(CO_2) produced by sending a letter by post. However, because of the ease and convenience of email, this advantage is offset by the huge quantity of email that comes and goes every day. According to research conducted by the Institute for Climate Change Action, a company with a hundred employees sends about 58 emails and receives 33 every day, producing up to 13.6 tons of CO_2 a year. And of course, with longer messages, even more CO_2 is produced. Therefore, eliminating unnecessary email can help protect the environment.

Q6: Is eating beef bad for the environment?
A: In order to produce lots of cheap beef, people have to cut down trees to make pastures. In some countries, rainforests are being damaged in order to raise more cattle. As part of their natural digestive process, cattle also release methane, which is one of the causes of global warming. It is clearly advisable that we reduce beef consumption.

Q7: If two thirds of the Earth's surface is covered in water, why is there danger of a water crisis?
A: Most of the water that covers the Earth is salt water which we can't drink. Human beings need fresh water for drinking, household uses and irrigation. Also, much of the fresh water that is available in rivers and lakes is polluted. In many places, as in Korea for example, rainfall is concentrated in one rainy season. During the rest of the year, these places often suffer from drought. It is important that we find better ways to reduce water pollution.

Q8: Someone told me that keeping houseplants helps purify the air. Is that really true?
A: Research conducted by NASA and the Associated Landscape Contractors of America showed that common houseplants actually do help purify the air. Everyone knows that plants take in carbon dioxide and let out oxygen, but this study found that certain plants also remove harmful chemicals from the air.

Q9: In public bathrooms, is it better to dry your hands with paper towels or with an electric hand dryer?
A: Much less energy is used by an electric hand dryer than it takes to make paper towels and deliver them. Did you know that nine trees have to be cut down to supply an average fast-food restaurant with paper towels for a year?

Q10: Which saves more energy: turning your computer off at night or putting it in sleep mode?
A: Putting your computer in sleep mode does save lots of energy, but shutting it down completely saves even more.

Q11: If you leave a charger plugged in after it's fully charged, does it still consume electricity?
A: You may be surprised to learn that phone chargers, DVD players, TV sets and other devices that are turned off but plugged in use up lots of energy every year.

02 수업 계획서와 교실 활동

1 Period 1

- **Date & Hour**: The ____class hour, _____, _____ , 20____
- **Class**: The _____ class of the _____ grade
- **Material**: Textbook (Listening & Speaking Zone)
- **Objectives**:
  1. Students can express sympathy or pity.
  2. Students can answer questions for specific information after listening.
  3. Students can pronounce "What are you" and "What do you".
- **Teaching Aids**:
  1. Textbook
  2. Computer, DVD-ROM, Worksheet

Procedures:

Steps	Activities	Time
Warm-up	1. **Exchange greetings and have small talk** ⓣ Good morning, everyone! ⓢ Good morning. How are you? ⓣ Fine. Thanks. 2. **Introducing today's new topic and lesson goals** ⓣ Open your books to page 94. What's today's topic? ⓢ "Saving Lives" ⓣ Right. Today we're going to listen to dialogues about endangered plants and animals and how to save them. Are you ready? ⓢ Yes. ⓣ Okay, let's get started.	2′
Build-up	Topic 1. Saving Lives Get It Ready 1. **Listening to an announcement and checking if the students understand it** ⓣ The picture shows a map of a park and some environmental signs. Now we will listen to an announcement. Listen carefully and check the sign you're not likely to see in the park. *(Listening)* Okay, let's check if your answer is correct. What do you think is the sign you're not likely to see in the park? ⓢ I think the answer is "c". ⓣ That's right.	10′

Steps	Activities	Time
Build-up	**Small Talk** **2. Having a conversation and sharing an interesting idea** ⓣ Here are three questions at the bottom of the page. Now talk about the three questions with your partner. *(Talking)* Are you done? ⓢ Yes, teacher. ⓣ Why don't we talk about question number three together? I'll pick three students to give us their answers. Student number 21. Okay, Jinsu, why do you think certain animals or plants become endangered? ⓢ I think animals and plants become endangered due to climate change, illegal hunting, human behaviors, etc.	10′
	Learn It **A** **3. Listening in and choosing the right picture** ⓣ First, look at the pictures quickly. Okay, tell me what the pictures are. ⓢ Picture a is "pink flowers", b is "pandas", and c is "various animals". ⓣ Good. Now we'll listen to three short dialogues about endangered animals or plants. Listen carefully and try to match each picture with the right dialogue. *(Listening)* Okay, let's check the answers together. Is there a volunteer? Good, Minsu, which picture does number 1 dialogue match? ⓢ Picture c ⓣ That's right. What about number 2 and 3 dialogues? ⓢ Number 2 is "picture b", and number 3 is "picture a".	10′
	B **4. Listening to a conversation and checking the answers.** ⓣ This time we'll listen to a conversation between a man and a woman. First, listen carefully and think about what the speakers are going to do after the conversation. *(Listening)* Are you done? Let's check if your answer is correct. Let's hear from everyone. What is the answer to the first question? ⓢ The answer is "a". ⓣ Yes, that's right. Listen again and find out what the man says is a way to protect flowers. *(Listening)* Okay, let's check the answers together. What's the answer for the second question? ⓢ I think it's "b". ⓣ Good.	10′

Steps	Activities	Time
Build-up	**Sound in Use** **5. Listening to examples and understanding the rule.** ⓣ Let's move on to Sound in Use. Look at the bold-faced words, "What are you" and "What do you". Listen carefully to how these are pronounced. *(Listening)* ⓣ In normal spoken American English, the contraction "what're" usually sounds something like "whadda". The "t" in the word "what" is somewhere in between a [t] and a [d] sound, but probably closer to [d]. And the "r" in "what're" is often not pronounced at all. Okay, let's listen again and repeat the sentences. ⓢ Yes, teacher. *(Repeating)* ⓣ Now, listen to the two sentences and fill in the blanks. *(Listening)* Did you get all the answers right? ⓢ Yes, we did.	5′
Wrap-up	**1. Reviewing today's lesson** ⓣ Today we talked about what a nature reserve park was and listened to several dialogues about endangered plants and animals. I hope you enjoyed today's class. ⓢ Yes, teacher. **2. Setting an assignment and informing students about the next lesson** ⓣ Next class, we're going to listen to a public service advertisement about endangered species and talk about this topic some more. See you next class. ⓢ Bye.	3′

2 Period 2

- **Date & Hour:** The ____ class hour, _____, _____ ____, 20____
- **Class:** The _____ class of the _____ grade
- **Material:** Textbook (Listening & Speaking Zone)
- **Objectives:**
  1. Students can listen to an advertisement and figure out the details.
  2. Students can learn express sympathy for someone or something.
  3. Students can review and practice communicative functions.
- **Teaching Aids:**
  1. Textbook/
  2. Computer, DVD-ROM, Worksheet

Procedures:

Steps	Activities	Time
Warm-up	1. Exchanging greetings and having small talk ⓣ Hello, everyone. How are you? ⓢ Great! How about you? ⓣ I'm feeling great, too. Thanks. 2. Introducing today's lesson and lesson goals ⓣ Open your books to page 96 and tell me what part we will study today. ⓢ "Listening & Speaking Zone (Use It)" ⓣ Good. How many endangered species do you think exist in this world? What causes them to become extinct? Today, we're going to listen to a public service announcement about animals becoming endangered and talk about the causes. Also, we'll learn how to express sympathy for someone or something. Okay, shall we start? ⓢ Yes, teacher.	2′
Build-up	Topic 1. Saving Lives Step 1 1. Checking what the pictures are about ⓣ Look at the pictures of animals. Tell me what they are. ⓢ They are "lions", "bluefin tuna", "whales", "polar bears", and "owls". ⓣ Good. They're all endangered animals, so what do you think are the causes of their becoming endangered? Guess and share your thoughts with your partner. ⓢ (Talking)	5′

Steps	Activities	Time
Build-up	**2. Listening to an advertisement and checking if students understand it** ⓣ Now we will listen to the public service advertisement. Listen carefully and try to fill in the blank of for each animal with its cause of extinction. Okay, let's listen. *(Listening)* Let's check the answers together. ⓢ Number 1 is "c", number 2 is "e", number 3 is "a", number 4 is "d" and number 5 is "b". ⓣ Good job. Now, let's listen again and answer the questions below. *(Listening)* Let's check the answers together. What are the answers to question number 1 and 2? ⓢ I think for question number 1, "they" is "endangered species" and "we" is "humans". And the answer to question number 2 is "forty". ⓣ Great. **Step 2** **3. Filling in the missing information** ⓣ Now, let's talk about the world's most endangered species. What you're going to do is called "information gap" activity. Let's play rock-paper-scissors first with your partner. The winner is going to be Student A and the other is to be Student B. Now, I'd like Student B to turn to page 244. ⓢ *(Doing the activity)* **4. Having a conversation based on the sample dialogue** ⓣ Okay, now we will listen to the example dialogue. *(Listening)* Then, practice the dialogue with your partner. Change your roles and keep practicing. *(Talking)* Are you done? ⓢ Yes, we are. ⓣ Then, I want you to fill in the blanks by having a conversation using the information you have. Talk with your partner about the world's most endangered species. Your partner has different parts of information that you have. ⓢ *(Talking)*	10′ 20′ 10′
Wrap-up	**1. Reviewing today's lesson** ⓣ Let's wrap up the class, everyone. Today we learned how to express sympathy for someone or something. What is the expression? ⓢ "I feel sorry for …." ⓣ Yes, exactly. Also, we talked about endangered species and how to save them. You did a good job. **2. Setting an assignment and informing students about the next lesson** ⓣ Next time, we'll listen to some dialogues about saving the environment and learn how to remind someone to do something. I hope you have a wonderful day. See you next class.	3′

3 Period 3

- **Date & Hour:** The ____ class hour, _____, _____ ____, 20____
- **Class:** The _____ class of the _____ grade
- **Material:** Textbook (Listening & Speaking Zone)
- **Objectives:**
  1. Students can tell how to remind someone of something.
  2. Students can answer questions for specific information after listening.
  3. Students can use the expression "speaking of which".
- **Teaching Aids:**
  1. Textbook
  2. Computer, DVD-ROM, Worksheet

Procedures:

Steps	Activities	Time
Warm-up	1. **Exchanging greetings and having small talk** ⓣ Hello, everyone. How do you feel today? ⓢ Great. How about you? ⓣ It couldn't be better, thanks. 2. **Introducing today's lesson and lesson goals.** ⓣ Open your books to page 98. Do you see today's topic? Let's read the topic together. ⓢ "Saving Energy" ⓣ That's right. Today's topic is "Saving Energy". What do you think are some of the things that we can do for the environment in our daily lives? Today, we'll listen to a dialogue about ways to protect the Earth. Okay, shall we start?	2′
Build-up	**Topic 2. Saving Energy** **Get It Ready** 1. **Filling in the blanks using the given words** ⓣ The picture shows how energy is wasted. Okay, look at the pictures, and talk about how we are wasting our energy and how we can save it with your partner. ⓢ *(Talking)* ⓣ Good. Now look at the pictures and try to fill in the blanks with the appropriate words written below. *(Filling in the blanks)* Let's check the answers together. ⓢ Number 1 is "running", number 2 is "open", number 3 is "lights", number 4 is "paper", number 5 is "electricity", and number 6 is "unplugging". ⓣ Good Job.	10′

Steps	Activities	Time
	Small Talk **2. Having a small talk with your partner and sharing interesting ideas** ⓣ Look at the three questions on the page. Talk about the questions with your partner. *(Talking)* ⓣ Why don't we talk about question number three together? I'll pick two students to give us their answers. Okay, Juhee, what are some things we can do to save energy in our daily lives? ⓢ We can try to reduce food waste and unplug electric devices when they are not in use. ⓣ Excellent.	10′
	Learn It **3. Filling in the blanks and checking the answers by listening to a dialogue** ⓣ Minsik and Jinhui are talking about energy use. Can you read the expressions below first? ⓢ "turn the TV off", "you're done with", "complaining about" ⓣ Good. Now, let's complete the conversation using the expressions below. ⓢ Yes, teacher. ⓣ Are you finished? Okay. This time we're going to listen to the conversation. Listen carefully and while listening, check whether or not you got the answers right.	10′
	4. Listening again and practicing the conversation ⓣ Listen again and find out when we can use the expression "Don't forget to …." *(Listening)* Jinho, can you tell me when you can say "Don't forget to …."? ⓢ Yes, I think we can use it when we want to remind someone to do something. ⓣ That's right. Now, practice this expression with your partner using your own examples.	10′
	Speaking Strategy **5. Understanding "speaking of which" and practicing the expression** ⓣ Look at the bold-faced expression, "speaking of which". As the sample dialogue shows, you can use "speaking of which" when you want to say something related to what you were just talking about. Now, practice the expression with your partner using your own examples. ⓢ Yes, teacher.	5′
Wrap-up	**1. Reviewing today's lesson** ⓣ Today we listened to a conversation about saving energy. How about doing something to save energy at home? I'm sure small actions can make a big difference. Everyone seemed to enjoy the activity a lot. Right? Please go over what we learned in this lesson at home. **2. Setting an assignment and informing students about the next lesson** ⓣ Next class, we're going to listen to a lecture by an expert on energy saving. All of you did a good job today. Have a nice day. ⓢ You, too!	3′

4 Period 4

- **Date & Hour:** The ____ class hour, _____, _____ ____, 20____
- **Class:** The _____ class of the _____ grade
- **Material:** Textbook (Listening & Speaking Zone)
- **Objectives:**
    1. Students can say how to save energy.
    2. Students can answer questions for specific information after listening.
    3. Students can review and practice the communicative function.
- **Teaching Aids:**
    1. Textbook
    2. Computer, DVD-ROM, Worksheet

Procedures:

Steps	Activities	Time
Warm-up	1. Exchanging greetings and having small talk ⓣ Hello, everyone! Today the weather is so nice, isn't it? ⓢ Yes it is! How are you today? ⓣ I'm really good. Thanks. 2. Introducing today's lesson and lesson goals ⓣ Open your books to page 100. Today we are going to listen to a lecture by an expert on saving energy. Then, you're going to do an energy saving game with your group members. Are you ready? ⓢ Yes, we are ready. ⓣ Okay, let's get started.	2′
Build-up	Topic 2. Saving Energy Use It Step 1 1. Listening to a lecture and checking the answers ⓣ Let's look at the picture and the chart. Can you guess what you're going to hear? First, try to fill in the blanks with your own words before we listen to the lecture. *(Reading)* Okay, let's share our ideas with our partner. ⓢ *(Talking)* ⓣ Okay, now listen carefully and fill in the blanks. *(Listening)* Are you finished? Let's check if your answers are correct. Suji, what are the answers for the blanks? ⓢ The first blank is "hot water", the second is "Turn off", and the third is "showers", the fourth is "toilet", and the fifth is "print out". ⓣ Right. Good job.	15′

Steps	Activities	Time
Build-up	**Step 2** **2. Practicing dialogues** ⓣ Look at the example dialogue in your textbook and practice the conversation with your partner, switching roles. *(Talking)* Are you done? ⓢ Yes, we are. ⓣ Okay, now think of your own examples and practice them your partner.	10′
	Step 3 **3. Playing games as a group** ⓣ Now, I'd like you to do a group work activity, so make groups of four. There are many energy saving ways on the board. With your group members, take turns flipping a coin and moving around the board. Read the statements about saving energy. You get points for the energy-saving efforts you're practicing daily. ⓢ *(Playing games)* ⓣ Okay. Good job, everyone.	20′
Wrap-up	**1. Reviewing today's lesson** ⓣ Today, we listened to a lecture about saving energy. Why don't you take this opportunity to think about ways to help save energy and make our planet a better place? All of you did a good job. **2. Setting an assignment and informing students about the next lesson** ⓣ Next class, we'll learn some new words and read a part of the main text. I hope today's class was a good and meaningful time for all of you. See you next time. Bye. ⓢ Bye.	3′

5 Period 5

- **Date & Hour:** The ____ class hour, _____, _____ ____, 20____
- **Class:** The _____ class of the _____ grade
- **Material:** Textbook (Reading Lounge)
- **Objectives:**
    1. Students can match new words and expressions with their meanings.
    2. Students can guess the topic of the main text from the title and the given picture.
    3. Students can tell the specific details of the main text.
- **Teaching Aids:**
    1. Textbook
    2. Computer, DVD-ROM, Worksheet

Procedures:

Steps	Activities	Time
Warm-up	**1. Exchanging greetings and having small talk** ⓣ Hello, everyone. How are you today? ⓢ Not bad at all. How about you? ⓣ I'm feeling great. Thanks. **2. Introducing today's lesson and lesson goals.** ⓣ Today we're going to start reading the main text. Before we begin, we're going to learn some new words. Also, we'll do an activity related to the content. Are you ready? ⓢ Yes, we are ready. ⓣ Okay, let's start today's lesson.	2′
Build-up	**Before You Read** **A. Learn Key Vocabulary** **1. Learning key vocabulary** ⓣ Look at the headlines from a newspaper, which are about environmental problems. First, read through the headlines and guess what word will go in each blank. *(Reading)* Are you done? Okay, now let's look at the words and their definitions below. Can you read them aloud? ⓢ *(Reading)* ⓣ Great. Let's fill in the blanks in the newspaper headlines with the appropriate words. Is there any word or expression you don't understand? Okay, let's check the answers together.	8′

Steps	Activities	Time
Build-up	**B. Explore the Theme** **2. Exploring the theme** ⓣ First, read the three questions below about the environment. *(Reading)* Are you done? Okay, now talk about the questions with your partner. ⓢ *(Talking)* ⓣ Good job. Now, write down your answers on the survey board. ⓢ *(Writing)* ⓣ Okay. I'd like you to share your ideas with the class.	7'
	Reading **3. Guessing the topic of the story from the title and the given picture** ⓣ Why don't we read the main text now? Open your books to page 103 and read the title aloud. ⓢ "Greenquestions.org" ⓣ Yes, exactly. Now, look at the picture. What do you think the main passage will be about? ⓢ The picture shows the Green Earth, so I think the main text will be about the environment. ⓣ You made a good guess. Let's start to read.	5'
	4. Reading the passage and understanding the meanings of the new words ⓣ First, let's read the passage on page 103 and try to find out the answer to the As You Read question. *(Reading)* What are some hazardous materials found inside a cell phone? ⓢ "Cell phones contain lead, mercury and arsenic." ⓣ Correct. Now, let's study the new words and expressions below. Repeat after me. *(Reading)* Now, we're going to study the meaning of each new word and expression.	20'
	5. Listening to and reading the passage again ⓣ Now, we'll listen to the passage. Listen to the audio and try to understand the content. *(Listening)* Now, I need a volunteer to read aloud for us. Who wants to read? ⓢ I'll read it, teacher. ⓣ Oh, Jumin, thank you. Read aloud for us. *(Reading)* Good job.	5'
Wrap-up	**1. Reviewing today's lesson** ⓣ All right, that's all for today. Today we read the first part of the Qs and As about the environment. Do you realize why you need to recycle your used cell phones? ⓢ Yes, we do. ⓣ Okay. I hope you read the article at home again and try to fully understand the content. **2. Setting an assignment and informing students about the next lesson** ⓣ Next class, we'll continue to read more about the environment. See you next time. Bye.	3'

6 Period 6

- **Date & Hour:** The ____ class hour, _____, _____ ____, 20____
- **Class:** The _____ class of the _____ grade
- **Material:** Textbook (Reading Lounge)
- **Objectives:**
  1. Students can tell the contents of the main text from the given pictures.
  2. Students can define the meanings of new words and expressions.
  3. Students can state the main idea and specific information from the text.
- **Teaching Aids:**
  1. Textbook
  2. Computer, DVD-ROM, Worksheet

Procedures:

Steps	Activities	Time
Warm-up	1. **Exchanging greetings and having small talk** ⓣ Hello, everyone. How are you today? ⓢ We're doing fine. How about you? ⓣ I'm feeling great. Thanks. 2. **Introducing today's lesson and lesson goals.** ⓣ Open your books to page 104. Did you go over what we read in our last class? ⓢ Yes, we did. ⓣ Today, we're going to read more questions and answers about the environment. Before we begin today's lesson, let me ask you a few questions to remind you of what we learned in the previous class. Shall we start?	2′
Build-up	**Reading** 1. **Guessing the main topic from the given pictures** ⓣ Before reading let's take a look at the pictures on page 104. What can you see in the pictures? ⓢ We can see fish bones and a black T-shirt with creative designs. ⓣ That's good. And what can you see in the picture on page 105? ⓢ We can see a tank of CNG(Compressed Natural Gas) and the mark used in email addresses "@". ⓣ Good guess.	5′

Steps	Activities	Time
Build-up	**2. Reading the passage and finding out the main topic** ⓣ Now, read the passage on pages 104 and 105 as fast as possible. *(Reading)* Are you finished? ⓢ Yes. ⓣ As we guessed, the main topic of this passage is "new and interesting things about the environment". Now, look at the As You Read question on page 104. The second question is 'What is regarded as food waste?" Minhee, tell us your answer. ⓢ Yes. It is only waste that can be processed into food for animals. ⓣ Good. And look at the third question on page 105. Why is CNG considered better for the environment than other fuels? ⓢ Because it produces less pollution than other fuels. ⓣ That's right.	10′
	3. Understanding the meanings of the new words and expressions ⓣ Now, let's study the new words and expressions below. Repeat after me. *(Repeating)* Now, we are going to study the meaning of each word and expression. *(Explaining)* Do you have any other words that are not familiar to you? ⓢ No, not at all. ⓣ Okay, please try to memorize every new word and expression. ⓢ Yes, teacher.	10′
	4. Listening to the passage and reading the text again ⓣ Now, we're going to listen to the passage. Listen to the audio and try to understand the content. *(Listening)* Now, I need a volunteer to read aloud for us. Who wants to read? ⓢ I'll read it, teacher. ⓣ Oh, Sungho, thank you. Read aloud for us. *(Reading)* Good job. Now, we'll study the meaning of each sentence and its structure to understand more about the passage. Are you ready? ⓢ Yes, we're ready.	20′
Wrap-up	**1. Reviewing today's lesson** ⓣ Okay, class! Let's call it a day. Did you learn some new things about the environment? Please keep in mind that you should review what we've learned today after this class. **2. Setting an assignment and informing students about the next lesson** ⓣ Next time, we'll learn more interesting information. Okay. Have a great time and see you next class. Bye. ⓢ Bye.	3′

7　Period 7

- **Date & Hour:** The ____ class hour, _____, _____ ____, 20____
- **Class:** The _____ class of the _____ grade
- **Material:** Textbook (Reading Lounge)
- **Objectives:**
    1. Students can predict and tell the contents of the main text from the given pictures.
    2. Students can tell the meanings of new words and expressions.
    3. Students can tell the main idea and specific information of the text.
- **Teaching Aids:**
    1. Textbook
    2. Computer, DVD-ROM, Worksheet

Procedures:

Steps	Activities	Time
Warm-up	1. **Exchanging greetings and having small talk** ⓣ Hello, everyone. How are you today? ⓢ All is well. How are you? ⓣ I'm doing fine. Thanks. 2. **Introducing today's lesson and lesson goals.** ⓣ Open your books to page 106. Today, we're going to read the rest of the main text. Do you remember what we read before? What was the title of the main text? ⓢ "Greenquestions.org" ⓣ That's right. Shall we start the lesson?	2′
Build-up	**Reading** 1. **Guessing the main topic from the given pictures** ⓣ Good. Now take a look at the picture on page 106. What can you see in the picture? ⓢ We can see a cow with a chain around her neck. ⓣ That's good. And what can you see in the picture on page 107? ⓢ We can see house plants with a lot of green leaves. ⓣ Good guess.	5′

Steps	Activities	Time
Build-up	**2. Reading the passage and finding out the main topic** ⓣ Now, read the passage on pages 106 and 107 as fast as possible. *(Reading)* Are you finished? ⓢ Yes. ⓣ As we guessed, the main topic of this passage is "new and interesting facts related to the environment". Now, look at the As You Read question on page 106. The fourth question is 'Why is eating beef bad for the environment?' Minhee, tell me your answer. ⓢ Yes. "It is bad because people cut down trees to make pastures and because cattle release methane." ⓣ Good. And look at the fifth question on page 107. What is a benefit of keeping houseplants? ⓢ "Certain plants remove harmful chemicals from the air." ⓣ Right.	10′
	3. Understanding the meanings of the new words and expressions ⓣ Now, let's study the new words and expressions below. Repeat after me. *(Reading)* Now, we are going to study the meaning of each new word and expression. *(Explaining)* Do you see any other words that are not familiar to you? ⓢ No, we don't. ⓣ Okay, please try to memorize every new word and expression. ⓢ Yes, teacher.	10′
Build-up	**4. Listening to the passage and reading the text again** ⓣ Now, we're going to listen to the passage. Listen to the audio and try to understand the content. *(Listening)* Now, I need a volunteer to read aloud for us. Who wants to read? ⓢ I'll read it, teacher. ⓣ Oh, Sangmin, thank you. Read aloud for us. *(Reading)* Good job. Now, we'll study the meaning of each sentence and its structure to understand more details of the passage. Are you ready? ⓢ Yes, we are.	20′
Wrap-up	**1. Reviewing today's lesson** ⓣ Time's up. That's all for today. This class, we read the rest of the main text. I hope you fully understood the content and learned a lot of new expressions and structures. Do you have any questions? ⓢ No, not at all. ⓣ Okay. I hope you have a nice day. **2. Setting an assignment and informing students about the next lesson** ⓣ Next time, we will do the After You Read section. So, I hope you read this main text once again after this class and make sure you understand it fully. Thank you for your attention. See you next time. Bye. ⓢ Bye for now.	3′

8 Period 8

- **Date & Hour:** The ____ class hour, _____, _____ ____, 20____
- **Class:** The _____ class of the _____ grade
- **Material:** Textbook (Reading Lounge)
- **Objectives:**
  1. Students can answer the questions according to the main text.
  2. Students can review and tell the meanings of new words and expressions in the main text.
  3. Students can complete the sentences based on the main text.
- **Teaching Aids:**
  1. Textbook
  2. Computer, DVD-ROM, Worksheet

Procedures:

Steps	Activities	Time
Warm-up	1. **Exchanging greetings and having small talk** ⓣ Hello, everyone. Are you having a good day today? ⓢ Yes. We hope you are, too. ⓣ I'm having a good day. Thanks. 2. **Introducing today's lesson and lesson goals.** ⓣ Open your books to page 108 and tell me what part we will study today. ⓢ "After You Read" ⓣ Yes, exactly. Last class, we read the last part of the main text. Today, we're going to check if we fully understood the main text by doing some activities in After You Read. Are you ready? ⓢ Yes, we are. ⓣ Okay, let's get started.	2′
Build-up	After You Read A 1. **Filling in the blanks based on the text** ⓣ First, look at what the three people say. Then, read carefully and fill in the blanks based on the main text we've studied. If you don't know the answer you can refer to the main text. ⓢ *(Reading and filling in the blanks)* ⓣ Okay, Now, let's share the answers together. How about the first blank? Which word can you fill in the blank? ⓢ I think it's "hazardous". ⓣ ⓢ *(Continuing checking the answers together)*	10′

Steps	Activities	Time
Build-up	B **2. Doing the quiz map** ⓣ You can see a quiz map on the page. First, read the given sentences and find out the right answer to move around the map until you reach either Try Again or Good Job. ⓢ *(Reading and finding out the answers)* ⓣ Are you done? Before you check your answers, compare them with your partner's and see if you guys got the same answers. If they are different, explain your thoughts to your partner until you two agree with one answer. *(Talking)* Okay, now let's go through from sentence number 1 to 9 and check the answers together. ⓣ ⓢ *(Checking the answers together)*	10′
	C. Over to You **3. Being Dr. Green and giving advice on questions about the environment** ⓣ First, take a look at a few questions about the environment. Imagine you are Dr. Green and think about how you would answer the questions. Then, write your answers in the blanks. ⓢ *(Reading and writing)* ⓣ Are you done? Then, compare your answers with your partner's. ⓢ *(Sharing the answers with their partners)* ⓣ Okay, everybody seems to be finished. I want you to share your thoughts and ideas as a class.	15′
	D. Think More **4. Sharing your ideas on the 3Rs** ⓣ As you can see, three words, "Reduce, Reuse, Recycle", are written in the box on the left. This is the slogan of the "3R Campaign". First, talk with your partner about 3R Campaign to protect nature. Then, ask and answer the three questions on the right with your partner. ⓢ *(Reading and talking)* ⓣ Are you done? Then let's share our answers with the class.	10′
Wrap-up	**1. Reviewing today's lesson** ⓣ Today, we went through some comprehension questions and activities about the main text. Also, we talked about how to protect the Earth. Do you have any questions? ⓢ No, we don't have any. ⓣ Okay, you guys did a good job today. **2. Setting an assignment and informing students about the next lesson** ⓣ Next class, we will move on to Expressions for Writing and Sentences for Writing. See you next time. Bye.	3′

9 Period 9

- **Date & Hour:** The ____ class hour, _____, _____ ____, 20____
- **Class:** The _____ class of the _____ grade
- **Material:** Textbook (Writing Workshop)
- **Objectives:**
    1. Students can understand the usage of "environment" and write a sentence using it.
    2. Students can understand the usage of "help" and write a sentence using it.
    3. Students can complete a paragraph using some connectors.
- **Teaching Aids:**
    1. Textbook
    2. Computer, DVD-ROM, Worksheet

Procedures:

Steps	Activities	Time
Warm-up	1. **Exchanging greetings and having small talk** ⓣ Hello, everyone. How are you today? ⓢ Everything is going fine. ⓣ I'm glad to hear it. 2. **Introducing today's lesson and lesson goals.** ⓣ Today, we're going to learn some usages of the words "environment" and "help" from the main text. Okay, now open your books to page 110. Why don't we get started? ⓢ Okay, teacher.	2′
Build-up	**Expressions for Writing** **Point 1** 1. **Seeing how the words are used in sentences** ⓣ Let's take a look at the sentences with the word "environment" in them. Then, let's find the point. We can find "environment" in expressions such as "protect the environment" and "harmful to the environment". Do you see how the word is used in these examples? ⓢ *(Examining the examples)* ⓣ Is everyone finished? Now, let's search for more examples of phrases and words with "environment". Can you think of any other examples? ⓢ Yes, I wrote down "help" and "good for" in the blanks. ⓣ Good job.	10′

Steps	Activities	Time
Build-up	**Point 2** **2. Seeing how the structures are used in sentences** ⓣ Look at the pictures and guess how the word "help" is used in a sentence. Then read the example sentences and see if you can understand their meanings. ⓢ *(Examining the examples)* ⓣ Did you understand them all? Now, let's find some more examples of sentences using this word. Then, fill in the blanks and practice them with your partner. ⓢ Yes, teacher.	15′
	Sentences for Writing **A** **3. Completing the sentences** ⓣ First, look at the two speech bubbles and read the sentences. Then fill in the blanks using the given words in the parentheses. ⓢ *(Filling in the blanks)* ⓣ Are you finished? Let's check the answers together. ⓣ ⓢ *(Checking the answers together)*	7′
	B **4. Completing the sentences** ⓣ First, look at the Earth Hour website. Then, read through the passage and fill in the blanks using the given words in the parentheses. *(Writing)* Are you finished? Then let's check the answers together as a class. ⓢ ⓣ *(Checking the answers together)*	8′
	C **5. Finding the appropriate places for the connectors** ⓣ Look at the connectors in the box below. Are there any words that are unfamiliar to you? ⓢ No, there aren't. ⓣ Now, read through the paragraph and find the appropriate places for the connectors in the box below. Are you finished? Let's check the answers together. ⓣ ⓢ *(Checking the answers together)*	5′
Wrap-up	**1. Reviewing today's lesson** ⓣ Well, that's all for today. We've learned some key expressions and structures. However, if you don't review them, you won't be able to use them in a proper way. Always remember "Practice makes perfect". **2. Setting an assignment and informing students about the next lesson** ⓣ I hope you search for more examples of the expressions we learned today. Next class we will write a proposal for a new recycled product. See you again, everyone!	3′

10 Period 10

- **Date & Hour:** The ____ class hour, _____, _____ ___, 20____
- **Class:** The _____ class of the _____ grade
- **Material:** Textbook (Writing Workshop)
- **Objectives:**
  1. Students can talk about recycled products.
  2. Students can write their own proposal for their own recycled product.
- **Teaching Aids:**
  Textbook, Computer, DVD-ROM, Worksheet

Procedures:

Steps	Activities	Time
Warm-up	**1. Exchanging greetings and having small talk** ⓣ Hello, everyone. How is everything today? ⓢ We're doing fine. How about you? ⓣ I'm feeling great. Thanks. **2. Introducing today's lesson and lesson goals** ⓣ Open your books to page 112 and tell me what part we will study today. ⓢ "Writing It" ⓣ Yes, exactly. Today, you're going to have a chance to look at some recycled products and see what they are made from. Then with the ideas that you come up with, you will write a proposal for your own recycled product. Are you ready? ⓢ Yes, we are. ⓣ Okay, let get started.	2′
Build-up	**Write It** **Step 1** **1. Rearranging and matching the details based on the brochure** ⓣ First, take a look at the recycled products brochure. Then, read the scrambled sentences from "a" to "e" and rearrange them to complete the paragraph. *(Reading and writing)* Are you done? Okay, now Sangwoo, can you tell me your answer? ⓢ I think it is "b – d – c – e – a". ⓣ That's right. Okay, now, take a look at other products on the bottom of the page. Guess what they are made from and write down your guesses in the blanks. ⓢ *(Writing)* ⓣ Are you done? Okay, let's check the answers together.	15′

Steps	Activities	Time
Build-up	**Step 2** **2. Planning a new recycled product** ⓣ Now, it's time to make a plan for make your own recycled product. First, think about the material you want to recycle, what you are going to make with it and the benefits you will get. If you've come up with an idea, write it down in the blanks. ⓢ *(Writing)* ⓣ Are you done? First, share your ideas with your partner. Then, I'd like some of you to present your ideas to the class.	10′
	Step 3 **3. Writing a proposal** ⓣ Now read through the sample writing. Then, write your own proposal for your own recycled product, based on what you wrote in STEP 2. *(Writing)* Did you finish writing? ⓢ Yes, we did. ⓣ Okay, then read it again and see if all the information is clearly written and it has a natural flow and is supported with appropriate reasons and details. Then, take a look at the Self-check List below and see if your writing meets the shown criteria. ⓢ *(Reading and assessing their own writing)*	20′
Wrap-up	**1. Reviewing today's lesson** ⓣ Let's call it a day. Today, we looked at some great recycled products and saw what they were made from. Then each of you wrote your own proposal for a new recycled product. Did you all have fun writing it? ⓢ Yes, we did have a lot of fun. **2. Setting an assignment and informing students about the next lesson** ⓣ Our time's up for today. See you later. Bye. ⓢ See you next time. Bye.	3′

CHAPTER 04 중학 영어 2

01 Your Life is a Gift!

Listen & Talk 1 Listening Script

Listen and Choose

M Anna, do you have any special plans for this year?
W Well, I'm thinking of swimming every morning. How about you?
M I'm taking a Chinese class.
W That's great. I hope you enjoy your class.

Listen and Answer

M Mina, what are you looking at?
W It's a special class program.
M Is it? Which class are you going to take?
W I'm thinking of taking the computer or drawing class. Let's take one together!
M I'd like to, but I have Chinese class every Thursday.
W Then let's take the drawing class. It's on Saturdays.
M Okay. Let's sign up for that class.

Listen & Talk 2

Listen and Check

W Dad, I fell again.
M Are you okay?
W Yes. I didn't get hurt, but riding a bicycle is not easy.
M I know, but don't give up. You can do it.
W Okay. I'll try again.

Listen and Answer

M Kelly, I can't go on anymore.
W Oh, don't give up! We're close to the top of the mountain.
M But my feet really hurt.
W Then let's take a rest under that tree.
M Okay.

W At the top, we can have lunch in the fresh air.
M Good. And let's take pictures, too.
W Sounds great!

Do It Yourself

Listen

M Yuna, what are you looking at?
W It's a special class program.
M Is it? Which class are you going to take?
W I'm thinking of taking the writing or swimming class. Let's take one together!
M I'd like to, but I have violin lessons every Wednesday.
W Then let's take the writing class. It's on Fridays.
M Okay. Let's sign up for that class.

Reading

Your Life Is a Gift!

My name is Sean Stephenson. Do you think that I look a little different? Yes, I'm only ninety centimeters tall, but I'm a small giant! I want to talk to you about myself. I Am Different. I always knew I was different. When I was born, my bones were very weak. Doctors thought that I was going to die as a child. But now, I'm over thirty years old. When I was younger, my bones broke more than 200 times. Each time, the pain was terrible and it made me sad.

Look on the Bright Side!

One day my mother asked me, "Is your disease going to be a gift or a burden?" I decided to think of it as a gift. From that time, my life changed. I started to do many things. I wrote two books and was on a TV show. I started helping children with physical problems. All of these things were possible thanks to my parents. With their help, I changed my way of thinking. They said, "Look on the bright side, not the dark side."

Stop Saying 'But'!

My life is still difficult. In cars, I have to travel in a seat for children. I have to press the buttons on elevators with a stick. I usually need a lot of help from other people. But I can do many things. I can make myself happy. What about you? Are your problems worse than mine? Are you unlucky? Do you say, "But I'm afraid I'll fail," "But I'm not good enough," or "But there's no time"? Stop saying 'but,' or it will make you unhappy. Enjoy doing all your work. Your life is a gift.

02 수업계획서와 교실활동

1 Sub Plan

(1) Period: 1

- **Section**: Warm up, Listen & Talk 1 pp.8-11
- **Time**: 45 minutes
- **Objectives**:
  1. Students will be able to answer questions by using the given pictures.
  2. Students will be able to listen to the dialogs and answer questions about them.
  3. Students will be able to talk about science programs that they are interested in.
- **Teaching Aids**:
  1. Textbook
  2. Computer, DVD-ROM, Worksheet
- **Procedures**:

Steps	Activities	Time (mins)
Introduction	Introduce the objectives of the lesson	3
Development	Warm up - Students guess what this lesson is about from the title and the pictures. - Students think about what activities make them happy.	10

Development	Listen & Talk 1
	A. Get Ready
	  - Students write their plans.
	  - Students talk about their plans with others.
	B. Listen and choose
	  - Students describe what Anna is doing in the pictures.
	  - Students listen to a dialog and answer a corresponding question.
	  - Students check their answers with the teacher.
	C. Listen and Answer
	  - Students go though the activities quickly.
	  - Students listen to a dialog and do the follow-up activities.
	  - Students check their answers with the teacher.
	D. Talk Together
	  - Students read about the programs in the pictures and choose what they want to do at the museum.
	  - Students talk with their partners following the example.
		30

Consolidation	Wrap up and give homework	2

(2) **Period**: 2

- **Section**: Listen & Talk 2 pp. 12-13
- **Time**: 45 minutes
- **Objectives**:
  1. Students will be able to listen to the dialogs and answer questions about them.
  2. Students will be able to talk about what they want to do better.
- **Teaching Aids**:
  1. Textbook
  2. Computer, DVD-ROM, Worksheet
- **Procedures**:

Steps	Activities	Time (mins)
Introduction	Introduce the objectives of the lesson	3
Development	**Listen & Talk 2** **A. Get Ready** - Students describe what happens in the picture. - Students pick appropriate expressions for the picture. **B. Listen and choose** - Students describe each picture. - Students listen to a dialog and answer a corresponding question. - Students check their answers with the teacher. **C. Listen and Answer** - Students go though the activities quickly. - Students listen to a dialog and do the follow-up activities. - Students check their answers with the teacher. **D. Talk Together** - Students look at the pictures and think about what they want to do better. - Students talk with their partners following the example.	40
Consolidation	Wrap up and give homework	2

(3) **Period**: 3

- **Section**: Communication Task p.14
- **Time**: 45 minutes
- **Objectives**:
  1. Students will be able to ask and answer questions about their plans.
  2. Students will be able to talk about their plans and share them with the class.
- **Teaching Aids**:
  1. Textbook
  2. Computer, DVD-ROM, Worksheet
- **Procedures**:

Steps	Activities	Time (mins)
Introduction	Introduce the objectives of the lesson	3
Development	**Communication Task** − Students make groups of about four. − Students read the given plans and write their own plan. − Students take turns asking and answering questions about their plans. − Students complete the given chart. − Students listen to the model dialog and drill themselves on it. − Students follow the directions and practice talking in English. − Some students stand up and practice the dialog in front of the class.	40
Consolidation	**Wrap up and give homework**	2

(4) Period: 4

- **Section**: Before You Read, Read On pp.15-16
- **Time**: 45 minutes
- **Objectives**:
  1. Students will be able to check off sentences they believe describe them.
  2. Students will be able to find what the people in some pictures have in common.
  3. Students will be able to read the main text and explain how Sean Stephenson is different from others.
- **Teaching Aids**:
  1. Textbook
  2. Computer, DVD-ROM, Worksheet
- **Procedures**:

Steps	Activities	Time (mins)
Introduction	Introduce the objectives of the lesson	3
Development	**Before You Read** **A. Read and Check** – Students read the given sentences and think about which one describes them best. – Students check off sentences they believe describe them best. **B. Look and Guess** – Students look at the pictures and talk about the four people in them. – Students read the given sentences and find what the four people have in common.	15
	Read On – Students see the picture and describe what the person in the wheelchair looks like. – Students listen to the first part of the text and try to figure out the topic. – Students listen to the CD again and repeat after it sentence by sentence. – Students read the first question in the Let's Think! section on page 17 and find the answer from the text. – Students learn new words and expressions. – Students learn the usage of the grammatical structures used in the text.	25
Consolidation	Wrap up and give homework	2

(5) Period: 5

- **Section**: Read On p.17
- **Time**: 45 minutes
- **Objectives**:
  1. Students will be able to understand the main topic of the text.
  2. Students will be able to answer questions related to the text.
- **Teaching Aids**:
  1. Textbook
  2. Computer, DVD-ROM, Worksheet
- **Procedures**:

Steps	Activities	Time (mins)
Introduction	Introduce the objectives of the lesson	3
Development	**Read On** − Students listen to the second part of the text and try to figure out the topic. − Students listen to the CD again and repeat after it sentence by sentence. − Students read the second question in the Let's Think! section on page 17 and find the answer from the text. − Students learn new words and expressions. − Students study the sentence structures used in the text.	40
Consolidation	**Wrap up and give homework**	2

(6) Period: 6

- **Section**: Read On, After You Read pp. 18–19
- **Time**: 45 minutes
- **Objectives**:
  1. Students will be able to understand the main topic of the text.
  2. Students will be able to answer questions related to the text.
  3. Students will be able to check their understanding of the main text.
- **Teaching Aids**:
  1. Textbook
  2. Computer, DVD-ROM, Worksheet
- **Procedures**:

Steps	Activities	Time (mins)
Introduction	Introduce the objectives of the lesson	3
Development	**Read On** – Students listen to the third part of the text and try to figure out the topic. – Students listen to the CD again and repeat after it sentence by sentence. – Students read the question in the Let's Think! section on page 18 and find the answer from the text. – Students learn new words and expressions. – Students study the sentence structures used in the text.	20
	After You Read – Students complete the information about Sean Stephenson using the given words. – Students complete the interview by matching the questions to Sean's answers. – Students talk with their partners about what they learned from the main text.	20
Consolidation	Wrap up and give homework	2

(7) **Period**: 7

- **Section**: Language Focus pp. 20–21
- **Time**: 45 minutes
- **Objectives**:
  1. Students will be able to find words that describe some pictures well.
  2. Students will be able to understand the usage of expressions with "do."
  3. Students will be able to understand the usage of the grammatical structures presented in this lesson.
- **Teaching Aids**:
  1. Textbook
  2. Computer, DVD-ROM, Worksheet
- **Procedures**:

Steps	Activities	Time (mins)
Introduction	Introduce the objectives of the lesson	3
Development	**Focus on Words** **A. Word Review** – Students read the sentences and complete them with the appropriate words for the blanks. – Students complete the sentences and check their answers with the teacher. **B. Word Partners** – Students learn the meanings of expressions with "do." – Students read the sentences and complete them with the appropriate words for the blanks.	20
	Focus on Forms **A.** – Students read the example sentences while focusing on the words in bold. – Students learn verbs that use a gerund as an object such as "enjoy," "give up," and "finish." – Students fill in the blanks with the correct form and check their answers with the teacher. **B.** – Students read the example sentences focusing on the words in bold. – Students learn the structure "make, find, keep + object + adjective." – Students complete the paragraph and review it with the teacher.	20
Consolidation	Wrap up and give homework	2

(8) **Period: 8**

- **Section**: Think & Write pp. 22-23
- **Time**: 45 minutes
- **Objectives**:
  1. Students will be able to write about their dreams.
  2. Students will be able to evaluate their writing using the Self Check section.
- **Teaching Aids**:
  1. Textbook
  2. Computer, DVD-ROM, Worksheet
- **Procedures**:

Steps	Activities	Time (mins)
Introduction	Introduce the objectives of the lesson	3
Development	**Think & Write** **Step 1** - Students think about what they want to be and write it down. **Step 2** - Students briefly write about what they want to be, what they like to do, and what they will do to make their dreams come true. - Students are instructed to refer to the expressions in the Useful Expressions section. **Step 3** - Students read the sample essay and write their own essay using their information from Step 2. - Students do the Self Check, and evaluate their writing. - Students present their writing to the class.	40
Consolidation	Wrap up and give homework	2

(9) **Period**: 9

- **Section**: Project Work, Do It Yourself pp. 24-25
- **Time**: 45 minutes
- **Objectives**:
  1. Students will be able to make their own class rules and present them.
  2. Students will be able to review the lesson by answering the questions.
- **Teaching Aids**:
  1. Textbook
  2. Computer, DVD-ROM, Worksheet
- **Procedures**:

Steps	Activities	Time (mins)
Introduction	Introduce the objectives of the lesson	2
Development	**Project Work** − Students make groups of four and think about ways to make class better. − Students make a presentation like in the example. − Students present their ideas to the class.	20
	Do It Yourself − Students listen to the dialog and answer the question. − Students read the paragraph and answer the two questions. − Students fill in the blanks with the correct words and complete the sentence.	20
Consolidation	Wrap up and give homework	3

중학 영어 3

01 Change Your Life, Change the World

1 Master Plan

(1) General Aims

① Students can listen to and understand the dialogs about actions to improve environmental problems.
② Students can talk about the places using expressions for expressing agreement, reminding someone of what to do, and asking someone's opinion.
③ Students can read the text about a family's efforts to solve environmental problems.
④ Students can write a problem and solution essay about how to improve environmental problems.

(2) Communicative Functions

① Expressing agreement
② Reminding
③ Asking one's opinion and answering it

(3) Language Skills

① Confusing word pairs
② Various meanings and functions of 'as'
③ Use of prepositions and conjunctions

(4) Time allocation

10 periods, 50 minutes each

목 차	쪽 수	차 시	시 간	학습활동
Unit Preview	174-175	1/10	10	• 단원 소재와 학습 내용 확인하기
Listen	176-177		40	• '동의하기'와 '상기시켜주기', '의견 묻고 답하기'가 포함된 대화를 듣고 그 내용과 표현 이해하기
Talk	178-179	2/10	50	• '의견 묻고 답하기'를 사용하여 환경문제와 이를 개선하기위한 방안 말하는 대화 연습하기 • 만화 속 대화를 완성하고 짝과 역할극 하기
In the Spotlight	180-181	3/10	50	• 뉴스에 소개된 환경보호 운동의 사례를 듣고 이를 요약하는 표 완성하기 • 자신이 실천해 볼 수 있는 3-2-1 서약을 말하기 • 주어진 진술에 대한 자신의 의견을 '동의하기'를 이용하여 짝과 대화해 보기
Before You Read / Read	182-183	4/10	15	• 설문지를 통해 자신의 일상에서의 생활 습관이 환경에 얼마나 영향을 미치는지 생각해 보도록 한다.
Read	184-191		35	• 본문을 읽고 일상에서 당연하다고 생각했던 편리함의 소중함을 깨닫고 각 개인의 실천이 환경오염을 개선하는 데 얼마나 큰 영향을 줄 수 있는지를 이해한다.
		5/10	50	
		6/10	50	
After You Read / Check Your Words	192-193	7/10	25	• 본문 중심 내용을 요약하는 표를 완성하고 세부내용에 대한 질문에 답하기 • 비판적 사고 능력을 요구하는 질문에 답하기
			25	• 새로운 어휘의 의미와 쓰임을 이해하고 세부 질문에 답하기
Write	194-195	8/10	50	• 환경 문제 해결 방안에 대한 글 쓰기 • Self-Check List와 친구들의 의견 반영하여 글 수정하기

Language Focus	196-197	9/10	50	• 다음 표현들을 문맥에 알맞게 사용하기
				  - 혼동되는 어휘들
				  - take action, take it for granted, get rid of, on a regular basis
				  - 'as'의 다양한 기능과 유사한 의미를 가지는 전치사와 접속사

Teen Links	198-199	10/10	20	• 친환경 발명품의 용도와 유의점 이해하기 • 환경오염을 주제로 한 만화 완성하기
Wrap Up	200-201		30	듣기, 말하기, 읽기, 쓰기 문제를 풀고 단원 성취도 확인하기

02 수업계획서와 활동

Unit 7	Unit Preview / Listen	Page	174–177
		Period	1/10

Aims of This Period	<ul><li>to identify the topics and the learning points of Unit 7.</li><li>to understand the meanings and the functions of the target communicative expressions: expressing agreement, reminding someone of what to do and asking someone's opinion.</li><li>to learn the main idea and the details through listening to a long dialog which includes the target communicative expressions</li></ul>

Steps	Procedure (min.)	Teaching and Learning Activities	Materials & Remarks
Introduction	Greeting (2')	• Exchanging greetings • Checking attendance	
	Motivating (5')	• Introducing Unit 7 • Asking questions about the pictures • Reading Unit Preview to see what they will learn in Unit 7	textbook, CD-ROM
	Stating the Aims (3')	• Stating the aims of this period	″
Development	Get Ready (5')	• Students read the three examples in the box and choose the word from the poster that best represents each example.	″
	Listen and Choose (10')	• Students listen to a short dialog and choose the correct word for the blank. • Students listen to a short dialog and choose T if the statement is true and F if it is false. • Students listen to a short dialog and choose the correct statement.	″
	Listen for Ideas (10')	• Students listen to a long dialog and choose what they will do on the weekend. • Students listen to the dialog again and choose the correct words for the blanks.	″
	Listen and Summarize (10')	• Students listen to a long dialog and choose what the dialog mainly about. • Students listen to the dialog again and complete the summary.	″
Consolidation	Wrap-Up (3')	• Checking students' understanding of the contextual meanings of the two communicative functions	blackboard
	Assignment (2')	• Giving an assignment: Make a short dialog of four turns using the target communicative expressions.	″

Unit 7	Talk	Page	178–179
		Period	2/10

Aims of This Period	• to talk about the ways to improve the environmental problems in their daily lives • to complete a long dialog with the target communicative expressions and role-play it		

Steps	Procedure (min.)	Teaching and Learning Activities	Materials & Remarks
Development	Try It Out (15′)	• Students look at the picture and think about which problem each person is causing. • Students match the problem with the right solution. • Students are divided into groups of four and practice the given conversation, using their own information.	textbook, CD-ROM
	Act It Out (20′)	• Students read a comic strip and complete it by filling the speech bubbles with the correct expressions. • Students check their answers while listening to the dialog. • Students practice and role-play the dialog. • Students talk about what time of the day they would choose for Earth Hour and explain the reason.	〃
Consolidation	Wrap-Up (3′)	• Having 3-4 students share their experiences with the whole class • Checking students' understanding of the two communi- cative functions by asking questions	blackboard
	Assignment (2′)	• Giving an assignment: Research on the various events to encourage people to do something to improve environ- mental problems.	〃

Unit 7	In the Spotlight	Page	180–181
		Period	3/10

Aims of This Period	• to complete a summary while listening to a news report introducing an environmental movement • to make their own pledge to help solve environmental problems • to give their opinions on environmental issues

Steps	Procedure (min.)	Teaching and Learning Activities	Materials & Remarks
Development	Tune In (15′)	• While listening to the dialog, students fill in the blanks with the proper words and expressions. • Students make their own 3-2-1 pledge that they will practice to help solve environmental problems.	textbook, CD-ROM
	Voice Out (20′)	• Students read three students' opinions on the use of plastic bags. • Students give their own opinions on the theme using the communicative target expressions. • Students share their opinions on the use of straws and present their opinions to the class.	″
Consolidation	Wrap-Up (3′)	• Having students engage in a short conversation using the target communicative functions	blackboard
	Assignment (2′)	• Giving an assignment: Make a 3-2-1 pledge that your class will follow.	″

Unit 7	Before You Read / Read	Page	182–183
		Period	4/10

Aims of This Period	• to guess what the text will be about after reading some phrases from it • to understand the difficulties they would face without the modern conveniences they take for granted

Steps	Procedure (min.)	Teaching and Learning Activities	Materials & Remarks
Development	Take the Green Survey (5′)	• Students take the green survey to check how green they are.	textbook, CD-ROM
	Listen and Read (5′)	• Students check new words and phrases as they listen to the text (pp. 183–191) and compare the content with what they predicted	〃
	Listen and Answer (10′)	• Students listen to the reading text again and answer the teacher's questions to help them understand the text	〃
	Read (10′)	• Students read the text carefully and answer the teacher's questions • Students understand the words and expressions and the sentence structures presented in the text	〃
	Comprehension Check-Up (5′)	• Students answer the While You Read and the Over to You questions.	〃
Consolidation	Wrap-Up (3′)	• Having students summarize the text orally • Reviewing new words and expressions	blackboard, handouts
	Assignment (2′)	• Giving an assignment: Write about your own experience having difficulties because you could not use modern conveniences.	〃

Unit 7		Read	Page	184-186
			Period	5/10

Aims of This Period	• to understand the efforts of the Beavan family • to understand various functions and meanings of 'as' and comprehend the text precisely		
Steps	**Procedure (min.)**	**Teaching and Learning Activities**	**Materials & Remarks**
Development	Take a Guess (5′)	• Students go over the pictures in the reading text and try to predict what the text is about.	textbook, CD-ROM
	Listen and Read (5′)	• Students check new words and phrases as they listen to the text (pp. 184-186) and compare the content with what they predicted.	″
	Listen and Answer (10′)	• Students listen to the reading text again and answer the teacher's questions to help them catch the main ideas.	″
	Read (10′)	• Students read the text carefully and answer the teacher's questions. • Students understand the words and expressions and the sentence structures presented in the reading text.	″
	Comprehension Check-Up (5′)	• Students answer the While You Read and the Over to You questions.	
Consolidation	Wrap-Up (3′)	• Having students summarize the text orally • Reviewing new words and phrases	blackboard, handouts
	Assignment (2′)	• Giving an assignment: Watch one of Colin's videos on the website and write about your impression.	″

Unit 7	Read	Page	187–191
		Period	6/10

Aims of This Period	• to figure out what the Beavan family got from their experiment • to understand various sentence structures and comprehend the text precisely

Steps	Procedure (min.)	Teaching and Learning Activities	Materials & Remarks
Development	Take a Guess (5′)	• Students go over pictures in the reading text and try to predict what the text is about.	textbook, CD-ROM
	Listen and Read (5′)	• Students check new words and phrases as they listen to the text (pp. 187–191) and compare the content with what they predicted.	″
	Listen and Answer (10′)	• Students listen to the reading text again and answer the teacher's questions to help them catch the main ideas.	″
	Read (10′)	• Students read the text carefully and answer the teacher's questions. • Students understand the words and expressions and the sentence structure presented in the reading text.	″
	Comprehension Check-up (5′)	• Students answer the While You Read and the Over to You questions.	″
Consolidation	Wrap-up (3′)	• Having students explain what the Beavan family got from their experiment • Reviewing new words and phrases	blackboard, handouts
	Assignment (2′)	• Giving an assignment: Watch *No Impact Man* and write about some of the experiments in the movie that impressed you.	″

Unit 7	After You Read / Check Your Words	Page	192–193
		Period	7/10

Aims of This Period	• to fill in the blanks with the expressions used in the main passage • to decide whether statements concerning the text are true or not • to define new words and use them appropriately in new contexts

Steps	Procedure (min.)	Teaching and Learning Activities	Materials & Remarks
Development	Get the Main Ideas (5′)	• Students read the main passage again and fill in the blanks with the expressions used in the main passage.	textbook, CD-ROM
	Get the Facts Right (5′)	• Students read the statements that describe the content and decide whether they are true or not.	〃
	Critical Thinking (10′)	• Students talk about the changes they think are most the impressive.	〃
	Complete the Magic Square (5′)	• Students read the definitions and put the number of the definition in the box that matches each word. • Students check their rows and columns are add up to 15.	〃
	Read and Choose (10′)	• Students read the English definitions and fill in the blanks with the correct words from the box	〃
Consolidation	Wrap-up (3′)	• Having students orally summarize the main ideas of the text • Reviewing new words and phrases • Doing the Vocabulary Master	blackboard, handouts
	Assignment (2′)	• Giving an assignment: Make four sentences with new words or expressions.	〃

Unit 7	Write	Page	194–195
		Period	8/10

| Aims of This Period | • to write a problem and solution essay about how to help solve environmental problems
• to revise their writing based on Self-Check questions and peer feedback |

Steps	Procedure (min.)	Teaching and Learning Activities	Materials & Remarks
Development	Study the Model (5′)	• Students read through a sample paragraph, and then complete an outline.	textbook, CD-ROM
	Prepare to Write (10′)	• Students decide what is the most serious environmental problem. • Students answer questions to help them organize their thoughts.	〃
	Write Your Story (10′)	• Students write a short paragraph using the answers from Prepare to Write.	〃
	Self-Check List (5′)	• Students check their work according to the Self-Check list. • Students revise their writing as necessary after the Self-Check.	〃
	Share Your Story (5′)	• Students read their partner's work and give feedback. Then they talk about the best friend they wrote about. • Students make comments on the group members' work.	〃
Consolidation	Wrap-Up (3′)	• Students make a list of comments from their partners and think about the strengths and weaknesses of their work.	blackboard, handouts
	Assignment (2′)	• Giving an assignment: Write a new draft reflecting suggestions and hand in the draft.	〃

Unit 7	Language Focus	Page	196–197
		Period	9/10

Aims of This Period	• to understand the differences in spelling and meaning of the confusing word pairs • to identify the meanings and the usage of the target expressions: *take it for granted, take action, get rid of, on a regular basis* • to understand the various meanings and functions of 'as' and the differences between prepositions and conjunctions

Steps	Procedure (min.)	Teaching and Learning Activities	Materials & Remarks
Development	Word-Building Skills (5')	• Students understand the differences in spelling and meaning of the confusing word pairs. • Students match the definitions with words from the box.	textbook, CD-ROM
	Expressions in Context (10')	• Students read a comic strip focusing on the meanings and uses of the underlined expressions • Students complete each sentence in the exercise by filling in the blanks with the underlined expressions	″
	Language in Use (20')	• Students read the sentences in the box and focus on the expressions in bold. (as) • Go over the example sentences and explain the meaning and the usage of 'as.' • Students read a passage and understand the usage of 'as' from the context. • Students read the sentences in the box and focus on the expressions in bold. (instead / instead of) • Go over the example sentences and explain the form and the meaning of 'instead' and 'instead of.' • Students choose the correct one in the blank to complete the sentence.	″
Consolidation	Wrap-Up (3')	• Students check the answers of the exercises they did in class and ask questions	blackboard handouts
	Assignment (2')	• Giving an assignment: Make four new sentences that include 'as' with different meanings and find other pairs of preposition and conjunction that have similar meanings.	″

Unit 7	Teen Links / Wrap Up	Page	198–201
		Period	10/10

| Aims of This Period | • to figure out the uses and their cautions of environmentally friendly products
• to answer unit review questions to check their understanding |||

Steps	Procedure (min.)	Teaching and Learning Activities	Materials & Remarks
Development	Trivia (7′)	• Students look at the picture and think of the benefit of each environmentally friendly product. • Students match each product to the sentence that describes its warning label.	textbook, CD-ROM
	Think Outside the Box (8′)	• Students look at cartoons and think about what kind of problem each character is having. • Students complete the cartoon with their own ideas.	
	Wrap Up: Listen and Talk (10′)	• Students listen to the dialog and find the main idea • Students listen and find what is not mentioned and the result of global warming. • Students tell a story based on the six pictures using the expressions under each box.	″
	Wrap Up: Read and Write (10′)	• Students read the passage and answer the questions. • Students write a short paragraph about global warming. It should include the given information and be about 100 words.	″
Consolidation	Wrap-Up (3′)	• Checking the answers to Wrap Up and ask questions • Summarizing the communicative functions, the key structures, and the reading passage	blackboard, handout
	Assignment (2′)	• Giving an assignment: Do the unit test.	″

CHAPTER 06 고교 (문화 영어)

01　Korean Wave Around the World

W: Today we are meeting Korean Waves, the winner of this year's K-pop Dance Festival in London. Here is John, the leader of the dance team. Would you please tell us about the special features of your dance?

B: Sure. We love the hot beat of K-pop. We love the soft moves of traditional Korean dances, too. We want to put them together and create rhythmic waves.

W: You rap in Korean. Do you speak the language?

B: Yes, but my Korean is not very good. I'm studying it at the Korean Cultural Centre UK, but it's not easy.

W: You must be interested in not only Korean music but also the Korean language.

B: You bet! You know what? The centre had a special week on famous Westerners in the Korean Empire last month. One of them was Ernest Bethell.

W: Ernest Bethell had a deep love for Korea and Korean culture, didn't he?

B: Yes. He was born in Bristol, not far from here. I learned that he founded Daehan Maeil Sinbo, a newspaper in Korean and English. He loved the Korean language and culture, and so do I.

W: That's cool! You're going to come to Korea for the final round, aren't you?

B: Absolutely! We're now polishing our moves. We are looking forward to the final round, visiting the country, and enjoying the hot energy of K-pop and K-food.

W: I wish you good luck! What places do you want to visit?

B: My first stop will be Insa-dong. I've heard that there are many fun activities to do there and lots of street food to enjoy. I'd like to go on a hanbok photo shoot and try tteokbokki. Then I hope to stop by Namdaemun Market. I want to pick up character socks and popular Korean goods for my sister. They must have a wide selection there.

W: I hope you find some nice ones. Thank you for being with us today.

B: Thank YOU.

02 수업 계획서와 교실 활동

1 수업 전체 목표

A. Achievement Standards

(1) Listening
- Students can listen to utterances and conversations about daily life and familiar general topics, and grasp storylines, themes, and main ideas.
- Students can listen to utterances and conversations about daily life and familiar general topics, and infer the sequence and the context of events.

(2) Speaking
- Students can express their opinions and feelings about daily life.
- Students can ask and answer questions about familiar people and objects.

(3) Reading
- Students can read texts about daily life or familiar general topics, and grasp outlines, topics, and main ideas.
- Students can read texts about daily life or familiar general topics, and grasp detailed information.

(4) Writing
- Students can write sentences about their experiences and plans in their own lives.
- Students can write passages for invitations, thanks, congratulations, consolations, diaries, and letters.

(5) Culture
- Students can suggest creative globalized Korean dishes.

B. Language Skills
- Listening and Speaking: Students can ask for opinions and express possibility.
- Reading : Students can read and understand an interview with a teenager who loves Korean culture.
- Writing : Students can write an email to a friend living in the place where they want to visit.

C. Communicative Functions
Students can communicate with each other using the following communicative functions.

Asking for opinions	Expressing possibility
A: What do you think of *jegichagi*? B: I think it's fun.	A: Amy is having *japchae*. B: **It must be delicious**. She's eating it up.

D. Language Forms: Students can use the following language forms.
- To-infinitive: There are many fun activities to do.
- Must: You must be interested in Korean music.

2 Time Allotment (11 periods, 45 minutes each)

Periods	Contents	Activities	Aids
1st	Introduction Listen and Speak 1	• Introducing a new lesson • Writing study plans and goals • Learning how to ask for opinions	Textbook, CD-ROM
2nd	Listen and Speak 2 Conversation	• Learning how to express possibility • Listening to a conversation about K-fried chicken • Doing a role-play using the main dialog	Textbook, CD-ROM, Learning Log
3rd	Real-Life Task	• Listening to a presentation about the way to introduce K-culture • Talking about the parts of K-culture foreign friends will like and the ways to introduce them • Presenting the group members' ideas to the class	Textbook, CD-ROM, Worksheet 7-1
4th	Mission Across Cultures	• Matching dishes with foreign foods to their countries' flags • Thinking of a creative globalized K-dish in groups. • Presenting the groups' creative dishes to the class	Textbook, CD-ROM, Learning Log
5–6th	Before Reading Reading After Reading	• Studying new words and expressions in the reading text, *Korean Waves* • Reading and understanding important information • Doing after-reading and self-directed activities	Textbook, CD-ROM, Learning Log, Worksheet
7th	Language Detective	• Completing sentences about what John does and wants using the to-infinitive • Completing sentences about Yuna using *must* or *may*	Textbook, CD-ROM, Learning Log
8th	Let's write	• Reading an email written by John to a friend living in Korea • Deciding on a city or region where one wants to visit and thinking of the items to bring there • Writing an email to a friend living in the city or region where one wants to visit • Revising the email, reflecting on the partner's feedback and comments	Textbook, CD-ROM, Worksheet
9–10th	Project Across Subjects	• Deciding on a city or region in Korea that foreign friends would like • Making a travel plan and presenting it to the class	Textbook, CD-ROM, cellphone
11th	Check My Progress	• Reviewing the lesson by solving problems • Completing My Learning Diary and reflecting on learning progress	Textbook, CD-ROM

3 각 차시 수업 계획서와 교실 활동

(1) Sub Plan 1

- **Period:** First of 11 periods
- **Section:** Introduction / Listen and Speak 1
- **Specific Aims:**
    1. Students can answer the lesson question and preview the lesson aims.
    2. Students can make their lesson goals.
    3. Students can ask for opinions.
- **Class Materials:** Textbook, CD-ROM, My Study Planner
- Flow of the Lesson

Step	Procedure	Activities
Introduction	Greeting Roll Call	• Teacher greets the students. • Teacher checks the attendance. • Teacher introduces the lesson aims and activities.
Development	Introduction	• Students read the title of the lesson • Students look at the picture on the introduction page and talk about the lesson aims for this lesson. • Students read the lesson question "Which parts of Korean culture would you like to share with the world?" and think about possible answers. • Students talk about their ideas with their classmates. • Students look at the lesson map and write their own goals for this lesson.
	Listen and Speak 1	■ **Get Ready** • Students look at the picture and choose the answer. • Students check their answer with their partners. ■ **A. Listen and Number** • Students listen to the dialogs and number the pictures. • Students listen again and check their answers. ■ **B. Write and Talk** • Students watch the CD-ROM and practice the sample dialog. • Students write their ideas about Korean culture. • Students talk about their ideas and complete the table.
Consolidation	Wrap Up Preview Closing	• Students review how to ask for opinions. • Teacher tells students that they are going to learn about how to express possibility. • Students say goodbye to the teacher.

(2) **Sub Plan 2**
- **Period:** Second of 11 periods
- **Section:** Listen and Speak 2 / Conversation
- **Specific Aims:**
  1. Students can express possibility.
  2. Students can understand the main idea of the dialog and find out detailed information.
  3. Students can do a role-play using the dialog.
  4. Students can talk about Korean food that foreigners would like.
- **Teaching Materials:** Textbook, CD-ROM, My Learning Log
- **Flow of the Lesson**

Step	Procedure	Activities
Introduction	Greeting Roll Call Review	• Teacher greets the students. • Teacher checks the attendance. • Students review how to ask for opinions. 　e.g. What do you think of *jegichagi*? • Teacher introduces the lesson aims and activities.
Development	Listen and Speak 2	■ **Get Ready** • Students look at the picture and choose the answer. • Students check their answer with their partners. ■ **A. Listen and Match** • Students read the direction and look at the student names and facial expressions. • Students match each student's name to a facial expression. • Students listen again and check their answers. ■ **B. Look and Talk** • Students watch the CD-ROM and practice the sample dialog • Students talk about Amy's experience of Korean culture using the expressions provided. 　e.g. A: Amy is enjoying *pungmul*. 　　　　B: It must be exciting. 　　　　A: You're right. She's dancing to the music. • Teacher gives students feedback.

Step	Procedure	Activities
	Conver-sation	■ **A. Get Ready** • Students look at the picture and guess what Jason and Seho are looking at. • Students discuss and present their ideas to the class. 　*e.g.* They are looking at a menu on the phone. ■ **B. Listen and Do** • Students read the directions and the three pictures provided in 1. • Students listen to the dialog and choose what Seho and Jason will do right after the conversation. • Students read the directions and the choices in 2. • Students listen again and choose the answers. • Students listen again and check their answers. ■ **C. Do a Role-Play** • Students look at the script and read it aloud. • Students do a role-play in pairs. ■ **My Turn** • Students think about Korean food that foreigners would like. • Students share their ideas with their partners. • Teacher gives students feedback. ■ **Sounds in Use** • Students read the two sentences. • Students listen to the CD-ROM carefully. • Students listen again and read along with the CD-ROM.
Consoli-dation	Wrap Up Preview Closing	■ **My Learning Log** • Students review how to express possibility. • Students think and write about what they did and learned today. • Teacher tells students that they are going to talk about the ways to introduce Korean culture in the next class. • Students say goodbye to the teacher.

(3) **Sub Plan 3**
- **Period:** Third of 11 periods
- **Section:** Real-Life Task
- **Specific Aims:**
    1. Students can listen to and understand a short presentation about the way to introduce Korean culture.
    2. Students can talk about the parts of Korean culture their foreign friends will like and the ways to introduce them.
    3. Students can present their groups' ideas to the class.
- **Class Materials:** Textbook, CD-ROM, Worksheet 7-1, 7-2
- Flow of the Lesson

Step	Procedure	Activities
Introduction	Greeting Roll Call Review	• Teacher greets the students. • Teacher checks the attendance. • Students review how to express possibility. e.g. It must be delicious. • Teacher introduces the lesson aims and activities. • Students answer the question at the top of the page.

Development	Real-Life Task	■ **Step 1**
		• Students listen to a presentation and choose what the presenter is going to post on the blog this week.
		• Students listen again and check their answers.
		
		■ **Step 2**
		• Students think of the parts of Korean culture that their foreign friends will like and the ways to introduce them.
		• In groups, students talk about their ideas.
		  A: I'm wondering what parts of Korean culture our foreign friends are interested in.
		  B: I think they must be interested in the Korean language.
		  A: What can we do for them?
		  B: What do you think of teaching them some nice Korean words?
		  A: That's a good idea.

Step	Procedure	Activities
	Real-Life Task	■ **Step 3** • In groups, students give a presentation about their ideas on the ways to introduce Korean culture. *e.g.* What can we do to introduce Korean culture to our foreign friends? First, we can teach them a K-pop dance. Second, we can teach them some nice Korean words. Third, we can cook some nice Korean foods. • Students listen to other groups' presentations. • Teacher gives students feedback.
Consoli-dation	Wrap Up Preview Closing	■ **Stop & Think** • Students reflect on what they did and complete the table with their partners. • Students do the activities on the worksheets. • Teacher tells students that they are going to talk about creative globalized Korean dishes in the next class. • Students say goodbye to the teacher.

(4) **Sub Plan 4**

- **Period:** Fourth of 11 periods
- **Section:** Mission Across Cultures
- **Specific Aims:**
  1. Students can match the dishes with foreign foods to their countries' flags.
  2. Students can suggest their own creative globalized Korean dishes.
- **Class Materials:** Textbook, CD-ROM, My Learning Log
- Flow of the Lesson

Step	Procedure	Activities
Introduction	Greeting Roll Call Review	• Teacher greets the students. • Teacher checks the attendance. • Students review what was covered in the last class • Teacher introduces lesson aims and activities.
Development	Mission Across Cultures	■ **Globalized Korean Dishes** • Students read the title and look at the flags and the three globalized Korean dishes. • Students think about what foreign food is used in each dish and where it comes from. • Students match the dishes with foreign foods to their countries' flags. • Students check their answers with their partners. ■ **Mission!** • In groups, students search for foods from other countries that go well with Korean foods. • Students think of their own creative globalized Korean dishes. • Students complete the table provided. • Each group give a presentation about their own creative globalized Korean dishes. • Teacher gives students feedback.
Consolidation	Wrap Up Preview Closing	■ **My Learning Log** • Students review their work on creative globalized Korean dishes. • Students think and write about what they did and learned today. • Teacher tells students that they are going to read *Korean Waves*. • Students say goodbye to the teacher.

(5) Sub Plan 5

- **Period**: Fifth of 11 periods
- **Section**: Before Reading
- **Specific Aims**:
    1. Students can learn new words and expressions from the reading text Korean Waves.
    2. Students can read the reading text and find out its main theme.
    3. Students can find out details about John's plan in Korea in the text.
- **Class Materials**: Textbook, CD-ROM, My Learning Log
- Flow of the Lesson

Step	Procedure	Activities
Introduction	Greeting Roll Call Review	• Teacher greets the students. • Teacher checks the attendance. • Students review their work on globalized Korean dishes. • Teacher introduces the lesson aims and activities.
Development	Before Read	■ A • Students look at the three pictures and talk about Korean culture each person is interested in. • Students complete the blanks with the right words provided in the box. • Students talk about each person with their partners. ■ B • Students look at the invitation letter from the Korean Cultural Centre. • Students complete the sentences using the expressions provided. • Students check their answers with their partners.
	Read	• Students look at the title of the reading text and the pictures. • Students guess what the reading text is about. ■ The First Reading • Students quickly read *Korean Waves* to figure out what the interview is mainly about. • Students share their ideas. • Teacher gives students feedback. ■ The Second Reading • Students read the text more slowly and underline the activities that John wants to experience during his trip to Korea. • Teacher walks around the classroom and helps students continue reading. • Students give feedback to one another.
Consolidation	Read	■ While-Reading Questions • Students answer the questions at the bottom of each page. • Students check their answers with their partners.

(6) **Sub Plan 6**

- **Period:** Sixth of 11 periods
- **Section:** After Reading
- **Specific Aims:**
  1. Students can study key expressions and structures from the reading text.
  2. Students can do after-reading activities.
  3. Students can talk about John's plan with their partners.
- **Class Materials:** Textbook, CD-ROM, Worksheet 7-3
- Flow of the Lesson

Step	Procedure	Activities
Introduction	Greeting Roll Call Review	• Teacher greets the students. • Teacher checks the attendance. • Students recall the outline of the reading text. • Teacher introduces the lesson aims and activities.
Development	Read	■ **Study Key Expressions** • Students listen to the reading text. • Teacher asks more questions about the text and students answer them. • Students listen to the text again sentence by sentence. • Students pay attention to new expressions in the text. • Teacher tells students the meaning and use of new expressions.
	After Read	■ **A** • Students read the passage and the three expressions provided. • Students fill in the blanks of the passage with the right expressions. • Students check their answers with their partners. ■ **B** • Students read John's travel note and find two parts that have incorrect information and correct them. • Students refer to the reading text if necessary. • Students check their answers with their partners. ■ **My Turn** • In pairs, students talk about what they think of John's plan. 　A: What do you think of John's plan? 　B: I think it sounds fun. • Students share their ideas with their classmates. • Teacher gives students feedback.

Step	Procedure	Activities
Consoli-dation	Wrap Up Preview Closing	■ **Stop & Think** • Students reflect on what they did and complete the table with their partners. • Students do the activities on the worksheets. • Teacher tells students that they are going to study two grammar forms in the next class. There are many fun activities **to do**. You **must** be interested in Korean music. • Students say goodbye to the teacher.

(7) **Sub Plan 7**

- Period: Seventh of 11 periods
- Section: Language Detective
- Specific Aims:
    1. Students can write sentences using the to-infinitive.
    2. Students can write sentences using must.
- Class Materials: Textbook, CD-ROM, My Learning Log
- Flow of the Lesson

Step	Procedure	Activities
Introduction	Greeting Roll Call Review	• Teacher greets the students. • Teacher checks the attendance. • Students review the previous classes on *Korean Waves*. • Teacher introduces the lesson aims and activities. • Students look at the two target sentences in A and B and read them aloud. There are many fun activities **to do**. You **must** be interested in Korean music.
Development	to-infinitive	■ A 1. • Students read the cartoon and think about the content. • Students read the sentences, focusing on the words in bold. 　A: Grandma! I brought you something **to eat**. 　B: Oh, thank you, dear. • Students look at the detective's question and answer it. • Students share possible answers to the detective's question with their partners. 2. • Students look at the pictures and read the sentences to be completed. • Students complete the sentences using the expressions provided. • Some students present their dialogs in front of the class.
	must	■ B 1. • Students read the cartoon and think about the story. • Students read the sentences, focusing on the words in bold. 　*e.g.* He hasn't eaten all day. He **must** be hungry. 　　　Well, he **may** not be. • Students look at the detective's question and answer it.

Step	Procedure	Activities
		• Students share possible answers to the detective's question with their partners. • In pairs, students do a role-play based on the cartoon. 2. • Students look at Yuna's suitcase. • Students make guesses about Yuna and write sentences about her, using either *must* or *may*. • In pairs, students read out the completed sentences.
Consoli-dation	Wrap Up Preview Closing	■ **My Learning Log** • Students review the two grammar forms. • Students think and write about what they did and learned today. • Teacher tells students that, in the next class, they are going to write an email to a friend living in the city or region that they would like to visit during winter vacation. • Students say goodbye to the teacher.

(8) **Sub Plan 8**
- **Period:** Eighth of 11 periods
- **Section:** Let's Write
- **Specific Aims:**
  1. Students can read an email written by John to a friend living in Korea.
  2. Students can decide on a city or region they want to visit and think of the items to bring there.
  3. Students can write an email to a friend living in the city or region they want to visit during winter vacation.
- **Class Materials:** Textbook, CD-ROM, Worksheet 7-4
- Flow of the Lesson

Step	Procedure	Activities
Introduction	Greeting Roll Call Review	• Teacher greets the students. • Teacher checks the attendance. • Students recall the two grammar forms. • Teacher introduces the lesson aims and activities. • Students think about a city or region they want to visit during winter vacation.
Development	STEP 1	• Students read an email written by John to Neha. • Students read the email again and underline the items that John wants to bring to Korea. • Students check their answers with their partners.
	STEP 2	• Students decide on a city or region to visit during winter vacation and complete the note. *e.g.* I want to visit **the U.K.** • Students think of items to bring to the place and complete the rest of the note. *e.g.* something **to eat**: **cup noodle** 　　　something **to wear**: **rain boots** 　　　something **to share**: *hanji*
	STEP 3	• Students read the email. • Students complete the email using the answers in STEP 2. • Teacher walks around the classroom and helps students complete the email. • Students read their own emails and some students present theirs to the class.

Step	Procedure	Activities
Develop-ment	STEP 4	• Students exchange writings with their partners. • Students listen to how to do a peer review of their partners' writings. • Students read their partners' writings and think about the questions in the table. • Students complete the table and write comments on their partner's writings. • Students revise their writings, reflecting their partners' feedback and comments.
Consoli-dation	Wrap Up Preview Closing	• Students do the activities on the worksheet. • Teacher tells students that they are going to make a travel plan in the next class. • Students say goodbye to the teacher.

(9) Sub Plan 9

- **Period:** Ninth of 11 periods
- **Section:** Project Across Subjects
- **Specific Aims:**
    1. Students can choose a city or region in Korea they want to visit with their foreign friends.
    2. Students can decide on the places to visit, things to do, and foods to eat in the place they chose.
- **Class Materials:** Textbook, CD-ROM, cellphone
- Flow of the Lesson

Step	Procedure	Activities
Introduction	Greeting Roll Call Review	• Teacher greets the students. • Teacher checks the attendance. • Students recall their email-writing activities. • Teacher introduces the lesson aims and activities.
Development	STEP 1	• In groups, students read the title and guess what they are going to do for a project. • Students look at the map and think of a city or region they want to visit with their foreign friends. • Students decide on the city or region they want to visit with their foreign friends. *e.g. Jeonju*
Development	STEP 2	• Students search for the places to visit, things to do, and foods to eat in the city or region they chose. • Students complete the table with the information they get from the search. *e.g.* Places to Visit: Jeonju *Hanok* Village/ *Hanji* Museum Things to Do: go on a *hanbok* photoshot/ *hanok* stay Foods to Eat: *bibimbap/ hotteok* • Teacher walks around the classroom and gives assistance as needed.
Consolidation	Wrap Up Preview	• Teacher tells the students that they are going to make their own travel plans next time.

⑽ Sub Plan 10

- **Period:** Tenth of 11 periods
- **Section:** Project Across Subjects
- **Specific Aims:**
  1. Students can make their own travel plans.
  2. Students can present their travel plans to the class.
- **Class Materials:** Textbook, CD-ROM, cellphone
- Flow of the Lesson

Step	Procedure	Activities
Introduction	Greeting Roll Call Review	• Teacher greets the students. • Teacher checks the attendance. • Teacher introduces the lesson aims and activities.
Development	STEP 3	• Students make their own travel plans. • In groups, students present their travel plans to the class. 　*e.g.* Here's the plan for our one-day trip. We're going to go to Jeju. In the morning, we will have *haemul-ttukbaegi* for breakfast and climb up to Seongsan Ilchulbong. For lunch, we will have *gogi-guksu*. Then in the afternoon, we will look around the traditional houses of Jeju at Seongeup Folk Village and visit Hamdeok Beach. In the evening, we will have *bulgogi* for dinner. What do you think of our plan? • Teacher gives students comments and feedback.
	Stop and Think	• Students talk about the travel plans and presentations of other groups. • Students complete the table focusing on the following questions: 　*e.g.* Did all the members participate in the project work? 　　　Was the presentation interesting? 　　　Did all the members work together to make travel notes and make a presentation on them? • Students vote for the best group.
Consolidation	Wrap Up Preview Closing	• Teacher tells students that they are going to review the lesson and do wrap-up activities. • Students say goodbye to the teacher.

(11) Sub Plan 11

- **Period:** Eleventh of 11 periods
- **Section:** Check My Progress, Learning Diary
- **Specific Aims:**
  1. Students can review what they learned in the lesson.
  2. Students can check how well they achieved their goals.
- **Class Materials:** Textbook, CD-ROM
- Flow of the Lesson

Step	Procedure	Activities
Introduction	Greeting Roll Call Review	• Teacher greets the students. • Teacher checks the attendance. • Teacher introduces what students are going to do today. 　e.g. We're going to check our progress. 　　　We're going to review our learning experiences.
Development	Check My Progress	• Students listen to a conversation and choose what the boy and girl are talking about. • Students listen to a conversation and choose what the girl will say after the boy's comments. • Students complete the dialog and have a conversation with their partners. • Students read a dialog and choose the dish being talked about. • Students read the passage and choose the right question for the blank. • Students read the passage and choose what can't be answered after reading it. • Students read the passage again and find out where to put the sentence provided. • Students look at the picture and complete the sentence.
	Learning Diary	• Teacher gives students' My Study Planners back to them. • Students read their goals in the planner. • Students think about their learning experiences and complete the graphs. • Students check how well they achieved their goals. • Students talk about what they did well and what they need to study harder. • Students talk about how they can use what they learned in real-life situations. 　e.g. I'm going to write about Korean culture in English on my blog so that I can communicate with people around the world.

Step	Procedure	Activities
		• Teacher gives students tips for self-directed learning. 　*e.g.* It is very difficult to keep track of our learning experiences. It may be a good idea to use mobile applications to keep track of them.
Consoli-dation	Wrap Up Preview Closing	• Students answer the following questions and review what they did in Lesson 7. 　T: How did you like Lesson 7? 　T: What activity was most interesting? • Teacher provides students with a preview of the next lesson. • Students say goodbye to the teacher.

03 4기능을 위한 수업 실연 활동

1 Time and Me

What is our No. 1 treasure? Is it the most important thing in your life? Or is it the happiest memory in your heart? We asked the question online and there were many middle school students who posted their answers. Let's read some of the answers.

Germany, Steffani

My No. 1 treasure is my smart phone. I talk to my friends, send messages, and take pictures with it. I wake up to its alarm, and I go to sleep with it near my bed. I spend most of my walking hours with my smart phone. I cannot live without it.

Korea, Jeongho

My No. 1 treasure is this baseball. I'm a big fan of the Thunderbirds, and my favorite player is Jason O'Neil. This ball was a home run ball that Jason hit. I was very lucky to catch it. After the game, I met Jason and he signed his name on it. Wow! It was the most amazing moment of my life!

New Zealand, Stephen

My No.1 treasure is the beautiful memories which I have of my elementary school. I lived on a small island before I entered middle school. I went to an elementary school which had only two classes for my grade. There were only 5 teachers. I had a really good time there.

(1) 듣기활동

Unit		Lesson 5. Time and Me	
Period 1/8		Warm Up, Listening	
Aims		1. Students can play '20 Questions Game' about precious people, things, or memories. 2. Students can understand dialogs about asking abilities and expressing inabilities. 3. Students can understand dialogs about telling opinions.	
Procedure		Activities	Teaching Aids
Introduction (5′)		• T & Ss greet each other and introduce the lesson. • T review the last lesson.	
Development	Warm-up (5′)	• T tells Ss teacher's own No.1 treasure like favorite people, things, or events in life. • T has Ss think of their No.1 treasure and play '20 question game' in pairs.	CD-ROM
	Listen on Target (7′)	• T tells what the two people do in four pictures. • Ss listen to a short dialog and check what they will do next. • Ss listen to a short dialog and fill in the blanks.	
	Listen in Context (8′)	• T checks the food names one by one. • Ss listen to a dialog and check in the foods two people will eat. • Ss listen to a dialog one more time if students want to. • Ss work on the worksheet.	CD-ROM Work-sheet
	Listening Activities — S	Ss listen to the dialogs and number the pictures. Ss listen to the dialogs again and check T or F. Ss listen to the CD and repeat the dialog.	CD-ROM Work-sheet
	Listening Activities — B	Ss listen to the dialogs and choose the correct pictures. Ss listen to the dialogs again and fill in the blanks. Ss listen to the CD and number the sentences in the correct order.	
	Listening Activities — A	Ss listen to the dialogs and number the correct pictures. Ss listen to the dialogs again and answer the questions. Ss listen to the CD and fill in the blanks. Ss practice the dialog with partners.	
Closing (5′)		• T reviews the lesson. • T gives an assignment; Ss read aloud the dialog script in the worksheet 10 times and write down the script in the notebook once.	

S: Supplementary level, B: Basic level, A: Advanced level

(2) **Video 시청**

Unit	Lesson 5. Time and Me	
Period 2/8	Video In Action	
Aims	1. Students can listen and understand the dialog. 2. Students can answer the questions about the dialog. 3. Students can practice the dialog with their partners. 4. Students can summarize the dialog.	
Procedure	Activities	Teaching Aids
Introduction	• T & Ss greet each other and introduce the lesson. • T review the last lesson. • T checks the assignment.	(5′)
Development — Before Watching	T talks about the picture in the textbook. T talks about the title and guess what the dialog is about.	picture (3′)
Development — Watching	Ss watch the video. Ss watch the video once more. Ss answer the questions.	CD-ROM (10′)
Development — After Watching	Ss practice the dialog with partners (line by line). Ss learn about listening tips (listening tips).	(12′)
Development — Video Activities — S	Ss watch the video and fill in the blanks with the given words. Ss read the sentences and check T or F. Ss practice the dialog with partners.	
Development — Video Activities — B	Ss watch the video and write in words starting with the given alphabets. Ss fill in the blanks to complete the summary. Ss role-play the dialog.	
Development — Video Activities — A	Ss watch the video and fill in the blanks. T corrects the errors in the summary of the dialog. Ss make their own dialogs and talk with partners.	
Closing	T reviews the lesson. T gives an assignment; to read aloud the dialog script in the worksheet 10 times and write down the script in the notebook once.	

(3) 말하기 활동

Unit	Lesson 5. Time and Me	
Period 3/8	Speaking	
Aims	1. Students can ask someone's abilities using the expression "Do you know how to ~?" 2. Students can express their inabilities using the expression "I don't know anything about ~." 3. Students can tell their opinions using the expression "I think ~."	
Procedure	Activities	Aids
Introduction (5′)	T & Ss exchange greetings. T reviews the last lesson. T checks the assignment.	
Development — Talk Like This	• Ss understand the example dialog. • Ss practice the dialog with partners using the given pictures and expressions. • Ss make more dialogs about what they know how to do.	CD-ROM (7′)
Development — Talk in Context	• Ss understand the example dialog. • Ss understand the verb phrase under the each picture. • Ss practice more dialogs with partners.	(8′)
Development — Pronunciation Tips	• Ss practice the sounds of [e] and [i:].	(5′)
Development — Speaking Activities (17′) — S	• Ss understand the example dialog. • Ss practice dialogs of "what they know how to do" and "do not know anything about". • Ss play a game of telling opinions about others' likes using the expression "I think~".	
Development — Speaking Activities (17′) — B	• Ss understand the example dialog. • Ss practice dialogs of "what they know how to do" and "do not know anything about". • Ss play a game of telling opinions about group members using the expression "I think~".	
Development — Speaking Activities (17′) — A	• Ss understand the example dialog. • Ss talk with partners using the given expressions. • Ss play a game of telling opinions about group members and expressing agreement on the opinions.	
Closing (5′)	• T reviews the lesson. • T gives an assignment; Ss make and write down a dialog using the expressions students learned in this lesson.	

(4) **읽기 활동** (1)

Unit	Lesson 5. Time and Me	
Period 5/8	Reading(1) What's your No 1 Treasure?	
Aims	1. Students can read and understand the replies on the Internet bulletin board on teenagers' No 1 treasures. 2. Students can talk or write about their own No. 1 treasures.	
Procedure	Activities	Aids
Introduction	• Ss & T exchange greetings. • T checks the assignment and review the previous lesson.	(5′)
Development — Before Reading (5′)	• Ss talk about the most important things in life. • T checkz the answers of the pre-reading activity. • Ss look at the pictures on the book and guess what they are going to read about.	CD-ROM
Development — Reading (30′)	• T introduces the text briefly. • Ss read the passages on pages 70–73 quickly. • Ss listen to the CD. • Ss listen and repeat after the CD and read the text individually. • Ss read the text aloud together or in groups. • Ss summarize each passage. • Ss learn new words and expressions in the text. • Ss study the text in detail. • Ss answer some comprehension questions.	CD-ROM Worksheet
Closing (5′)	• Ss read the text aloud together one more time. • Ss find out each person's No. 1 treasure and underline the reasons. • T gives an assignment; to write about the students' No. 1 treasures in 5–6 sentences.	

(5) 읽기 활동 (2)

Unit			Lesson 5. Time and Me	
Period 6/8			Reading(2) What's your No 1 Treasure?	
Aims			1. Students can talk about the main idea of the text. 2. Students can scan the text for more specific information. 3. Students can understand other teenagers' ways of life. 4. Students can do reading activities according to their proficiency levels.	
Procedure			Activities	Teaching Aids
Introduction (5')			• Ss & T exchange greetings. • T checks the assignment and review the previous lesson.	
Development	After Reading (15')		• Ss read out the text together. • Ss complete the table on the text. • Ss find out and check incorrect statements. • Ss fill in the blanks of the dialog between Jeongho and Yena. • Ss ask three other students about their No. 1 treasures.	CD-ROM
	Reading Activities (15')	S	• Ss match the kinds of No. 1 treasure with the four persons. • Ss fill in the blanks with the given expressions to complete the dialog between Steffi and Chris.	CD-ROM Work-sheet
		B	• Ss match the kinds of No. 1 treasure with the four persons. • Ss find out appropriate sentences that are fit for the blanks of the dialog between Steffi and Chris.	
		A	• Ss complete the table of a survey on No. 1 treasures and write the treasures of Steffi, Jeongho, and Chris. • Ss fill in the blanks to complete the dialog between Steffi and Chris.	
Closing (5')			• T presents passages on the students' No. 1 treasures and check understandings. • T gives an assignment; to correct errors in the passages.	

(6) 쓰기 활동

Unit		Lesson 5. Time and Me	
Period 7/8		Forms in Action, Writing	
Aims		1. Students can understand the usage of subjective relative pronouns and use them. 2. Students can understand the usage of objective relative pronouns and use them. 3. Students can modify nouns with the definite article and superlative adjectives.	
Procedure		Activities	Teaching Aids
Introduction (5′)		• Ss & T exchange greetings. • T checks the assignment and review the previous lesson.	
D e v e l o p m e n t	Forms in Action (15′)	• Ss study the kinds and usage of subjective relative pronouns: 'who' and 'which'. • Ss study the kinds and usage of objective relative pronouns and make relative pronoun clauses. • Ss study the forms of superlative adjectives. • Ss study how to modify nouns with the definite article and superlative adjectives.	CD-ROM PPT Worksheet
	Write	• Ss look at the people and talk about their jobs. • Ss complete the sentences using relative pronouns.	CD-ROM (5′)
	Write in Context	• Ss look at picture and complete the sentences. • Ss describe the classmates with the definite article and superlative adjectives.	(7′)
	Writing Activities (10′) — S	• Ss write about a person who students want to marry and a house where they want to live with the given expressions. • Ss explain favorites using the given adjectives.	CD-ROM Worksheet
	Writing Activities (10′) — B	• Ss write about a person who students want to marry and a house where they want to live with relative pronouns and the given expressions. • Ss explain favorites using the given adjectives.	
	Writing Activities (10′) — A	• Ss write about a person who students want to marry and a house where they want to live with relative pronouns and the given expressions. • Ss complete the dialog of one's favorite food, sport, and teacher.	
Closing (3′)		• T sums up the lesson. • T gives an assignment; to write about what kind of people the students want to be in the future.	

(7) Portfolio 활동

Unit	Lesson 5. Time and Me	
Period 8/8	Wrap Up, Culture Portfolio, Self Check	
Aims	1. Students can wrap up the lesson by solving some review questions. 2. Students can practice the functions and structures of the lesson again. 3. Students can write replies about their No. 1 treasures on the Internet bulletin board.	
Procedure	Activities	Teaching Aids
Introduction	• Ss & T exchange greetings. • T checks the assignment and review the previous lesson.	(5′)
Development — Wrap Up	• Ss listen to the dialog and choose the proper picture. • Ss find the appropriate sentence for the blank of the dialog and practice with partners. • Ss read the passage about No.1 treasure and locate the given sentence in the passage. • Ss write an answer to the question about the most interesting subject.	CD-ROM (20′)
Development — Culture Portfolio	• Ss read replies on the Internet bulletin board. • Ss write their own replies on their No.1 treasures.	(15′)
Closing	• T checks the page Self Check and find out how much students have learned.	(5′)

PART III

수업실연 모의문제

모의문제 1

Lesson 4. Give the Earth a Hand

- 대상: Practical English II
- Level: Upper Intermediate
- Time: 100 minutes block time

1. Directions

Examinee's Response 1.	⟨Using material 1, teach a vocabulary activity⟩ A. Teach underlined three words using guessing strategy in the text. B. Check students' understanding of the key vocabulary, *protection*, *thrown away*, and *damage*.
Examinee's Response 2.	⟨Using material 1, design while Reading & Writing Activities⟩ A. Give questions to students to check their understanding of the reading text in Material 1. B. Have students find out specific information in pairs to complete. in ⟨Table 1⟩
Examinee's Response 3.	⟨Using material 2, engage students in speaking activity⟩ A. Make a group. B. Cooperate to solve the problems with their ideas in group. C. Have students write about one solution for each problem in groups.
Examinee's Response 4.	⟨Using material 2, encourage students in an Evaluation activity⟩ A. Have students present their writing, and provide a scoring rubric with 3 criteria for peer evaluation of each group's presentation. B. Give 2 feedbacks after the presentation. One should be a positive feedback and the other should be a negative feedback.

2. Lesson Procedure

Class	Skills	Objectives
1–3	Listening Speaking (지도안 작성)	Students will be able to: • give their opinions on how to save energy. • answer questions for specific information after listening. • review and practice the communicative function. • solve the problems.
4–5	Reading	
6–7	Reading and Writing	
8–9	Writing & Grammar	
10	Portfolio	

⟨Material 1⟩

Like many other people, you probably have a lot of questions about environmental protection but haven't been able to find the answers easily. Here are answers to some of the things you may be curious about.

Q1: What should I do with my old cell phone when I buy a new one?
A1: People usually just throw their old cell phones in the trash. In fact, according to the Ministry of the Environment of Korea, more than 18 million used cell phones were thrown away in 2010 in Korea alone. In the United States, more than 130 million cell phones are thrown away every year. Cell phones contain hazardous materials that damage the environment such as lead, mercury and arsenic. They also contain valuable metals such as gold, silver and copper. This makes it all the more important to recycle old cell phones. Manufacturers can repair them for resale or reuse some materials and parts.

Q2: Is eating beef bad for the environment?
A2: In order to produce lots of cheap beef, people have to cut down trees to make pastures. In some countries, rainforests are being damaged in order to raise more cattle. As part of their natural digestive process, cattle also release methane, which is one of the causes of global warming. It is clearly advisable that we reduce beef consumption.

⟨Table 1⟩

Question	Answer
1. How many cell phones are thrown away in Korea?	
2. How many cell phones are thrown away in United States?	
3. Why are cell phones dangerous?	
4. Why do we have to recycle old cell phones?	
5. Why do we have to cut down trees?	
6. Why do we reduce beef consumption?	

⟨Material 2⟩

Questions for Problem Solving
(1) I recently saw a T-shirt that was said to be "upcycled." What is upcycling?
(2) Is the exhaust of cars and buses that burn compressed natural gas (CNG) free of pollutants?
(3) Is email more eco-friendly than regular paper mail?
(4) Someone told me that keeping houseplants helps purify the air. Is that really true?

단계	교실 활동
	교수·학습 활동
수험생 작성 1.	
수험생 작성 2.	
수험생 작성 3.	
수험생 작성 4.	

모의문제 2

Chapter 10. See the Trees, Not the Forest

- 대상: 중학교 2학년
- Level: Lower Intermediate
- Time: 90 minutes block time

1. Directions

Examinee's Response 1.	Using 〈material 1〉, encourage students to involve in a Pre-Reading activity. A. Students brainstorm to predict the general meaning of the text from the title, '**See the Trees, Not the Forest**' B. Students guess the meaning of the new words through contexts: *details, represent, decision*.
Examinee's Response 2.	Using 〈material 1〉, design while Reading & Writing activity. A. Teacher gives questions to students to check their understanding of the reading text of 〈Material 1〉. B. Students find out specific information in pairs to complete 〈Table 1〉. for information for each number.
Examinee's Response 3.	Using 〈material 2〉, encourage students in a Speaking activity. A. Students in groups discuss one of twos in 〈material 2〉. B. Groups present their thoughts on comparison and other groups give a rubric with 3 criteria for peer-evaluation for content of each group's presentation.
Examinee's Response 4.	Using 〈material 2〉, encourage students to make a focus on form activity. A. Teacher observes the students' presentation. B. Teacher gives two corrective feedback on the students' language errors.

2. Lesson Procedure

Class	Skills	Objectives
1-2	Listening	
3	Speaking	
4-5	Reading	
6-7	Reading and Writing (지도안 작성)	Students will be able to • predict the meaning of the text and guess the meaning. • scan to find detailed information regarding each number. • read the main text and answer questions related to it. • understand the usage of the grammatical structures presented in this lesson.
8-9	Writing & Grammar	
10	Portfolio	

〈Table 1〉

Number	information
1.4	
1.6	
70	
85	

⟨Material 1⟩

Lesson 10. See the Trees, Not the Forest

When we compare groups, we often look at their averages. Averages can help us see the big picture. However, we have to think about the <u>details</u>, too. To Cross or Not to Cross? "General! Do you hear that? The enemies must be right behind us," a soldier shouted. "I know, but we can't jump into the river!" said the general. "On average, the river is 1.4 meters deep and we are 1.6 meters tall. We are tall enough to cross the river," cried the soldier. They started to cross the river, but when they reached the center of the river, some soldiers disappeared under the water. Why did that happen?

The average height of the soldiers was 1.6 meters, but that doesn't mean that every soldier was 1.6 meters tall. Maybe some were taller and maybe some were shorter. In the same way, not every part of the river was 1.4 meters deep. Who did better, Jinsu? My average score is higher. So I did better! Yunho, what? I did better in every subject except for History. How can you say that? Jinsu's average is certainly higher than Yunho's. Still, it seems strange to say that Jinsu did better. Why is that?

Look at Yunho's report card. His average score without History is 85. His average score with History is 70. Because his History grade is much lower than his other grades, the average score of 70 doesn't really represent his generally high grades.

An average is usually good enough to represent a group as a whole. However, it doesn't represent each part. When some parts of the group are too different, the average does not <u>represent</u> the group well. "Try to see the forest, not the trees," they say, but sometimes we need to see the trees as well! If we let the forest hide all of the trees, we may make the wrong <u>decision</u>.

⟨Material 2⟩ Group activity

Who is a better friend and why?	
Which one is more considered when you buy a mobile phone?	

단계	교실 활동
	교수·학습 활동
수험생 작성 1.	
수험생 작성 2.	
수험생 작성 3.	
수험생 작성 4.	

모의문제 3

Lesson 7. Something about Korea

- 대상: High school 1, intermediate, 30명
- 수업실연: development 부분 (20분)
- Time: 90 minutes block time

⟨Directions⟩

Examinee's Response 1.	⟨Using material 1, teach a Pre-Listening Activities⟩ A. Students brainstorm to identify one hot place to introduce and promote 'Korean Visit' for overseas tourists with their group members. B. Students learn three essential vocabulary: *tribe, expert, demand*
Examinee's Response 2.	⟨Using material 1, design while-Listening and Speaking Activities⟩ A. Students listen to the ⟨material 1⟩ and complete a ⟨table 1⟩ to make comprehension better with group members. B. Teacher provides comprehension questions to the whole class. C. Students find out specific information in pairs for the questions.
Examinee's Response 3.	⟨Using material 2, encourage students in a post-Speaking and Writing Activities⟩ A. Students choose one of tourist spots in ⟨Material 2⟩ in groups. B. Students write to design a pamphlet about their tourist spot where they want to recommend for their foreign friend who visit Korea for the first time.
Examinee's Response 4.	⟨Using scoring rubric, encourage students in an Evaluation activity⟩ A. Students present their pamphlet to class. B. With ⟨scoring rubric⟩, students give peer evaluation of each group's presentation. C. Teacher gives two corrective feedback on the students' language errors.

⟨Material 1⟩

[STEP 1]

W: Welcome to *Korea in the World*. In today's news, *Hangeul* is being used by a tribe in Indonesia. The tribe has decided to use the Korean alphabet to write their spoken language. The leader of the tribe said they chose *Hangeul* because it is better suited to the sounds of their language than any other alphabet. We'll be right back with more on Korea's impressive international achievements after a short break.

[STEP 2]

W: This is *Insight Korea*. Korea has been ranked as having the best wireless Internet services out of the OECD countries. Experts say the spread of smartphones and tablet computers has quickly driven up demand for faster and wider wireless Internet services. Also, We're about to discuss three reasons why Korea is a great place to live. Number one, Korea has a very convenient public transportation system. You can get around easily and quickly. Number two, there are many shops that are open 24 hours, so you can shop any time you want. Number three, Korean restaurants provide a lot of free side dishes. If you are interested in learning more about Korea, visit our website: www.insightkorea.org.

⟨Table 1⟩ For Promotion of Korean Tourism

Item	Features
Korean Hangeul	
Korea Insight	1.
	2.
	3.

〈Material 2〉

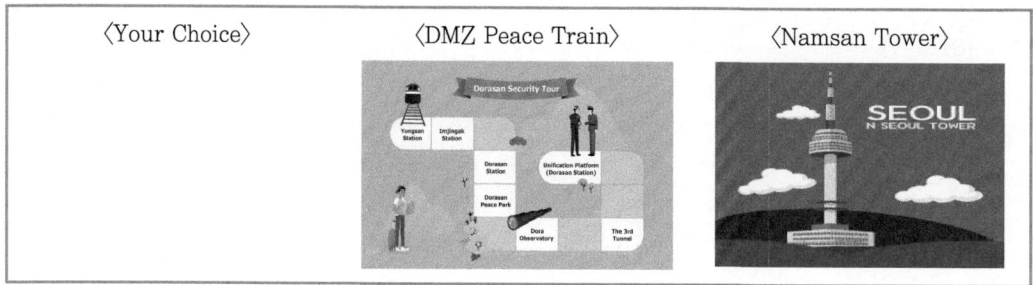

〈Your Choice〉　　〈DMZ Peace Train〉　　〈Namsan Tower〉

〈Rubric〉

Group Name	Evaluation Item	Grade			
		A	B	C	D
	Completion				
	Organization				
	Tourist Interests				
A: completely agree, B: agree, C: not really, D: needs repair					

단계	교실 활동
	교수 · 학습 활동
수험생 작성 1.	
수험생 작성 2.	
수험생 작성 3.	
수험생 작성 4.	

모의문제 4

Chapter 5. From School Project to World News

- 대상: 고등학교 1학년
- Level: Upper Intermediate
- Lesson Objectives: Ss will be able to ~
  - talk about their ideas to write the ads for some products with the organizer.
  - focus two grammar points in reading and practice them in use.
  - write a complaint letter if you bought a product that was not satisfied.

〈Directions〉

Examinee's Response 1.	〈Using Material 1, design a pre-reading activity〉 A. Encourage students to activate their background knowledge related to Material 1. B. Encourage students to read for the main idea of the text. C. Teach one of the three underlined words in the text.
Examinee's Response 2.	〈Using Material 1 and 2, design a post-reading activity〉 A. Ask students to do pair reading and find details using Material 1 and 2. B. Confirm with students for their comprehension after reading of the text.
Examinee's Response 3.	〈Using survey, Encourage students in a speaking activity〉 A. Design a survey speaking activity. B. Act as a facilitator while speaking activity. C. After the speaking activity, give feedback on either content or language use.
Examinee's Response 4.	〈Engage students in writing.〉 A. Design a group writing activity. B. Provide the teacher's modeling before students' writing.

〈Material 1〉

Everyone knows that advertisements rarely tell the whole truth, but how much truth do they tell? We generally assume that advertisements deliver the facts when it comes to numbers. After all, we can confirm numbers. Two students in New Zealand attempted to confirm an advertising claim with a scientific experiment. The following is an account of what happened three years after their experiment.

TUESDAY, MARCH 27, 2007 : Giant Company Cornered by Two Students

New Zealand – A high school science experiment by two 14-year-old girls has put GlaxoSmithKline in court. GSK is the world's second largest food and drug company. It has been charged with breaking New Zealand's Fair Trading Act. Representatives of the company will appear in court.

The situation arose from a school science project by Anna Devathasan and Jenny Suo. In 2004, the students wanted to make sure that their favorite juice contained the vitamin C it claimed to contain. They tested the vitamin C content in Ribena, which is made from black currants. For comparison, they also did tests on orange juice products. They found that regular orange juice contained about 72mg of vitamin C for every 100ml. Each 100ml of Ribena contained only 22mg of vitamin C.

The girls were surprised at the low vitamin C levels of Ribena. The company had promoted the product by claiming that the black currants in Ribena had four times the vitamin C of oranges. The ads were successful, and the drink became very popular with teenagers. "We thought we were doing it wrong and that we must have made a mistake," Anna said. They were convinced that they were right only after repeating the experiment a number of times.

〈Material 2〉

Numbers	Meaning
100ml	
72ml	
22mg	

〈Survey〉

Your giant company	Advertisement you remember	Reasons
Samsung	smartphone	creative color and designs

219

단계	교실 활동
	교수·학습 활동
수험생 작성 1.	
수험생 작성 2.	
수험생 작성 3.	
수험생 작성 4.	

모의문제 5

Lesson 7. Korean Wave Around the World

- 대상: 중학교 2학년
- Level: Lower Intermediate
- Lesson Objectives: Ss will be able to
  - listen to a presentation about the way to introduce Korean culture.
  - talk about the parts of Korean culture foreign friends will like and the ways to introduce them.
  - present the group members' ideas to the class.

〈Directions〉

Examinee's Response 1.	〈Using material 1, teach a vocabulary activity〉 A. Teach three underlined words by guessing strategy, founded, polishing, goods. B. Activate students' schema of the various Korean culture.
Examinee's Response 2.	〈Using material 1, design a listening activity〉 A. Let students listen to the speakers talking about the culture. B. Make a summary of the dialogue.
Examinee's Response 3.	〈Encourage students in a speaking activity〉 A. Design a group speaking activity showing the picture cards about Korean culture. B. Let students introduce their choice of culture to a foreign friend who doesn't know anything about Korean cultures. C. In groups, students give a presentation about their ideas on the ways to introduce Korean culture. D. Give feedback on content.
Examinee's Response 4.	〈Engage students in language-focused activity〉 A. Let students practice some target phrase they have difficulty using in speaking. B. Provide formative assessment that checks if students have achieved the objectives of using the target phrase.

〈Material 1〉

I: Today we are meeting Korean Waves, the winner of this year's K-pop Dance Festival in London. Here is John, the leader of the dance team. Would you please tell us about the special features of your dance?

J: Sure. We love the hot beat of K-pop. We love the soft moves of traditional Korean dances, too. We want to put them together and create rhythmic waves.

I: You rap in Korean. Do you speak the language?

J: Yes, but my Korean is not very good. I'm studying it at the Korean Cultural Centre UK, but it's not easy.

I: You must be interested in not only Korean music but also the Korean language.

J: You bet! You know what? The centre had a special week on famous Westerners in the Korean Empire last month. One of them was Ernest Bethell.

I: Ernest Bethell had a deep love for Korea and Korean culture, didn't he?

J: Yes. He was born in Bristol, not far from here. I learned that he <u>founded</u> Daehan Maeil Sinbo, a newspaper in Korean and English. He loved the Korean language and culture, and so do I.

I: That's cool! You're going to come to Korea for the final round, aren't you?

J: Absolutely! We're now <u>polishing</u> our moves. We are looking forward to the final round, visiting the country, and enjoying the hot energy of K-pop and K-food.

I: I wish you good luck! What places do you want to visit?

J: My first stop will be Insa-dong. I've heard that there are many fun activities to do there and lots of street food to enjoy. I'd like to go on a hanbok photo shoot and try tteokbokki. Then I hope to stop by Namdaemun Market. I want to pick up character socks and popular Korean <u>goods</u> for my sister. They must have a wide selection there.

I: I hope you find some nice ones. Thank you for being with us today.

J: Thank YOU.

Note: I=interviewer, J=Jack

단계	교실 활동
	교수·학습 활동
수험생 작성 1.	
수험생 작성 2.	
수험생 작성 3.	
수험생 작성 4.	

모의문제 6

Chapter 8. Dos and Dont's of Gift-giving

- 대상: 고등학교 1학년
- Level: Intermediate
- Lesson Objectives: Ss will be able to:
  - understand some precautions when buying gifts.
  - appreciate the differences of customs in other countries.
  - use the new language form and new vocabulary in context.
  - write the composition of comparison.

⟨Directions⟩

Examinee's Response 1.	Using ⟨material 1⟩, teach a vocabulary activity. A. Teach underlined three words using guessing strategy in the text. B. Check students' understanding of the key vocabulary.
Examinee's Response 2.	Using ⟨material 1⟩, design while Reading & Writing Activities. A. Give questions to students to check their understanding of the reading text in Material 1. B. Have students find out specific information in pairs to complete Table 1.
Examinee's Response 3.	Using ⟨Table 1⟩, engage students in Writing activity. A. Make a group. B. Present a model writing to help them to write with. C. Have students write in groups about your traditions of giving gifts in a process-based writing. D. Make sure that students not concentrate on language use.
Examinee's Response 4.	Encourage students in an evaluation activity. A. Have students present their writing, and provide a scoring rubric with three criteria for peer evaluation of each group's presentation. B. Give feedback after the presentation. One should be a positive feedback and the other should be a negative feedback.

⟨Material⟩

What gift would you like to receive? We tend to buy gifts that we would like to receive. Gift-giving, however, can be a little tricky in cross-cultural situations. Gift-giving customs and rules vary from culture to culture.

If you send flowers in Europe, be sure to send them in odd numbers. Also, roses are far too personal, and used for funerals. In China, try to give things in pairs because Chinese philosophy stresses harmony and balance. Clocks are not a good gift for the Chinese; the word in Mandarin for clock is very similar to the word for death. In general, avoid any gift that may be even indirectly connected with death. Be aware, also, of the host country's religious rules and customs. Leather products are not good in India, where Hindu traditions hold the cow sacred. Avoid leather picture frames and wallets if you plan to visit India. Fine wine is appreciated in many cultures around the world, but it is unacceptable in Muslim countries, where drinking is prohibited. Good gifts for Muslim friends would be silver compasses; no matter where in the world they might be, they can always locate Mecca to perform their daily prayers.

Generally, the best gift is something that is unique to your country. It does not need to be especially valuable or rare. Possibilities include a book about your country, an inexpensive piece of art, or something else that reflects your culture. If the children of your host country collect coins and stamps, they would be pleased with a set of your country's coins or a selection of new stamps. Also, it is not wise to bring things that are common in that country as gifts. For example, don't take something made of silver to Mexico, where silver is plentiful.

⟨Table 1⟩

Country	You should.....	You should not.....

단계	교실 활동
	교수·학습 활동
수험생 작성 1.	
수험생 작성 2.	
수험생 작성 3.	
수험생 작성 4.	

모의문제 7

Chapter 9. Can you Hear What I hear?

- 대상: 고등학교 1학년
- Level: Lower Intermediate
- Lesson Objectives: Ss will be able to:
  - talk about their ideas to make the ads for some products with the organizer.
  - understand the new vocabulary by guessing the meaning in context.
  - focus two grammar points in reading and practice them in use.
  - write a complaint letter if you bought a product that was not satisfied.

〈Directions〉 (지도안 작성 2-5)

Examinee's Response 1.	〈Using material 1, teach a vocabulary activity〉 A. Teach three underlined words, invention, audible, disturbing by guessing strategy. B. Check students' understanding of the key vocabulary.
Examinee's Response 2.	〈Using material 1, design a post-reading activity〉 A. Let students use the underlined phrase, stand it. B. Make a summary of the reading text.
Examinee's Response 3.	〈Encourage students in a writing activity〉 A. Design a group writing activity showing the picture card. B. Provide the teacher's modeling of story writing. C. Let students write about students' own worries and advice using the target phrase. D. Give feedback on both content and language use.
Examinee's Response 4.	〈Engage students in speaking activity〉 A. Make a group. B. Plan a speaking activity that students will promote students' participation. C. Let students talk about their own worries and advice using the target phrase. D. Make sure that students not concentrate on language use.
Examinee's Response 5.	〈Closing activity〉 A. Provide formative assessment that checks if students have achieved the objectives of using the target phrase.

⟨Material 1⟩

Can You Hear What I Hear?

"Tom's phone is ringing, and Ms. Lewis doesn't hear a thing," said Belinda as she laughed to herself. "Yes, she is going on with the lesson," her friend replied. Their classmates started laughing, and Ms. Lewis had no idea what was going on. "When I heard about it, I couldn't believe my ears," said Donna Lewis, a high school teacher in Manhattan. "But one of the kids gave me a copy of the ring tone. My colleague and I played it for some first graders. They could all hear it, but we couldn't."

The ring tone that she couldn't hear is called the Teen Buzz. It makes use of an <u>invention</u> called the Mosquito. The Mosquito is an annoying 17kHz buzzer. It was first designed to keep teenagers from hanging around in front of stores.

The high-pitched sound made by the Mosquito is so <u>disturbing</u> that young people cannot <u>stand it</u> and go away. Since it is <u>audible</u> only to kids, adults use the Mosquito to keep them away.

The <u>invention</u> is based on a scientific fact related to hearing loss. Humans can generally hear sounds with frequencies between 20Hz and 20kHz. However, the range of <u>audible</u> sounds varies with age. When you are younger, you are able to hear high-pitched sounds. When you get older, it is likely that you will no longer hear these sounds. The Mosquito makes a high-frequency noise that usually only people under the age of 20 can hear.

⟨Worries and Advices⟩

Student Name	Worry	Advices

단계	교실 활동
	교수·학습 활동
수험생 작성 1.	
수험생 작성 2.	
수험생 작성 3.	
수험생 작성 4.	

모의문제 8

Chapter 9. Change for the Better

- 대상: High School I, low intermediate, 32명
- Level: Lower Intermediate
- Time: 100 block time
- 수업실연: development 부분 20분 (examinee's responses 2-5)

1. Directions (지도안 작성 2-5)

Examinee's Response 1.	⟨Encourage students in a Warm-up activity⟩ A. As motivation pre-activity, students do a group discussion activity regarding the today's topic, 'Change for the better'. B. Students do a brainstorming.
Examinee's Response 2.	⟨Using material 1, encourage students in a function-based activity⟩ A. Teacher asks students to guess the meaning and function of the underlined target phrase, '**I can't agree more**' in ⟨Material 1⟩. B. Students are encouraged to make a list of ⟨table 1⟩ what they can do for the better world, choose the ONE item and do a role play using the target phrase.
Examinee's Response 3.	⟨Using table 1, encourage students in a Reading activities⟩ A. ⟨Material 2⟩ is an introduction of the main text. As a pre-reading activity, students complete ⟨table 2⟩ to understand the whole meaning of the text in their group. B. Students in group choose one character in 'The Help' who they think the most impressed one and write with two reasons.
Examinee's Response 4.	⟨Encourage students in a Writing activity⟩ A. Teacher provides the model writing about his/her own friend. B. Students write a story about their best friend.
Examinee's Response 5.	⟨Encourage students in a focus on form activity⟩ A. Teacher gives two corrective feedback for each group regarding one for content and the other for language for the students' writing.

2. Lesson Procedure

Students will be able to:

- think about and share their ideas about 'living together'.
- guess the meaning of key phrases in the listening text.
- understand characters and settings of 'The Help' and write about a person.

⟨Material 1⟩

Listen and Check

G: Hey, John. What happened to your leg?
B: I broke my leg while playing soccer. I have to be in this wheelchair for two weeks.
G: Oh, no. That's too bad. Do you want me to help you with your bag?
B: Thank you very much. That would be really helpful.
G: How's life in a wheelchair?
B: It's very difficult, actually. There are many stairs at school, but no elevator. I realized that physically challenged people face great inconveniences in their everyday lives.
G: Maybe we should have more elevators for them.
B: Right, I <u>can't agree more</u>.

⟨Table 1⟩

To do list for the better world

Group name:

1. Use less electricity to save energy on the Earth.
2. _____
3. _____

⟨Material 2⟩

The Help

The Help is a novel by an American author named Kathryn Stockett. It is a story about African-American maids working in white households. The book is set in Jackson, Mississippi, just before the Civil Rights Act was passed in 1964. The story is told mainly by three women: Skeeter, Aibileen, and Minny. Skeeter is the daughter of a rich white family. Her mother wants her to get married like her friends, but Skeeter wants to be a journalist. It is beyond what was expected of a Southern white woman in the 1960s. Aibileen is an African-American maid. She raises white families' children only to see them grow up and leave her. Minny, Aibileen's friend, also works as a maid. These three women work together and write a book, The Help, to tell the stories of African-American maids. While they are working together, a friendship develops across races and social status.

Meet the Main Characters
Aibileen's heart is so big, we just might all fit inside it. If you're lucky, she might even write you into her prayers, which are known to be particularly powerful. Minny and Aibileen are the two primary women representing "the help" – the black women who make life so nice and comfy for their white employers. In many ways, these two women are not alike but best friends. Skeeter is a bundle of surprises. She's a 23-year-old white woman with a college degree. She lives at home on her family's cotton farm. And she devotes herself, at considerable risk, to a book featuring the real stories of the black women who work for the white families in her hometown of Jackson, Mississippi.

⟨Table 2⟩

Characters	Relationship	What to do
Aibileen		
Minny		
Skeeter		

단계	교실 활동
	교수·학습 활동
수험생 작성 1.	
수험생 작성 2.	
수험생 작성 3.	
수험생 작성 4.	

모의문제 9

Chapter 5. The Two Faces of SNS

- 대상: Middle School 3
- Level: Lower Intermediate, 30명
- Time: 90 minutes block time

1. Directions

Examinee's Response 1.	Using 〈Worksheet 1〉, design brainstorming activity for debate. A. Students do a brainstorming activity to talk about their experiences on SNS. B. Students debate about the advantages and disadvantages of SNS using the phrases given in the 〈table 1〉.
Examinee's Response 2.	Using 〈Material 1〉, encourage students to do Pre-Reading and While-Reading activities. A. Teacher teaches the THREE underlined words, *functions, spread, damage* using the context to let students guess the meaning in the reading 〈material 1〉. B. Students understand general ideas and details of the functions of SNS in 〈material 1〉.
Examinee's Response 3.	Using 〈Worksheet 2〉, implement Writing activity. A. Students in group choose one side of using SNS and write their own ideas of reasons of likes or dislikes. B. Note that this writing will be connected to the activity of (Examinee's response 1).
Examinee's Response 4.	Encourage students in a Grammar Check-up in their writing. A. Teacher gives TWO corrective feedback for each group regarding their grammatical errors on the summary writing. B. Students discuss to discover the rule from the examples.

2. Lesson Procedure

Students will be able to :

- discuss the advantages and disadvantages about using SNS.
- answer the questions to complete their comprehension.
- write a summary on comprehension.
- find out the rule of the target forms.

⟨Worksheet 1⟩

advantages	disadvantages
I think SNS websites give ……	SNS websites may harm …..
I believe SNS websites help ……	SNS websites can cause …
SNS websites may allow ….	I doubt if ….

⟨Worksheet 2⟩ My Social Networking Service

Social Networking Service	
Likes	Dislikes

〈Material 1〉 Functions of SNS

T: Social Networking Service (SNS) websites have become popular with many Internet users. It is SNS websites that allow each person to connect with others all over the world. They have many helpful functions, but sometimes cause some problems. Now, we will discuss the effects of using SNS websites. Nuri, what's your opinion of SNS websites?

S1: I think SNS websites give us many benefits. We can quickly exchange information when we use SNS websites. We can post and check whatever we want to share online in real time. For example, if you ask about good places to shop online, you can get comments quickly.

S2: I think that's a good point, but I believe that it is the powerful spread of information that causes serious problems. I mean that SNS websites can be the source of false information and unpleasant words which may harm people. These bad words can hurt someone's feelings.

T: Nuri and Mike both made good points about SNS websites. What do you think, Amy?

S3: I believe SNS websites help us keep good relationships with people we don't meet often. It is amazing that I can connect with my friend Jane in America. I can keep in touch with her online whenever I want.

S2: I'm not sure if people we meet online can be true friends. If they contact us only online, it will be difficult to keep sincere relationships with them.

S3: I see your point, but SNS websites help us remember whenever there are important events. For example, they tell us about our friends' birthdays or school festivals. That is, SNS websites play a very important role in human networking.

T: OK, Susan, do you agree with Amy?

S4: Well, I doubt if social networking always serves that purpose. As far as I know, SNS websites are not safe, no matter what we do to protect our personal information. We need more privacy. Strangers may steal our ID and use our personal data, such as our names, e-mail addresses, and photos.

S1: That's possible, but I want to tell you about another good effect of SNS websites. I think they help us find hope in a disaster. For example, when a bad storm hit the U.S.A. news reporters, doctors, and other local people began to post information about the damage and ways to help on SNS websites. Lots of other SNS users tried to give whatever they could to help the victims.

T: Everyone did a good job. We can see that Social Networking Service websites have two faces: they can help or harm us. So it's important for us to make good use of SNS websites and be more careful when we use them.

Note: T=teacher, S=student

단계	교실 활동
	교수·학습 활동
수험생 작성 1.	
수험생 작성 2.	
수험생 작성 3.	
수험생 작성 4.	

모의문제 10

Chapter 5. The Long and Winding Road to Marriage

- 대상: 고등학교 2학년
- Level: Upper Intermediate
- Lesson Objectives: Students will be able to:
  - put the dialogue between Jina and Bomi in order.
  - understand the key expressions in the passage.
  - predict the first impression related to the main passage.
  - focus two grammar points in reading and practice them in use.

〈Directions〉

Examinee's Response 1.	〈Using Material 1, design a listening activity〉 A. Let students listen and put the dialogue between Jina and Bomi in order. B. Let students predict the conclusion of story.
Examinee's Response 2.	〈Using Material 2, design a reading activity〉 A. Ask students to do pair reading and find details using Material 2. B. Let students understand the key expressions in the passage. C. Ask students to predict the first impression related to the main passage.
Examinee's Response 3.	〈Engage students in post-reading activity.〉 A. Confirm with students for their comprehension after reading of the text. B. Check the answers with their group members.
Examinee's Response 4.	〈Ask students in focus-on-form activity.〉 A. Discuss their linguistic problems in understanding reading. B. Focus two grammar points in reading and practice them in use for feedback.

〈Material 1〉

〈Jina〉	〈Bomi〉
• How did you like the movie, Bomi?	• Maybe not, but I'll keep looking.
• Oh, you're wrong about him.	• You don't agree with me?
• No, I think he's really honest and nice. He's my type.	• Yes. He should be smart, nice, handsome, rich and ...
• Have you ever thought about the perfect man for you?	• Not me. If I were Elizabeth, I would turn down his proposal.
• Ha, ha. There is no one like that.	• Well, I think Darcy is arrogant and selfish.

〈Material 2〉

Elizabeth and Darcy met at a ball and got married within a year, but it was not love at first sight. When his friend, Mr. Bingley, suggested Darcy dance with her, he commented: "She is all right, but not beautiful enough for me." Elizabeth overheard this remark and quickly formed a bad impression of him. His first impression of her, however, changed very quickly. He soon found her to be quite beautiful, and then irresistible.

However, he believed that marriage was out of the question because her family was from a lower social class. Darcy even advised his best friend, Mr. Bingley, who was in love with Elizabeth's elder sister, Jane, to leave the neighborhood with him. When Elizabeth learned that Darcy was responsible for her sister's unhappiness, her impression of his hardened into prejudice.

Despite all his efforts, he found it impossible to forget her. When they met again, he proposed to her. It was far from a romantic proposal. He told her in plain words that he loved her in spite of her family background and against his own will. Angry, she told him that he was the last man in the world that she would marry.

Since he had been sure of his success, he was shocked when she said no. He thought any woman would be delighted to marry a rich, handsome, and intelligent man like him. Elizabeth, however, did not find him attractive at all. She told him he was arrogant and selfish, with no consideration for the feelings of others. He was hurt, but had to agree that there was some truth in her words.

단계	교실 활동
	교수 · 학습 활동
수험생 작성 1.	
수험생 작성 2.	
수험생 작성 3.	
수험생 작성 4.	

PART IV

심층면접

CHAPTER 01 심층면접 기출 문제

　　인성교육의 중요성이 대두되면서 교사임용시험에서 심층면접의 비중이 점점 더 강화되고 있다. 일찍이 개정안이 발표된 경기, 강원, 대구와 서울에서 인성교육을 위한 교사가 필요하다는 공고문을 내면서 다른 지역에서도 그 흐름을 함께 하고 있다. 영어교사 임용시험을 보는 수험생들은 자신의 인성을 가다듬고 문제에 대한 실제적인 해결이 되는 답안을 만들어 내는 연습을 해야 할 것이다. 기출문제를 파악하고 연습하는 과정에서 기계적인 말하기 연습이 되어서는 안되고 실제로 학교 현장에서 만나는 학생, 학부모, 동료교사와 교장 선생님과의 문제점과 해결책을 이해하고 설명하려는 노력이 보여야 하겠다.

　　교육부가 초·중등 교원임용 2차 시험에서 면접과 수업실연의 중요성을 강조하면서 각 시·도 교육청은 2차 시험 배점을 변경했다. 교육부는 교육과정 개정에 맞게 수업과 평가역량을 갖춘 교사를 선발하기 위해 교원 임용시험에 대한 개선방안을 마련한다고 밝힌바 있다. 이에 따라 개별 시도교육청은 임용 2차 시험에 심층 면접, 수업실연 비중을 확대했다. 중등 교사 임용고시는 서술형 필기시험인 1차 시험(100점 만점)과 심층면접, 수업실연, 학습과정안 작성 등으로 구성된 2차 시험(100점 만점)으로 구성된다.

서울	서울시교육청은 초·중등 임용 2차 시험 개별면접에서 추가질문을 포함시켰고 수업지도안은 한국어로 작성하며, 초등 임용 시험에서는 수업실연에 반성적 성찰면접을 추가했다.
세종	세종교육청은 2025년부터 자체 문제출제에서 평가원 문제로 변경하였으며 총 4문항으로 구상과 즉답형 합하여 10분의 면접을 실시하게 되었다.
인천	인천광역시교육청도 초등 임용에서 교수·학습과정안 작성 배점을 20점 만점을 10점으로 줄이는 대신 교직적성·심층면접 점수를 30점에서 40점으로 늘려 비중을 강화했다. 중등 임용에서는 교수·지도안 작성 점수를 아예 폐지하고 교직적성·심층면접과 수업실연 점수를 각각 올려 변별력을 높였다.
전남	전라남도교육청은 중등교사 임용고시 2차 시험에서 교수학습 지도안 작성 배점을 없앤 대신 수업실연 50점, 교직적성 심층면접 50점으로 비중을 확대했다. 초등교사 임용에서도 교수안 작성 점수를 없애고 수업실연, 심층면접 배점을 각각 5점씩 올려 비중을 높였다.
강원	강원도 교육청은 2025년부터 수업실연을 20분으로 평가하고 심층면접은 10분으로 개편 실시하게 되었다.

　　한국교육과정평가원은 보통 임용 1차 필기시험 문제와 수업실연, 면접 등 2차 시험문제를 출제한다. 각 시도별 교육청은 평가원이 출제한 2차 시험문제를 자율적으로 선택해 반영한다. 평가원이 출제한 2차 시험 문제를 적용한 시도교육청의 경우, 임용시험에서 2차 시험 최저점이 80점에서 60점으로 낮아지게 된다. 2차 시험에서 가장 낮은 편차점이 80점이었던 규정이 60점으로 낮아지면서 점수의 편차가 커지고 그에 따라 2차 시험에서 합격 여부가 정해지므로 그 중요도 또한 높아지게 되었다.

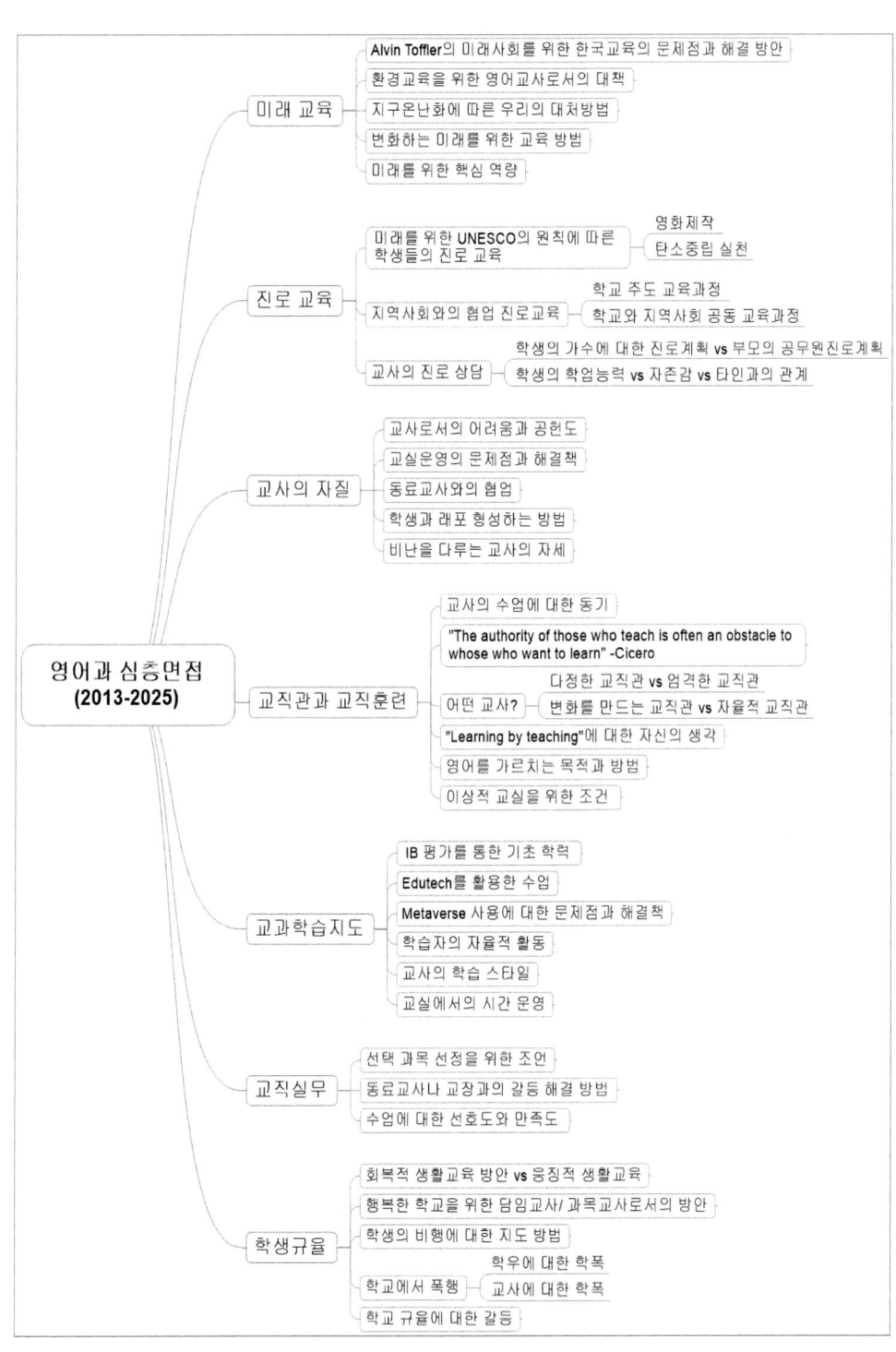

기출 문제와 예상답안

Q1. 학교 규칙의 이해 *2025년 구상형*

Minsu has been arriving late to school because he does not fully understand the school rules and expectations. As his teacher, how would you address this issue from both (1) an individual perspective—providing guidance and support directly to Minsu—and from (2) a whole-class perspective—ensuring that all students clearly understand and follow the school rules?

예상답안

(1) Individual perspective (Supporting Minsu directly)

- Clarify expectations: Meet with Minsu one-on-one to explain the school rules in simple language or with visual aids if needed, making sure he understands what "being on time" means and why it's important.
- Provide reminders and strategies: Suggest practical steps such as setting an alarm earlier, preparing his school bag the night before, or arranging transport.
- Check-in support: Follow up regularly to encourage him and see if he is making progress, showing that the teacher cares about his improvement.

(2) Whole-class perspective (Supporting all students)

- Review rules together: Conduct a short class session where school rules are explained clearly, using posters, role-play, or visual organizers so all students can internalize them.
- Connect rules to real-life benefits: Discuss why punctuality matters—such as respect for others, readiness to learn, and developing responsibility.
- Promote a positive culture: Instead of just enforcing rules, encourage students to support one another (e.g., peer reminders, praise for punctuality). This way, rules feel like shared responsibilities rather than punishments.

Q2. 수업 설계 *2025년 구상형*

As a beginning teacher, you are responsible for designing lessons that align with curriculum learning standards and support student achievement. How would you approach lesson planning from two perspectives: (1) your own personal preparation as an individual teacher, and (2) collaborative planning with peer teachers to ensure consistency, shared expertise, and effective learning outcomes?

예상답안

(1) Personal perspective

- As a beginning teacher, I would first study the national curriculum standards and my school's guidelines to identify the key learning outcomes for each unit. I would then break these outcomes into smaller, achievable lesson objectives. To plan effectively, I would choose teaching methods that reflect my students' needs and learning styles, such as scaffolding tasks, integrating multimedia, and designing formative assessments. I would also prepare reflection notes after each lesson to evaluate what worked well and what needs improvement for future planning.

(2) Collaborative peer-teacher perspective
- In addition to my own preparation, I would actively collaborate with colleagues to ensure my lessons are aligned with the broader goals of the grade level. This might involve participating in co-planning sessions, sharing teaching materials, and discussing classroom challenges with more experienced teachers. Working with peers allows me to gain insights into effective strategies, adapt lesson pacing to match the grade-level sequence, and maintain consistency across different classes. Collaboration also fosters innovation, since teachers can combine their expertise to design engaging activities and real-life tasks that better achieve the learning standards.

Q3 미래 교육　　　　　2025년 구상형

Based on (가), suggest the teacher's abilities to achieve future education and describe the teacher's roles for the students A and B.

> (가) UNESCO advocates for inclusive, equitable education by leveraging local resources and digital learning platforms. Key principles include:
> - Local capacity building – Strengthening community-based schools, teachers, and materials to address regional needs.
> - Digital inclusion – Expanding online learning while ensuring accessibility for marginalized students (e.g., low-tech solutions for areas with poor connectivity).
> - Equity over equality – Tailoring solutions to bridge gaps for disadvantaged groups (rural, disabled, or low-income learners).
> - Public-private partnerships – Collaborating with governments, NGOs, and tech companies to scale affordable digital tools.
>
> "Education is a human right—innovation and localization must combine to leave no one behind."

Student A: I'm interested in film-making and want to learn it, but our school doesn't offer a program for it. So I'm afraid there's no course or place available at school.

Student B: After learning about carbon neutrality, I want to work with other overseas students on a project.

예상답안

(1) Two teacher abilities for future education based on (가) can be explained with the two abilities:
① Capacity-building ability – Teachers should be able to connect local resources and opportunities to student needs, creating alternative pathways when the school curriculum lacks certain programs.

② Digital integration ability – Teachers should skillfully incorporate digital platforms and online collaboration tools to ensure students can access learning beyond physical limitations.

(2) Two teacher roles for student A and B can be suggested:
① For Student A (film-making interest): The teacher acts as a learning facilitator, guiding the student to local resources such as community workshops, online film-making courses, or partnerships with local organizations, thus overcoming the school's program limitations.
② For Student B (carbon neutrality project): The teacher acts as a global connector, helping the student collaborate with international peers through digital platforms, while providing guidance on how to manage cross-cultural teamwork and project-based learning.

Q 4 인터넷을 통한 괴롭힘 2025년 구상형

Based on the statistics in (가), suggest ONE campaign name and lesson method to solve the problems while developing digital literacy and real-life tasks in English class. Explain the FOUR reasons your method would be effective in your own language.

The statistics of cyber bullying reveal the types of problems students face as a result of cyber attacks.

(가) cyber bullying	
violent language	42%
personal data leak	25%
defamation	22%
deep fake	11%

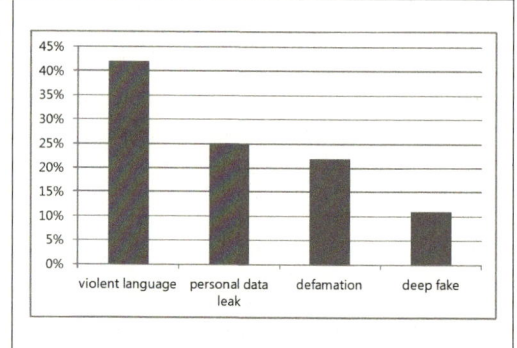

예상답안

1. 캠페인 이름과 수업방법

- Based on the data in (가), a highly effective lesson method would be:
- Create a "*Digital Citizenship Public Service Announcement* (PSA)" Campaign.
- This method directly addresses the most prevalent issues (violent language, data leaks, defamation) by having students proactively create solutions, thereby developing crucial digital literacy skills through a real-life task.

First, I can let students analyze & discuss to understand the problem. Students examine the provided statistics (가) to identify the most common forms of cyberbullying. In groups, they discuss and research real-world consequences of these actions, for example, *How does violent language escalate? What happens when personal data is leaked?* or, *How can defamation affect a person's life?* Second, students research how to prevent and respond to these specific cyber threats. They must evaluate online sources for credibility. Each group chooses one cyberbullying type. For example, Group 1, for violent language, collaboratively writes a script for a short (60-90 second) video PSA. The script must be in English and clearly explain the problem, its impact, and a positive call to action, for example, "Think before you post," "Report abusive behavior," or, "Protect your passwords". Third, using smartphones or school equipment, students film and edit their PSAs. Then students can improve English communication through authentic, problem-based tasks and develop critical digital literacy skills of recognizing risks, suggesting safe practices.

2. 효과적인 이유
- The method can be used as educational material for students in the school. The first reason this method is effective is it directly forces students to engage deeply with the specific problems of violent language, data leaks, and defamation, moving them from passive victims or bystanders to active, empowered digital citizens. Second, it also develops multiple digital literacies. Students practice information literacy (researching), media literacy (creating media), critical thinking (analyzing problems and crafting solutions), and collaboration (working in groups). Third, authentic real-life task. Creating a PSA for a real audience is a meaningful task with purpose, far more engaging than a hypothetical worksheet. It mirrors real-world marketing and advocacy campaigns. Fourth, integrating English learning. The entire project is conducted in English—from group discussion and research to scriptwriting, filming, and presenting—promoting fluency and practical language use. In this way, classroom learning can be connected to real-life digital experiences students actually face.

Q5 진로 교육 · 2025년 구상형

진로교육을 위하여 다음과 같은 두 가지 방법이 제시되고 있다. 이 중 한 가지를 선택하여 실제 교육 현장에서 어떻게 적용할 수 있을지 구체적으로 서술하시오. 선택한 방법을 중심으로, 학생들의 진로 역량 강화뿐만 아니라 학교와 지역사회의 상호 발전이라는 관점에서 어떻게 기여할 수 있을지도 함께 서술하시오.

A. 학교 주도 교육과정 개발 및 운영 - 지역사회 자원 활용
B. 학교와 지역사회가 공동으로 교육과정을 개발 및 운영 - 교육 발전과 지역 발전의 상생

예상답안

저는 B. 학교와 지역사회가 공동으로 교육과정을 개발 및 운영하는 방안을 선택하겠습니다. 학교와 지역사회가 협력하여 진로교육 과정을 설계한다면, 학생들은 보다 현장감 있는 경험을 통해 자신의 진로를 탐색할 수 있습니다. 예를 들어, 지역의 기업, 공공기관, 문화센터 등과 협력하여 직업 체험 프로그램이나 멘토링 활동을 운영한다면, 학생들은 교실 안에서 배우기 어려운 실제 직업 세계를 경험할 수 있습니다. 또한, 지역사회의 다양한 전문가들이 수업에 참여하면, 학생들은 다양한 진로 모델을 접할 수 있고, 지역사회는 차세대 인재를 육성한다는 점에서 상생효과를 얻을 수 있습니다. 나아가 이러한 공동 운영은 단순히 학생 개인의 진로 역량 강화에 그치지 않고, 학교 교육의 질적 발전과 지역사회의 지속 가능한 성장에도 기여합니다. 즉, 학교는 지역사회의 교육적 자원을 효과적으로 활용하고, 지역사회는 학교와 함께 지역 발전의 기반을 넓힐 수 있게 됩니다.

Q6 교사의 학교 업무   2025년 즉답형

교사 A는 현재 담당하고 있는 행정 및 일반적인 학교 업무에 대해 불만을 가지고 있으며, 대신 학생과 직접적으로 관련된 업무를 맡고 싶다는 의사를 보이고 있다. 이때, 학교 관리자는 교사 A에게 기존의 업무를 그대로 맡게 할지, 아니면 학생 관련 업무를 새롭게 배정할지를 결정해야 한다. 이에 대해 본인의 입장을 밝히고, 그 이유를 세 가지 근거를 들어 구체적으로 서술하시오. 자신의 의견을 논리적으로 전개할 수 있도록 하시오.

예상답안

선택 ① 기존 업무를 맡게 해야 한다 (교사 A는 기존 업무를 계속 맡는 것이 바람직하다.)

- 학교 운영의 안정성 유지 – 기존 업무는 학교 전체 운영에 필수적인 부분이므로, 갑작스럽게 교체하면 혼란이 발생할 수 있다. A 교사가 업무에 익숙한 만큼 안정적 운영을 위해 맡기는 것이 필요하다.
- 공정성 확보 – 교사의 업무는 개인적 선호보다는 학교의 필요와 균형에 따라 배분되어야 한다. 만약 A 교사의 희망만을 반영한다면, 다른 교사들에게 불공정하게 느껴질 수 있다.
- 점진적 조정 가능성 – 당장은 기존 업무를 유지하되, 학생 관련 업무에 점차 참여할 기회를 제공함으로써 A 교사의 동기 부여와 전문성 향상을 동시에 이끌 수 있다.

선택 ② 학생 관련 업무를 맡겨야 한다 (교사 A는 학생 관련 업무를 맡는 것이 바람직하다.)

- 교사의 동기 부여 강화 – 교사가 선호하는 업무를 맡을 경우, 더 큰 열정을 가지고 학생 지도에 임할 수 있으며 이는 학습 효과에도 긍정적인 영향을 준다.
- 학생 중심 교육 실현 – A 교사의 관심과 역량을 학생 업무에 활용하면 학생들의 요구에 맞는 세심한 지원이 가능해지고, 학생 중심 교육의 목표를 실천할 수 있다.
- 업무 효율성 증대 – 불만이 있는 업무를 억지로 수행할 경우 효율성이 떨어질 수 있으나, 관심 있는 영역을 맡게 되면 생산성과 만족도가 함께 높아질 수 있다.

Q7 가정통신문 이해   2025년 즉답형

제시문의 문제상황 원인을 밝히고 이를 해결하기 위한 지도 방안을 담임교사와 교과 교사 측면에서 말하시오.

> 제시문: 학생들이 가정통신문 내용을 이해하지 못한다. 이유가 특히 "미진" "상비약 지참" 등의 표현의 뜻을 알지 못하기 때문이었다.

예상답안

(1) 문제상황 원인 분석

- 어휘 이해 부족: 학생들이 가정통신문의 한자어 및 공식적 표현(예: "미진", "상비약 지참")을 이해하지 못함.
- 가정통신문의 형식적 언어: 교육기관에서 사용하는 관용적 표현이 일상언어와 괴리되어 있음.
- 학생-학교 간 소통 단절: 학생 스스로 내용을 해석할 기회가 부족하고, 교사의 사전 설명이 미비할 가능성.

(2) 지도 방안: 담임교사 측면

- 사전 설명 및 시각 자료 활용: 가정통신문 배포 전, 주요 용어(예: "미진" → "미처 준비하지 못한 것", "상비약 지참" → "필요한 약 가져오기")를 구체적인 예시와 함께 설명. 퀴즈 형식으로 중요 내용 확인 (예: "상비약 지참은 언제 필요한가요?").
- 학생 참여형 안내: 학생들이 통신문 내용을 동료와 함께 요약해 발표하도록 유도. 이해도 낮은 학생을 위해 개별 상담 실시.

(3) 지도 방안: 영어 교사 측면
- 어휘 지원 및 쉬운 언어 제공: 주요 용어 사전 교육: 가정통신문 배포 전, 어려운 단어(예: "미진" → "준비하지 못한 물건", "상비약 지참" → "응급약품 지참")를 플래시카드나 간단한 정의로 설명합니다. 학생 수준에 맞는 영어/한국어 요약본 제공: 시각 자료(예: "약품", "마감일" 아이콘)와 함께 쉬운 언어로 재구성된 통신문을 배포합니다.
- 능동적 이해 활동: 질의응답 시간: 통신문 읽은 후, 학생들이 자신의 언어로 설명하도록 유도합니다(예: "'상비약 지참'이 너에게 무슨 의미야?"). 역할극 활동: 실제 상황(예: 여행 준비 물품 챙기기)을 연기하며 용어를 자연스럽게 습득합니다.
- 담임교사와의 협력: 다과목 연계 학습: 가정통신문을 영어 수업 자료로 활용해 언어 학습과 실생활 이해를 결합합니다. 피드백 공유: 학생들이 자주 오해하는 내용을 담임교사와 공유해 향후 통신문 개선에 반영합니다.
- 디지털 및 학부모 협력: 학교 플랫폼에 오디오 설명이 포함된 간단한 통신문을 업로드해 비원어민 학생을 지원합니다. 학부모용 영어 요약본으로 집에서 논의할 수 있도록 핵심 내용을 영어로 정리해 보냅니다.

Q8 교육적 가치   2024년 구상형

Choose one educational value that you think it important and explain it with reasons. Name of your character education brand and explain TWO ways to implement it as a homeroom teacher in middle school.

예상답안

Educational value that I think is Respect. For this, I can make brand name "Respectful Minds." I think respect is a fundamental value in character education that promotes positive relationships, social harmony, and personal growth. It encourages students to treat others with kindness, consideration, and empathy, fostering an environment where everyone feels valued and understood. Teaching respect in our school is essential because students are at a critical stage in developing their social identities and learning how to navigate complex interpersonal relationships. Respect not only builds a positive classroom culture but also helps students develop self-respect, responsibility, and tolerance for diversity.

I have two ways to implement "Respectful Minds" as a homeroom teacher.

1. Classroom respect agreement

    As a homeroom teacher, I would start the year by having students co-create a "Classroom Respect Agreement." This agreement would be a set of guidelines that every student has to follow in the class. The process of creating the agreement will allow students to reflect on what respect means to them and gives them ownership over the classroom culture. For this, I can facilitate a discussion on respect, asking questions like "What does respect look like in our classroom?" and "How can we show respect in our daily interactions?" I collect ideas from the students and draft a collective agreement that everyone signs, symbolizing their commitment to upholding these values. Lastly, I display the agreement on board in the classroom as a daily reminder and refer to it when they have moments of conflict or when I need to reinforce positive behaviors.

2. Respect journals and weekly reflections

    Another way to implement "Respectful Minds" is through weekly reflection journals. Each student would keep a personal journal where they reflect on their experiences of showing and receiving respect throughout the week. This reflection process encourages students to practice mindfulness and reinforces respectful behavior. For example, every Friday, I can dedicate 10 minutes to journal writing. Students can reflect themselves with questions like, "How did I show respect to a classmate this week?" or "When did I feel respected, and how did that make me feel?" Using this time, students can share their experiences in small groups to promote peer discussion about respect. This way I can help them recognize their own growth and areas for improvement.

Through the "Classroom respect agreement" and "Respect journals," my students will develop a deeper understanding of respect as both a personal value and a social practice. These activities provide opportunities for reflection, dialogue, and accountability, and help to create a respectful and inclusive classroom culture.

Q 9 환경교육을 위한 영어교사로서의 대책 *2024년 구상형*

> Our environment is at a critical moment. Now is a pivotal time for governments, businesses, and individuals to make significant changes, like reducing carbon emissions, adopting sustainable practices, conserving natural habitats, and promoting education on environmental issues. Without immediate and coordinated action, the consequences will be increasingly severe for future generations. As a global citizen, we should all collaborate to save our earth and build solidarity. For ecological and environmental education, suggest TWO practical ways you can do with your students as a subject teacher.

예상답안

As an English teacher, there are several practical ways to integrate ecological and environmental education into language learning. Here are two effective methods that not only teach English but also raise awareness about environmental issues, fostering global citizenship and a sense of responsibility toward the planet.

1. Eco-Themed Project-Based Learning (PBL)

    First of all, I can incorporate project-based learning where students collaborate on research and presentation projects related to environmental issues. Topics such as pollution, climate change, and endangered species can be explored. To do this, three steps can be implemented. In Step 1, I divide students into small groups and assign them to choose eco-related topics such as "How plastic affects marine life" or "The impact of deforestation." In Step 2, I have students research their topic, using articles, videos, or documentaries in English. I can guide them in writing reports or essays on their findings. In Step 3, students can present their findings to the class, creating visual aids like posters or digital presentations. So, I think this method not only helps students practice English but also deepens their understanding of pressing environmental issues. It encourages teamwork and critical thinking while fostering a sense of responsibility and global citizenship.

2. English Writing Campaign: Letters for Change

    Secondly, I can organize a letter-writing campaign. Students can practice formal letter writing by thinking about real-world environmental problems. They can write to local government officials, businesses, or international organizations advocating for eco-friendly policies, or they can create persuasive essays to raise awareness within the school community.

To do this, I can suggest THREE steps. In Step 1, students learn the format and style of formal letter writing in English, focusing on persuasive techniques and respectful tone. In Step 2, I assign students to write letters or essays on environmental topics, such as urging Starbucks to reduce plastic use, supporting renewable energy, or promoting recycling programs for Burgerking. In Step 3, I encourage students to send their letters to actual recipients or publish their essays in the school newsletter to amplify their voices. I believe that this activity empowers students to actively participate in environmental advocacy while improving their English writing skills. It connects language learning with meaningful real-world action, demonstrating how their voices can contribute to positive change globally.

By engaging with ecological topics and participating in environmental advocacy, students become more aware of their role as global citizens, fostering a collective effort to protect the earth and build solidarity in addressing environmental challenges.

Q 10 두 교사의 교육관 — 2024년 구상형

다음과 같이 서로 다른 관점을 가지고 있는 두 교사가 있다. 자신의 교육관에 더 적합한 관점을 선택하고 이를 실천할 방안 2가지를 서술하시오.

> A관점 : 교사는 학생들에게 변화하는 사회에 대해 가르쳐야한다.
> B관점 : 교사는 학생들에게 그동안 축적되어온 중요한 진리를 가르쳐야한다.

예상답안

저는 A 관점, 즉 "교사는 학생들에게 변화하는 사회에 대해 가르쳐야 한다"는 관점이 제 교육관에 더 적합하다고 생각합니다. 빠르게 변화하는 사회 속에서 학생들이 필요한 역량을 기르기 위해서는, 교사가 최신 사회적, 기술적, 경제적 변화에 대한 이해를 제공하고 학생들이 미래 사회에 적응할 수 있도록 준비시켜야 한다고 봅니다. 이 관점을 실천할 수 있는 방안 두 가지를 제시하겠습니다.

1. 미래 역량 강화형 수업 운영

    학생들이 변화하는 사회에서 성공적으로 살아가기 위해 필요한 미래 역량, 즉 문제 해결 능력, 창의적 사고, 협업, 디지털 리터러시 등을 강화하는 수업을 운영해야 합니다. 이를 위해 전통적인 주입식 수업을 넘어, 실생활 문제를 해결하는 프로젝트 기반 학습(Project-Based Learning)을 도입하여 학생들이 실제 사회에서 직면할 수 있는 문제를 창의적으로 해결할 수 있는 기회를 제공합니다. 그를 위해서 실제 사회 이슈를 기반으로 수업 주제를 선정하여, 예를 들어 환경 문제, 인공지능(AI), 디지털 기술 발전 등을 주제로 한 프로젝트를 통해 학생들이 실질적인 사회 변화를 탐구할 수 있도록 합니다. 팀별로 다양한 해결책을 모색하고 발표하도록 하여 협업 능력을 기르고, 디지털 자료를 활용한 프레젠테이션과 논문 작성 등을 통해 실전에서 필요한 기술을 습득하도록 돕습니다.

2. 시사 교육 및 비판적 사고 훈련

    학생들이 급변하는 사회에서 자신의 입장을 비판적으로 사고하고, 다양한 관점을 이해하며 스스로 결정을 내릴 수 있도록 시사 교육을 강화해야 합니다. 이를 통해 학생들이 단순히 지식을 받아들이는 것을 넘어, 변화하는 사회 속 문제를 분석하고 올바른 판단을 내릴 수 있는 능력을 기를 수 있습니다. 실천 방안으로는 매주 시사 토론 시간을 마련하여, 최근의 사회, 경제, 정치 이슈에 대해 학생들이 토론할 수 있는 기회를 제공합니다. 이를 통해 학생들이 다양한 관점을 배우고, 자신의 의견을 논리적으로 정리할 수 있도록 돕습니다. 미디어 리터러시

교육을 통해 학생들이 가짜 뉴스나 편향된 정보를 비판적으로 분석할 수 있도록 훈련합니다. 이를 통해 변화하는 정보 환경 속에서 스스로 판단하는 능력을 기를 수 있습니다.

결론적으로 변화하는 사회에 대한 교육은 학생들이 미래 사회에서 요구하는 역량을 키우고, 급변하는 환경에 적응하는 데 필수적입니다. 미래 역량 강화형 수업과 시사 교육을 통해 학생들이 변화를 수용하고 비판적 사고를 발전시킬 수 있는 기회를 제공함으로써, 변화하는 사회 속에서 자신감을 가지고 살아갈 수 있도록 지원하겠습니다.

합격을 위한 TIP

미래 역량 강화형 수업은 학생들이 변화하는 사회에서 필요한 다양한 역량을 키울 수 있도록 하는 교육 방식을 포함한다. 이러한 수업 방식은 문제 해결 능력, 창의성, 비판적 사고, 협업 능력, 그리고 디지털 리터러시 등 미래 사회에서 중요한 역량을 강화하는 데 중점을 둔다. 구체적인 미래 역량 강화형 수업의 예로는 다음과 같은 것들이 있다:

1. **프로젝트 기반 학습 (Project-Based Learning, PBL)**
   - 특징: 학생들이 실생활과 관련된 문제를 해결하기 위해 스스로 프로젝트를 계획하고 수행하면서 학습 목표를 달성한다.
   - 역량 강화: 문제 해결 능력, 자기주도 학습, 창의적 사고 및 협업 능력
   - 예시: 환경 보호 프로젝트에서 학생들이 지역 환경 문제를 조사하고, 해결책을 제시하며, 실제로 실행 가능한 방안을 도출해 발표한다.

2. **협력적 학습 (Collaborative Learning)**
   - 특징: 학생들이 함께 학습하며 서로의 아이디어를 공유하고 피드백을 주고받는 방식으로 진행된다.
   - 역량 강화: 의사소통 능력, 협업 능력, 사회적 책임감
   - 예시: 모둠 활동에서 여러 문화나 시사 문제에 대해 토론하고 각자의 입장을 논리적으로 설명하면서, 타인의 의견을 존중하는 연습을 한다.

3. **문제 해결 학습 (Problem-Based Learning, PBL)**
   - 특징: 실제 생활에서 직면할 수 있는 문제 상황을 설정하고, 이를 해결하기 위한 다양한 방안을 모색한다.
   - 역량 강화: 비판적 사고, 창의적 문제 해결 능력, 실천적 응용력
   - 예시: 에너지 절약 문제를 주제로 한 수업에서 학생들이 에너지 절약 방안을 모색하고, 가정과 학교에서 실천할 수 있는 구체적인 방안을 만들어 발표한다.

4. **디지털 리터러시 및 코딩 교육**
   - 특징: 학생들이 디지털 도구와 프로그램을 활용하여 정보를 분석하고 창의적으로 표현하는 법을 배운다.
   - 역량 강화: 디지털 리터러시, 논리적 사고, 창의적 문제 해결 능력
   - 예시: 기본적인 코딩과 데이터 분석을 배우며, 소셜 미디어 사용법 및 인터넷상의 정보 분석 능력을 키웁니다.

5. **디자인 씽킹 (Design Thinking)**
   - 특징: 학생들이 창의적 사고를 통해 문제를 이해하고, 아이디어를 탐색하고, 시제품을 만들어가며 해결책을 모색하는 과정이다.
   - 역량 강화: 창의성, 문제 해결 능력, 사용자 중심의 사고
   - 예시: "미래의 교실"이라는 주제로 학생들이 직접 교실을 설계하고, 필요한 기술이나 학습 도구를 구상해 발표한다.

이와 같은 미래 역량 강화형 수업은 학생들이 다가올 미래 사회에서 더 유연하고 적극적으로 대응할 수 있는 능력을 키우는 데 필수적이며, 단순한 지식 습득을 넘어선 응용력과 융합적 사고를 장려한다.

Q 11. 학생지도의 문제점과 해결 방안

2024년 즉답형

각 교사의 입장에서 학생지도의 문제점을 인식하고 해결하는 방안을 제시하시오.

A교사	면학분위기 저해하는 학생 있어 학생지도에 어려움을 겪고 있다.
B교사	학교폭력 업무가 처음이어서, 업무에 부담을 느낀다.

예상답안

각 교사가 겪고 있는 상황에 맞춰 해결 방안을 제시하겠습니다.

A 교사: 면학 분위기를 저해하는 학생 지도 방안

1) 긍정적 행동 강화 전략 도입
- 문제 해결 방안으로 학생의 부정적 행동보다는 긍정적 행동을 강화하는 전략을 사용합니다. 예를 들어, 학생이 수업에 집중하는 모습을 보일 때마다 작은 칭찬이나 격려를 주어 긍정적인 행동을 강화합니다. 이는 학생의 자기 효능감을 높이고, 면학 분위기를 자연스럽게 형성하는 데 도움이 됩니다.
- 실행 방법으로는 수업 참여도에 따라 작은 보상 제도를 운영하거나, 칭찬 노트를 사용하는 등 학생에게 긍정적인 피드백을 지속적으로 제공하는 방식입니다.

2) 교사-학생 간의 상담 및 관계 개선
- 면학 분위기를 저해하는 학생과의 개별 상담을 통해 교사-학생 간의 관계를 개선하고, 학생의 행동 배경을 이해하는 것이 필요합니다. 학생의 어려움이나 불만을 들음으로써 그들의 행동 원인을 파악하고, 함께 해결책을 찾는 과정을 거칠 수 있습니다.
- 수업 후 시간을 내어 학생과 1:1 면담을 진행하고, 학업에 대한 어려움이나 개인적인 문제를 파악하여, 지원할 수 있는 방법을 모색합니다. 또한, 학생이 수업에 더 적극적으로 참여할 수 있도록 동기 부여하는 구체적인 목표를 함께 설정합니다.

B 교사: 학교폭력 업무 부담 해결 방안

1) 학교 내 지원 체계 활용 및 협업
- 학교폭력 업무는 처음이므로, 혼자 모든 업무를 처리하려고 하기보다는 학교 내 지원 체계와 협력하는 것이 중요합니다. 학교폭력 전담 부서나 선배 교사, 상담교사 등과의 협력을 통해 업무에 대한 부담을 나누고, 필요한 정보를 얻습니다. 특히, 학교폭력 대응에 경험이 많은 교사와의 협업을 통해 업무를 단계적으로 이해할 수 있습니다.
- 실행 방법으로 주기적인 팀 회의에 참석해 정보를 교류하고, 각 상황에 맞는 적절한 조치를 안내받습니다. 필요한 경우 외부 전문가의 도움을 요청하거나, 관련 연수를 추가로 받는 것도 업무 이해를 높이는 방법입니다.

2) 학교폭력 관련 연수 및 자료 활용
- 학교폭력 업무가 처음인 만큼, 관련 연수를 통해 업무 지식을 체계적으로 습득하고, 최신 사례와 법적 절차에 대한 이해도를 높이는 것이 중요하며, 이를 통해 업무에 대한 자신감을 기를 수 있습니다.
- 실질적으로 교육청이나 학교에서 제공하는 학교폭력 관련 연수에 적극적으로 참여하고, 관련 법률이나 절차에 대한 매뉴얼을 정리하여 참조할 수 있도록 합니다. 또한, 업무 처리 중 궁금한 점이 생기면 즉시 상급자나 학교폭력 전담 기관에 문의하여 상황에 맞게 대응합니다.

Q 12 행복한 학생들을 위한 교육방안　　　　　2024년 즉답형

중·고등학교 학생들을 대상으로 행복감을 조사해보니, 다음과 같은 결과가 나왔다.

> 맛있는 급식〉 교우관계〉 교과수업〉 교사와의 관계〉 진로, 진학

학생들은 학교에서 자신의 삶의 절반을 보내는 만큼 학교라는 공간은 행복된 배움터여야 한다. 위의 결과에 의하면 학생의 행복감이 교사와의 관계와 진로진학에서 낮게 나타나고 있음을 알수 있다. 학생들의 행복감 증대를 위해 교과교사, 담임교사의 측면에서 교육 방안을 각각 2가지씩 제시하시오.

예상답안

학생들의 행복감을 증대시키기 위해 교과교사와 담임교사 측면에서 각각 교육 방안을 제시하겠습니다.

1. 교과교사의 교육 방안
- 학생 중심의 수업 운영: 교과 수업이 학생들의 행복감에서 상대적으로 낮은 순위로 나타난 만큼, 학생 중심의 수업 운영이 필요합니다. 학생들의 흥미를 고려한 수업 자료와 실생활과 연계된 활동을 통해 수업을 더욱 재미있고 의미 있게 만들 수 있습니다. 예를 들어, 토론, 프로젝트 수업, 실험 등 다양한 방식으로 학생들이 적극적으로 참여할 수 있는 기회를 제공합니다.
- 개별 피드백 제공: 학생들에게 개별적이고 구체적인 피드백을 제공함으로써 학생들이 자신이 성장하고 있음을 느낄 수 있게 해야 합니다. 성적 향상뿐만 아니라 노력과 발전에 대한 긍정적인 피드백을 제공함으로써 학생들이 자신감을 얻고 교과 수업에서 더 많은 동기 부여를 느낄 수 있습니다.

2. 담임교사의 교육 방안
- 정서적 지지 제공: 담임교사는 학생들과의 관계에서 중요한 역할을 합니다. 학생들이 심리적 안정감을 느낄 수 있도록 정서적인 지지를 제공하는 것이 중요합니다. 이를 위해 정기적인 상담 시간이나 개인 면담을 통해 학생들의 고민을 듣고 도움을 제공하는 체계적인 지원이 필요합니다.
- 진로, 진학 상담 강화: 진로 및 진학에 대한 불안감이 학생들의 행복감에 부정적인 영향을 미칠 수 있습니다. 담임교사는 진로, 진학과 관련된 현실적이고 구체적인 정보를 제공하고, 학생들의 관심사와 적성에 맞는 진로 방향을 찾을 수 있도록 돕는 상담 시간을 정기적으로 운영할 필요가 있습니다. 예를 들어, 전문가 초청 강연이나 직업 체험 프로그램 등을 통해 학생들이 다양한 진로 선택의 기회를 가질 수 있도록 지원합니다.

　교과교사와 담임교사는 각각의 역할에서 학생들의 학습과 정서적 지원을 강화할 수 있으며, 이를 통해 학생들의 학교 생활에서 느끼는 행복감을 크게 높일 수 있습니다. 교과 수업의 흥미 유발과 개별 피드백, 정서적 지지와 진로 상담은 학생들의 전반적인 만족도와 행복감에 긍정적인 영향을 줄 것입니다.

Q 13 회복적 생활교육 방안　　　　　2023년 구상형

Explain your actions under this situation as below.

> (가) At the group chatting room, Student A uploaded some negative comments about Student B. Student C told Student B about that, and angry Student B went to Student A to address the issue and express his grievances. But A strongly denied that he didn't do it.
>
> (나) Student A was worried about his record for school violence.

(1) Three measures as a homeroom teacher
(2) Four Conditions for the Implementation of "School-Based Conflict Resolution" (학교 자체 해결체가 실시되기 위한 조건 4가지)
(3) One method for "Rehabilitative Life Education Strategies" (회복적 생활교육방안)

예상답안

(1) Three measures to solve the problems as a homeroom teacher:

As a homeroom teacher, it is essential to address and resolve the issues arising from this situation:

① Mediation: First and foremost, I would initiate a mediation session between Student A and Student B, facilitating a constructive dialogue where they can express their concerns and feelings. This would allow for a better understanding of the situation and potentially lead to a resolution.

② Involvement of school counselor: I would engage the school counselor to provide support and guidance to both students. The counselor can help them navigate their emotions, provide conflict resolution strategies, and address any underlying issues, such as Student A's worries about his school violence record.

③ Restorative practices: Implementing restorative practices within the classroom and school community would be crucial. This involves fostering a sense of responsibility and accountability among students and creating opportunities for them to make amends and rebuild trust. Restorative circles and conferences can be used to facilitate this process.

(2) Four conditions for the implementation of "School-based conflict resolution":

To effectively implement "School-based conflict resolution," the following four conditions must be met:

① Clear procedures: There should be well-defined and transparent procedures in place for addressing conflicts within the school. These procedures should outline the steps to be taken when conflicts arise, including mediation, counseling, and disciplinary actions if necessary.

② Trained staff: School staff, including teachers and counselors, should receive training in conflict resolution and restorative practices. They should be equipped with the skills and knowledge needed to facilitate productive dialogues and support students in resolving conflicts.

③ Supportive environment: The school should foster a supportive and inclusive environment where students feel safe and comfortable discussing their grievances. Open communication channels and a non-judgmental atmosphere are essential.

④ Follow-up and evaluation: After conflicts are addressed, it is crucial to follow up and evaluate the effectiveness of the resolution process. This feedback loop ensures continuous improvement in conflict resolution practices within the school.

(3) One method for "Rehabilitative life education strategies":

One effective method for "Rehabilitative life education strategies" is implementing mentorship programs. These programs pair students with positive role models or older peers who can provide guidance and support. Mentors can help students set goals, develop life skills, and make better choices. They also serve as a source of encouragement and accountability, promoting positive behavior and personal growth among students. Mentorship programs contribute to creating a rehabilitative and nurturing educational environment.

합격을 위한 TIP

	응보적 훈육	회복적 훈육
잘못이란	규칙 위반	인간과 관계에 대한 침해
잘못의 결과	처벌	피해발행 → 책임질 의무 → 책임 이행 → 피해 회복
책임자	개인	개인과 공동체
주요질문	어떤 규칙을 위반했는가? 누가 범인인가? 어떤 처벌이 합당한가?	누가 피해자인가? 어떤 피해가 발생했는가? 피해자의 요구는 무엇인가? 피해를 회복하기 위해 무엇을 할 필요가 있는가?

Q 14 IB 평가를 통한 기초 학력 *2023년 구상형*

(가) Through the student's learning log, it was found out that the lesson was difficult to understand and lack of interests because the lesson mainly consisted of the teacher's explanation.
(나) Through the teacher's reflection log, it was difficult to design multiple choice final exam.
(다) IB Assessment

- To solve the problems in (가), (나), IB approaches to teaching can be implemented.
(1) Explain the reasons IB assessment is needed.
(2) Two qualities of IB assessment

예상답안

(1) The need for IB assessment arises due to the identified issues in the student's learning log and the teacher's reflection log. The lesson was challenging to comprehend, and students lacked interest primarily because it relied heavily on teacher-centered explanations. IB assessment is necessary to address these problems because it promotes a student-centered approach to learning, emphasizing inquiry-based methods that engage students actively in their education. It encourages critical thinking, problem-solving, and independent learning, fostering a more holistic and meaningful learning experience.

(2) Two qualities of IB assessment are:
① Authenticity: IB assessments are designed to reflect real-world challenges and scenarios. They assess students' ability to apply knowledge and skills in practical situations rather than mere memorization. This authenticity ensures that what students learn is relevant and applicable beyond the classroom.
② Reflective of Learner Diversity: IB assessments are sensitive to the diverse needs and abilities of learners. They recognize that students have different strengths and learning styles, and assessments are designed to accommodate these differences. This inclusivity allows for a more equitable evaluation of students' abilities and potential.

Q 15 메타버스 사용에 대한 문제점과 해결책 2023년 구상형

I used 'metaverse' in my lesson but students don't like it with some complains. Discuss the solution for each problem of the students.

> Student A: I'm not very familiar with metaverse. When I logged in, it kept unconnecting for an unknown reason, which was quite irritating.
> Student B: Screen layout is too complicating to understand what it is.
> Student C: The lesson seems not different from our old lesson except for the quizznet, even though it is called metaverse-based lesson.

예상답안

(1) Student A (Solution: Provide a clear introduction and troubleshooting)
- Start the lesson with a clear and concise introduction to the metaverse concept. Explain its relevance to the lesson and how students can benefit from it.
- Offer detailed instructions on how to log in, including troubleshooting tips for common issues like disconnection. Create a step-by-step guide or video tutorial that students can refer to if they encounter problems.
- Assign a technical support or IT resource that students can reach out to for immediate assistance if they face connectivity issues during the lesson.

(2) Student B (Solution: Simplify the User Interface)
- Simplify the layout of the metaverse platform, reducing unnecessary clutter and visual distractions. Focus on the essential elements that students need for the lesson.
- Provide an orientation or walkthrough at the beginning of the lesson to explain the layout and the functions of different elements on the screen.
- Ensure that icons, buttons, and menus are intuitively designed, and consider using tooltips or pop-up explanations for any unfamiliar features.

(3) Student C (Solution: Enhance Engagement and Interactivity)
- Incorporate more interactive and immersive elements into the metaverse-based lesson. For example, you can use 3D simulations, virtual field trips, or collaborative projects that make use of the metaverse environment.
- Highlight how the metaverse enhances specific aspects of the lesson, such as fostering collaboration, offering real-time feedback, or providing a unique learning experience.
- Collect feedback from students to identify areas where the metaverse can be better integrated to create a distinctive and engaging learning experience. By addressing these concerns and making adjustments to your metaverse-based lesson, you can create a more positive and engaging learning environment for your students while using this innovative technology.

합격을 위한 TIP

메타버스(Metaverse)란?

메타버스를 활용한 교육의 지향점은 다음과 같다. 첫째, 학습자의 주도성을 회복하고 성장시켜나갈 수 있는 공간으로서의 메타버스 활용 교육이 필요하다. 스스로 만든 세상에서 아이들은 주체로서 소통하고 교류하고 배우고 성장한다. 메타버스 세계에서 아이들은 세상의 문제에 대해 토론하고, 문제해결을 위한 전략들을 함께 모색하고, 문제해결을 위해 능동적 참여자로 활동한다. 이는 OECD의 교육 2030과 2022개정 교육과정에서 중요하게 다루어지고 있는 '학습자 주체성'의 일면이며, 우리 교육에서 오랫동안 구현하고자 했던 학습자 중심 교육, 배움 중심 교육의 모습이기도 하다.

둘째, 메타버스 활용이 기존 매체 활용 수업에 대한 대체재라기보다 기존 매체가 가지고 있는 문제나 제약점을 보완함으로써 교육의 질을 높이고자 수업에 메타버스 활용을 시작했음을 알 수 있는 대목이다. 화상강의는 대규모 전달식 수업에 강점이 있고, 메타버스는 모둠 소통이나 협력 기반의 문제해결형 수업에 더 적절하다. 또한, 교실 수업이나 화상강의에서 학습에 어려움을 가지는 활동형 학습자, 게임형 학습모델을 선호하는 학습자, 실감형 콘텐츠와 기기들이 구비된 교육환경에 있는 학습자들에게는 메타버스 적용이 좋은 교육적 대안 모델이 될 수 있을 것이다.

셋째, 누구도 소외 없는 포용적 공간으로서의 메타버스 활용을 지향해야 한다. 앞선 조사에서 학습자들은 메타버스를 학습의 흥미와 주도성을 높여주는 교수 학습 공간으로서의 가치를 높게 평가한 바가 있다. 메타버스를 활용한 수업의 아바타 꾸미기, 가상공간 창작 활동, 게임 기반의 학습 방법 등은 기존의 학습에 흥미가 없거나 소외된 학습자들을 학습의 장으로 초대하는 장치들이 될 수 있다. 이 과정에서 다른 문화에 대한 호기심을 높이고 상호 존중의 태도를 배울 수 있다. 또한 메타버스 가상세계의 시민으로 살아가는 경험과 메타버스가 제공하는 높은 몰입감은 포용적이고 지속가능한 미래를 함께 만들어나가는 데 필요한 지식과 기술, 태도와 가치를 개발시킬 수 있는 기회를 제공해줄 수 있을 것이다.

Q 16. 에듀테크를 활용한 수업 *2023년 구상형*

(1) Based on the purpose of (가), explain the lesson with THREE smart device-based classroom activities and explain their pedagogical effects to the parents.

(2) Based on the situation in (나), explain what Teacher Kim should consider to use Edutech in class in TWO ways.

> (가) Parents find out that their children use the 'smart device' at home and are curious what their children learn at school.
>
> (나) Teacher Kim designs the lesson using the 'smart device.' However, he spends too much time to explain how to use Edutech tools and runs out of time when he has teach the main content. He doesn't even have time to check and monitor students' progress.

예상답안

(1) Three Smart device-based classroom activities and their pedagogical effects for parents:

① Activity 1: Interactive Digital Quizzes: Interactive quizzes engage students actively with the lesson content. These quizzes can be designed to assess their understanding of key concepts, reinforce learning, and provide immediate feedback. Parents can benefit by seeing their child's progress and understanding how well they grasp the material.

② Activity 2: Virtual Field Trips: Virtual field trips allow students to explore and learn about various subjects in an immersive way. Parents can appreciate how their children use smart devices to visit historical landmarks, ecosystems, or cultural sites, enhancing their understanding of the world beyond the classroom.

③ Activity 3: Online Collaborative Projects: Collaborative projects promote teamwork, problem-solving, and communication skills. Parents can witness their child's ability to collaborate with peers, share ideas, and create digital presentations or reports, showcasing their creativity and 21st-century skills.

(2) Considerations for Teacher Kim when using Edutech in Class:

① Prioritize essential tools: Teacher Kim should prioritize and introduce essential Edutech tools that align with the main learning objectives. This ensures that students spend more time on meaningful content rather than on excessive tool explanations.

② Pre-training and simplified instructions: Before the lesson, Teacher Kim can provide pre-training materials or videos that demonstrate how to use the selected Edutech tools. During the lesson, he should offer simplified, step-by-step instructions, focusing on the key functionalities that students need for the task at hand. This approach saves time and keeps students focused on learning rather than tool navigation. By considering these strategies, Teacher Kim can effectively integrate Edutech into the classroom while maximizing instructional time and monitoring student progress.

합격을 위한 TIP

인공지능·에듀테크 활용 영어수업 지원 (2023. 6. 19)

울산광역시교육청(교육감 천창수)은 중등 영어수업에 인공지능과 교육 정보기술 활용을 지원한다. 울산시교육청은 17일 시교육청 컴퓨터교육실에서 울산 지역 중등 영어교사 37명을 대상으로 '영차!영차!(영어프로젝트, ChatGPT) 활용'을 주제로 인공지능(AI) · 교육 정보 기술(에듀테크) 활용 영어교사 직무연수를 한다. 이번 연수는 인공지능을 활용한 영어 수업과 미래 교육에 대한 이해도를 높여 영어교사의 역량을 강화하고자 기획됐다. 영어프로젝트 수업 운영과 챗GPT를 활용한 영어 수업을 나눠 진행된다. 영어프로젝트 수업은 '말하기, 쓰기 활동을 위한 온라인 협업 도구, 쌍방향 프리젠테이션 협업 도구, 프로젝트 활동을 위한 협업 도구'에 대해 강의한다. 챗GPT와 함께하는 영어수업은 '챗GPT는 무엇인가, 챗GPT로 학교 업무하기, 챗GPT로 영어 수업하기'에 대해 강의한다. 연수에 참가한 한 교사는 "생성형 인공지능을 활용한 영어수업으로 학습자가 스스로 질문을 하고 답을 찾는 것이 중요하다는 것을 공감하게 돼 의미있는 시간이었다"고 말했다. 울산시교육청 관계자는 "챗GPT 활용으로 개인별 맞춤 영어교육의 확대, 대화형 영어 학습 확대, 영어 글쓰기 교육 혁신이 앞당겨질 것이다"며 "앞으로도 영어교사들의 전문성 신장 연수를 확대해 영어수업에 활기를 불러일으킬 수 있는 다양한 프로그램을 지원하겠다"고 말했다.

Q 17   탄소저감 정책 수업에 대한 갈등 해결책   2023년 즉답형

To teach the theme, "Carbon Reduction Policy," Teacher A wants to implement an event program, while Teacher B wants to deal with it as a part of a regular class. Because of the issue, the two teachers have a conflict.

(1) If you are Teacher A, how would you persuade Teacher B to follow your ideas?

(2) Any notable points when persuading Teacher B?

(3) If you are to mediate between Teacher A and Teacher B, how would you mediate them to solve the problem?

예상답안

(1) To persuade Teacher B to implement the event program for teaching the theme of "Carbon Reduction Policy," I would approach the discussion with a collaborative and persuasive strategy:

- Highlight the Benefits: Emphasize the potential benefits of the event program. Explain how it can make the learning experience more engaging and memorable for students. Mention that events can create a real-world connection to the topic, which can lead to better comprehension and retention.

- Align with Learning Objectives: Show how the event program aligns with the learning objectives and curriculum standards. Illustrate that it can enhance the students' understanding of the subject matter while meeting educational goals.

- Share Success Stories: Provide examples or case studies of schools or teachers who have successfully used event programs to teach similar topics. Highlight any positive outcomes, such as improved student engagement and knowledge retention.

- Offer to Collaborate: Express willingness to collaborate with Teacher B in planning and executing the event program. Assure Teacher B that their input and expertise in the classroom will be valued and incorporated into the event.

(2) When persuading Teacher B, it's important to:

- Listen Actively: Begin by listening to Teacher B's concerns and perspective. Understand their reasons for preferring the regular class approach. This will help tailor your persuasion strategy to address their specific concerns.

- Be Flexible: Be open to compromise and adjustments in your event program proposal. Show that you are willing to accommodate Teacher B's preferences and ideas to find a middle ground.

- Respect Their Expertise: Acknowledge Teacher B's expertise in classroom management and pedagogy. Show that your goal is to complement their teaching methods, not replace them.

- Highlight Student Engagement: Emphasize how the event program can boost student engagement, which can lead to better learning outcomes. Teacher B may be more receptive if they see the potential benefits for students.

(3) Mediating between Teacher A and Teacher B involves facilitating a constructive dialogue and finding a mutually acceptable solution. Here's how I would mediate:

- Organize a Meeting: Arrange a meeting between the two teachers in a neutral and collaborative setting. Create an agenda that allows both teachers to express their perspectives.

- **Active Listening**: Ensure that both teachers have the opportunity to actively listen to each other's viewpoints without interruption. Encourage them to share their concerns, preferences, and goals.
- **Identify Common Ground**: Help both teachers identify areas of agreement or common ground. This could include shared educational objectives or a desire to provide the best learning experience for students.
- **Generate Compromise Solutions**: Facilitate a brainstorming session to generate compromise solutions that incorporate elements of both Teacher A's event program and Teacher B's regular class approach. Encourage creative ideas that blend the best of both worlds.
- **Commit to Collaboration**: Encourage both teachers to commit to collaboration and teamwork. Emphasize the benefits of working together to create a more enriched learning experience.
- **Establish Evaluation Criteria**: Develop criteria for evaluating the success of the chosen approach. This can include measures of student engagement, comprehension, and achievement of learning objectives.
- **Monitor Progress**: After implementing the agreed-upon approach, monitor progress and gather feedback from students. Use this feedback to make further adjustments and improvements.

The goal of mediation is to find a solution that respects both teachers' perspectives while prioritizing the best interests of the students. It's essential to create an atmosphere of collaboration and compromise to achieve this outcome.

Q 18 교실운영의 문제점과 해결책 *2023년 즉답형*

Teacher A is experiencing TWO problems. State those problems and suggest FOUR solutions for the situations.

> Teacher A shows Youtube videos, TV shows, and movies that are irrelevant to what students are learning. Also, Teacher A lets students do self-study time throughout most of the semester and etc., which brings the class disorder.

예상답안

Problem 1: Irrelevant video content (Solutions)

① Align content with learning objectives: Teacher A should align the video content with the learning objectives of the course. Before showing any video, ensure that it directly relates to the topic being taught. This will make the content more meaningful and engaging for students.

② Preview videos: Before showing any video in class, Teacher A should preview it in advance to ensure its relevance and appropriateness. This allows for the removal of any content that does not contribute to the educational goals.

③ Seek student input: Involve students in the selection of video materials by asking for their input or suggestions. This not only engages students in the learning process but also ensures that the content is of interest to them.

④ Provide context: Before showing a video, Teacher A should provide context and set clear expectations for what students should focus on while watching. Encourage students to take notes or engage in a discussion afterward to reinforce the educational value of the video.

Problem 2: Disordered class structure (Solutions)

① Establish clear classroom routines: Create a structured daily routine that includes defined time slots for various activities, such as instruction, group work, self-study, and breaks. Consistency in the schedule helps maintain order in the class.

② Set expectations: Clearly communicate classroom expectations and behavior guidelines to students from the beginning of the semester. Establish consequences for disruptive behavior and consistently enforce them.

③ Interactive learning activities: Incorporate interactive and engaging learning activities throughout the semester. Encourage active participation, group discussions, and hands-on exercises to keep students focused and minimize disorder.

④ Regular monitoring: Actively monitor and manage classroom dynamics during self-study time. Teacher A should circulate among students, provide support, and address any issues as they arise. This active presence can help maintain order and ensure productive self-study sessions.

By implementing these solutions, Teacher A can address the problems of irrelevant video content and classroom disorder, creating a more engaging and organized learning environment for students.

Q 19 모둠활동 운영 방안
2023년 즉답형

Explain how you would administer the group work to be more effectively managed.

> Student A: During group work, all the students just say what they want to say, not listening to the others.
> Student B: I cannot participate our group work since it is difficult to follow.
> Student C: I don't like to join in the group work. I feel that the active participants get disadvantages.

예상답안

To address the students' concerns and administer group work more effectively, I would implement the following strategies:

1. Clear Guidelines and Roles:
- Before starting any group work, I would establish clear guidelines for collaboration. These guidelines would include active listening as a crucial component. Students should be encouraged to actively engage in discussions by listening to their peers' contributions.
- Assign specific roles to each group member. For example, designate a "facilitator" responsible for ensuring everyone has a chance to speak, a "timekeeper" to manage the discussion time, and a

"recorder" to document key points. Having defined roles can help students stay on track and ensure equal participation.

2. Structured Discussion Format:
- Implement a structured discussion format, such as "Think-Pair-Share" or "Round Robin." These formats provide a framework for students to take turns speaking and listening, ensuring that everyone has an opportunity to contribute.
- Encourage students to summarize their group's discussion and share it with the whole class. This promotes active participation and ensures that each group member's input is valued.

3. Differentiated Tasks:
- Recognize that some students may find the group work challenging to follow (as mentioned by Student B). To address this, assign differentiated tasks within the group. Some students can tackle more complex aspects of the task, while others focus on foundational elements. This ensures that all students can contribute meaningfully, regardless of their proficiency level.

4. Individual and Group Accountability:
- Balance individual accountability with group accountability. Ask each student to submit an individual reflection or response related to the group's work. This ensures that even quieter or less active participants contribute their thoughts.
- Evaluate group dynamics and provide constructive feedback on how well the group worked together. Encourage students to reflect on their own contributions and discuss ways to improve collaboration in the future.

5. Encourage Active Participation:
- Address the concern expressed by Student C about active participants potentially having disadvantages. Encourage active students to facilitate discussions, guide their peers, and ensure that quieter students have opportunities to share their ideas. Active participants can also serve as mentors or coaches to help their peers succeed.

6. Reflect and Adjust:
- After each group work session, hold a debriefing discussion with the whole class. Encourage students to share their experiences and suggest improvements. Use this feedback to make adjustments and refine the group work process for future activities.
- By implementing these strategies, I aim to create a more inclusive and effective group work environment where all students actively participate, listen to one another, and benefit from collaborative learning experiences.

Q 20 학생들의 수업에 대한 불만에 대한 해결책 2023년 구상형

Describe the common problem from the students' comments as below, and the suggestions to solve the problems in FOUR ways.

> The school administered the survey to the students about the satisfaction about the lesson. The following is the comments of some students.
> - We used the newspapers in the classes of Maths, Korean, and Social studies but it didn't give us any interests or fun.
> - During the half-year exam, we have to prepare performance tests, too.
> - We like to monitor what other teachers teach in their lessons.

예상답안

Common Problem: Lack of interest and engagement in lessons

Suggestions to solve the problems:

① Incorporate interactive activities: To address the issue of using newspapers without sparking interest, teachers can integrate interactive activities into the lessons. For example, in Math, students can solve real-world problems using data or statistics from newspaper articles. In Korean, they can analyze and discuss news stories, and in Social Studies, they can explore current events and their implications. These hands-on activities make the content more engaging and relevant.

② Diversify assessment methods: If students are concerned about performance tests during half-year exams, teachers can diversify assessment methods. While traditional written exams are necessary, consider adding performance-based assessments that allow students to demonstrate their understanding through projects, presentations, or practical applications of knowledge. This approach caters to different learning styles and can reduce test-related stress.

③ Promote cross-subject learning: To address the desire to monitor other teachers' lessons, consider introducing cross-subject collaborative projects. For example, teachers from different subjects can work together to create interdisciplinary lessons or projects that showcase the interconnectedness of subjects. This not only enriches the learning experience but also satisfies students' curiosity about what other teachers are doing.

④ Introduce technology and multimedia: To make lessons more engaging, teachers can incorporate technology and multimedia resources. In my English class, podcasts, online debates, or multimedia presentations can add variety. Some virtual field trips, documentaries, or data visualization tools can make language learning more authentic and appealing.

By implementing these suggestions, teachers can create a more engaging and interactive learning environment, addressing the students' concerns and fostering a more positive and enriching educational experience.

Q 21　동료교사의 불만에 대한 대처 방법

2023년 추가질문형

If your peer-teachers complain that your students are causing trouble, how would you deal with that?

If my peer-teachers complain that my students are causing trouble, I would take a proactive and collaborative approach to address the issue. Here are the steps I would follow:

- Listen Actively: I would listen carefully to my peer-teachers' concerns, allowing them to express their observations and feelings. It's essential to be open to their feedback and understand their perspective.
- Acknowledge the Issue: I would acknowledge the issue and take responsibility for the behavior of my students. It's important to show that I value their input and take the matter seriously.
- Gather Information: I would seek specific details about the incidents or behaviors causing trouble. Understanding the context, frequency, and severity of the issues can help in devising an effective solution.
- Meet with the Peer-Teachers: I would arrange a face-to-face meeting with my peer-teachers to discuss the concerns in more detail. This meeting would provide an opportunity for constructive dialogue and collaboration in finding solutions.
- Involve the Students: Depending on the nature of the issues, I may involve the students in addressing the problem. This could include having a classroom discussion about behavior expectations, consequences, and the impact of their actions on others.
- Implement Classroom Management Strategies: I would review and adjust my classroom management strategies if necessary. This might involve setting clear expectations, establishing consistent consequences for disruptive behavior, and implementing positive reinforcement for good behavior.
- Communicate with Parents: If the issues persist, I would communicate with the parents or guardians of the students involved. A collaborative effort between teachers and parents can often lead to improved behavior and accountability.
- Seek Support: If the problems continue despite interventions, I might seek support from the school's counseling or behavior intervention team. They can provide additional strategies and resources to address the challenges effectively.
- Monitor Progress: I would continuously monitor the students' behavior and communicate with my peer-teachers to keep them updated on the progress made. It's essential to maintain open lines of communication.
- Reflect and Adjust: Finally, I would regularly reflect on my teaching methods and classroom management techniques. Continuous improvement is key to addressing behavior issues effectively.

In dealing with such situations, maintaining a positive and collaborative attitude is crucial. By working together with my peer-teachers, the students, and other support resources available, we can create a more conducive learning environment and address behavior issues effectively.

Q 22   다정한 교직관 vs 엄격한 교직관   2023년 구상형

Ms. Park gives some advices to a new teacher, Mr. Kim about the class management but the following situation occurred:

> Ms. Park, an experienced teacher, advised Mr. Kim to adopt a strict and authoritative approach to classroom management at the beginning of the semester. Her reasoning likely stemmed from the belief that setting clear rules and boundaries early on establishes a sense of order and respect, which can later provide a foundation for more flexibility and openness as students understand the teacher's expectations.
>
>   Contrary to Ms. Park's advice, Mr. Kim decided to take a friendly and student-centered approach. He prioritized building rapport with the students by creating a relaxed and inclusive classroom atmosphere. By accepting students' opinions and ideas early on, he aimed to foster mutual respect and trust, assuming that such a relationship would naturally lead to cooperative behavior over time.
>
> By April, the students were no longer listening to Mr. Kim's instructions, as they might have interpreted his friendly demeanor as a sign of weakness or inconsistency. This lack of discipline would have caused:
> - Difficulty in maintaining focus during lessons.
> - Frequent disruptions or disregard for class activities.
> - Struggles for Mr. Kim to regain control, as attempts to enforce rules later might have been met with resistance or confusion from students who were used to the earlier leniency.

Based on the situation, describe TWO advantages and TWO disadvantages about Mr. Kim's management methods in class.

예상답안

(1) Advantages of Mr. Kim's management methods:

① Friendly teacher-student relationship: Mr. Kim's approach of being friendly and open to students' opinions and ideas from the beginning of the semester fosters a positive teacher-student relationship. This can create a more welcoming and inclusive classroom atmosphere where students feel comfortable expressing themselves and seeking help when needed.

② Student empowerment: By allowing students to share their opinions and ideas, Mr. Kim empowers them to take ownership of their learning. This can lead to increased engagement and a sense of responsibility for their education, as they feel that their voices are valued.

(2) Disadvantages of Mr. Kim's management methods:

① Loss of classroom control: As the semester progresses, Mr. Kim's leniency in enforcing rules and expectations can result in a loss of classroom control. Students may perceive him as less authoritative, leading to a lack of discipline and a chaotic learning environment, as described in the situation in April.

② Inconsistency in behavior expectations: Shifting from a strict approach to a more lenient one mid-semester can confuse students and create inconsistencies in behavior expectations. Students may struggle to adapt to the changing classroom environment, leading to disruptions and a breakdown in classroom management.

In summary, striking a balance between friendliness and maintaining a structured learning environment is crucial for effective classroom management. This situation highlights the importance of balance in classroom management. While building rapport and being approachable are valuable, they must be complemented by clear expectations and firm boundaries, especially early in the academic year. Without this balance, students may struggle to respect authority or adhere to classroom norms, leading to behavioral challenges and a less productive learning environment.

Q 23. 지구 온난화에 따른 우리의 대처방법 2022년 구상형

Our environment has some problems as Text 1 explains. Based on the Text 3, identify the TWO problems that you can find in the Text 2. Then suggest the concrete solutions.

Text 1.
Global warming is the long-term heating of Earth's climate system observed since the pre-industrial period due to human activities, primarily fossil fuel burning, which increases heat-trapping greenhouse gas levels in Earth's atmosphere. The term is frequently used interchangeably with the term climate change, though the latter refers to both human- and naturally produced warming and the effects it has on our planet. It is most commonly measured as the average increase in Earth's global surface temperature.

Since the pre-industrial period, human activities are estimated to have increased Earth's global average temperature by about 1 degree Celsius, a number that is currently increasing by 0.2 degrees Celsius per decade. It is unequivocal that human influence has warmed the atmosphere, ocean, and land.

Text 2.
Accordingly, our school decided an Monthly Activity Plan to make an effort to preserve the environment as below.

1. May	One day/ School Statement Announcement, Petition for environment preservation
2. July	1-2 weeks/ Environment Campaign of students participation
3. September	1-2 weeks/ Environment Campaign of students participation
4. November	One day/ Discussion session with watching polar bear in Arctic video clip

Text 3.
"One swallow does not make a summer, neither does one fine day; similarly one day or brief time of happiness does not make a person entirely happy." -Aristotle

예상답안

We should understand that we cannot be sure that a situation is going to improve immediately even though one good thing has happened. So, if I observe our school plan, in May and November, there is just one day promotion plan to preserve environment. Environment conservation does not happen in just one day but we have to make constant and continuous efforts to make it happen on a long-term plan. And students should understand after the announcement or discussion session, there should be consequent actions to do something to preserve environment. We can make daily plans to practice easily at home or school, such as using a handkerchief instead of paper tissue, using stairs instead of elevator, using a tumbler instead of disposable cups and etc. With these simple actions, we can start our little step for our environment conservation.

Q 24. 혁신적 교육을 위한 교사와의 갈등 *2022년 구상형*

Describe one common problem of two teachers, A and B, 1) in terms of school culture 2) in terms of individual teacher. And suggest the solutions of each teacher A and B, respectively. Two situations show the conflicts with other peer teachers as below:

Teacher A	I want to implement subject-integrated curriculum but other peer teachers object to the theme-based teaching. They claim that it is hard to be consistent with the theme since our subject has our own specialty.
Teacher B	In post-pandemic, we are able to have the in-person class and I want to maintain online class with blended learning. But other teachers in our English department object to it. Instead, they want to go back to the traditional teaching methods, as the same teaching method as that of pre-Covid.

예상답안

I can see a common problem of two teachers. In terms of school culture, two teachers have difficulty implementing new teaching methods. Most teachers don't want to have change or innovative thinking in teaching but keep using the traditional teaching methods that is more comfortable and convenient for them. In terms of individual teacher, I believe that some of teachers make an effort to improve their teaching methods to benefit the students' learning. But there is a school system and curriculum that school should abide by. So, they cannot just change on their own. As for the solutions, teacher A wants to implement an integrated lesson with other subjects. She can start with an authentic material from English magazine, Utube, news and etc that she can continue with our subject specialty. The material can be a good source of the various themes as long as the students are interested in. Teacher B wants to implement blended learning integrated with online class.

> **추가질문** 교원학습 공동체와 이유 구체적인 계획
>
> 교사가 되면 서로 나눔의 태도가 중요합니다. 교사가 되어 만들고 싶은 교원학습공동체와 이유, 구체적인 계획을 말하세요.

예상답안

한국어 전통적으로 '혼자서' 수업을 진행하고 문제를 해결해왔던 교사들이 그 한계를 인식한 후, 수업을 개선하기 위한 기술과 방법을 배우고, 교육에 대한 열정과 가치를 나누기 위해 모여 만든 것이 바로 교사학습공동체입니다. 교사학습공동체는 교과 지식 획득, 상담 기법 공유 등 구체적인 목적을 가지고 소규모로 운영되는 공동체부터 실제 수업에서 사용하는 수많은 자료들을 온라인으로 함께 개발하는 대규모의 공동체까지 목적과 운영방식에 따라 굉장히 다양한 종류가 존재합니다. 배움과 나눔, 그리고 협력을 실천하고 싶은 교사들 누구나 학습공동체에 들어가 함께 할 수 있습니다.

영어 Traditionally, teachers implemented the class 'on their own' and solved the problems without any collaboration or help. Therefore, a 'teacher training community' is formed when teachers want to share their passion and value on teaching and some expertise of teaching techniques with their co-teachers. Any teachers who want to share learning and collaborative work can join the 'teacher training community.'

After I become a teacher, I want to design a 'reading club for teachers.' It can sound a little old and boring but I'm sure it's easy for any teachers to access without a big preparation. Reading a book can be a good resource to people who live in a modern society. But we have hundreds of reasons that cannot read a book even one book a month. While we are reading a book and sharing our ideas to each other, we can think of new ideas and methods that can benefit both teachers and students.

Q 25 Alvin Toffler의 미래사회를 위한 한국교육 2022년 즉답형

Describe your opinions about each situation 1 and 2 as below, suggest THREE methods that the Korean schools should move forward. (상황 〈1〉과 〈2〉에 대한 자신의 의견을 밝히시오. 그리고 향후 한국교육이 나아가야 할 방향 3가지를 제시하시오.)

> **Situation 1**
> Student A: I don't know any differences between school online classes and Internet lectures.
> Student B: I'd better watch the lectures on social media, which helps me more than in school.
> Student C: If I could not receive a graduate diploma, I might quit the school.
>
> **Situation 2**
>   Futurist Dr. Alvin Toffler, currently visiting Korea, pointed out the need for diversification in educational systems and curricula instead of sticking to the old system, which is long a legacy of the post industrial age. The government, clinging to the myth of the equality code and hampering diversification, should listen to Dr. Toffler's words attentively. Dr. Toffler further argued, What Korea needs most right now is to get rid of the evils of bureaucracy and to push

> for innovations in education, Korean education is in a way a victim of bureaucratic meddling, with the government nagging at private schools all the time curtailing their independence and interfering with how universities should select their students. Unless the Korean education is freed from the evils of bureaucracy, it will remain the way it has been in the industrial age.

예상답안

In situation 1, I can understand the current education situation of our students. The students don't have trust our educational system but just think the school of an institute that gives grades or goes through for the next level. They don't come to school to learn or work together with teacher and other students. In situation 2, Albin Toffler pointed out the problem of our education system, bureaucracy. Korean bureaucracy system interfered our students' creativity and diversification in schools. So if we want to improve our educational system, we need to be out of the old system. In situation 3, the student pointed out that school is just to get the diploma that he might need for further education or employment.

Korean schools need to focus more on the current students' needs and interests. The schools should respect each teachers' innovative ideas and methods in teaching. The schools need to have a certain level of freedom that the government bureaucracy cannot touch.

Q 26 교사의 자질 — 2022년 추가질문

> Discuss your teaching principles and TWO qualities that you should be prepared for, if you want your students to grow up a type of person that you wish in future. (내가 가르치는 학생이 어떤 사람으로 성장하길 원하는지, 이를 위해 필요한 교사의 자질 2가지를 말하세요.)

예상답안

I think I need to have expertise and awareness on ethics as a teacher. I want my students to grow up a person that the society needs in future whatever area they are. For that, I can support them with my expertise they need. In addition, even though they are in a high status in their position, they should be equipped with moral values. Otherwise, their social status will be meaningless and even plunged to the bottom in any case.

Q 27 선택 과목 선정을 위한 조언   2022년 구상형

As a homeroom teacher, suggest some advices or methods to support each student A, B, and C, respectively.

(1) Student A has to choose one elective subject matter for next year.
(2) Student B has not decided his future career and been confused what subject matters have to be chosen among so many subject matters.
(3) Student C has no subject matters to choose since there is no subject matters that she is interested in.

예상답안

First, student A wants to choose one elective subject for next year. Elective subject is different from the compulsory subjects that everybody should take. So he has to consider his own interests and future career that he pursues. Student B also has difficulty which subjects he has to take since he is not sure about his future career. During the school years, many students are still considering and changing their future career, which is very natural. So, even though they have no definite plan for future, they don't have to be worried about but just choose any subjects they are interested at the moment. Student C has no subjects she wants to choose. Unluckily, the school cannot afford to provide all the subjects students want. So, she could choose an alternative subject that can be similar to her interests.

Q 28 사회성 향상을 위한 활동   2022년 구상형

Under the Covid-19 situation, students have very little opportunities to develop socializing. As a teacher, choose ONE activity as below to develop the students' sociability and suggest the reasons of doing the activity.
- Peer activity
- Creativity-based experiential activity
- Theme-based experiential activity

예상답안

During Covid-19, students have very little opportunities to meet with friends in and out of school. To develop their sociability skill, peer activity can be recommended. Peer activity can be easily applied in any type of peer works. For example, when I give an assignment, the work should be completed only in pair. Then, the peer should work together to complete the assignment. They can first start reluctantly, but they become like socializing with their peers. Later, they might work together voluntarily above the assignment.

Q 29 학급규칙을 통한 자율성 신장   2022년 구상형

Describe the methods to improve the students' independence or autonomy considering the students' opinions about the class rules for students' conduct.

> (1) Student A: We have to decide the class rules through our discussion.
> (2) Student B: I don't know the reasons the class rules should be made again. Can't we use the school rules instead of making the class rules?
> (3) Student C: Last year, I made a duty to clean the class after school every day due to the rule of tardiness. I wish we could change the rule this year.

예상답안

For student A, when we make our class rules for students' conduct, they prefer deciding through their discussion in class. This way, they want to abide by the rules they made rather than others' orders or instructions. For student B, they don't want to make separate class rules other than school rules. But every class has their own characters and personalities. So, if they make their own class rules to make use of their personalities, the rules will be their own that they want to follow. For student C, he complains that he has to follow the rule he doesn't want. If the rule was decided by whole class, he might have a different attitude towards the rule. Since he and his classmates agreed to follow the rule, he couldn't afford to complain any rewards and punishment.

Q 30 학생과 과목교사의 갈등시 담임교사로서 처리 방법   2022년 즉답형

If you have a conflict between the teacher and student as in the situation below, describe what you would do as a homeroom teacher.

> You are a homeroom teacher. And one subject teacher brought one of your students to the teacher's room and asked you to do some discipline on the student's misbehavior after the class. Previously, you told the student off several times on the teacher's behalf, but you were also exhausted after the recurrence of the same incidents.

예상답안

I believe that the subject teacher had no intention to leave the whole responsibility to me, a homeroom teacher. But he might think that the student was hard to handle himself and it would be better to hand the student over to me. So, even though it would make me exhausted to take care of the student, that could be one of my responsibilities as a homeroom teacher. I'm sure that the subject teacher would appreciate me and would take better care of our class.

Q 31 교사의 자질과 계획 2021년 구상형

Describe two qualities that Teacher A showed as below. And discuss your own plans to develop each quality as a teacher.

> Teacher A found out that a student of his homeroom class was depressed. He suggested the student join a drama club, where he showed a real talent and passion in writing a drama script and well adjusted to the school life. Something crossed his mind that some other students also went through the same problem that he couldn't find.

예상답안

Teacher A showed interests in each student and took a good look at their problems. When we had care and affection towards a person, we could see the person's strength and weakness better. From the viewpoint, he also made an effort to find out what the student was good at. So, he discovered the student's real talent, which led to a better school life.

When I become a teacher, I also want to be a teacher who truly cares about each student and understand their problems. For that, I will share the journal with the students. They write a journal entry about anything that comes to their mind, and I write back to them with my comments. In addition, if I want to find out the students' talent, I also need to be open minded for various areas. I will attend some educational or career seminars to learn from. Then I could recommend the exact area that the students maximize their potentials.

합격을 위한 TIP

매년 출제되는 교사의 자세, 교사가 갖추어야할 자질에 대한 문제이다. 올해는 좋은 동료 교사를 보고 배울 능력이 있는지에 대한 출제의도라고 볼 수 있다. 학생에게 '관심'을 많이 두고 있는 점, 그리고 학생이 잘할 수 있는 영역을 '발견'해준 점, 그리고 다른 학생들도 잘 챙기고 있는지 '성찰'하는 점 등을 포인트로 잡아서 교사의 자질을 이야기하고, 이런 자세를 기를 수 있는 방안을 추상적 방안 보다는, 자신만의 특색있는 방법으로 구체적으로 제시하는 것이 중요하다.

Q 32 　교사의 가치관　　　　　　　　　　　　　　2021년 즉답형

(1) Under the circumstances, choose one teacher that you think has the most important teaching principles and discuss the reason based on your teaching principles, and (2) Suggest a type of person you want your students to grow up to be through your education. ((1) 다음 상황에서 가장 중요하다고 생각하는 가치관을 지는 교사 선택하고, 그 이유를 자신의 교사상에 비추어 제시하고, (2) 자신의 교육을 통해 학생을 어떤 인간으로 길러낼 수 있는지 제시하시오.)

> A교사: It's important to develop the students' basic academic abilities.
> B교사: It's important to develop the students' self-confidence.
> C교사: It's important to help students build up good relationship with friends.

예상답안

Teacher C is the one that matches with my teaching principle. I believe that our education has many ways to help students to grow up to be a well-rounded human being. For that, we teachers have a responsibility to support and help them to be a better person for our society. The students can develop creative thoughts and information processing on problem solving. And they can socialize friends or people around them in a community when necessary.

합격을 위한 TIP

몇가지 중에서 선택하는 문제를 대할 때는 그 중에 정답은 없다는 것이다. 그 중에서 자신의 신념과 교육관을 가지고 충분한 논리적 근거를 가지고 설명하는 것이 중요하다. 교육과정에서 찾는다면 기초학력은 창의적 사고 역량이나 지식정보처리역량과 연결할 수 있고, 자신감은 자기관리역량과, 그리고 교우관계는 공동체 역량과 연결하여 설명할 수 있다.

Q 33 　업무 과중한 교사의 동료교사와의 갈등　　　　　　　　　2021년 즉답형

1) From teacher A's viewpoint, describe the reason of the behavior of teacher A.
2) According to the teacher's professional ethics, criticize teacher A's rejection.
3) If you are teacher A, how would you deal with the problem?

> Teacher A had excellent ability in online teaching and passion on teaching. A senior teacher let him take a charge of online-related lessons in school. His own lessons and students' disciplines were affected by overworking of the online lesson work. Under the circumstances, peer teachers also asked him to help their online teaching. In the end, teacher A declined all the teachers' requests and announced that 'I cannot help you, since it's not my duty.'

> 예상답안

(1) I can understand the teacher A's situation. He might think he ran out of time for his students and lesson management if he spends too much time for teachers' online training. (2) But rather than just refusing the other teachers' request, he could think of the teachers' responsibility towards making a better community first. He could consider some better ways to help the teachers with the collaboration. (3) If I were teacher A, I would hold a regular training session for online teaching for teachers rather than individual coaching. That can give me a good opportunity to develop my expertise in the area as well as help teachers.

합격을 위한 TIP

거의 매년 출제가 되고 있는 '동료교사와의 갈등' 문제이다. 읽어보면 A교사가 업무도 몰아서 받은 것도 힘든데 동료교사까지 도와야 하는 상황이 힘들 수 있으므로 A교사를 이해할 수 있다. 다만 문제에서는 교직윤리측면에서 '비판'을 하라고 했으므로 어떻게든 비판을 기본으로 가지고 있어야 한다. A교사는 학생에게까지 피해가 갈 수 있는 상황이므로 거절을 했겠지만, 교사 '공동체'가 중요하므로 '거절'을 하기 보다는 시간을 많이 뺏기지 않고 효율적으로 동료교사까지 도울 수 있는 방안을 고려해서 답변으로 제시하는 것이 중요하다. 동료교사와의 갈등에 관한 문제는 항상 공동체적인 측면에서 협조적인 방향으로 답변을 구성하는 것이 필요하다.

Q 34 학교폭력의 피해 후 관계 회복 · 2021년 구상형

Give advice on Student A and student B that the teacher can provide to improve their relationship. Make sure to include specific action plans on empathy, apology, and rebuilding the relationship of the whole class students.

Class Record on School Violence	
Date	Descriptions
3월 15일	Student A accidently collided with student B, but did not apologize. Student B got upset, and punched student A on his stomach. Also, student B swore loudly at student A. Many other students in the classroom witnessed it.
4월 15일	This school violence case was concluded as a minor one.

Student A	Although B didn't hurt me a lot, other students in the classroom watched me getting punched. And B was swearing hard at me, and it damaged my self-esteem. Although B apologized, I'm still uncomfortable and don't want to face B.
Student B	I feel like everything has been messed up since A didn't apologize to me in the first place. Because of that, I had a trouble with my parents, and I think other students consider me as weird.

예상답안

First of all, I should say to every student 'violence should not be allowed, under any circumstances.' So I should let all the students aware that we keep 'zero tolerance for violence' in our school. In this incident of school violence, both students can be victims. In the first place, when they collided, both of them were responsible and should have apologized politely to each other. Student B DID apologize but student A was still upset about the incident. So, student B has to keep expressing his sincere apology until student A accepts his apology. If they still have a difficult time, professional counseling is recommended to revive their relationships and heal their minds.

Q 35 온라인 수업에서의 학생들 출결과 수업태도의 문제점   2021년 구심형

Several problems occurred regarding online classes. Provide problems of each case. Then, suggest their resolution.

(1) [Case A] Youngmi showed good achievements in offline class. However, in online learning, she shows low participation since it is lecture-based online class. Also, she sometimes cannot understand material.
(2) [Case B] Hansu does not participate in online class. He comes only for attendance grading. The teacher keeps calling him to stay in the online class.
(3) [Case C] Sunam doesn't like online based process-oriented evaluation. This is because some students get help from others and share the answers.

예상답안

Youngmi lost her interests in online lesson since it was a lecture-based class. She needs to be provided with some active lesson she can participate. She learns more from experience-based or discovery-based learning, where she can find out a new rule from her experiences. Hansu doesn't participate in online class but just check his attendance. For him, he needs some type of initiative for him to want to come to online class. For example, he can bring his own topic or question to discuss in online class. Sunam doesn't like online process-oriented evaluation since some students cheat in a test. Then teacher has to make sure with the student that we are not allowed to cheat in a test. The teacher should show a strict attitude towards the students' unethical behavior.

Q 36 문제학생을 위한 인지적, 정의적 지원 방법   2021년 즉답형

Describe your teaching principles and rationales why you have to help student A. Suggest the methods of supporting students A in terms of cognitive and affective aspects. (자신이 가진 교육관을 설명하고, 이에 따라 A학생에게 도움이 주어져야 하는 필요성에 대해 설명하세요. 그리고 A학생의 인지적 영역과 정의적 영역 각각에 대한 지원을 제공하는 방안을 제시하세요.)

> Student A
> 1. Lack of learning abilities in Korean language, English, Mathematics
> 2. ADHD (정서 산만)
> 3. Low self esteem and difficulty socializing with friends (자존감이 낮고 친구 관계 어려워함)
> 4. Irregular habit of everyday life and skipping of the meals (기초생활습관 잘 잡혀있지 않고, 끼니를 거르는 경우가 많음)

예상답안

I believe that every student needs to be safe and supportive in school. When we have a close look at each student, we can see their worries or problems. Then we can be more involved in their lives to solve the problems. Student A doesn't seem to have any protection from school and home. So she has a low level of basic learning abilities and shows learning disorder. She can use after school activities or mentoring system to catch up with missed parts in the subjects. In addition, she has no friends to get along and low self esteem. Through regular and consistent counseling, I can more closely monitor and find out her situation. If necessary, I can associate with the school supporting team to provide the student with financial support. Peer mentoring will be a good method for socializing. Once they build up a good relationship, the student will have self confidence in making friends and extend the relationship to other friends.

Q 37 기초학력 지원사업을 꺼리는 학생 대처방법   2021년 추가질문

Discuss the THREE concrete methods you would do to solve the problem, if the student doesn't want to participate in 'Basic learning support center.' (이와 같은 기초학력지원사업에 대상 학생이 참여하기를 꺼리는 경우, 이를 해결하기 위한 3가지 구체적인 방안을 제시하세요.)

예상답안

If the student doesn't want to participate in basic learning supporting, I would start with talking with the student to find out the reasons. I should build up rapport with the student to give him trust in me. I will let him know that I am the person who can wait for and offer my support in any way. I can introduce a student mentor who had the same experience with him. He received the learning support and now he is a college student with high achievement. Lastly, I will let the student understand the basic learning support is one of their essential aspects to live in the society. Without basic learning, it would be hard to go to college or to get a job in future.

Q 38 수행평가의 문제점과 해결책 | 2020년 구상형

The following is the students' feedback on their performance assessment. Identify the problems and their solutions for each student. (다음은 수행 평가에 대한 학생의 피드백이다. 여기에서 드러나 수행 평가의 문제점을 3가지 찾아, 각각해결 방안을 말하시오.)

> Student A: I cannot complete the performance task since the task is too long.
> Student B: I've already have four performance tasks from the other classes.
> Student C: I don't know what I have to do. I'd rather go back to the multiple choice tests.

예상답안

① Student A has difficulty completing the task since the task is too long. I would adjust the amount and time for the performance task considering the students' needs and proficiency levels. As for the solution, before starting the semester, need analysis for the students can be implemented to set up the appropriate amount and contents of the task.

② Student B has multiple tasks across the curricular even within one day. The subject teachers need to cooperate and decide the tasks across the curricular so that students can have consistent tasks to integrate and develop integrated knowledge.

③ Student C has a lack of understanding performance task. Students can prefer simple multiple choice tests. As for solution, performance task can develop the students' higher order thinking and a well-rounded learning.

Q 39 교사의 지도에 순응하지 않는 학생 지도방법 | 2020년 구상형

Under the circumstances as below, explain the TWO essential qualities that the teacher needs and the efforts related to the qualities.

> Chulsu in my class often comes late or is absent. I'm concerned about your attendance. "Chulsu, don't be late at school. I'm having a hard time. If you keep late and absent like this, you might have to stay in the same class next year due to your attendance rate." But Chulsu came late again today as if he didn't mind the teacher's advice at all.

예상답안

The teacher needs some qualities for the student who doesn't cooperate with school disciplines. First, we need to understand the reasons and purposes of the student's misbehaviors. The reasons of misbehaviors could be low school grades, family problems, teachers' negligence, alienation of peer groups and etc. Without the reflection of the problems, if the teacher just emphasizes the discipline, the student would revolt against the teacher's authority. The teacher's expectation towards the student and warm and kind talks will affect his probable behaviors. Through 'after-school counseling session' or 'having lunch together', the teacher can empathize with the student's difficulties and talk about some solutions for the problems. The teacher can observe any changes, give him some praise, share the teacher's stories to build up rapport and encourage him to change into the more positive person.

합격을 위한 TIP

회복적 생활교육을 이해하기 위한 기본 개념 : 응보적 정의와 회복적 정의

⊙ 응보적 정의 (Retributive Justice)	⊙ 회복적 정의 (Restorative Justice)
• 잘못된 행동이 있을 때 그에 상응하는 고통(처벌)을 부여하는 것 • 사회를 통제하고 사람의 행동을 변화시킬 수 있음 • 사회의 안전성의 한계 대두	• 정의는 처벌이 아니라 가해자와 공동체 구성원의 노력으로 피해가 온전히 회복될 때 성취됨 • 회복적 정의는 삶의 새로운 패러다임 • 회복적 정의는 회복적 실천으로 확장 • 회복적 생활교육은 회복적 정의 운동에 속함 • 회복적 생활교육은 결과보다는 과정에 집중

Q 40 자율성과 교사에 의한 학습 비교   2020년 구상형

Based on the passage below, suggest the example case for 1) and 2) respectively, describe your principles on education related to 1) and 2).

> 1) You can lead a horse to water, but you can't make it drink. Let it drink by itself.
> 2) But, if the horse doesn't drink by itself, it should be forced to drink.

예상답안

Some school activities for 1) could be student-oriented discussion, debate lesson, problem solution learning, project learning, cooperation learning, restorative education and etc. Some school activities for 2) could be teacher-oriented memorization and textbook-based teaching, school or teacher-oriented class management, retributive education.

I support for students-oriented education as shown in 1). The students are capable of growing up by themselves with unlimited potential. The teacher should be a supporter or facilitator to help the students develop into a well rounded person. The teacher can motivate and guide the students to involve any challenging tasks considering the developmental stage, characteristics, environment of the students.

Q 41 부장교사와의 갈등 해결법
2020년 즉답형

1. 아래 본문의 두 부장교사 중 본인이 선호하는 교사와 그 이유를 말하시오.
2. 자신이 선호하지 않는 부장교사와 함께 일을 하면서 갈등이 발생하였을 때 어떻게 대처할 것인지 말하시오.

> 부장교사 A : 저는 어느 상황에서든 그것이 좋은 일이든, 어려운 일이든 상관없이 얼굴을 보고 소통하는 것을 좋아 합니다. 그래서 업무관련 일도 만나서 이야기 하는 것을 선호합니다.
> 부장교사 B : 저는 메신저로 소통하는 것이 좋습니다. 요즘은 디지털 시대잖아요. 업무 관련 이야기 역시 메신저로 하는 것을 선호합니다.

예상답안

1) 부장교사 A의 경우를 선호한다. 메신저로만 하는 소통하는 경우에는 오해가 생길 수 있다. 의사소통에서는 언어적, 비언어적 요소가 모두 중요하므로 서로 직접 만나 이야기를 하는 것이 불필요한 오해를 막을 수 있다.

2) 부장교사 B의 경우를 선호한다. 수업과 행정업무에 모두가 바쁘고 일이 많아서 항상 직접 만나 소통하는 것은 비효율적이다. 일단 메신저를 최대한 활용해서 업무를 완수하고, 꼭 필요한 경우에만 대면하는 것이 더 효율적이라고 생각한다.

3) 의사소통은 매우 중요한 일인데, 선호하지 않는 부장교사와 갈등이 발생하였을 때 빠르게 대처해야 한다. 우선은 부장교사가 선호하는 방식에 맞추어 적극적으로 소통하고 협력을 강화해 갈 것이다. 그 과정에서 충분한 신뢰가 형성되었을 때 적절한 방법으로 부장교사에게 자신이 바람직하다고 생각하는 소통방식도 제안해 볼 수 있다. 학교 현장에는 다양한 가치관과 성향을 지닌 교사들이 있으므로 나 자신이 선호하는 방식만 고집해서는 소통과 협력이 불가능할 거라 생각된다. 또한 부장교사가 가지고 있는 경험과 능력을 존중하고 그와 맺는 관계는 효과적인 직무수행을 위해서 갈등은 해결되어야 한다고 생각한다.

Q 42 급식질서를 위한 해결방법
2020년 구상형

다음은 A중학교에서 실시한 설문조사 결과이다. 다음 설문조사 결과를 바탕으로 A중학교의 문제를 해결하기 위한 방안을 3가지 말하시오.

(A중학교 설문조사 결과)

1. 학생 대상 질문 : 우리학교의 급식시간에 급식질서가 잘 지키고 있다고 생각하나요?

매우 그렇다	그렇다	보통이다	아니다	매우 아니다
10%	10%	25%	35%	20%

2. 교사 대상 질문 : 우리 학교의 급식시간에 급식 질서가 잘 지키고 있다고 생각하나요?

매우 그렇다	그렇다	보통이다	아니다	매우 아니다
10%	15%	25%	35%	15%

예상답안

급식시간의 급식질서에 대한 설문조사 결과 학생과 교사 모두 부정적인 의견을 보여주는 수치가 50% 이상을 차지하고 있다. 이를 해결하기 위해서 학생들이 중심이 되어 급식질서 지키기 캠페인을 실시하거나 포스터 제작등을 통해 급식실 질서의 필요성을 스스로 인식하도록 한다. 급식실을 학생들을 위한 다목적성, 유연성, 다양성을 갖춘 공간으로 혁신하여 질서유지를 학생 스스로 지켜 나갈 수 있도록 한다. 급식실은 학생들의 정서적 안정과 스트레스 해소를 위해 안락하고 편안한 분위기를 조성하고 학생들의 눈높이에 맞는 휴게 공간을 제공하도록 한다.

거시적인 측면으로, 학교, 교사, 학부모의 연합 토론회를 실시할 수 있다. 이 토론회에서는 급식 질서와 관련된 규칙 제정 등을 위한 종합적 해결책을 합의할 수 있다. 불합리한 학교공간과 동선이 급식 질서의 혼란을 만들어 낼 수 있으므로 학교 공간을 개선하여 질서를 유지할 수 있도록 한다.

Q 43 행복한 학교를 위한 교수법 *2020년 구상형*

Every student in school should have a 'happy learning.' From this viewpoint, discuss the THREE teaching methods that student A lives a happy school live based on the counseling note as below:

> **Counseling note for Student A**
> - April: Student A received a lowest level of academic achievement.
> - May: Student A complained that he doesn't have any interests and want go to school.
> - June: Student A bandaged on his wrist from injuring himself.

예상답안

Student A doesn't feel safe or happy in school at all. So, we have to take an urgent action for him to live a happy school life. First, when he received a lower level of underachievement, we have to find out the reasons and individual factors to plan a program tailored to his situation. Some planning can be supported, such as learning consulting, after school support, learning mentoring, or intense learning program. When the student doesn't have any interests in school, there might have some reasons. Some interesting programs such as alternative classes, WEE class, mentoring or trip programs can be included. And most importantly, in June, the student self-harmed to show that he needs an urgent measurement. With the association with professional counselors, he should be checked for emotional or behaviroal features, such as ADHD, depressions, or anxiety. In school, whole class or pair meeting can be helpful to make friends. A various club activities can improve his self-esteem and the teacher's compliments or encouragement will help him to develop the sound identity.

Q 44 개인정보 보호법에 따른 조치 *2020년 즉답형*

Some of the following cases can violate 'Personal Information Protection Act.' Describe which cases violate the Act and the reasons you think.

> - (Case 1) I wrote down the students' personal information on my diary to use counseling.
> - (Case 2) I hand over the students' contact numbers to the parents' representative to promote the parents' meeting without the consent.
> - (Case 3) I put the result of volunteering work on the class notice board, like "Excellent work, 오O서", "Needs effort, 김O수."

예상답안

한국어 (사례1)은 개인정보보호법 위반이 아니다. 교사는 학생의 정보를 알 수 있으며 이러한 정보를 활용하여 원활한 교육활동을 진행하기 위한 목적이므로 개인정보법 위반은 아니다. 단 교사는 어떠한 순간에도 학생의 개인정보를 외부에 노출하거나 노출 위험이 발생하지 않도록 유의해야 한다.

(사례 2)는 개인정보보호법 위반이다. 전화번호는 개인을 식별할 수 있는 정보이며 사전 동의없이 다른 사람에게 배포하는 것은 위반이다. 교육적 목적을 위해서라도 사용하기 위해서는 사전에 학부모 동의를 받아야 한다.

(사례 3)은 개인정보법 위반이다. 가운데 이름을 가리더라도 학급의 다른 학생들은 학생들의 이름을 쉽게 인식할 수 있다. 학사행정에 불가피한 정보공개가 아닌, 개인정보를 공개하여 타인에게 수치심을 유발하였으므로 개인정보 보호법 위반이다.

영어 (Case 1) didn't violate the 'Personal Information Protection Act.' Teacher needs to know the students' personal information for the purpose of educational activities. But she has to have an extra care not tp reveal the information to the third parties in any moment.

(Case 2) violates the Act. Students' contact numbers are the personal information and cannot hand over to others without the consent. Even though it is an educational purpose, it should not be allowed.

(Case 3) violates the Act. Even though the middle name was hidden, other students could easily recognize the students. In addition, this is a violation since this is not a part of Academic Administration and can humiliate some of students.

Q 45. 무임승차 현상의 문제점과 해결방안   2020년 즉답형

In group work, not all the students participate in the work but some of students just sit around to get the same group score as the others. Describe the problems and solutions of the free riders.

예상답안

한국어 모둠학습에 참여하지 않은 학습자가 성과를 공유하는 무임승차현상은 반대로 학습능력이 높은 학습자가 자기로 인해 성과가 공유되는 것을 꺼려 적극적으로 참여하지 않는 봉효과까지 만들 수 있는 문제점이 있다. 그래서 학생들이 개개인의 노력을 보상받지 못한 다고 생각하여 모둠학습에 필수적인 협상활동을 하지 않으려고 할 수 있다. 이를 위한 해결 방안으로 협동하여 모둠 학습 점수도 주어지지만 동시에 개인보상을 실시한다. 모둠 안의 동료평가를 실시하고 결과를 활용하여 새로운 모둠을 구성할 수 있다. 개인별 책임감을 가질 수 있는 활동이나 긍정적 상호의존도, 협력기술, 모둠별 평가방법을 개선하여 협동하면서도 개별의 책임감을 강화할 수 있다.

영어 The phenomenon of free riders brings about the sucker effects that high achieved students also don't want to participate in the group work. Because they don't think they get enough rewards for their efforts, they don't want to participate the group work. For solution, the students need to get grades from individual work as well as the group work. Peer evaluation in a group can be used to design a new group. Some activities can be used to enhance individual accountability by developing interdependence, cooperation skills, or new evaluation methods.

Q 46 학습권 침해하는 학생과 무례한 태도의 학생 — 2019년 구상형

1. Under the circumstances, identify the TWO problems and discuss how to immediately deal with the problems as a teacher.

> The two students were always making a fuss in class. They haven't had good manners in class and paid attention to the lesson. Mr. Kim told them off but it wasn't long before they made a noise again to interrupt the lesson. When Mr. Kim disciplined them again, Minsu, who was a highly academic student, rudely complained with an irritated look on his face, 'Sir, we are behind the other classes and just need to catch up.'

예상답안

한국어 수업상황의 문제점을 살펴보면 두 명의 학생이 수업시간에 반복된 문제행동을 보이고 있어서 정상적인 수업 흐름을 방해하고 있다. 같은 교실안에서 학습권을 침해받고 있다고 생각하는 학생이 거칠게 불만을 표현하고 있다. 그 과정에서 성적은 좋으나 교사에 대한 존중이 없는 무례한 태도로 표현하는 민수로 인하여 교사와 감정적 대립으로 사태가 커질 수 있는 가능성이 있다. 즉각적인 대처방안으로 첫째, 문제행동을 일으키는 두 학생에게 문제행동 관리가 길어지다 보면 정상적인 수업 진행이 어렵기 때문에 학급규칙을 상기시키고, 교실밖에서 개별적으로 타임아웃을 실시하여 생각할 시간을 준다. 민수에게는 어떠한 상황에서도 교사나, 혹은 다른 친구들에게도 거칠게 표현하여 무례하게 하는 것은 좋지 않음을 언급하고 수업후 개별 면담시간을 가진다. 면담에서는 여러 상황을 제시하여 스스로 무엇이 문제였는지를 인식할 수 있도록 한다. 그룹 역할극등을 통해 무례한 태도로 자신의 의사를 표현하지 않고 존중의 태도를 갖추면서도 자신의 의사를 전달할 수 있는 방법을 익히도록 하는 상담시간을 가진다.

영어 The problems are that the two students interrupt the class with repeated misbehaviors. One academic student, Minsu rudely complains his learning right is interrupted by the two other students. Even though he is a high achiever in class, he doesn't show any respect towards teachers and other students. For measurement to solve the problem, first, for the two students, I will give 'time out' session out of class or individually. Then, they have some time to think about their misbehaviors. For Minsu, I will let him know that he is not allowed to speak rudely to anyone in any situation and have separate counseling session. During counseling, he needs to realize his problems and learn how to express his opinions and feelings without being rude.

Q 47 오지 전보에 대한 교사의 태도 — 2019년 구상형

After reading the situation, 1) Describe whether you want to apply "transfer to 함경도" or not with reasons, 2) Regardless of the situation, discuss what attitudes you will have towards the transfer to the remote place.

> It has been three years since we were reunified with North Korea. 함경도 has experienced a shortage of English teachers.

전공영어 2차 수업실연

예상답안

한국어

1) 전보 신청을 한다.
   - 국민의 교육 기본권을 실현을 책임진 교사로서 특히 취약지역에 정의로운 차등이 적용되어야 한다고 생각하는 교육철학에 입각해서 한다.
   - 가정배경이 다르고 지역이 다르고 배움의 속도가 달라도 모든 학생에게 교육이 희망이 될 수 있도록 한다.
   - 남북통일을 이루어가는 시점에 기여하고 싶어서 한다.

2) 마음가짐
   - 단 한 명의 학생도 포기하지 않는 책임 교육을 한다는 마음으로 통일시대에 교육이 도움이 될 수 있도록 한다.
   - 경청, 공감, 존중하는 마음으로 신뢰관계를 형성한다.
   - 소통하고 협력하면 이룰수 있다는 마음을 가진다.
   - 새로운 환경에서 도전을 이겨내면서 더 성장하고 싶어서 한다.

영어   I would like to apply for the transfer to 함경도. As a school teacher, I want to follow the principle that every child has the fundamental right of learning. Especially, the children in a remote place should have the same fair amount of education. Education can make it difference to anyone, even though all the students come from different background, place, and level of learning. I also want to challenge myself and grow to be a better person in a new and difficult environment.

I have the strong opinion towards this offer. I should not give up one single student. I want to contribute myself to make the era of reunification. I should build up trust with empathy, attention and respect. If we share and cooperate to each other, I believe that we can achieve anything.

Q 48 성실한 교사 vs 교수방법이 좋은 교사 선택   2019년 즉답형

1. Among the two teachers as below, choose one teacher with integrity and describe the teacher from your experiences.
2. Discuss your chosen teacher in terms of the role and responsibility.
3. If you have to do cooperative teaching, which teacher would you do with?

> Teacher A does not get along with other teachers. He doesn't do research on the materials but is good at improvisation and flamboyant speaking skills. So, his class has popularity from the students. Teacher B has a good relationship with other teachers. He does sincere research on the lesson materials but is not popular among students because of the boring teaching methods.

예상답안

한국어   성실성의 측면에서 B교사를 선택했다. B교사는 수업 준비도 열심히 하고 교사 공동체 안에서 잘 협력하지만 경험의 부족이나 기술적인 면의 부족으로 수업전반에 있어서 학생들의 호응도를 끌어내지는 못하고 있다. B교사는 상호작용이 없는 교사중심의 진도 나가기 식 수업이나 학생의 요구나 특성을 고려하지 못한 수업을 진행하여 지루하고 단편적인 지식만 전달하고 끝나는 수업이나 피상적 이해에 끝나는 수업을 진행할 수 가 있다. 그래서 협력수업을 하게 될 때는 A교사를 선택하여 A교사의 도움을 받을 수 있다. A교사는 학생의 특성, 능력,

요구나 부족함등을 잘 이해하고 상호작용을 잘 진행할 수 있다. 상호 보완적인 측면으로 두 교사가 힘을 합하면 함께 성장할 수 있는 기회가 될 수 있다고 생각한다.

영어 In terms of integrity, I will choose teacher B. Teacher B is a hard worker to prepare his lessons and cooperate in teachers' community, even though he has a lack of experiences and skills and doesn't get students' satisfaction. Teacher B might lead a boring lesson since he has no interaction between students and delivers lecture-based teaching without considering the students' needs and characteristics. If I have to do a cooperative teaching, I have to choose teacher A. Teacher A understands the students' needs, levels, lacks and characteristics to cooperate with them. The two teachers can work together to complement to each other by compensating for their weaknesses.

Q 49 미래를 위한 혁신 교육 2019년 구상형

After reading the passage below, 1) Describe your thoughts and the rationales according to your educational viewpoints; Which one can give better teaching, a human teacher or a robot instructor? 2) Describe how you guide the students to grow into a well-developed human being.

> With the 4th Industrial Revolution, the development in technology is expected to bring a relatively big change to school education. Recently, the interactive robot came out. In addition, a robot can be a substitute for a teacher to do a lesson. While some teachers welcome the change, others are concerned that the school system would collapse in no time.

예상답안

한국어 미래를 준비하는 학교혁신의 교육은 교사가 담당할 수 있다.
1) 혁신되어가는 기술은 어떤 수준의 사람이 어디에서, 어떻게 사용하느냐에 따라서 달라질 것이다. 기술의 발전이 축복이기보다는 재앙이 될 수 있다. 2) 계산능력과 정보처리능력에서 탁월한 능력을 보이는 교육로봇 역시 교육받고 경험있는 교사의 통제 아래 있을 때 모든 학생의 잠재력을 최대한 발휘하게하고, 더불어 살아가는 공동체에 기여하는 삶을 가꾸는 교육에 기여 할 수 있다. 아이들은 성장 단계에 맞는 사회적 관계 맺기가 필요한데 학교는 아이들에게 이런 것들을 제공해 줄 수 있는 총체적인 삶의 장이다.

영어 I believe that the teacher should be responsible for the next generation to prepare the 4th industrial revolution. First of all, the changing technology will be dramatically different depending on who, how or where it is used. Otherwise, the development in technology can not be a blessing, but a disaster. Second, a robot instructor needs to be under control of a trained and experienced teacher. Even though the robot is apt at calculation and information processing, the most important thing is the students' well-being and well-rounded education to live together in the community.

전공영어 2차 수업실연

Q 50 공동체 생활을 위한 협력적 교실 문화
2019년 구상형

There are some students who have no interest in class work and participation in group work. They are usually egocentric, without showing any interests in group issues. Discuss how you can organize interaction and cooperation under the circumstances in FOUR ways.

학급 일에 관심이 없고 모둠활동 참여에 소극적인 학생들이 많다. 또한, 자기 일에만 관심이 있으며 공동의 일에 관심이 없다. 이러한 교실에 소통과 협력적 교실문화를 어떻게 만들 것인지 4가지를 말하시오.

예상답안

한국어 공동체 생활을 위한 협력적 교실 문화를 형성하기 위해서 몇가지 방법을 제안할 수 있다. 첫째, 학생자치활동을 활성화하도록 한다. 학생이 주도하는 아침조회를 실시하거나, 학생이 만드는 학급규칙을 명시화하거나, 정기적인 학급회의를 개최하여 소통하고 협력하는 태도를 배워나갈 수 있다. 둘째, 1인 1역의 활성화를 도모한다. 그 안에서 학생들은 협력적 인성과 책임감을 높여갈 수 있다. 셋째, 학급문화와 예술 활동을 장려한다. 음악, 미술, 문예창작을 할 수 있는 시간을 마련하여 학급이 함께 성취할 수 있는 문화를 만들어 나간다. 함께 문화를 창작하면서 심미적 감수성이나 협력적 인성을 함양할 수 있다. 마지막으로, 학급봉사활동을 함께 해나갈 수 있다. 작은 봉사활동이더라도 그 안에서 보람을 찾고 봉사의 가치, 공동체 의식, 민주시민의식, 협력적 인성 체득할 수 있게 될 것이다.

영어 I can suggest some ways to design a cooperative class culture to live together as one community. First, self-regulated activities for students should be promoted. For example, they can organize a class gathering once a week or hold a regular class meeting to learn how to interact and cooperate. Second, each student can be given one role in class. Students can develop cooperative attitudes and responsibility doing the role. Third, class culture and arts activities should be recommended. Students can participate in music, fine arts, or creative writing to develop class culture that all the classmates can cooperate. Lastly, students can do a volunteer work all together. They can find a value of volunteering, a sense of community, or cooperative attitudes while working together.

Q 51 교육과정에서 꿈, 인성교육, 진로교육을 위한 지도방안
2019년 구상형

After finishing the National College Entrance exam, describe how to instruct the 3rd grade of high school students to develop their dreams, talents, creative education, or career training.

예상답안

한국어 첫째, 대학수학능력시험 이후 입시 위주의 수업으로 인해 소홀했던 진로 교육, 독서활동, 교양강좌 등의 활동을 실시하여 다양한 학습 경험을 제공하고자 한다. 둘째, 학생이 배움의 주제가 되어 스스로 선택하고 경험하는 다양한 교육 기회 제공을 통한 학생 중심의 교육을 실현하고자 한다. 학생이 이끌어가는 학습 경험의 기회를 제공하여 주도적 진로 설계 역량을 함양하고자 한다. 셋째, 지역사회의 다채로운 문화사업과 지역교육공동체에서 구축한 사업을 학교 교육활동과 적극 연계하여 학생들의 성장을 지원하도록 한다. 교내외에서 실행 가능한 체험활동 프로그램을 운영하되 지역사회와 협력하여 체험활동 안전망을 구축하도록 한다.

영어 First, after finishing the National College Entrance exam, students can participate in new curriculum, such as career training, reading literature, or cultural studies. Second, students can be the owner of learning to choose and learn various types of educational experiences. Students can plan and design their own curriculum they need in future. The experience-based learning can help them to apply their learning to real life immediately. Third, some of local community plans can be associated with the school educational activities. Students have a chance to experience real-life activities in a safe atmosphere.

Q 52. 다문화 가정학생의 문제점과 해결책 — 2018년 구상형

Through the counseling sessions, a homeroom teacher realized that the student A had been going through hard times during the school life. Identify the TWO reasons student A had a problem and suggest the solutions related to the problem based on the passage below.

> Student A is from a multi-cultural family, who has settled in Korea not long ago. Student A is not familiar with Korean culture and Korean language. In addition, he usually takes longer to warm up to new people and unfamiliar situations. He has a rather delicate and shy personality, which has difficulty to get along with the classmates.

예상답안

한국어 친구들과 어울리지 못하는 학교부적응 상태를 다음과 같이 원인 분석할 수 있다. 첫째, 한국문화와 한국어를 잘 모른다. 둘째, 개인적 성향으로 소극적인 성향을 가지고 있다. 해결책으로 한국문화와 한국어에 서투른 것이 문제이므로 방과후 학습을 통해 언어능력향상 프로그램, 문화적응 프로그램을 활용한 한국문화 및 한국어 학습기회를 제공할 수 있다. 조금 더 큰 프로젝트로 학교에 오지 않는 토요일을 이용하여 근교의 문화체험학습 등을 함께할 수 있다. 또한 학생을 잘 이해할 수 있는 그들 고국 출신 대학생 멘토를 연계하여 기초학습, 학생 전화상담, 체험학습을 통해 긍정적인 정체성을 확립할 수 있도록 한다. 또한 학생이 다른 학생들과 차별화하여 잘하는 것을 이용하여 다른 학생들을 가르쳐 주는 시간등을 마련하여 존재감을 부각시키면 자신감과 자아확립에 도움이 될 것이다.

영어 The student's state of maladjustment in school can be explained as below: First of all, he is not familiar with Korean culture and Korean language. Second, he has an introverted personality, which makes a bit difficult to adjust to new place and new people. So, we can suggest some solution for the student. First, if he could improve his Korean language level, he could communicate about their daily lives with his Korean classmates. So, we can provide some of after school programs to support for Korean language and Korean culture awareness. Or, we can prepare the weekend field trip to explore Korean culture in our neighborhood. In addition, if possible, we can introduce the college mentors from the same home country. They can understand the student's difficulties better than us. They can regularly counsel with the student about school lives, academic difficulties and etc to develop their self-identity in Korea.

Q 53. 학습자 중심을 위한 교사의 자질

2018년 구상형

Below is the students' responses towards the Mr. Kim's lesson. Answer each questions for the students' problems as below.

1) Suggest the Mr. Kim's quality as a teacher.
2) Discuss your efforts to be prepared with the quality.
3) If you become a teacher, what would be your plans in the future?

- Our teacher does not give fair attention to all the students in class.
- I get stressed out with the students who don't participate in group work.
- Project work is interesting but I don't know what I learned after class.
- Self-directed learning takes lots of effort. I wish our teacher gave the lesson with exam-oriented content.

예상답안

한국어 첫째, 김 교사에게 필요한 자질은 학습자 중심의 수업을 위하여 다양한 학생들의 피드백을 성찰하면서 자신의 수업을 어떻게 개선해야 학생들의 삶과 관련된 핵심역량을 길러줄 수 있을지 고민해야 할 것이다. 둘째, 본인은 이러한 자질을 갖추기 위해 지금까지 대학수업, 교생실습, 교육 봉사등의 동아리 활동을 통하여 계속 노력해 왔다. 마지막으로 교사가 된 후 그러한 자질을 갖추기 위한 계 으로 우선 배움이 즐거운 교육과정 수업과 평가의 일체화의 관점을 가질 필요가 있었다. 영어교과의 성취기준을 고려한 학생 참여형과 협력형 수업 능력을 갖추려고 노력할 것이며 학생들의 성장과 발달 과정에 초점을 둔 과정중심 평가가 필요할 것이다. 학생중심의 수업능력 함양을 위한 전문적 학습공동체에 적극적인 참여를 하려고 계획하고 있다. 그를 위해서 학생과 수업나눔의 시간을 가지고, 수업성찰, 수업협의, 공개수업 나눔 시간을 통해 수업에 대한 공동설계, 실천, 평가, 개선할 수 있도록 해야 할 것이다.

영어 First, Mr. Kim should raise awareness on how to improve his lesson for student-oriented learning and how to develop the students' core competencies related to the students' lives. Second, I've made efforts to be a good teacher through participating a various activities such as community volunteer work, school sports club, school mentoring program and etc. When I become a teacher, I have some plans to achieve this. Above all, curriculum and evaluation should be consistent and appealing to the students to become students-oriented learning. I will prepare for students-oriented and collaborative learning based on Achievement Standards and will implement process-based evaluation to evaluate the students learning process. Lastly, I have a plan to participate the professional learning community to improve my skills in managing the students-oriented learning. I also want to share my previous lessons with my students and support my lesson with reflection notes, lesson consulting, open class and etc.

Q 54 학생성적을 교원평가에 반영하는 것에 대한 찬반의견 2018년 구상형

Below is a part of Mr. Choi's teaching journal. Read and discuss the questions.
1) Discuss your view of humanity.
2) Explain the reasons you agree or disagree with the opinions of Mr. Park with some rationals.

> In some foreign countries, teacher evaluation includes the students' achievement in school grades. Based on this, Mr. Park claims that we need to include the students' school grades in the teacher evaluation system. But I cannot agree with that. If we adopt this system, the teacher would be treated just as a exam scorer. Students should be educated to grow up a well-rounded human being.

예상답안

한국어 첫째, 학생에 대한 인간관으로 학생은 자율적이며, 책임을 가질지 알며, 무한한 잠재력을 가진, 지정의가 종합된 존재이며 개개인의 실존적 경험을 바탕으로 삶을 가꾸어가는 존재이다. 따라서 학교교육의 임무는 학생의 개성을 존중해주고, 학생이 전인적 발달의 주인공이 될 수 있도록 자기 주도적이고 협력적인 배움의 환경을 제공해서, 학생들이 4차 혁명시대를 주도적으로 살아갈 수 있는 바른 인성을 갖춘 창의융합인재로 커나가게 하는 것이다. 그리고 교사는 입시위주의 교육에서 벗어나 모든 학생이 실제 학력, 즉, 4차 산업혁명 시대가 요구하는 삶의 역량을 갖출 수 있도록 돕는 조언자 혹은 안내자가 되어야 한다. 둘째, 학생 성적 결과를 교원 평가에 반영해야 한다는 박 교사의 의견에 반대한다. 박교사가 가지고 있는 학력관은 과거 산업발전을 위해 학력에만 초점을 맞춘 입시위주의 교육관에 머물러 있다. 그것은 실제 학생의 삶과 동떨어져 있어서 학생의 내적 동기를 불러일으키지 못하는 단편지식을 암기하는 입시위주의 교육을 강화한다. 이러한 산업화 시대의 교육관으로 4차 산업혁명 시대가 요구하는 바른 인성을 갖춘 창의융합인재를 길러내기는 어려울 것이다.

영어 First, the students are one independent, responsible and capable human being, who live a life based on their experiences. The school needs to respect the students' personality, provides the independent and cooperative atmosphere, and help students become a person with convergence talents and good attitudes. For the student to become an independent human being, the teacher needs to be a guide or facilitator to support them to be prepared for the era of 4th industrial revolution. Second, I don't agree with the Mr. Park's. His viewpoint of teaching remains the past, when entrance exam was the most important educational value for industrial development. The education didn't intrinsically motivate the students but just enhanced entrance exam to encourage fragmented knowledge.

Q 55 융합 교육과정을 위한 협업의 필수 요건 　　　2018년 즉답형

다음은 융합교육과정을 만들기 위한 상황에 대한 글이다. 다음 지문을 읽고 아래 항목들을 설명하시오.
1) 내가 연구부장이라면 왜 그러한 행동을 하였는지 연구부장의 입장에서 설명하시오.
2) 교사가 협업을 할 때, 연구부장에게 필요한 측면을 바람직한 교사의 인성적 자질, 태도의 측면에서 설명하시오.
3) 위와 같은 상황이라면, 최 교사가 보여야 할 태도에 대해 설명하시오.

> 융합교육과정을 만들기 위해서 두 교과의 두 교사가 함께 일을 하게 되었다. 연구부장인 교사는 신임교사 최 교사의 의견을 묻지 않고 의사결정을 내릴 때가 많다. 이에 최 교사는 자신의 의견을 묻지 않는 것에 서운하면서도 연구부장 교사가 부담이 될까봐 질문조차 하지 못하고 있는 상황이다.

예상답안

한국어 첫째, 연구부장의 입장에서 신임교사의 의견을 묻지 않고 의사결정을 내렸다면 몇 가지 이유가 있을 거라 생각된다. 신임교사의 능력에 대한 저평가가 첫째 원인이 될 것이다. 신임교사는 경험과 전문성이 부족하여 교육과정에 대한 타당한 견해를 갖기에는 역부족이라고 판단했기 때문에 의견 수립 과정을 생략하고 신속하게 일을 처리하려고 했을 것이다. 또한 시간이 부족했을 것이다. 과목을 책임지는 연구부장 교사로서 다양한 행정업무가 많다 보니 의견을 조정할 시간이 없어 의견수렴 과정을 생략했을 것이다. 둘째, 협업을 위해 연구부장에게 필요한 자질과 태도는 무엇보다도 구성원에 대한 존중이 요구된다. 존중은 신뢰하는 관계를 구축하여 활발한 의사소통과 협력을 가능하게 하는 핵심 요소이기 때문이다. 그리고 학교 구성원의 의견을 충분히 수렴하는 태도가 중요하다. 학교는 미래의 민주시민을 길러내는 곳이기에 민주적 조직 (부서) 운영이 무엇보다 중요하다. 그래서 민주적인 조직 운영의 핵심은 의사결정 과정에 모든 구성원을 참여시키는 것이므로 단독적으로 의사결정을 하게 되면 구성원이 수동적이 되고, 불만이 발생할 수 있다. 허용적인 분위기를 조성해서 누구나 자유롭게 의견을 제시하여 최선의 의사결정이 되도록 해야 한다. 셋째, 어려운 입장이지만 신임교사, 최 교사가 보여야 할 태도는 자신의 입장을 솔직하게 표현해서 협업을 이끌어낼 수 있는 태도가 중요하다. 대화의 방식으로 자신의 의견을 표현하고, 구체적인 목표를 공유하고, 적절한 과제분담과 역할분담이 주어질 수 있도록 한다. 또한 이러한 과정이 어렵지만 개인적인 성장과 집단지성의 힘을 경험하는 계기로 삼는다면 신임교사가 미래 연구부장의 위치에 있을 때 훌륭하게 임무를 수행해 갈 수 있을 것이다.

영어 First, from the side of the head teacher, there would be some reasons. He wouldn't trust the capabilities of the new appointed teacher. Since the new teacher has a lack of experiences and expertise, he might pass the cooperation processes to expedite the plan. Or due to running out of the time, he could pass all the cooperation processes. Second, the head teacher needs to respect each member to work together. Above all, he needs to accept any critical ideas of the teachers, which is a value of democratic society, since the school is a place to bring up the democratic citizens in future. The core value of democratic organization is to involve all the members. If the head teacher makes a decision on his own, the fellow teachers would become passive in any tasks to lead to complaints. Permissive atmosphere will help them to speak out their ideas freely to result in the best resolution. Lastly, the newly appointed teacher, Mr. Choi, could have a candid conversation with the head teacher to bring up cooperation although it is not an easy job to do. He could express his stance towards the problem, share some suggestions, and say that he would be willing to share any tasks or roles. To Mr. Choi, this could be an opportunity to experience the personal growth and collective intellectuals to lay a cornerstone to become a fine head teacher in near future.

Q 56 교사의 혁신방법의 어려움   2017년 구상형

Analyze the reasons why the teacher Kim fails to innovate his class based on ⟨A⟩. Suggest the THREE solutions regarding the problem.

⟨A⟩ "The authority of those who teach is often an obstacle to those who want to learn."
— Cicero

⟨Situation⟩
Teacher Kim is very passionate about teaching. He has always studied and researched for better teaching methods. And his colleague teachers complimented all his efforts for the students. However, it turned out that his performance report was not satisfactory. He was shocked to know that his students were not satisfied with his class on a general term. The students actively participated in group activity, engaged in the class, and as a result, they achieved the lesson goals. He had still been in distress and disbelief that what the problems were.

예상답안

Teacher Kim tries to innovate his class a lot but fails to get much satisfaction from the students. I believe the main reason for his failure is that he couldn't let go of his authority as a teacher. I doubt he ever asked his students what they really want to learn. To solve this problem, I'd suggest the following three measures. First of all, he should start from the students' needs. That is, he needs to find out what the students want and need to learn. He may conduct needs analysis and base his class entirely on what the students need to learn. Secondly, he should cooperate with other teachers and get advice from them. It might be difficult from he himself to see his problems. He can ask peer teachers, especially senior teachers to sit in his class and monitor it, or he can participate in some club to discuss class ideas with other teachers. Lastly, he can give the students some choices. It is natural that people become satisfied when they are given a choice. Through such classes as project work, teacher Kim can let the students choose what they want to learn, how they want to learn, or how they want to be evaluated, and thus increase their satisfaction about his class.

Q 57 미래 역량 발전시키는 방법   2017년 구상형

Based on the belief of 'I' in ⟨A⟩, identify how valid the statement of ⟨B⟩ is. Suggest TWO pedagogical methods in order to develop the 'future core competencies' in ⟨B⟩.

⟨A⟩ I believe that the students have their own right to choose what to wear in school.
⟨B⟩ I believe that it is important to develop 'future core competencies'. In the future, this is not just to accumulate knowledge but apply the knowledge in real life. Many advanced countries have already adopted the education innovations in many areas.

예상답안

The question about whether school students can choose what they want to wear is related to the future core competencies. I believe the question is closely related to self-regulation. If the students have a right to choose what they want to wear, it can be a little start to improve their self-management skills and critical thinking ability. As they are given choices, they might be responsible for the consequences of their behavior and actions accordingly.

To improve future core competencies, I would suggest the following two methods. First, it is to implement a project class. In this class, students make a decision the topic they want to research and come to their own conclusion based on their experiences and research. Through the process, they will able to develop their self-management skills. Second method is implement a real life, authentic task. By participating in real-life tasks, they will be able to apply their knowledge to the task and improve the problem solving skills.

Q 58 교과지도와 창의적 체험활동 지도 측면에서 교육관 *2017년 즉답형*

A: 교사가 적극적으로 개입하여 학생의 변화를 이끌어 내야 함
B: 학생들이 스스로 변화할 수 있도록 기다려야 함

예상답안

저는 B에 나타난 교사관이 더 바람직하다고 생각합니다. 왜냐하면 A에서 말한대로 교사가 적극적으로 개입해서 학생들을 변화시키는 것이 가능하다면 A가 맞지만 사실 이것은 불가능하기 때문입니다. 학생들은 학생들만의 존재이고, 따라서 교사의 역할은 학생들의 성장을 지원하는 조력자에 그친다고 생각합니다.

B 교사관을 실현하기 위해 교과지도 측면에서 저는 먼저 포트폴리오 평가 방식을 사용하고 싶습니다. 포트폴리오는 학생들이 수행한 과제들을 모두 모아놓은 작품집이기 때문에 학생들의 성장을 가장 잘 보여준다고 생각합니다. 다음으로 B 교사관을 실현하기 위해 창의적 체험활동 측면에서는 연극 수업을 꼭 진행해보고 싶습니다. 대학교 때 연극 동아리 활동을 했었는데, 연극만큼 협동이 필요한 작업이 없다고 생각했고, 교사가 되면 꼭 한번 학생들과 해보고 싶었습니다. 협동을 통해 작품을 무대에 올리는 과정에서 학생들이 많이 배울 수 있다고 생각합니다.

Q 59 어려움과 해결방안 *2017년 추가질문*

위에서 본인이 선택한 교직관을 따랐을 때 예상되는 어려움과 이를 극복하기 위한 방안을 제시하시오.

예상답안

B 교사관을 따르기 위해서는 많은 인내심이 필요하다고 생각합니다. 생각대로 학생들이 변화해주지 못할 때 큰 좌절감을 느낄 것이기 때문입니다. 저는 이 어려움을 극복하기 위해서는 먼저 학생들의 어려움을 파악하는 것이 필요하다고 생각합니다. 모든 학생들은 성장하고 싶어합니다. 그들이 그러지 못할 때에는 이유가 있을 것이라고 생각합니다. 예를 들어, 공부를 잘하고 싶지만 공부하는 방법을 모를 수도 있고, 친구들의 관계로 어려움을 겪고 있을 수도 있으며, 심각하게는 가정 폭력에 시달리고 있을 수도 있습니다. 저는 자주 학생들과 상담하고 얘기하여 학생들이 가진 어려움들을 파악하고 해결해주기 위해 노력할 것입니다.

Q 60 수업의 문제점 개선방법 2016년 구상형

Identify two problems of Mr. Park and the solutions based on the situation below.

> Mr. Park (less experienced teacher), and Mr. Kim (experienced teacher) teach the students of the same grade with cooperation. Not like Mr. Kim, Mr. Park has difficulty keeping up with class schedule of the academic year and has not completed the assigned units before the midterm exam. While the students of Mr. Kim are satisfied with the lesson, the students of Mr. Park complain about their lesson, saying that they don't understand contents and main points.

예상답안

(1) Problem 1: Difficulty managing class schedule and pacing
- Problem: Mr. Park is falling behind the academic calendar and has not finished the assigned units before the midterm exam. This creates inconsistency and affects students' preparation.
- Solution: Mr. Park can collaborate more closely with Mr. Kim to align lesson pacing, create a shared unit plan with clear checkpoints, and use time-management strategies (e.g., prioritizing core content, setting weekly goals). Observing Mr. Kim's class could also help him see how to balance depth with pacing.

(2) Problem 2: Students' lack of understanding and dissatisfaction
- Problem: Students complain they do not grasp the content or main points, suggesting that Mr. Park's explanations and lesson delivery are unclear or not sufficiently scaffolded.
- Solution: Mr. Park should focus on clearer lesson objectives, provide summaries of main points, and use more scaffolding techniques such as guided practice, visual aids, or formative checks (e.g., quick quizzes, comprehension checks). Feedback from students can also guide him to adjust teaching methods to better meet their needs.

Q 61 교사의 사명감과 역량 2016년 구상형

다음과 같은 상황에서 필요한 교사의 사명감에 대해 말하고, 이 교사에게 필요한 역량을 교과지도와 생활지도 측면에서 한 가지씩 말하시오.

> 상황1. A교사는 개별적으로 학생들을 신경 쓰지 않고 집단적으로만 신경 쓴다.
> 상황2. 문제를 잘 푸는 학생이든 그렇지 않은 학생이든 한 반에서 섞인채로 수업한다.
> 상황3. 문제행동을 하는 학생만 신경을 쓰다 보니 조용한 학생들이 소외감을 느낀다.

예상답안

(1) 교사의 사명감

교사는 모든 학생을 균형 있게 지도해야 할 책임과 사명감을 가지고 있다. 특정 학생에게만 관심을 집중하거나 집단만을 고려한 수업 운영은 학생 개개인의 성장을 저해할 수 있다. 따라서 교사는 개별 학생을 존중하고, 교과와 생활 양 측면에서 균형 잡힌 지도를 실천해야 한다.

(2) 교과지도 측면의 필요 역량과 생활지도 측면의 필요 역량
- 먼저, 교사의 사명감은 학급 내 모든 학생이 소외되지 않고 자신의 잠재력을 발휘하도록 돕는 데 있다. 이는 학생 개개인을 존중하고, 학습과 생활을 균형 있게 지도하는 태도라 할 수 있다.
- 교과지도 측면에서의 역량은 개별화 수업 설계 능력이다. 수준이 다른 학생들이 한 반에 섞여 있는 상황에서, 교사는 난이도 조절 과제나 차별화된 학습 자료를 제공하여 모든 학생이 학습 성취를 경험할 수 있도록 지도해야 한다.
- 생활지도 측면에서의 역량은 관계 형성과 상담 역량이다. 문제행동 학생뿐만 아니라 조용한 학생, 눈에 띄지 않는 학생에게도 긍정적 피드백과 개별적 관심을 제공하여 모든 학생이 교사로부터 존중받는다고 느끼도록 해야 한다.
- 결국 교사는 학생 개개인의 다양성과 특성을 존중하는 사명감을 바탕으로, 수업에서는 맞춤형 지도를, 생활지도에서는 관계 형성을 통해 학급 모두가 성장할 수 있도록 이끌어야 한다. 이러한 균형 잡힌 지도가 진정한 교사의 역할이 될 것이다.

Q 62 벌점 부과에 따른 학생 지도 — 2016년 구상형

교복지도에 있어 A교사는 엄격하게 규칙을 적용하여 벌을 부과하고 B교사는 학생이 스스로 행동을 고칠 수 있도록 지도한다. 어느 교사를 선호하는가, 그리고 그 이유가 무엇인가요?

> A: 규칙에 따라서 어긴 학생들에게 벌점을 준다.
> B: 마구 벌점을 주지 않고 학생들이 스스로 규칙을 깨닫도록 한다.

예상답안

B교사의 방식을 더 선호하는 이유는 학생 지도의 궁극적인 목표는 단순히 규칙 준수가 아니라, 학생이 스스로 책임감을 갖고 행동을 개선하도록 돕는 것이기 때문이다.

- 첫째, 자율성과 내적 동기를 기를 수 있다. 단순한 벌점보다는 스스로 잘못을 깨닫고 행동을 고치는 과정에서 학생들은 자기 주도적인 태도를 배우게 된다.
- 둘째, 교사-학생 관계 개선에 효과적이다. 벌점 위주의 지도는 학생에게 반발심을 키울 수 있지만, 대화와 지도는 신뢰를 쌓고 긍정적인 관계를 유지할 수 있다.
- 셋째, 장기적 생활지도 효과를 기대할 수 있다. 벌점은 순간적인 제재에 그치지만, 스스로 규칙을 지키는 습관은 생활 전반에서 지속적으로 이어질 수 있다.
- 결론적으로, 규칙은 분명히 중요하지만 지도는 학생 스스로 깨닫고 행동을 변화시키는 방향으로 나아가는 것이 더 교육적이라고 생각한다.

Q 63 협동 학습
2016년 즉답형

> 학생들이 협동학습을 해야 하는 상황이다. 하지만 학생 B가 자신의 조원들과 협동하지 않고 독자적으로 과제를 해 와서 발표를 하겠다고 한다.
>
> 1. 협동학습의 의미가 무엇인가?
> 2. B학생이 왜 저러한 행동을 보인다고 생각하는가?
> 3. 만약 자신이 해당 교사라면 B학생에게 발표할 기회를 주겠는가?

예상답안

1. 협동학습은 다양한 강점을 지닌 학생들이 서로 협동하여 공동의 과제물을 만드는 과정이다.
2. 공동체 의식의 부재, 배려심 부족, 이기적인 생각일 수 있으나 동시에 협동 학습을 해 본 경험이 없어서 협동학습에서 오는 장점을 이해하지 못하고 있을 것이다.
3. B학생에게 발표의 기회를 줄 것이다. B학생이 혼자서 열심히 준비를 하였고 만약 발표의 기회를 주지 않는다면 학습동기를 꺾을 수 있기 때문이다. 하지만 개별점수에는 반영하지 않을 것이다. 그리고 협동학습의 중요성과 의의를 설명하고 이후에 협동학습에 잘 참여하도록 격려한다면 B학생도 이후에는 협동학습에 참여하게 될 것이다.

Q 64 교사의 벌로 상처받은 학생 문제 해결
2015년 구상형

Suggest FOUR methods in this situation. You are the homeroom teacher of the student called Sumi. You want to solve the problem that Sumi goes through.

> Sumi often takes a specific class off and instead go to a nursing room saying that she is not well. But it has already been fourth time this month. I asked her the reason. According to her, Mr. Park, a writing teacher, gave her the harsh comment, "Didn't you say that your writing skill is good? But is this all you can do?" The classmates of her thought that the teacher's comments were somewhat funny but at the same time they were too cruel.

예상답안

1) 학생과 individual counseling을 통해 정확한 이유를 파악한다.
2) 학생이 writing에 관심이 많으므로, writing skill을 향상시킬 수 있는 자료를 더 제공해 준다.
3) 학급 전체를 대상으로, 교사의 teaching styles와 그로부터 상처받은 다른 학생이 없는 지를 파악한다.
4) Park 교사에게 공손히 학생들의 감정을 전달해주고 다른 방식의 교수 방식 제안한다.

합격을 위한 TIP

1번과 2번은 영어문제로 3번과 4번은 한국어문제로 발표하는 방식입니다. 한 반에 30명씩 배치되었어요. 평가실에는 심사위원 세 분의 책상과 마주보고 수험생의 책상이 있습니다. 여자선생님 한분, 남자선생님 두 분이었는데 제가 답변을 하면 중간 중간 고개를 끄덕여 주셨고 우호적인 분위기였어요.

Q 65 협동하지 못하는 학생 문제 해결 2015년 구상형

What would you say to Minsu if he were present in front of you? Counsel with Minsu in the following situation.

> Sunwoo got his leg injured riding an motorbike. He was hospitalized for a while and back to the school on crutches. The class members got a class meeting to decide to help him. All the classmates take turns to pick him up from his home and take him back after school on the schedule.
>
> Minsu "Tomorrow is a day when I have to take care of Sunwoo. But our final exam is coming soon. And I have no enough time to study but even have to help Sunwoo. So, to be frankly, I don't want to help Sunwoo at the moment. What do I have to do?"

> **Conditions**
> (1) Understand and empathize with Minsu.
> (2) Persuade him with "a sense of community" or "consideration of others".
> (3) Guide Minsu to voluntarily help Sunwoo.

예상답안

1) empathy를 한다. 열심히 한 것을 인정하고 이번 시험을 학생이 얼마나 중요하게 여기는 지를 공감해 준다.
2) 다른 학생들이 injured student을 도와주는 데 모두 열심히 participate & cooperate하고 있음을 이야기한다.
3) 다른 학생들과 순서를 바꿔 보자고 제안해 보는 것은 어떨까?
4) 그것이 여의치 않다면 다른 방식으로 생각해 보자 (네가 이번에 도움을 주면 다음 번 네가 어려움에 처했을 때 도움을 받을 수도 있을 것이다. 삶은 혼자 사는 것이 아니기에 이번 일을 통해서, 서로 돕고 사는 것의 중요성을 느껴보는 것도 좋을 것 같다)

Q 66 학생 문제 상담 2015년 구상형

생활지도에 힘쓰고 있던 윤 교사는 자신의 교사일지를 보다가 다음과 같은 상황을 돌이켜 보았다. 윤 교사에게 필요한 역량을 제시하라.

> **교사일지**
> - A가 계속 무단결석을 했다. A가 무단결석을 하는 상황까지 오도록 하지 않을 순 없었을까
> - 우울증을 가진 학생이 있어서 그 학생을 돕기 위해 혼자 전문서적을 읽었지만, 제대로 문제를 해결하지 못했다.
> - 나는 학생들 앞에서 감정을 숨기고 언행을 조심히 한다고 했는데, 아이들이 나에게 거리감을 둔다.

예상답안

1) 아이들의 사소한 고민도 정확히 파악하도록 평소에 상담을 자주해야 한다.
2) 전문적 상담 스킬을 높이려 교사연수 프로그램을 활용해야 한다 + 선배교사의 조언 구해 실천한다.
3) 감정을 아예 드러내지 않는 것은 좋은 태도가 아니다. 학생과의 진정한 소통을 위해 노력한다. (떡볶이 파티 or 운동장 캠핑)

Q 67 교학상장
2015년 구상형

강 교사는 자신의 능력을 계발하기 위해 힘쓰고 있지만, 이미 학생들을 가르치기에는 충분한 능력을 갖추었다고 생각한다. 다음은 강교사가 들은 한 강연의 일부이다. 강 교사에 대한 의견을 말하고, 당신이 원하는 교사상을 제시하라.

> 우리는 다 알고 있다고 생각하지만 ………… 이것이 바로 교학상장(教學相長)이다.

예상답안

1) 교학상장의 관점에서 보기의 교사의 마음가짐은 바람직하지 않아 보임
- 교사는 가르치면서 자신의 부족한 부분을 더 많이 발견하게 되며, 그를 통해 보다 더 완벽한 수준으로 도달할 수 있는 계기를 가져야 함
- 인생의 길을 함께하는 동반자로서, 학생과 함께 보다 더 발전돼 가는 마음가짐을 가지는 것이 중요함

2) 개인적인 교사상
- 학생들에게 안내자와 같은 교사가 되고 싶다.
- 학생을 보다 바른 길로 인도 하는 이정표가 되고 싶다.
- 교학상장의 의미에서 나 역시 학생과 함께 발전해 나가면서 그들을 보다 바른 길로 인도하고 싶다.

합격을 위한 TIP

강선생님이 자신은 학생을 가르치기에 충분하기 때문에 더 이상 공부할 필요가 없다고 생각하는 것이 문제로 보입니다. 그런데 그 아래 박스에 교학상장의 뜻이 제시되므로 배우는 일은 끝이 없으며, 가르쳐 보니 배우는게 더 중요하다고 느낀다고 생각합니다. 저는 이 박스의 내용이 강선생님이 처음에는 자신이 충분하다고 자만하였으나 나중엔 이렇게 생각이 바뀌었다고 이해하여, 강선생님의 바뀐 생각에 동감한다고 말했습니다. 그리고 이와 관련해 본인의 교직관을 말하는 것이었어요. 그런데 박스의 내용을 또 다른 교사의 생각으로 잘못 이해한 사람들도 있는 것 같습니다.

Q 68 Group Activity
2014년 구상형

Mr. Choi tries to use group activity in his English class. However, some students would not be willing to participate in the activity and rather avoid it. Discuss THREE methods you can make them participate.

예상답안

① Analyze students' needs, interests - utilize multimedia or learning materials - develop intrinsic motivation
② Grouping strategy - mixed levels: high and low ability Ss - participation with feedback or scaffolding
③ Awareness of the value of cooperation - develop individual accountability (eg) team leader, idea collector, reporter…

합격을 위한 TIP

제가 앉는 자리에 책상 따로 없고 의자만 있었어요. 의자에 앉은 자세에서 왼손에 구상지 들고 오른손으로 살짝살짝 제스추어 했어요. 구상지를 바짝 들어서 제 얼굴에 가져가지 않고 거의 무릎에 구상지 붙여서 했습니다. 의자에서 구상지 들고 하는 연습 미리 해 두시면 좋을 것 같아요.

Q 69 친구들과의 문제 해결
2014년 구상형

A student of yours, Minsu came up to you to talk about his problem with Nayoung. He asks you to change his seat in the class because she always talks to him even during the class hours and sometimes copy his homework to hand it out. You can start by empathizing with his feelings.

예상답안

"Minsu, You go through some difficult time with Nayoung. You know, I also had very similar experience as yours. I had a friend who talked to me in class time to make both of us punished. I got so irritated and angry with her. But, later I found out that she was a real kind and generous person. So I tried to help her with some homework and classwork. My teacher found it out and gave me a big compliment. You know, my school grade couldn't be better after that. Now, you are very worried that Nayoung copied your homework. I also heard that from some others. Let me talk to her that she wouldn't do it again. So from now on, you just enjoy your work and friends around you. Minsu, I really want to tell you how much I appreciate your courage to speak out your problems to me. So any time you're very welcome to talk to me."

합격을 위한 TIP

민영이가 문제점이 있다는 것을 알고 있지만 도와주면 오히려 너에게 도움이 될 수 있다는 점을 논리적으로 이해시키려고 했습니다.

Q 70 학교 생활에서의 책임감
2014년 구상형

Describe what you should do as a novice school teacher in school. Discuss from three points of class management, teaching, and administration.

예상답안

① Class management: Ss should have responsibility in class management. (eg) making class rules, checking class rolls, erasing blackboard…

② Teaching: S-centered class (eg) Project, Discussion teamwork…

③ Administration: Putting priority of importance, making balance between lesson preparation, counseling, administration, asking for advices from senior teachers

Q 71 Self-Study Room 사용   2014년 구상형

You have a responsibility to allot students to self-study room in school. However, the number of students is limited as the space is not enough for everyone. There are two choices, either using lottery system or according to financial needs. Describe which choice would be better for this case and why. After that, suggest TWO methods of using the self-study room more effectively.

예상답안

① For Ss with financial difficulty: Low economic-status family → opportunity to academic achievement, Pleasure of self study
② Effective Use
- Ss plan how to use, present the methods, manage in their Ss' community
- If extra room in school, change to self-study ones.

Q 72 수업중 교사에 반항하는 학생 지도 방법   2013년 구상형

Discuss FOUR measures you could take for the student who used the smart phone during the class. The student is very stubborn to insist not having used the smart phone wouldn't hand out the phone to the teacher, even though you said that you saw him using the phone during the class.

예상답안

① 문제학생을 개별적으로 데리고 나온다. 다른 친구들 앞에서는 영웅심리로 더 반항하고 좋지 않은 태도 취할 수 있기 때문이다.
② 학생에게 핸드폰을 하는 것을 분명히 봤다고 확실한 어조로 설명한다.
③ 학부모에게 도움을 요청하여 학교 등교시 스마트 폰을 소지하지 않도록 지도한다.
④ Disciplinary measure로서 봉사활동, reflection paper쓰라고 해서 반성할 기회를 준다.

Q 73 학생의 꿈과 부모의 직업이 다른 경우 부모 상담   2013년 구상형

A parent rings up to you to discuss about the conflict with her son. The student, Chulsu, wants to be a singer and the parents want him to be a public servant when he grows up. The mother asks you to make him give up his dream of being a singer and back to study. Suppose that you are the teacher in the situation. Decide which position you would take; either to tell the parent to support her son's dream or to dissuade him from becoming a singer as the parent wishes.

예상답안

① 우선은 학생이 원하는 singer가 되는 것을 supporting 해달라고 요청한다.
② 요즘에는 학생들의 specialty, talent, trait discovery하는 게 더 중요한 시대이다. 이미 학생은 talent를 찾았으니 더 발전시킬 수 있게 부모로서 도와주는 것이 우선이라고 생각한다.

③ public servant가 되도 아이가 원하는 삶이 아니면 즐거운 삶을 살 수가 없음을 인지하도록 한다.
④ 비용이 문제라면 after school을 통해 학교에서 배우고 지도가 가능하다. 많은 학교에서 outside instructor를 초청하여 전문적인 교육이 가능하기도 하다. 혹은 local community와 연계해서 program 참여하게 할 수 있다.

Q 74 학교업무운영에 대한 조언 — 2013년 구상형

Suppose that you are in the position of Mr. Kim and discuss the THREE measures what to do in this situation.

> ⟨Mr. Kim's Blog⟩
> I am a newly-employed teacher and go through a hard time in school. I'm so worried that I have no time for students' counseling and teaching preparation as there are pileup of administrative work and participation of teacher training and so on. I wanted to get some tips about this situation from my peer or senior teachers but they seem to be so busy and I'm afraid that they don't wanna be bothered by this.

예상답안

① experienced T, senior T에게 자문을 구할 수 있다. 경험 많고, 초임 때 나와 같은 상황을 겪었을 것이기 때문에 적절한 도움 줄 것이라고 생각된다.
② 방학이나 주말을 활용해 T-training program에 참여한다. 수업 후 시간을 이용할 수 있다. 수업연구나 학생상담 등의 시간으로 활용이 가능하다.
③ 쉬는 시간 등을 이용해 학생들이랑 rapport를 형성할 수 있다. 상담할 시간이 부족해도 학생들의 현재 상황을 체크 가능하고, 애정과 관심을 보여주고 친한 관계를 형성할 수 있다.

Q 75 이해하는 교사 vs 동등하게 대하는 교사 — 2013년 구상형

Which type of teacher do you want to become?
- Type A: Teacher who understands students
- Type B: Teacher who treats every student equally

Choose one of them and discuss the reasons of the choice and suggest what efforts you can make to become the type of teacher.

예상답안

교사 A를 선택한다.
- 이해하는 교사는 good rapport, good relationship 형성이 가능하다.
- 학생들을 이해해야 학생들의 specialty discovery 용이, 적절한 future job 제시 가능하다.
- director가 아니고 facilitator, helper라고 생각하기에 문제 상황 시 주저 없이 찾아와 조언 구하고 교사도 적절한 도움 줄 수 있다.

Q 76 'penalty point' 시행에 대한 원인과 해결책 제시   2012년 구상형

The 'Penalty Point System' is currently being implemented at your middle school. You found out that one student was passing by with abusing his friend verbally at the corridor. You reprimanded the student but he just uttered, "You can just give me penalty. I still have 10 points left to be used." without any hint of reflection on his conduct. Describe the two reasons why the 'Penalty Point System' is not effectively used at the school and discuss the measures to solve the problem.

예상답안

The penalty point system is not effectively implemented at the school because of the following reasons. First, the teacher is considered as a mere penalty point assignor to students. This means that the teacher fails to be a role-model for students, therefore, loses respect from them. Second, since students are forced to obey the school policy, they are neither autonomous nor responsible for their behaviors. To solve this problem, the teacher should take counsel with students whenever they get penalty points. As a way of expressing empathy, the teacher shows that they are willing to help them to improve their behavior. And this counseling system will make students accept their teachers as a respectful supporter rather than just a point giver. Moreover, students should be given opportunities for reflecting their misbehaviors. They may be assigned to write a reflection paper in reflection room whenever they get a penalty point. Through this alternation, students will be more autonomous and responsible for what they behave.

Q 77 남의 험담을 좋아하는 학생 상담   2012년 구상형

Student A has received a word of praise with good school report and manners. She, however, likes to gossip of others. She starts spreading the bad words about a newly appointed English teacher. You are supposed to counsel the student A. Consult with her using the criteria below.
1) Start discussing with the story that she would empathize with.
2) Counsel considering the part of student A
3) Explain with precision and easy to understand

예상답안

I actually had a similar experience with you when I was a middle school student. I had a very close friend, but we had a small trouble at the end of the semester. Instead of talking to each other, we talked to others about each other in bad ways. I never knew this would make our trouble worse. With the help of our homeroom teacher, we could finally talk to each other openly and understand each other's true feeling. What you are doing right now is not the right way to solve the problem with the new English teacher. Try to put yourself in her shoes. How would you feel? You would never feel good, would you? If you have complaints about her, you need to go and see her to talk about it. Otherwise, she never knows what you are thinking. I am sure that your new English teacher will listen to you and try to solve the problem with you.

합격을 위한 TIP

교사가 상담을 하는 상황이므로, 부드럽게 자신의 이야기로 시작하여 학생의 입장을 공감하는 것이 중요하다고 생각한다. 학생 A의 입장을 공감하고, 자세하고 구체적이면서도 예시 등을 이용하여 이해하기 쉽게 설명한다.

Q 78 공동체업무를 등한시하는 이기적인 교사 대처법   2012년 구상형

You are strict about self-management but got some criticism from colleague teachers as following. Discuss your measures according to the ethics of teaching.

A : You seem greatly concerned about students' group bully but you are actually meddling in everything with too much nagging.

B : You are so engaged with self-development, such as teachers' training, study at graduate school and etc. But other teachers feel pressure on the work share because of making up for your position.

예상답안

A teacher should not be overly engaged in students' own affairs. For situation A, I would try to be a friendly environment creator for students. I would show them movies or documentaries which contain messages about precious friendship. So that they can figure out the importance of getting along with others by themselves. I would also adopt a lot of group works, where students can co-operate each other for one specific goal. By working in groups, students will find out the value of helping and living with each other. A teacher also needs to be responsible for one's work in groups. Since the whole school is one team with one educational goal, all members should be devoted to their assigned roles. By making a self-check list, I would try to remind myself of the list of work that I need to complete for the whole school, before I spend time for my individual development.

Q 79 특별전형을 위한 학생 선택과 이유   2012년 구상형

You take charge of 3rd grade of high school students in a rural area. University A would suggest that they would give a special admission on one student in order to promote the 'Balanced Regional Development' in the area. There are two students who can be recommended for the special admission. The principal entirely entrusts you with the task of selecting one student. 1) Which student would you recommend? Explain with rationales? 2) What would you explain for the student who is not selected?

- Student A : school grade 96 points, school representative, son of county governor
- Student B : school grade 98 points, no experience in school representative, son of poor farmer

예상답안

I would recommend student A for a special admission to university A. Since both of the students live in the same rural area, family background can not be considered for the choice. Also, in terms of academic achievements, their school grades are almost the same. So, the teacher should concern about their speciality in the other areas. for example, Student A has been a school representative while student B has no experience for that. So, the teacher would assume that the student A has higher leadership who can become potential candidate for a special admission. The teacher can cheer up the student B to give advice for another opportunity. As the students has no experience in extracurricular activities, the teacher can suggest him to experience diverse things and participate in club activities.

Q 80 다문화가정 학생 bully문제에 대한 해결책   2012년 즉답형

A student from multi-cultural family has got bullied and picked on by other classmates. He said that he wanted to quit the school and even commit suicide. Discuss the two measures to guide the student in problem and his classmates respectively.

예상답안

In the case of the student in problem, a specialized expert needs to consult him to prevent his committing a suicide. Suicidal issues are not easy for the teacher to handle because more expert knowledge about counselling. In addition, he should participate in a group work so that he can adapt to the cooperative school environment. For example, project work about what students like in school can be recommended. By doing so, they will collaborate to complete the project and the problematic student will enjoy the school life. For the classmates, group counselling must be done by an expert counsellor too. Thus, they can understand what they have done to the student from a multi-cultural family is wrong. Also, collaborative work such as simulation or role play can be employed to raise their sense of multi-culture. For example, some students are assigned roles of students from multi-cultural families and then they experience some hardship those students have undergone.

Q 81 교사인기도에 집착하는 박교사에 대한 조언   2012년 즉답형

Mr. Park is a teacher with two-year experiences in the school. He teaches students with a great enthusiasm, volunteering in the after-school program for free of charge and even buying some sweets after the program. He becomes the most popular teacher in the school. He, however, does not consider the other teachers' circumstances and, thus, gets criticized for striving for populism.

예상답안

First, as a member of teacher community, Mr. Park should suppress his desire to give too much care to the students because his too much enthusiasm has caused students to have unbalanced perspectives on other teachers. Specifically, students think that other teachers are not good because they have not bought any sweets for them. Second, he should not buy sweets for students because this makes students not intrinsically motivated but extrinsically. If this no intrinsic motivation continues, students are not wiling to study without more extrinsic rewards and they are demotivated in other teachers' classes that do not provide any extrinsic rewards. Third, he should stop providing the after-school program for free of charge because the free program has a bad influence on the regular after-school programs. Also, some students and parents who have paid for the program will obviously complain about why they have paid for the after-school classes.

Q 82 급식실에서 싸운 학생 조치 방법 — 2011년 구상형

In the school lunch cafeteria, students had a big fight and, as a consequence, a few students were hurt and some facilities were broken. If you were the very first one to witness the scene, describe the three measures you could take.

예상답안

First, the most important measure for me to take is to react upon the situation with a calm, composed manner, not getting students perplexed. Since the fight happened in school cafeteria, I will take proper measures for other students to finish their school meal. Also, I'll take an action to make the two students who are involved in the fight go to the teacher's room because I do not want other students to be disturbed by the trouble. Second, I will take an emergency measures if there are seriously injured students because of the fight. If it is not enough, I'll call 911 and send him to the general hospital in order to secure the student's safety and health condition. Lastly, I will consult with teachers who are directly in charge of the involved students and try to solve the problem in collaboration with them because they are well aware of the students. Once I notify them of the fight briefly, I will discuss next measures with them. During the discussion, I will find out who started the fight, what happened to them and what are the consequences. Then I will share the information with other teachers.

Q 83 특별활동 - 적극적으로 동아리에 가입할 수 있는 방법 — 2011년 구상형

At the beginning of the semester, each student should be allocated to one extra-curricular club each. However, some clubs have exceeded the number of students they could accommodate. So, many of students were forced to join the clubs that they did not want. Even worse, teachers also have to take charge of the clubs they have not volunteered. All these led to students' complaints with inactive participation. Discuss three measures to make the club activity more variable and active.

예상답안

To make the club activity more varied and active, I will take the following three measures. First, I will carry out a research on students' interest and aptitude and open the extra-curricular activities that correspond to theirs. They should accommodate students needs, wants and lacks. If students' needs are disregarded and if they are arranged into the activities that they didn't want, it violates the principle that club activity should cultivate students' autonomy and self-motivating habit. Second, if the activity is essential in educational aspect but if it is not preferred by students, teacher should derive students' participation by telling them the features of the club that are related to career, personality, and educational achievement. Club activities should be carried out with the perspective of students, not of teachers. In learner-centered club activities, students get useful advice and knowledge which help them choose right passage of career that properly corresponds to their specialty and aptitude. If students aren't aware of this fact, teachers should notify them of the exploitation of the club in a long perspective. For example, students can be offered some kind of project work in order to present it during school festival or club activity exhibition. Through those chances, students learn the real value of the activity and thus students' participation will be greatly enhanced. Third, the quality of the club activity can be promoted with the guidance of excellent teachers. Even if students show interest in the area of the activity, they turn away if the quality of the activity is low. Not to mention the case of uninterested one. Thus, the teacher who is in charge of the club activity should operate the club properly with maximum expertise. The teacher should provide students with variable contents and informative advice. Not only the guidance teacher but also parents or experts in the related area can be nominated as an adviser of the club. Students' participation of the club activity will increase accordingly.

Q 84 체험 학습을 함께 하도록 동료교사 설득 — 2011년 구상형

Your school is planning to do 'career field-trip day' to enhance the career training education. However, teacher A is against the plan because the field-trip results in a loss of class hours and heavier workload. Suggest the three measures to meet with the following guidelines.
- Teacher A: "Our school is currently teaching the subject of 'career and future' and regularly holding 'career counseling'. On top of that, if we have to have 'career field-trip day' and spend a whole day, we have a loss in other subject matters, which will aggravate our workload."
- Condition: Supposing that the examiner were your colleague, discuss your opinions to persuade your colleague.

예상답안

I agree with your opinion. I have considered the problem from that aspect, too. We do have the subject matter of 'career and future' and currently hold 'career counseling'. However, if the students go field trip and experience the life and work of the professionals by themselves, it will bring more positive impacts than a number of in-class instructions. This opportunity will help the students to choose their future career and ultimately motivate them to study harder. Field trips will surely compensate for the regular class hours. We may need some supplementary class hours, but the students' active participation will make it easier to manage the lessons.

Q 85 교원 평가 문제에 대한 해결책 제시 2011년 구상형

Mr. Kim has received some feedback from his students for the 'Teacher's Performance Evaluation'. Describe his problems shown on the following feedback and suggest some solutions.
- Student 1: I don't know what I learnt from Mr. Kim's lesson.
- Student 2: Mr. Kim always finishes the class about 5 minutes late and we have less break time.
- Student 3: Mr. Kim doesn't know my name even after one semester.

예상답안

I can suggest three ways to deal with Mr. Kim's problem. First, the student 1 mentioned that he or she doesn't know exactly what has been taught in class. I think this problem has been caused because Mr. Kim didn't notify students of the lesson objectives well. In order to solve this problem, I will recommend Mr. Kim that he make sure of letting students know the lesson objectives at the beginning and the end of the lesson. Second, the student 2 complained that Mr. Kim always finishes the class about 5 minutes late so students cannot have enough break time. This also can affect the next class negatively. I believe the best way to solve this problem is to practice. As the old saying goes, 'practice makes perfect.' This practice can be performed in various ways. One of the ways is to analyse the lesson plan carefully and to record teaching performance, and to monitor it by oneself. To ask some advices from more experienced senior teachers is recommendable too. Third, the student 3 is not satisfied with the fact that Mr. Kim doesn't know their name even after one semester. To deal with this problem, Mr. Kim should make a various efforts to memorize their names. For example, he should take some time to get familiar with students' names and faces at the beginning of the semester. Or, he can match students' names and their faces in the classroom by calling their names instead of just calling "student," "hey" or "you."

Q 86 교사가 회사 로고 찍힌 물품을 거절하는 이유 2011년 구상형

There will be an orientation for new students. Ms. Kim takes charge of planning an 'orientation day'. A company of school uniforms suggests that they provide the three students from low-income family with scholarships and prestigious stationery sets inscribed with the company's logos. She asks the vice principal if the school would accept the offer. And he asks about her opinion on that offer to follow it. If she is to decline the offer, describe the three reasons why she has to decline.

예상답안

I appreciate the company's suggestions, but can not accept the offer for the three reasons. First, giving the students company-supported scholarships or stationary sets is against my faith and teaching philosophy. I have always taught students that they should be careful and have a critical attitude when they are exposed to a commercial. Then, giving those scholarships and stationary sets with company logos for free at school may confuse students. Second, those scholarships and stationary sets with school uniform company logos can impart a wrong impression that the company officially supports our school. This would cause students to choose a certain company blindly when they buy their school uniforms. Third, it is inappropriate for schools to be involved with a certain profit-making organization. This is because schools are public sectors and need to take a neutral stance. Of course, donating some money or giving financial supports without any advertising purposes may be welcomed. Otherwise, any donations with intentions should be carefully considered.

Q 87 학급경영에서 rapport 형성을 위한 조언   2011년 즉답형

Teacher A has established a close rapport with her students. Teacher B has complained some difficulties. "My students has no goals to live by and some of them do not even study at all. Some are late for class, some do not complete for clean-up duty and just run away." What advices could Teacher A give Teacher B?

예상답안

I think it's important to make a good relationship with students. With trust, a teacher should be a role model to them first and have them act upon the standard. For example, planning and making daily objectives through the morning assembly and end-day meeting can be a good way to build good relationship with students. This would help teacher to figure out their characters and circumstances. I'm sure your disciplines should be based on good relationship with students. Then, they will listen to your guidance and reward with good actions.

Q 88 일반 + 장애아동이 함께 소풍 - 부모 설득   2011년 즉답형

There is a mixed class of normal and retarded students. They have decided to do some field trip activity all together. However, they have to rearrange time and schedule because of the retarded students. Some parents with normal students has appealed the rearrangements caused by the retarded students. What would you explain the parents to deal with the problem?

예상답안

I would suggest that the parents teach their children to be unbiased and open to everyone including retarded students. Living with other people equally is a very important virtue in the society. Working collaboratively with retarded students can teach this virtue. With helping the retarded students, students would be in their shoes and consider how difficult they feel. As a result, this experience would make the students grow up with strong moral and responsibility, which is necessary for all of us.

CHAPTER 02 심층 면접 핵심 개념 정리

1. 학교 교육에 대한 교육관

성적순으로 한 줄 세우는 교육이 아니라 학생의 특기와 적성을 성장시키는 학교	Develop students' specialty and aptitude rather than evaluate them with one criteria or school ranking.
건전한 인성과 창의력을 갖춘 글로벌 인재가 키워지는 학교	upright character and creativity to become global leaders
왕따와 폭력이 없이 서로 존중하고 사랑하는 공동체 학교 문화가 구현된 학교	Build communal school culture that students respect and love apart from bullying and violence.
성적, 가정환경, 외모, 장애 등을 이유로 차별받지 않고 교육 받을 수 있는 환경이 실현된 학교. 특히 소외계층 자녀들과 다문화 가정 자녀들의 학습권이 보장된 학교	Never discriminate students on the ground of grade, family background, appearance, disability. Especially guarantee right for learning of students from neglected and multi-cultural family.

2. 교직이 전문직인 이유

교직은 전문적인 지식과 기술, 이론적 배경을 갖추고 있다.	Equipped with professional knowledge, skill and theoretical background
교직에 종사하고자 하는 사람은 전문적인 지식과 기술을 획득하기 위하여 오랜 훈련과 교육기간이 필요할 뿐만 아니라, 엄격한 자격기준 또는 표준이 요구된다.	To be occupied with teaching, require not only long discipline and education duration to acquire professional knowledge and skill but strict criteria of qualification
교직은 지속적인 이론 연구를 통해 그 전문성을 표준 이상으로 신장시켜야 한다.	Develop professionality over the standard through continuous study.
교직 수행에서 자율성과 그에 대한 책임은 필수불가결한 요소이다.	Autonomy and accountability are indispensable in carrying out teaching.

3. 교사의 사명 - 오지 학교로 발령 받았을 경우 교육을 어떻게 할 것인가?

제 교육철학은 학생이 성적이나 외모 그리고 가정환경이나 거주지역 등을 이유로 차별받아서는 안 된다는 것입니다.	I should never discriminate students according to their grade, appearance, background or economic status.
교사는 봉사정신을 가져야 합니다.	I have a strong sense of public duty.
참된 스승이 되려면 남이 싫어하는 힘든 일, 어려운 일에 도전하라고 은사님께서 늘 강조하셨고 저도 그 말씀에 공감하기 때문입니다.	One of my teachers stressed the need for hard and tough work that everybody hesitates to do if I want to be a true teacher.

4. 교직과 다른 직업과의 차이점

인간 자체를 대상으로 하는 직업이며, 주로 미성숙자를 대상으로 하는 직업이다.	We have to deal with human beings, who grow into future citizens.
교직은 소명의식을 가지고 사회에 봉사하기 위한 직업이다.	Vocation for teaching to serve the society
교직은 다른 어느 직업보다 국가와 사회에 지대한 영향을 미치는 공공사업이다.	Public work that brings about more positive influence on the nation and society than any other occupation

5. 고등정신능력을 길러주는 학력신장 방법

학생중심의 지식구성식 교육을 할 수 있는 능력이 필요하다.	Require ability to enhance students' construction of knowledge in student-oriented approach
ICT활용교육을 할 수 있는 능력이 필요하다.	Require ability to educate the use of ICT

6. 건강한 인성을 길러주는 인성교육 방법

이론중심의 인성교육과 강압적인 생활지도에서 벗어나 체험중심의 인성교육과 민주적인 생활지도를 할 수 있는 능력이 필요하다.	Ability to experience-based personality education and democratic school guidance instead of theory-based and coercive guidance
정보윤리를 철저히 가르칠 수 있는 능력이 필요하다.	Ability to teach information ethics thoroughly
다원화 사회에 맞게 다양한 문화를 이해하고 소개할 수 있는 능력이나 세계화 시대에 맞는 어학능력이나 평생학습사회에 꼭 필요한 자기주도적 학습능력이 필요하다.	• Ability to understand and introduce diverse culture according to multi-cultural society. • Language abilities in the age of globalization • Self-directed learning ability for lifelong learning

7. 오늘날 인성교육이 필요한 이유와 해결책

1) 원인

가정적 차원: 핵가족이 되어 가정교육 약화, 맞벌이 가정 증가, 문제가정 (결손, 위기, 빈곤가정) 증가, 부모의 출세 지향적 교육	lack of home discipline due to a nuclear family/ parents working family/ broken family/ parents' ambitions for success
학교교육적 차원: 입시위주의 지식교육으로 과도한 경쟁의 분위기 속에서 성적만 강조하고 인성교육 소홀, 이론중심의 도덕	neglect moral education, too much competition because of university entrance exam, do Ethics focusing on the theory
사회적 차원: 물질주의, 개인주의, 사치향락풍조, 정보화의 역기능 만연	materialism, egotism, trend toward extravagance, side effects of informatization

2) 해결책

(체험의 원리) 지식 전달 중심에서 벗어난 학생의 동기화를 강조하는 실천 중심의 교육으로 전환해야 체득하기 쉽고 습관화가 될 수 있다.	(Learning by doing) Focus on practice and experience, so that students can build good habits: Emphasize the importance of experience to motivate students, not from the theory.
(통합성의 원리) 전 교육과정에서, 모든 교사가: 통합적 인격교육: 교과지도, 창의적 체험활동, 생활지도 등의 전 영역을 통해서, 잠재적 교육과정까지도 포함	(Principle of integration) All teachers should do their best in all areas: a regular class, an extra-curricular activities, guidance counseling, latent curriculum.
일상생활을 통해서 도덕 경험을 하도록 (지속성의 원리) 꾸준하게 실천할 때 내면화, 습관화를 성취	Students have moral experience through daily life: put them into practise continuously/ internalize the act and make them habits.
(관계성의 원리) 다양한 프로그램 (자치활동, 청소년 활동, 봉사활동, 1일1선 운동, 효도일기 등등)을 통해 공동체 의식을 함양하고, 민주의식을 기초로 공동체 발전에 기여하는 사람 양성, 통제 위주의 생활지도 방식을 개선하고 교사와 학생이 인격적인 관계를 형성하는 것을 우선하는 방향으로 교사는 자상한 안내자의 역할을 해주어야 한다.	Implement a various of programs to promote community spirit; volunteer/ extracurricular activities/ one good thing every day/ letter to parents. Current counseling to control students, should be changed: Teachers can make a good rapport with students: a good guide.
(자율성의 원리) 학생이 스스로 문제에 대해 결정하고 실천할 수 있는 기회를 제공하는 방향으로	Give students opportunities which they can decide on their matters by themselves and put it into practice.

8. 교실의 바람직한 변화

• 학생중심의 수업 실현과 면학 분위기 조성	• Establish student centered teaching and create an academic atmosphere.
• 함께하는 학습 분위기	• Learning atmosphere with every student's participation
• 쾌적하고 안전한 교실환경	• Clean and safe classroom environment

9. 교사의 자질

• 이러한 변화를 교사가 주도하는 것이 아니라 학생과 적극적인 상호작용을 통해 이뤄가는 자질	• Interact with students through their active participation rather than teacher-led change.
• 학생의 잠재력을 믿어주면서 학생에게 자주인, 창조인, 세계인으로서 미래상을 늘 강조하고 촉구하는 자질	• Believe in students' potential and encourage them to be an independnt, creative and globalized person.
• 학생의 작은 변화에도 민감하고 긍정적인 변화를 격려하는 자질	• Be sensitive to students' little change and encourage it.

10. 20년 후 원하는 교사상

• 올해보다 시간이 지나면서 더 나은 교사	• Want to be a better teacher by increasing the teaching skill over the years.
• 가르치는 일을 즐기는 교사	• Enjoy teaching itself.
• 학생과 소통을 잘하는 교사	• Communicate effectively with students.
• 어렵고 힘든 처지에 있는 학생에게 더 큰 관심을 쏟고 살피는 교사	• Pay more attention to the students from unfavorable background.

11. 되고 싶은 바람직한 교사상

• 학생을 사랑하고 민주적으로 대하는 교사	• Have affection and treat students democratically.
• 유머감각이 풍부하고 개방적이고 다원적인 가치를 지닌 교사	• Have a sense of humor and open mind and diversified value.
• 확고한 윤리의식을 가지고 늘 인간성 향상에 힘쓰는 교사	• Have a strong work ethics and help to enhance their humanity.
• 전인교육의 관점을 바탕으로 인성함양과 학력신장을 조화롭게 추구하는 교사	• Based on well-rounded education, harmonize building an upright character with learning ability.
• 늘 연구하고 학습하는 교사	• Study and learn steadily.

12. 교사로서 지녀야 할 자질

• 교직적성을 갖추어야 한다. • 교과전문성을 갖추어 자신이 담당하는 교과지식에 정통해야 하고, 학습주제에 맞는 효과적인 교수방법에 능숙해야 한다. • 교사는 사회변화에 따라 스스로 자기의 교직능력을 향상시켜야 한다. • 교직에 대한 자부심을 가져야 한다. • 봉사적이어야 한다.	• Have an aptitude for teaching profession. • Have specialty on the subject they teach and should be tactful in their teaching. • Enhance competence in teaching according to the change of the society. • Have self-esteem in teaching profession. • Should have dedication and commitment

13. 이질적인 학급을 이끌어가는 데 필요한 교사의 자질과 실천계획

• 이질적인 학생을 다 포용하면서 차별 없이 맞춤식 지도를 하는 자세가 가장 필요한 자질이다 • 전천후 상담능력을 기른다. • 학생에게 설문조사를 실시하여 담임의 학급운영에 가장 절실하게 느끼는 무엇인지 파악한다. • 방과후 다문화 가정 자녀나 학부모를 대상으로 한 프로그램에 참여한다. • 이질적인 학급운영과 관련된 다양한 연수와 연구에 적극적으로 참여한다.	• Offer the best tailored training and mentoring in the industry embracing every student without discrimination. • Develop all-weather capability in consultation. • Find out what is desperately needed in manage the class through conducting a survey. • Participate in a after school program for children and parents from multi-cultural family. • Actively participate in a diverse training and study related with running a heterogeneous class.

14. 리더십 있는 교사의 특징

자신과 관련해서 투철한 교육관과 사명감을 가지고 부단히 자신을 성장시켜 가는 면학수행에 힘쓰는 교사이다.	Regarding teacher oneself – with clear work ethics and full commitment, work at it constantly.
학생과 관련해서 윤리적인 측면에서 학생을 사랑하고 인격적으로 대해주며 비밀을 보장해 주고 민주적으로 대해주는 교사이다.	Regarding students – in ethical aspect, love students, treat them democratically and respectfully, keep their secret in confidence.
학생과 관련해서 전문성이라는 측면에서 학습지도와 생활지도에 능통한 교사이다.	Regarding students – be professional in guiding learning and counseling.

타 교원과 관련해서 늘 인화에 힘쓰고 굳은 일도 마다하지 않고 업무에 협력하고 갈등을 잘 조절하는 교사이다.	Regarding other teacher – Try to mingle with other teachers, take the tough task voluntarily, cooperate and control the conflict.
학부모와 관련해서 학부모를 예의 바르게 대하고 학부모의 이야기를 경청하고 학생의 상황을 공유하면서 함께 협력해서 학생을 이끌어가는 교사이다.	Regarding parents – Treat parents with courteous manner, share students' stories, and cooperate to lead students.

15. 학급담임의 역할

• 학급의 책임자로 학생에게 새로운 지식과 기능을 습득시키고, 바람직한 사회성을 길러주는 일	• As a person who is in charge of the class, let students acquire knowledge and skill and develop their desirable sociality.
• 학급의 모든 일을 학생과 공동으로 참여하여 계획, 실천하는 일	• Participate in all the class tasks with students together and plan and implement them.
• 학부모와 협력하여 가정생활의 기초과정을 습득시키는 일	• Cooperate with parents and help students acquire the basic process of the family life.

16. 학급담임으로서 갖추어야 할 교사의 자질

• 협동적인 민주적인 생활태도를 지닌 교사	• Have collaborative and democratic lifestyle.
• 유능한 지도능력과 왕성한 책임감을 지닌 교사	• Have full responsibility and competent at teaching.
• 교과에 대한 학식과 교수법이 특출한 교사	• Have professional knowledge and teaching method.
• 원만한 대인 관계, 인정과 칭찬하는 교사	• Have well-integrated relationship with co-workers who get the credit for commendation.
• 학생 문제에 적극적 관심과 흥미를 보여주는 교사	• Show concern and interest actively in students' troubles.

17. 학급담임 회피와 교사 이기주의 극복: 학급담임을 맡지 않으려는 이유

• 윤리적인 측면에서 교사 개인의 사명감이 부족하기 때문이다. • 구조적인 측면에서 보면 무엇보다 학급담임의 핵심 역할은 생활지도인데 갈수록 생활지도가 어려워지고 있기 때문이다. • 행정업무가 많다. • 수업시수의 부담이 크다.	• Lack of a sense of duty in ethical aspect • School counseling, which is the major role of the homeroom teacher, is getting difficult in structural aspect. • Have lots of administrative tasks. • Too heavy a burden of class hours per week

18. 교사가 되었을 때 교사 이기주의 극복방안

• 초임교사로서 확고한 교원윤리를 확립한다. • 초임교사로서 학급담임을 맡을 수 있도록 생활지도 기술을 확보한다. • 초임교사로지만 다른 선생님들이 회피하는 기타 특별업무를 자발적으로 맡아보겠다.	• Establish teaching ethics for teachers. • Secure the expertise of school counseling to be in charge of homeroom teacher. • Voluntarily take the special task that other teachers tend to avoid.

19. 학급담임회피 문제의 종합적 해결책

• 학급당 학생 수 감축 (작은 교실 만들기) • 수업시수 법제화 • 행정 업무 경감 • 학급담임에게 인센티브 제공 • 교사 자신의 사명감 제고와 생활지도 능력 신장	• Decrease students number per class. • Legislate the lesson hours per week. • Alleviate the administrative task. • Provide homeroom teacher with incentives. • Improve teachers' own sense of duty and school counseling.

20. 학부모와 갈등이 생겼을 때 대응방안

흥분하지 않고 침착한 자세로 예의 갖추고 학부모를 대하고, 자녀에 대해 애정을 가지고 지도하고 있다는 자세를 보여준다.	Treat parents with calm and courteous manner and show you are guiding students with affection.
갈등에 대한 학부모의 입장을 경청하면서 표면적인 대화 내용보다는 내면에 있는 감정과 생각을 읽을 수 있도록 노력한다.	Pay attention to the parents' position regarding conflicts and try to determine what's in their minds instead of just looking at the superficial part of their conversation.

교육과정 운영과 관련된 문제라면 교사의 교육관을 정확하게 알려주어서 부당한 간섭을 하지 않도록 한다. 그러나 참견이 아닌 참여는 존중되어야 한다.	When it comes to the management of curriculum, it's important to inform the teacher's educational thoughts to the parents in order not to be interfered in any way. However, their involvement should be respected.
학습지도와 관련된 문제라면 가정학습 과제를 제시하여 학부모가 학생의 수준을 알고 함께 지도할 수 있도록 한다.	When it comes to the course of study, let the parents know the student's level and take a part in teaching, providing home study assignment.
생활지도와 관련된 학부모의 과민 반응이라면 자녀의 학급생활을 구체적으로 알려 자녀에 대한 객관적 이해를 유도한다. 예컨대 학교 생활모습을 영상물로 만들어 보게 하거나 직접 교실생활을 참관해 볼 수 있는 기회를 제공한다.	If the parents overreact regarding the way the teacher guide the student, try to lead them to understand objectively by telling them their children's class behavior. For instance, you may show video clips of students' school life or give them a chance to visit the class in person.

21. 학부모의 불만 문제 처리

문제행동을 하는 학생에게 생활지도 차원에서 지도를 했는데 학부모가 불만을 표시해왔다. 어떻게 대처하겠는가?	Suppose the parents show dissatisfaction with your discipline in student's misbehavior at school. How would you respond?
• 가장 우선적으로, 공손하게 학부모가 어떤 불만을 왜 품게 되었는지 경청한다. • 불만사항을 경청할 때는 표면적인 이야기보다는 내면의 감정과 목소리에 주의한다. • 학부모의 심정을 이해한다고 공감을 표시해 준다. • 사건이 발생한 원인과 진행과정, 그리고 취한 조처를 자세히 알려주고 그 조치가 어디까지나 교육적인 조치였음을 이해시킨다.	• Listen to the reasons why the parents have the dissatisfaction. • When listening to the dissatisfaction, pay attention to their emotion and voice tone. • Let them know you empathize with their feelings. • Let them know the reason, procedure, and measures of your discipline and make sure that was implemented on the educational principles.

22. 과도한 체벌에서 비롯된 학부모의 항의

• 교육적 차원에서 한 체벌이었지만 불상사가 일어난 데 대해 진심으로 사과한다.	• Apologize for such an unfortunate incident to happen despite it's an educational punishment.
• 모든 치료를 책임지겠다고 말한다.	• Tell them you will be in charge of every treatment.
• 선배교사나 부장교사 교감과 상의하여 조언을 구한다.	• Discuss with senior teacher or vice principal and ask advice from them

23. 창의적인 학급을 운영하기 위한 담임교사의 역할

전인적인 인간 (배려와 나눔을 실천하는 창의적 인재)을 양성하는 것을 목표로 학급 운영계획을 수립해야 한다.	Should establish classroom management plan with the goal of fostering the whole-person education.
자애로우면서도 공동체적 관계가 살아 있는 학급 분위기를 조성해야 한다.	Should foster classroom atmosphere which encourages benevolent and communal relationship to be found.
학생의 학습과 생활을 주도하는 위치가 아니라 안내하고 조력하는 역할을 해주어야 한다.	Should play a role of guiding and assisting rather than leading students' learning and living.
학생의 관심과 흥미, 그리고 필요와 능력을 고려하여 학급을 운영해야 한다.	Should manage the class considering students' interest, concern, necessity and ability.
모든 교육활동을 학교 목표 달성에 집중해야 한다.	Every school activity should concentrate on achieving within the school goal.

24. 학생 생활 지도

• 결석, 지각, 조퇴 등의 근태 지도	• Guidance of attendance, tardiness, taking an early leave (from school)
• 학급 일 한 가지 분담하여 맡기	• Dividing up the class work
• 청소, 주번 활동의 유의점	• A note on cleaning, class duty
• 안전지도	• Safety guide

25. 학부모와의 원활한 대화를 위한 방법

• 학급 신문이나 유인물로 학교와 학급 소식을 전한다.	• Deliver school and class news via class newspaper and printed materials.
• 학부모와의 상담은 주로 전화를 이용하는 게 좋다.	• The consultation with the parents are recommended through the phone.

• 학부모와의 대화는 개별적 접촉보다는 학급 전체를 대상으로, 다수의 학부모가 참여할 수 있도록 일정한 시간과 공적 장소를 정해 사전 예고 후 하도록 한다.	• When it comes to parent consultation, deal with the whole class instead of personal contact and inform the fixed time and place beforehand so that most parents can participate.

26. 중학교 신임교사로서, 자신만의 특별한 학급운영 방안

함께 하는 학급분위기를 만들어가는 기본생활습관과 공동체의식 함양에 주력한다.	Promote fundamental habit and communal spirit for building classroom atmosphere with the whole class.
사이버 공간에서도 민주시민의 정체성을 유지할 수 있도록 정보윤리교육에 힘쓴다.	Strive to enhance the information and ethics education to maintain the identity of civics on the virtual space.
자기주도적 학습능력을 바탕으로 창의력을 신장하는 방안으로 모둠별 독서활동을 이끌어간다.	Lead a group reading activity as a way of increasing the creativity based on the self-directed academic ability.
학습부진아 제로운동을 벌인다.	Campaign for 'We have zero underachievement.'
학생이 주인의식을 가지고 모든 과정에 참여하는 민주적인 학급경영을 하겠다.	Operate the democratic classroom management that students participate in every process with a sense of ownership.
모든 학생을 공평하게 대하고 언제든지 대화의 창구를 열어놓는 학급경영을 하겠다.	Treat every student fair and implement open communication.
함께하는 학급분위기를 창출하는 (공동체 의식을 길러주는) 학급경영을 하겠다.	Make a cooperative classroom atmosphere that every student takes part in together.
자기주도적 학습능력과 창의력을 키우는 학급경영을 하겠다.	Promote self-directed learning skills and creativity.
상을 많이 주는 학급경영을 하겠다.	Give awards to the students who make the most efforts and improvement.
(학부모에게) 학부모님들이 학교생활을 잘 알 수 있고 관심을 가지고 지원할 수 있는 학급경영, 부모님과 제가 협력해서 우리 아이들이 밝은 인성과 실력을 갖출 수 있는 학급경영을 하겠다.	Inform parents of students' school life so that they care and support the students at most. Cooperate with students so that they build good character and competence.

27. 교장이 예고없이 수업참관을 하고 수업협의를 요청할 때 교사의 견해

수업 장학은 교육/ 학교 경영 등 학교를 전반적으로 파악하는 데 필요한 정보를 수집 할 수 있으나, 수업 장학이 효과가 있으려면 교사와 교장의 상호작용이 잘 일어나야 한다. 그러기 위해서는 교장이 정해진 일정으로 수업 장학을 해줘야 하며, 교사는 적극적으로 수업장학을 활용해서 수업과 학습활동을 개선해갈 수 있다.	The supervision implemented by school principal can be helpful considering that we can get information about teachers' instructions and school management. The principal should plan his supervision and let teachers know in advance. For teachers, they respect the supervision and try to amend their weaknesses in more active way.

28. 교사 발령 후 지식 정보화 사회에 알맞은 자기 계발 방법

자신의 수업을 녹화, 녹음 분석, 평가	to videotape or record our lessons and then assess our lessons with analysis of contents and methods
교직, 교양, 전공과목과 관련된 문헌 자료, 정보자료 활용하기	to utilize much information though many literatures in teaching subjects or guiding students
방송매체/ 교원연수 프로그램 힘을 빌리기	to participate in teacher training programs or get information or great ideas through the media
학교 상호방문 프로그램 적극 참여 – 강연회, 시범수업, 교과연구회	to take part in various programs like project classes or lectures given by expert in education field, we can also improve our teaching skills and apply proper methods to our classes

29. 동료장학 활성화 방안

협의 형태를 다양하게 만들기 예를 들어, 프로젝트 중심 협의회/ 체험중심 교사모임 등	to make various conferences with fellow teachers is recommendable. For example, we can design the project-based conference or experience-centered meetings proceeded by teachers' community
교사들 사이의 상호불간섭주의 같은 문화적 요인 개선	to get rid of non-reciprocal principle and instead build supportive atmosphere together
수업을 Youtube에 담아 동료에게 평가 받고, 동료의 충고를 귀담아 듣고 개선하려고 노력하기	to make our efforts to improve our teaching skills by reflecting our classes based on feedback provided by other co-teachers

30. 학교장이 학교 홈페이지에 교사의 수업 동영상을 올리려고 할때의 찬성 혹은 반대

1) 찬성답변

동료장학이나 자기장학이 가능해 수업능력을 향상시킬 수 있기 때문입니다. 교육의 수요자인 학부모의 만족도를 제고 할 수 있기 때문입니다. 대부분의 경우, 학부모가 수업을 볼 수 없기에 수업 동영상을 통한다면 시간,장소에 구애 받지 않고 교사의 태도, 아이들의 학습 태도 등을 볼 수 있다. 공교육을 정상화 할 수 있는 좋은 방법이라 생각합니다.	If we videotape our classes, we can improve our teaching skills considering that it can be used practically for co-supervision and self-supervision. In most cases, children's parents cannot participate in the classes with limitation of time and place. So, with the videotape posted online, they can watch their children's classes and also know their children's learning progress and attitude. This could be a good opportunity to improve the quality of public education.

2) 반대답변

물론 자기장학/ 동료장학에 활용하는 것은 아주 좋은 방법이며, 온라인 수업공개도 폭넓게 전문적인 피드백을 받을 수 있다는 면에서는 좋습니다. 하지만 모든 이에게 공개하는 것은 신중해야 한다고 봅니다. 자칫 학부모와 학생이 교사의 수업을 평가하고 점수를 매기는 수단으로 오용될 수 있기 때문입니다. 따라서, 동료장학/ 자기장학에 활용하는 취지에 맞게 교사들만 볼 수 있게 공개해야 한다고 생각하며, 모든 이에게 공개여부는 협의회를 통해 모든 교사의 의견을 반영해야 한다고 생각합니다.	Without a doubt, the demonstration classes can be very useful for co-supervision and self-supervision. And through this, teachers get meaningful feedback on their classes. But, I wonder whether we should open our class video to all parents and students, because this can be used for the means of assessing teachers subjectively. For this reason, to execute this system, you should have a conference with all teachers and reflect their opinions enough.

31. 학부모에게 공개하는 공개수업의 장점

• 다양한 피드백을 통해서 수업의 질 향상	• We can give the high-quality instructions from feedback on my lessons.
• 학부모가 자녀의 학습태도를 알 수 있다.	• Parents are aware of their children's learning attitude/school life.
• 교사가 수업지도 능력 향상에 더 노력을 기울일 수 있다.	• Based on feedback, teachers can realize their weaknesses and improve teaching ability.
• 교사와 학부모의 유대감을 늘려서 공교육에 대한 신뢰감 향상할 수 있다.	• We can build rapport/ good relationship with parents to gain trust on public education from parents
• 정확하게 교사를 평가할 수 있는 근거를 제공한다.	• The demonstration classes provide the objective basis for teachers' assessment.

32. 자신의 수업공개를 반대하는 교사의 이유와 수업능력 향상을 위해 취할 조치

1) 이유

연령대가 다르고 교육관이 다 다르므로, 평가하는 타 교사에 대한 불신이 있을 수도 있다. 동료교사의 평가가 자신의 교육권을 침해한다는 인식이 팽배하다. 자신의 능력이 드러난다 생각하여 부담을 느낀다.	Every teacher can have different view of educational philosophy, so some of them do not trust others' assessment. They think the assessment can infringe their right for lessons. They can feel uncomfortable because their ability as a teacher comes out to the public.

2) 조치

적극적으로 수업공개를 하고 다양한 형태의 자기장학 및 동료장학을 하겠다.	I'll take an initiative in demonstrating my classes. And, I'll use various types of supervision for my successful teaching performance.

33. 교장의 연구수업 지시에 대한 준비 방법

지도안/ 티칭 method측면에서 경험이 많은 선배교사(멘토)에게 자문을 받기	I'll ask some advices from experienced teacher or mentor on my lesson plan and proper teaching methods.
주제선정→ 주제에 관한 교재연구 → 학생의 지도방법논의 → 수업형태에 알맞은 학생조직/ 점검→ 효율적 자료활용/ 판서 점검→ 수업 안 설명과 검토 → 모의수업을 통한 수업 문제점 논의 → 사전협의 과정을 거치기	The first thing I should do is to select the lesson's topic. And then, I'll consider how to teach the topic to achieve the lesson's goal. Diagnosing students' levels and designing proper group activities and materials are also crucial. With specific lesson plan, I'll demonstrate class and get some advices and feedback from my mentor, and amend weaknesses.

34. 컨설팅 장학

사전협의회, 공개수업, 사후협의회, 결과내기 4단계에 걸쳐 이뤄진다. 수업개선을 위해 전문성을 갖춘 사람들이 학교의 요청에 따라 제공되는 독립적인 자문활동을 펼친다. 이는 수직적 장학이 아니라 수평적 장학이다.	Consulting Supervision proceed in main 4 stages from pre-conference, demonstration classes, post- conference, to assessment stage. This is implemented by education experts to improve teaching performances. The relationship between expertise and teachers is build up based on equal principal.

35. 임상장학

5년 미만의 저경력 교사에 대한 특별 장학	This is implemented for less- experienced teacher under 5 years, so it can be considered as special type of supervision.
장학자가 초임교사와 전임교사들의 수업형태를 관찰하여 수업의 질 향상 도모	School inspectors inspect teachers' classes and provide some feedback on the class to help teachers give high-quality instructions.
교실현장에서 교사와 장학자의 친밀한 일대일관계 속에서 계획된 협의회, 수업관찰 및 분석, 피드백 협의회라는 절차를 거치면서 교사의 전문성 및 수업 기술 향상을 도모	This kind of supervision proceeds in the classroom and teachers have one to one conference with expertise. They can plan their instructions to improve teaching skills based on feedback.

36. 초임교사에게 Mentoring이 필요한 이유

전문성 신장	Developing teaching ability/ skills as a teacher
정서적 안정도모- 자신감/ 자아효능감을 높임으로써 교사의 지도능력과 학생들과의 관계를 높여갈 수 있다.	Mentoring program is beneficial for teachers, especially new-appointed teachers because it can contribute to improve teachers' ability to teach and interact with students. It can make teachers have more self-confidence and self-efficacy.

37. 교사 멘토와 멘티에서의 문제점과 해결방안 각각 1가지

1) 멘토

문제점: 수업공개내용을 멘티와 협의없이 제시해버림- 자신의 입장만 강조	Suggesting her idea without discussing with mentee
해결방안: 멘티의 의견/ 고민을 경청하고 상호협의에 의해 조언과 안내를 제공해야한다.	To solve this problem, mentor should listen to and respect the mentee's opinions, and through the conference, she should guide the mentee to implement the classes more effectively.

2) 멘티

문제점: 수업계획안을 작성해야 하는지 의문을 표하는 것을 볼 때, 교수능력 제고하려는 적극성이 부족하다.	For a mentee, she queries necessity of making lesson plan and does not want to make it. She does not take any initiative to improve her instructions.
해결방안: 초임교사로서 전문성이 부족하다는 것을 인정하고, 멘토링에 적극적으로 임하기	So, the teacher (mentor) should recognize her lack of specialty and try to take mentoring system more actively.

38. 옷차림이 교사의 본분에 어긋난다고 교장선생님에게 지적을 받았을 경우

교사로서 기본적인 몸가짐은 중요한 사항이다. 학생의 동일시 대상이 되는 처지인 만큼 때와 장소에 맞는 옷차림이 중요하나. 따라서 교장 선생님이나 동료 교사에게 지적 받을 정도의 옷차림이면 고쳐야한다.	As teachers can be a role model or an example for students, they are expected to behave properly and be conservative about manners all the time. If we are given feedback on dress, we should reflect that and follow the proper dress codes.

39. 자기장학의 정의와 방법

자기장학은 스스로 교사가 계획을 세워 실천하고 자기 반성에 의한 자기 향상교육이다.	Self-supervision is necessary for improvement of teachers' instructions.
자신의 수업을 녹화, 녹음 분석, 평가	First way is to video or record our lessons and then estimate our lessons with analysis of contents and methods.
교직, 교양, 전공과목과 관련된 문헌 자료, 정보 자료 활용하기	Teachers can utilize much information though many literatures in teaching subjects or guiding students.
방송매체/ 교원연수 프로그램 이용하기	We can participate in teacher training programs or get information or great ideas through the media.
학교 상호방문 프로그램 적극 참여- 강연회, 시범수업, 교과연구회	By taking part in various programs like project classes or lectures given by expert in education field, we can improve our teaching skills and apply proper methods to our classes.

40. 동료장학 참관 시 중점해서 볼 사항

• 교사의 매체활용 기술	• We can check the teacher's ability to utilize digital technologies.
• 학습자와의 상호작용	• The teacher's interaction with students is essential.
• 교사의 비언어적 행위- 수업의 효과성	• Teachers' non-verbal communication is also influential on students' academic achievement.
• 수업 내용/ 전개방식의 적절성	• Teacher has to proceed her lesson effectively with the appropriate methods.

41. 동료장학을 받는 교사의 태도

• 수업을 피드백을 통해서 개선하려는 자세	• We should have attitude to reflect their feedback on the lesson and improve the lesson.
• 동료가 객관적으로 관찰 할 수 있게 유도	• We should induce fellow teachers to watch my class and give advices and feedback on my lesson objectively.

42. 신규교사로서 수업지도 및 생활지도 측면에서 동학년 교사와 협력할 방법

• 생활지도 방법이나/ 수업방법에 대해 질문을 나누면서 다양한 의견 교환	• I have to exchange opinions with co-teachers about how to teach and guide students.
• 수업을 녹화해서 자기점검표를 기록하며, 동교과/ 동학년 협의회에서 조언을 받는다.	• I can get some advices on my classes from other teachers, especially who teach same subject with me. I can improve teaching skills by self-assessing the lesson with the checklist.
• 수업연구대회 형태로 수업을 youtube로 만들어 사이버공간에 게시하여 전문가들로부터 조언을 받을 수 있다.	• By uploading my class youtube on the Internet, I can get feedback from teachers and expertise.
• 경험이 많은 교사와 짝을 맺어 멘토링 장학으로 수업진행 노하우를 터득할 수 있다.	• I'll ask the experienced teacher to be mentor. With mentoring supervision, I can learn what the effective and successful teaching is.

43. 학교에서 교사들 사이에 일어날 수 있는 갈등사례와 이를 해결할 방안

1) 갈등 사례

현장학습 계획 시 동료교사와 의견 충돌이 있을 것 같다.	When we plan the field trip, disagreement among teachers can arise.

2) 해결

감정적인 대응은 삼가고 함께 협력해야 할 동료로 생각하고 갈등을 해결	We should not react emotionally with my fellow teacher because they are my co-teachers who I have to cooperative with, rather than competitors.
동료교사의 의견을 경청하고 옳다면 의견을 수용	I should listen to them saying and respect their opinions. If their idea is more reasonable, I'll follow their opinions.
갈등의 원인을 파악하고 가능한 해결책을 함께 구상해서 도출하고 최대한 서로가 공감하는 해결책 찾기	I should perceive the reason of our conflict and find the best solution with my fellow. The solution should reflect our opinions fully to make all of us feel satisfied.
갈등이 되는 사안에 대해 경험 많은 선배교사에게 조언을 구하기	If we cannot resolve the conflict, I'll ask some advice to the experienced teacher.
동료교사와 관계를 돈독히 할 수 있는 자리마련	I'll have a special time with my fellow teacher to build a rapport/ good relationship.

44. 학교장과의 의견 충돌시 해결방법

경험많은 선배교사에게 교장과 의견이 다를 때 어떻게 문제 해결하는지 자문해본다.	I'll consult experienced teachers with conflict between the principal and me and seek advices on solutions.
교장에게 개별 면담을 요청한다. 면담 시 교장의 의견을 경청하고 의견이 다른 이유가 무엇인지 파악하고 나의 잘못된 판단이 있는가 파악한다.	I'll ask to have separate meeting with the principal to understand his thoughts and argument more deeply. By doing so, I can reflect myself to figure out any misjudgement.
교장의 견해가 옳다면 자신의 의견 철회하고 초임교사로서 부족한 점을 인정하고 앞으로도 좋은 조언을 많이 해 달라고 부탁한다.	If the principal's opinion is more resonable, I'll admit my fault and lack of experience as a teacher and I'll ask him to give more advices.

교장의 생각이 잘못 되어 보이더라도 굽히지 않는다면 따르겠다. 왜냐면, 그는 더 경험이 많고 학교 운영을 거시적으로 볼 줄 아는 안목을 지녔기 때문이다.	If he doesn't back down his point, I'll follow him. This is because he has more experiences in teaching and school management. The principal must have insight in dealing with school's various situations.

45. 신임교사로서 자신만의 특별한 학급 운영방안

함께 하는 학급분위기를 만들어가는 기본생활 습관과 공동체 의식 함양에 주력한다.	I would focus on building the awareness about cooperation and daily habits which make the class atmosphere done together.
사이버 공간에서도 민주시민의 정체성을 유지할 수 있도록 정보윤리교육에 힘쓴다.	I try to focus on information ethics education in order for students to maintain identity as a democratic citizen in cyber space.
자기주도적 학습능력을 바탕으로 창의력을 신장하는 방안으로 모둠별 독서활동을 이끌어간다.	I would organize reading clubs as a way to improve creativity based on students' self-directed learning ability.
학급을 민주시민의 자질과 창의성을 길러주는 방향으로 이끌어 갈 것이다. 다음과 같은 방안을 가지고 나가겠다.	I would encourage students to build creativity and the sense of citizenship.
학생이 주인의식을 가지고 모든 과정에 참여하는 민주적인 학급경영을 하겠다.	I would let the students to take part in the whole process with a sense of ownership.
모든 학생을 공평하게 대하고 언제든지 대화의 창구를 열어놓는 학급경영을 하겠다.	I would treat all the students fairly. Also, I would often have a time to talk with other students.
함께하는 학급분위기를 창출하는 학급경영을 하겠다.	I would create the class atmosphere every students could take part in.
학생들의 의견을 최대한 반영하고 학생 한사람 한사람을 존중하고 그 가능성을 발휘할 수 있도록 민주적인 운영방식을 취한다.	I would choose democratic way so as to reflect students' opinion and respect every student.
교사라는 권위를 내세우지 않고 열린 경영, 투명한 경영을 한다. 모두가 학급의 주체로서 인정받고 자신의 능력을 발휘하게 한다.	I would not insist on the authority as a teacher. I would try to develop each student's ability by accepting them as the subjects of the class.
학급을 하나의 공동체로 만들어 너와나의 관계를 형성하여 서로 존중하는 인격적인 관계를 유지 발전시켜 나가겠다.	I would respect each student by making the class as one of community

46. 학령인구 감소가 중등 교육에 미칠 영향과 교사의 대응방안

1) 긍정적인 면

개별화 수업과 수준별 수업을 할 수 있는 여건을 제공한다.	It provides the environment to establish individual class and differentiated class.

2) 부정적인 면

학생들의 공동체 의식은 더 위기를 맞을 것이다.	Students' awareness about cooperation is difficult to be built.

3) 대응방안

공동체의식이 충만한 함께 하는 학급분위기를 조성하는 데 총력을 기울여야 한다.	People should try to establish the class atmosphere in which cooperative awareness are fully built.
저출산 문제와 관련된 다양한 주제를 교육내용에 담아야 한다.	Various themes related to low birth rate should be included in the educational content.

47. 교원 평가에서 동료교사가 점수를 낮게 준 것을 알게된 후 대처방법

동료교사가 악감정이 있거나 불편한 관계여서 의도적으로 낮은 점수를 주었다는 판단이 들면 본래 취지에 맞게 공정한 평가를 해달라고 부탁하고 악감정이나 불편한 관계를 해소할 수 있는 방안을 마련해서 개인적인 관계가 공정한 평가를 왜곡시키지 않게 한다.	If you think that co-teacher intentionally give lower grade because he has ill feeling towards you, you can ask him to do fair assessment whatever reason it is or you can prepare some ways to resolve a conflict.
동료교사가 좋은 관계인데 나름대로 소신대로 평가를 했다는 판단이 들면, 왜 그런 점수를 주었는지 이유를 파악하고 동료교사가 생각하는 더 좋은 방안들을 경청하고 적용해본다. 수업공개와 같은 형태나 공동연구 형태로 동료장학에 힘쓴다.	If you think that co-teachers who have good relationship with you, evaluate fairly, you should find out the reason why he gave lower grade and try to listen to better ways the co teacher thought. You should make an effort to learn through open class or collaborative study.
어떤 경우라도 감정적으로 대응하지 않고 합리적으로 문제를 해결한다.	You should try to solve the problem rationally not to react emotionally in any circumstances.

48. 외국유학을 상담해 온 학부모 상담

• 유학을 보내려는 이유에 대해서 물어본다.	• We should ask some specific reasons they want their child to study abroad.
• 학교교육에 대한 불만사항을 확인하면 학교와 교사가 해결할 수 있도록 노력하겠다고 한다.	• We should address the complaints that the parents have for the school, if they chose to go abroad with some school-related problems.
• 부모의 이직이나 이민으로 유학이 불가피한 상황이라면 현재 학생의 학업성취도 상황, 평소 학교생활에 정보를 제공하여 바람직한 유학에 도움이 되도록 한다.	• If the given situation is inevitable, we should encourage students to have an advisable study abroad.

49. 양성평등교육 방안

• 교육과정에 '남성다움'과 '여성다움'에 대한 성 고정관념에서 벗어날 수 있는 내용을 반영한다.	• A teacher should reflect the content which can make students break their gender stereotypes of maleness and femaleness in curriculum.
• 교육활동 중에 성별로 분리하여 팀이나 조를 짜는 것을 가능한 피한다.	• A teacher avoids making groups according to gender as much as possible in curricular activity.
• 재량활동시간의 일부를 활용하거나 연간 수업시수를 늘려 양성평등교육을 실시한다.	• A teacher implements education for gender equality by making use of a part of extra-curricular activity.

50. 독서논술교육 방안

• 독서 분위기를 조성한다.	• A teacher is able to create an atmosphere for reading books.
• 독서논술 프로그램을 다양하게 추구한다.	• A teacher is able to pursue the program for reading books and writing an essay in various ways.
• 인터넷을 통해 독서교육을 활성화한다.	• A teacher is able to activate reading education through the internet.

51. 교실 독서교육 방안

• 학급문고를 운영하다. • 학년별 필독독서 목록을 제공해준다. • 신의 수업에서 교과와 연계한 독서교육(독서-토론-논술)을 실시한다.	• to run class library. • to provide a list of a must read books according to students' needs and wants related to their future dreams. • to implement reading education related to regular curriculum in the lesson. Reading education consists of reading a book, discussion and writing an essay.

52. 국제 이해교육 활성화 방안

교과활동, 창의적 체험활동 시간을 이용하여 국제 이해교육을 실시한다.	A teacher is able to implement education for international understanding by making use of curricular activity and creative activity class.
교실수업보다 체험활동 형식을 통한 국제이해교육을 실시하다.	A teacher can implement education for international understanding through the form of the experience program. (volunteering program for foreign workers, participation in festivals for foreign workers)
외국인과 함께 하는 문화교실을 열어 일반학생에게 다문화 체험학습의 기회를 제공한다.	A teacher is able to provide the opportunity to experience multiple cultures for students and to open Cross-Cultural Awareness Programme where students will spend time getting along with foreigners.

53. 통일교육 지도

학생들이 관심 있는 북한 또래 아이들의 학교생활과 가정생활을 중심으로 교육한다.	We should teach the subject matter, using north korean students' school and domestic life that our students are interested in.
교사중심의 주입식 교육에서 벗어나 학생중심의 참여식, 체험식 교육을 지향한다.	Putting aside teacher-centered lesson, we should be able to have student-centered and experience-oriented lesson for the benefit of students.
다양한 학습방법과 학습보조수단을 활용해야 한다.	If a variety of teaching style and material is used for the lesson, the lesson will be more motivated for the learners.

54. 농산어촌 학교 소규모 학교 약점과 강점 살리기

1) 약점

학생 수가 적어 학생이 상호작용을 할 수 있는 기회가 적다. 따라서 협동심, 사회성, 성취감, 자신감을 기를 수 없어 학력향상과 인성함양에 어려움이 크다. 복식수업을 해야 하는 경우가 많아 수업의 질이 떨어진다.	Small number of students makes students have less opportunity to interact each other. Thus, students cannot well develop their spirit of team work, socialization, the sense of achievement, and confidence. Usually, those schools are supposed to have a class with all different graders, which harms the quality of classes.

2) 장점

학생 수가 적어 개별화 교육을 적용할 수 있다. 사교육 의존도가 낮으므로 교사가 소신껏 교육철학을 펼칠 수 있다.	Small number of students make it possible to apply individualized education to every student. With less private education, teachers can teach students with the teachers' own educational philosophies.

3) 농산어촌 약점 극복방안

• 정규수업에서 학생수가 적다는 이점을 살린 개별화 지도	• In regular classes, making use of the small number of students, individualized teaching can be administered.
• 이러닝 활용으로 사이버 학습 포털 사이트를 활용하여 비 전공교사, 복식수업의 문제점 해결	• E-learning should be utilized to complement the problem of lack of subject teachers and one class with different graders.
• 인근 소규모 학교와 방과후 학교 공동운영	• Schools can co-operate after-school classes with nearby schools.
• 인근에 대학이 있는 경우 연계: 대학생 멘토링 (학습지원, 상담)	• If there are universities nearby, mentoring program can be implemented by using college students.
• 도서관의 교수학습 센터화 및 놀이터화: 도서관을 현대화하여 문화적 교육적 사각지대에 있는 학생들이 다양한 자료와 정보에 접하면서 학습할 수 있는 장으로, 건전한 오락과 휴식을 즐길 수 있는 놀이터로 전환해야 한다.	• School libraries should be a center of various educational materials for students and students' play space.

55. 활기찬 학교 문화 형성

남을 배려하는 생활을 실천하게 한다.	Students should be disciplined to be considerate of other's feelings in their school life.
전 교과 지도를 통한 타인 배려의식 지도, 나부터, 지금부터, 작은 일부터 실천하기	Through every subject classes, students should be taught how to care for others' feelings. They should respect others' feelings like their own, from the trivial occasions.
친구사랑 운동을 전개한다: 친구의 장점, 선행 등을 찾아 칭찬하기, 친구사랑의 날 제정운영, 칭찬 마일리지 운영 및 칭찬 대상 수여하기	The campaign of "love friends" can be conducted: Finding friends' merits and good deeds and giving praise to them
인터넷 중독 예방, 치료교육으로 건전한 사이버 문화를 조성한다.	Schools conduct the prevention campaign of computer addiction and offer remedial treatment to establish healthier online culture.
인터넷 중독 학생 개인별 자가 진단 실시, 중독 예방 치료 프로그램 운영 (교육과정, 상담 중심)	Schools can offer self checklist of computer addiction for students and prevention program for the addiction through operating counseling and regular classes.

56. 학생이 오고 싶은 좋은 학교

수업(교과와 창의적 체험활동)이 재미있고 유익할 때 학생이 오고 싶어 합니다. 교사중심이 아니라 학생중심의 수업을 하는 학교일 때 오고 싶어 합니다.	When classes, that is, regular subject classes and creative hands on activities are interesting and useful then, they will be motivated to come school. Classes should be student centered.
공부하는 것이 자기 수준에 맞고 (일제식 수업에서 맞춤형 수준별 수업일 때), N세대에 맞게 재미있게 가르칠 때 (칠판과 분필에 의존하는 수업이 아니라 새로운 세대에 맞는 ICT를 활용한 다양한 수업)	If classes fit students' interest and needs with appropriate levels to each individuals, they want to go to school. Considering the new generations, students want to learn lessons through various and interesting ICT utilization.
함께 하는 분위기, 즉 서로 존중해 주고 아껴 주는 공동체적 관계가 학교에 살아 있을 때; 폭력과 왕따 없는 학교 = 공동체 의식을 심어주는 실천중심의 인성교육	If students can feel the congenial atmosphere and community spirit in school, where students respect and care for each other; where there is no bullying and violence among students; Students should learn the value of community spirit through strengthening the education that builds students' characters.

쾌적하고 청결한 환경 조성으로 공부할 마음이 솟구치게 하는 학교 환경이 조성되어 있을 때; 집처럼 편안함을 주면서도 집중할 수 있는 분위기가 조성된 학교	When school is well equipped with comfortable and clean learning environment; schools are comfortable and suitable for concentrating their study, students are motivated to go to school readily.

57. 사교육을 통한 선행학습

1) 선행학습의 원인

• 입시에 대한 학생과 학부모의 강박관념, 불안심리 (학벌주의, 출세주의적 교육관)	• Students and parents suffer from college entrance competition due to their cult of success and their status seeking.
• 학원수업이 학교수업보다 좋다는 그릇된 맹신	• They have blind faith in private lessons, considering private lessons are more effective than public education.
• 불충분한 공교육 서비스	• Insufficient service of public education causes them to rely more on private lessons.

2) 학원 선행학습 (문제풀이식, 주입식, 암기식, 반복식 학습)이 학생에게 끼치는 폐해

• 학교수업 내용을 이미 알고 있다고 생각하고 불성실한 학습태도를 보인다.	• Students may think that they know the lesson already and do not concentrate on the regular classes in school.
• 자기주도적 학습능력을 상실한다.	• Too much reliance on private education deprives students of their creativity and self-directed learning.
• 암기 학습만으로 창의력을 상실한다.	• To learn in advance by cramming method of teaching causes students to lose their creativity.

3) 선행학습 문제점 해결방안(학교차원)

• 학교수업을 교과내용을 전달하는 방식에서 탐구력을 통해서 개념과 원리를 이해하고 이를 새로운 상황에 적용하는 기회를 많이 제공한다.	• Teachers try to teach lessons through discovery instruction, where students can find basic concepts and principles by themselves. They can apply those into their life and new circumstances.
• 학교 수업을 일제식에서 수준별 맞춤식으로 바꾼다.	• Whole-class teaching should be modified into level-differentiated classes to tailor to each student's different educational needs.

• 다양한 학습기회와 방법을 제공한다.	• Various kinds of method of teaching and flexible learning environment should be provided.

4) 지도 방안

• 모르면서도 안다고 생각하고 수업에 집중하지 않는 경우 많은데 원리나 개념에 대한 정확한 이해가 없는 문세풀이식 선행학습의 문제점 일깨워주고 신시한 태도 수업에 임하게 한다.	• There are many students who think they know the content of lesson and do not concentrate on the regular classes. However, they just did rote-memory without understanding concepts, or principles. Teachers should let them know what the problem is in their understanding and pay attention to the class by giving more advanced learning.
• 수업내용이 선행학습을 받은 학생이 이미 알고 있는 내용이라면 심화학습 과제(응용문제)를 주어 학습하게 한다.	• Teachers give them additional advanced tasks if students can put their theory into practice.
• 또래 교수의 역할을 수행하게 하여 교학상장의 기쁨을 알게 한다.	• By experiencing mutual teaching experiences through teaching peer group, they can feel a sense of achievement and rewards altogether.

58. 수업시 학습지도 측면의 원인과 해결방안

1) 원인

• 개인차를 무시한 일제식 수업을 하였기 때문이다.	• The teacher is negligent of students' differences in their ability in learning and their needs while doing a whole class teaching.
• 교사 중심의 주입식 암기식 수업을 하였기 때문이다.	• The teacher did a rote learning and teacher-centered class instead of student-centered one.
• 칠판과 분필만 사용해서 수업했기 때문이다.	• Only with traditional blackboard, chalk and lecturing. The simplest form of teaching.

2) 해결책

• 과목의 특성을 살려 흥미와 능력을 고려한 적절한 수준별 수업을 실시한다.	• Teacher should implement level differentiated classes, considering each student's interest and ability.
• 자기 주도적 학습능력과 창의성을 키워주는 다양한 교수, 학습전략을 활용한다. 토론학습, 문제해결학습, 탐구학습 등	• Various types of teaching that builds self- and creativity-based learning should be implemented; discussion, problem solving projects or discovery activities
• 다양한 교육매체를 활용하되 특히 ICT 활용수업을 적극 도입한다. 특히 N세대인 것을 고려해서 사이버 가정학습과 결합된 온오프 혼합형 수업으로 학생의 흥미를 유발하고 자기주도적 학습을 이끈다.	• Various types of educational media should be implemented. ICT should be integrated into classes because N-generations have strong interest and familiarity in using technologies everyday. Cyber-home learning programs and off classes can be blended to attract students' strong interest and motivation to study on their own.

59. 생활지도 측면의 원인과 해결방안

1) 원인

• 학생이 수업의 규율을 몰라서 지키지 않을 수 있다.	• Students may not know the class rule well.
• 강화와 벌을 적절하게 활용하지 못했기 때문이다.	• Teacher did not make use of the reward and the punishment properly.

2) 해결방안

• 수업의 규율을 학생과 합의하여 만들고 일관되게 집행한다.	• Rules should be made by students and teacher together in class assembly to give them a sense of responsibility and fairness without exception.
• 토큰법, 프리맥의 원리, 타임아웃 같은 잘못된 행동을 수정해 주는 기법을 적정하게 사용한다.	• We can make use of the principles of token or time-out to guide students' misbehaviors depending on the situation.
• 자치활동, 봉사활동, 모둠활동을 통해 남을 배려하는 마음, 질서를 지킬 줄 아는 마음을 길러준다.	• Through volunteer work, and community work, I will instill the importance and value of respecting others and keeping the order.
• 면학분위기를 조성할 수 있는 규칙을 학기초에 학생과 함께 협의 하여 결정하고 일관되게 적용하겠다.	• To keep good study atmosphere, at the start of the semester, students can set up our class rules.

60. 공교육의 중요성

공교육이 살아나야 학력과 부가 되물림되는 사회현상을 극복할 수 있다: 사교육비가 엄청나서 가계의 허리가 휘고 있다. 더 큰 문제는 사교육에 의존한 교육이 계속되다 보면 부모의 소득격차가 교육격차로 이어지고 또다시 이것이 학력격차와 소득격차로 이어지면서 가난과 부가 되물림되는 불평등한 사회가 된다는 사실이다. 공교육이 살아나야 이러한 악순환의 고리를 끊을 수 있다.	When public education is regularized, we can break the vicious cycle of the inheritance of wealth and academic background: The private education expenditure is increasing and takes up the households' major spending. The bigger problem is that if we continue to rely on the private education, this will deepen the gap between the affluent and poor families, making our society unfair, where there is a transfer of wealth and poverty. Therefore, public education should be revived so that this vicious cycle should be stopped.
진정한 글로벌 인재를 길러내려면 공교육이 중요하다: 공교육은 전인교육을 지향한다. 그러나 사교육은 당장 상급학교 진학에 도움이 되는 성적 올리는 데 초점을 맞추고 있다. 그래서 문제풀이식 반복식 교육으로 지식 정보화 시대를 끌고 가는 데 가장 중요한 창의력과 자기주도적 학습능력을 소멸 시키고 있다. 그러나 공교육은 지덕체를 골고루 발달시키면서 균형잡힌 차세대 인재를 길러낼 수 있는 구조를 가지고 있다.	To foster the true global leaders, we need public education: Public education is in line with the whole person education. However, private education only focuses on getting good scores for entering prestigious colleges. Rote-memory skills or skill based problem solving can harm our students' creativity and self disciplined learning ability. But public education is designed to develop students to a whole person.

61. 학교에서 안전사고 대처방법

• 당황하지 말고 다친 학생을 안정시킨다. • 보건교사의 응급치료를 받고, 상태에 따라 병원으로 후송하여 정밀치료를 받게 한다. • 담임교사는 교감, 교장에게 알리고 피해학생 부모님께 연락한다. • 가해학생이 있는 경우에는 부모님께 연락하여 피해학생에 대한 책임을 지도록 한다.	• Remain calm and relieve an injured student. • Get an injured student to have emergency medical treatment at school and if his injury is serious, send him to the hospital to get a thorough medical treatment. • A homeroom teacher informs the principal and the parents. • If there is an attacker, call his parents and ask them to take responsibility for the whole treatment if necessary.

62. 안전지도 방안

• 이론중심이 아니라 실행중심의 안전생활지도를 강화해야 한다. • 체험활동, 모의 훈련 등 실천 중심의 안전교육을 실시해야 한다. • 현장지도를 통해 교통사고 예방교육을 강화해야 한다. • 가정과 지역사회와 연계하여 안전사고 예방교육을 생활화해야 한다.	• Reinforce practice-based safety education, not knowledge-based one. • Carry out practice-based safety education such as hands on activities and mock exercises. • Through field lesson, reinforce preventive discipline for traffic accident. • Make preventive discipline on safety daily routine by establishing ties with family and community.

63. 형식적인 봉사활동의 문제점 지도방안

• 봉사활동의 필요성을 알려준다. • 봉사활동의 필요성과 방법을 알려주면서 다양한 사례를 소개한다. • 학생들이 참여할 수 있는 여러 가지 활동을 다양하게 할 수 있도록 정보를 충분히 수집하고 구체적인 계획을 세운다. • 봉사활동이 끝나면 활동의 과정과 결과를 평가하여 다음 봉사활동에 대한 동기를 유발하게 한다. • 지역 사회 유관 기관과 봉사단체와 긴밀한 협조체제를 유지하여 효율적인 봉사활동을 한다.	• I would remind the reason volunteering work is required. • I would introduce various example cases of volunteering along with explanation of necessity and ways of volunteering work. • I would plan in an explicit way after pooling enough information to help students to participate in a variety of activities. • I would trigger expectations toward the next volunteer work by giving students a chance to evaluate process and product of the work they have done. • With the cooperation of community centers or organizations of volunteers, volunteer work can be more efficient.

64. 다양한 동아리 활동 활성화 방안

학생 선택권을 존중하면서도 다양한 동아리 활동을 활성화하는 방안을 말하겠다. 학생을 대상으로 수요조사를 실시하여 학생이 원하는 동아리를 다양하게 만들어 학생의 선택의 폭을 넓혀 주어야 한다.	Let me tell you how to activate various club activities respecting students' rights. Through the survey, I would pool all the club information they are interested in. Students can have more options to choose from a variety of clubs provided.
동아리에 학생들이 고르게 참여하게 하려면, 각 동아리의 특색과 참여할 때 얻을 수 있는 효과를 알리는 홍보를 수행해야 한다.	For the even participation of each club, students should have detailed information about the effects of clubs.
동아리 활동을 활성화하려면 교내외의 인적 물적 자원을 적극 활용해야 한다.	To activate club activities, personal and physical resources inside and outside the school should be utilized.
우수지도교사를 확보해서 동아리 활동의 질을 높여 주어야 한다.	Qualified instructors should be provided in order to improve the quality of club activities.

65. 성공적인 학급회를 위한 지도방법

특정학생이 발언을 독점하지 않도록 지도한다.	Teacher prevents one specific student from dominating the class meeting.
다수의견을 수용하고 반대의견 존중하고 예의있게 자신의 입장 개진하도록 지도한다.	Teacher encourages students to accept the majority's opinion, respect different opinions and suggest their opinion in a polite way.
학생이 자발적으로 학급회의를 진행한다.	The class meeting should be run voluntarily.

66. 인터넷 게임 중독 문제점과 지도방안

1) 게임중독의 문제점

• 정신발달에 장애가 생긴다.	• hamper mental development.
• 신체발달에 문제가 생긴다.	• hinder their physical development.
• 대인관계가 파괴된다.	• make it impossible for students to socialize with other people.
• 인터넷 범죄에 빠지기도 한다.	• make students get involved in cyber crimes.
• 학습부진 현상이 나타나고 정상적인 일상생활을 하기 힘들어진다.	• make their academic performance and daily lives difficult.

2) 지도방안

• 정기적으로 정보통신윤리교육을 실시한다.	• Teacher teaches ethics on information communication on a regular basis.
• 학교가 인터넷 게임보다 더 재미있는 일을 제공해 줄 수 있어야 한다.	• School should be able to offer more fun activities than games.
• 중독에 빠진 학생이 원만한 대인관계를 회복하도록 지도한다.	• Teacher guides them to restore good relationships with other people.
• 게임중독에 빠진 원인 (부모의 자녀 방임, 가까이 지내는 친구의 영향 등)을 함께 진지하게 찾아보고 해결을 모색한다.	• Teacher investigates the cause of the addiction such as neglect from parents or influence by close friends and finds the solutions accordingly.
• 해야 할 일을 반드시 한 뒤에 적절한 시간만 인터넷을 하는 습관을 길러준다.	• Teacher guides them to make it a habit to complete assignment first and uses Internet for specific amount of time.

67. 과목 수업도중 문을 발로 차고 수업시간에 나간 학생에 대한 담임교사의 조치

1) 원인

• 철수가 보이는 공격성은 다양한 원인에서 비롯되었을 수 있다. 가정불화, 부모의 이혼, 경제적 빈곤 등 학생을 둘러싼 가정환경이 만족스럽지 못해서 불만이 공격적 행동으로 표출되는 경우가 있다.	• His aggression can originate in various causes. His environment such as family troubles, parents' divorce, or adverse economic environment can cause a student to do aggressive behaviors.
• 대중매체로부터 공격성, 폭력성 등을 학습하는 경우가 있다.	• A student can pick up violence and aggression from mass media.
• 욕구충족이 안되면 공격적 행동을 보이기도 한다: 불만족스러운 상황을 말보다 행동으로 표현 (ADHD): 욕구를 표현하지 못해 마음속에 분노가 쌓여 공격적인 행동을 보일 때 가 있다.	• A mentally challenged student tends to show aggressive operations when his desire is not satisfied: A student with ADHD expresses their dissatisfaction with aggressive operations, not with words.

2) 지도방안

• 쉽게 화를 분출하는 철수에게 지속적인 사랑과 관심을 표현한다.	• Express constant love and attention.
• 화를 누그러뜨릴 수 있는 공간을 만들어 준다.	• Make a place where he can calm himself down.
• 감정을 참을 수 있는 기술을 알려주자.	• Instruct skills with which he can control his feelings.

68. 중도 탈락자 예방 방안

담임교사와 생활지도 담당교사는 학생 개개인의 가정 사정 및 교우관계를 면밀히 파악하여 알맞는 지도를 적극적으로 실시한다.	A teacher and counselor should provide appropriate guidance for students based on their background and friends' relations.
중도탈락 예상 학생에 대해서는 개인별로 상담교사를 지정하여 졸업할 때까지 진로지도와 개인상담을 실시하여 중도탈락을 예방한다.	Assign individual counselor to expected dropouts and carry out career and individual counsel until those students graduate from school.
즐거운 학교를 만든다.	Make a school safe and pleasant to students.
학생들의 다양성과 개별성을 존중하고 그들의 적성에 맞는 교육과정을 운영한다.	Respect students' diversities and uniqueness and provide educational curriculum to their aptitude.
학습부진아 해소를 위한 수준별 수업과 특기와 적성을 신장해주는 체험활동과 특별활동을 장려한다.	Encourage level-differentiated class which works off school underachievement and encourage extra-curricular activities to boost students' aptitude and specialty.
교내 문화공간을 확충하고 학생 단체활동, 사제동행 수련활동 등을 활성화하여 부적응 학생의 참여를 유도한다.	Expand cultural spaces in school and participate maladjusted students by encouraging group activities or retreats.

69. 가출경험이 있는 학생 지도

가출의 근본 원인이 되었던 학생의 욕구나 바람을 정확히 파악하여 다른 방법으로 충족할 수 있는 방법을 찾아보도록 한다.	Find the fundamental desire of running away from home and help the student to meet the desire with other ways.
학생의 주변인물에게 협조를 구한다. 학생이 건전한 생활을 할 수 있도록 돕는 지지자가 되어줄 것을 부탁한다.	Ask the student's acquaintances for help and become supporters who help the student live healthy lifestyle.
학교생활에 흥미를 가질 수 있도록 적절한 역할을 부여하고 다른 학생과 자연스럽게 어울릴 수 있도록 소집단 활동의 기회를 준다.	Give the student opportunity to be motivated in school life and provide group work through which the student can mix naturally with other students.

70. 자살충동을 느끼는 학생

학업문제, 건강문제, 가정환경, 교우관계 등을 종합적으로 살펴 우울증과 자살충동이 어떤 이유 때문에 발생했는지 분석하여 그에 맞는 종합적인 처치를 계획한다.	Analyze the reason a student feels like committing suicide and gets depression by considering the problems of study, health, family, or friends. After that, plan a comprehensive measure.
항상 학생에게 관심을 가지고 배려를 하되 자립심과 극기심을 길러준다.	Care for the student while bringing up independence and the spirit of self-restraint.
가정과 연계하여 지도한다.	Guide the student by establishing ties with his or her family.

71. 문제행동아 (학교부적응아) 지도 방안

열린 대화를 나눔으로써 친밀한 관계를 형성한다.	Form a close relationship with a student through a heart-to-heart talk. Developing a bond of sympathy and loving attention can contribute to relieving maladjustment.
적절한 칭찬과 보상을 활용한다.	Use proper compliments and rewards as a behavior reformation technique. Proper praises and rewards can lead to good deeds since maladjusted students get used to scolding.
가정, 상담전문가, 특수교사와 연계해서 지도한다.	To understand the cause of problem behaviors, guide them by establishing ties with family, counselor, teachers.

72. 학급에 집단 따돌림을 당하는 학생 예방과 대처방안

1) 예방

• 평소에 상담을 지속적으로 실시하여 학생에게 공동체의식을 길러주고 인권교육도 정기적으로 실시한다.	• Promote communal (team) spirit by counseling students consistently and provide human rights education to students regularly.
• 쪽지 상담과 설문조사를 수시로 실시하여 왕따 학생을 파악한다.	• Figure out a bullied student by conducting message counsel and a survey frequently.
• 학생회 주관으로 집단 따돌림 예방을 위한 다양한 행사를 실시한다.	• Implement 'student council' to offer diverse events for preventing bullying, role play, day of reconciliation.

2) 대처방안

• 가해학생을 데리고 양로원, 고아원 등 수용시설 방문하여 봉사활동 실시함으로써 자신보다 어렵고 불편한 사람들을 도와주면서 심적 변화 유도	• A teacher can induce emotional change of bullying-group students by doing various volunteer works together for orphans or elderly people.
• 자치회의 시간 및 특활시간에 따돌림에 대한 토론 및 역할극 등을 실시해 피해자의 고통을 가해자가 느껴 볼 수 있도록 한다.	• A teacher can make bullying-group students realize how bullied-group students suffer from by carrying out discussion or role play.
• 학생이 따돌림의 피해에 대해 이야기를 할 때 진지한 태도로 받아주어야 한다.	• If a student speak out the problems of bullying, teacher should listen carefully and take the problem seriously.

73. 학생 갈등 (의견대립, 싸움) 해결방안

갈등 해결의 원칙을 정한다: 상호존중, 욕하지 않을 것, 경청한 다음 의견 말하기	Set rules for resolving conflicts such as respect each other, do not use swear words, listen carefully to others first.
상대방의 입장을 이해하도록 한다: 불만사항, 갈등요인을 솔직하게 토로	Put themselves in others' shoes: talk honestly about their complaint or causes of conflict.
문제해결을 위한 각자의 입장을 말하도록 한다. - 상대방의 의견을 비판 없이 경청	Tell their own position to solve the problem and listen others' opinion without judgements.
하나 혹은 그 이상의 해결방법을 합의하도록 한다.	Reach an agreement on more than one solution.
합의사항을 문서로 기록하고 보관한다.	Prepare a written note about agreement and then keep it.
약속이 잘 지켜지는가를 점검해보는 다음 만남시간을 정한다.	Set a next meeting to check the fulfillment of promise

74. 기초 기본 생활 습관이 지켜지지 않는 이유와 교사의 지도방안

1) 잘 지켜지지 않는 이유

• 학교차원: 학력신장에 치중한 나머지 인성교육과 생활 지도를 소홀히 했다.	• At school level: A school highlights only on students' academic ability rather than personality.
• 가정차원: 모든 것을 허용하며 과잉보호 했다.	• At family level: Parents are overprotective of their children.
• 사회차원: 편의주의와 무질서, 학력제일주의가 만연해있다.	• At social level: There are pervading opportunism, disorder and academic elitism.

2) 지도방안

• 실천 중심적이고 자율적인 지도를 수행한다.	• Teacher should provide experience-based teaching.
• 모든 교사가 전 교육과정에서 기본 생활 습관을 지도해야한다.	• All teachers should teach basic attitudes through whole curriculum.
• 학생이 지켜야 할 기본 생활 규칙을 학생과 함께 협의하여 명확히 결정하고 학년 초부터 지키게 한다.	• Teacher and students decide the rules together, and teacher lets students follow the rules from the beginning of the semester.
• 교사가 실천의지를 가지고 솔선수범하는 모습을 보여주는 것이 중요하다.	• A teacher should be a role-model for students.

75. 학습에 흥미를 잃은 학생에 대한 동기유발 방법

수준에 맞는 맞춤형 학습을 실시한다.	Implement tailored learning that matches with students' their own level.
학습부진이 능력에 있지 않고 노력 부족에 있음을 일깨워준다.	Make retarded students realize that low achieving in their study is not from their ability but from their efforts.
작은 성공의 경험을 제공하고 칭찬해 준다.	Provide a chance to experience little successes in their life and praise them.

76. 인터넷을 학교교육에 활용할 수 있는 방안

수업과 연계한 온라인 학습, 사이버 가정 학습을 통해서 학력 제고에 활용	E-learning can be used to improve students' academic performance through Online learning combined with classroom based learning and cyber home learning.
학교, 학급 홈페이지 및 교사 개인 홈페이지 형태로 학교와 학급경영에 활용	It can be used for managing school and class in forms of school, class or teacher homepages.
교류와 협력의 장으로 사용	We can use e-learning as a place for interaction and cooperation.
온라인을 통해 학습, 생활, 진로상담을 비롯한 전문상담 활성화에 활용	We can use e-learning to activate professional counselling as well as learning, life design, and career counselling.

77. 교사가 모르는 질문을 받았을 때 처리방법

교과내용과 관계없는 질문내용이면 간단하게 답하든지 수업 후에 개별적으로 질문하게 한다.	If the question is unrelated to the contents, teacher answers briefly or after class.
교과 내용과 관련된 내용은 먼저 전체학생에게 질문을 돌려 같이 생각해 보는 기회를 갖게 한다.	If the question is related to the lesson, let the whole class think about the question.
이 문제를 푸는 데 필요한 기본지식이나 원리를 설명해 줄 수 있다.	Tell about basic principles or concepts that are required for the question.
다음 시간까지 연구해 오기로 하고 다음 학습과제를 지도한다.	Teacher will look over the question and give the right answer in the next lesson.

78. 교사가 열심히 지도하였으나 학생의 학업성적이 낮을때 원인과 대책

학생의 답안을 확인하고 분석한다. 특별히 정답률이 낮은 문제는 그 내용을 제대로 설명했는지, 지도방법은 옳았는지 살펴본다.	Teacher checks students' answers and analyze the reasons why the class got lower scores. Teacher look at closely teaching methods.
학습 부진의 원인을 정확히 파악하여 부진을 해소할 수 있는 방법을 찾아본다.	Teacher find the reasons of underachievement of the class and find a way to improve their weaknesses.
부정적인 예언은 학생의 학습의욕을 꺾고 부적응행동을 증가시킨다: 출발점행동 진단 오류 여부, 적절한 교재 선택 여부, 수업목표와 내용 파악 부실에서 온 교재 연구 미비 여부, 학생 실태 파악 소홀에서 비롯된 개인차 무시 여부, 교사의 책임감 결핍 여부	Negative prediction will discourage students from learning and increase maladjusted behavior: misjudgment in students' initial ability by diagnostic test, inappropriate learning materials to goals and objectives, ignorance of individualized differences and lack of teacher's responsibility.
개별화 학습과 수준별 학습을 적극적으로 실천한다.	Teacher carries into practice individualized learning and level differentiated learning.
평소에 자신의 지도방법이 부적절한 것은 아니었는지 반성해 본다.	Teacher regularly reflects on her teaching to know whether her teaching methods are appropriate.

79. 교직생활의 공식적, 비공식적 행사에서 개인의 의사를 고려하지 않는 경우 대처 방법

교직은 공동체 생활을 전제로 하는 것이기 때문에, 개인의 의사가 반영되지 않더라도 상급자의 지시나 다수결로 내려진 결정이라면 존중하고 따른다.	Although teachers' group is professional one, they work as a team in the community, teachers have a duty to have supportive manners to one another and follow the direction of superiors.
적절한 기회가 있으면 개인의 의사가 최대한 반영되는 것이 행사의 질과 의미를 높일 수 있다는 점을 얘기하면서 설득한다.	But, if we have a proper chance to discuss the way about making decision on school events, I can suggest the better way to reflect all members' opinions. At this time, but, I should persuade other teachers politely.

CHAPTER 03 한국어 면접 핵심문제와 답안

1 미래 사회는 4차 산업혁명과 AI 기술의 발전으로 급격한 변화를 겪고 있으며, 이러한 변화 속에서 도전적이고 창의적인 인재가 더욱 중요해지고 있다. 전통적인 지식 전달 중심의 교육 방식은 더 이상 미래 사회의 요구를 충족시키지 못하기 때문에, 미래 사회에 대비한 학교교육의 방향은 학생들이 창의적 문제 해결 능력과 비판적 사고력을 갖출 수 있도록 하는 방향으로 나아가야 한다. 도전적이고 창의적인 인간을 기르기 위한 미래사회에 대비한 학교교육의 방향에 대해 구체적으로 말해보세요.

1. 창의적 문제 해결 능력 함양
    - 프로젝트 기반 학습(PBL): 학생들이 실생활 문제를 해결하는 과정을 통해 창의적 사고력을 기를 수 있는 프로젝트 기반 학습이 필요하다. 학생들은 팀으로 구성되어 다양한 문제에 도전하고, 자신들의 아이디어를 구현해보는 과정에서 창의성과 협동심을 키울 수 있다. 이 과정은 실제 문제를 해결하는 방식으로 이루어져 학생들이 비판적 사고와 문제 해결 능력을 자연스럽게 습득하도록 도와준다.
    - 융합 교육(STEAM): 과학, 기술, 공학, 예술, 수학을 융합한 STEAM 교육을 통해 학생들이 다양한 학문 간의 경계를 넘나들며 창의적으로 사고할 수 있는 능력을 길러야 한다. 이를 통해 학생들은 다양한 관점에서 문제를 바라보고, 혁신적인 해결책을 찾는 능력을 갖출 수 있다.

2. 비판적 사고와 정보 활용 능력
    - 미디어 리터러시 교육: 정보화 시대에서는 학생들이 정보를 분석하고 평가하는 능력이 매우 중요하다. 단순히 지식을 습득하는 것을 넘어서, 학생들이 올바른 정보를 선택하고 활용할 수 있는 비판적 사고 능력을 길러야 한다. 이를 위해 미디어 리터러시 교육을 강화하여 학생들이 다양한 정보의 진위를 판별하고, 이를 창의적으로 활용할 수 있는 역량을 키우는 것이 필요하다.
    - 디지털 기술 활용 능력: 미래 사회에서는 디지털 기술 활용 능력이 필수적이다. 프로그래밍, 데이터 분석, AI 활용 등 다양한 디지털 기술을 학교 교육에 통합하여, 학생들이 이러한 기술을 창의적이고 실용적으로 사용할 수 있는 능력을 갖추도록 해야 한다.

3. 자기주도 학습과 평생 학습 태도 형성
    - 학생 중심의 자기주도 학습: 교사는 학생들이 스스로 학습할 수 있는 환경을 제공하고, 학생들이 자기주도적으로 학습 목표를 설정하고 달성할 수 있도록 도와야 한다. 플립 러닝(Flipped Learning)과 같은 방식으로 교실 밖에서 개별적으로 학습하고, 교실에서는 학습한 내용을 바탕으로 토론하고 문제를 해결하는 학습 방법을 통해 학생들의 자율성을 높일 수 있다.
    - 평생 학습 태도 함양: 빠르게 변화하는 사회에서는 평생 학습의 중요성이 강조된다. 학생들이 지속적인 학습을 통해 새로운 기술과 지식을 습득할 수 있는 태도를 기르도록 교육해야 한다. 이를 위해 학교는 학습에 대한 내적 동기를 자극하고, 끊임없이 성장하고 도전할 수 있는 학습 문화를 조성해야 한다.

4. 협동과 사회적 책임의식 강화
    - 협동 학습: 미래 사회에서는 협력이 중요한 덕목이기 때문에, 학생들이 팀원들과 함께 목표를 이루기 위해 소통하고 협력하는 경험을 쌓는 것이 중요하다. 팀 프로젝트나 협동 과제를 통해 학생들은 서로의 의견을 존중하며 협동하는 방법을 배우고, 이를 통해 리더십과 협업 능력을 기르게 된다.
    - 사회적 책임의식: 또한, 사회적 책임감과 윤리적 의식을 갖춘 인재를 양성하는 것도 필수적이다. 학생들

이 자신의 능력을 사회에 기여하고, 지구와 인류를 위한 지속 가능한 발전에 이바지할 수 있도록 환경 교육이나 사회적 문제 해결 프로젝트 등을 통해 책임 의식을 고취시켜야 한다.

5. 글로벌 시민 교육
- 다문화 이해 및 글로벌 마인드: 글로벌 시대에는 다문화 이해와 국제적 감각이 필수적이다. 학생들이 다양한 문화와 관점을 이해하고 수용할 수 있도록, 다문화 교육 및 국제 교류 프로그램을 강화해야 한다. 또한, 글로벌 사회에서 필요한 외국어 능력과 커뮤니케이션 능력을 기르는 것이 중요하다.
- 지속 가능 발전 교육: 환경 문제와 사회적 불평등 같은 글로벌 이슈를 다루는 지속 가능 발전 교육을 통해, 학생들이 글로벌 시민으로서 윤리적 책임과 문제 해결 능력을 갖추게 해야 한다. 이를 통해 학생들은 세계적인 시각을 가지고, 공동체 발전에 기여하는 인재로 성장할 수 있다.

6. 창의적 사고를 위한 실패 경험의 기회 제공
- 실패에서 배우기: 학생들이 도전하고, 실패할 기회를 제공해야 한다. 창의적 사고는 실패를 통해 발전하기 때문에, 학생들이 실패를 두려워하지 않고 다양한 도전에 나설 수 있는 안전한 학습 환경을 마련해야 한다. 교사는 학생들에게 실패도 중요한 학습 과정이라는 것을 알려주고, 실패를 통해 무엇을 배웠는지 스스로 성찰하도록 도와야 한다.

미래 사회에 대비한 학교 교육은 창의적 사고와 비판적 문제 해결 능력을 길러내는 데 초점을 맞추어야 한다. 학생들은 스스로 학습하고, 협력하며, 글로벌 이슈에 책임감 있게 대응할 수 있는 능력을 갖추어야 한다. 이를 위해 학생 중심의 교육, 융합적 학습, 디지털 기술 활용 등을 통해 미래 인재로 성장할 수 있는 환경을 마련해야 한다. 지속적인 자기주도 학습과 협동 학습, 그리고 실패를 통한 학습이 가능하게 함으로써 학생들이 도전적이고 창의적인 인재로 성장하도록 돕는 것이 학교 교육의 중요한 방향이 되어야 한다.

2 추가질문 위와 같은 미래 교육을 실천하기 위하여 21세기를 향한 미래지향적 교사의 교사상을 말해보세요.

21세기를 향한 미래지향적 교사상은 급변하는 사회와 교육 환경 속에서 학생들이 창의적이고 도전적인 인재로 성장할 수 있도록 다양한 역할을 수행하는 교사이다. 미래 사회의 요구에 부응하고, 학생들의 잠재력을 극대화하기 위해 교사는 단순한 지식 전달자가 아니라, 학생들의 학습 가이드, 코치, 멘토로서 다양한 책임과 역할을 맡게 된다. 다음은 미래지향적 교사의 교사상과 이를 실천하기 위한 주요 특성이다.

1. 창의적이고 융합적인 사고를 지닌 교사
- 융합적 사고: 교사는 다양한 학문과 기술을 통합하여 새로운 가치를 창출하는 융합적 사고를 지녀야 한다. 이를 통해 학생들에게 과목 간 경계를 넘나드는 창의적 문제 해결력을 가르칠 수 있다. 예를 들어, STEAM 교육을 도입하여 과학, 기술, 공학, 예술, 수학을 융합하는 학습 경험을 제공하며, 학생들이 현실 세계의 문제를 창의적으로 접근하도록 돕는다.
- 비판적 사고 촉진: 단순히 지식을 전달하는 것을 넘어, 학생들이 스스로 사고하고 문제를 해결하는 비판적 사고력을 기를 수 있도록 지도한다. 교사는 질문을 통해 학생들이 깊이 있는 사고를 하도록 유도하고, 문제를 다양한 관점에서 분석하는 능력을 길러준다.

2. 디지털 기술을 능숙하게 활용하는 교사
- 디지털 리터러시 역량: 미래 사회에서는 디지털 도구와 기술의 활용이 필수적이다. 교사는 최신 디지털 기술을 활용하여 효과적인 학습 도구를 제공하고, 학생들에게 디지털 리터러시를 교육할 수 있어야 한다. 이를 위해 온라인 학습 플랫폼, 가상현실(VR), 증강현실(AR) 등을 수업에 도입하여 학생들이 디지털 기술을 자연스럽게 익히도록 지원한다.

- 플립 러닝과 하이브리드 수업: 교사는 플립 러닝이나 블렌디드 러닝과 같은 학습 방식을 통해 학생들이 자기주도적으로 학습하고, 교실에서는 토론과 프로젝트 활동에 집중할 수 있도록 학습 환경을 조성한다. 이는 교사의 디지털 도구 활용 능력과 수업 설계 능력을 요구한다.

3. 평생 학습을 실천하는 교사
   - 끊임없는 자기 개발: 미래지향적 교사는 평생 학습자로서, 끊임없이 새로운 지식과 기술을 습득하고 자신을 발전시킵니다. 이를 통해 교사는 최신 교육 트렌드와 혁신적인 교수법을 습득하며, 학생들에게 더 나은 교육을 제공할 수 있다. 연수 프로그램과 전문적 학습 공동체(PLC)에 적극 참여하여 동료 교사들과 협력하고, 학습자 중심의 교육을 실천할 수 있도록 자신을 계속해서 업그레이드해야 한다.
   - 실험적이고 도전적인 수업 설계: 교사는 전통적인 교육 방식을 뛰어넘어 새로운 교수법과 학습 전략을 실험하는 데 주저하지 않아야 한다. 실패를 두려워하지 않고 다양한 시도를 통해 창의적이고 혁신적인 수업 방법을 도입하는 교사가 되어야 한다.

4. 학생 중심의 학습 촉진자
   - 자기주도 학습 촉진: 교사는 학생들이 자기주도적으로 학습할 수 있도록 도와야 한다. 학생 스스로 목표를 설정하고 학습 과정을 계획하며 문제를 해결하는 능력을 키울 수 있도록 학습 환경을 설계한다. 학생의 흥미와 관심을 반영한 프로젝트 기반 학습(PBL)이나 문제 기반 학습(Problem-Based Learning) 등의 방식을 통해 학생들이 학습의 주도권을 가질 수 있게 한다.
   - 개별화된 피드백 제공: 미래지향적 교사는 학생 각자의 학습 수준과 필요에 맞는 개별화된 피드백을 제공하여 학생들이 자신의 학습 방향을 조정하고 발전할 수 있도록 지원한다. 이를 위해 교사는 학생의 강점과 약점을 파악하고, 이를 기반으로 한 맞춤형 지도와 학습 자료를 제공해야 한다.

5. 협력적이고 소통하는 교사
   - 학생과의 소통: 교사는 학생들과의 신뢰 관계를 구축하고, 상호작용을 통한 소통을 강화해야 한다. 학생들이 자신의 생각과 감정을 자유롭게 표현할 수 있는 환경을 조성하고, 이를 통해 교사와 학생 간의 협력을 촉진한다. 교사는 학생들의 의견을 경청하고, 그들의 학습 과정에 대한 피드백을 제공하며, 학생들이 스스로 문제를 해결할 수 있도록 지원해야 한다.
   - 협력 학습 촉진: 교사는 학생들이 팀으로 협력하여 학습하는 협력 학습(cooperative learning)을 적극 도입해야 한다. 학생들이 서로의 의견을 존중하고, 공동의 목표를 위해 협력하는 과정을 통해 사회적 기술과 문제 해결 능력을 함양할 수 있도록 돕는다.

6. 정서적 지원과 공감 능력 있는 교사
   - 정서적 지원 제공: 교사는 학생들이 겪는 학습 및 정서적 어려움을 이해하고, 이들에게 정서적 지원을 제공하는 것이 중요한다. 심리적 안정감과 자기 효능감을 느낄 수 있도록 격려하며, 교사는 학생들의 정신적, 정서적 건강을 우선시하는 교육을 실천해야 한다.
   - 학생들의 개별성 존중: 교사는 학생들의 개별적인 요구와 특성을 존중하고, 이를 반영한 수업을 설계해야 한다. 학생마다 학습 스타일, 속도, 관심사가 다르기 때문에, 이러한 다양성을 인정하고, 차별화된 학습 경험을 제공하는 것이 중요하다.

7. 글로벌 시민 의식을 함양하는 교사
   - 지속 가능성과 글로벌 이슈 교육: 교사는 학생들에게 지속 가능한 발전(SDGs) 및 글로벌 이슈에 대한 교육을 제공함으로써, 학생들이 글로벌 시민으로서의 의식과 책임감을 가질 수 있도록 도와야 한다. 환경 문제, 인권 문제 등 글로벌 이슈에 대한 수업을 통해 학생들이 공동체에 기여하고, 사회적 책임감을 느끼는 인재로 성장할 수 있도록 교육해야 한다.
   - 다양성과 포용성 교육: 미래 사회에서 중요한 덕목인 다양성과 포용성을 교육하는 역할도 중요하다. 교사는 학생들이 다양한 문화와 배경을 이해하고, 타인과의 차이를 존중하는 태도를 기를 수 있도록 지도해야 있다. 이를 위해 다문화 교육과 세계 시민 교육을 포함한 수업을 적극적으로 도입할 수 있다.

21세기를 향한 미래지향적 교사는 창의적이고 혁신적인 사고를 바탕으로 학생들의 잠재력을 극대화할 수 있는 학습 촉진자이자 평생 학습자로서 끊임없이 자기 발전을 추구하며, 도전적이고 창의적인 학습 환경을 조성하여 학생들이 미래 사회에서 성공적으로 성장할 수 있도록 도울 것이다.

3 양성평등교육의 중요성을 설명하고, 기본적인 방안을 4가지 말하시오.

① 중요성
- 각자의 개성과 능력을 충분히 발휘하기 위하여
- 자립적인 마음과 태도 능력을 배양하기 위하여
- 타인의 특성과 개성을 존중하는 마음을 가지게 하기 위하여
- 사회국가적으로 잠재되어 있는 인력을 개발하기 위하여

② 기본방안
- 교수학습 자료의 선정 시 활용목적의 적합성과 더불어 교재의 내용 및 구성 등이 학생들에게 성 고정관념이나 편견을 강화시킬 우려가 있는지 점검한다.
- 남녀학생간의 협력을 격려하는 교실활동을 조직하고 남녀학생 모두에게 지도력 계발의 기회를 제공한다.
- 교과활동 중 성별로 모둠이나 팀을 분리하여 조직하는 것을 가능한 한 피한다.
- 혼성학급에서 남학생 또는 여학생이 수업을 주도적으로 이끌어갈 우려가 높다고 판단되는 경우에는 성별로 집단을 분리하여 수업하는 것이 좋다.
- 교원자신이 성 고정관념에 따른 기대를 갖고 언어를 사용하는지 또는 이에 따른 교수활동을 하고 있는지를 점검한다.

4 정보화 시대에 교사가 갖추어야 할 자질은 급변하는 기술 환경과 학습자의 요구에 부응하기 위해 매우 중요하다. 교사는 단순한 지식 전달자가 아니라, 디지털 리더이자 촉진자, 평생 학습자로서의 역할을 수행해야 한다. 이를 통해 학생들이 정보화 사회에서 필요로 하는 다양한 역량을 키울 수 있도록 돕는 것이 중요하다. 정보화 시대에 교사가 갖추어야 할 자질에 대해 구체적으로 말해보세요.

정보화 시대에 교사는 학생들이 필요로 하는 다양한 역량을 키울 수 있도록 돕는 것이 중요하다. 이를 위해서는 아래와 같은 교사가 갖추어야 할 핵심 역량이 있다.

- 디지털 리터러시: 디지털 도구와 기술 활용 능력은 필수적이다. 교사는 컴퓨터, 스마트 기기, 인터넷, 소프트웨어 및 다양한 교육 플랫폼을 사용하여 수업을 계획하고 운영할 수 있어야 한다. 이는 학습 자료를 제작하거나 학생들과의 소통을 위해 필수적이다. 예를 들어, 온라인 학습 관리 시스템(LMS), 화상 회의 도구, 소셜 미디어, 교육용 앱 등을 사용해 효율적이고 상호작용적인 수업을 운영할 수 있어야 한다.
- 비판적 사고와 정보 평가 능력: 정보화 시대에는 방대한 양의 정보가 넘쳐나기 때문에 교사는 학생들에게 비판적 사고를 가르칠 수 있어야 한다. 교사는 정보의 출처를 평가하고, 신뢰할 수 있는 자료를 선별하는 능력을 가지고 있어야 하며, 이를 학생들에게 전수해야 한다. 특히 가짜 뉴스나 잘못된 정보에 대한 인식과 올바른 정보 사용법을 가르치는 것이 중요하다.
- 창의적 문제 해결 능력: 빠르게 변화하는 기술 환경 속에서 교사는 창의적으로 문제를 해결할 수 있는 능력

을 갖추어야 한다. 이는 다양한 디지털 도구를 활용하여 수업을 설계하고, 학습자의 개별적인 요구를 충족시키는 맞춤형 학습 전략을 개발하는 것을 포함한다. 예를 들어, 학생들이 지식을 실생활에 응용하도록 프로젝트 기반 학습이나 문제 해결 학습을 창의적으로 설계할 수 있어야 한다.
- 평생 학습 역량: 정보화 시대에는 교사도 지속적으로 배우고 성장하는 자세가 필요하다. 새로운 기술이나 교육 트렌드가 끊임없이 등장하기 때문에 교사는 자기계발과 전문성 향상을 위해 평생 학습자로서 역할을 해야 한다. 최신 교육 기술, 새로운 교수법, 데이터 분석 도구 등 교육 혁신에 대한 학습을 지속해야만 학생들에게 최신의 교육을 제공할 수 있다.
- 학생 중심의 수업 설계 및 관리 능력: 정보화 시대의 학생들은 다양한 학습 스타일을 가지고 있으며, 교사는 이를 고려하여 학생 중심의 수업을 설계하고 운영해야 한다. 디지털 도구를 활용한 개별화된 학습과 협력 학습 환경을 제공함으로써 모든 학생들이 자신의 학습 목표에 도달할 수 있도록 해야 한다. 예를 들어, 온라인 학습 자료, 퀴즈, 게임 등을 활용하여 학생들이 스스로 학습할 수 있는 기회를 제공할 수 있다.
- 효과적인 소통 및 협력 능력: 디지털 시대의 교사는 학생, 학부모, 동료 교사들과 효과적으로 소통할 수 있는 능력이 필요하다. 이는 온라인 플랫폼을 통한 원활한 의사소통, 학부모와의 협력, 동료 교사들과의 협업을 포함한다. 또한 학생들이 서로 협력하며 학습할 수 있는 환경을 조성하고, 협동 학습을 촉진할 수 있는 디지털 도구와 방법을 활용해야 한다.
- 윤리적 책임감: 정보화 시대의 교사는 디지털 윤리와 책임에 대한 명확한 인식을 가지고, 이를 학생들에게 교육할 수 있어야 한다. 온라인 안전, 저작권 준수, 개인 정보 보호 등과 관련된 이슈를 다루는 것이 중요하다. 학생들이 인터넷 사용 규범을 이해하고, 윤리적으로 디지털 공간을 활용하도록 지도하는 것도 교사의 중요한 역할이다.
- 데이터 활용 능력: 정보화 시대에는 교육 데이터를 수집하고 분석하여 수업을 개선하는 능력이 중요하다. 교사는 학생들의 학습 데이터를 바탕으로 학습 진도와 성취도를 평가하고, 그 결과에 따라 맞춤형 피드백을 제공할 수 있어야 한다. 학습 분석 도구를 통해 학생의 학습 패턴을 파악하고, 개별화된 학습 계획을 수립하는 데 유용하게 사용할 수 있다.

5 ICT(정보통신활용교육)의 의미와 목적을 간단히 제시하시오.

ICT 활용교육은 CD-ROM 타이틀을 이용하여 수업을 하거나 혹은 인터넷 등을 통한 웹 자료를 활용하여 교수-학습을 하는 것과 같이 각 교과시간에 정보통신 기기를 활용하여 교과의 목표를 가장 효과적으로 달성하기 위한 교육활동이다. 즉 정보통신 기술을 도구적으로 활용하여 학습자의 학습동기를 유발하고 자기 주도적인 학습능력을 신장시키려는 교육활동을 의미한다. ICT 활용교육의 목적은 학생들의 창의적 사고와 다양한 학습활동을 촉진시켜 학습목표를 효과적으로 달성할 수 있도록 지원하는 데 있으며 보다 궁극적으로는 이러한 정보통신기술을 이용하여 학습과 일상생활에서 당면하는 문제를 효과적으로 해결할 수 있도록 하는 데 있다.

6 컴퓨터 보조수업의 장점과 단점에 대해 말해보세요.

■ 장점
- 개별화 수업을 전개할 수 있다.
- 컴퓨터가 설치된 곳이면 어디에서든 학습을 전개할 수 있으므로 원격교육이 가능하며 학생중심의 수업이 가능하여 자기 주도적 학습을 실현시킬 수 있다.

- 다량의 정보를 신속하게 처리할 수 있는 능력을 배양할 수 있으며 결과에 대하여 즉각적인 피드백이 이루어지므로 학습속도와 양을 조절할 수 있다.
- 다양한 영상과 음향을 활용함으로써 학생의 학습욕구를 자극하며 주의를 집중시켜 능동적인 학습이 이루어진다.

■ 단점
- 컴퓨터의 설치, 학습자료, 제작 등에 경비가 많이 든다.
- 컴퓨터에 의한 학습 분위기는 딱딱해지기 쉽고 비인간적이 될 수 있다.
- 컴퓨터가 교사를 완전히 대치할 수 없다.

---

7 우리나라 교육의 가장 큰 문제점은 교사중심의 획일적인 주입식 교육이라고 보며 이 같은 교육으로는 미래의 지식기반 사회에 걸맞은 창의적인 인간을 길러낼 수 없다. 그러므로 발표수업을 통한 토론 중심의 수업과 같이 학생이 직접 활동하고 체험할 수 있는 방법을 활용해야 한다. 선생님이 생각하는 문제점과 이에 대한 효과적인 교육방법에 대하여 구체적으로 말해보세요.

우리나라 교육의 가장 큰 문제점 중 하나는 교사 중심의 획일적인 주입식 교육이다. 주입식 교육은 교사가 주로 일방적으로 지식을 전달하고, 학생들은 그 내용을 수동적으로 받아들이는 방식이다. 이 방식은 암기 위주의 교육으로 이어지며, 학생들이 문제 해결 능력이나 창의력을 발휘하기 어렵게 만든다. 결과적으로 학생들은 비판적 사고 능력과 창의적인 사고력을 키우기보다는, 주어진 정보를 반복적으로 외우고 시험을 대비하는 데 집중하게 된다.

(1) 문제점의 구체적인 영향:
- 학생의 능동적 참여 부족: 주입식 교육은 학생들이 수동적인 학습자로 머물게 하며, 질문을 하거나 자신의 생각을 표현하는 기회를 제한한다. 이는 학생들이 자신의 생각을 논리적으로 정리하고, 타인과 소통하는 능력을 키우는 데 한계를 둔다.
- 창의성 저해: 창의적 사고를 키우려면 다양한 방법으로 문제를 탐구하고, 새로운 아이디어를 만들어 내는 과정이 필요하다. 하지만 주입식 교육은 정해진 답을 찾는 데 집중하기 때문에 학생들이 스스로 탐구하거나 창의적으로 생각할 기회를 제공하지 못한다.
- 비판적 사고 부족: 주입식 교육에서는 정답만이 중요시되기 때문에, 학생들이 비판적으로 생각하거나 문제를 깊이 탐구하는 시간이 적습니다. 이는 21세기 사회가 요구하는 창의적이고 융합적인 사고 능력 개발에 한계를 주게 된다.

(2) 효과적인 교육 방안: 이러한 문제점을 해결하기 위해서는 학생 중심의 활동적이고 체험적인 학습 방식으로 전환하는 것이 중요하다. 그 중에서도 발표 수업과 토론 중심의 수업은 효과적인 대안이 될 수 있다.
- 토론 수업: 토론 중심의 수업은 학생들이 주어진 주제에 대해 자신의 의견을 논리적으로 표현하고, 다른 학생들과 의견을 교환하며 사고력을 확장할 수 있는 기회를 제공한다. 이는 비판적 사고와 문제 해결 능력을 향상시키는 데 효과적이다. 토론을 통해 학생들은 다양한 관점을 이해하고, 자신의 생각을 정리하며, 논리적으로 설득하는 능력을 기르게 됩니다. 이는 단순한 암기를 넘어서 사고의 폭을 넓히는 데 도움을 준다.
- 프로젝트 기반 학습 (PBL, Project-Based Learning): 프로젝트 기반 학습은 학생들이 주어진 문제를 해결하기 위해 스스로 탐구하고, 협력하며 결과물을 만들어가는 학습 방식이다. 학생들은 실제 문제 상황을 경험하면서 지식을 체득하고, 창의적으로 해결책을 모색할 수 있다. 이 방법은 학생들에게 주도적으로 학습할 수 있는 기회를 제공하며, 학습 내용을 실생활에 연결하여 이해도를 높이는 효과가 있다.

- **발표 수업**: 학생들에게 자신의 학습 내용을 발표하도록 하는 수업 방식은 학생들의 자신감을 키우고, 의사소통 능력을 향상시키는 데 매우 효과적이다. 발표 과정에서 학생들은 학습 내용을 정리하고, 전달하는 법을 배우며, 자신의 의견을 설득력 있게 표현하는 능력을 기르게 됩니다. 발표는 단순 암기가 아니라 깊이 있는 이해를 요구하기 때문에, 학생들이 학습 내용을 보다 깊이 탐구하고 자기 주도적으로 학습할 수 있도록 하다.

21세기 지식기반 사회에서는 창의적이고 비판적인 사고력, 문제 해결 능력, 그리고 의사소통 능력이 매우 중요하다. 이를 위해서는 기존의 주입식 교육에서 벗어나, 학생들이 능동적으로 학습에 참여하고, 토론과 발표, 프로젝트 기반 학습과 같은 체험적이고 참여적인 방법을 직용하는 것이 필요하다. 이러한 방법은 학생들이 단순히 지식을 암기하는 것을 넘어, 학습 내용을 이해하고, 스스로 사고하는 능력을 기르는 데 크게 기여할 것이다.

8 [추가질문] 중고등학교에서 재량활동이 미래 교육과 관련하여 중요한 이유와 중요성에 대해 아는 대로 말해보시오.

재량활동은 미래사회를 주도적으로 이끌어 갈 수 있는 자기 주도적인 능력과 창의성을 신장시켜 학교교육의 궁극적인 목표인 인간교육을 실현하고자 하는 것이다. 학생들의 발달단계상 흥미를 중요시하고, 자기주도성을 길러야하는 특성을 가지고 있는 중고등학교 단계에서 학생의 흥미와 요구를 중시하는 재량활동은 큰 의미를 가진다고 할 수 있다. 또한, 자기표현의 기회를 많이 제공하여 자신의 취미와 소질을 계발할 수 있도록 한다는 점에서도 재량활동은 큰 의의를 가진다고 할 수 있다.

9 현재 공교육이 변화하는 시대를 따라가지 못한다는 비난을 받고 있다. 교육프로그램을 현대화하고 주입식 교육방법에서 벗어나 학생중심의 교육이 되게 하며 교사가 교육과정과 생활지도의 전문가가 되도록 자질을 함양시켜야 한다. 이를 위해서는 교사 스스로가 끊임없이 자기 연수를 하고 부단히 실천해야 하며 교사들을 위한 다양한 연수프로그램을 마련해야 한다. 아울러 대학 입시제도를 개혁하고 교사와 학생 간의 끊임없는 상호작용이 있어야 할 것이다. 이러한 공교육의 구체적인 활성화 방안에 대해 말해보세요.

공교육의 활성화를 위해서는 현재의 교육 시스템을 현대화하고, 주입식 교육에서 벗어나 학생 중심의 교육으로 전환하는 것이 중요하다. 이를 위해 교사와 학생 모두에게 지속적인 발전의 기회를 제공하는 체계적인 교육 프로그램과 제도 개혁이 필요하다. 아래에서 공교육 활성화를 위한 구체적인 방안을 제시하겠다.

1. 학생 중심의 교육환경 조성
- **활동 중심의 수업**: 학생들이 스스로 학습에 참여할 수 있는 프로젝트 기반 학습(PBL), 토론 및 발표 수업 등 학생들이 주도적으로 학습을 진행할 수 있는 환경을 조성해야 한다. 교사는 가르치는 사람에서 촉진자로서의 역할을 수행하여, 학생들이 다양한 문제를 해결하고 창의적 사고를 기를 수 있도록 도와주어야 한다.
- **맞춤형 학습 제공**: 학생들은 각자의 능력과 흥미에 따라 학습 속도와 수준이 다르기 때문에, 이를 고려한 개별화 학습이 필요하다. 온라인 플랫폼과 멀티미디어를 활용한 개별 맞춤형 학습 자료를 제공하여 학생들이 자기주도 학습을 할 수 있도록 지원해야 한다.

2. 교사 역량 강화 및 연수 프로그램

- 교사의 전문성 향상: 교사는 교육과정 설계와 학생 지도의 전문가로서, 지속적인 연수를 통해 자신의 역량을 강화해야 하다. 교사 스스로가 평생 학습자가 되어 최신 교육 트렌드와 교수법, 그리고 디지털 기술을 습득하고 학생들에게 효과적으로 적용해야 한다.
- 교사 연수 프로그램의 다양화: 교사들을 위한 다양한 연수 프로그램이 마련되어야 한다. 예를 들어, 디지털 리터러시 교육, 창의적 문제 해결 능력 개발 연수, 학생 상담 기법 등 교사가 실질적으로 수업에 활용할 수 있는 프로그램들이 필요하다. 또한, 교사 간의 협력 학습을 장려하여 서로의 경험과 노하우를 공유하는 기회를 제공해야 한다.

3. 대학 입시제도 개혁
- 지식 암기 중심에서 역량 평가 중심으로 전환: 현재의 대학 입시제도는 지식 암기에 치우친 경향이 크다. 그러나 학생의 창의력, 문제 해결 능력, 협동심 등 다양한 역량을 평가할 수 있는 입시 제도로의 개혁이 필요하다. 수능이나 내신 성적만이 아닌, 학생부 종합전형이나 포트폴리오 등 다양한 평가 방식을 통해 학생의 전인적 성장을 반영하는 입시 제도가 마련되어야 한다.
- 입시 스트레스 완화: 입시의 높은 경쟁으로 인해 학생들은 많은 스트레스를 받으며, 창의적 사고보다는 정해진 답을 찾는 데 집중하게 된다. 이를 해결하기 위해 대학 입학 정원의 확대, 다양한 진로 탐색 기회 제공, 적성 기반 입시 등의 개혁이 필요하다.

4. 교사와 학생 간의 상호작용 활성화
- 상호작용을 촉진하는 수업 방식: 교사와 학생 간의 의사소통을 활발히 할 수 있는 환경을 조성해야 한다. 이를 위해 질문 중심 수업이나 피드백 중심 수업을 통해 학생들이 자신의 생각을 자유롭게 표현하고, 교사가 적절한 피드백을 제공하는 방식이 필요하다. 교사는 학생들에게 개방적이고 친밀한 소통을 장려하여, 학습에 대한 동기부여를 높일 수 있다.
- 학생 상담 및 멘토링 강화: 교사는 학생들의 학업뿐만 아니라 정서적 지원과 진로 지도에도 중요한 역할을 해야 한다. 정기적으로 학생들과 1:1로 상담하고, 멘토링 프로그램을 통해 학생들의 개인적 성장을 돕는 것이 필요하다. 학생의 강점과 약점을 파악하고 이를 바탕으로 맞춤형 교육을 제공함으로써, 학생들이 스스로 성장할 수 있는 환경을 만들어야 한다.

5. 디지털 기술을 활용한 공교육 혁신
- 온라인 학습 플랫폼의 활성화: 정보화 시대에 걸맞게 온라인 학습 플랫폼을 적극적으로 도입해야 한다. 이를 통해 교사는 언제 어디서나 학생들이 학습할 수 있는 환경을 제공하고, 학생 개개인의 학습 상황을 실시간으로 모니터링할 수 있다. 또한, 온라인 자료를 통해 학생들은 자신에게 필요한 지식을 자기주도적으로 습득할 수 있다.
- 하이브리드 학습 모델 도입: 온라인과 오프라인 수업을 혼합한 하이브리드 학습 모델을 도입함으로써 학습의 유연성을 높일 수 있다. 이는 특히 다양한 학습 스타일을 가진 학생들에게 효과적이며, 교사도 학생들의 개별적 요구를 충족시킬 수 있다.

공교육 활성화를 위해서는 교사와 학생 모두가 변화하는 시대에 적응할 수 있도록 교육환경의 현대화와 교육과정 개혁이 필수적이다. 학생 중심의 참여적 학습을 강화하고, 교사의 전문성을 끊임없이 개발하는 연수 프로그램이 뒷받침되어야 하며, 대학 입시 제도 역시 다양한 역량을 평가할 수 있도록 개혁이 필요하다. 이를 통해 학생들은 창의적이고 능동적인 학습자가 되고, 교사들은 전문가로서의 자질을 갖추게 되어, 공교육의 질을 향상시키고 21세기 인재를 양성하는 데 기여할 수 있을 것이다.

10 (추가질문) 멀티미디어를 이용한 수업의 장점을 말해보세요.

- 시각적·청각적 자극을 통한 학습 동기 유발: 멀티미디어는 텍스트, 이미지, 동영상, 음성 등 다양한 매체를 활용하여 학습자에게 흥미를 유발하고 학습에 대한 동기를 높인다. 이를 통해 학생들은 더 재미있고 몰입도 있게 학습에 참여할 수 있다.
- 개인화된 학습 지원: 멀티미디어 자료는 학습자의 수준과 학습 속도에 맞춰 개인화된 학습을 제공할 수 있다. 학생은 자신의 학습 능력에 맞게 자료를 반복 학습하거나 다양한 자료를 선택해 학습할 수 있다.
- 복합적인 이해 촉진: 텍스트와 이미지, 음성을 함께 제공함으로써 학습자에게 복합적인 정보를 통합하여 이해할 수 있게 도와준다. 예를 들어, 실험 영상이나 3D 애니메이션을 통해 추상적인 개념을 더 쉽게 이해할 수 있다.
- 상호작용성 강화: 멀티미디어는 상호작용을 통해 학생들이 수업에 능동적으로 참여하도록 한다. 예를 들어, 인터랙티브 퀴즈나 시뮬레이션을 통해 실시간으로 피드백을 받고, 자신의 학습 내용을 즉각 확인하고 수정할 수 있다.
- 언제 어디서나 학습 가능: 온라인 멀티미디어 자료는 시간과 장소에 구애받지 않고 학습할 수 있는 장점을 제공한다. 학생들은 교실 밖에서도 인터넷만 있으면 쉽게 자료에 접근하고 학습을 이어갈 수 있다.
- 다양한 학습 스타일에 적응: 멀티미디어는 시각적, 청각적, 동작적 학습 스타일을 모두 지원하기 때문에 다양한 학습 유형을 가진 학생들이 자신에게 맞는 방식으로 학습할 수 있다. 이는 개별 학습자의 이해도와 성취도를 향상시키는 데 큰 도움이 된다.
- 복잡한 개념의 시각화: 특히 수학, 과학, 역사 등에서 복잡한 개념이나 과정을 시각적으로 표현함으로써 학생들이 쉽게 이해할 수 있도록 돕는다. 예를 들어, 역사적 사건의 타임라인을 시각적으로 나타내거나, 과학적 현상을 애니메이션으로 설명하는 방식이다. 멀티미디어는 다양한 학습 방법을 제공함으로써 학습자들의 이해를 돕고, 학습 경험을 더 풍부하게 만들어준다.

11 최근 TV, 컴퓨터 등 각종 매체의 보급으로 인해 학생들의 독서량이 급격하게 줄고 있다. 이러한 현실에서 바람직한 독서지도의 원리와 방법을 말해보시오. 방법으로는 구체적인 방법으로 2가지 이상 말하시오.

① 독서교육의 원리: 독서교육의 근본적인 원리는 알맞은 책을 골라 알맞은 시기에 목적에 맞게 스스로 읽게 하는 것이다.
- 성장발달과 개인차에 알맞은 지도
- 독서능력과 흥미 및 습관개선에 알맞은 자료를 선택하여 지도
- 성장과정에 텍스트와 방법을 적절히 배치한 발달단계에 맞는 덕서지도
- 자발적인 동기유발에 의한 습관적 독서지도

② 독서교육방법
  ㉠ 개인별 맞춤 독서교육프로그램
    적합한 책을, 적합한 학생에게, 적합한 시기에 제공하는 맞춤독서로서 학생의 독서능력을 진단하여 수준에 맞는 도서를 선정하여 제공해 주며, 도서별 독서 확인평가문제를 통해 독서상태를 평가하고, 그 결과를 지속적으로 관리해 주면서 독서에 대한 동기부여와 함께 독서습관을 길러줌으로써 개인의 독서능력을 효과적으로 향상시켜주는 개인별 맞춤 독서교육프로그램

ⓒ 독후감을 탈피한 독서 감상표현지도
　지금까지 독서교육하면 으레 독후감과 연계시켜온 것이 사실이다. 그러나 획일적으로 이루어지는 독후감이 학생들에게 오히려 독서에 대한 동기유발을 저해하고 독서의 장애물로 여겨지고 있다. 그래서 이를 개선하기 위해 독서 감상표현을 다양화 했다. 독서 감상표현의 영역을 한정하지 않고 자신의 개성과 취미에 맞게 표현하도록 지도하였다. 독서 감상표현의 다양화로 그 동안 개발된 표현방법을 세분하면 100여 가지가 된다.

　예) 방송프로그램을 활용한 독서 감상표현, 콩트쓰기를 통한 독서 감상표현, 숨은그림찾기를 통한 독서 감상표현, 내용 요약을 통한 독서 감상표현, 자유연상을 통한 독서 감상표현, 광고 형식을 통함 독서 감상표현 등

12

지식정보화 사회에서 멀티미디어가 중고등학교 학생들에게 제공하는 독서교육의 교육적 가치는 다양한 측면에서 긍정적인 영향을 미칠 수 있다. 독서교육과 멀티미디어의 결합은 학생들에게 보다 흥미롭고 효과적인 학습 경험을 제공하며, 이는 독서 능력뿐 아니라 전반적인 사고력, 창의력, 그리고 비판적 사고를 키우는 데 중요한 역할을 한다. 지식 정보화 사회에서 멀티미디어를 통한 독서교육의 교육적 가치에 대하여 설명하세요.

1. 흥미와 몰입도 향상
   - 멀티미디어를 활용한 독서교육은 시청각 자료, 애니메이션, 영상, 음성 자료 등 다양한 형식을 통해 학생들의 흥미를 유발할 수 있다. 특히 디지털 네이티브로 불리는 중고등학생들은 전통적인 텍스트 중심의 독서보다는 시각적 자료나 음성 자료에 더 친숙하므로, 멀티미디어가 결합된 독서 활동은 학습 동기를 크게 높일 수 있다.
   - 예를 들어, 전자책(eBook)이나 오디오북을 통해 책을 읽거나 들으면서 멀티미디어적 요소를 추가함으로써 학생들이 책에 더 깊이 몰입할 수 있다.

2. 이해력과 상상력 증진
   - 텍스트만으로 이해하기 어려운 내용을 시각화하거나 영상화하여 제공함으로써 독서의 이해를 돕고, 학생들이 스토리나 정보를 보다 쉽게 파악할 수 있게 한다. 예를 들어, 문학 작품의 등장인물 분석이나 주제 설명에서 영상을 활용하여 학생들이 보다 생동감 있게 내용을 접할 수 있다.
   - 또한 멀티미디어 자료가 독서 내용을 보강하거나 확장하여 상상력과 창의력을 자극할 수 있다. 가령, 특정 소설의 배경이 되는 역사적 사건에 대해 다른 다큐멘터리나 애니메이션을 보면서 텍스트의 맥락을 더 풍부하게 이해할 수 있다.

3. 다양한 학습 스타일 충족
   - 시청각 학습 스타일을 선호하는 학생들이나, 독서를 통해 배운 정보를 실제 사례나 영상을 통해 체험하고자 하는 학생들에게 멀티미디어는 매우 유용하다. 다양한 멀티모달(multimodal) 학습 자료가 텍스트의 내용과 결합됨으로써 학생들의 학습 스타일에 맞춘 개별화된 학습이 가능하다.
   - 예를 들어, 시각 자료(이미지, 비디오)와 청각 자료(오디오북, 팟캐스트)를 결합해 제공하는 독서 프로그램은 복합적인 학습 경험을 통해 학습 효과를 극대화할 수 있다.

4. 비판적 사고 및 정보 해석 능력 향상
   - 멀티미디어 자료는 단순히 정보를 제공하는 것을 넘어 학생들이 비판적으로 사고하고 정보를 분석하는 능력을 기르는 데 도움을 줄 수 있다. 예를 들어, 멀티미디어 자료에서 제공되는 뉴스 기사나 다큐멘터리의 내용을 텍스트와 비교하고, 이를 통해 정보를 분석하거나 의견을 형성하는 훈련을 할 수 있다.

- 이는 학생들에게 미디어 리터러시(media literacy)를 함양하게 해주며, 오늘날 정보화 시대에서 필수적인 정보 해석 능력과 비판적 사고를 길러줍니다.

5. 다양한 주제와 문화 경험 제공
   - 멀티미디어를 통해 다양한 주제와 관련된 자료를 접할 수 있으므로, 독서활동을 더욱 다양화할 수 있다. 예를 들어, 환경문제, 사회적 이슈, 세계 문화와 관련된 다양한 멀티미디어 자료가 학생들에게 풍부한 지식과 새로운 관점을 제공한다. 이는 독서 범위를 확장하여 학생들이 글로벌한 시각을 갖게 하는 데 도움이 됩니다.
   - 이러한 멀티미디어 자료들은 학생들이 전통적인 독서 텍스트 외에도 더 넓은 범위의 콘텐츠를 접할 수 있게 하여, 더 깊이 있는 사고를 가능하게 한다.

6. 참여와 협력 증진
   - 멀티미디어를 활용한 독서 교육은 학생들이 협력 학습(collaborative learning)을 하게 만드는 데 유리하다. 예를 들어, 학생들이 한 문학 작품을 읽고, 관련된 동영상 자료를 보며 토론하거나, 디지털 플랫폼을 통해 독서 일기나 독서 관련 프로젝트를 함께 완성하는 방식으로 협력적인 학습 환경을 조성할 수 있다.
   - 소셜 미디어나 온라인 학습 도구를 사용하여 학생들이 자신의 독서 경험을 공유하거나, 작품에 대한 의견을 나누는 과정에서 협력적이고 상호작용적인 독서 경험을 확대할 수 있다.

멀티미디어는 중고등학생들에게 독서의 교육적 가치를 높이는데 필수적인 도구로 자리 잡고 있다. 이를 통해 학생들은 단순히 텍스트를 읽는 것 이상의 경험을 하며, 학습에 대한 흥미와 몰입을 높이고, 다양한 학습 스타일에 맞춘 맞춤형 교육을 받을 수 있다. 동시에 비판적 사고력과 정보 해석 능력까지 기르며, 독서를 통해 보다 넓은 세상과 연결될 수 있다.

---

13 중고등학교에서 인성교육은 매우 중요한 문제로 부각되고 있다. 효과적으로 인성교육을 수행하기 위해서는 학생들이 실제로 체험하고 적용할 수 있는 다양한 프로그램이 필요하다. 이러한 인성교육에 활용할 수 있는 구체적 프로그램을 중고등학생의 발달 단계와 사회적 요구에 맞춰 제시하시오.

---

1. 또래 멘토링 프로그램: 학년별로 상급생과 하급생을 연결하여 상급생이 하급생의 멘토가 되는 프로그램이다. 상급생은 자신의 경험을 바탕으로 하급생을 지도하고, 하급생은 상급생에게 궁금한 점을 물어보며 유대감을 형성한다.
   - 활동 내용: 정기적으로 만나는 시간을 정해 학교 생활, 학습 방법, 진로 고민 등을 이야기하면서 서로의 경험과 가치를 공유하는 시간을 갖습니다. 예를 들어, 학기 초에 멘토-멘티 짝을 정하고, 매월 주제별로 대화를 나누며 활동을 진행한다.
   - 기대 효과: 상급생은 리더십과 책임감을, 하급생은 신뢰감을 형성하고 학교생활 적응력을 높일 수 있다. 서로 간의 소통을 통해 공감 능력과 배려심을 기를 수 있다.

2. 사회봉사 프로젝트: 학생들이 학교 내외에서 다양한 봉사활동을 기획하고 실행하는 프로그램이다. 지역사회와 협력하여 봉사활동 기회를 마련하고, 학생들이 자발적으로 참여하도록 한다.
   - 활동 내용: 예를 들어, 노인 요양원 방문, 환경 정화 활동, 장애인 지원센터 봉사 등 다양한 활동을 통해 실질적인 봉사 경험을 제공한다. 활동 후에는 리플렉션(reflection) 세션을 통해 활동의 의미와 느낀 점을 공유하는 시간을 가진다.
   - 기대 효과: 사회적 책임감을 고취하고, 배려와 봉사의 가치를 체득하게 하며, 학생들이 사회 구성원으로

서 긍정적인 역할을 수행하도록 도와준다.

3. **역할극(Role Play)과 상황극 프로그램**: 학생들이 일상에서 마주할 수 있는 다양한 갈등 상황을 역할극으로 연출하고, 그에 대한 해결 방안을 모색하는 프로그램이다. 이를 통해 학생들이 공감 능력과 문제 해결 능력을 기를 수 있도록 한다.
   - 활동 내용: 예를 들어, 친구 간의 갈등, 학교폭력 예방, 가족과의 소통, 진로 고민 등의 상황을 주제로 역할극을 준비한다. 각 역할을 체험하고 상황 속에서 자신의 감정과 타인의 입장을 이해하는 기회를 제공한다. 이후에는 역할극에 대한 피드백을 주고받으며 서로의 생각을 공유한다.
   - 기대 효과: 타인의 입장을 이해하는 공감 능력과 상황을 평화롭게 해결하는 문제 해결 능력을 키울 수 있다. 학생들은 실생활에서 발생하는 갈등 상황에 대해 올바르게 대처하는 연습을 할 수 있다.

4. **독서와 토론을 통한 가치관 형성 프로그램**: 인성교육에 적합한 도서나 기사 등을 읽고, 그 내용에 대해 학생들이 토론하는 프로그램이다. 주제는 다양하게 선정할 수 있으며, 예를 들어 우정, 존중, 자아 존중감, 협동 등 다양한 인성적 주제를 다룰 수 있다.
   - 활동 내용: 한 달에 한 권씩 독서 주제를 정하고, 이를 읽고 난 뒤 소그룹 토론을 진행한다. 토론을 통해 각자의 의견을 나누고 타인의 생각을 존중하며, 인성적 가치에 대한 개인적 견해를 깊이 있게 탐구할 수 있다.
   - 기대 효과: 비판적 사고와 타인의 의견을 경청하는 태도를 기르고, 협력적 소통 능력을 향상시킨다. 독서를 통해 다양한 삶의 가치와 인성적 요소를 깊이 이해할 수 있다.

5. **감사 일기 및 긍정 일기 작성**: 학생들이 매일 감사한 일이나 긍정적인 경험을 일기로 작성하는 활동이다. 이를 통해 매일의 일상에서 긍정적인 부분을 찾아내고, 감사함을 느끼며 자아 존중감을 높인다.
   - 활동 내용: 학생들이 하루에 감사한 일 3가지를 매일 기록하는 감사 일기를 작성하거나, 긍정적인 경험을 기록하는 긍정 일기를 작성하도록 한다. 매주나 매월 모여 학생들끼리 작성한 내용 중 일부를 공유하며 서로 긍정적인 피드백을 주고받는다.
   - 기대 효과: 학생들이 감사와 긍정의 마음을 키우고, 스트레스를 관리하며 자아 존중감을 향상시킬 수 있다. 정서적으로 안정된 학교 생활을 돕는 데 중요한 역할을 한다.

이와 같은 인성교육 프로그램은 학생들의 발달 단계에 맞춰 설계되어야 하며, 정서적 공감 능력, 사회적 책임감, 협동과 배려 등 다양한 인성적 요소를 균형 있게 기를 수 있도록 설계되어야 한다.

---

14 '한명의 아이도 낙오되지 않도록 한다'라는 기치아래 모든 학생과 함께 가기 위한 교육이 중시되고 있다. 학업부진아의 성적부진 원인에 대해 간단하게 요약하고 학업 부진아를 지도하기 위한 교사의 태도에 대해 말해보세요.

---

① 원인
- 낮은 지능과 신체 건강상의 원인
- 학습 흥미와 동기 부족
- 정서적 불만이나 불안, 갈등 등의 정서적 원인
- 결손가정, 가정의 빈곤에서 오는 열등감, 가정 내 불화와 부모의 비교육적 태도 등

② 교사의 태도: 학업 부진아에 대한 교사의 태도는 학생의 학습 동기와 자신감에 큰 영향을 미치기 때문에 특히 중요하다. 교사는 다음과 같은 태도를 유지해야 한다.
- 이해와 공감: 학습 부진의 원인이 학습 능력 외에도 다양한 배경적 요인(가정환경, 심리적 요인, 학습 기

회 등)에서 비롯될 수 있음을 이해하고, 학생의 입장을 공감하는 태도가 필요하다. 학생의 학습 어려움에 대한 깊이 있는 이해를 통해 신뢰 관계를 형성하고, 학생이 교사의 관심을 느낄 수 있도록 하는 것이 중요하다.

- 긍정적인 기대와 격려: 학습 부진 학생에게 지나치게 낮은 기대를 가지거나 부정적인 시각으로 바라보기보다는, 긍정적인 가능성을 보고 격려하는 태도가 중요하다. "할 수 있다"는 믿음과 격려를 통해 학생이 스스로에 대한 긍정적인 태도를 가지게 하고, 작은 성취도 칭찬하며 학습에 대한 동기부여를 지속적으로 제공한다.
- 개별화된 학습 접근: 학습 부진 학생에게는 개별적이고 맞춤형 접근이 필요하다. 교사는 학생의 수준과 속도에 맞춘 개인화된 학습 목표와 자료를 제공하여, 학생이 수업을 따라가고 성취감을 느낄 수 있도록 돕는다. 예를 들어, 수준별 과제나 단계적인 피드백을 통해 학생이 자신의 학습을 점진적으로 발전시킬 수 있도록 해야 한다.
- 실패를 허용하는 환경 조성: 학생들이 실패를 두려워하지 않고 시도할 수 있도록, 실수와 실패를 학습 과정의 일부로 받아들이는 분위기를 조성해야 한다. 교사는 실수를 발전의 기회로 인식하도록 지도하고, 실패에서 배우는 경험을 통해 점진적으로 성장할 수 있는 환경을 만들어 준다.
- 협력적인 지원 제공: 학습 부진아의 성장을 위해서는 교사뿐만 아니라 가정과 학교가 협력해야 한다. 담임교사나 특수교육 교사와의 협업을 통해 학습 부진 학생을 위한 다각적 지원을 제공할 수 있으며, 학생의 발전 상황을 공유하면서 통합적인 지원 환경을 조성하는 것도 중요하다.

이와 같은 태도를 통해 교사는 학습 부진 학생이 스스로 학습에 대한 자신감을 회복하고, 긍정적인 학습 경험을 쌓아갈 수 있도록 지도할 수 있다.

---

15 현대의 교육에서는 단지 학교에서 제공하는 지식을 암기하는 것이 아닌 창의적 인간을 육성하는 것이 중요해지고 있다. 이를 위해서는 학생들이 비판적 사고와 문제 해결 능력, 새로운 아이디어를 탐구하는 능력을 키울 수 있는 다양한 교육 방법이 필요하다. 이러한 창의적 인간을 기르기 위한 구체적 방안에 대해 말해보세요.

1. 문제 해결 중심 학습(PBL: Project-Based Learning): 문제 해결 중심 학습은 학생들에게 현실적인 문제를 제시하고, 그 문제를 해결하기 위한 프로젝트를 수행하도록 하는 교육 방법이다. 이 과정에서 학생들은 비판적으로 사고하고, 협력하며, 창의적으로 해결책을 제안하게 됩니다. 예를 들어, 환경 보호를 주제로 학생들이 팀을 이루어 지역 사회의 문제를 연구하고, 해결 방안을 발표하도록 할 수 있다. 이를 통해 학생들은 스스로 문제를 정의하고, 다양한 해결책을 탐색하며, 창의적인 사고를 발휘할 수 있다.

2. 융합 교육(STEAM 교육): STEAM 교육은 과학(Science), 기술(Technology), 공학(Engineering), 예술(Arts), 수학(Mathematics)을 융합한 교육 방법으로, 다양한 학문 간의 연계를 통해 창의적인 사고를 길러준다. 이를 통해 학생들은 과학적, 논리적 사고뿐만 아니라 예술적 표현 능력도 함께 발달시킬 수 있다. 예를 들어, 수학 수업에서 기하학적 원리를 배운 후, 미술과 연계하여 이를 활용한 창작 활동을 하는 프로젝트를 진행할 수 있다.

3. 개방형 질문과 탐구 기반 학습: 창의적인 사고를 촉진하기 위해서는 개방형 질문을 활용하여 학생들이 자신의 생각을 자유롭게 표현하고, 깊이 있는 탐구를 할 수 있도록 해야 한다. 단순히 정답이 있는 질문보다는, 학생들이 다양한 관점에서 문제를 탐구하고 독창적인 아이디어를 제시할 수 있는 기회를 제공한다. 예를 들어, "지속 가능한 에너지를 활용한 미래 도시의 모습을 상상해 보라"는 질문을 통해 학생들이 새로운 아이디어를 창출하고 발표하도록 할 수 있다.

4. **실패를 학습의 일부로 받아들이기**: 창의성을 기르기 위해서는 실패를 두려워하지 않는 환경이 필요하다. 교사는 학생들이 도전하고, 실수하고, 그 실수를 통해 학습할 수 있는 분위기를 조성해야 한다. 실수는 배움의 과정이라는 것을 강조하고, 학생들이 실패 속에서도 창의적인 해법을 찾을 수 있도록 격려하는 것이 중요하다.

5. **협력적 학습 환경 조성**: 창의적인 아이디어는 다양한 사람들과의 협력에서 나올 때 더욱 풍부해진다. 팀 프로젝트나 협동 학습을 통해 학생들이 다양한 의견을 나누고, 서로의 아이디어를 결합하여 새로운 해결책을 찾는 경험을 제공해야 한다. 이러한 과정을 통해 학생들은 타인의 시각을 존중하고, 공동의 목표를 위해 창의적으로 문제를 해결할 수 있는 능력을 기르게 된다.

6. **자기 주도적 학습 환경 제공**: 창의성을 길러주기 위해서는 학생이 주도적으로 학습할 수 있는 환경을 제공하는 것이 중요하다. 학생들이 자신의 관심사와 호기심에 따라 주제를 선택하고 탐구할 수 있도록, 다양한 자원과 도구를 제공하여 스스로 학습하는 능력을 키워준다. 이를 통해 학생들은 자신의 속도에 맞춰 학습하며, 창의적인 사고를 더 잘 발휘할 수 있게 된다.

위와 같은 방법들을 통해 학생들이 학교 교육을 통해 단순히 지식을 암기하는 것이 아니라, 창의적인 사고를 바탕으로 문제를 해결하고 새로운 아이디어를 창출할 수 있는 능력을 길러낼 수 있다. 창의적 인간을 기르기 위한 교육은 단순한 지식 전달이 아닌, 학생들이 능동적으로 사고하고 탐구하는 과정을 지원하는 방향으로 나아가야 한다.

합격을 위한 TIP

STEAM이 뭘까?
- 즐거운 수업, 재미있는 수업, 살아있는 수업
- 융합인재교육 | 통합교육 | 인성교육 | 예술교육 | 창의력 | 감성 | 협동

2010년 초에 인터넷 포털사이트 다음(www.daum.net)에서 어린이들의 장래 희망을 조사한 결과 과학자는 19위였습니다. 대통령, 의사 등과 함께 과학자가 항상 상위권을 차지하던 것을 생각하면 많이 달라진 모습입니다. 더는 우리 아이들에게 과학자는 매력적인 직업이 아닌 듯합니다. 이러한 현상의 단면은 2009년 OECD 국가들을 대상으로 한 2009년 '국제 학업성취도 평가(PISA)'에서 드러납니다. 조사 결과 우리나라의 학업성취도는 중국과 핀란드에 이어 3위의 성적을 기록했습니다.

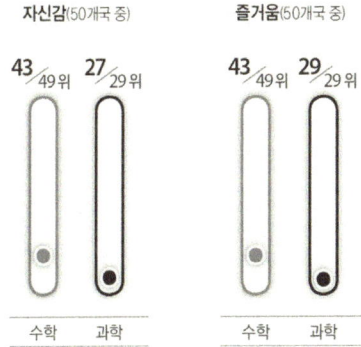

| 우리나라 학생의 수학·과학 학습에 대한 태도(TIMSS, 2007)

2007년 실시한 '제3차 수학·과학 성취도 비교연구(TIMSS)'에서는 우리나라가 싱가포르, 대만, 일본에 이어 4위를 차지했습니다. 문제는 높은 학업성취도에도 불구하고 학습에 대한 흥미, 자발성에서는 중하위권 수준을 벗어나지 못하고 있다는 점입니다. 2006년 PISA에서는 과학에 대한 흥미가 57개국 중 55위를 기록했고, 2007년 TIMSS에서는 수학 과목의 자신감과 즐거움 점수가 50개국 중 43위였습니다. 과학 과목도 자신감이 27위, 즐거움이 29위에 머물렀습니다

이러한 현상에는 여러 가지 이유가 있겠지만, 학교에서 진행되는 일방적인 지식 전달식, 암기식 과학 수업도 하나의 원인이라 할 수 있습니다. 주입식·암기식 문제 풀이 중심의 수업 방식으로는 시험지를 통해 측정하는 성취도는

높일 수 있었지만, 해당 과목을 학습하려는 동기와 흥미는 이끌어 내지 못한 것입니다.

학생들의 학습하려는 동기와 흥미를 높이기 위해 STEAM(융합인재교육)이 우리나라 교육과정에 도입되었습니다. 창의적인 과학기술인재를 육성하고자 추진되는 STEAM 교육은 Science, Technology, Engineering, Arts & Mathematics의 약칭으로 과학, 기술, 공학, 예술, 수학 교과 간의 통합적인 교육 방식을 의미합니다. 한마디로 STEAM(융합인재교육)은 "과학기술에 대한 학생들의 흥미와 이해를 높이고 과학기술 기반의 융합적 소양과 실생활의 문제 해결력을 배양하는 교육"이라고 생각하면 됩니다.

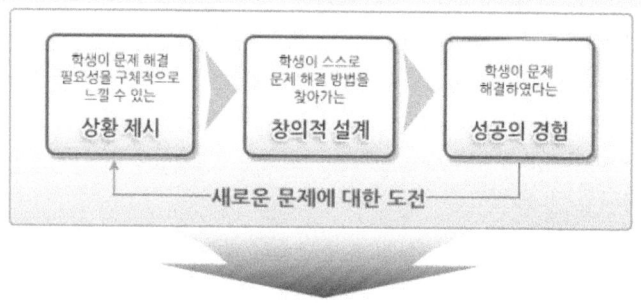

STEAM(융합인재교육)은 위 사진과 같은 체계를 갖추고 있습니다. 학생에게 [상황을 제시]하여 자기 문제로 인식하게 한 다음, [창의적 설계]로 문제 해결력을 배양합니다. 마지막으로 [감성적 체험]으로 학생에게 새로운 도전을 권합니다. 3가지 과정을 거쳐 과학기술 분야에 관한 흥미와 동기를 부여하는 것이 STEAM(융합인재교육)입니다. 위 사진은 학생들이 목재구조물을 만들어 보는 수업입니다. 학생들에게 어려운 개념인 '구조역학'을 목재구조물을 통해 알아보는 과정입니다. 목재구조물을 만들기 위해 '지진에도 견딜 수 있는 건축물'을 가지고 [상황제시]를 하고, 학생들이 모여 [창의적 설계]를 합니다. [창의적 설계] 과정에서 학생들은 다양한 의견을 주고받으며 목재구조물의 구조에 관하여 생각을 짜냅니다.

이처럼 STEAM(융합인재교육)이 적용된 수업을 학생들과 함께 1년 정도 하다 보니, 학생들이 과학 수업시간을 좋아하고 기다리고 있었습니다. 특히 실생활과 연계된 주제를 가지고 STEAM(융합인재교육)이 시행되다 보니, 학생들은 자신들의 문제가 수업의 주제로서 다뤄지는 것에 흥미를 느끼고 관심을 가지기 시작했습니다. 또한, [예술] 분야에 강점을 가진 학생들도 STEAM(융합인재교육)이 적용된 수업에 흥미를 느끼고 자신감도 가지기 시작했습니다. [감성적 체험] 단계에서는 아무래도 [예술]과 관련된 능력이 필요로 하기 때문인 것 같았습니다.

STEAM(융합인재교육)은 학생들이 [협동]하지 않으면 안 되게 구성되어 있습니다. 학생들이 서로 머리를 맞대고 고민하지 않으면 다양한 산출물이나 결과물이 나올 수가 없습니다. 학생끼리 서로 이야기를 나누고 협동하는 과정에서 STEAM(융합인재교육)의 효과가 더 커집니다. 이러면서 학생끼리 서로 친해지고 관계도 좋아지는 등, STEAM(융합인재교육)은 [인성교육] 면에서도 보탬이 된다고 생각합니다. STEAM(융합인재교육)에 참여한 학생들에게 STEAM(융합인재교육)의 의미를 물어보면 그 의미는 정확히 모르지만, '즐거운 수업, 재미있는 수업'이라고 말합니다. 그만큼 학생의 학습에 관한 흥미와 동기를 유발하는 데에는 STEAM(융합인재교육)이 효과가 있다고 생각합니다. 학부모의 반응도 낮지 않습니다. 처음에는 STEAM(융합인재교육)이 무슨 수업인지 몰랐던 학부모가 대다수였는데, 지금은 STEAM(융합인재교육)에 관한 관심이 많아졌습니다. 특히 자녀가 학교에서 즐겁게 공부하고 오는 모습을 보면서 STEAM(융합인재교육)의 효과에 긍정적으로 반응하는 학부모가 많이 생겼습니다. 지난 세기 우리 사회 눈부신 발전의 가장 큰 원동력은 교육을 통한 인재 육성이었습니다. 그간 우리 교육은 짧은 시간에 정확한 지식을 효율적으로 전달하는 임무를 수행하며 시대가 요구하는 인재를 성공적으로 키워냈습니다. 이제 산업화, 정보화를 넘어 창의력이 경쟁력의 핵심이 되는 새로운 시대가 도래하고 있습니다. STEAM(융합인재교육)은 학생들이 과학기술 소양을 바탕으로 인문학이나 예술 등 타 분야를 연계하여 공부하고 이를 실생활에서 직접 활용할 수 있도록 하는, 살아있는 교육입니다. 이를 통해 학생들은 스스로 학습에 흥미를 갖고 즐겁게 공부하며 융합 마음을 갖춘 창의 인재로 성장하게 됩니다.

16 학교에서 실천할 수 있는 효과적인 안전교육의 방향은 학생들의 안전 의식을 높이고 위기 상황에서 적절하게 대처할 수 있는 능력을 기르기 위해 체계적이고 실질적인 교육 방안을 마련하는 것이 중요하다. 학교에서 실천할 수 있는 효과적인 안전교육의 방향에 대해 말해보시오.

1. 실습 기반의 체험형 안전교육
   - 이론 중심 교육보다는 체험과 실습을 통해 학생들이 직접 위기 상황을 경험하고 대처법을 익힐 수 있는 기회를 제공해야 한다. 예를 들어, 소방 훈련, 응급처치 실습, 화재 대피 훈련 등을 주기적으로 시행하여 학생들이 위기 상황에서의 행동 요령을 몸으로 익히도록 해야 한다.
   - 가상 현실(VR)이나 시뮬레이션 기술을 활용하여 다양한 위기 상황을 체험하게 함으로써 현실적인 대처 능력을 키우는 것도 효과적이다.

2. 교과와 연계된 통합형 안전교육
   - 안전교육을 단순한 한 차시의 교육으로 끝내지 않고, 교과 수업과 통합하여 일상적인 교육 과정에서 자연스럽게 안전의식을 함양할 수 있도록 한다. 예를 들어, 과학 수업에서 화학 실험 안전을 강조하거나, 체육 수업에서 운동 중 부상 예방을 주제로 다룰 수 있다.
   - 프로젝트 기반 학습(PBL)을 통해 학생들이 팀을 이루어 특정 안전 문제에 대한 해결책을 찾는 방식으로 안전의식을 내재화하는 교육 방법도 적용할 수 있다.

3. 일상 생활 속에서 실천하는 안전습관 형성
   - 학생들이 일상 생활 속에서 자연스럽게 안전한 행동을 실천할 수 있도록, 생활 속 안전교육을 지속적으로 실시해야 한다. 예를 들어, 등하교 시 교통안전 교육, 학교 내 화재 대피 경로 숙지 등은 학생들이 매일 실천할 수 있는 부분이다.
   - 또한, 가정과 연계한 안전교육도 중요하다. 학교에서 가르친 내용을 가정에서 부모와 함께 실천하거나 점검할 수 있도록, 안전 체크리스트나 가정에서의 안전교육 자료를 제공하여 학교와 가정이 협력할 수 있는 시스템을 구축해야 한다.

4. 학생 주도적 안전 교육 프로그램
   - 학생들이 직접 안전 모니터링이나 안전 캠페인에 참여하도록 하여 주도적 안전 의식을 함양한다. 예를 들어, 학교 내 안전관리단을 운영하여 학생들이 자율적으로 학교 내 위험 요소를 발견하고 보고하거나, 안전 캠페인을 기획하는 프로그램을 통해 학생들이 적극적으로 안전 문제에 관여하도록 유도할 수 있다.
   - 또래 교육(peer education)을 통해 학생들이 서로에게 안전 수칙을 가르치는 방식도 효과적이다. 학생들끼리의 교육은 보다 쉽게 공감하고 실천할 수 있게 만드는 요소가 된다.

5. 정서적 안전과 심리적 안전 강조
   - 안전교육에서 정서적 안전과 심리적 안정도 매우 중요한 요소이다. 학교 폭력 예방 교육, 사이버 폭력 예방 교육 등을 통해 학생들이 심리적 안전을 지키는 방법을 배울 수 있도록 해야 한다. 이를 위해 정신 건강 교육을 정기적으로 시행하고, 교사와 상담교사의 긴밀한 협력을 통해 학생들의 심리적 위기 상황에 적절히 대응할 수 있는 체계를 구축해야 한다.

이와 같은 방법들을 통해 학생들이 안전에 대한 경각심을 높이고, 실제 위기 상황에서 대처할 수 있는 능력을 길러주는 실질적이고 체계적인 안전교육을 실현할 수 있다.

17 선생님이 생각하는 훌륭한 교사의 자질에 대해 말해 보시오.

교사는 교육자에게 필요한 학생관과 교육에 대한 사명감을 지녀야 한다. 교사는 학생을 하나의 인간으로서 존중하고 그의 주체적 학습 능력에 대한 확신을 지녀야 한다. 즉, 학생은 나름대로의 적극적 학습 능력을 지니고 있으며 교사는 이를 촉진하는 조력자 또는 안내자 역할을 수행한다는 관점을 지녀야 한다. 또한 교사는 교직에 대한 신념과 사명감을 지녀야 한다. 교직을 생계유지 수단으로만 보지 말고, 미래의 주체에 대한 교육을 미래 사회를 창조하고 변화시키는 최고의 수단으로 인식하여야 한다. 이러한 확신 또는 사명감은 평생동안 지속해야 하는 것인 바, 때로는 자신감이 떨어지고 회의가 생길 수도 있다. 그럴 때마다 교사는 관련 인문과학 서적을 탐구하거나 동료 교육자들과 적극적으로 교류함으로써, 자신의 확신과 사명감을 굳게 유지하여야 한다.

교사는 학생에 대한 이해와 애정을 지녀야 한다. 교사는 학생의 지적·정의적·신체적 발달에 대하여 상식이나 개인적 경험에 입각한 지식을 넘어서는 전문적 지식과 이해를 지녀야 한다. 아동 개인을 이해하기 위해서는 그 학생이 속한 사회의 특성과 변화 방향에 대한 수준 높은 식견을 가져야 함은 물론이다. 또한 아동의 성장 발달을 기대하고 그것을 위하여 적극적으로 조력하려는 의지, 즉 아동에 대한 헌신적 애정을 지니고 있어야 한다. 이러한 애정을 지니고 있는 교사는 아동의 부정적 측면을 강조하기보다는 긍정적 측면과 능력을 강조하고 신장시키는 노력을 전개하게 된다. 그 결과 교사와 아동의 상호작용이 더욱 원활하게 되어 최대한의 교육적 효과를 거둘 수 있다.

교사는 교육내용에 대한 이해와 교수 능력, 그리고 탐구 능력을 지녀야 한다. 교사는 평소에 가르치고자 하는 내용에 대한 연구를 꾸준히 하여야 하며, 이는 초등학교 교사에게도 예외가 되지 않는다. 교사의 교육내용에 대한 이해가 피상적 수준에 머무르게 되면, 그 교사는 아동들에게 핵심적이고 필수적인 내용 요소와 주변적인 내용 요소를 구분하여 제시하지 못하게 된다. 본래 강조를 두어 가르쳐야 할 개념이나 원리 등에 대해서는 피상적 제시에 그치고, 중요하지 않은 주변 활동에 지나치게 많은 교수-학습 시간을 소모한다. 또한, 교사는 교육내용을 아동들에게 효과적으로 제시하고 효과적인 학습을 도와주는 기법을 내면화하고 있어야 한다. 같은 교육내용이라도 아동의 특성에 따라, 교수-학습 여건에 따라 다른 교수법을 필요로 할 수 있다. 다양한 교수법을 상황에 적절하게 제시하는 교사의 능력이야말로, 기능이 아니라 예술의 영역에 속하는 것이다. 뿐만 아니라, 교사는 다방면에 대한 탐구 의지와 탐구 능력을 지녀야 한다. 교사의 탐구능력은 스스로의 성취도를 높일 수 있을 뿐 아니라, 교사로부터 행동의 모델을 찾는 아동들의 탐구 능력을 향상시키는 데 중요한 요소가 된다.

교사는 적극적인 행동 의지와 항상 노력하는 자세를 지녀야 한다. 교사는 대체로 매우 다양한 역할과 과다한 업무를 수행해야 하는 형편에 있다. 과다한 업무에 시달리다 보면, 자칫 모든 업무에 소극적이 되고 최소한의 노력만을 전개할 수 있다. 무엇보다도 교사 본연의 업무인 교재 연구와 아동 이해를 위한 연구, 교수-학습 자료 수집 등을 소홀히 하게 될 가능성이 있다. 교사 역할의 중요성에 비추어 볼 때, 교사들은 교육 환경의 어려움에 매몰되지 않고 오히려 적극적으로 그 어려움을 극복해야 한다. 여러 번 언급했다시피, 교사들의 이러한 삶의 자세와 행동양식은 아동들의 행동과 인생관에 귀감이 되기도 한다. 따라서 교사는 평소에 축적해 온 삶의 자세와 아동관에 일관된 행동을 적극적으로 실천하고 그러한 노력을 지속적으로 전개하여야 한다.

교사는 학부모와 지역사회 인사, 선후배 교사들과 효과적으로 상호작용할 수 있는 의사소통 능력과 인격적 감화력을 지녀야 한다. 교사는 필요에 따라 학부모와 아동에 대한 면담을 수행한다. 때로는 다른 기관과 접촉하여 청소년 선도를 위하여 협의하고 공동 노력을 전개하기도 한다. 그리고, 교사는 공식적인 학교 조직의 일원으로서 선후배 교사들과 교재 연구, 또는 학교 환경 개선을 위한 다각적인 협의를 하게 된다. 교사는 이러한 다양한 상호작용의 상황에서 설득력 있는 의사소통을 전개하여야 한다. 그럼으로써 주어진 문제에 대하여 여러 사람이 짧은 시간 내에 최선의 결론을 도출할 수 있다. 특히 현대 사회에서 개인적 경쟁이 심화되고 물질숭배 의식이 높아질수록, 아동들과 더불어 순수한 삶을 살며 자신을 갈고 닦는 노력을 전개하고 있는 교사들에 대한 기대와 존경이 더욱 높아지게 된다. 이러한 점을 고려하여, 교사는 평소에 다른 사람들과의 상호작용에서 교육자로서의 품위를 견지해야 한다.

18 잠재적 교육과정의 연구 배경과 개념에 대해 말해 보시오.

잠재적 교육과정은 최근에 논의되기 시작하였으며 따라서 이의 개념정립은 아직 탐구단계에 있다고 할 수 있다. 잠재적 교육과정이라는 용어는 Merton이 사회제도의 적응에 관련된 의도하지 않았던 결과를 잠재적 기능이라고 부른 데서 기인하고 있다. Merton은 미국남서부의 원주민인 호피인디언의 기우제에 대한 풍습을 연구하여 사회적 제도와 행동의 표면적 기능과 잠재적 기능을 구분하였다. 표면적 기능의 관점에서 보면 기우제는 비를 내리게 하는 기능으로 이것은 근대적 과학의 입장에서 보면 하나의 미신이나 전통적인 타성에 불과하다. 그러나 잠재적 기능의 관점에서 보면, 기우제는 가뭄으로 인하여 들뜬 민심을 가라앉히고 부족간의 집단의식과 단결을 강화해주는 기능을 한다. 표면적 기능의 관점에서 보면 비합리적이고 미신에 불과한 기우제가 잠재적 기능의 관점에서는 새로운 의미로 관찰되고 해석된다.

Merton의 사회제도와 관련된 잠재적 기능이라는 생각은 교육학 분야에 적용되기 시작하였다. 교육과정에 대한 논의가 전문화되면서 학교의 교과활동에서 의도한 바와 관련이 없는 또는 상반되는 학습결과에 주목하게 되었다. 교과의 범위를 벗어난 일상의 학교생활에서 학교에서는 의도하지는 않았으나 학생들이 갖게 되는 경험이 허다하며 이러한 경험들은 학교교육의 역기능과 순기능에 모두 관련되어 있음에 관심을 갖게 되었다. 잠재적 교육과정은 학교교육의 전 사태에 관련된다. 학교의 물리적 조건과 제도 및 행정조직뿐만 아니라 사회심리적 상황 등을 포함하여 잠재적 교육과정의 요소를 담고 있지 않은 학교 사태는 거의 없다.

19 학습지도자로서의 구체적인 교사의 역할은?

- 수업 전개자로서의 행위
- 교육과정 구성자로서의 행위
- 수업연구 수행자로서의 행위
- 교육평가자로서의 행위
- 일정의 교과내용의 사실을 모순 없이 학생들에게 구체적으로 명확히 가르친다.
- 교육과정 운영의 과정에서 학생들에게 건전한 삶의 방향을 고취하고 가치관의 형성을 고취시킨다.
- 교사의 전문성을 고취한다.
- 학생들에게 적절한 과제를 제시하여 학습에 동기유발을 시킨다.

20 교사가 갖고 있는 권리는 무엇인가?

교사가 갖고 있는 권리는 크게 두 종류로 구분할 수 있다. 교사가 교육이라는 전문적 활동을 수행하는 데 필요한 적극적 권리로서 교육자유권(자율성), 생활보장권, 근무조건의 개선, 복지후생의 이익추구 등을 포함하는 개념이다. 이것은 주로 물질적 내지 물리적 측면으로서 교사들이 그들의 본연의 임무인 교육 활동에 전념할 수 있도록 보장받아야 할 권리다. 교육자유권은 결국 교사의 자율성 신장을 목표로 한다. 현행 헌법 제 31조 4항에는 교육의 자주성, 정치적 중립성, 교육의 전문성 보장이 명시되어 있다. 교원의 자율성이 강조되는 것은 전문직으로서의 직능이 유감없이 발휘되고 업무 수행이 온전하게 이루어지도록 하기 위해 요청되는 전제 조건이기 때문이다. 생활보장권은 교원이 안정된 생활기반 위에서 가르치는 일에 몰두할 수 있는 여건을 마련해 주는 것이다. 모든 교원이 교직에 전념하기 위해서는 건강을 유지할 권리, 자녀교육의 권리, 거주할 주택의 권리, 노후를 안락하게 생활할 권리가 보장되어야 한다. 교사의 전문적 활동을 수행하기 위한 소극적 권리가 있다. 이것은 주로 법적인 측면으로서 신분보장, 쟁송제기권, 불체포특권, 교직단체활동권 등이 있다. 교육 공무원은 국가공무원 법에 의한 신분보장은 물론 교육 공무원법에 의하여 일반 공무원보다 더 강력한 신분상의 권리를 보장 받고 있다.

21 (추가질문) 교원의 의무와 권리에 대해 말해보세요.

- 적극적 의무 : 교육 및 연구 활동의 의무, 성실 복종의 의무, 품위 유지의 의무, 비밀엄수의 의무 등
- 소극적 의무 : 정치활동 금지, 집단행위의 제한, 영리업무 및 겸직의 금지
- 적극적 권리 : 자율성의 신장, 생활보장, 근무조건개선, 복지후생제도의 확충
- 소극적 권리 : 신분보장, 불체포특권, 교직단체 활동권

22 학생에게 자애로운 교사와 교과교육에 실력 있는 교사가 반드시 일치하지는 않을 수도 있다. 학교 교사로서 어느 쪽이 더 중요하다고 생각하는가?

두 가지 모두 학교 교사로서 중요한 자질이고, 끊임없이 노력해야 하는 부분이나, 둘 중에 비중을 더 두라고 한다면 자애로운 교사, 즉 인간적인 교사가 학교 교사에 더 적합하다고 생각한다. 학교 교육목표는 비단 높은 학업성취에만 있는 것이 아니다. 학교교육은 전인교육을 목적으로 하고 있기 때문에 지나친 학업위주의 교육은 학생들의 전인적 발달을 저해할 수 있다. 또한 청소년기의 학생들은 인성이나 자아정체감이 형성단계에 있기 때문에 이에 대한 기초적인 관심과 교육이 매우 중요하다.

23 최근 학생들의 영양불균형을 유발하는 편식 등의 식습관으로 인해 아동 성인병이나 비만 등이 사회문제로 대두되고 있다. 학생들에게 올바른 식습관을 가지도록 하기위한 지도방안을 말하시오.

① 가정에서의 올바른 지도-학부모와의 연계지도와 학교 차원에서의 프로그램 마련을 위해 하루 식생활의 대부분을 차지하는 가정에서부터 올바른 식습관 지도가 이루어질 수 있도록 하는 것이 중요하다.
② 나의 식생활 바르게 알기-학생들로 하여금 자신의 식생활을 되돌아보게 하고 좋지 않은 식생활을 유지할 경우 발생할 수 있는 위험을 알리고, 바른 식습관을 실천할 수 있도록 관리하는 방법을 알려주는 것이 중요하다.
③ 급식지도-학교에서 밥을 먹을 때 직접 올바른 식습관을 형성할 수 있도록 먹을 만큼의 음식을 받게 하는 것이나 잔반을 남기지 않도록 하기, 자신의 먹은 음식 영양 체크리스트 만들기 등의 활동을 실천함으로써 실생활에서 직접 올바른 식생활을 할 수 있는 경험을 준다.

24 쉬는 시간에 잠시 교무실에 다녀온 사이 교실에서 아동들이 심하게 폭력을 사용하며 싸우고 있는 장면을 목격하였다. 교사로서 이 아동들을 어떻게 지도할 것인가?

　우선 싸우고 있는 상황을 멈추게 하고, 감정을 가라앉힐 시간을 준다. 그런 후 학생들로 하여금 자신의 의견과 상대의 의견을 듣고 말하는 시간을 주어 학생들의 의견을 충분히 들어본다. 이 때, 교사는 중립적 태도를 유지하고 되도록 의견 표명을 자제하고 학생의 말에 귀를 기울이는 것이 중요하다. 학생들이 서로의 이야기를 차례로 얘기하는 과정에서 서로를 이해할 수 있도록 돕는다. 그런 후 폭력이 아닌 정당한 의사표현방법을 알려주고 먼저 폭력을 휘두른 학생에게는 폭력은 어떠한 경우에서도 잘못된 것이라는 것을 확실히 주지시키도록 한다. 그런 후 반드시 사과하고 화해하는 시간을 가지도록 한다. 이 후 싸운 것에 대한 벌을 주어야 할 경우에는 두 사람이 같이 청소를 하게 하는 등 친밀해 질 수 있도록 배려한다.

25 자신의 수업스타일에 대해 지나치게 간섭을 많이 하는 선배 교사 또는 교장선생님이 있다. 그 선생님들께 자신의 그동안의 수업방법에 대한 입장을 꼭 전달해야 할 때가 왔다면 뭐라고 하겠는가? (직접 말하는 방식으로 서술하시오)

　이 상황에서는 저의 존중과 이해를 바탕으로 하면서도 저의 교육 철학과 방법론을 분명히 전달하는 것이 중요하다고 생각합니다. 이러한 점들을 고려하여 다음과 같이 표현할 수 있습니다. "선생님들께서 저의 수업에 관심 가져 주시고 조언해 주시는 점에 감사드립니다. 선배님들께서 주신 조언을 통해 제 수업이 더 발전하고 있다는 것을 느낍니다. 다만, 저는 학생 중심의 수업을 통해 학생들이 스스로 생각하고 경험을 통해 배워나가는 과정을 중시하고 있습니다. 이러한 방식이 아직은 익숙하지 않거나 조금 더딜 수 있지만, 학생들이 주도적으로 참여하면서 배움의 깊이를 스스로 만들어 갈 수 있는 장점이 있다고 믿습니다. 물론, 선생님들께서 그동안 축적하신 귀중한 경험과 조언을 소중히 여기며, 제 방식과 잘 융합해 나가도록 노력하겠습니다. 제 수업 방법에 대해 지속적인 이해와 격려를 부탁드리며, 저 역시 발전을 위해 계속 배우고 성장해 나가겠습니다."

26 집에서는 부모님께 천사 같은 학생 박 군이 사실 학교에서는 다른 아이들을 괴롭히고 불량스러운 학생들과 어울리는 학생이다. 어느 날 학생들의 불만을 들은 황 교사는 부모님과 상담하기로 마음먹었다. 당신이 황 교사라면 부모님과의 대화를 어떻게 이끌어 가겠는가?

　상담을 위해서는 평소 학생의 행동습관이나 교우관계, 성격 등에 대한 기초자료를 꼼꼼하게 관찰하여 기록해 놓는 것이 중요하다. 충분한 자료가 모아졌다면, 학부모와의 면담을 요청하고, 먼저 가정에서 학생의 모습을 학부모로부터 더 자세히 듣는 것이 필요하다. 이후, 기초자료를 토대로 사례를 들어가며 학생의 학교생활 모습을 학부모에게 전달한다. 이때, 직설적으로 전달하는 것 보다는 사례를 통해 학부모가 실제 학생의 모습을 느끼도록 하고, 되도록 완곡한 표현을 사용하도록 한다. 사례와 더불어 교사가 생각하는 행동변화의 원인을 설명하고 학부모의 의견을 듣는다. 상담 이후에도 학부모와 지속적으로 정보를 주고받으며, 학교와 가정에서 연계지도가 이루어질 수 있도록 하며, 체계적으로 학생의 행동을 바로잡을 수 있도록 한다.

27. 학습이나 생활상에 문제가 있는 아동을 잘 지도하려면 다른 학생에게 소홀해 질 수 있다. 이 딜레마를 어떻게 해결하겠는가?

학습이나 생활상에 문제가 있는 아동을 따로 지도하는 시간을 마련하려고 생각한다면, 다른 학생에게 많은 시간을 할애하지 못하여 소홀해 질 수 있는 현상이 발생할 수 있다. 그러나 생활 속에서나 수업 중에 작은 노력을 통해서 지도하려고 한다면 큰 무리 없이 모든 학생을 지도할 수 있을 것이다. 우선 중요한 것은 쉬는 시간이나 방과 후 잠시 동안의 시간 등 자투리 시간을 이용하여 문제학생과의 대화를 많이 시도하는 것이다. 이를 통해 학생에 대한 보다 많은 정보를 수집하고 학생이 교사가 배려하고 있다는 것을 느끼게 하는 것이 중요하다. 이를 통해 가정과 지속적인 상담활동을 하는 것도 중요할 것이다. 그리고 학습에 문제가 있는 아동의 경우에는 자신감을 잃은 경우가 많으므로 아동의 수준에서 대답할 수 있는 발문을 많이 제공하여 발표하게 하고, 답을 하면 크게 칭찬해주어 자신감을 높이는 것이 중요하다. 또 수준별 활동을 활용하는 방법도 효과적일 것이다. 생활에 문제가 있는 아동은 문제가 있는 행동의 이유를 관찰하여 해결할 수 있도록 하고, 아동에게 책임을 부여함으로써 해결할 수 있다.

28. 교사가 학생평가 전문가로서 갖추어야 할 능력을 서술해 보세요.

- 평가방법을 선정하는 능력이 있어야 한다. 교사는 학습목표의 평가의 목적을 확인하고 명확히 해야 하며 거기에 맞는 평가방법을 선정해야 한다.
- 교사는 평가도구를 개발할 수 있는 능력을 갖추어야 한다. 교사는 평가의 목적과 내용에 적합한 평가도구를 개발하거나 선택해서 사용해야 하며, 평가도구를 개선해야 한다.
- 평가를 실시하고 채점하고 성적을 부여하는 능력이 있어야 한다. 교사는 평가계획에 부합하도록 평가를 실시하면서 정확하게 채점하고 평가목적에 맞도록 성적을 부여해야 한다.
- 교사는 평가결과를 분석하고 해석하고 활용하고 그것을 토대로 다양한 관련자들과 의견을 나누어야 한다.
- 학생의 인격을 존중하고, 특성과 배경을 고려하여 공정하게 평가하고, 평가의 적절성을 판단해야 한다.

29. 교사를 따르지 않는 학생이 있을 수 있다. 지도방안을 서술하시오.

- 학생에게 반에서 중요한 업무를 맡겨 책임감을 느끼게 하여 학급일에 협조하게 한다.
- 학생에게 일을 지시하기 보다는 학생 스스로 일을 처리해 나갈 수 있도록 학생에게 협조한다.
- 학생이 학습에서 중요한 사람이라는 것을 깨우쳐주고, 지속적인 믿음을 보여주어 학생이 점차 교사를 믿고 따르게 한다.

30   학업에 흥미를 느끼지 못하고 무단결석을 할 때 지도방안을 말해보시오.

- 가장 먼저 학업에 흥미를 느끼지 못하는 원인을 찾아본다. 동시에 부모가 모르는 경우도 있기 때문에 부모에게 무단 결석 사실을 알려 사유를 알아본다.
- 결석한 학생에 대해 학급전체가 관심을 보이는 것이 중요하므로 급우들의 관심을 유도한다.
- 무단결석이 계속되면 학부모에게 내교 통지서를 보내어 면담을 하고 원인을 알아 적절한 지도를 한다. 면담이 어려운 경우에는 가정방문을 한다.
- 학부모에게 학부모와 학생에게 결석생에 대한 징계규칙을 설명하고 그대로 무단결석을 계속하면 고지한대로 징계하여 잘못을 고치도록 한다.
- 무단결석은 금품갈취, 성폭력, 윤락 등 청소년 비행으로 이어질 수 있다. 그러므로 담임이 취한 모든 지도 내용을 지도일지에 남겨 문제가 발생했을 때를 대비한다.

31   자기주도적 학습에 대해 아는 대로 말해보세요.

정보의 홍수로 새로운 지식이 매일 쏟아져 나오고 기존지식의 수명이 점점 단축되어가는 정보화 사회에서는 산업사회와는 달리 기존지식만으로는 삶을 살수 없기 때문에 자기 스스로 학습을 할 수 있는 자기주도적 학습능력이 필요하다. 자기주도적 학습능력이란 학생들 스스로 목표를 세우고 그 목표를 달성하기 위해 자유로운 탐색이나 정보수집과 같은 활동을 함으로써 자신의 학습활동을 진행시켜 나갈 수 있는 능력이다. 자기주도적 학습능력은 교육 본연의 목적 실현에 기여하며 창의력을 신장하여 국가발전을 꾀할 수 있고, 정보인 육성과 평생학습의 신장을 위해 필요하다. 이러한 자기 주도적 학습에 있어서의 교사의 역할에 대해 살펴보면 우선 학습자들이 자신감과 신념을 가지고 스스로 계획을 세워 공부할 수 있도록 철저히 지도하고 격려해야 한다. 그리고 창의성 계발을 위하여 기초기본능력을 함양시키고 학생에 맞는 목표와 내용 방법을 수립할 수 있도록 도와주는 역할을 해야 하며 아울러 학습하는 방법을 가르쳐 주어야 한다.

32   협력학습의 학습효과에 대해 말해보세요.

- 모든 학생을 학습에 참여시킬 수 있다.
- 학생들에게 책임감을 길러줄 수 있다.
- 학교생활 자체를 즐겁게 만들 수 있다.
- 학생들의 학업성적 향상에 더욱 효과적이다.
- 학생들의 인종적, 문화적 편견을 감소시키고 동료들 사이의 우정을 돈독하게 해 준다.
- '할 수 있다'는 적극적이고 능동적인 가치관을 지니게 한다.
- 학습 장애아, 학습부진아, 미진아들에게 더욱 효과적인 흥미와 동기를 불러일으킬 수 있다.

33 수행평가에 대해 말해보세요.

객관식 평가로는 질적인 평가나 충고형 평가가 어려운 것을 보완하기 위해 도입된 수행평가는 기존의 평가와는 달리 학생 스스로가 직접 만들거나 행동으로 나타낸 실제 수행한 결과를 평가하는 방식으로 학생의 창의력이나 문제해결력 등 고등사고기능을 파악하고 개별적인 학습을 신장하기 위해 강조되는 평가방식이다. 수행평가의 종류에는 서술 및 논술검사, 구술시험, 찬반토론법, 실기시험, 실험, 실습법, 면접법, 관찰법, 포트폴리오, 자기평가보고서 등이 있으며 이러한 수행평가는 선택형 평가에 비해서 실시하기가 어렵고, 인적·물적 자원이 많이 소요되며 학습목표를 포괄하여 평가하기 어렵다. 또한 타당성, 신뢰성, 비교가능성, 공정성의 확보에 많은 어려움이 따른다.

34 수업을 방해하는 학생에 대한 교사의 대응 방안에 대해 말해보세요.

- 교사가 모든 학생을 잘 볼 수 있고 학생 근처로 쉽게 이동할 수 있도록 좌석배치를 한다. 문제행동에 대한 교사 개입의 영향이 감소시키고자 하는 방해 행동보다 오히려 큰 부정적 영향을 주어서는 안된다.
- 문제행동이 발생할 때 첫 단계는 조용하게 그 학생과 접촉하는 것이다 : 학생들이 어기고 있는 학급규칙이나 절차를 상기시킨다.
- 적절하지 못하게 화를 내는 교사의 반응은 학생들의 긴장과 불복종, 방해 행동을 증가시키므로 교사가 조용하고 신속하게 문제행동에 대처하여 다른 학생들이 그들의 행동을 개선하도록 한다.
- 발생 가능한 문제들이나 사소한 수업방해 행동에 대해 주목하고 반응할 수 있도록 교실을 자주 살펴본다 : 한두 명의 학생이 심하게 혼란을 일으키는 경우 다른 학생들은 과제수행에 몰두하도록 하고 소란을 피우는 학생과 개인적으로 이야기 한다.

35 바람직한 발문의 내용과 방법에 대해 말해보세요.

- ■ 발문의 내용
  - 질문이 수업 목표와 관련된 것인지를 확인한다.
  - 학생들이 언제나 올바른 대답을 할 수 있는 질문을 한다.
  - 교과의 특성에 따라 다양한 질문을 한다. (낮은 수준의 질문과 높은 수준의 질문을 적절히 구사)
  - 질문의 용어는 직접적이고 명확하며, 학생들에게 익숙한 어휘와 어법을 사용한다.
  - 학생의 지식이나 경험 및 능력에 적합한 질문을 한다.
  - 한 번에 하나의 요점만을 질문하며, 구체적이고 간단히 답할 수 있는 질문을 한다.
  - 학생의 능력을 고려해서 다양한 수준의 질문을 하고 모든 학생이 정확하게 답할 수 있도록 응답기회를 준다.
- ■ 발문방법
  - 구체적인 목표에 따라 적절한 순서로 질문계획을 세운다.
  - 논리적 계열을 만들어 질문한다.
  - 학생들은 처음 질문이 잘 알고 있는 것이면 자신감을 갖게 되므로 쉬운 것부터 어려운 것으로 차례로 질문한다.

- 학생들이 답하기 전에 계속하여 여러 가지 질문을 하게 되면 당황하게 되므로 한 번에 한 가지만 질문한다.

36. 학습동기를 유발하기 위한 바람직한 전략에 대해 말해보세요.

- 목표를 구체적으로 인식시킨다.
- 협동과 경쟁을 적절히 활용한다.
- 상과 벌을 적절히 활용한다.
- 학습결과에 대한 정보를 제공한다.
- 주의를 집중시킨다.
- 학습자의 욕구와 목표 및 과제내용을 일치시킨다.
- 긍정적인 자아개념을 형성시킨다.
- 성취감을 느낄 수 있도록 한다.

CHAPTER 04 영어 면접 핵심문제와 답안

1 List your THREE strengths as a teacher and explain each one.

① Dynamic: I am a high energy person who likes to use many different types of teaching techniques to instruct students.
② Compassionate: I understand that students have a lot of pressure and stress in their lives and I like be flexible in my attitude and work with them in order to help them succeed.
③ Responsible: I am an organized and detailed person who brings a mature and disciplined approach to my studies and teaching work.

2 What causes you to lose your temper?

① Students who insult other students in the classroom
② Students who are constantly late for class
③ Students who refuse to take accountability for their own behaviour but instead want to blame others
④ Students who spread rumours are all suitable responses

3 What is the reason to have you decided to become a school teacher among many other jobs?

I've wanted to be a school teacher because I like to work with young people alot. They are pure and so cute so I think I'll never be bored if I'm with them. And secondly, school students are very flexible, so they are easily changed by my teaching. In other words, teaching affects their lives quickly and greatly.

4 Give any examples of role models of a good teacher or someone who impressed you a lot in your life.

My role model as a teacher is my mother. She has been an elementary school teacher for 30 years. Even after so many years, her passion about teaching has never gone down but instead become much stronger. She always treats students with respect and think and see the world on the students' side.

---

5 Have you had any experiences in your life that never forget? Explain about your experience and the reason why you think that.

The time when my grandfather died was the most shocking and memorable experience in my life. Since I was the only child for my parents, I was also the only and the most beloved grandchild of my grandfather. He wasn't a very sweet grandfather, but he was the most generous man on earth. He always cared about me and thought about me alot. So, even if he didn't tell me so, I could feel that and he loved me. However, at that time I didn't express my feelings much to my grandfather. I realized that I loved him as much as he did love me at the moment he passed away. I regretted but it was too late. From that experience I learned that there is a right time to say something. And, until now, I always miss my grandfather.

---

6 Explain about a difficult situation you have encountered during teacher-training, and how you have resolved it.

When I was on the second teacher training in 2006, I took responsibility of 4th grade students. One day, during the break time, a parent suddenly came into the classroom and beat one of the girls without saying a word. I was really shocked and looked for a homeroom teacher of my class but she wasn't there. So, I tried to stop the parent and told her to calm down and talk to me in the teacher's room. I succeeded to drag out her from the classroom but she was too angry to talk so I waited. She calmed down within a minute and told me that the girl kept beating her own son, so he got bruises. So, I told her that I could understand the mother but it is a wrong way to punish her by beating, and also it would have been better to talk to teacher first before doing that. She agreed with me and I promised that I will tell that girl not to do that. So, the parent went back home.

---

7 What are the teachers' other roles or responsibilities except for teaching?

- To be a role model of behavior and thoughts: Students can learn from teachers behavior and expressions without teaching.
- To be a counselor: Teachers must be a friend so that they can tell the problems or their thoughts so that teachers can help them.
- To be a leader: As a leader of the class, teachers should lead their students to the right way.

8 What is your greatest attribute or quality that you can bring to a class of students?

① My passion and enthusiasm for the English language
② My dynamic and creative personality
③ My patience and understanding of the challenges of learning a second language
④ My understanding and ability to integrate technology into the classroom

9 What is your biggest weakness?

I have many creative ideas and activities for my students but class time is limited. It can be difficult to use all the activities that I would like, but over time I have realized what lessons are most important to improve my students learning. I now realize I cannot do everything that I would like to do.

10 What do you like most and dislike most about teaching?

What I like most about teaching is the ability to help a student achieve academic and personal success in their lives. What I dislike most about teaching is that classroom time is limited. Therefore, I am not able to utilize all the lessons and activities that I would like for teaching the students.

11 What is your first summer vacation plan on next year after you get appointed as a school teacher? This will be your first vacation as a school teacher.

I want to travel for a while because I really like to travel but I couldn't for several years of studying. And I want to take a extra classes for teacher in vacation. I heard that there are plenty of classes provided only for teacher which is very useful. I hope that I can teach better for taking those classes. And I will study English in Great Britain's Culture Center.

12 Do you consider yourself a risk taker? Provide a real life example.

YES. I resigned from an important and good paying job as a Corporate Manager so I could return to University and attend graduate school in order to become a teacher. There were no guarantees I would succeed at graduate school or find work as a teacher. I took a large financial risk in order that I could pursue my dream and true passion of becoming a teacher. Successful teachers are those who take risks.

13 If a student said you were the worst teacher they ever had, what would you say?

I would thank them for being honest with me and providing me with their feedback. I would ask them the reason why they felt that way. I would ask them the ways I could be a better teacher. I would try to find a compromise solution between what the student wanted and what I was responsible for delivering to the class.

14 How can teachers prepare their students for globalization in English class?

① **Teach various kinds of cultures**: The differences and similarities between Korea and other countries in aspects of language, non-language and culture.
② **Use the computer in the classroom**: Show students many countries' life and thoughts through computer and projection TV system. Multimedia can help students feel other countries vividly and closely.
③ Give students some theme about world news in these days.
④ Show different kinds of pronunciation and intonation of English.

15 What do you think are the teachers' roles for students of multicultural families?

① Help them to learn korean
② Teach other students not to do some bad behaviors to them like race discrimination.
③ Make intimate atmosphere in class and school.
④ Connect school and educational facilities which are related to muticulturalism.

16 What can you offer your school that other candidates cannot?

① Leadership experience (coaching, student clubs)
② Other languages that you can teach
③ Other subjects you could teach if required
④ Organizational skills or Business skills that you possess from previous career

17 What is your long-range objective? Where do you want to be 5 or 10 years from now?

Within five years, I would like to become one of the very best teachers in my school. My personal ambition is to become a top level teacher in the education industry. I will work toward becoming the teacher that the other teachers in the school can depend upon for assistance. Be fully prepared to take on any greater responsibilities that might be presented to me in the long term.

18 Are you a team player? Or do you like to work alone?

I am a team player. For example I have had opportunities in academics (group work, tutoring), athletics, scouts, club activities, student politics etc. to develop my skills as a team player. I always try to help others achieve their best. In academics, I've worked on several team projects, serving as both a member and team leader. I understand the value of working together as a team to achieve a greater goal than any one person could have achieved individually.

19 Have you ever had a conflict with a Manager/ Superior or Principal? How was it resolved?

Yes, I have had conflicts in the past. Nothing serious, but certainly there have been situations where there was a disagreement that needed to be resolved. I've found that when conflict occurs, it's because of a failure to see both sides of the situation. Therefore, I ask the other person to give me their perspective and at the same time ask that they allow me to fully explain my perspective. At that point, I would work with the person to find out if a compromise could be reached. If not, I would accept their decision because they are my superior. In the end, you have to be willing to submit yourself to the directives of your superior, whether you are in full agreement or not.

20 If you had to live your life over again, what would you change?

It can be very easy to continually look back and wish that things had been different in the past. But I understand that things in the past cannot be changed, that only things in the future can be changed. I continually strive to improve myself each and every day and that's why I'm working hard to continually increase my knowledge in the education field. I want to become the very best teacher in a school and to make positive change. There isn't anything in my past that I would change because I look only to the future to make changes in my life.

21 How do you react to stress and pressure?

I find that I work better under pressure. I enjoy working in an environment that is challenging. I am the type of person that is able to use the nervous energy created by stress to motivate and fuel myself to complete my work/projects. I am used to working in a demanding environment with deadlines, and enjoy the challenges.

22 Tell me how you handled an ethical dilemma.

I worked part-time in a bank and a long-time and valuable customer wanted a cheque cashed right away but didn't have the money in his account to cover the amount of the cheque in case the cheque was invalid. The bank's policy prohibited cashing cheques in that manner, if I cashed the cheque I would have been violating bank policy if I did not I would be upsetting a good customer. It was a real dilemma so I went and spoke to the supervisor, explained the situation, and asked for their advice.

23 Are you a self-starter?

① Yes, I am definitely a self-starter. When I was a University student it was my policy to find out early on what projects, assignments or essays needed to be submitted for each of my courses. I would then quickly create a working group of fellow students and devise a list of roles and responsibilities for the project/assignment. OR for individual work I would go to the library to locate the best source materials possible for completing the assigned work. Having a quick and rapid response to my work allowed me to produce high quality work in an organized and time efficient manner.

② Yes, I am a self-starter when I worked at Acme Corporation, I was positive that the firm would be adopting a new operating system within a year, so I started taking classes at the local university at night in order to prepare myself. I was the only one in the office that knew how to operate the equipment when it was installed, so I was appointed trainer and subsequently trained 200 co-workers.

24 How do you balance career and family?

I haven't had a problem balancing my work and private life. One has never interfered with the other. I am capable of getting my work done without it interfering with my personal life." "I can easily balance my career and family life as my children are now in school and my wife/husband is starting a new career. We both work hard and have flexible schedules and have a good personal life, spending time with friends and family every week." OR "I am not married and have no children so I have more time to dedicate to my teaching work while still being able to pursue my personal interests and hobbies.

25 Do you like to be challenged?

YES. The teaching profession is full of challenges on a daily basis, for example, student behaviour, problems with multi-media equipment, lesson plans that don't work, etc. I understand and accept that I will not always be able to predict or control situations and that I will have to react quickly to these challenges. When I am challenged it has the effect of bringing out my best qualities and that I enjoy being a problem solver and quickly creating effective solutions to challenge.

26 Are you an empathetic person? Give an example?

I am a compassionate and understanding person because these are important qualities a successful teacher must possess. For example, I shouldn't force the student who had a speech problem to speak in front of the class. I gave the student who was having problems at home more time to finish their work assignment, gave them extra help to complete their work.

27 How often do you miss deadlines?

It happens VERY infrequently with me. While there is a possibility of not achieving every deadline, it is however my experience that proper planning, organization and prioritization of your work can enable a person to avoid missed deadlines.

28 Describe your philosophy of teaching. Describe what you think is the purpose of teaching and how you can achieve it.

① Purpose : to encourage students to increase their knowledge, improve their ability and develop their creativity
② How : stimulating their imagination and desire to achieve success using individual and co-operative learning methods and sharing ideas

29 How can you tell that a person is a good listener?

① When they are looking or watching you when you are speaking
② If they are writing down important facts of information as you speak
③ If they provide visual or facial clues that demonstrate understanding or confusion
④ If they demonstrate a willingness to ask thoughtful questions

30 What is your attitude concerning student deadlines for handing in their work?

① A teacher should demonstrate a level of flexibility towards deadlines.
② Students should always be encouraged to hand in their work even if it is late. (assessment purposes)
③ Teachers should work with the students to help them meet their deadlines. For example, after hours help, constant reminders of the deadline, encourage students to speak to teacher in advance of deadline about why they need a time extension.

31 Do you believe you should build a rapport with students? If yes... how?

YES... absolutely! I'll show an interest in the work in my class. I'll show an interest in the work in other subjects and their other school activities. I'll show an interest in their lives outside of school. I'll encourage students to visit me whenever they want to talk about something or open lines of communication.

32 Describe an ideal classroom that you think.

① A place where all students are motivated and engaged in the process of learning
② A place free from ridicule, intimidation, negativity and fear
③ A place where students and teacher work as partners to achieve their educational goals
④ A place where all students feel safe, comfortable and confident to participate in all aspects of the class

33 How would you describe a successful principal?

It is important that a successful principal has the ability to bring the teachers together to form a co-operative team and motivate them to reach the school districts goals and objectives. The principal should be visible and easily accessible to both students and teachers. The principal should relate well to a diverse group of individuals has compassion for the students, teachers and parents.

34 What qualities do you feel a successful teacher should have?

① The key quality should be leadership.
② A teacher should have the ability to provide both creativity and the intellectual stimulus to motivate their students to learn.
③ A teacher should also be a positive role model for the students to follow.
④ A teacher should be able to inspire students to reach the highest of their abilities.

35 If there are students who say that they don't want to study English, what rationales would you say that English language is important for them to study?

① It helps students prepare for life in the "Global Village" where English is the International language of communication
② It can provide accelerated career opportunities for students entering the work place and looking for good paying jobs both inside and outside of Korea
③ It can help students in their academic life at University and College

36 How do you measure 'success' as a teacher?

As a teacher, I measure success by the level of academic success that my students are enjoying in my class. I also measure success by the level of interest and enthusiasm that students display in my classroom. I measure success by the level of partnership that occurs between myself and my students. I measure my own personal success by how well I've achieved the goals I set myself. I feel I've been successful to date because I have attended my University of choice, I have graduated with my Degree in English and I have also acquired valuable teaching/ leadership experiences. The key in being successful is to set challenging yet attainable goals. My current goal is to succeed at this interview.

37 How would you encourage creative thinking in your classroom?

① Use some teaching methods for creation: Brainstorming, Brainwriting, six hats, and so on
② Praise when students get their own ideas and present them.
③ Give students time to interact with each other and communicate creative theme.
④ Overlook students' slips from time to time

38 In what ways do you encourage creativity in the classroom?

① **Student centered activities** : focus is on allowing the students to express or discover their creativity and their individual interests when completing assignments
② **Multi-media** : use movies, computers, internet, photographs, hands-on materials are all tools to excite the students imagination and increase their interest levels.

39 Talk about teaching and learning methods to develop students' creativity.

The most important tool a teacher can bring to class is a respect for the student's interest. If a student is doing something that they are interested in, they are more likely to be creative. Teachers also need to be flexible. Contents and methods should be changed according to the characteristics of the individuals in the classroom. Teachers should also be trained in their specialty area for more productive teaching. It's very important that education does not become confined to the classroom. Expand the places of learning to include libraries, local community centers and anything else that is suitable.

40 Talk about the necessity of creativity in education with respect to the knowledge information-oriented society and desirable classroom environment to promote creativity of students. Can you talk about a desirable classroom environment to promote the creativity of students as a teacher?

Teachers need to be responsible for implementing creativity in the classroom. A desirable class atmosphere is psychologically stable, open and permissive. A closed atmosphere makes students feel uncomfortable in opening up. The students need to know that making mistakes and failure is OK. Assessing students' creativity should be based on their individuality. And new ways of learning, such as discovery learning, inquiry learning and project learning need to be encouraged. Students should be given as many as various opportunities as possible.

41 Can you talk about the characteristics of creative students?

Creative students tend to be very curious and honest. They see things for how they are and accept that, but continue to ask questions about their surroundings. They have an attachment to finding the solution to issue that other students don't have. They find solutions on their own accord. There's a voluntariness in these students that is not found in other students.

42 How do you measure student performance in your classroom?

① Collecting assigned work and marking it
② Class participation marks
③ Co-operation and classroom behaviour
④ Attendance

43 Describe some methods of 'positive reinforcement' that you may use in your classroom.

① Allow students to choose the topic or activity for a part of the next class lesson.
② Offer public praise for students who are working to the best of their abilities.
③ Create a reward system.

44 What are some ways you can avoid behaviour problems?

① Recognizing that all students are different
② Dealing with them according to their individual situation, background and needs
③ Working with the class to isolate bad behaviour and create an environment that does not accept it
④ Paying close attention to the mood of students in the class and react accordingly

45 How do you feel about noise in your classroom?

It does not disturb me if students make noise when students are working in groups or when students are working in groups or are helping their neighbour. Students making noise between activities in the lesson plan is acceptable. But, I do not tolerate students making noise when the teacher is speaking or when a student is answering a question or reciting a sentence.

46 How do you handle a student who is talented but has a discipline problem?

① Have this student sit at the front of the class so that you can monitor them more closely.
② Frequently request the student to answer questions or read stories out loud to the rest of the class.
③ Have this student perform teacher assistance tasks or give them a type of leadership role.
④ Provide the student with extension work that will keep them busy learning while the rest of the class complete the work.
⑤ Offer them praise for good work and good behaviour.

47 How would you respond to the student who continually acted up, or distractions, in your classroom?

① Ignore the student, tell the class to ignore the student.
② Move the student to the front of the class.
③ Discuss the matter with the student's other teachers and find out how they manage the situation.
④ Create a teacher-student contract that details the teachers expectations and student's responsibilities.
⑤ Outline the punishments for not following the contract.
⑥ Inform parents of the situation.
⑦ Enlist their support.

48 Many school students enjoy playing the computer games. But some of male students get in worse situation than just enjoy the games. What are the reason so many students are in game addiction? How to overcome it?

Gaming in PC has been a way of life nowadays and most children are playing this kind of online, roll playing, shooting & action, strategy & simulation and sports game in pleasure. Many children are grown to be absorbed in the PC game rather than the important missions they really have to achieve in early years.

① **Reasons**: Students are alone with a computer at home. Many parents are all in their workplace in these days. Friends all talk about the game when they come to school. The game has become the essential point among them.

② **Solutions**: Students can have more quality time with parents and family. They do activities in real world and feel that they are more exciting than the games, to play a soccer, baseball and basketball in the ground, or to do the game of Korean chess or Paduk which was the replacements of PC game. Educational Campaign can be held in the school. Teachers and schools have to do some kinds of campaigns against the life of only games and for the public relations about good activities for them like an exercise.

49 One student hits another student. What would you do?

First of all I'd remind the class that violence has no place in our classroom and that I have a zero tolerance policy towards hitting or throwing objects at each other. I'll take both students out into the hallway to discuss the situation. I shouldn't choose sides. I'll tell them if they continue with this type of behaviour they will be punished severely, such as removal from class, parents' notification and etc. I'll bring both students back into the class and separate them so that they are sitting at the front of the class and on opposite sides of the room.

50 An irate student begins to yell and insults you. It is the last hour of the day with fifteen minutes left to go in the hour. How would you respond?

First of all, I would pause and breathe not to get angry and then make eye contact with the student. I would take the student aside (back of classroom / hallway) where I can speak privately and ask the student if it has been a bad day. I'd ask what is making him angry and if I can help. When the student is calm, I'd inform the student that as he has chosen to break rule #1, respect towards the teacher, what the consequence of their action is (the punishment they will receive for their behaviour).

51 A student confides in you and provides information to indicate they are victim to abuse. What would you do?

① Offer feelings of empathy towards the student, ask them if they want help.
② Ask for guidance from your Department Head or a trusted senior teacher.
③ Request to speak to the Principal about the situation and let Principal decide what should or should not be done. Obey your Principal, they have the experience and training for properly handling these situations… don't involve yourself more than necessary!

52 An angry parent calls you because they are upset about their child's low grades. What would you say to the parent?

① First thing to do is let the parent calm down about the situation.
② Remain calm and don't get defensive.
③ Arrange an interview with the parent and student.
④ Bring students marks, work and other supporting documentation to the meeting.
⑤ Discuss a strategy for improving the students grades that can involve the concerned parent.
⑥ Ask the parent to bring the student with them for a follow-up meeting in 3-4 weeks time.

53 How do you keep parents informed of their child's progress?

① Send home a letter once a semester that details students progress in the class.
② Parents sign it and their child returns the letter to the teacher.
③ Make phone calls to parents once a semester letting them know about their child's progress.
④ Encourage the parents to visit on parent-teacher night.
⑤ Encourage parents to contact you to arrange a meeting if they desire a meeting.

54 A parent comes to you and complains that what you are teaching his child is irrelevant to the child's needs. How would you respond?

First I would let the parent vent their feelings and I would agree with the parent's concern about the child's education. I would voice my concern for what's best for the student and their academic progress. Then I would ask for specifics. The problem may have nothing to do with what I'm teaching. I would bring a copy of the course curriculum that was designed and approved by the Education Ministry and explain that I am following the guidelines. If the parents were still not satisfied I would refer the matter to the school Principal and let them handle the situation.

55 If you are teaching a lesson and the students just do not seem to understand, what do you do?

① Stop and find out what is confusing them.
② Slowly repeat the part of the lesson that was creating confusion with the students.
③ Change to a new part of the lesson plan.
④ Review previous lesson.

56 Can a student be forced to learn? How do you encourage a student to learn?

① NO... a student can never be forced to learn.
② Find out what the students are interested in outside of school and try and design lessons that incorporate these interests.
③ Use multi-media in your classroom (variety).
④ Design student-focused lessons.
⑤ Assign team-based work and let the students choose their own teams (encourages peer tutoring and co-operation).
⑥ Design lessons that allow students to use computers and the internet as learning tools.

57 How do you give your students recognition? Do you think a student can have too much recognition?

① Provide them with small rewards in front of the class.
② Call them to the front of the class to receive their marked work and/or reward.
③ Use them as an example to motivate the rest of the class to work hard and achieve good results.
④ Let other teachers know about their good work/ behavior.
⑤ A teacher needs to be very careful not to create feelings of jealousy or separation between students.

58 How would you motivate a lazy student?

　First step is determine why the student is lazy. There may be a medical problem. The student may find the lesson boring. Or they may be confused with the material. Ask the student what type of lesson they enjoy and then try and design lessons that include these type of learning styles. Students have many different styles and methods for learning.

59 What would you consider to be the characteristics of a good listener?

① A person who allows people to express and explain themselves without interruption.
② A person who listens carefully and politely to the information that people are providing to them.
③ A person who does not get defensive or over-emotional when listening to people's criticisms of them.
④ A person who is willing to have an open and flexible mind and try to understand the other person's opinion and feelings.
⑤ A person who will take the opinions of others and use this information to make positive change within themselves.

60 If a student came to you and said, "None of the other students like me," what would you tell him/her?

First of all, as a step one, I would talk in private with the student and ask them WHY they felt this way and if they had any ideas WHY the other students didn't like them. Second, carefully monitor the behaviour of the other students towards the disliked student. Next, I'll have the disliked student included in different groups when team work is assigned to the class. Finally, let me try and match the student with another student in the class who is more tolerant and patient.

61 How do you want students to remember your class?

① That they learned a lot about the subject and had fun at the same time
② That they found the class to be interesting
③ That they enjoyed my lessons and teaching style
④ That they were glad to have taken the class and it motivated them to continue taking this subject in their future studies

62 Describe your ideal lesson.

① Lesson plan has clear instructions and attainable goals for the students.
② Students are enjoying what they are learning and feel motivated to complete the work to the best of their ability, class works as well as individuals, in their teams and or as an entire group.

63 What have you learned from your mistakes?

① That the best teachers are willing to take risks and experience mistakes…
② That no matter how hard you design a lesson and try to teach it, sometimes your lessons will not work or be accepted by the students… that is OK!
③ A teacher needs to recognize and accept when a lesson is not working well and quickly transition to a new learning activity in these situations.
④ Always be prepared with extension activities or a backup lesson in case your original lesson is not working.

64 What works best for you in classroom control?

① Self-confidence
② Maintaining the students' interest the students interest
③ Being prepared and organized
④ Being consistent in my behaviour
⑤ Being flexible in my attitude
⑥ Being open-minded and responsive to student feelings and allowing them some level of input

65 How do you structure your time to manage all of the school duties associated with teaching?

① Prioritize my responsibilities.
② Multi-task to meet deadlines.
③ Avoid too many extra-curricular activities.
④ Begin my day early to maximize my productivity (early to bed & early to rise).

66 Tell me about a time you had to handle multiple responsibilities. How did you organize the work you needed to do?

While attending University, I also worked at an academy(etc). I was successful because I practiced good time-management skills and I made a priority list of tasks every day. As I completed each task, I checked it off the list. It is amazing how something very simple can keep you very organized. As a result of my priority lists, I was able to visualize my daily progress and get my work done on time.

67 What have you gained from your work experiences?

My work at the academy/ company really helped me develop my interpersonal skills and learn how to lead people. When I was teaching English, it was my responsibility to give my students a sense of confidence, motivation and the tools necessary for them to succeed.

68 What motivates you?

① Helping students to learn, to maximize their potential and achieve their individual level of academic and personal success
② My sense of caring and responsibility to my work
③ Setting goals/ambitions for myself and achieving them
④ Working hard to be successful at anything and everything that I am involved with or engaged in

69 You are assigned the special English class. But this class has no textbook to be used. And some of innovative schools have no specific textbooks. All depend on the teachers who are in charge of the class. What do you think about the class without textbook?

I think the textbook is necessary in class. There are so many teaching materials except textbook these days, and sometimes they are much more effective than textbook. However, textbook contains other basin meanings that materials cannot provide. It should be kind of guidelines to teaching materials that suggests core contents and the direction of teaching. So, I believe that textbook is necessary in class.

70 Which teacher is more appealing to you? Is it a teacher whom students like or is it a teacher whom students respect?

I believe that it is more important for the student to respect me. The student-teacher relationship is a professional one. That a student likes me would be nice, but that doesn't mean the student will consider me as someone that can be learned from. The best situation would be both.

71 What kind of relationship do you want with your students?

① Trust & Respect: Exchange of ideas and an energetic rapport
② Open lines of communication
③ Willingness to understand each other
④ Encouragement to try new things
⑤ Freedom and confidence to share ideas

72 Tell us about some of the challenges you expect to face as a teacher and the probable solutions for them.

A) Do you understand the nature of the teaching profession
B) Your management style for solving these types of "challenges"
　① List out the obvious challenges like: 1) difficult students, 2) angry parents, 3) multiple deadlines for work, 4) co-teaching with foreign English teacher.
　② Then list a quick solution you have for managing these types of challenges: 1) effective classroom rules and management, 2) communicating with parents (phone calls, progress reports etc.) 3) prioritizing your work and maintaining a detailed daily schedule 4) open communication

73 What interests you most about the teaching profession?

　I am motivated by the opportunity to help students achieve academic success and that I'm honoured to have the chance to be a positive role model in students lives. I believe that teaching is a sacred and special responsibility that allows me to help the next generation prepare for their future and strengthen their communities. Teaching offers me a huge amount of personal satisfaction and strong feelings of self-fulfillment.

74 Describe a professional skill that you have developed within yourself.

① Computer skills: I have learned how to use various software programs and that they will enable me to provide extra value to my students.
② People skills: I have learned to be a better listener and moderator in times of conflict and that these skills will help me create and maintain effective classroom management.

75 How would you react if I told you that your interview, so far, was terrible?

Well, I'd be quite surprised and rather disappointed. I have put a lot of work into preparing for this interview and getting this job is very important to me. But may I ask you, what parts of my presentation did you consider were not up to an acceptable standard? If you could pinpoint these areas to me, maybe I could go over them again and clear up any misunderstandings that might exist. I'm sure that's where the problem lies.

76 Do you make mistakes? Can you share your mistakes with others?

Yes of course on occasions, but I obviously try not to, and I always try to correct them and learn from them. Absolutely I can share them. By sharing I can get the guidance I need, gain another perspective or opinion and it may help prevent others from making the same mistakes.

77 Do you intend to further your education?

Yes, I am always taking classes at the local college/ university to keep current on the latest in classroom computer technology so I can continue to offer creative and interesting lessons for my students. Yes, I intend to eventually go back to school part-time at night and earn my master's degree in English etc. However, I want to take a year off and get settled in a new job and home before starting.

78 Describe a situation in which you found that your work/ results were not up to your professor's or supervisor's expectations. What happened? What action did you take?

I was asked to put together a proposal for a new print management system. Misunderstanding my boss, I thought it was just an informal paper. When I presented it to him days later, he was upset with the quality of the paper because it had to be presented to our Vice-President of Finance. I explained my misunderstanding, apologized, reworked the paper, and had it back to him with enough time for him to review it before he presented it successfully at the meeting.

79 How well do you accept criticism? Failure? Defeat? What is your response to it?

There is always room for improvement. I need feedback. I know that I cannot please everyone. There is no such thing as failure as long as I learn from it. I use criticism to motivate myself to work harder and become better than before. Avoid taking it personally and getting emotional, instead I use it as a learning tool for self-improvement.

80 What difficulties have you faced on the job?

While teaching at the private academy, I had to balance a lot of completing demands from the parents, the children, the teachers and the administration. It really taught me how to view all sides of any situation, and how to prioritize my time. I found that differences of opinion usually occur because two people can't see both sides of the situation. I learned to see the other person's side and explain my position.

81 These days, many school students attend a private institute after school. What effects do you think private institutes have on the educational system?

In the most private institutes, students pre-study comparing to what they are learning now in school. That can make student feel confidence in school, but that can also make students feel bored. So, they can lose the right attitude for studying and that can influence their further study in bad way. In private institutes, they also teach students almost the same contents with school. In this situation, if students don't get the skills what they need to learn in something, students might think that they know that skills when they learn in school because they are familiar with the contents. This can cause serious loss of learning for students.

82 What extracurricular activities did you participate in while attending University?

I participated in the Student English Association. We met weekly, studied together, discussed English language books and topics of interest, held fund raising events and socialized with foreign English students. I was also a member of the University Student Newspaper. I wrote articles using the English language about various events that were happening on Campus and in the city where I was studying.

83 How will you handle the parts of this job you like the least?

I will perform all of the tasks my job requires on time and to the best of my ability regardless of whether or not I enjoy them. Generating high quality work no matter what the task, is very important to me on a both a professional and personal level.

84 What influenced you to choose this career?

My past experiences have shown me that I enjoy working with. Without doubt, once I have created and practiced my lesson plans and prepared myself for potential questions or objections, I feel very confident teaching students. Lastly, I like teaching because my potential for success is limited only by how much of myself I dedicate toward my goal. If any profession is founded on self- determinism, it surely must be teaching.

85 During a parent/teacher interview, a parent is angry with their child because their child had not performed well in the last examination. What would you say to the parent?

I'll say "Calm down." first. And then I'll tell them it is true that their child performed badly in the exam but that is nothing to angry about. Because I knew he/she is much better than this and it is a mistake for onetime. And I'll tell them not to blame him/her about the score, but help him/her to study about what they got wrong, so that he/she can do better next time.

86 In English education, what is the good point of the game?

① Game can easily motivate students.
② Games have uncertainty so that students can concentrate.
③ Games can get rid of burden to study.
④ Games can make students participate eagerly in english class.

87 How do you plan and organize your work?

Planning and writing a plan is very important. I like to strategize how best to do things before I do them. If it is work that is new for me I'd ask for advice from senior teachers or mentors. I try to learn from previous examples. I always prioritize my work, I manage my time, and I understand the difference between urgent and important. For very complex or detailed projects, I produce quite a detailed schedule and include review stages so I can measure my progress.

88 Do you consider yourself to be organized?

I manage my time very well. I routinely complete tasks ahead of schedule. For example, offering the interviewer proof of your organizational skills by telling him about a major project/assignment that you organized and completed on time at University or at work.

89 Why were your grades not excellent in school?

① I know my grades weren't that excellent in school, but I've never been very good at taking tests. I don't think my grades are an accurate reflection of my ability. I feel that I know this field as well as any new graduate. I just don't perform well on tests.

② I made A's in English, but C's and D's in my other classes that I was required to take to earn my degree. I've just never enjoyed these other classes, so I wasn't particularly good at researching and writing the many essays that were required in these classes, so my grades were average as a result.

90 Do you plan and organize before you start working?

I like to create a framework for any work assignment I am responsible for. After I have established a framework, I then develop a detailed "action plan" for achieving results. I usually use a day planner to keep myself focused on the tasks at hand and to monitor me to progress towards achieving my goals. I often review a mental checklist of important details every morning as I prepare myself for coming to work. This helps me motivate myself and to stay focused on the important tasks at hand.

91 Which type of teacher are you? Do you anticipate problems or just react to them?

I always try to anticipate problems and resolve them before they occur. For example, I was working on a very important group project at school and after a couple of weeks I realized that several of the group members were not comfortable with their roles and responsibilities within the group. I spoke with them to find out their feelings and was able to work with the other group members to switch some of our roles and responsibilities in order to accommodate the needs and wishes of all group members. By being sensitive and observant to the feelings and behaviour of all the group members I was able to anticipate a serious problem and come up with a satisfactory solution and avoid a potential disaster on our group project.

92 Do you think that the principal has the right to tell the teachers how to dress?

I believe that the principal has a right to tell the teachers to dress in a professional manner. How people dress affects other people's and students impression of them. The clothes a teacher wears can be an effective tool for dealing with students. A teacher should be a role model and demonstrate project a clean and professional image to their students.

93 What would you do if the principal asked you to do something the wrong way?

If I was aware that there was a more efficient or better way to perform a task, I would tactfully(carefully) point this out to the supervisor. However, if he or she still wanted me to do it his or her way, I would do as they wished.

94 Today, some native English teachers from your sister school in Canada will visit your school to stay in your school for a few days. Explain to them about the daily schedule of your school. Greetings have already done.

Usually, students come to school by 8:30am. And, first class starts at 9, so each class has their own activity before the class. Each class will last 40 minutes, and lower grades like 1st or 2nd grades have 4 classes for a day and upper grades from 3th to 6th grades, have 6 classes. After 4th class, students have lunch time for an hour. In addition, students can participate in extracurricular if they want. Our school is providing variety kinds of activity to students.

95 There are some students in your class who had lived overseas a while. So, there is significant gap between students' English skills. How can you handle this situation?

In this case, I think collaboration work is useful to run English class effectively. Some other students, except those students from abroad, can be timid and not willing to participate eagerly. And the students from abroad can be bored during the class. However, using collaborating method, students from abroad can play the role of assistant teacher, so they can participate in class with pleasure. Moreover, the other students can learn from students from abroad, so they can improve their english skills ,much more, and they can participate during class. And for the students from abroad, teacher can offer other activities or supplies that is appropriate for their English ability.

96 One of your students keep making language mistakes while communicating in English the class. Explain how you would correct that student.

I will not correct directly if it is not damaging the fluency of English. If I correct that immediately and directly, students might lose confidence in speaking English and they also can lose their interest about English. I think to correct them without these side effects, teacher need to observe the mistakes of students and make a note about them. And at the end of the class, teacher can correct mistakes about pronunciation or expressions to the whole class and make them practice or speak.

97 Classroom noise has been becoming a big problem in the school. How would you encourage your students to reduce the volume? Present at least 3 ways.

For the first way to make students quiet, making signs with children can be good way. Make a promise with students if teacher give them a sign, students do acting as promised. Like ringing a bell once, raise hands. Second way is make rules with children. These rules can be used not only when students are noisy but all the other situations in class. Rules must contain the students' consent so that they are willing to keep it. And for the last, reducing teachers own voice should be a good method. Students tend to be noisier if teacher shouts or yells at them. If teacher reduce his or her own voice, students can be noisier for a while. However, when the time passes, students will notice they can hear teacher's voice, and they will reduce their voice enough to hear teachers.

98 How can teachers improve students' English fluency in the class?

- Give a lot of speaking opportunities in English during class
- Provide them a situation that students can communicate with fun like games, role plays
- Do not correct errors or mistakes if it is not interrupt communication or fluency.

99 Today is your first day of class. What rules would you say to students as an English teacher? Present as if you speak to your students in class.

I am your English teacher. English is not a difficult subject matter. If you have any problem with English, I will help you with great interest. So I want you to come to me anytime when you have an question or want to learn more things about English. My room is the first on 3 floor. I want to tell you three rules of my class. First, you should speak even a word in English in a class.

I will check it. Second, you should follow my actions for being quiet and talking with your partner. You should be quiet when I show you this warning sign and talk about your words about some themes when I show you this sign. Last, Don't tease your friend who cannot speak English. You should respect and teach each other

---

100 How would you get parents involved in the learning process?

I would have several strategies to get parents involved in the learning process. Firstly, I would initiate the first casual contact with parents at the beginning of the school year. Secondly, I would also continue communicating to parents via a web page. Lastly, I would organize formal meetings with the parents through out the year. Those 3 strategies could be helpful for getting parents involved in the learning process.

---

101 People say that these days, school teachers have been losing their authority from the students in the classroom and from the parents. What degree do you agree with the statement, and why?

I think teachers are losing their authority and it's becoming worse. One of the biggest reason that causes is because parents are losing their faith about public education. Because of this parents wants to involve in educational situation so deep enough to infringe teachers authority. Parents participation is very important in class. However that is acceptable only when this is happening in right time, right situation and with optimum levels and teachers request. another main reason that cause losing power of teachers is media. Media tends to broadcast issues about education exaggeratingly so people might think things in wrong way.

---

102 One of you students, Sunny is afraid of speaking English. To make her speak more naturally in English, how can you teach her? Present at least 3 ways to teach.

First of all, the most important thing is to make students feel speaking in English is not difficult but comfortable and fun. Song, chant and game are very useful in that situation. These activities can make students fun and comfortable, and it is very effective way to improve English in natural situation. Next thing is apply Total Physical Response for young students. Students can improve their English skills following teachers physical acting. It contains less pressure of speaking, so this method can reduce the fear for English. And during class, teacher should not correct every error of students, because it can increase the fear for English class. Errors don't have to be corrected unless it is disturbing communication.

103 The number of English teachers from overseas are on the rise these days. Present your opinion about the English class by native English teachers.

In a way, English class by foreign teachers are good because they can give students meaningful input with their qualified English skill. However, I think Korean teachers are also very important in a secondary school. Because most of students have no or little experience of meeting with foreign culture and people and, thus, are not good at understanding them. Moreover, their identity as a Korean has not been completed so if they meet foreign culture directly, they can have confusion about their cultural identity. In that situation Korean teachers can help not to lose their own identity. So, I think to satisfy improving English ability and cultural identity, it is good to teach children with cooperation between Korean teacher and native teacher of English.

CHAPTER 05 임용 면접 모의문제와 답안

Q1 학교에서 괴롭힘을 당하는 학생을 위한 학급과 개인 차원의 지도 방법

One day, you found out a student, Junha had gone through hard times in school through his friend's diary. Discuss the FOUR methods to help this student, Junha, from the different perspectives.

> **Student's Diary**
>
> *I have a friend called Junha for my 3rd grade. He is from a poor family. When he comes to my place, my mom takes good care of him and treat him nicely. But other classmates make fun of him and even beat him for the reason of him being poor. Whenever I see that, I feel sorry for him. He often takes some days off. I am worried that he is absent today.*

예상답안

When the problem of bullying or violence in the school is concerned, we should approach it very tactfully to avoid any worst case. So I can suggest some solutions from the four points of perspective; the cause of problem, the victim student, the whole class and the parents.

(1) I should diagnose the cause of the problem. If it results from financial problem as mentioned in the diary, I would look for a method to support him financially such as scholarship without feeling shame. I also support him in order to build up good relationship with other friends.

(2) I can handle this problem on behalf of Junha.
- I empathize the sufferings of Junha that got bullied from his classmates. And then I promise to him that this incident wouldn't happen again and make an action for the students who bullied him by the school regulation.
- I introduce a case of successful life to go through the time of discrimination and contempt, such as Barak Obama and Steve Jobs.

(3) I can guide the class for several ways.
- Students should understand that beating and bullying are against school regulations. Those who involve in abuses must apologize to Junha and makes sure that this will not happen again.
- Students can have a spirit of community through voluntary or group work.
- Experiential-humanity education should be continued not to discriminate due to family background.

(4) I have to cooperate with his parents.
- I apologize to the parents for the accident that shouldn't have occurred in school.
- I send them the message that I would do my best that he adjust to school.
- I let them know the problem that he had to go through at school and ask them to encourage him to stand in dignity.

답안 키워드

class	student
① Ss should understand that beating and bullying are against school regulations. ② Ss can have a spirit of community through voluntary or group work. ③ I have to cooperate with his parents for further counseling.	① I should diagnose the cause of the problem. ② I can handle this problem on behalf of Junha. I empathize the sufferings of Junha that got bullied from his classmates. ③ I introduce a case of successful life to go through the time of discrimination and contempt.

한국어 예상답안

학교상황에서 일어날 수 있는 구상형문제로서 문제 분석과 지도방안 범주를 설정하여 준하를 도울 수 있는 방안은 대상별로 (준하, 학급, 준하 부모) 나누어 접근하는 게 요령이다.

1. 개인	• 따돌림과 폭력에 시달리고 있는 준하의 아픔을 진심으로 이해해주고 그런 일이 반복되지 않도록 교사가 책임지고 다른 학생들을 지도하겠다고 약속한다. 긍정적인 예언과 칭찬과 격려를 통해 준하의 자아존중감을 높여준다. 불우한 가정환경에서 자라면서 차별과 모멸을 견디어내고 훌륭한 삶을 살아간 사례를 소개한다. • 준하가 밝은 모습으로 적극적으로 교우관계를 개선해 가도록 관심과 지원을 보내준다. 준하가 경제적인 어려움 때문에 좌절하지 않도록 물질적 지원(장학금)을 해줄 수 있는 방법을 찾아 제공해준다. 대학생 멘토를 소개해주어 학습지원과 정서적 지원을 해줄 수 있도록 조치한다.
2. 학급	• 준하를 따돌리고 때리는 아이들에게 학칙에 어긋난 일이며 학생의 본분을 망각한 일이라는 것을 분명히 일깨워주고, 준하에게 사과하고 다시는 그런 일이 재발하지 않도록 지도한다. • 자치활동, 봉사활동, 모둠활동을 통해 공동체의식을 심어준다. 가정환경이나 성적, 그리고 장애를 이유로 친구를 차별하는 일이 없도록 체험중심의 인성교육을 지속적으로 실시한다. 학급에서 준하를 돕고 지켜줄 수 있는 특별 친구, 도우미를 만들어 준다.
3. 가정	준하 학교생활이 원만하지 못한 것에 대해 죄송하다는 마음을 전한다. 최선을 다해서 준하가 학교생활에 잘 적응할 수 있도록 도와주겠다는 뜻을 전한다. 준하가 학교에서 겪고 있는 문제를 알려주고 가정차원에서도 준하가 당당하게 학교생활을 할 수 있도록 용기를 주고 자신감을 북돋아 달라고 부탁한다.

Q2 학부모상담: 성적부진학생과 인터넷게임중독학생에 대한 조치

Read the dialogues of the parents A & B and analyze their needs and demands and explain the solutions to solve the problems for the parents B. Suppose that you are talking to the parents who come to see you about their kids' problems.

학부모 A:	My kid does computer games a lot at home and thus achieved a very low school performance at school.
학부모 B:	Our kids' school grades are very low. We spend too much money on private tuition fees. We believe that school teachers have to be more responsible for the students' academic achievement.

예상답안

Korean parents are well-known to be passionate about their children's study and school reports. There should be some solutions to make up for the low grades.

(1) Level-differentiated studies should be added to regular classes such as heterogeneous group work, division lessons in the class and etc...
(2) After-school activities should be more activate and have some variety of its kind to different proficiency and themes.
(3) Cyber home schooling could be used for extra work.
 - Online level-differentiated class during a subject matter classes
 - Online self-study at home (chosen subject and level)
(4) Foundation studies on a subject matter should be completed thoroughly under the charge of a homeroom teacher and subject matter teachers.

답안 키워드

① Level-differentiated studies
② After-school activities to different proficiency and themes
③ Cyber home schooling
④ Foundation studies on a subject matter

한국어 예상답안

(1) 게임 중독에 빠진 학생에 대한 해결책	(2) 학습부진과 사교육비 부담 해결방안
① 부모가 학생을 무조건 비난하거나 야단쳐서는 안된다. 반항심으로 역효과가 생길 수 있다. ② 학생이 왜 인터넷에 빠지게 되었는지 현실적인 원인을 찾아내어 개선책을 시도해 보도록 한다. ③ 게임을 하면서 생기는 좋은점과 나쁜점을 함께 이야기하여 스스로 문제점을 인식하도록 한다. ④ 학생이 할 수 있는 흥미있는 활동을 개발할 수 있도록 북돋운다.	① 정규 수업에서 수준별 수업을 강화해야 한다: 수준별 이동수업, 학급 내 분단수업 ② 방과후 학교를 활성화해야 한다: 수준별 교과를 통한 과외 흡수 ③ 사이버 가정학습을 활용해야 한다: • 교과수업에서 온라인 수준별 수업 • 가정에서 방과후 온라인 자율학습 (원하는 과목, 원하는 수준으로) ④ 기초학력 책임지도제를 철저히 실시한다: 학급담임+교과담임+지도교사

> **Q 3** 수업을 학교 홈페이지에 올리겠다는 교장선생님에 대한 찬반 의견
>
> Your school principal plans to put your lesson on the school website to promote the teachers' teaching performance. He asks your opinion about this consideration as he has been considering a while for self-administration. Express your opinions from the viewpoints of appropriateness, logic, and language fluency. The examiner would be your school principal.

예상답안

- I agree with the idea that our lessons are uploaded on the website for the following reasons.
  (1) If self or peer supervision is available, teaching skills may be strengthened. As a fresh teacher, my teaching ability is relatively less skillful than the experienced. Therefore, if other teachers can monitor my class in record, they can suggest a variety of precious advices to me, and even I can check my strengths and weaknesses to improve my teaching in class. Vice versa, I can also learn a lot from teaching of other peers and senior teachers.
  (2) Parents would be satisfied if they can see the class in progress, as they hardly have a chance to do it. If the class is uploaded on the site, they are able to monitor the teacher and students' learning attitudes. They, then, can put their trust in the school as their needs wanting to know the school would be fulfilled.
  (3) In conclusion, I believe that this method is one of the most progressive self-supervision because this can help to promote the teacher's expertise, recover the parents' credibility and return our public education back to normal.

- I don't believe that upload of the lesson on the website is a very good idea for the following reasons. Recording the class in progress can be a good method for self- and peer-supervision. Class observation can be an effective strategy to promote teachers' expertise even though this doesn't keep the 'principle of reciprocal non-interference' in teaching profession. However, it should be more careful to put the class on the school homepage open to public. It could be used to put each teacher in competition for the order of superiority. If a teacher receives a lower score, he or she then can be discouraged to create unnecessary sense of rivalry. If it is to be uploaded on the homepage, it should be classified only to use for self- and peer supervision for teachers themselves. Whether it should be open or not is put on question to discuss through the open referendum, to minimize side-effects.

답안 키워드

Agree	Disagree
• I agree with the idea that our lessons are uploaded on the website for the following reasons. ① If self or peer supervision is available, teaching skills may be strengthened.	• I don't believe that upload of the lesson on the website is a very good idea for the following reasons. ① It should be more careful to put the class on the school homepage open to public.

② Parents would be satisfied if they can see the class in progress, as they hardly have a chance to do it. ③ I believe that this method is one of the most progressive self- supervision because this can help to promote the teacher's expertise, recover the parents' credibility and return our public education back to normal.	② It could be used to put each teacher in competition for the order of superiority.

한국어 예상답안

면접관을 학교장이라고 생각하면서 답변해야 한다는 조건에 유의해서 대답해야 한다. 찬성과 반대의 논리적 설명이 구체적으로 서술될 수 있도록 한다.

찬성	① 동료장학이나 자기장학이 가능해 수업능력을 향상할 수 있기 때문입니다. 저는 초임교사로 수업능력은 떨어집니다. 따라서 다른 교사가 제 수업을 동영상으로 볼 수 있다면 제가 발전할 수 있도록 다양한 조언을 해 줄 수 있을 것입니다. 또 제 자신도 제 수업에서 나타난 장단점을 체크해서 수업개선에 활용할 수 있습니다. 이뿐만 아니라 저도 다른 동료나 선배교사의 수업을 언제든지 다양하게 볼 수 있어 여러 가지를 배우고 여러 모로 도전을 받을 수 있을 것 같습니다. ② 교육의 수요자인 학부모의 만족도를 제고할 수 있기 때문입니다. 학부모가 수업장면을 볼 수 있는 기회는 거의 없습니다. 간혹 공개 수업을 한다고 여러 시정 때문에 참여할 수 있는 학부모는 극소수에 불과하다. 그런데 수업 동영상을 홈페이지에 올려놓으면 학부모가 시간과 장소에 구애 받지 않고 궁금해 하던 교사의 가르치는 모습과 학생들의 학습태도를 볼 수 있습니다. 따라서 학부모의 알 권리가 충족되어 학교생활에 대한 이해와 관심이 높아지고 학교에 대한 신뢰가 커질 것이라고 생각합니다. ③ 결론적으로 수업동영상을 홈페이지에 올리는 것은 적극적인 자율장학으로서 교사의 전문성을 신장하고, 학부모의 신뢰를 회복하고 공교육을 정상화할 수 있는 좋은 방법이라고 생각합니다.
반대	물론 수업동영상을 찍어 동료장학과 자기장학에 활용하는 것은 좋은 방법이라고 생각합니다. 수업공개가 교직의 오랜 관행인 상호불간섭주의를 깨고 교원의 전문성을 신장할 수 있는 강력한 수단이기 때문입니다. 수업공개도 오프라인에서 일회적인 공개수업을 하는 것보다는 수업동영상을 찍어 교류하는 것이 좀 더 쉽고 폭넓게 전문적인 피드백을 받을 수 있다는 면에서 훨씬 좋다고 생각합니다. 하지만, 홈페이지에 올려 모든 이에게 공개하는 것은 신중해야 한다고 봅니다. 학부모와 학생이 교사의 서열을 매기는 수단으로 오용될 수 있기 때문입니다. 그렇게 되면 낮은 등급을 맞은 교사가 교수의욕을 잃을 수 있고 교사 사이에 불필요한 위화감이 조성될 수 있기 때문입니다. 따라서 올리려면 교사만 볼 수 있는 교사방에 올려서 수업능력을 향상하자는 본래의 취지대로 동료장학과 자기장학에 활용하도록 하는 것이 바람직하다고 생각합니다. 그리고 홈페이지에 올려 모든 이에게 공개할 것인가는 전체 교사의 다양한 협의를 거쳐 부작용을 최소화하는 방향으로 신중하게 결정하는 게 좋다고 생각합니다.

Q 4. groupwork를 원하지 않는 학생을 설득

You are doing groupwork for the topic of Information Technology. Jisung doesn't want to participate in the groupwork but solve problems on the paper by himself. He believes that the teacher's thoughtful explanation would be more helpful than the groupwork and therefore, solves the problems to improve his exam result for the next week. Explain the methods of discipline guidance. Think that the examiner is Jisung.

예상답안

Jisung, I understand that you prefer my explanation of the material. Surely, some lessons could be more effective in learning from the lecture, but others from the groupwork of each other. If you learn from the teacher's explanation, you can learn more material faster but you don't have a chance to express your opinions and to memorize on long-term. On the other hand, cooperation learning has such advantages as the other lecture-style learning cannot give.

First of all, you can learn the cooperation strategies to solve a problem. Even though you can't solve the problem by yourself, you can easily solve it through scaffolding with others. You can have pleasure to learn to discuss and share the work. If you teach with each other, you can have self-satisfaction through peer-teaching.

Secondly, you will learn such cooperation skills as communication skills, conflict adjustment skills, and respect and leadership skills in the process of completing a task with others. These skills could be even more helpful than just getting good school reports to live your life in the future. Lastly, the most important thing could be study for the exam without distraction for some students. But, if you ignore the stuff that you think that is not directly related to the exam, you will end up losing the main parts of learning.

답안 키워드

① You can learn the cooperation strategies to solve a problem.
② You can have pleasure to learn to discuss and share the work.
③ You will learn such cooperation skills as communication skills, conflict adjustment skills, and respect and leadership skills.
④ You could study for the exam without distraction for some students.

한국어 예상답안

📌 면접관을 지성이라고 생각하고 답변하라는 조건이 있으므로 거기에 맞추어야 한다. 답변의 형식은 지지하고 동의하지만 반대의견을 제시해준다.

지성이 학생이 선생님이 설명하는 식으로 수업했으면 더 좋겠다고 했는데 그게 아주 틀린 말은 아니에요. 하지만 수업의 주제마다 강의식으로 하는 게 좋을 때도 있고, 지금처럼 협동학습이 더 좋을 때도 있어요. 강의식 수업은 어떤 주제를 맨 처음 소개하거나 많은 내용을 주마간산 격으로 빠르게 훑어보는 데는 장점이 있지만 선생님이 일방적으로 수업하는 것이어서 학생들이 의사를 표현하기 힘들고 개별적으로 공부해야 한다는 한계가 있어요. 하지만 지금 수업처럼 주제의 특성을 살려 협동학습을 하면 여러 가지 장점이 있어요.

① 지성이나 학생이 함께 협력해서 문제를 풀어가는 기술(긍정적인 상호의존성)을 배울 수 있어요. 혼자서는 풀 수 없는 문제도 여러 사람의 힘과 지혜를 합하면 쉽게 풀려요. 그리고 선생님이 다 지시해주지 않고 서로 의논하고 작업을 분담해서 스스로 하는 것이니까 공부하는 재미도 더 있습니다. 예를 들어 지성이가 과제를 풀어가면서 다른 친구보다 더 잘 아는 것은 가르쳐주고 모르는 것은 배울 수 있으니까 또래교수의 기쁨도 맛볼 수 있어요.

② 협력해서 과제를 풀어가는 과정에서 의사소통기술. 갈등조정기술. 남을 존중하고 배려하는 기술. 혹은 리더십을 배울 수 있어서 협동학습이 좋은 거예요. 강의식 수업에서는 그런 기술을 배울 수 없잖아요. 어떻게 보면 남의 의견을 들어주고 갈등이 생겼을 때 대화를 통해 잘 해결하고. 다른 친구들의 리더가 되어보는 경험은 단순히 시험성적 잘 나오는 것보다 나중에 지성이가 직장생활을 하고 가정을 꾸려가는 데 훨씬 도움이 될 거예요.

③ 마지막으로 시험 공부하는 게 중요하다고 했는데 맞는 말이지만 수업 시간에는 그 수업에 충실해야 되요. 당장 시험이 걱정되어서 시험과목이 아니라고 외면하는 것은 결국 악순환을 되풀이하는 행동이에요. 수업시간에는 그 과목에 집중하지 않으면 그만큼 그 과목의 내용을 놓치는 게 되니까 나중에 만회하는 데 훨씬 더 많은 노력과 시간이 필요해요.

Q 5. 학교행사에 참여하지 않으려는 학생에 대한 교실운영

In your middle school class, you have a student who is shy and introvertive and don't get along with other students. A school trip is coming soon but she does not want to come along. Her parents, however, want to send her daughter to the trip since this will be a good chance to make friends with. As a homeroom teacher, what discipline would you implement to let her participate in the school activity? Describe your two kinds of classroom management from the standpoints of the student and the whole class.

예상답안

I can solve this problem from the two standpoints, individual student and whole class.

(1) I would persuade the student to join the trip to have an opportunity to get to know classmates through counseling.

- I would show my willingness to help her make school life better if she has any specific needs from the school. I would tell her my experiences of having a great time with my classmates during my school trip.
- I would try to find some reasons why she couldn't get along with other classmates such as family, personality, or learning impairment. Then, I would do comprehensive and ongoing counseling to deal with it.
- I would give the student some responsibility or task to complete during the trip. Then, she would facilitate her potential fully. For example if she can sing or dance, she would have a chance to perform her talents, to make her proud of herself and furthermore her classmates look at her differently.
- During the school trip, the student could actively interact with other classmates by implementing some tasks, even though they are trivial.

(2) As for the whole class, I would focus on the importance of the school trip to make friends with.

I'd encourage all the students in the class to participate in any of the activities or preparation for the trip. And then I would put all the students in a group of four or five to work with during the school trip as the group activity helps to build a sense of cooperation and integrity.

답안 키워드

① I would persuade the student to join the trip to have an opportunity to get to know classmates through counseling.
② I would give the student some responsibility or task to complete during the trip.
③ As for the whole class, I would focus on the importance of the school trip to make friends with.

한국어 예상답안

🔔 수학여행이 얼마 남아 있지 않으므로 평소에 바람직한 친구관계를 어떻게 형성해갈 것인가가 아니라 수학여행을 계기로 어떻게 지도할 것인가에 초점을 두고 답변한다.

학생 차원

① 상담을 실시하여 수학여행이 친구를 사귈 수 있는 절호의 기회임을 설득한다.
- 상담을 통해 원하는 학교생활을 물어보고 좀 더 즐거운 학교생활을 위해 교사가 적극적으로 돕겠다는 의지를 표명한다. 그리고 이번 수학여행이 친구를 사귀어 즐거운 학교생활을 만들어 가는 데 좋은 기회가 될 것이라고 구체적인 예를 들어 참여를 설득한다. 특별히 교사 자신의 경험담이 있다면 소개한다.
- 동시에 상담과정에서 다른 친구들과 어울리지 못하는 원인(가정환경, 성격, 학습부진)을 찾아 종합적이고 중장기적인 대처방안을 찾아 지속적으로 지도한다.

② 외톨이 학생에게 수학여행에서 친구관계를 개선할 수 있는 과제나 역할을 부여하여 수행하게 한다.
- 외톨이 학생이 자신의 잠재력을 한껏 발휘할 수 있는 숨은 개인기가 있다면 준비하게 하여 수학여행 장기자랑 때 발표하게 하면 다른 친구들의 인식을 개선하고 관계형성을 도모할 수 있다.
- 수학여행 기간에 소극적인 성격을 고려해서 사소한 일이지만 외톨이 학생이 할 수 있는 몇 가지 과제를 맡겨 다른 아이들과 활발한 상호작용이 일어나게 한다.

학급 차원

① 수학여행이 특별히 친구를 사귀는 절호의 기회임을 강조하고 그 취지에 맞는 수학여행 프로그램을 반 전체 학생이 함께 짜도록 지도한다.
- 재량활동 시간이나 훈화를 통해 수학여행이 체험학습의 의미도 있지만 단체생활을 통해서 협동심을 기르고 평소 몰랐던 친구를 사귀는 좋은 기회라는 점을 강조한다. 동시에 실제로 친구관계를 확대하고 강화할 수 있는 프로그램을 학생이 스스로 구상하고 적용해 보게 한다.

② 교사가 미리 모둠을 짜서 수학여행 때 모둠별로 활동하도록 지도한다.
- 모둠활동은 협동심과 단결심을 길러주는 데 효과가 크다. 따라서 수학여행 가기 전에 미리 모둠을 짜서 조별로 할 수 있는 활동이나 조별대항 경쟁프로그램(사진 콘테스트, 장기자랑)을 마련한다. 그러면 외톨이 학생이 적극적으로 같은 조의 학생과 협동하고 대화할 수 있는 기회를 제공할 수 있다.
- 모둠장(또래 도우미)에게는 수학여행 전에 특별히 외톨이 학생이 소외되지 않고 친구를 사귀는 좋은 기회가 될 수 있게 배려하도록 지도한다.

③ 수학여행에서 서로 우정을 쌓을 수 있는 프로그램을 실시한다.
- 예를 들어 마니또 게임을 실시하면 외톨이 학생을 포함하여 전체급우가 남모르게 친절과 선행을 베풀게 하면 서로 가까워지는 기회를 얻을 수 있다.

Q 6 방과후 수업의 부정적인 견해에 대한 문제점과 해결책

Students, parents and teachers are all negative about the ideas about the after-school classes shown as the following dialogs. After reading the dialogs, analyze the problems and suggest some solutions to strengthen the after-school activities.

S1 :	After the normal class hours, I have to go to the private institute.
S2 :	I simply don't like to be left for the after school activities.
Parents:	The school doesn't systematically manage the students as the private institute does.
Teacher:	I have lots of regular class hours and extra administration work more than I can handle.

예상답안

As a whole, after-school activities are not favored by students, parents and even teachers. Some problems and probable solutions could be suggested.

(1) The program is not welcomed by students and parents because of its low quality and less variety. Therefore, a program with more variety and high quality is needed.
- We have to introduce various academic subject matters and meet with special aptitudes, and so students can take tailored courses in their favor.
- It is important to operate level-differentiated classes, for example, supplementary class for low-level and essay class for high-level. In this way, students will stop rushing to private institutions.
- Through preparing special aptitude education program, we should develop their autonomous learning. In addition, consulting programs should be added to protect and guide students in a right course.

(2) Second, we are short of distinguished teaching staff for a specific area. If we could secure the number of excellent teachers, students will come back to join the school programs.
- We need to utilize local personnel assets such as local celebrities or university student groups as after-school instructors .
- Proper monetary reward is necessary to secure excellent teachers.

(3) They are negative about the program in that the program operates only in weekdays. Therefore, the time management of the after-school program should be flexible -we should also consider operating the program not only during the weekdays but also on weekends and vacations.

(4) Although the tuition fee is lower than that of private institutions, still parents need to pay extra money on that. Thus, the course should be more widely offered for free so that the financial burden can be lessened. Especially, for the children from the low-income family, the classes should be more provided free of charge to ensure them equal opportunity for education.

(5) Some teachers don't agree with the program because of their heavy workload. Practical solution to decrease their workload should be suggested, such as arranging administration staff, office computerization and etc. On top of that, universities or non-profit organization can take charge of the after-school project to create the more improved management of the program.

답안 키워드

문제점	해결책
① The program is not welcomed by students and parents because of its low quality and less variety.	① Therefore, a program with more variety and high quality is needed.
② We are short of distinguished teaching staff for a specific area.	② If we could secure the number of excellent teachers, students will come back to join the school programs.
③ They are negative about the program in that the program operates only in weekdays.	③ The time management of the after-school program should be flexible.
④ Although the tuition fee is lower than that of private institutions, still parents need to pay extra money on that.	④ The course should be more widely offered for free so that the financial burden can be lessened.
⑤ Some teachers don't agree with the program because of their heavy workload.	⑤ Practical solution to decrease their workload should be suggested, such as arranging administration staff, office computerization and etc.

한국어 예상답안

제시문은 결국 수요자인 학생과 학부모 입장에서 방과후 학교가 학원보다 질 낮은 프로그램을 제공하기 때문에 신뢰할 수 없다는 것이고 정규수업을 담당하고 있는 교사 입장에서는 필요성은 인정하지만 업무 부담 때문에 방과후 학교를 꺼린다는 말이다. 따라서 이런 문제를 해결할 수 있는 종합적인 활성화 방안을 제시한다.

문제점
① 프로그램 질이 낮고 다양하지 못하기 때문에 학생과 학부모가 외면한다. 따라서 다양하고 질 높은 프로그램을 운영해야 한다.
② 우수한 강사가 없기 때문에 학생과 학부모가 외면한다. 따라서 우수한 강사를 다양한 방법으로 확보할 수 있다면 학원으로 갈 이유가 없다.
③ 평일에만 방과후 학교를 운영하는 취약점 때문에 학생과 학부모가 외면한다.
④ 방과후 학교의 수강료가 학원에 비교하여 저렴하기는 하지만 수요자 부담의 원칙이라는 문제점이 있어서 학생과 학부모가 외면한다.
⑤ 교사의 입장에서 보면 프로그램이나 행정업무처럼 교사가 맡아야 할 일이 많아지기 때문에 교사가 부담스러워한다.

해결책
① 교과 프로그램, 특기적성 프로그램, 돌봄 프로그램 등을 다양하게 마련하여 누구나 원하는 과목을 맞춤식으로 수강할 수 있게 해야 한다.
  - 특히 교과 프로그램에서 학습부진아를 위한 수준별 프로그램, 적성 상위자를 위한 특별 프로그램(예:논술반)을 질높게 운영하는 것이 중요하다. 그래야 학원으로 가는 발걸음을 멈출 수 있다.
  - 특기적성교육 프로그램도 마련해소 자기 주도적 학습능력을 신장해야 한다. 또 인성과 정서함양 프로그램과 청소년을 보호하고 선도할 수 있는 상담 프로그램도 반드시 구비하는 것이 중요하다.
② 지역에 우수한 자원을 방과후 학교의 교사로 확보하는 방안을 강구해야 한다. (예컨대 지역인사, 대학생 조직 등등)
  - 적정한 금전적 대우를 병행해야 우수한 강사를 확보할 수 있다.
③ 방과후 학교의 운영시간을 탄력적으로 적용해야 한다.
  - 평일에만 하는 것이 아니라, 토요 휴업일, 방학에도 운영하는 방안을 고려해 봐야 한다.

④ 금전적인 부담없이 수강할 수 있도록 자유수강권을 확대해야 한다.
  - 특히 사교육을 받기 힘든 저소득층 자녀에게 균등한 교육기회를 보장한다는 취지를 살려 원하는 강의는 마음껏 들을 수 있는 자유수강권을 대폭 확대해야 한다.
⑤ 교사의 업무 부담을 줄여줄 수 있는 실질적 조치를 취해야 한다.
  - 전문요원을 배치하고, 업무를 전산화해야 한다. 이와 더불어 운영 주체를 꼭 학교장만 할 것이 아니라 대학이나 비영리단체로 위탁해서 더 좋은 방과후 학교를 운영할 수도 있을 것이다.
  - 이러한 점들을 보안한다면 방과후 학교가 학교 교육을 보안해주고 학생과 학부모를 만족 시키는 수요자 중심의 교육정책으로 자리 잡을 것이다.

Q7 시험 상황에서 특정 학생에게 추가시간을 주는 것에 대한 이유

> Taewoo is a maladjusted student in learning. He has been gradually improving as a result of your efforts of counseling and out-of-class teaching. His self-confidence has also been on increase. However, at the final test, he marked wrong on the answer paper and changed to the new one five minutes before the end of the exam. Taewoo wanted to have one more minute to finish marking after finishing the exam. By the school regulation, he should not be allowed to have the extra time. Explain the three pedagogical grounds if you are to permit the extra time for Taewoo.

예상답안

(1) I would give permission to allow some extra time for the following reasons. First of all, Taewoo could be highly motivated and get some confidence in learning thanks to the good school report. In other words, he will build up "success experienced." If a teacher did not give extra time, Taewoo would have lost his self-confidence he has built so far and come to fall into "learnt helplessness." However, when he can be saved from this crisis with the teacher's care, he will be confident that he can change and do better with his schoolwork. Consequently, he will aim for the higher achievement based on that confidence.

(2) To give an extra time is more meaningful as to following the primary purpose of an assessment. Assessment also includes students' ability not only to make a mistake in marking, but to understand and apply the learning material. Therefore, to maintain the most primary purpose of the test, it is sometimes needed to make a flexibility on other peripheral rules such as the time limit on marking. However, a special condition should be given. If he will use one extra minute, he can mark only pre-decided answers under supervision. It will not harm the main purpose of the test.

답안 키워드

① It can be a good opportunity to build up good rapport with a student. (Build up trust, S will try to study harder)
② If I don't give the extra time, the S will be discouraged from trying harder (poor result- he cannot be rewarded for his effort, self efficacy & self respect & confidence↓)
③ It does not violate the original purpose of the test (The purpose of the test is to check Ss' overall understanding about the lesson, by not giving the extra time Ts cannot see Ss' comprehension about the lesson, T might have difficulties guiding Taewoo's further study)

한국어 예상답안

'추가시간을 더 준다고 할 때'라고 이미 조건이 나와 있으므로 추가 시간을 더 주는 것 자체를 반대한다면 문제의 핵심을 잘못 잡게 된 것이다. 다음과 같은 교육적 근거에서 추가시간을 줄 수 있다고 설명해야 한다.

Q8 학생의 시험답안 문제제기에 대한 대처법

After finishing mid-term exam, a student claimed against your scoring criteria. The answer was based on the textbook, but the student brought another outside-material. What would you do? Describe the FOUR possible methods from your position as the teacher.

예상답안

① 그냥 정답이라고 하니까 수용해버리는 자세가 아니라 적극적으로 더 옳은 답을 찾아보려고 노력한, 문제제기한 학생의 자세를 격려해준다.
② 학생이 근거로 제시하는 자료의 타당성을 검토하여 기존의 답이 정답이 아니라고 결론이 나왔다면 모든 학생에게 그 이유를 설명해주고 채점결과를 수정한다.
③ 교사가 제시한 답안이 맞다고 결론이 나면 문제를 제기한 학생에게 그 학생이 주장하는 바가 왜 오류인지 체계적으로 설명해준다.
④ 정답의 오류 여부를 판단하는 문제는 개인적으로 처리하지 않고, 동료교사, 선배교사, 교사협의회를 통해 신중하게 결정한다.

답안 키워드

① to praise S's active attitude of finding the alternative answer and shows flexible attitude. (compare other Ss' passive attitude, passion for his own study)
② to hold the teacher conference to discuss the problem and get advice from the senior or experienced teacher
③ T's Answer X - give S reasonable explanation and inform all the students the revised answer
④ T's Answer O - give S detailed and reasonable explanation with reliable resources

Q9 인사자문 위원회/ 교장과의 의견 충돌시 대처법

Human Resource Committee were against appointing teacher A as a head teacher but the principal appointed him. Suggest your opinions on the principal's implementation from the viewpoint of regulation and leadership.

예상답안

① 법규적 차원에서는 운영규약을 어떻게 정했느냐에 따라 달라진다. 만약 인사자문위원회의 운영규약에 위원회에서는 의견을 낼 수 있는 것이고 교장이 최종 임명권을 가지고 있다고 정해져 있다면 임명한 것이 문제가 되지 않는다. 그러나 운영규약에 위원회의 결정을 받아 교장이 임명하게 되어 있다면 법규 위반이다.
② 지도성의 측면에서는 민주적 운영이라고 볼 수 없다. 교장이 인사 자문위원회의 결정에 문제가 있다고 생각하면 재심을 요청하고 그래도 자신의 의견이 받아들여지지 않으면 인사자문위원회의 의견을 따르는 것이 민주적인 운영이라고 생각한다. 인사자문위원회 설치 취지가 인사에 민주적이고 객관적인 의견을 반영하는 데 있기 때문이다.

답안 키워드

① Regulation – Depending on the policy; if a principal has the right to appoint a head teacher, we should respect his decision, if the committee has the right to decide, it should not be accepted.
② Leadership – His implementation is not democratic. The leader should respect the public opinion, but he ignored it. He should accept and follow the committee's conclusion. Otherwise, he will lose other teachers' respect.

Q 10 교사수당 없이 진행하는 특별 아침반 실시에 대한 찬성의견

> Your school is planning to do morning special self-study session one hour before the normal class hours. But you get told that you won't get any extra pay for this. Discuss this implementation 'for' and 'against'.

예상답안

아침자율학습을 하는 것을 찬성한다. 추가 수당을 지급하지 않는 것은 분명히 교사의 노동권을 침해한 것이다. 하지만 학생의 학습권 역시 중요하다. 노동권과 학습권이 다 보장될 수 있는 것이 이상적인 형태이다. 하지만 이 예에서처럼 충돌하는 경우도 있다. 그럴 때 교사는 노동권보다는 학습권을 우선 고려해야 한다고 생각한다. 아침자율학습을 시행하기로 결정한 배경에는 충분한 교육적 의미가 있었을 것이다. 교사의 권익도 중요하지만 그보다 더 중요한 것은 학생의 권익이다. 왜냐하면 진정한 학교는 학생이 행복한 학교이다. 학교는 있어도 교육은 없고, 교사는 있어도 스승은 없다는 지탄의 목소리가 높은 요즘 이런 문제의 해법을 제대로 찾는 것이 공교육의 질과 교사의 권위를 회복하는 첫걸음이라고 생각한다.

답안 키워드

- Agree – Even though not giving extra pay infringes teacher's right to work, Ss' right to learn is more important.
  ① Ss can establish a good habit of getting up early in the morning. (Early birds catch the worm; extra time to study, successful people get up early)
  ② Ss can be an autonomous leaner (responsible, manage their own study, preview, review)
  ③ By showing EBS program about twice a week regularly, Ss' academic achievement will be increased. (reduce private expense, reinforce public education)

⚠ 답안작성 유의점

찬반을 묻는 문제로서, 개인적인 의견에 어긋난 교육부의 방침이나 일반적인 학교의 관행이 있을 수 있으므로 조심하여 답변해야 한다. 면접관의 보수적인 성향을 고려한다면 왠지 보수적으로 답변해야 할 것 같은 압박을 받을 수 있다. 이 문제 같은 경우에는 논리적으로 답변하되 너무 극단적으로 가지 말고, 논리적으로 답변한다는 것은 우선 자신의 주장(결론)을 분명히 밝히는 것이다. 시작 부분에서 찬반의견을 확실히 표명해야 하고 난 후에 찬반의 근거를 다양하게 대도록 한다. 그리고 반대편의 주장에도 일리는 있다는 입장을 표명하고 자기주장을 내세우는 것이 중도적인 입장에서 필요하다.

Q 11. Performance-based assessment의 문제점에 대한 해결책

English tests have recently brought many different types of direct tests including spoken and written tests. Students and parents are all very concerned about their results. There are some students in your class who claim against their performance test result. Describe FOUR precautionary measures not to occur this problem.

예상답안

평가의 다양성, 신뢰성, 공정성을 확보하기 어려워 수행평가의 결과에 이의를 제기하는 경우가 있다. 따라서 이를 막으려면 다음과 같은 방법으로 투명성을 높여야 한다.
① 채점 기준표를 명확히 정해야 한다.
② 평가 내용과 기준을 학생과 학부모에게 미리 공개한다.
③ 공동출제, 공동채점 방식을 취하여야 한다.
④ 평가결과를 공개하고 학생에게 이의신청 기회를 주어야 한다.

- 채점의 객관도(신뢰도)가 부족한 것은 교과협의회나 학년협의회, 그리고 성적관리위원회의 심의를 거쳐 명료한 채점 기준표를 마련하고 정확한 평가를 할 수 있도록 평가자가 소양을 갖추어야 한다.
- 과제의 타당도가 부족한 것은 학습목표에 맞게, 배운 내용으로, 가장 중요한 내용으로 출제할 때 해소된다.
- 평가의 공정도 부족한 것은 채점 기준을 미리 공포하고, 공동출제, 공동채점 방식을 취하고 학생의 이의제기를 접수해야 해결할 수 있다.
- 교사의 전문성이 부족한 것은 교육부에서 평가의 기준과 자료, 그리고 프로그램을 개발, 보급해주어야 하고 교사 자신은 장학과 연수에 열심히 참여하고 교과협의회를 활성화해야 해결할 수 있다.

답안 키워드

① Make clear criteria (T & Ss know what to assess and measure)
② To increase the validity - make test questions with co-teachers (The test can contain overall contents that the Ts taught-not subjective)
③ To increase the reliability - more than two teachers assess the same student. (T can secure the objectivity of the test result)
④ Open the criteria to the Ss and parents (Ss and parents will accept the result without any doubt)

Q 12. 아침 특별반 실시를 반대하는 부모와 학생 설득

You agree with the morning special self-study session but parents and students do not like it. What would you do? Explain to persuade them to participate the class in FOUR ways.

예상답안

First of all, if the morning special self study is carried out based on reasonable educational purpose, I would explain to parents and students its intent, content and effect. To be specific, I would notify them of its intent through newsletters or school webpage. As for students, I will try to converse with them and have time to listen to their opinions. If they insist that they do not get the session, I'd choose to respect their opinions, rather than pushing them to follow it. I believe that class management should reflect not only teachers' part but also students' and their parents' stance in a cooperative atmosphere. Still if there are the parents or students who oppose to it, I will start carrying out the session only with students who volunteer to participate the morning special self-study session. If they have experienced the positive effects of it, other students will participate in it later on.

답안 키워드

① I'll show understanding about their positions. (not everyone has the same opinion, every S has different learning styles)
② I would explain to parents and Ss the session's educational purpose.
③ I would inform the parents of its intent through school newsletters or by posting on school webpage.
④ For Ss, I will try to converse with them and have time to listen to their opinions. If they insist that they do not want the session, I will not push them hard, because class management should reflect students' and their parents' stance sufficiently.
⑤ Still, if there are parents or Ss who oppose to it, I will carry out the session only for Ss who want to participate. If people see the positive effect of the session, Ss will voluntarily participate in it.

한국어 예상답안

먼저, 아침자율학습이 충분히 교육적 의미를 담고 시행되는 것이라면 그 취지와 내용, 그리고 효과를 학부모와 학생에게 설득하겠다. 구체적으로 학부모에게는 학부모나 가정통신문이나 학급 홈페이지를 통해서 그 취지를 알리겠다. 학생과는 대화의 시간을 마련해서 취지를 소개하고 학생의 입장을 들어보면서 학생을 설득하겠다. 그래도 학부모나 학생의 반대가 완강하다면 무리하게 추진하지 않겠다. 왜냐하면 학급운영은 교사의 입장도 중요하지만 수요자인 학생과 학부모의 입장을 충분히 반영해야 하기 때문이다.
* 혹은 그래도 학부모나 학생이 많이 반대한다면 우선 원하는 학생들로 아침자율학습을 실시하겠다. 이것을 통해서 효과가 있다는 것이 전해진다면 차차 더 많은 학생이 아침자율학습에 참여할 것이다.

Q 13 자녀의 저조한 성적으로 화난 부모 대응방법

You have an angry mother who calls on you in the school because they are upset about their child's low grades. She complains about the contents you are teaching in class. She also insists that your lesson is not related with the students' current needs and levels. Discuss the way you respond to the mother in FOUR steps.

예상답안

Let the parent vent their emotions about the situation. Remain calm and don't get defensive. Empathize the parents' concern about the course. Bring students marks, work and other supporting documentation to the meeting. Discuss a strategy for improving the students grades that can involve the concerned parent. Ask the parent to bring the student with them for a follow-up meeting in 3-4 weeks time.

답안 키워드

① Remain calm and don't get defensive.
② Bring students marks, work and other supporting documentation.
③ Discuss a strategy for grades.
④ A follow-up meeting

> **한국어 예상답안**

학교 현장에서 빈번히 일어나는 사례이므로 현실성있는 답변이 필요하다.
① 우선 학부모에게 차분하게 이야기 할 수 있음을 설명하고 건설적인 의미의 참여는 충분히 고려하고 존중된다는 것을 알린다.
② 학생의 성적에 근거가 된 자료와 과제물 등을 가져와서 정확하게 채점되었음을 알린다.
③ 차후에 학생의 성적을 올리기 위한 전략과 교사와 부모가 도와 줄 수 있는 방법을 토의한다.
④ 4주 후에 부모와 학생이 함께 할 수 있는 meeting을 구성하여 발전상태를 점검한다.

Q 14. 특별활동 - 원치 않는 동아리에 가입함 : 적극적으로 만들 3가지 방법

At the beginning of the semester, each student should be allocated to one extra-curricular club each. However, some clubs have exceeded the number of students they could accommodate. So, many of students were forced to join the clubs that they did not want. Even worse, teachers also have to take charge of the clubs they have not volunteered. All these led to students' complaints with inactive participation. Discuss three measures to make the club activity more variable and active.

예상답안

To make the club activity more varied and active, I will take the following three measures. First, I will carry out a research on students' interest and aptitude and open the extra-curricular activities that correspond to theirs. They should accommodate students needs, wants and lacks. If students' needs are disregarded and if they are arranged into the activities that they didn't want, it violates the principle that club activity should cultivate students' autonomy and self-motivating habit. Second, if the activity is essential in educational aspect but if it is not preferred by students, teacher should derive students' participation by telling them the features of the club that are related to career, personality, and educational achievement. Club activities should be carried out with the perspective of students, not of teachers. In learner-centered club activities, students get useful advice and knowledge which help them choose right passage of career that properly corresponds to their specialty and aptitude. If students aren't aware of this fact, teachers should notify them of the exploitation of the club in a long perspective. For example, students can be offered some kind of project work in order to present it during school festival or club activity exhibition. Through those chances, students learn the real value of the activity and thus students' participation will be greatly enhanced. Third, the quality of the club activity can be promoted with the guidance of excellent teachers. Even if students show interest in the area of the activity, they turn away if the quality of the activity is low. Not to mention the case of uninterested one. Thus, the teacher who is in charge of the club activity should operate the club properly with maximum expertise. The teacher should provide students with variable contents and informative advice. Not only the guidance teacher but also parents or experts in the related area can be nominated as an adviser of the club. Students' participation of the club activity will increase accordingly.

답안 키워드

① students' interest and aptitude
② students' participation by telling them the features of the club
③ learner-centered club activities

한국어 예상답안

① 학생들의 관심과 적성을 고려할 수 있도록 한다.
② 특별활동이 교육적 환경에 필수적이라면 학생들이 선호하지 않더라도 교육적 가치를 가지고 설득할 수 있도록 한다.
③ 좋은 특별활동을 만들기 위해서 우수한 교수진이 필요하다.

Q 15 Penalty point system의 문제점과 해결방안

Many schools implement reward and punishment system. Parents are concerned about the punishment system on students' violating school rules, which most of the students are against. Explain the problems of reward and punishment system and the solutions.

예상답안

Despite its advantages at school, the reward and punishment system has some problems. First of all, it deprives students of their autonomy and responsibility. As students are forced to obey the rule under the suppression of the system, they are likely to be passive rule-followers. To increase their autonomy and responsibility, it is important to reflect their opinions when setting up the rules. Teachers should give them opportunities to participate in the process of school policy making. Second, ambiguous criteria of the reward and punishment system cause problems. The criteria active participation reward in class may vary from teacher A to teacher B. To this problem, teachers need to observe successful cases of this system in other schools. Carefully looking at the successful implementation, teachers may be able to clarify their own criteria for the system. Third, teachers may be considered as a mere point assignors under this system. Failing to be role models for students, they may lose their dignity and respect from students. To prevent this problem, teachers should counsel with individual students whenever they get penalty points. Rather than just giving them points, teachers have to let students reflect about their behaviors not repeat it again. Similarly, teachers are expected to encourage students with compliments whenever they get rewarding points.

답안 키워드

문제점	해결책
① It is too superficial. (complicated procedure, T is not trained well on using this system) ② The criteria is vague and ambiguous. (If the criteria is not clear, giving point is very subjective depending on different teachers) ③ It is not well informed to the students and parents (They don't know when, why, and how to get the rewarding points or to get rid of the penalty points. They don't know the future effect of this penalty point system)	① T training program on this system should be prepared more practically. (not just the head teacher but, all school teacher should be trained) ② Make the criteria more specific. (The exact situation and the points should be specified. For example, for the late students, the teacher gives 2 penalty points) ③ By using school newsletter or web-pages, Ts can inform Ss and parents of the system and its effectiveness more specifically.

한국어 예상답안

현행 상벌점제 시행 과정의 문제점
① 아날로그식 관리로 상벌점제 운영을 담당하는 교사의 업무가 너무 많아 상벌제가 형식적으로 운영되고 있다.
② 상벌점제 기준 선정의 문제점이 있다. 교사의 판단기준으로 모호한 규정 (예 학급일에 적극적으로 참여했을 때 등). 두발 및 복장 규정이 과다하게 많고, 상점규정보다 벌점규정이 많아 상쇄 효과가 적음
③ 상벌점제 운영과 관련된 학부모 교육과 학부모 연계지도가 미흡하다.

해결방안
① 학교의 상벌점제 규정을 재정비한다.
  • 상벌점제의 기준안을 제공
  • 두발 및 복장은 생활지도규정에 어긋날 경우에만 적용
  • 상정규정과 벌점규정의 균형 유지 (각 10개 이내로 규정)
② 교육공동체의 의견을 수렴하여 규정을 제정한다.
③ 홍보활동을 강화한다. (학교홈페이지, 가정통신문 발송, 교실에 홍보물 게시, 학부모회 개최하여 고지, 조종례 학급자치 수시로 환기)

Q 16 동료교사와의 갈등 & 해결책

School is another small community. As a newly employed teacher, you could have some troubles or problems with your colleagues or senior teachers. Describe some probable cases of conflicts that could happen among the teachers at school and suggest the solutions when they occur.

예상답안

There are some conflicts among the teachers at school. I would suggest three solutions for this problems. First, newly appointed teacher cannot control his students skillfully. Thus experienced teacher can have complaints about the chaotic situation. To deal with this, the teacher can participate in teacher training and get some skills about classroom management. Also the teacher can get advice from his senior teachers to solve the problem. second. some teachers try to avoid his duties in school. To address this problem. the teacher can use his own checklist to check whether or not he completed assigned duties. Third, teachers strive for populism to be the most popular teacher in the school without considering other teachers' circumstances. Expecting to get some sweets, the students think that the other teachers are not as generous as the popular teacher. To deal with it, teachers should have to make strict rules about reward. By doing so, teachers can keep their dignity and respect from their students.

답안 키워드

갈등	해결책
① Newly appointed Ts cannot control their Ss skillfully, and thus it can disturb co-teachers and other classes. ② Ts do not complete duties in school. ③ Some Ts strive for getting Ss' favors. ex) giving too much sweets to Ss.	① T training program – Ts can learn skills about class management and get advice from senior T or experienced T. ② School can make checklists about each T's duties on the board so that all the Ts do not delay or forget what are supposed to do. ③ Ts should make a strict rule about giving reward.

한국어 예상답안

갈등	① 신임교사로서 학생지도나 학교지도에 능숙하게 행하지 못한다. ② 교사가 학교에서의 의무를 완수하지 못한다. ③ 교사가 학생의 인기를 얻으려는 정책에만 의존한다.
해결책	① 감정적인 대응을 삼가고 함께 협력해야 할 동료이고 역지사지하는 자세로 갈등을 바라보고 해결한다. ② 동료교사의 판단의 근거가 되는 내용을 경청하고 옳다면 동료교사의 의견을 수용한다. ③ 상대방의 의견이 잘못되었다는 판단이 들더라도 따져서 감정을 상하기보다는 서로 입장을 공유하고 함께 일해 나가야 할 동역자라는 관점을 잃지 않는다. ④ 갈등이 되고 있는 문제를 정확히 파악하고 가능한 해결책을 함께 구상해보고, 도출한 해결책을 평가해 본다. 그래서 서로 공감하는 최선의 해결책을 찾는다. ⑤ 동료교사의 의견대로 정리되었다고 알아서 하라는 식의 태도를 버리고 일단 결정된 계획이 잘 시행될 수 있도록 힘과 지혜를 실어준다. ⑥ 갈등이 되고 있는 사안에 대해 경험 많은 선배교사에게 조언을 구한다. ⑦ 이후에 동료교사와 관계를 더 돈독히 할 수 있는 자리를 마련한다.

Q 17 교사의 집단이기주의의 발생 이유와 해결책

At the beginning of the year, many teachers don't want to take a duty of homeroom teacher due to various reasons including all the extra burden in school. Explain THREE reasons for this teachers' collective selfishness and THREE efforts to overcome this as a newly-employed teacher.

예상답안

There are three reasons for the teachers' collective selfishness. First, becoming a homeroom teacher causes heavy extra workload. To resolve this problem, more administrative staff need to be hired and homeroom teachers' work should be focused on the classroom management. Second, every year, the growing number of teachers have conflicts with parents of their students. Some parents even attack and swear at teacher in front of many students. Many of those parents insist that the teachers treat unfairly to their children. As these tragedies are caused by miscommunication between the teachers and the parents, both of them need to meet regularly and share their opinions on about student guidance. By doing so, the teacher can understand more deeply about their students as well as their problems at home. Third, it is hard for teachers to control and manage the class because there are too many students in one class. Moreover, there are always some students who never listen to the teachers. From individual teachers' perspective, getting practical advices from the senior teacher is recommended. Since they are more experienced with class management, senior teachers can give the other teachers useful tips. The government also needs to try to lessen the number of students in one class for the teachers' better classroom management and more effective education for students.

답안 키워드

이유	해결책
① Lack of the sense of responsibility ② Heavy extra workload ③ Conflicts with parents of their Ss	① A sense of community spirit ② More administrative staff need to be hired and homeroom teachers' work should be focused on the classroom management. ③ Meet regularly and share their opinions.

한국어 예상답안

학급담임을 맡지 않으려는 이유
① 윤리적인 측면에서 교사 개인의 사명감이 부족하기 때문이다. 힘들고 어려우면서도 건지는 것은 없다는 이유로 학급담임을 회피하고 있다. 그러나 학급담임은 학생지도를 수행하는 가장 기본적인 직위이자 학생과 가장 광범위하게 상호작용 할 수 있는 직위이다. 그런데 어렵고 힘들다고 학급담임을 회피하는 것은 교사로서 윤리를 확립하지 못했기 때문이다.
② 구조적인 측면에서 보면 무엇보다 학급담임의 핵심역할은 생활지도인데 갈수록 생활지도가 어려워지고 있기 때문이다. 교사가 통제할 수 없는 문제행동아가 증가하고 있다. 부모의 과잉보호에 길들여지거나 부모의 무관심 속에 방치된 아이들이 지도에 따르지 않는다. 생활지도 문제로 학부모와 갈등이 발생하고 민원이 제기되는 사례도 많아지고 있다. 이렇듯 교권이 땅에 떨어진 상태이므로 교사가 학급담임이나 생활지도 담당보직을 기피한다.

③ 행정업무가 많다. 학급담임을 맡으면 행정업무가 급격히 늘어나고 그래서 수업과 상황지도에 제대로 신경 쓸 겨를이 없다. 마지막으로 수업시수의 부담이 커지면 자연스럽게 학급담임을 회피하게 된다.

교사가 되었을 때 교사 이기주의를 극복할 방법
① 초임교사로서 확고한 교원윤리를 확립한다. 교직은 봉사직이다. 투철한 헌신성을 바탕으로 수행해야 하는 전문직이다. 따라서 교육과 학생을 내 자신의 권익이나 편안함보다 우선해야 한다는 가치관을 정립한다.
② 초임교사로서 학급담임을 맡을 수 있도록 생활지도 기술을 확보한다. 학급담임을 회피하는 구조적인 이유는 생활지도가 어렵기 때문이다. 어렵다고 포기하면 학교는 무너진다. 그리고 그런 상황에서 교사를 한다는 것은 사명은 던져버리고 밥그릇만 챙기는 일이다. 따라서 학생에 대한 애정을 바탕으로 섬세하고 지혜롭게 학생을 지도할 수 있는 생활지도 기술을 습득한 데 힘쓰겠다.
③ 초임교사지만 다른 선생님들이 회피하는 기타 특별업무를 자발적으로 맡아보겠다. 그래야 초임교사로서 부족한 경험과 기술을 더 빨리 터득할 수 있고 다른 교원들과의 인화에도 도움이 된다고 본다. 편안한 것만 선호하고 어려운 일은 다른 동료에게 떠넘기려는 교사는 누구도 선호하지 않을 것이다.

Q 18 교사 수행평가의 주제내용

Teacher Performance Evaluation assesses THREE aspects in the part of teacher's 'Teaching Management'. Describe the three aspects and the rationales.

예상답안

There would include lesson preparation, implementation, and evaluation and application for the criteria of teacher performance evaluation.

(1) First of all, for the preparation, you have to check if you understand the curriculum and make an effort to improve the teaching methods, if you analyze the contents and students' needs, and if you build up the teaching and learning strategies.

(2) In the second place, for the implementation, you have to be concerned with how the introduction is, if the leading questions and teacher's attitude are proper, how the teacher-student interaction is, if teaching material is utilized well, and if the closing of lesson is acceptable.

(3) Lastly, for the evaluation and application, you are to consider if the way to evaluate students and the content of tests are valid and the outcomes are well-applied. Once you test these three aspects evenly, the whole constructs of classroom management can be holistically evaluated and the lesson can be more professional.

답안 키워드

① lesson preparation
② implementation
③ evaluation and application

한국어 예상답안

질문 분석의 틀-무엇을 묻고 있는가? (학력, 인성, 전인)

수업지도 현장에서 평가해야 할 3가지 요소는 수업준비, 수업실행, 그리고 평가 및 활용이다.
① 수업준비 요소는 교육과정을 이해하고 학습방법을 개선하려고 노력했는가, 학습자 특성과 교과내용을 제대로 분석했는가, 교수학습 전략을 적절하게 수립했는가를 체크한다.
② 수업실행 요소는 도입부가 어떠한가, 교사의 발문이 적절한가, 교사의 태도가 적절한가, 교사학생의 상호작용은 어떠한가, 학습자료는 잘 활용하는가, 수업진행은 어떠한가, 학습정리는 잘했는가를 체크한다.
③ 평가 및 활용 요소는 평가의 내용과 방법이 적절한가, 평가 결과를 잘 활용하는가를 체크한다. 이렇게 3 요소를 고르게 평가하면 수업지도의 전반적인 요소를 종합적으로 평가할 수 있어서 수업의 전문성을 높일 수 있다.

Q 19. 교사가 외부지원을 위해 자신의 수행능력을 확대보고하면 안 되는 이유

You are an English teacher in an English-specialized middle school. If you over-evaluated your performance, you would've received more financial support from the private and public organizations but you did not. Explain the THREE rationales that you chose not to do so.

예상답안

I decided not to over-evaluate my performance for three reasons. Most of all, it violates the principle of honesty and integrity as a teacher. Teachers must be sincere and honest in their workplace, and it is regulated as a duty of every educator. Even if I cannot get more financial support from my report, I must obey the regulation to keep report as truly as possible. Second, a falsified report may distort the original purpose of the evaluation. The reason of reporting my performance is to diagnose the strengths and weaknesses of my own performance as an English teacher and find ways to develop my teaching skills. But if I do over-evaluate, not only I cannot have any chance of improvement, but my students will not get better education from me. Moreover, my false report may harm the other teachers and schools that are also engaged in the evaluation. The third reason is that I should behave as a role-model for my students. I am not just a transmitter of academic knowledge for them but I have a duty to show them desirable humanity and morality to follow. If I deceive others and get financial profit for myself, my students will imitate my wrong-doings. That would be an unacceptable and inappropriate behavior. So I must keep morality and honesty for my students.

답안 키워드

① It violates the teacher's sense of integrity. (As a public servant, the teacher should be sincere and honest.)
② The falsified report distorts the original purpose of the teacher performance evaluation.
③ A teacher will fail to become a role-model with morality.

한국어 예상답안

① 교직윤리 가운데 하나인 성실의 의무 관점에서 볼 때 이 교사의 행동은 정당하다. 교사에게 최소한의 법적 윤리 가운데 성실의 의무가 있다. 교사는 주권자인 국민 전체에 대한 봉사자로서 국민에 대해 책임을 지며 공공복리를 위해 법령을 준수하며 성실히 직무를 수행해야 한다. 성실히 직무를 수행해야 한다는 말은 정해진 기준에 따라 비록 자신이 속한 학교나 자신에게 불이익이 오더라도 사실을 속이지 않고 보고한다는 의미이다. 따라서 과장하여 보고하는 것은 교사의 최소한의 법적 의무인 성실의 의무를 위배하는 것이다.

② 성과 부풀리기는 원래 교육청에서 평가하는 취지를 왜곡하는 행태이기 때문에 당연히 하지 않아야 한다. 일전에 교사의 무책임한 내신 성적 부풀리기가 대학에서 내신 성적을 평가의 기준으로 불신하는 계기를 제공한 적이 있다. 성과에 기초하여 잘 한 학교는 교육청에서 더 지원해 주자는 것이 성과 보고의 원래 취지인데 성과를 조작하는 것은 성과측정을 하는 원래 취지에서 벗어나 공정한 경쟁을 벌인 다른 학교에 피해를 주는 것이다. 윤리불감증은 다른 교사에도 빠르게 확산되어 성과 측정 자체가 무의미해지고 교육의 질을 향상하고자 하는 노력은 수포로 돌아갈 것이다. 정직하게 보고하고 미흡하거나 잘못된 점을 찾아 개선하는 데 힘써야 한다.

③ 교사는 학생뿐만 아니라 모든 국민의 사표가 되어야 한다. 학교는 단순히 지식을 전수해주는 기관이 아니라 바람직한 인성과 도덕성을 함양하는 장이다. 그런데 교사가 목전의 이익을 위해 반칙과 부정을 마다하지 않는 표리부동한 행동을 한다면 그것은 고스란히 교육과정에도 스며들 것이다. 말과 행동이 달라 전혀 학생들에게 감동을 주지 못하면 교사로서 자격이 없다. 교권은 먼저 교사가 높은 윤리의식을 지니고 있을 때 비로소 확립된다.

Q 20 교사가 되고자 하는 이유

There are many occupations in the society you can choose from. Now you are taking a Teacher's Admission Test to enter a teaching profession. Explain TWO reasons why you want to be a teacher.

예상답안

(1) I want to be a teacher because I have the qualities needed in a teacher. Every individual has their own interests and talents. When a person chooses a job based on their talents and aptitudes, they will be able to realize their full potential.

(2) Being a teacher would give me a chance for self-achievement. I enjoy teaching as well as learning. Also, I have learned English since I was very young and tried hard to be equipped with as the best capabilities as I can. Teaching others is a great way to express myself. I will do my utmost to become a great teacher.

(3) I want to be a teacher because I think it's my calling. Currently a teacher is one of the most preferred careers among job applicants. Maybe it's because being a teacher is more stable than other jobs and reasonably well-paid. Surely that can be a good reason, but I have better reasons for being a teacher. To me, teaching is very rewarding and meaningful because I can lead students to grow as a mature individual with excellent personality and academic ability. I am sure that I could become a teacher who helps the students to change and improve their lives.

답안 키워드

① fit to my aptitude and identity
② have a chance for self achievement
③ become a calling – value of teaching, guide to young people

> **⚠ 답안작성 유의점**
>
> 개방형 문제이다. 정해진 답이 있는 것이 아니므로 최대한 창의적으로 답변하는 것이 좋은 점수를 받는 방법이다. 교직이 자신의 적성에 맞다는 것과 교직이 보람 있고 가치 있는 직업이라는 것을 설명하여 교사가 되려는 이유를 말하면 무난하겠다.

① 교사가 제 표현이기 때문에 교사가 되려고 한다. 사람은 각기 적성과 특기와 재능이 있다. 자신의 재능과 적성에 맞는 직업을 택했을 때 무한한 잠재력이 계발되고 그것을 통해 자아실현 및 사회봉사의 책임을 다한다고 생각한다. 나는 가르치는 일에 매력을 느껴왔다. 그래서 교사가 되려고 한다. 또 나의 전공인 영어에 무한한 애정을 가지고 있고 그쪽에 누구보다도 전문적인 역량을 갖추기 위해 노력해왔다. 그래서 영어교사가 되려고 한다. 영어교사는 내 존재를 표현하는 창이다. 끝까지 도전해서 반드시 영어교사가 될 것이다.

② 교사가 제 사명이기 때문에 교사가 되려고 한다. 요즘은 교사가 선호하는 직업 가운데 하나이다. 다른 직장에 비해 안정되고 있고 넉넉한 보수를 받을 수 있기 때문이다. 물론 그런 이유도 내가 교사가 되려는 이유 가운데 하나이겠지만 결코 그것이 중심은 아니다. 나의 적성과 재능이 단지 나를 표현하는 것에만 그치고, 필요한 물질을 공급해 주는 것에만 끝난다면 그건 너무 허무하다고 생각한다. 아이들이 좋은 품성과 실력을 갖춘 성인으로 자랄 수 있도록 안내자가 되어주는 것, 거기에 보람이 있고 의미가 있고 가치가 있다.

③ 그밖에 잊을 수 없는 은사, 자기 인생의 결정적인 경험, 가정환경 등을 매개로 말하든 교사가 적성에 맞고 스스로 가장 의미 있는 일이라고 생각한다는 점을 부각시킬 수 있다면 좋은 답이 될 수 있다.

Q 21 교사의 자질 및 리더십

> Mr. Kim is all respected by the principal, vice principal and students and parents. He shows a model of the best leadership for a school teacher. What are the features of this kind of good teachers? When you become a school teacher, what would you do to exercise good leadership. Describe FOUR features of good teacher with leadership and TWO measures to do as a newly-employed teacher.

예상답안

(1) 좋은 교사의 자질

The leadership of teachers can be characterized with five distinctive features. Firstly, teachers should have professionalism in their work. They develop their own educational ethics with responsibility on students and classes. Secondly, teachers should respect their students. So the students can feel comfortable when they talk with teachers in private. Thirdly, teachers should be knowledgeable and talented enough to teach subjects and guide students' behavior. These teachers can foster students' individual learning styles and their senses of the community as well. Fourthly, the teacher's leadership comes from establishing the good relationship with students and other co-workers. Although there are many unexpected conflicts in school, the teacher with leadership can handle this well. Lastly, teachers should be good listeners. To bring operation from students and parents, they should be polite and empathize with what they are saying.

(2) 리더십을 발휘하기 위해 초임교사로서 할 일

As a novice teacher, there are two ways to show leadership at school. Firstly, I could strive on self-supervision. Through this, I can diagnose strong and weak points of my teaching approach to improve myself in school and class management. Secondly, I will communicate with co-teachers, senior-teachers, parents, and students to improve any kind of elements of my class. So I can notice what really needs but at the same time, change those aspects.

답안 키워드

① T should have professionalism. (expert in their own subject, develop own teaching skills, participate in teacher training program)
② T should establish a good rapport with Ss. (compassionate, understanding good listener, show empathy)
③ T should have the collaborative attitude toward their co-teachers. (help others, set a good example, do their duties on time)
④ T should always behave morally to become a role-model for the Ss. (As a leader of the Ss, Ts should keep their sense of integrity)

한국어 예상답안

🔔 리더십 있는 교사라는 용어를 사용했지만, 좋은 교사의 정의를 묻고 있다. 교사 주체들과 수요자에게 신망 받는 교사(좋은 교사)는 교사의 권위를 완비한 교사, 곧 윤리성(도덕성)과 전문성을 갖춘 교사이다.

1. 그런 리더십이 있는 교사의 특징은 한 마디로 교사로서 윤리성과 전문성을 갖춘 교사이다. 첫째, 자신과 관련해서 투철한 교육관과 사명감을 가지고 부단히 자신을 성장시켜 가는 면학수행에 힘쓰는 교사이다. 둘째, 학생과 관련해서 윤리적인 측면에서 학생을 사랑하고 인격적으로 대해주며 비밀을 보장해주고 민주적으로 대해주는 교사이다. 셋째, 학생과 관련해서 전문성이라는 측면에서 학습지도와 생활지도에 능통한 교사이다. 매년 쓰던 수업지도안 그대로 다시 사용하는 교사가 아니라 부단히 자신의 전공과 관련해 해박한 지식을 쌓아가고 늘 어떻게 가르치면 더 학생들이 잘 배울 수 있을까 고민하는 교사이다. 그래서 학원교사보다 월등히 뛰어난 실력을 가지고 학생의 수준에 맞게 맞춤식 수업을 할 뿐만 아니라 다양한 교수·학습 기법으로 수업 시간에 잠이 오지 않게 하며 학습부진아만큼은 제로로 만드는 교사이다. 한편 생활지도를 할 때는 바쁜 일정 속에서도 꾸준한 상담을 통해 학생의 실태를 정확히 파악하고 학습, 진학, 생활에 관련된 제반문제를 적절하게 풀어갈 수 있도록 지도해주는 교사이다. 또 기본생활 습관과 공동체의식을 길러주어 함께 하는 학급분위기를 만들어 주는 교사이다. 넷째, 타 교원과 관련해서 늘 인화에 힘쓰고 궂은 일도 마다하지 않고 업무에 협력하고 갈등을 잘 조절하는 교사이다. 다섯째, 학부모와 관련해서 학부모를 예의 바르게 대하고 학부모의 이야기를 경청하고 학생의 상황을 공유하면서 함께 협력해서 학생을 이끌어 가는 교사이다.

Q 22 학습분위기 향상을 위한 방안 (+ 교실붕괴 상황 및 극복방안)

You often spot the students who doze off and chat during the class. When they get told off about the misbehavior, they just utter that they've already learned the things at a private school. They do not seem to be interested in the lesson to participate the class. You need to analyze the reasons of the situation and solve the problems. Describe FOUR reasons and suggestions why the students are not interested in lesson academically and TWO reasons and suggestions from the viewpoint of behavioral management.

예상답안

(1) 학습지도 측면의 원인과 해결방안

① The reason for low participation in class stems from the traditional way of teaching. To cope with the problem, the teacher should prepare her class considering individual differences. By figuring out students' interests and proficiency, the teacher can provide tailored instruction. In this way, students will be willing to engage in the class more actively.

② The problem results from teacher-centered instruction where students are required to memorize what they've learned. As an alternative to this method, it is recommended that the teacher utilizes teaching strategies promoting self-directed learning. Students will be able to develop autonomy in their learning by taking part in various activities such as discussion, problem-solving learning, cooperative learning and discovery learning.

③ The problem lies in lack of varieties in teaching methods. To deal with the problem, employing multimedia tools can be an effective way since it can contribute to stirring up students' interest. Conducting blended learning can be another way because it can lead students to becoming autonomous learners.

④ The problem is attributed to the teacher's failure in promoting students' motivation. Thus, the teachers have to devise methods to encourage their motivation to learn. For example, teachers can arouse students' curiosity by introducing materials interesting and relevant to their real life. Also, she can build up their confidence and makes them feel a sense of success by providing level-appropriate tasks. In addition, students would be more willing to be involved in class if teachers provide them with complement and rewards about what they have successfully achieved.

(2) 생활지도 측면의 원인과 해결방안

① It is possible that students are not fully informed of classroom rules. Or, students probably violate the class regulations without awareness of how important following the rules is. To cope with this problem, teacher and students should make classroom rules collaboratively. Since the rules are constructed based on their opinions, students will take responsibility for their misbehavior. Thus, they'll strive to abide by the regulations.

② The teacher seems not to utilize reinforcement and punishment properly in her class. Thus, she needs to compliment students on their achievement to promote their motivation to learn. But, if they put on a black hat, she should inflict punishment as a way of correcting their misbehavior.

답안 키워드

문제점	방안책
① Teacher-centered class tends to make such situations. (too much teacher talk, lack of interaction with Ss, T does not monitor Ss' works) ② Mixed-level classes; the levels of each S in one classroom are different. (low - too difficult, high - too easy ⇨ low motivation) ③ T does not use diverse materials (just textbook and board) ④ T gives unclear direction for guiding Ss. (Ss cannot follow the class, lose concentration)	① Student-centered로 바꾸자. ② organize level differentiated tasks ③ utilize multimedia equipment such as video clips and PPT ; Use authentic materials such as realia and pictures ④ T should use diverse body language and intonation, so that they can draw Ss' full attention.

한국어 예상답안

교실붕괴 상황을 극복하는 문제이다. 특별한 조건이 없으므로 학습지도 측면과 생활지도 측면으로 나누어 접근하여 원인과 해결책을 제시한다. 답변 방식은 원인과 해결책을 일대일로 대응시키는 방법과 원인과 해결책을 별도의 집합으로 묶어서 답변하는 방식이 있다. 내용을 잊지 않고 구술하기 쉬운 방식은 원인과 해결책을 일대일로 대응시키는 방식이다.

학습지도 측면과 원인과 해결방안

① 개인차를 무시한 전통적인 수업을 하였기 때문이다. - 영어 과목의 특성을 살려 흥미와 능력을 고려한 적절한 수준별 수업을 실시한다.
② 교사 중심의 주입식 암기식 수업을 하였기 때문이다. - 자기 주도적 학습능력과 창의성을 키워주는 다양한 교수 학습 전략을 활용한다. 토론학습, 문제해결학습, 탐구학습, 포트폴리오 수업, 협동학습 등등
③ 칠판과 분필 그리고 입만 사용해서 수업했기 때문이다. - 다양한 교육매체를 활용하되 특히 ICT 활용수업을 적극 도입한다. 특히 N 세대인 것을 고려해서 사이버 가정학습과 결합된 온 오프 혼합형 수업으로 학생의 흥미를 유발하고 자기 주도적 학습을 이끈다.
④ 학습동기를 유발하지 못했기 때문이다. - 학생과 관심과 호기심을 끄는 사례를 제시하고, 나도 할 수 있겠다는 자신감을 불어 넣어준다. 또 칭찬과 보상을 통해 학습에 능동적으로 참여하도록 이끈다.

생활지도 측면의 원인과 해결방안

① 학생이 수업의 규율을 모르거나 지키지 않기 때문에 발생할 수 있다. - 수업의 규율을 학생과 합의하여 만들고 일관되게 집행한다.
② 강화와 벌을 적절하게 활용하지 못했기 때문이다. - 토큰법, 프리맥의 원리, 타임아웃 같은 잘못된 태도를 교정해 주는 기법을 적정하게 사용한다.

Q 23. 학교폭력 예방방안 (학교측면/ 가해학생측면)

You found out during a counseling session that a student of yours had got beaten and bullied from other students for money in school over last semester. What would you do with the abuser students not to occur these incidents again? Describe your measures from the standpoints of the whole class and the abuser students. Describe them for FIVE measures from each standpoint.

예상답안

(1) 학교폭력 예방방안

To solve the school violence problem, I suggest some methods in terms of school and the abuser students. In case of school, we can deal with the violence problem in various manner.

First, I'll make the cooperative classroom atmosphere by raising the sense of community. The school violence happens because students do not know how to work together. Also, they need to think others first. To do these, experiential learning will be good such as youth-training activities and volunteer activities. These activities help them recognize themselves as a member of the community. Consequently, the feeling that all of us belong to the same group will help to prevent the violence problem. Second, students should try to prevent the violence by themselves. As the main reason of the violence is the conflict between students, they can handle the problem on their own and it's the most effective way. For example, they can make the students' committee to make the solution for the violence. Another way is to make the peer counseling club. In the club, they can share their difficulties and help each other. Third, I will set the regular discussion session to make school life better. The conversation with open mind helps students to understand each other deeply. It also provides the chances for them to think about why violence cannot be tolerated. Specially, after watching the video related to the violence, students can make a discussion or do the role play activities. Through this, they can understand and empathize with the students who are bullied. Fourth, it is difficult for me to expect all the incidents in advance to prevent it, Instead, I will hold the regular class conference. In the conference time, students set the weekly rules to prevent the violence problem by themselves. This make them have responsibility to keep the rules. As a result, it will contribute to protect themselves from any violence. Fifth, systematic counseling is necessary. Counseling can be preformed in various ways such as individual counseling or group counseling. This helps me to figure out students' school life. So when the problem happens, I can find out the main reasons of the problem and settle it immediately. Lastly, I'll build up the network between school, parents and local community to prevent the school violence. This network will be helpful to monitor and guide students so they cannot bully or beat other students easily. Also, the network can be used to correct their misbehavior in and outside of the school more effectively.

(2) 가해학생 지도

I also take a measure for the abuser students so they cannot repeat the misbehavior in the future. First, I will find out the surrounding situations of the abuser students and the bullied students both. And I'll ask the abuser students why they did that. Their violence can have various reasons in complex way. Some problems can come from the issues of family or the friendship. Or some can be a mixture of having more than one problem. So as s teacher, I will analyze what makes the students bully others and according to the results I will treat them differently. Second, I'll let the abuser student stand in the part of the bullied students through role-exchange counseling. During the counseling, they can recognize negative aspects of school violence and why such violence cannot be accepted in any situation. Third, the abuser students should be given the chance to reflect their misbehavior. So I'll make them write down what they did and what is the result. During that, they can think about their action more carefully and reflect it. This will lead them to apologize the bullied students. Fourth, I'll let them know they can get the extra penalty if they make the violence problem once more. This will prevent them from bullying or beating another students. Fifth, I should care for the abuser students with affection. If I just scold or punish them excessively, it will make the counter effects. For instance, they will bully other students more as a way of expressing their anger of being punished. So instead of scolding, I'll take care of them with love. Sixth, I'll contact with the parents of the abuser student. I'll inform them the seriousness of the incident that their children caused to other students. And I'll make a meeting to talk to each other and to apologize the parents of the bullied students and pay for the necessary medical care if necessary. Next, I'll watch the abuser students and the bullied students consistently with careful attention. This will help the same problem do not happen again. If the abuser students do not change their wrong behaviour and repeatedly bully other students, I'll punish them more severely. I need to notice the other students that violence cannot be tolerated. Also, I can make connection between the abuser students and their favorite seniors or teachers. It will be useful to deal with their aggressive actions. Field-trip is also a good way. For example, I can do the voluntary work with them. While helping others, they are encouraged to empathy with other people who are in the bad situation. Lastly, I need to ask for help to specialized experts because I'm a fresh teacher. I lack of experiences, so their professional way to guide the abuser students is definitely helpful to deal with this situation.

답안 키워드

학교측면	학생측면
① School implements special programs to develop Ss' collaborative spirits. (club activity, experiential learning, volunteering work) ② School builds up the network between school, parents and local community to prevent the school violence. • Abuser Ss – it will be helpful to monitor and guide abuser Ss not to bully others • Victim Ss – it can be an open door for them, visit whenever they want, say whatever they want	① T takes disciplinary measures on the abuser Ss' misbehavior. (volunteering works inside or outside of the school) ② Systematic counselling • T talks with him to know S's family background and current situations. • T shows understanding • T makes the Ss realize the seriousness of their misbehavior. ③ As a long term measure, T can have Ss write dialogue journal. (monitor Ss' emotion and Ss' current situation, build up a good rapport with the Ss) ④ T gets some helps from the specialized expert (get professional treatment)

한국어 예상답안

(1) 학교폭력 예방방안

1. 체험중심으로 공동체의식을 심어주어 함께하는 학급분위기를 조성한다. 학교폭력이 일어나는 근본적인 원인은 학생들 사이에 공동체의식, 타인을 배려하는 의식이 결여되어 있기 때문이다. 따라서 평소에 학급에서 자치활동, 수련활동, 봉사활동, 조별활동 같은 체험을 통해서 공동체 의식을 심어주어야 한다. 그래서 급우 사이에 친밀도가 높아져 학교폭력을 예방할 수 있다.
2. 특히 학생자치활동을 통해 학생이 스스로 자율적으로 학교폭력을 예방하는 것이 중요하다. 학교폭력은 주로 학생 사이에 갈등이 생겨서 발생한다. 따라서 서로 존중해주는 가운데 자율적으로 풀어가는 것이 가장 효과가 크다. 따라서 힉생이 학교폭력 예방도우미 조직을 만들어 학교폭력 예방과 또래 보호활동에 자발적으로 참여하고 학교의 폭력 실태를 정확하게 파악하여 문제해결을 주도하게 만들어야 한다. 동시에 학생들이 쉽게 접근해서 고민을 털어놓을 수 있는 또래 상담 반을 만들 수 있다.
3. 즐겁고 행복한 학교생활을 할 수 있도록 토론문화를 정착시킨다. 진실한 대화는 학생들이 서로 신뢰하고 좀 더 깊이 상대방을 이해할 수 있게 하여 인간의 존엄성과 학교폭력의 문제점을 깨닫게 한다. 학교폭력 영상물을 보고 토론하는 것이나 역할극을 해보는 것도 유용한 방법이다. 또 평소에 서로 칭찬하기 운동을 벌인다.
4. 학교폭력은 돌발적으로 일어나는 사건이므로 예방을 위해서는 정기적인 학급회를 개최해야 한다. 최소 1달에 한 번씩 학급회의를 열어 학교폭력 예방을 위한 학급규칙을 제정하고 지키도록 학생들을 지도한다.
5. 지속적이고 체계적인 상담활동을 강화한다. 쪽지상담, 개별상담, 집단상담, 또래상담 설문조사를 통하여 학생실태를 늘 정확히 파악해야 한다. 그리고 상담이 발생하면 신속하게 상담을 통해 원인을 파악하고 종합적인 대책을 수립한다. 조, 종례를 반드시 실시하고 학생의 얼굴이나 복장을 살핀다. 학부모와 지역사회가 함께 하는 학교폭력예방 네트워크를 구축하고 운영한다.

(2) 가해학생 지도

1. 가해학생이 폭력을 행사한 주변상황과 원인을 정확히 파악하여 사안별로 지도방법을 결정한다. 즉 폭력이 일회성 폭력인가 아니면 가정문제, 교우관계, 성격장애와 같은 구조적인 원인이 누적된 것에서 발생한 것인가 따져서 원인에 맞는 처방을 내온다.
2. 피해학생의 피해상황과 고통을 깨닫게 하고 피해학생의 입장에서 서보도록 한다. 이 과정에서 폭력의 부당성을 분명하게 이해시킨다. 반성문 작성 같은 방법을 통해 가해학생이 잘못을 뉘우치도록 하고, 피해학생을 함께 찾아가 사과하도록 한다. 다시 폭력을 쓰면 가중처벌을 받는다는 것을 주지시킨다. 심한 야단이나 처벌은 보복과 다른 문제를 야기하므로 애정과 관심을 가지고 지속적으로 지도한다.
3. 가해학생 부모에게 사건을 알려서 가해 학생 부모가 피해학생 부모에게 정중히 사과하고 치료에 대해 책임을 지도록 한다. 피해학생과 가해학생을 지속적으로 관찰하여 폭력이 재발하지 않도록 한다. 가해자가 행동을 교정하지 않고 계속해서 따돌림을 할 경우 그에 따른 적절한 벌을 주어 다른 학생들이 폭력을 행사하면 안 된다는 것을 인식하도록 한다. 가해자가 좋아하는 선배나 교사와 결연을 시켜 지도할 수 있도록 한다.
4. 가해학생을 데리고 체험학습을 실시한다. (양로원, 고아원 등 수용시설 방문하여 봉사활동을 실시함으로써 자신보다 어렵고 불편한 사람들을 도와주면서 심적 변화를 유도)
5. 교사의 힘이 부족할 경우는 전문가에게 도움을 청해 조속히 문제를 해결하도록 한다.

Q 24 교직관에 따른 교실운영 방안

You are newly employed as a middle school teacher. You are assigned a role of homeroom teacher at a high school. Now, you are planning the methods how to organize the class at the beginning of the semester as you believe that your students would be changed according to your pedagogical principles. Discuss your own classroom management in FIVE ways.

예상답안

① I'll make cooperative classroom atmosphere where students can feel a sense of community. For example, some collaborative activities can be suggested such as volunteer work, training activities and student school committee.

② To help students to build their own identity in the cyber-space, I will teach them netiquette. This new type of education can prevent students' game addiction and misbehavior in cyber-space.

③ To encourage students to do self-directed study, I will make a class library. Students can be motivated because they can choose what they want to read. And at the end of the semester, I'll collect the book report for assessment.

④ I will diagnose the problems of retarded students through continuous counseling. After that, I will suggest some advices for them. At the same time, after-school curriculum and homework can be utilized to make up for their educational needs according to their different proficiency.

⑤ I'll encourage students to participate in all the process of classroom management. In deciding how to manage classroom, the teacher should respect and collect students' various opinions about the class regulations. This way can be effective since students will take responsibility for their decision as a member of the class.

⑥ I'll treat my students fairly. Specifically, I won't evaluate students depending on their grades. Instead, I'll try to see their strength in various fields and encourage them to develop their specialties. Also, I'll enable students to easily access to me whenever they want to seek assistance about their problems.

답안 키워드

① T tries to build up collaborative atmosphere. (ample group activities, emphasize the sense of unity, mini-olympics)

② T helps Ss to become an autonomous learner (self-check list, direct/manage their own study, responsibility, independence)

③ T has Ss take part in setting the class rules at the beginning of a semester. (democratic way, Ss will follow the rules well)

④ T holds rewarding ceremony every months. (self-efficacy, confidence)

⑤ T can take part in the class as a co-partner. (not a director but a facilitator)

> ⚠️ **답안작성 유의점**
>
> 📖 창의성을 발휘해서 답변해도 좋은 개방형 문제이다. 따라서 교사 자신의 특성과 교육관을 자유롭게 표현할 수 있는 구체적인 답변을 구상하라.

① 함께 하는 학급분위기를 만들어가는 기본생활습관과 공동체의식 함양에 주력한다. 그 방안으로 봉사활동, 수련활동, 자치활동을 내용으로 달마다 특색 있는 프로그램을 운영한다. 그리고 학급부서를 모둠별 활동으로 대체하고 모둠별 일기를 쓰게 한다.
② 사이버 공간에서도 민주시민의 정체성을 유지할 수 있도록 정보윤리교육에 힘쓴다. 그 방안으로 악플금지, 세임숭 독예방, 네티켓 지키기 운동을 벌인다.
③ 자기 주도적 학습능력을 바탕으로 창의력을 신장하는 방안으로 모둠별 독서활동을 이끌어 간다. 모둠별 독서활동은 학년말에 학급문집 형태로 그 결과를 수렴할 계획이다.
④ 학습지진아 제로운동을 벌인다. 지속적인 상담으로 학습부진의 원인과 해결책을 찾아 처방하되 수업 때 수준별 지도와 함께 방과후 보충학습과 방과후 온라인 가정학습을 적극적으로 활용하여 학습부진아를 제로로 만들 예정이다.
⑤ 학생이 주인의식을 가지고 모든 과정에 참여하는 민주적인 학급경영을 하겠다. – 교사중심 지양, 학생 한 사람 한 사람 의견을 존중, 학급회 활성화, 학급 홈피 게시판을 통해 다양한 의견 수렴, 학급규칙도 학생과 합의해서 스스로 지킬 수 있도록 지도한다.
⑥ 모든 학생을 공평하게 대하고 언제든지 대화의 창구를 열어놓는 학급경영을 하겠다. – 학생을 편애하지 않을 것이다. 성적으로 평가하지 않을 것이다. 언제든지 학생과 학부모님과 고민을 함께 나누고 문제해결을 지원하는 학급경영, 대화의 시간을 많이 갖는 학급경영을 할 것이다.
⑦ 함께하는 학급분위기를 창출하는 (공동체 의식을 길러주는) 학급경영을 하겠다.
   예 특색 있는 봉사활동, 수련활동 등등
⑧ 자기 주도적 학습능력과 창의력을 키우는 학급경영을 하겠다.
   예 동기부여 (자기 비전 세우기) 독서습관 형성을 위한 환경조성, 사이버가정학습
⑨ 상을 많이 주는 학급경영을 하겠다.
   예 노력상, 변화상, 선행상, 칭찬상, 스마일상, 대기만성상
⑩ (학부모에게 한다면) 학부모님들이 학교생활을 잘 알 수 있고 관심을 가지고 지원할 수 있는 학급경영, 부모님과 제가 협력해서 우리 아이들이 밝은 인성과 실력을 갖출 수 있는 학급경영을 하겠다.

Q 25 부모들이 사교육을 맹신하는 이유 & 해결책

There are some parents who are doing two jobs for their children's private tuition fee and other parents who ask to decrease the amount of assignment because of Hagwon assignment. Describe the reasons and countermeasures.

예상답안

1. The causes in school are as follows.
- The excessive educational structure fosters the private educations. Students are searching for private institutes teaching by rote and cramming for good grades.
- Students are going to private institutes because of the schools which can't meet the need of the students. Public schools don't have any effective educational system where students can learn depending on their level. To bridge the gap, more students would go to private institutes, which

causes a vicious circle.
- Thirdly, Students are searching for private institutes due to the teachers who don't have professionalism and a strong sense of responsibility. These teachers are very coy about students and parents' needs.
- Finally, poor educational environment makes students go to the private institutes. In school, tailored teaching are difficult and tons of administrative duties don't allow teachers to have enough time to prepare classes.

2. The causes out of school are as follows.
- In Korea, the academic elitism runs widespread. It causes people to think educational background is more important than real ability.
- Parents believe blindly in the private institutes with wrong belief of education. Parents let their children enrol the private institutes to get better scores and enter a prestigious university.

As for the solutions,

1. The fundamental countermeasure to improve the quality of public education
- We should keep qualified teachers available. We could make quality talents come to schools and gone them better treatment and improve in-service training and professional development for teachers. There is a need to expand level-differentiated instructions and settle the culture of basic standards to help slow learners.

2. Short term countermeasure to absorb existing private education into the public education
- We should utilize the after school hours. special ability aptitude education, non-graded system could be employed to meet the needs of students and parents.
- Secondly, we could activate e-learning. Through school homepage, we can help students study whenever they want at their own pace. From this, we can help slow learners or the children of lower-income groups.
- Thirdly, we can use college student mentoring. It could not only relieves the underachievement of students but also makes students to get a career counseling.

3. Long-term countermeasure to root out the private educations
- We should dissolve the academic elitism and settle the ability system. We also make an effort to help students to develop their own talents and interests.

답안 키워드

이유	해결책
① School cannot meet Ss' needs. • not follow current educational trends • not give the level-differentiated instructions • not consider every S's interest and own talents ② Poor educational environment • T's too much work load besides teaching jobs • Too many Ss in one class • Poor equipment (not enough computers or audios)	① Needs analysis : interest, motivate, Low Ss- supplement time/ High Ss - further study, level-differentiated class ② Hire assistant Ts: lessen the work, Main subject T can put more effort on teaching

> ⚠️ **답안작성 유의점**
>
> 📺 사교육 해소방안을 묻고 있는 문제이다. 원인 1과 2의 항목을 그대로 일대일 대응시켜서 대책을 구술할 수 있다. (논리적일 뿐만 아니라 쉽게 답할 수 있는 방법이다.) 예시답안에서는 근본대책, 현존 사교육을 흡수하는 단기대책, 장기대책으로 구분하였다.
>
> ---
>
> **(1) 원인**
>
> 〈학교 안〉
> ① 시험석차 위주의 교육경쟁구조(입시를 위한 성적 중심의 한 줄 세우기 교육)가 사교육을 조장하고 있다. 학생들은 학교 석차 상승과 입시에 필요한 더 좋은 성적을 얻기 위해 단기간에 문제풀이식 반복식 교육을 하여 성적을 올려주는 학원을 찾는다.
> ② 학생의 욕구를 충족시키지 못하는 학교교육 때문에 학원에 간다. 학습능력이 다른 이질적인 학습집단을 수준별로 끌어줄 수 있는 교육시스템이 없어서 사교육이 발생하고 학원에서 선행학습을 받은 학생 때문에 다시 학력격차가 더 벌어지는 악순환이 되풀이 되고 있다.
> ③ 학생과 학부모의 교육요구에 소극적으로 대처하는 전문성과 책무성이 없는 교사 때문에 학원을 찾는다.
> ④ 교육환경이 열악한 것이 학원을 찾게 한다. 다인수 학급이어서 맞춤식 지도가 어렵고, 교사가 처리해야 할 행정업무가 많아 그것을 처리하다보면 수업을 연구하고 준비할 시간이 없다. 그래서 수업이 질이 떨어지고 학생들이 더 질 높은 수업을 해주는 학원을 찾는다.
>
> 〈학교 밖〉
> ① 사회에 능력보다는 출신학교가 중요하다는 학벌주의가 널리 퍼져있다. 명문대학 졸업장이 능력보다 우선되는 학벌주의 사회풍조가 조성되어 있고 이에 맞물려 대학에 등급이 매겨져 있기 때문에 이유를 불문하고 성적을 올려 명문대학에 가야 한다는 관행이 생겼다.
> ② 학부모가 왜곡된 교육관을 가지고 사교육을 맹신하기 때문에 자녀를 학원에 보낸다. 자녀의 특기와 적성을 무시하고 무조건 명문상급학교에 진학해야 한다고 교육관을 지닌 부모가 많고, 공교육은 다 받는 것이지만 내 자녀가 좀 더 앞서 가려면 학원에 가서 더 배워야 한다고 생각하는 부모도 많다.
>
> **(2) 대책**
>
> 〈학교의 질을 근본적으로 개선하는(학생과 학부모의 신뢰를 회복하는) 대책〉
> ① 우수교원을 확보해야 한다. 교원의 처우를 대폭 개선하여 우수한 인재를 교원으로 유입시키고, 교사 양성체제를 체계화하고, 현직교사 연수 제도를 개선해야 한다. 그리고 교원능력개발평가를 안착시켜서 교사의 전문성을 신장해야 한다.
> ② 학생의 개인차를 반영한 수준별 수업을 확대한다. 수학, 영어 교과에 대한 수준별 이동수업을 확대하고 국어, 사회, 과학 교과는 학급 안에서 수준별 분단 학습을 강화한다. 즉, 상위학생들을 위한 수준별 이동수업을 확대 실시하고, 학습부진아를 위한 기초학력 책임지도제를 정착시킨다.
>
> 〈현존하는 사교육을 공교육 체계로 흡수하는 단기대책〉
> ① 방과후 학교를 활용해야 한다. 방과후 학교에서 수준별 교과 프로그램, 무학년제, 상위권 학생을 위한 특별 프로그램, 특기적성교육 프로그램을 다양하게 실시하되 학원보다 더 질 높은 프로그램을 더 저렴하게 공급해서 학생과 학부모의 욕구를 충족시켜주어야 한다.
> ② e-learning(사이버 가정학습)을 활성화 한다. 학교 홈페이지에 사이버 가정학습체계를 구축해서 학생들이 활용할 수 있도록 교사가 안내해주고 사이버 가정학습을 수업과도 적극 연결시킨다. (온/오프 혼합형 수업) 또 EBS 방송을 효과적으로 이용할 수 있도록 안내한다. 이러닝을 이용하면 학생이 원하는 과목을 원하는 수준으로 가정에서도 학습할 수 있다. 즉, 얼마든지 학습부진해소나 선행학습이 가능하고 저소득층 자녀도 금전적인 부담 없이 공부할 수 있다.
> ③ 대학생 멘토링을 활용한다. 이를 활용하면 학습부진 해소에 도움을 줄 뿐만 아니라 생활상담, 진로상담까지 겸할 수 있어 1석 2조 효과가 있다.

〈사교육을 완전히 제거하는 장기대책〉
① 사회 차원에서 학벌주의를 제거하고 능력주의를 정착시키고 대학의 서열을 없애고 특성화 대학으로 전환해 간다.
② 자녀의 적성을 무시한 채 명문대만 가라고 하는 출세주의적 사고방식에서 적성과 특기를 살려 진학하는 적성중심의 교육관으로 교육관을 바꾸어 나간다. 또 문제풀이식, 반복식 학원교육이 학생에게 반드시 있어야할 자기 주도적 학습능력과 창의성을 빼앗아 가는 것을 인식시킨다.

Q 26 학습자 중심학습 방법의 종류와 유의점

These days, many classes administer learner-centered activities. Even in English classes, there are many types of learner-centered activities. First, discuss the various types of learner-centered activities. Second, specify ONE type of learner-centered learning activities and describe the procedure of the activity and some precautions students should take to get the activity more facilitated.

예상답안

- There are diverse learner-centered learning methods such as individualized learning, discussion activity, CAI, problem solving, inquiry learning, project learning, NIE, Internet-based learning, cooperative learning, and experiential learning.

- To specify more on discussion activity, the following procedure is required. First plan the lesson and the next, create comfortable and cooperative atmosphere among students. Thirdly, select the discussion theme and the way of distributing the chances of talking. If the discussion is not activated well or the students are too much emotionally involved in the discussion, the teacher should mediate the conflict and further promote active discussion. Fifthly, after the discussion, the teacher needs to ask questions to check what the students learned from the discussion, and finally the teacher assesses the students' performance based on her observation during the students' talk.

In addition to procedure to follow, there are also precautions for the discussion activity. First of all, the purpose of the talk should be clearly settled, so that students can know what their discussion is for. Second, the content of the discussion should be based on the fact not unreliable sources. When giving students materials to be used in the discussion, the teacher needs to find the materials in trustable sources. Third, teacher should encourage every student to participate in the discussion, so that no one is excluded or left behind. Every student should receive opportunity to speak. Fourthly, appropriate attitude is required to the students for good discussion flow. They should respect other's opinion with rational mind and should not react emotionally or use abusive language to opposite team. Fifthly, the students need to learn how to present their argument clearly and talk persuasively backing up their opinions with good reasons. Finally, the students should try to derive the best conclusion about what they discussed. They should try their best to arrive at the most reasonable and socially acceptable conclusion.

답안 키워드

Discussion activity
- Procedure: plan the lesson, select the discussion theme, check what the students learned from the discussion, and assess the students' performance
- Precautions: purpose of the talk should be clearly settled, every student to participate in the discussion, respect each other's opinions and try their best to arrive at the most reasonable and acceptable conclusion

한국어 예상답안

① 개별화(수준별) 수업, 토론수업, CAI(학습의 개별화, 즉각적인 피드백, 학습 진전도의 지속적인 추적과 확인, 오류의 개선), 문제해결학습, 탐구학습, 프로젝트학습, NIE, 인터넷활용수업 협동학습, 체험학습 등등

② 토론식 수업의 절차
- 토의 학습을 계획한다. 원활한 토의 진행을 위해 서로 이해하는 분위기와 자유로운 분위기를 조성한다.
- 주제를 선정하고 형태와 방식을 결정하는 과정을 안내한다. 화제가 빈약하거나 토의 도중 감정적으로 대립하거나 갈등상황이 연출되었을 때 이를 적절히 조정한다.
- 적절한 질문과 발문으로 토의 과정에 참여하는 학생의 사고를 평가한다.
- 토의 과정을 면밀히 관찰하여 자료를 수집하고 평가한다.

③ 토론식 수업의 유의사항
- 토의의 정확한 목적을 세워야 한다.
- 토의 내용과 자료는 사실에 근거를 두어야 한다.
- 소외되는 학생이 없이 모두 적극적으로 토의에 참여해야 한다.
- 서로 의견을 존중하고 타인의 의견을 수용할 줄 아는 태도를 가져야 한다.
- 타당한 논거로 뒷받침 된 분명한 주장으로 상대방을 설득해야 한다.
- 최선의 결론을 도출할 수 있어야 한다.

Q 27 다른 교원으로부터의 비난에 대한 대책

You are strict about self-management but got some criticism from colleague teachers as following. Discuss some measures according to the ethics of teaching.

A : You seem greatly concerned about students' group bully but you are actually meddling in everything with too much nagging.

B : You are so engaged with self-development, such as teachers' training, study at graduate school and etc. But other teachers feel pressure on the work share because of making up for your position.

예상답안

A teacher should not be overly engaged in students' own affairs. Concerning students' private affairs, I'd better make a friendly environment for students rather than provide all the little details. I would show them some documentaries in class which contain messages about precious friendship, so that they can figure out the importance of getting along with others by themselves. I would also adopt a lot of group works, where students can co-operate each other for one specific goal. By working in groups, students will find out the value of helping and living with each other. A teacher also needs to be responsible for one's work in the teachers' community. Since the whole school is one team with one educational goal, all members should be devoted to their assigned roles. By making a self-check list, I would try to remind myself of the list of work that I need to complete for the whole school, before I spend time for my individual development.

답안 키워드

① A: meddling into students' affairs too much : showing videos or group work
② B: no responsibility in teachers' community : completing check-list

한국어 예상답안

① A: 교사는 학생을 위한 따뜻한 환경을 조성해주고 그를 위한 동기부여를 해주는 것이 중요하다. 개인적인 사생활에 너무 간섭하는 것은 바람직하지 않다. 구체적인 방법으로 우정에 관한 영화를 보여주어 중요성을 인식시키거나 그룹활동을 통해 같이 달성할 수 있는 일의 기쁨을 깨닫게 한다.
② B: 교사는 학교사회의 일원으로서 책임감을 가지고 역할을 다해야 한다. 구체적인 방법으로 check-list를 작성하여 개인의 일을 하기 전에 그룹에서의 자신의 의무를 완료했는지 살펴야 한다.

Q 28 인성교육과 생활지도의 부족에 대한 이유와 대책

You found that many students do not keep the good manners for everyday lives in school. One student does not greet the teachers properly, another student often swears at his classmates, another student does not complete their duty when they are given a cleaning duty. Describe TWO reasons for these misbehaviors and FOUR measures to solve the problems.

예상답안

- There are two main reasons that students cannot keep the good manners. First of all, at the school level, teachers ignore moral education and life guidance because the school curricular mostly focuses on assisting students to have great academic achievement. Second, in terms of the home education, as one facet, some parents are too busy to teach students the rules of etiquette, and as the other, some parents' overprotection of their children leads them to be spoiled and not to keep the good manners.
- As for the countermeasures, first, the teacher should have students be familiar with the basic courtesy by having them exposed to the model behaviors and reflecting theirs. It can be done through the entire education at school. To be specific, the teacher should continuously guide the students to obtain the fundamental manners not just during the class but extracurricular activity as well. Second, at the beginning of the semester, both a teacher and students should work together to set the class manners that the students must obey. By letting students take part in the procedure,

students will be motivated to follow the rule and keep the basic manners more efficiently. Third, students can habituate themselves to basic manners more practically when it is continued at home by cooperating with the parents. To activate home based moral education, the school would be better to offer effective guidance materials to the parents. Last, since teachers have the responsibility to guide their students onto the right path, they must take the initiative and set an example all the time for their students to follow.

답안 키워드

Reasons	① School education : T ignore personality education and just focus on increasing Ss' academic achievement. ② Home education : nucleus family, both parents are working – lack of communication ③ Social environment : many places which can have bad influence on Ss (karaoke, pub, PC rooms – easy to access)
Measures	(School and family should cooperate for instructing the good manners.) ① School education : School should focus on moral education. • T gives Ss opportunities to be aware of the importance of basic courtesy (shows video about model behaviors, gives reflecting time for their pre-behaviors, rewarding time for the model Ss) • School implements the mentoring program considering the Ss' talents and traits (university Ss, outside lecturer) ② Home education • Parents should try to talk with their child as much as possible (have dinner together, take care about Ss' current emotion, establish a good rapport) ③ School can build up the network with local communities (monitor Ss' behaviors)

한국어 예상답안

〈원인〉
① 학교 차원에서 보면 학력신장에 치중한 나머지 인성교육과 생활지도에 소홀히 했기 때문이다.
② 가정 차원에서 보면 자녀수가 적다보니 모든 것을 허용하며 과잉보호하거나 부모가 맞벌이를 하거나 가정 형편이 어려워 자녀를 돌볼 시간이 없어서 학생들이 기본생활습관을 제대로 배우지 못한 경우가 많다.

〈해결책〉
① 기초기본생활습관을 지키게 하는 교사의 지도방안
  • 기본생활습관 지도의 대전제는 교사가 이론 중심적이고 타율적인 지도를 지양하고 실천 중심적이고 자율적인 지도를 수행하는 것이다.
  • 기본생활습관 지도와 관련된 특별한 프로그램으로는 학교방송을 통한 훈화교육, 아침다짐회, 마침 반성회 시간 등이 있다.
② 학생이 지켜야 할 기본생활규칙을 학생과 함께 협의하여 명확히 결정하고 학년 초부터 지키게 한다.
  • 기본생활규칙은 아침활동, 교실출입, 준비시간 활동, 학습활동, 소집단활동, 점심시간활동, 정리정돈, 등하교 수칙시 지켜야 할 일, 규칙 등을 학생과 함께 협의하여 결정한다. 그리고 학생이 정한 규칙을 지키도록 계속 주의를 환기하고 적절한 강화를 한다.

- 정해야 할 규칙: 대인관계 규칙(비품이나 자료 잘 사용하기, 남의 물건 사용할 때 허락 받기, 인사 예절 지키기, 상대방 존중하기, 고운 말 쓰기, 서로 도와주기)
- 각자 맡은 일인 일역, 당번 같은 활동을 통하여 봉사하는 생활습관을 길러준다.
- 각자 활동한 학습장소 정리하기, 물건치우기, 개인 사물함 정리정돈하기를 습관이 되게 하여 항상 다음을 준비하는 태도가 몸에 배도록 한다.

③ 기본생활지도는 학교교육활동만으로 성공할 수 없으므로 가정과 연계하여 지도해야 한다. 학부모가 참여하는 좌담회를 개최한다든지 가정통신을 통해 지도 자료를 제공한다든지 학교와 가정이 함께 제정한 시상을 실시하는 것이 여기에 속한다.

④ 기본생활습관 지도의 중점 지도덕목을 선정하여 실제로 실천할 수 있는 기회를 제공해야한다. 인사 잘하기, 질서 지키기, 남을 방해하지 않기(큰소리 지르지 않기, 다른 사람 괴롭히지 않기, 화장실 조용하게 다녀오기)와 같은 두세 가지 중점 지도덕목을 선정하여 집중적으로 지도함으로써 바람직한 습관을 형성하게 한다. 이때 중점 지도덕목 실천을 앞서서 선도하는 학생 도우미 제도를 실시하거나 학생 스스로 다짐한 내용을 실천하고 평가하게 함으로써 체험학습의 기회를 확대하고 자율적인 실천을 유도할 수 있다. 이 과정에서 교사는 실천 결과에 따라 상찬으로 동기를 부여하는 것을 잊지 않아야 한다.

⑤ 모든 교사는 이 교육의 필요성을 절감하고 몸소 표본을 보이는 데 앞장서야 한다. 이 모든 것과 더불어 교사가 실천의지를 가지고 솔선수범하는 모습을 보여주는 것이 중요하다. 기본생활지도는 몇몇 교사에게 맡겨진 일이 아니다.

Q 29 학교일제고사에 대한 찬성/반대 의견 (Performance Achievement Tests)

Describe your opinions on 'Performance Achievement Tests' that has currently been administered throughout the country. Make your decision for "For" or "Against" along with its rationales.

예상답안

(1) 찬성 (positive effect)

I agree with it because it improves the quality of school education. There are five reasons that show how it improves the quality of school education.

① It enables the students and the parents to realize the result of the education. It fulfills their right to know.

② It makes the competitions in good faith among the teachers and the schools, because the objective information is opened to the students and the parents. This enhances the teaching ability.

③ The direction of education is established by analyzing the result of the tests.

④ It narrows the gap among the districts and the schools.

⑤ The problem of school underachievement can be minimized at national level.
- How? The competent teachers are placed at the lower-achieving schools.

(2) 반대 (the problems and the limitation)

I disagree with it for the following reasons.

① The multiple-choice questions in the test do not actualize the purpose of the education, whole-rounded education.

- It excludes the primary objective in assessment that our 7th curriculum and constructivism in education emphasize. Thus, if the genuine evaluation that is suited for the purpose of the education is necessary, a variety of assessment including performance-based assessment should be implemented over a long-term basis.

② The result of the test is open to public.
- The schools will be graded
- The school will focus on answering the questions on the workbooks, repetition, memorization, teaching by rote for 'Performance achievement test'. (일제고사)
- Personality education and speciality aptitude education would not be done well. The students will be under of a lot of stress. The private education market will be growing.

③ The reason for the gap of level of education among the schools and the districts is the financial gap among the parents. The districts with the vulnerable and farming and fishing villages need more support and investment.

답안 키워드

Agree	① At the level of student & parents • Ss' current level of academic achievement. ② At the level of Ts • T can supplement the Ss' weakness and reinforce their strong point. ③ School/ Educational administration's level • curriculum by considering the average Ss' weaknesses • financial support for schools to organize after-school programs
Disagree	① test of multiple choice items - not be able to achieve pedagogical objectives ② competitiveness among the schools ③ forcing Ss to private schools for advanced study

한국어 예상답안

(1) 찬성 (긍정적인 효과)
학교교육의 질을 개선하는 방안이므로 찬성한다.
① 교육결과를 알 수 있어 학생과 학부모의 알 권리를 충족시켜준다.
② 이렇게 학생과 학부모에게 객관적인 정보가 공개되면 교사 간, 학교 간 선의의 경쟁을 촉발하여 결국은 수업능력이 향상된다.
③ 평가결과를 분석하여 교육방향을 수립한다.
④ 지역 간, 학교 간 격차를 해소한다.
⑤ 학습부진 문제를 국가 차원에서 최소화할 수 있다. 어떻게? 부진학교에 우수교사 배치. 보충학습 자료를 개발 보급

(2) 반대 (문제점, 한계)
① 일제고사의 성격이 선택형 지필평가로는 전인교육이라는 교육목표를 실현하기 어렵다.
- 7차 교육과정과 구성주의 교육관이 강조하고 있는 주요한 평가를 배제하고 있다. 따라서 교육목표에 맞는 진정한 평가를 원한다면 표집을 선정하여 수행평가를 포함한 다양한 평가방식으로 장기간에 걸쳐 평가하는 것이 옳은 길이다.

② 평가의 결과가 공개되면
- 학교의 등급이 매겨지고 학교는 일제고사를 위한 문제풀이식, 반복식, 암기식, 주입식 교육에 매달릴 것이다.
- 인성교육과 특기적성교육은 허울만 남고 학생들은 과중한 학업 스트레스에 시달릴 것이다.

③ 학교별 지역별 학력격차가 나는 이유는 학부모의 경제적 차이가 주요 원인이다: 취약계층이 많은 지역과 농어촌에 더 집중적인 지원과 투자가 필요하다.

Q 30 학업성취도 평가결과 공개에 대한 문제점

If you are in the committee to support for the "Performance Achievement Tests", what would you say to the other side of the people? Point out their concerns of the result of the tests and suggest the countermeasures in THREE ways.

예상답안

① Many people worries that the competition among the students would be intense and the private education would be expanded to get good marks in the Performance Achievement Tests. Also, they worried that the education gap would be intensified by the zeal for students' education and educational background. The Performance Achievement Tests, however, do not prompt the private education and the intense competition among the students, because they are not reflected on the academic records. It is used to assess the students' current abilities. The tests should be used to check the students' current levels. Whole-rounded education that is the principal objective of the education should be ensured. along with humanity education. Also, the dependence on the private education will be decreased as after-school and students-centered classes are popular among students.

② If the result of the tests is open to public, the gap among the schools will be revealed. The important point is that the parents, the teachers, the government and the local community should be developed together by facing the situation of their school education. The ranking of the schools should not discourage the teachers and the students. It, instead, will open the way to support the schools with underachievement. The competent teachers should be placed on these schools. The environment of the schools should be improved and the financial support is necessary for them.

③ The result of the Performance Achievement tests should be utilized only to figure out the number of students with underachievement and improve its states and to improve the teaching skills.

답안 키워드

① Society: It can lead to competitive atmosphere for students to get high academic achievement. (private education expense↑, neglect moral education, pursue Elitism)

② School: Students will be reluctant to enter the schools which got poor result from the test. (unbalanced number of students in each school)

③ Students: Inferior students will be discouraged when the test result is open. (demotivated, low self-esteem, lose confidence)

한국어 예상답안

① 학업성취도 평가 점수를 올리기 위해 과열경쟁을 하거나 사교육이 더 심해지는 건 아닌지, 왜곡된 교육열과 학벌주의가 결합해 교육 양극화나 사회 양극화를 조장할까 걱정하지만 학업성취도 평가는 내신에 반영되지 않고 학생들의 실력을 측정하는 도구이므로 별도의 사교육이나 과열 경쟁이 필요하지 않다. 자신의 성적이 어느 정도인지를 점검하는 계기로 삼는 것이 바람직하다. 대책으로는 우리교육의 목표는 전인교육이라는 사실을 분명히 하고 인성교육을 충실히 해야 한다. 동시에 학력신장 측면에서도 정규수업과 방과후 학교를 통해 학생 중심의 맞춤식 교육과 학습부진아 해소에 힘을 쏟아 사교육 의존도를 줄여야 한다.
② 학업성취도 평가 결과를 공개하면 학교서열화를 초래하지 않을까 걱정이 될 수 있겠지만 학업성취도 평가 결과가 공개되면 학교간의 차이는 어느 정도 드러날 수 있다. 하시만 중요한 것은 학교 교육의 정확한 현실을 파악해 학부모, 교원 정부 및 지역사회가 함께 고민하면서 발전하자는 것이다. 대책으로는 학교의 서열공개가 다니는 학생에게 낙인효과를 주거나 교사의 교수 의욕을 꺾는 것이 아니라 원래 취지대로 열악한 학교를 전폭적으로 지원하는 것으로 나가야 한다. 우수교사 배치, 학교환경 개선, 재정투자 등을 실제로 시행해야 한다. 그렇지 않으면 무책임하게 학교 등수만 정해서 갖가지 부작용을 초래하는 결과를 낳을 것이다.
③ 학업성취도 평가를 공개했을 때 자료는 다음과 같이 활용될 수 있다.
- 기초학력 미달학생을 파악하고 학습부진을 해소하기 위해서
- 수업능력을 개선하기 위해서

Q 31 봉사활동을 활성화하는 방안

Secondary schools put some 20-hour-volunteer activities in practice but they become routine with losing their true values. Describe some guidance methods to find the solution.

예상답안

In secondary schools, volunteer activities become routine with losing their true values. To resolve this problem, there are four methods. First, the teacher invites the guest speaker who has lots of volunteer experience influence on her life. Second, the teacher makes volunteer activities more practical through cooperation with local organizations. Many students spend their voluntary working times on meaningless activities such as cleaning the fire stations. If the volunteer activities are associated with local organizations, the activities will be diverse, and practical. Third, making group volunteer project could be another solution. If the project is chosen by students' own preference, it will promote students' motivation to do voluntary activities, since they decide their projects, and they have freedom to design the project. Finally, if the teacher does the volunteer activities together, it will not only enhance students' motivation, but also provide good model of volunteer activities. Students can learn from the teacher's behavior not from the teacher's words.

답안 키워드

① learn from others' experiences
② associate with local communities
③ make their own group
④ learn from teacher's model

한국어 예상답안

① 봉사활동의 필요성을 알려준다. 왜 봉사활동을 해야 하는지 알아야 행동을 유발할 수 있기 때문이다.
- 특히 거창한 봉사활동이 아니라 우리 주변에서 할 수 있는 조그만 봉사활동을 하는 것도 매우 중요하다는 것을 알려준다.
- 이러한 봉사활동이 봉사 대상자에게도 도움을 주지만 봉사하는 학생에게도 공동체의식과 민주시민의식을 체득하고 다양한 직종을 폭넓게 접할 수 있으므로 진로선택에도 도움이 되고, 나눔을 통해서 더 풍성해지는 기쁨을 체험하게 한다는 것을 알려준다.

② 봉사활동의 필요성과 방법을 알려줄 때는 다양한 사례를 소개한다. 이때 교사가 일방적으로 설명하는 방식을 지양하고 예를 들면 특별활동 시간을 통해서 학생들이 스스로 사례를 찾아보게 하는 방식을 취한다.
③ 학생들이 참여할 수 있는 여러 가지 활동을 다양하게 할 수 있도록 정보를 충분히 수집하고 구체적인 계획을 세운다.
④ 지역 사회 유관 기관과 봉사 단체와 긴밀한 협조체제를 유지하여 효율적인 봉사활동을 한다.
- 복지관, 양로원, 보육원 같은 사회 복지시설/ 경찰서, 우체국, 소방서, 동사무소 같은 행정기관/ YMCA, 청소년 자원봉사 센터 같은 시민단체

⑤ 봉사활동 증명서와 같은 활동의 결과보다 교사도 함께 참여하는 등 실질적인 봉사활동이 되도록 하고 봉사활동이 끝나면 활동의 과정과 결과를 평가하여 다음 봉사활동에 대한 동기를 유발하게 한다.
⑥ 궁극적으로는 학생들이 스스로 봉사활동 조직을 만들어 자율적으로 봉사활동을 해가도록 지도한다.

Q 32. 20시간의 봉사활동은 충분한가? 추천할만한 봉사활동은?

> The current volunteer hours are 20. Is this appropriate amount of time or not sufficient? If there are any activities for volunteer work, please recommend some, along with concrete reasons for voluntary activities.

예상답안

I think 20 hour voluntary activity is not enough to realize the true meaning and value of voluntary activities. 20-hours per year means five times four-hour activities during a year. What they can feel and how they can find the meaning of voluntary activity by unconnected five-time activities. Thus I recommend a yearly group voluntary project which is designed by students by themselves. I will motivate students' to participate more actively and project will more meaningful since they design the project.

한국어 예상답안

① 시간을 더 늘려야 한다. 인성교육의 측면에서 탁월한 효과가 있기 때문이다.
② 공동체 의식과 민주시민의 자질 함양, 진로에 대한 경험의 폭 확대, 리더십 함양, 나눔의 기쁨 체험, 자발적인 봉사활동을 통해 더불어 사는 사회구현, 사회전반에 봉사활동이 활발해지면 자신이 힘들고 어려울 때 자립, 자활할 수 있는 손길로 돌아온다는 것을 인식하게 한다.

Q 33 학원의 소수 정예반에 대처하기 위한 학교의 방안들

Nearby private institutes administer small number classes of advanced students. How would your school deal with this? Discuss some countermeasures to implement.

예상답안

It is a serious problem that private institutes are often considered more effective than schools. Many advanced students feel they gain little from school lessons and place greater trust in private institutes. To address this issue, we need to consider how school faculty are utilized. I understand that teachers already have many responsibilities, such as student counseling and administrative work, in addition to teaching. However, to improve our teaching skills, we should make better use of vacation periods or other breaks for professional development.

Another solution is to implement level-differentiated classes for advanced students. This way, advanced learners can avoid repeating content they have already mastered, while lower-level learners can receive instruction that is more appropriate to their needs. Such an approach would make classes more effective for all students.

한국어 예상답안

① 정규수업에서 학교상황과 학생의 요구를 고려하여 수준별 수업을 할 수 있다. 예컨대 능력별 집단편성을 하여 수준별 이동수업, 학급 내 분단수업을 한다.
② 패스트 러너에게 정규수업시간에도 수준에 맞는 별도의 과제를 부과하여 자기 주도적 학습 형태로 개별 지도하거나 또래 교수자로 지명하여 교학장의 기쁨을 맛보게 한다.
③ 학교에서도 방과후 학교 시간을 이용해서 선수학습과 학업능력의 차이가 있는 학생들을 수준별로 얼마든지 가르칠 수 있다.
④ 방과후 학교에 예를 들어 상위권 학생을 위한 통합논술수업을 개설해서 적절한 팀티칭을 한다면 얼마든지 학원수업을 능가하면서 상위권 학생들의 요구를 충족할 수 있다.

Q 34 환경교육을 위한 문제점과 해결책

You are a middle school teacher in a rural farming area. You've opened some classes of environment conservation for the parents because of the environmental contamination nearby but not many parents wanted to participate in the programme. Explain the problems from viewpoints of 1) current situation 2) problem diagnosis 3) solutions along with some examples.

예상답안

1) I think the current situation is like followings. Parents do not put much value on conservation of school environment. To be more specific, supportive atmosphere is not created. For example, parents don't participate in volunteer work.

2) The reason of the problem is on the below two dimensions. First, the parents in rural agricultural

area do not have enough time to participate in school work, because of their long working hours. Also, comparing th the parents in the cities, their low expectation of their daughters and sons is another reason. Second in terms of school dimension, there was no negotiation of setting the schedule of school activities between parents and school. In addition to that, the promotion wasn't provided for parents to get to know about the programs.

3) In order to solve this problem, there are three solutions. First of all, when the school plans to carry out this kinds of activity, parents' opinion should be reflected. For this, there should be opportunity for parents to engage in decision making and administration. Then, parents can develop the sense of ownership. For instance, they can organize volunteer group for eco-village which improve the school environment. Secondly, we can combine their interests with this program. For example, career counseling programs in a festive atmosphere with free lunch.

Last, enough promotion should be conducted to get parents aware of the programs. To be more specific, we can make them notice the environment issue of out community problem through school letter and school web pages.

한국어 예상답안

1) 현 상황은 다음과 같다고 생각한다.
   학부모가 학교환경 교육에 참여할 필요를 느끼지 못하고 있다. 좀 더 확장해서 본다면 학부모 교육을 비롯한 자원봉사나 학교행사에 학부모가 협력하고 지원하고 자문하고 조언하는 분위기 조성이 되어있지 않다.

2) 문제의 원인은 다음과 같이 2차원에서 진단할 수 있다.
   ① 학부모 차원을 보면 먼저 농촌지역 학부모들임을 고려할 때 학교행사참여가 생업에 지장을 초래할 가능성이 많다. 다음으로 농촌지역 학부모들은 도시지역 학부모에 비해 자녀에 대한 관심이나 기대가 낮아 상대적으로 학교와 협력하는 일에 소홀하다.
   ② 학교 차원의 원인을 보면 먼저 학부모 참여를 배제하고 부적절한 시기를 선택한 학교의 일방적인 교육추진이 잘못되었다. 다음으로 사전 홍보를 다양하게 하지 못한 것을 원인으로 들 수 있다.

3) 이런 문제점을 해결하려면 다음과 같은 조치를 취해야 한다.
   ① 학교가 일방적으로 행사를 정하고 통보하는 식이 아니라 학부모의 의사를 최대한 반영한 환경교육 프로그램을 마련해야 한다. 그러려면 학부모가 의사결정과정과 집행과정에 참여할 수 있는 공간을 제공해야 한다. 예를 들어 일방적으로 프로그램의 내용과 시기를 정해서 통보하는 식으로 하지 말고, 사전에 설문조사를 통해서 행사의 의도와 시기, 그리고 방식에 대해서 의견을 수렴하거나, 학부모 대표와 간담회 자리를 마련하여 의사결정과정에 적극적으로 학부모를 참여시킨다. 그래야 과거의 실수를 되풀이하지 않고 교육내용과 형식을 결정할 수 있고, 학부모들이 주인의식을 가지고 참여한다. 예를 들어 학부모들이 자발적으로 생태마을 가꾸기 봉사단을 조직하여 학교주변 환경교육을 성공시킬 수 있는 좋은 방법이다.
   ② 환경교육과 다른 관심 있는 주제를 결합시켜 행사를 개최한다. 학부모의 참여를 유도하려면 가능하면 식사를 제공해주고 자녀에 대한 기대와 관심을 높일 수 있는 진학안내 프로그램이나 축제적인 요소를 가미한 프로그램과 병행해서 환경교육을 실시하는 것도 좋은 방법이다.
   ③ 사전에 환경교육에 대한 충분한 홍보를 실시한다. 환경문제가 지역사회의 공동문제라는 것을 부각시키는 내용을 담은 가정통신문을 꾸준히 발생하고 학교홈페이지를 통해서 도지역 환경문제의 심각성을 충분히 홍보한다. 또 학교 운영회를 활용하여 지역주민의 관심과 참여를 독려한다.

전공영어 2차 수업실연

Q 35 방과후 특기반을 위한 코스선택

If you are to be in charge of an after-school extracurricular class, what subject would you like to teach?

예상답안

If I am to be in charge of an after-school class, I would like to lead the chamber orchestra. There are two reasons for my choice: capitalizing on my hands-on experience and providing students with more chances to develop themselves. First of all, when I was a college student, I belonged to the amateur chamber orchestra. As a leader of the cello part, I managed people to cooperate each other and abide by the rules for the orchestra. This experience has taught me how to encourage people to behave in a harmonious way. Secondly, by utilizing my experience, I can encourage my students to get interested in music other than academic subjects such as mathematics and history. This after-school class will broaden my students' interests so that they can enjoy their lives with different perspectives.

⚠ 답안작성 유의점

자신의 특기적성을 고려해서 전공과목 외에 방과후 학교에서 맡을 수 있는 프로그램을 구상해두어라. 예를 들면 상담반, 스포트 댄스, 네일 아트 담당 같은 것은 전공에 관계없이 맡을 수 있는 프로그램일 것이다.

Q 36 교수방법을 향상시키기 위한 방안

After being appointed a teacher, what would you do to improve yourself in the society of information technology. (=What efforts would you make to improve your teaching techniques?) Describe some of your methods with concrete examples.

예상답안

To begin with, I'll be devoted myself to self supervision. First, I'll monitor my teaching in record. Second, I'll get feedback from my students on my teaching, discipline and classroom management. Thrid, I'll utilize the articles and resources related in my major subject. Fourth, I'll attend the graduate school or correspondence college in order to enhance my proficiency. Lastly, I'll be actively involved in seminar, conference, forum and so on.

Additionally, peer supervision is another way to motivate me. Frist, I'll willingly hold the research class and demonstration class that can be uploaded on Utube. Second, as a newly appointed teacher, through the mentoring supervision, I can learn a lot from experienced senior teachers as well as my colleagues. Lastly, I'll actively ask both the principal and vice principal to monitor my teaching.

한국어 예상답안

첫째, 자기장학의 형태로 다음과 일에 힘쓴다.
- 자신의 수업을 녹음·녹화하여 분석·평가한다.
- 자신의 학습지도, 생활지도, 학급경영 등과 관련하여 학생들을 대상으로 의견조사를 한다.
- 교직 교양 전공과목과 관련된 문헌자료와 정보자료를 활용한다.
- 야간대학 방송통신대학 등의 과정, 대학원과정의 수강을 통해서 전문성을 신장한다.
- 각종 연구, 교과연구회, 동학년협의회, 학습발표회, 강연회, 시범공개회 그리고 학교 상호방문 프로그램에 적극 참여한다.
- 인터넷을 이용해서 사이버 장학을 실시한다.
- 전문기관, 전문가 현장방문 견학을 실시한다.

둘째, 동료장학의 형태로 다음의 일을 할 수 있다.
- 수업연구와 수업공개(Youtube로 수업을 만들어 사이버공간에 올리는 것도 방법)장학을 실시한다.
- 멘토링장학을 받는다. 초임교사로서 경험이 풍부한 선배교사를 멘토로 정해 지도와 조언을 받음으로써 자신 있게 수업을 진행하고 교직 노하우를 터득한다.
- 학교장 및 교감에게 수업참관을 의뢰한다.

Q 37 창의적 재량활동을 운영하는 데 있어서의 문제점과 해결 방안

There are some school activities between 1st year of Middle School and 1st year of High school at your discretion. They are both for subject matter and creative activities. Creative activities are administered for one hour a week but become too routinized. Suggest some problems and solutions to make them substantial.

예상답안

As for administering the creative activities, there are three main problems. First, the teacher faces the difficulties of preparing the appropriate programs and standardized materials for creative activities. Second, the teachers cannot secure the enough time for the creative activities, as flexible time planning is not easy. Third, professional teachers in diverse field are insufficient who can offer the various experiences to the students.

As solutions, first, teachers should collaborate in developing activities and materials. It can be done with teachers of same grade or same subject. Second, by making connection with the local communities, teachers should facilitate the range of experiential activity. By allying with the local communities, teachers can offer students the chance of experiencing various creative activities. Also, they can reduce their workload. Third, there should be more teachers' training that they can develop their talent and expertise continuously. By exploiting the each teacher's specific talent and expertise, varied and active extracurricular activity can be planned.

답안 키워드

문제점	해결방안
• preparation of the programs • insufficient time • lack of teachers with expertise	• collaboration • local communities • teachers' training

한국어 예상답안

1. 문제제기

창의적 재량활동을 운영하는 데 핵심 장애는 프로그램과 자료가 부족하고 시간표 편성이 어렵고 전담교사를 확보할 수 없어 한 학급을 1명의 교사가 전담하여 다양한 영역의 창의적 활동을 지도하고 있다는 것이다. 이런 운영 방법은 교사의 전문성을 발휘하기 힘들고 통일된 프로그램과 자료제작도 어렵다. 통일된 프로그램과 자료를 확보한다고 하더라도 획일적인 내용에 그치게 되어 창의적 재량활동의 내실을 꾀하기 힘들다.

2. 활성화 방안

따라서 이런 문제를 해결할 수 있는 방안을 찾아보아야 한다. 예를 들어 이런 방안을 시도해볼 수 있다.

- 창의적 재량활동 시간표를 융통성 있게 짜서 교사 1명이 한 주제씩 분담하여 그 내용을 가지고 모든 학급을 순회하면서 지도한다.

한 학생의 창의적 재량활동을 특정한 요일의 특정한 시간으로 배정하여 지도교사가 1년 동안 한 학년의 모든 학급을 순회하게 하고 교사는 자신이 개발한 창의적 재량활동 프로그램만을 지도하므로 전문성이 높아지고 학생은 다양한 내용으로 전문성을 갖춘 교사를 번갈아 맞이하므로 같은 질의 창의적 재량활동을 할 수 있다. 이 방법을 취하면 평소에 교사들이 자신의 교과나 특기를 살려서 학습내용을 선정하고 자기연수나 동호회를 조직하여 자신만의 전문적 영역을 구축할 수 있다. 교사의 교육적 신념과 관심, 특기, 소질 등을 발휘할 수 있도록 지원하여 학생들이 특색 있는 학교교육의 기회를 접할 수 있도록 한다. 이런 활동의 결과물로 각 학년별로 교재를 발간할 수도 있다.

결론적으로 시간을 융통성 있게 편성하여 모든 교사가 주제 분담 식으로 전 학급을 순회하면서 창의적 재량활동을 진행하면 교사는 교과 외의 자신의 전문성을 개발할 수 있어서 좋고 학생은 흥미와 관심을 충족시켜주는 신선하고 질 높은 수업을 할 수 있어서 좋다.

- 이 밖에도 창의적 재량활동의 본래 취지를 살려 유의미한 시간이 되게 하려면 각종 프로그램과 거기에 따른 교수, 학습 자료를 확보해야 한다. 그 방법을 알아보면;
  - 창의적 재량 활동의 원래 취지대로 학생의 흥미와 관심을 끌 수 있는 주제 탐구 활동과 기타 자율 활동(자율 연구, 현장체험학습, 학교 특성화 프로그램 등)을 강화해야 한다.
  - 동학년협의회와 교과협의회를 통해 창의적 재량활동 프로그램과 자료를 개발하여 활용한다.
  - 지역 교육청의 교수학습센터 기능을 확대한다: 교수학습센터를 통해 학교끼리 프로그램, 교육자료, 정보교환, 우수사례 발굴 보급
  - 범교과 학습은 학습 내용에 해당하고, 자기 주도적 학습은 학습 방법으로 볼 수 있으므로 양자를 구분할 것이 아니라 통합하여 운영하는 방법도 모색하여야 할 것이다.
  - 창의적 재량활동을 특별활동의 계발활동과 봉사활동 시간과 통합하여 운영하는 방안도 모색해야 한다. 이러면 창의적 재량활동의 내용을 개선하고 시간 운영에서 오는 교사의 부담을 줄일 수 있다.
  - 연수를 통해 교사의 전문성을 신장한다.

Q 38. 말썽을 피운 학생을 처벌한 것에 대해서 학부모가 불만을 제기한 경우

You've done some disciplines on the student who had made some troubles at school. The parent paid a visit to complain against your punishment on the student. How would you deal with this? Discuss your solutions for the angry parents with concrete examples.

예상답안

I would listen to their complaints carefully, showing empathy toward their feelings. I would make it sure that as a homeroom teacher, I always treat the student with deep affection. I would explain to the parents the incident in detail and let them know that my discipline was only for the educational purpose. If the parents' complaints stem from their overreaction, I'll let them know how the student has behaved at school so that they can understand that the discipline was acceptable. If the discipline was too strict, I would apologize to the parents and promise that I'll guide the student with a sense of respect and understanding. I'll ask the parents to encourage the student to adjust his misbehaviors. I would try to establish a close relationship with the troubling students through continuous counseling so that I can prevent any troubles or misunderstandings in advance.

답안 키워드

① listen to their complaints
② let them understand that my discipline
③ encourage the student to adjust his misbehaviors
④ continuous counseling

한국어 예상답안

① 공손하게 학부모가 어떤 불만을 품게 되었는지 경청한다. 불만사항을 경청할 때는 표면적인 이야기보다는 내면의 감정과 목소리에 주의한다. 학부모의 심정을 이해한다고 공감을 표시해준다. 담임으로서 학부모의 자녀에 대해 애정을 가지고 지도하고 있다는 것을 알려준다.
② 사건이 발생한 원인과 진행과정, 그리고 취한 조처를 자세히 알려주고 그 조치가 어디까지나 교육적인 조치였음을 이해시킨다. 학부모의 과민반응이라면 자녀의 학교생활을 구체적으로 알려서 오해를 풀게 한다.
③ 자신의 지도가 비교육적이었거나 강압적인 면이 있었다면 정중하게 사과하고 좀더 인격적이고 민주적인 생활지도를 하겠다고 약속한다.
④ 학생의 문제행동이 교정될 수 있도록 부모의 관심과 협조를 당부한다. 학부모가 불만을 표시해 온 것은 자녀가 전달하는 내용을 들은 것에 기초했을 것이므로 평소에 문제학생과 더 많은 상담을 통해 친밀한 관계를 형성하고 불필요한 오해나 갈등의 소지를 없앤다.

Q 39. 영어교사로서 학생들의 창의적 사고력을 길러줄 수 있는 교육 방법 구상하기

Thinking skills and exploration and global human resources are pivotal elements in this knowledge-based society. Describe your teaching methods to improve a sense of creativity related to the subject of English.

예상답안

As an English teacher, I will help my students to develop their creative thinking skills in several ways.

1) First, I can design level-differentiated lesson based on the language proficiency of my students. The high-level students can express their ideas freely when their learning material is a little bit challenging. And the low-intermediate level students are also able to interact with their peers when they can understand the lesson fully.

2) Secondly, I will teach them to think both creatively and critically. For one example, a task which requires students to think about one topic in many aspects enables them to draw out diverse range of answers. And for another example, discussing in groups and reflecting on the result can motivate them to think critically.

3) The third way is to promote their self-directed learning. Students can participate in the lesson actively and autonomously when they work on project-works, hands-on activities, and problem-solving. While they complete those activities, they can find their unique way to solve certain problems.

4) Next, I should make my students intrinsically motivated. I believe that my students can develop their creativity best when they find the purpose of learning from themselves. So I will advise them to set their own goals and objectives of learning.

5) To develop students' creativity, it is also important to make open and accepting atmosphere for my students. If students feel easy and comfortable when they express their opinion in front of others, they can generate a creative outcome. And as a teacher, I should tell them to accept others' opinion with open mind.

답안 키워드

Teacher	Students
• design level-differentiated lesson	• do self-directed learning
• accept diverse range of answers	• set their own goals and objectives of learning

한국어 예상답안

1. 개인차를 반영한 수준별 수업을 진행한다.
   - 학생 개개인의 흥미와 관심을 존중한다. (하고 싶은 일을 할 때 창의력 증진이 된다.)
   - 개인의 특성에 따라 학습 내용과 방법을 달리한다.
2. 유창성, 융통성, 독창성을 기반으로 새로운 아이디어를 생산해주는 확산적 사고와 나온 아이디어의 유용성과 적절성을 판단하는 비판적 사고를 다양한 방법으로 균형 있게 길러준다.
   - 창의성을 유발하는 발문을 자주 한다.

- 다양한 사고 훈련 기법을 활용한다.
  - 예 확산적 사고 : 브레인스토밍, 체크리스트, 마인드 맵
  - 예 비판적 사고 : 역브레인스토밍, 하이라이팅
3. 창의력을 신장해주는 다양한 교수, 학습 방법을 적용한다.
   - 문제해결학습, 탐구학습, 프로젝트학습, 독서-토론-논술수업, NIE, 자기주도적 학습에 바탕을 둔 수업, 인터넷 활용수업, 협동수업, 경험의 기회를 넓혀주는 체험학습
4. 내적 동기유발에 힘쓴다.
   - 창의력은 어떤 과제에 흥미, 만족감 같은 내적인 동기가 높을 때이다. 이러한 내적 동기를 유발하려면 교사 주도적 학습에서 벗어나 학생의 자기 주도적 학습을 강화해야 하는데 학생이 스스로 학습과제와 학습방법을 선택하도록 길을 열어 줄 때 학생의 자발성과 집착력은 가장 커진다.
5. 창의성을 조장하는 심리적, 물리적 환경을 구축해야 한다.
   - 결과보다는 과정에 중심을 두고 학생들의 실수와 색다른 아이디어의 가치를 인정해주는 개방적이고 허용적인 심리적인 풍토 속에서 창의성이 자란다. 그리고 다양한 자료가 배치되어 활용할 수 있는 교실 환경을 조성하고 도서관, 지역사회로 학습의 장을 확산시켜 학생들의 경험의 폭을 넓혀준다.
6. 교과와 연계한 독서-토론-논술 교육으로 창의성을 신장한다.
   - 단원이나 학습목표에 맞는 독서자료를 제시하거나 탐구하게 하여 독후활동을 펼치고 때때로 주제를 택해서 토론 수업을 전개하고 그 결과는 글쓰기로 연결시켜 수행평가에 방영하는 방법으로 학생들의 탐구력, 사고력, 표현력, 창의력을 길러준다.

Q 40 자기표현이 어렵고 학업 성취도가 낮은 우울증 학생이 극단적 시도

There is a student A, who is passive in self-expression and low academic achievement, and very quiet with no troubles at school. Recently, he has been very depressed and not got along with his classmates. A few days ago, his suicide note was found. How would you deal with the problem? Describe four methods to solve the problem with concrete examples.

예상답안

① First of all, the teacher must stop the student's impulsive suicide attempt. Many students show self-destructive behaviors because of excessive stress. Teachers need to let the students know that they are well-cared for and emotionally supported. Then, the teachers should instruct the students to learn how to control their emotion and impulsive behaviors.

② Through an intensive counseling, the teacher should find out the cause of the problem and take appropriate measures. They must examine the students' personal background such as school works, health, family, and relationship with classmates.
(General causes of depression and suicide attempts are stress, frustration, low academic achievement, choosing a career, lack of communication with parents and friends, overprotection of the parents, highly competitive school environment, low self-esteem, and lack of problem-solving ability.)

③ Teachers should have the student get appropriate treatment for his depression. Teachers should find out the negative thoughts and beliefs that cause the student to feel depressed. Then they should help the student to change those thoughts into more realistic and rational ones. In this way, the teachers will guide the student to think more positively and rationally.

④ The teacher should cooperate with the parents. The teacher lets the parents know about the situation and asks them to work together in instructing the student. High expectation from the parents can be a burden to the student. On the contrary, the parents' ignorance toward their child could also make the student feel frustrated. Therefore, the teacher should ask the parents not to force their child but to guide him to choose a career based on his aptitude and talent. Also, the parents should take care of their child with deep love and spend more time talking to each other.

⑤ The teacher can make a peer counseling class so that the students can share their common concerns and build up a friendly relationship. Also, the teacher helps the students carry out self-directed learning, make new friends, and participate actively in whatever they do. The teacher could also provide a number of opportunities for success with words of encouragement and compliment. If the student is suffering from financial difficulty, the teacher could introduce people who carried out a successful life despite their poor family background. Another way is to have the students participate in club activities in order to make new friends and become equipped with ability to express themselves. The students also can get help through individual, intensive counseling and treatment programs.

답안 키워드

① stop the student's impulsive suicide attempt
② intensive counseling with teacher or professional counselors
③ appropriate treatment
④ cooperate with the parents

한국어 예상답안

① 우선 충동적인 자살기도를 막는 것이 급선무다: 스트레스를 견디지 못하고 돌이킬 수 없는 자기 파괴적인 행동을 취할 가능성이 있으므로 먼저 따뜻한 관심과 정서적 지지를 제공한 후 점차 학생이 감정과 행동에 대한 충돌조절 능력과 대처 능력을 습득하도록 지도해 준다.

② 상담을 통해 원인을 정확하게 파악하여 대처한다. 학업문제, 건강문제, 가정환경, 교우관계 등을 종합적으로 살펴 우울증과 자살충동이 어떤 이유 때문에 발생하였는지 분석하여 거기에 맞는 종합적인 처치를 계획한다. (일반적인 우울증과 자살 충동의 원인 : 스트레스와 좌절경험-부정적인 생활사건-학습부진, 진로문제, 부모나 친구와 의사소통 붕괴, 과잉보호, 부모의 지나친 기대, 진학경쟁, 낮은 자존감, 문제해결능력 부족)

③ 우울증에 가장 효과가 큰 인지치료 방법을 적용한다 : 학생을 우울하게 만드는 부정적 생각과 역기능적 신념을 찾아내어 그러한 생각을 더욱 현실적이고 합리적인 사고로 대치할 수 있도록 돕는다. 즉, 사건-부정적인 생각-우울한 기분의 연결고리를 분명하게 파악하게 하여 그 사건에 대해 다르게 생각해볼 수 있도록 유도하고 부정적이고 자기 패배적인 생각보다는 긍정적이고 합리적인 생각을 하도록 도와준다.

④ 가정과 연계하여 지도한다 : 학부모에게 학생의 상황을 알리고 협력해서 지도할 것을 요청한다. 가정에서 자녀에게 지나치게 높은 기대를 하면 부담 때문에, 반대로 전혀 무관심하면 좌절감 때문에 자살충동에 빠질 수 있다. 따라서 과잉기대를 하는 학부모에게는 부모의 입장을 너무 강요하지 말고 학생의 적성과 능력에 맞는 진로를 선택할 수 있도록 지도해 달라고 한다. 또 자녀의 생활고 진로에 무관심한 학부모에게는 관심을 가져주고 대화시간을 늘려달라고 당부한다.

⑤ 그 밖에 병용할 수 있는 방법
- 또래 상담을 활용한다. 또래상담을 통해 고민을 함께 나누고, 친구관계를 적극적으로 형성해가도록 지도한다.
- 학업성적 때문에 의욕을 잃고 있다면 자기 주도적으로 학습할 수 있는 방법을 알려주고 공부를 조금 못하더라도 친구를 잘 사귀고 어떤 일에든지 적극성을 가지고 참여할 때 성공적인 인생을 살아갈 수 있음을 일깨워준다.

- 성공의 기회를 제공하여 주고, 긍정적인 예언을 해주고 칭찬을 자주하여 긍정적인 자화상을 확립하게 하고 자신감을 갖게 한다.
- 가정형편이 어려워 좌절하고 있다면 역경을 이겨낸 구체적인 사례를 들려주거나 그런 내용이 담긴 책을 선물한다. 또 함께 어려운 상황에 있는 이들을 체험한다. 그러면서 희망과 용기를 잃지 않게 한다.
- 학생에게 관심을 가지고 배려를 하되 자립심과 극기심을 길러준다. 과잉보호에 물든 학생은 어려움이 약간만 있어도 쉽게 포기하는 경향이 있다.
- 적절한 동아리 활동을 소개해주어 친구도 사귀고 자기표현력도 기르게 한다.
- 전문가와 연결시켜 심층상담을 받거나 치료 프로그램에 참여하도록 한다.

Q 41 학습 의욕이 부족해 수업을 방해하는 학생과 일탈학생 지도

You joyfully start off a beginner teacher. But you have many students who have lack of motivation to interrupt the class. How would you deal with these students? And you want to get some advices from your peer teachers but have no opportunities for that. Describe how you would improve your teaching skills.

예상답안

- 교과지도 측면

First, I will make the class student-centered rather than teacher-centered. If they feel the class is focusing on them, they will be motivated and participate it more actively. Second, I will plan the course which leads to students' creativity and self-regulation. Meaningful learning can be done if the students are able to free from the rote learning. Third, I will support the innovative use of ICT in education. ICT will give the students a range of choices for the learning material and methods, not just blackboard and textbook. For example, each student can use computers and do self-study through the Internet. In addition to these ways, it may be a good way to give the students the lesson which generates their interest. Project work, NIE and cooperative learning can be involved in the lesson.

- 생활지도 측면

As the matter of student guidance, democratic and humane guidance is required because teachers' authority and commands can't draw on students' voluntary behavior and just provoke disobedience. Next, through the volunteer work and group work, I can make them the people who are considerate of others' feelings and who keeps the rules. Third, in the beginning of the semester, students will discuss and decide the rules of creating academic atmosphere by themselves and then apply the rules with fairness. Lastly, I will carry out ongoing and systematic counseling.

After school program can be an effective way to solve this problem. It's a good way to involve low-achievers in supplementary program after school. Club activities and personality development programs will give the students a sense of community and cultivate their moral character.

답안 키워드

To deal with the problem, I would guide delinquent students and the students who have lack of motivation in the following ways.

교과지도 측면	생활지도
• student-centered class • meaningful learning • use of ICT	• democratic and humane guidance • volunteer work and group work • decide the rules by themselves

한국어 예상답안

1. 학습의욕이 부족해 수업을 방해하는 학생과 일탈학생에 대한 지도는 다음과 같은 방법으로 하겠다.
   먼저 교과지도 측면에서,
   - 일제식 수업에서 벗어나 맞춤식 수업을 하겠다. + 부연설명
   - 주입식 암기식 수업에서 벗어나 창의력과 자기주도적 학습능력을 길러주는 수업을 하겠다. + 부연설명
   - 칠판과 교과서 중심에서 벗어나 N세대에 맞는 ICT활용수업을 확대강화 하겠다. + 부연설명
   - 다양한 자료와 교수 학습 방법으로 재미있는 수업 (프로젝트 수업, NIE수업, 협동학습, ICT활용수업) + 부연설명

   다음으로 생활지도 측면에서
   - 권위주의적 강압적인 생활지도에서 벗어나 민주적이고 인격적인 생활지도를 하겠다. + 부연설명
   - 자치활동, 봉사활동, 모둠활동을 통해 남을 배려하는 마음, 질서를 지킬 줄 아는 마음을 길러준다.
   - 면학분위기를 조성할 수 있는 규칙을 학기 초에 학생과 함께 협의하여 결정하고 일관되게 적용하겠다.
   - 상담을 지속적이고 체계적으로 시행해 가겠다.

   마지막으로 방과후 학교를 적극적으로 활용하겠다.
   - 방과후 수준별 교과 보충수업 프로그램에 학습부진아를 참여시킨다.
   - 동아리 활동이나 정서계발, 심성계발 프로그램에 참여하게 하여 기본생활습관을 기르고 안정된 정서를 함양하게 한다.

2. 동료교사의 조언이 어려운 상황에서 다음과 같은 방법으로 수업능력을 계발하겠다.
   - 교과협의회, 동학년협의회에 열심히 참여한다.
   - 선배교사 멘토를 구해서 다양한 자문과 지도를 받는다.
   - 수업연구에 참여하고 수업을 공개한다.
   - 다양한 자기 장학활동을 해간다.
   - 수업능력을 계발할 수 있는 동호회에 참여하여 활동한다.
   - 학생지도를 어떻게 해야 하는지 늘 문제의식을 가지고 다른 교사의 사례를 눈여겨보고, 우수사례를 수집 분석 연구해서 창의적으로 적용해보는 데 힘을 쏟겠다.

Q 42 동료교사의 조언이 어려운 상황에서 수업능력을 계발하는 방법

Describe FOUR methods you can improve your class management when you are in a school where you have no peer teachers to talk to about your class.

예상답안

With no opportunities to get advice from colleague teachers, I would firstly try to develop my teaching skills by eagerly attending the teachers' conference of the curriculum. Also, I can ask for help to senior teacher and get some advice from him. Observing others' classes and opening my class to other teachers or parents can be effective way to improve the teaching skills. At the same time, self-monitoring will give opportunity of objective reflection. In addition to these ways, I can join the club that helps to improve teaching skills with keeping on how other teachers do. And then, if I collect and analyze outstanding cases and apply what I learned in a creative way, I would improve the teaching skills without peer teachers' feedback.

답안 키워드

- attending the teachers' conference
- asking for help to senior teacher
- observing other teachers' classes
- self monitoring

Q 43 소외계층 아이들을 위한 e-learning 활용방안

Some areas in your community has got a big discrepancy between students' proficiency levels. The students in less-privileged areas have less opportunities to learn and access to diversity of culture. If you are to teach at a small school in this low economic-financial area, what would you do to decrease the gap between these advanced areas and status and decrease private tuition fee? Explain four things to do this.

예상답안

There are four ways that decrease the private tuition fee and effectively lowers the gap between advanced area and low economic-financial area.

① First, e-learning can be one way to lower gap between different level of economy. To make e-learning happen, school should build up hardware infrastructure that includes high-tech equipment. At the same time, school can create e-learning system on the school web page so that students can learn at home as well. If these conditions are met, there are four advantages that students can benefit from. First of all, when there is shortage of optional class instructors especially in islands and isolated areas, regular class of advanced area can be presented through webpage. Second, students can self-direct their learning through blended learning, which makes the learning more satisfactory. Third, e-learning can allow students to get further learning to support level-differentiated class. Lastly, e-learning provides students with EBS program or cyber home learning as a tailored class, which helps low achievers to preview and follow the course. Also, in this type of class, students can ease the burden of private tuition since they do not have to pay for it.

② We can utilize school library as a resource of educational information. School library can open new possibilities to students who lack the chances to experience cultural facilities. If the library is well equipped with various resources and media and if it provides students with space for group work, libraries can function as cultural facilities that satisfy the aesthetic needs and offer spaces for study.

③ Schools can conduct useful after-school program. They can open classes like level-differentiated subject program, various specialty aptitude program, stress management program, and career education program.

Such programs can be consigned to universities or nonprofit organization. Besides, school can also supply students with high-quality instructor from local human resource. Then students' needs that were not fully met from regular class can be effectively satisfied. In this way, after-school program can compensate the function of education in school and relieve the burden of private tuition. Also, it can actualize education welfare.

④ School should actively develop Saturday field trip and summer camp. We should consider the condition of rural area where students hardly have time to experience such activities with their parents. By doing so, we can expect students' academic progress.

⑤ We can utilize university students as mentors. They can conduct individual learning and moral education by meeting rural area students on a regular basis. In that way, students' gap between classes, areas, and education can be narrowed. University students as mentors can offer various programs such as foundation program for basic learning, specialty & aptitude program, and career education program. Especially in rural areas where there are not enough university students during semester, schools can employ college students who visit their hometown during vacation. It will be a lot of help for students if their mentors give them advice periodically.

답안 키워드

- learn from school web page
- self-direct their learning
- support level-differentiated class
- participate in field trip

한국어 예상답안

1. 이러닝을 실시할 수 있도록 학교에 하드웨어 인프라를 구축하고 최첨단 미디어실을 마련한다. 동시에 학교 홈페이지에 사이버 가정학습 지원체계(이러닝 체계)를 구축한다. 이러한 조건을 갖추게 되면;
   - 정규교과를 보완하는 형태로 선택교과의 교사가 부족할 때, 농어촌 도서벽지 학교의 정규교과 운영을 사이버 학습형태로 실시할 수 있다.
   - 온 오프 혼합형 수업을 실시하여 학생이 자기 주도적으로 참여하는 가운데 더 충실한 수업을 할 수 있다.
   - 수준별 교실수업 지원형태로 인터넷을 이용하여 심화 보충 수업을 실시할 수 있다.
   - 수준별로 공부할 수 있는 EBS 방송수업이나 사이버 가정학습을 안내하여 맞춤식 수업을 받도록 한다. 이러면 학생이 원하는 과목을 원하는 수준으로 학습할 수 있기 때문에 학습부진해소와 선행학습에 도움이 되고 무료로 수강할 수 있기 때문에 사교육비 부담에서 벗어나 마음껏 공부할 수 있다.

2. 학교 도서관을 활용하여 교육정보 자료관으로 활용한다.
   문화시설이 부족하고 학교교육 외에 학습의 기회를 접할 수 있는 기회가 부족한 학생들에게 학교 도서관은 새로운 가능성을 제공해준다. 도서관에 다양한 자료와 매체를 구비하고 있고 모둠학습을 할 수 있는 공간을 마련하면 도서관이 단순히 도서대여점 기능을 하는 데서 벗어나 문화적 욕구를 충족하고 학습할 수 있는 공간과 기회를 제공하는 장으로 변모할 수 있다. 즉 학교 도서관이 자료 및 정보 제공의 장이자, 독서활동의 장이자, 건전한 휴식을 취하는 문화의 장이자, 학습과제를 스스로 풀어가는 학습활동의 장이 되어야 한다. 또 교사도 적극적으로 도서관 활용 수업을 펼쳐야 한다.

3. 내실 있는 방과후 학교 프로그램을 운영한다.
   수준별 교과 프로그램, 다양한 특기적성 프로그램, 스트레스 매니지먼트와 진로교육 프로그램을 개설하여 대학교나 비영리단체에 위탁운영을 하거나 지역 자원을 활용하여 질 높은 강사를 공급해준다. 그러면 정규수업에서 채울 수 없었던 학생의 다양한 욕구를 채워줄 수 있으므로 학교교육기능을 보완하고 사교육비를 경감하고 교육복지를 실현하는 효과가 있다.
4. 토요체험학습과 방학캠프를 적극적으로 개발한다. 부모와 함께 체험학습을 갈 수 있는 여유가 없는 논산어촌 실정을 고려하여 학력신장을 꾀한다.
5. 대학생 멘토를 활용한다. 학생을 정기적으로 만나 개별화 학습과 인성지도를 실시하는 대학생 멘토를 활용하여 계층 간, 지역 간, 교육격차를 해소한다. 대학생 멘토는 기초학습 교과 지도, 특기 적성지도, 진로 학교생활 상담 등 다양한 활동을 해 줄 수 있다. 농산어촌 지역에서도 방학 중에 귀향한 대학생을 멘토로 활용하여 멘토링을 지속적으로 실시하게 하면 농산어촌 학생들에게 큰 도움이 될 것이다.

Q 44 학교를 더욱 생동감 있게 만들 수 있는 방법

Explain THREE methods to build up lively school culture to get every student to want to attend.

예상답안

① Students should get consideration for others. I would like to guide them to be aware of caring others through all the subjects they learn and set up a moto like "from me, from now, and from little things"

② I will conduct a campaign for friendship. As a part of the campaign, I will let them praise others' good deed and strong point, and make the day of friendship. Also there is compliment mileage so that the best student who receives compliment a lot can get rewards.

③ I will make a prevention and treatment program for the Internet addiction to form a sound online culture. By using self-check list, both the teacher and students are aware of if they are addicted or not.

④ I will run a volunteering team for caring school. The team consists of students, local leaders and parents. Also I will connect maladjusted students to the member of the volunteering team. In addition to this, students who do well in volunteering services will get rewards this will lead to their active participation. I will encourage students to participate in various activities and lively school festival.

⑤ The school should enhance the counseling program for students. For example, peer counseling could be helpful so I will promote this counseling program. Also the school needs to help teachers to improve their counseling ability.

⑥ I should make school environment safe. We will present safety education during semester regularly and run courses for prevention of safety accidents, and for preparations for a catastrophe.

⑦ We should hold career education. We will present career education regularly during semester in order to help students to find their way in the future. In addition, vocation-experience program would help them to decide what to do in the future.

답안 키워드

① Build up Cooperative spirits (implement various group activities and club activities, naturally establish close friendship)

② Implement counseling system (open door for all students, visit whenever they want without time limit, say whatever they want)
③ Carry out career education program (good opportunities for various experiences which can help to find their future career)
④ Make Ss actively participate in organizing school events and policy to grow up as a democratic citizen. (activate school union)

한국어 예상답안

① 남을 배려하는 생활을 실천하게 한다 : 전 교과 지도를 통한 타인 배려 의식 지도, 나부터, 지금부터, 작은 일부터 실천하기(기본생활관 형성, 질서의식 고취, 민주시민 의식 고취, 문제행동 근절)
② 친구 사랑 운동을 전개한다: 친구의 장점, 선행 등을 찾아 칭찬하기, 친구 사랑의 날 제정 운영, '칭찬 마일리지' 운영 및 '칭찬 대상' 수여하기 (왕따, 학교폭력 근절, 함께 하는 학급 학교 분위기 조성)
③ 인터넷 중독 예방 치료교육으로 건전한 사이버 문화를 조성한다: 인터넷 중독 학생 개인별 자가 진단 실시, 중독 예방 치료프로그램 운영 (교육과정, 상담중심)
④ 학교사랑 자율 봉사단을 만들어 운영한다: 학생 학부모 지역인사 참여 학교 사랑 자율 봉사단 조직, 학교생활 부적응 학생 결연지도, 봉사활동 우수사례 발굴 홍보. 다양한 동아리 활동을 장려하고 어울림과 사랑이 넘치는 학생축제를 운영한다.
⑤ 학생상담활동을 강화해야 한다: 또래 상담을 활성화하고 교사의 상담능력을 신장한다.
⑥ 안전사고 없는 학교를 만들어야 한다: 교육과정과 연계한 안전교육을 실시하고, 안전사고 예방활동을 하며, 재난 대비 교육을 실시하여 안전생활을 습관화한다.
⑦ 진로교육을 활성화해야 한다: 교육과정과 연계한 진로교육을 실시하고, 부모 직업체험을 비롯한 직업체험학습을 실시한다.

Q 45 독서교육을 위한 방법

Describe the guidance methods for reading education as an English teacher with concrete examples.

예상답안

- A teacher carries out reading education related to each subject. After providing students with a reading text that is related to each lesson in their subjects, a teacher lets the students role ply based on their reading. Also, writing an essay can be recommended as an after-reading activity. In addition, students discuss the contents of the book and have an NIE activity. And then, all the results of these activities are reflected in their performance test.
- A teacher utilizes the library as resources in his or her class.
- A teacher provides the lists of books recommended for each grader.
- Students can make a classroom library.
- After students make group-reading journals, a teacher gives an award to the best group every semester.
- A teacher lets them introduce the book they read to other classmates in one-minute speech

- A teacher creates a section for reading on the school homepage and let students post various reading essays.
- Both a teacher and students read books together during the morning self-study session.

답안 키워드

- role play based on their reading
- library as resources
- group-reading journals
- reading on the school homepage

한국어 예상답안

1. 자신의 수업에서 교과와 연계한 독서교육(독서토론논술)을 실시한다. 교과별 단원(주제)별 읽기 자료 제시 – 독서를 바탕으로 역할놀이, 감상문 쓰기 같은 다채로운 독후활동 시행 – 주제를 정해 토론수업이나 NIE수업 실시 – 그 결과는 자신의 주장을 정리한 논술 쓰기와 수행평가로 연결
2. 자신의 수업에서 도서관활용수업을 실시한다.
3. 학년별 필독도서 목록을 제공해준다.
4. 학급문고를 운영한다.
5. 모둠별 독서일기를 작성하게 해서 가장 우수한 모둠을 학기마다 시상한다.
6. 1분 스피치를 통해 학생이 자신이 읽은 책을 소개하게 한다.
7. 학교 홈페이지에 독서코너를 만들어 다양한 독서 및 독후활동을 하게 한다.
8. 아침자율학습시간을 사제동행 독서시간으로 활용한다.

Q 46 다문화 가족 학생 지도

Describe your guidance methods for the children from multicultural families, who cannot adjust to new school and environment.

예상답안

To deal with the students from multicultural families, the teacher can concern about guidance methods in several ways. First of all, having special lessons about multi-culturalism for all the students can be useful. As a teacher I can show appropriate documentary and video clips about multiculralism and have my students discuss about this issue. By doing so, I would be able to enhance students' understanding about their friends from multicultural family. I may also design a role-play or a simulation for students to be more open minded toward those who are from different cultural background.

Second, I would counsel with students from multicultural families. Through intensive counseling, I can figure out the area students need help and provide appropriate assistance for them. For example, for those who have difficulties in Korean language, the school can provide after school language programs. Leaning Korean, they will be able to achieve higher academic goals and enjoy their school lives more. To help them to be familiar with Korean culture, the school can offer them a buddy assistance program, in which they can make Korean friends and learn about Korean culture by visiting various traditional places such as Kyung-bok Gung and cooking traditional food like Kim-bob together.

Third, I will hold a multicultural festival where students and parents are invited to introduce their culture and this will help students to aware of the various aspects of culture. Specifically, there will be some sections or booths for each country. Participants are expected to walk around and experience what other families have prepared. In this way, not only parents but also students can raise their awareness of diverse culture.

답안 키워드

- documentary and video clips about multiculralism
- counsel with students from multicultural families
- multicultural festival

한국어 예상답안

1. 모든 학생을 대상으로 다문화 교육을 실시해야 한다. 모든 학생을 대상으로 다문화 이해 교육, 반편견교육, 세계시민교육을 체계적으로 실시한다. (창의적 재량활동, 방과후 학교, 다문화 체험프로그램을 활용) 그럴 때 일반 학생들이 다양한 문화를 수용하고 존중함으로써 순혈주의와 배타주의를 극복하고 사회적 약자인 다문화 가정의 자녀를 포용하는 태도를 배우며, 다문화 가정의 자녀들도 건전한 정체성과 인간관계를 형성할 것이다.
2. 다문화 가정 자녀를 위한 보상교육을 실시한다. 다문화 가정 자녀는 언어능력이 떨어지고 정체성 혼란을 겪고 있으며, 대인관계 형성에 어려움을 느끼고, 대부분 학습부진에 시달리므로 이 문제를 해결하려면 방과후 학교에 다문화 가정 자녀를 위한 보충학습을 실시하고 상담 프로그램을 운영하거나, 동급, 1:1도우미를 맺어주거나, 대학생 멘토링을 실시하거나, 다문화 가정 자녀를 종합적으로 지도해주는 전담교사를 배치해주어야 한다.
3. 다문화 가정 부모를 위한 사랑방을 운영한다. 사랑방은 한글교육, 우리문화 이해, 자녀교육

Q 47 다양한 배경의 학생을 다루는 데 요구되는 자질

Your class is mixed with students from all different backgrounds such as parents' social and economic status, single-parents family, multi-cultural family, and all different school performances, and etc. Describe one teacher's quality to manage this kind of heterogeneous class and give two concrete examples to make it practice.

예상답안

To manage heterogeneous class, which consists of students from all different backgrounds, the teachers need to have understanding and empathy towards their students. Then what they have to do to make it practice. First of all, the teacher can use journal writing where students can freely express their feelings and experiences during classes. After reading the students' journal, the teacher can add comment on the journal. By doing so, the teacher can be empathized with their students and improve their understanding toward them. secondly, the teacher can visit his students' families. This will be beneficial for teachers to know more about his students especially about their academic problems, and troubles in their family. thus the teacher can become more open-minded toward his students.

답안 키워드

- empathy toward their students
- use journal writing
- open-minded toward his students

> ⚠️ **답안작성 유의점**
>
> - **문제분석** : 이 질문은 교사가 갖추어야 할 자질과 그 자질을 향상하는 실천계획을 구체적으로 말해야 하는 문제이다.

이질적인 학생을 다 포용하면서 차별 없이 맞춤식 지도를 하는 자세가 가장 필요한 자질이다. 다시 말해 학부모의 재력, 가정환경, 학생의 성적과 외모에 상관없이 모든 학생을 공명정대하게 대하는 자질과 동시에 이질적인 학생들이 서로 잘 어울리고 잠재력을 꽃피워갈 수 있도록 맞춤식 지도를 할 수 있는 자질을 갖추어야 한다.

자질을 향상하는 실천계획

1) 전천후 상담능력을 기른다.
    이질적인 학생들을 차별하지 않고 맞춤식으로 지도하려면 더 전문적인 학습, 생활, 진로상담의 기법과 시스템을 배우고 적용해야 한다. 따라서 학생상담과 관련된 다양한 서적을 학습하고 상담관련 세미나, 워크샵, 연수 또는 이러닝을 활용해서 상담기술을 제고하고 학생상담 시스템을 구축한다.
2) 학생에게 설문조사를 실시하여 담임의 학급운영에 가장 절실하게 느끼는 것이 무엇인지 파악한다. 이질적인 학생들을 편견 없이 잠재성을 최대한 살려주는 방향으로 지도하려면 학생들이 마음 문을 열고 자신의 문제와 욕구를 솔직하게 드러내는 게 중요하다. 설문조사를 실시하면 학생이 담임과 학급운영과 관련하여 바라는 바를 정확하게 파악할 수 있다.
3) 방과후 다문화 가정 자녀나 학부모를 대상으로 한 프로그램에 참여한다. 다문화 가정 자녀 지도 문제는 점점 더 담임교사의 업무의 중요한 분야로 잘 잡아갈 것이다. 또 다문화 가정 자녀는 교육의 사각지대에 놓여 있는 아이들의 전형이기도 하다. 따라서 방과후 다문화 가정 자녀나 학부모를 대상으로 한 프로그램에 참여하여 일정한 역할을 맡아 봉사하면 이질적인 학생들을 차별 없이 이끌어 갈 수 있는 경험을 폭넓게 갖출 수 있을 것이다.
4) 이질적인 학급운영과 관련된 다양한 연수와 연구에 적극적으로 참여한다. 단위 학교나 지역 차원에서 이질적인 학급운영과 관련된 연수나 연구가 있다면 적극적 참여한다. 그래서 다양한 운영사례를 배우고 연구에 참여하여, 실제로 맡고 있는 학급에 적용할 수 있는 구체적인 방안을 도출하여 적용하는 데 힘쓴다.

Q 48 수행평가 고유의 취지를 살리기 위한 대책

Performance-based assessment becomes routine to lose their own values. Describe the four assessment methods to be implemented in the classroom to solve this problem.

예상답안

To keep the own values of performance-based assessment, the following four assessment methods need to be adopted in appropriate ways. First, essay writing should require students to think and express their own ideas creatively and logically. Second, discussion sessions allows students to exchange opposing opinions of students. In the process of expressing their thoughts and listening to other students' opinions, they can learn how to adjust contrasting ideas. Third, students can participate in project works where they can cooperate together to achieve one common goal. Interacting with each other, students can scaffold each other and develop their social skills. Fourth, portfolio can be effectively implemented to assess students' process of learning. Since it collects every single work of students throughout the semester, it allows for both teachers and students to observe each learning step of individual students.

답안 키워드

- essay writing for creative and logical thinking
- discussion to exchange opinions
- project work for cooperation

한국어 예상답안

① 서술형검사: 문제의 답을 학생이 직접 서술하도록 한다.
② 논술형검사: 개인의 생각이나 주장을 창의적이고 논리적이면서도 설득력있게 조직하여 작성하도록 한다.
③ 구술시험: 특정내용이나 주제에 대해 자신의 의견이나 생각을 발표하도록 하여 표현력, 의사소통력, 판단력 등을 평가한다.
④ 토론법: 서로 다른 의견을 제시할 수 있는 주제를 가지고, 찬성과 반대의견을 토론하는 과정에서의 준비성, 충실성, 논리성, 반대의견에 대한 태도, 토론 진행방법 등을 평가한다.
⑤ 면접법: 학생과 직접 면담하여 질문하고 대답하는 과정을 통해 평가한다.(말하기, 생활문제)
⑥ 보고서: 하나의 주제를 가지고 자료를 수집하고 분석종합하여 보고서를 작성하게 한다.

Q 49 학교 정보 공시제도의 장점

'Public Announcement Provisions of School Report' consists of faculty status, facilities, statistics of school violence, school hygiene, financial status, school meals, students academic achievement and etc. Discuss four advantages of enforcing 'Public Announcement Provisions of School Report' in secondary schools.

예상답안

There are four advantages of enforcing Public Announcement Provisions of School Report. First, it can fulfill the students and parents' right to know. Both students and parents can acquire objective information about their schools. And it can help them to choose a certain school and attend the school education. Second, based on the feedback from the Public Announcement Provisions of School Report, the quality of a school will improve. For example, if a school is evaluated low in handling students' violence, the school can implement follow-up measure to fix the problems. And this will result in students and parents' high satisfaction. Third, after the evaluation of Public Announcement Provisions of School Report, the government investment and local community assistance are provided. And this helps to narrow the gap among schools. Lastly, information from Public Announcement Provisions of School Report will foster the research on education. For example, if researchers find that the low rates of school violence results in high academic achievement, other schools will try to reduce school violence so that students can focus on studying.

답안 키워드

- students and parents' right to know
- the quality of a school to increase
- government investment and local community assistance

한국어 예상답안

1. 학생과 학부모의 알권리가 충족된다. 학생과 학부모는 학교에 대한 객관적인 정보를 정확히 알 수 있으며 이를 바탕으로 학교를 선택하고 학교 교육에 참여할 수 있다.
2. 단위학교에서는 학교 전반의 책무성과를 알 수 있다. 기초학력 미달학생에 대한 관심이 높아져 교육성과에 대한 교사들의 책임감을 높이고, 재정운영을 비롯해 경영의 투명성을 높여 학교의 신뢰도를 높이는 기회가 된다. 아울러 다른 학교들과 비교하여 강점은 더욱 강화하고 약점은 보강함으로써 여러 학교가 함께 성장할 수 있는 발판이 마련될 것으로 기대한다.
3. 지역사회에서는 지역 공교육에 대한 관심과 투자를 높여 나갈 수 있다. 객관적인 자료에 기초해 성장의 주요 인프라인 초·중·고등학교의 지원을 위한 근거가 제공되기 때문이다.
4. 학계에서는 그간 자료 부족으로 겪었던 어려움이 해소되어 각종 연구가 활기 있게 진행될 것으로 보인다. 정보 공시를 통해 객관적이고 다양한 자료가 제공되면 교육 현안과 관련된 여러 주제에 대한 정책 및 학술연구가 가능하다.
5. 지역 간, 학교 간 교육격차를 해소하는 데 기여한다. 시도교육청에서도 학교나 지역별 특성을 고려한 정책수립과 지원이 더욱 활발히 이루어 질 것으로 전망한다. 정부도 부족한 부분에 대한 지원을 강화해 교육경쟁력을 높이는 계기가 될 것이다.

Q 50 교사로서의 교육에 대한 전망

You are given a part of Martin Luther King's speech 'I have dream' (… *I have a dream that one day even the state of Mississippi, a state sweltering with the heat of injustice, sweltering with the heat of oppression, will be transformed into an oasis of freedom and justice. I have a dream that my four little children will one day live in a nation where they will not be judged by the color of their skin but by the content of their character.*…) Discuss your vision on education including pedagogical principles, aims, maxims and portraits of teachers and students.

예상답안

Education is not just another career but more of a mission to raise young people to a whole-grounded person. So, any of the students should not be discriminated for a reason of school grades, family background, or even disability in school. In this way, we should have a school where every student and teacher can be proud of attending. For this purpose to be achieved, teacher should have integrity and pride in raising future leaders and keep professionalism to teach their major areas.

답안 키워드

① Education to focus on discovering Ss' talent, specialty and traits. (부모님이 원하거나, 인기 있는 직업을 passive하게 선택하기 보다는 하고 싶은 일에 종사 할 수 있게 한다.)
② Education to focus on building up Ss' cooperative spirits (더불어 사는 사회)
③ Education should provide Ss with fair opportunity on achieving social status. (학생들이 노력을 하면 무엇이든 그들이 원하는 것을 할 수 있다.)
④ Education to establish Ss' morality and humanity (학교는 학력신장 뿐만 아니라, 학생의 personality, good attitude 형성에 노력하고 도움을 줄 수 있다.)

> ⚠️ **답안작성 유의점**
>
> - **문제분석** : 개방형 질문이다. 전인교육이라는 관점을 유지하면서 자신의 비전(교육철학, 교육목표, 교사관, 학생관, 교육과 관련된 좌우명)을 풀어나간다.

- 성적순으로 한 줄 세우는 교육이 아니라 특기와 적성으로 여러 줄 세우는 학교
- 건전한 인성과 창의력을 갖춘 글로벌 인재가 키워지는 학교
- 왕따와 폭력이 없이 서로 존중하고 사랑하는 공동체적 학교 문화가 구현된 학교
- 성적, 가정환경, 외모, 장애 등을 이유로 차별 받지 않고 교육 받을 수 있는 환경이 실현된 학교, 특히 소외계층 자녀들과 다문화 가정 자녀들의 학습권이 보장된 학교
- 교사의 권위가 서고 전문직의 교직풍토가 자리 잡아 교사가 전문성과 긍지를 가지고 보람을 느끼며 가르칠 수 있는 학교
- 교육공동체의 각 주체들이 민주적인 관계를 바탕으로 서로 존중하고 협력하는 학교

Q 51 소외학생 지도방안

Describe how you would guide the students who are isolated from other classmates in your class.

예상답안

To guide the isolated students to adjust to the classroom, I suggest the following ways. First, I'll help them recognize themselves in a positive way. When they respect themselves, they can be respected from others. To do that, I'll find out their strengths and make a compliment to them. For example, I can give them some easy mission. When they complete the mission, I will provide a reward. Through this, they will build their self-confidence. This is the first step to make the friendship with other students.

Second, I'll give some tips how to communicate well with others. It will be useful because miscommunication is the main reason of the conflict between people. So the isolated students should be able to think on the part of others. They have to know how to catch the others' needs and wants. Then, they can react to their partners properly in conversation. Once they become the effective communicator, they can appeal to other students' friendliness.

Finally, I believe it is essential to help students build up a sense of community. It is because community spirit enables them to understand and respect others. To give them chances to put themselves in someone else's shoes and make a close relationship with others, I'll implement a variety of activities in my class. For example, a field day, training activities, voluntary work and student committee can be effective ways to foster cooperative classroom atmosphere.

답안 키워드

① T encourages and praises Ss through counseling. (self-efficacy and confidence↑)
② T makes Ss aware that he is the important person in the classroom. (T gives Ss specific roles in the classroom: group leader, collecting the assignments)
③ T help Ss to establish collaborative spirits. (a lot of group activities and volunteer activities, mini Olympic)
④ T teaches Ss effective communicate skills.
- How to start the conversation
- How to response appropriately
- How to show their empathy to their interlocutor
- How to end the conversation

한국어 예상답안

1. 칭찬과 격려를 통해서 자아정체감을 형성해준다(자아존중감을 높여준다). 칭찬은 고래도 춤추게 한다고 했다. 그 아이의 장점을 발견하고 (의도적으로 심부름을 시키거나 또래지도자가 되는 경험을 갖게 하는 것도 한 가지 방법) 칭찬해주면 자기방어와 열등감, 그리고 막연한 죄의식에서 벗어나 자신감을 갖고 자신을 사랑하게 된다. 자신에 대한 존중과 긍정이 풍부하고 만족스러운 친구관계의 첫걸음이다.
2. 긍정적인 의사소통법을 알려준다.
진정한 의사소통은 다른 사람을 배려하는 것으로부터 시작된다. 다른 사람의 감정 상태를 읽고, 상대가 원하는 것이 무엇인지 알아서 이를 배려할 줄 아는 기술을 습득하게 하면 그 학생은 어디에서나 환영을 받을 것이다. 그 중에서도 다른 아이들과 대화할 때 긍정의 언어를 사용하며 상대방의 기운을 북돋아주는 훈련을 집중적으로 시키면 다른 아이들의 친근감을 느끼고 다가올 것이다.
3. 평소에 아이들에게 공동체 의식을 길러준다. 공동체 의식이 있어야 서로 마음을 열고, 이해하고, 존중하고 가까워질 수 있다. 따라서 반 체육대회, 조별활동, 수련활동, 자치활동, 봉사활동, 칭찬릴레이, 선플달기 같은 다양한 체험을 중심으로 함께하는 학급 분위기를 조성해준다.

Q 52 방과후 수업참여율을 높이는 방안

Students do not participate in after-school class implemented by school. Describe the reasons of the low participation and its solutions.

예상답안

The low participation of after-school classes is derived from three different reasons. First of all, the after-school classes cannot satisfy students' various needs. Each of the students has different learning styles and English proficiency. So, we should survey what they want and what their proficiency level is through needs analysis. Secondly, the after-school classes are considered to be just another form of the regular classroom activities. As a result, students get easily bored what they learn in the after-school classes. To motivate students, the school can let students know that the after-school classes will be exciting with various programs. Lastly, the school can change parents' negative attitude toward the after-school classes through inviting them to a model class. If they monitor how teachers teach their children, parents would send their children to the after-school classes.

답안 키워드

이유	해결책
① Not various programs (only focus on academic achievement not developing Ss' specialties) ② Lack of qualified Ts • There are not many Ts who can manage the diverse fields as they have knowledge only about their subject matters. • They do not have time and opportunities to learn special fields to guide Ss. ③ Parents are not well informed of the program. • parents who don't know the existence of the program itself and don't know how to sign up for the lesson ④ Poor school environment • not various materials, poor facilities (no swimming pool, lack of science labs)	① Needs analysis • 학문뿐 아니라 흥미/trait 고려한 프로그램 마련 (sports, cooking, music) ② Teacher training • Subject matter Knowledge만 키우기 위한 연수 뿐 아니라, diverse experience를 제공하는 연수 마련 ③ Outside instructor/local community network • 모든 것을 학교에서 다 준비 X : For some programs, school invites specialist on those fields. ④ More financial supports • So that schools can be equipped with special facilities (swimming pool, cooking room) ⑤ regular school correspondences to the parents or caretaker

한국어 예상답안

특히 참여율을 제고하려면
1. 다채로운 방과후 학교 홍보
2. 수요자의 요구조사 및 반영 (가정통신문, 학교 홈피, 방과후 학교 설문지, 방과후 학교 학부모 공개수업, 방과후 컨설팅을 통해 조언과 평가를 수집하여 반영)
3. 교직원과 학부모 연수(긍정적인 마인드 형성, 협조체계 구축)와 같은 방법이 있다.

Q 53 체벌반대의견

Do you agree or disagree with corporal punishment?

예상답안

I disagree with the corporal punishment implemented on students because of several reasons. Firstly, the corporal punishment might change students' misbehavior for a short period of time, but actually, it will make the situation worse. Second, students would feel frustrated and fear by the corporal punishment. Moreover, there are some possibilities that their intrinsic discovery learning will be prohibited by the punishment. For the third reason, the corporal punishment would reinforce students' aggressive behavior. Fourthly, we cannot guarantee that the corporal punishment is always conducted reasonably. If teachers get too much emotional, we cannot say that the punishment is educationally appropriate. Lastly, the school should always respect each of the students as a human being. But the corporal punishment is not the way to respect their self-identity.

답안 키워드

① only temporal effect : It cannot be the fundamental method and does not help correct Ss' misbehavior in the long term.
② It will interfere with building up a good rapport between T and Ss.
  - Forming a close rapport is very important for Ss to enjoy their school life.
  - Physical punishment will make Ss feel apathy against their T.
③ It will make Ss have negative ego.
  - low self efficacy, confidence↓, self respect↓
④ S cannot become an autonomous learner.
  - Ss are not likely to actively participate in the class.
  - In order to avoid the punishment, Ss just respond passively.
⑤ Corporal punishment most often produces in Ss' anger, resentment.
  - It teaches violence and revenge as solutions to problems.

한국어 예상답안

- 체벌은 일시적인 효과는 있을지 모르나, 체벌의 계속적인 사용은 문제행동의 악화를 초래하기도 한다.
- 체벌은 학생의 공포심을 자극하여 자발적인 탐구정신을 억압함으로써 학습과정에 지장을 초래한다.
- 체벌을 받은 학생은 교사와 사회에 대한 공격성이 증가하고 폭력을 학습하게 된다.
- 체벌은 상당히 교사의 감정에 좌우되고 감정이 격한 상태에서 이루어질 가능성이 많기 때문에 체벌이 합리적이고 온건하게 이루어진다는 보장이 없다.
- 체벌은 인간의 존엄성을 해치고 부정적인 자아개념을 형성한다. 인간의 이성적 가치를 가르쳐야 할 교육기관에서 교사의 체벌은 오히려 학생들에게 이성적인 문제해결이 아니라 불합리한 문제해결 방법을 가르치게 된다.

Q 54 학습의욕이 없는 학생을 참여시키는 방법

If your student asks "Why do I have to study English" on the first day of first year of middle school, what would you answer? Discuss your answers with concrete examples.

예상답안

It is important to make students aware of the significance of learning English to encourage students' motivation. First of all, I'll introduce various examples that show how English is related to their real life. By recognizing correlation between learning English and their real life, they will be more interested and engaged in English class. Secondly, I'll let them know students can benefit from learning English when they choose their occupation in the future. To be specific, as the world is globalized, English competence is one of the prerequisite ability in the job market. If they are proficient enough to communicate in English, they would be a competitive candidate for their career in the future.

Thirdly, I'll explain that English language proficiency might have a great influence on students' academic success in universities whatever their major is. There are lots of cases that the books and articles about almost all fields are written in English. Thus, to expand knowledge, they should learn English to build on and share expertise in their field.

Finally, students can broaden their view of the world by communicating with others in English. If students are able to interact with foreigners in English, they can have opportunities to share their opinion about what they are interested. Also, they can understand various cultures of different countries better. In this way, students can improve their quality of life and have a competitive power in the globalized society.

답안 키워드

① Culture
- a lot of opportunities to encounter various cultures (In this globalized era, by using the international language, English, we can communicate with people from different cultures, Ss can broaden their eye-sight)

② In-depth study for their major
- many books are published in English. So, if you can speak English you can get up-to-date knowledge without waiting until it is translated into Korean can enter university abroad

③ Future career
- There will be much more opportunities to select their future career. (There are a lot of companies which share technology with other global companies—such companies require fluent English speaking employees)

④ Volunteering
- Ss can do rewarding works in developing countries.

한국어 예상답안

① 배우는 교과가 학생의 실제 생활과 어떻게 연관되어 있고 적용되고 있는지 구체적인 사례를 통해서 알려줌으로써 흥미와 학습동기를 유발하겠다.
② 배우는 교과에서 습득하는 지식과 기술이 학생의 진로와 어떻게 연결될 수 있는지, 즉, 교과와 관련된 직업세계는 어떤 모습을 띠고 있는지 구체적인 사례를 통해 알려줌으로써 학습동기를 유발하겠다.
③ 꼭 학생이 선택할 진로나 직업에 직접적으로 연관되지 않더라도 자기를 실현하고 행복한 삶을 살아가는 데 배우는 교과의 지식과 기술이 중요한 역할을 한다는 것을 설득하여 흥미와 학습동기를 유발하겠다.
④ 이 교과를 열심히 배우면 좋은 점 10가지라는 형태로 다양한 측면(전인발달의 측면, 생활과 직업의 측면)으로 필요성을 접근하여 흥미와 학습동기를 유발한다.

Q 55 학생들의 이기주의 극복을 위한 건강한 가치와 태도를 가르치는 방법

These days, students are over-protected by their parents and become egocentric and selfish. Describe the ways how you guide the students to keep healthy values and attitudes in themselves with concrete examples.

예상답안

1. I will help students to develop living habits, community spirit, and information ethics through various activities, training, and volunteer activities.
   - It is more important for the students to internalize healthy values and attitudes from a variety of experiences than cognitive understanding.
   - I will help the students to develop their autonomy and democratic decision-making while they collaborate and solve the problems in the class and school by reinforcing the independent student activity.
   - I will teach the students information ethics focusing on experience in order to build healthy society that people understand and collaborate each other in cyberspace.
2. I will employ more group activities in the school so that the students can be more considerate and polite to each other and respect others' opinions.
3. I will make the students write a journal about filial behavior and do some campaign so that the students can be aware of the value of family, respect the elders, have good relationship with frients, and care for juniors.
4. I will help the students to form a habit of saving by doing the campaign that leave the used uniforms and textbooks.
5. I will make the students have a moment of meditation in the morning. Also, I will do the campaigns such as compliment relay, writing good comments, and using polite language.

답안 키워드

- Build up cooperative spirits. (club activities, group activities, close relationships, develop social skills)

- Activate volunteering activities (help Ss have rewarding experience of helping others, make peaceful society)
- Create a special session for praising. (For example, each S says 3 good points about their pairs → lively atmosphere, form a good habit of looking on the bright side)

한국어 예상답안

① 기본생활습관, 공동체의식, 정보윤리를 자치활동, 수련활동, 봉사활동 같은 실천과 체험을 통해 길러주겠다.
  - 인지적 이해보다도 다양한 체험을 통한 내면화가 중요
  - 학생자치활동을 내실화하여 학급과 학교에서 일어나는 제 문제에 적극적으로 협의 실천하는 가운데 자주성과 사회성, 민주적 의사결정을 기르게 한다.
  - 다양한 봉사활동을 경험하게 하고 궁극적으로 사율적인 봉사활동 소식을 만들어 운영하게 하여 서로 협력하는 태도, 타인을 배려하는 너그러운 마음, 더불어 살아가는 공동체의식을 길러준다.
  - 사이버 공간에서도 서로 배려하고 협력하는 건강한 문화를 조성해갈 수 있도록 정보윤리 교육을 체험 중심으로 실시한다.
② 학교생활에서 모둠활동을 많이 시켜 남을 배려할 줄 알고, 민주적으로 의사소통할줄 알고, 서로 예절을 지킬줄 아는 습관이 형성되게 하겠다.
③ 효행일기 쓰기와 효행의 달 행사를 통해 가족의 소중함을 알고 어른을 존중하고 친구와 우애하고 아래 학년을 사랑하는 품성을 길러주겠다.
④ 교복과 교과서를 물려주는 운동을 벌여 아껴 쓰고, 나눠 쓰고, 바꿔 쓰고, 다시 쓰는 절약정신을 길러주겠다.
⑤ 아침 명상의 시간을 운영하고 칭찬 릴레이 운동, 선플 달기 운동, 고운말쓰기 운동 등을 실시하겠다.

Q 56 교장에게 혼자 해결하기 어려운 업무를 배정받을 경우

This is your second-year in your teaching. Your principal suggests you organize the mid & long-term plan for school. You believe that this would be over your limits. How would you accept the principal's suggestion? Suppose that you are explaining it to your principal.

예상답안

- I would tell the principal that I will do my best to organize the plan because there must be a reason for him to ask to me. So, it could be an opportunity for self-development and for contributing to the school administration.
- However, I think it is impossible and inappropriate to make the plan by myself since I'm only in my second year. So, I will consult with senior teachers and experts so that I could build the network with those people to get advice about making the plan.
- After that, I will analyze the previous plan to list the problems and what to improve, and collect the applicable exemplary causes. Also, in the process of organizing the plan, I will modify and complement the plan by receiving experts' advice and then summit the final plan.

답안 키워드

- An opportunity for self-development and for contributing to the school administration.

- Consult with senior teachers and experts.
- Analyze the previous plan to list the problems and improvements.

한국어 예상답안

- 최선을 다해 짜보겠다고 말씀드리겠다. 왜냐하면 2년차인데 학교 중장기 계획을 짤 것을 부탁했다면 그럴 만한 이유가 있을 것이다. 그래서 비록 자신에게 버거운 일이라 할지라도 한편으로는 자기발전의 계기로 삼고 또 한편으로는 학교 교육행정에 이바지한다는 각오로 열심히 도전해 보겠다.
- 그런데 초임교사 혼자의 힘으로 중장기 계획을 짠다는 것은 불가능한 일일 뿐만 아니라 바람직하지도 않은 일이므로 가장 먼저 교장, 교감, 부장교사, 선배교사, 학원위원, 그리고 기타 전문가에게 자문을 구하겠다. 그래서 업무를 수행하는 데 꼭 고려해야 하고 참고할 만한 내용이 무엇인지 파악하고 향후 다양한 자문을 해줄 지원 네트워크를 구성하겠다.
- 그 다음에 학교에서 이전에 수립했던 중장기 계획을 분석하여 문제점과 개선점이 무엇인지 정리해보고, 관련 자료와 다른 학교의 우수사례도 수집하여 적용 가능한 것이 있는지 검토해 보겠다. 계획을 수집하는 과정에서도 수시로 다른 교원과 전문가에게 자문을 받아 수정 보완하여 최종안을 올리겠다.

Q 57 학업성적이 높은 학생과 낮은 학생 모두 수업에 집중할 수 있도록 만드는 방법

There are mixed students who achieve high academic-performance and vice versa in a class. Describe the teaching and learning methods that students from both sides all achieve the learning objectives. (When you manage the class, you can find some students are interested in the lesson and actively involve the activities but some other students are passive and not interested in the class. Are there any methods to guide these low motivated students to reach the lesson aims?)

예상답안

① In terms of school lessons, student-centered lessons should be employed instead of teacher-centered ones. In order to do that, first of all, level-differentiated learning needs to be promoted to satisfy both the advanced and the low-level students. Level differentiated learning can be done by ability grouping or group activities. Secondly, students' self-directed learning is recommended. In the self-directed learning, the teacher should not teach by rote or emphasize memorization during the teaching. In contrast, students' experiences are expected and student-led discussion occurs accompanying problem solving, inquiry learning, NIE, cooperative learning. Furthermore, various multimedia and information communication technology can effectively raise students' interest and promote blended learning, in which students take the active role in learning. Thirdly, it is important to stimulate students' motivation. The teacher can build in students' confidence by introducing examples about overcoming difficulties and have students actively engage in learning.

② Outside the class, after-school activity should be utilized for successful level-differentiated learning by complementing or deepening students' knowledge according to their level.

③ In addition, the teacher may focus on the students' attaining fundamental academic ability. Lastly, cyber teaching and learning center can be employed on the school website to support tailored learning.

답안 키워드

- Level differentiated learning can be done by ability grouping or group activities. Secondly, students' self-directed learning is recommended.
- Outside the class, after-school activity should be utilized.
- The teacher may focus on the students' attaining fundamental academic ability.
- Cyber teaching and learning center can be employed on the school website.

한국어 예상답안

① 정규 수업에서 교사 중심의 수업에서 벗어나서 학생 중심의 수업을 해야 한다.
- 일제식 수업을 지양하고 수준별 수업을 강화해야 한다.
  - 교과의 특성을 살려 능력별 집단편성을 하여 수준별 이동수업, 학급 내 분단수업을 적극적으로 활용 한다.
- 교사 중심의 주입식, 암기식 수업을 지양하고 학생중심의 자기주도적 학습을 강화해야 한다.
  - 학생의 경험을 존중하고 학생이 학습주도권을 질 수 있는 토론학습, 문제해결학습, 탐구학습, NIE 수업, 협동학습과 같은 다양한 교수 학습 방법을 활용한다.
  - 다양한 교육매체를 활용하되 특히 ICT활용수업을 적극 도입한다. 특히 학생이 N세인 것을 고려해서 사이버 가정학습과 결합된 온 오프 혼합형 수업으로 학생의 흥미를 유발하고 자기 주도적 학습을 이끈다.
- 학습동기를 적극적으로 유발한다.
  - 학생과 관심과 호기심을 끄는 사례를 제시하고, 나도 할 수 있겠다는 자신감을 불어넣어준다. 또 칭찬과 보상을 통해 학습에 능동적으로 참여하도록 이끈다.
② 방과후 학교를 활성화해야 한다.
- 수준별 교과 프로그램을 마련하여 학생이 자기 수준에 맞게 심화 보충 수업을 받게 한다.
③ 기초학력 책임 지도제를 철저히 실시한다. 학교 홈페이지에 사이버 교수 학습 센터를 구축하여 가정에서도 인터넷을 이용하여 원하는 분야를 원하는 수준으로 맞춤식 수업을 받을 수 있게 한다.

Q 58 학교폭력을 당한 학생에 대한 피해자 대처방법

There were incidents of school violence and extortion of money. The student who got suffered from the incidents reported this to you. Describe the ways how you would guide these both students as an assault and a victim.

예상답안

① I will relax him and check his physical and mental states first.
② After that, I will try to talk with him by guaranteeing personal security and secrecy. Most of the victims tend to be afraid of telling what happened due to the fear of revenge. Teacher should show the students the strong will to protect them and let them know there are many organizations to help them such as police office and school faculty.
③ As the victims start talking, we should think on his position and give him the full support about this situation.
④ We should tell him that we will pay more attention to this problem and do our best to help the victim to adapt to the school life.

⑤ The victim is intimidated under the fear and negative thinking. Teacher should calm the victim and seek for objective circumstantial judgement and reasonable solutions.
⑥ If the problem is slight, we can help the victim to solve this problem by himself. Encourage the victim to express his strong will to the bully and get the bully's apology. If necessary, suggest the victim to accompany his friends when he comes to school and goes back home. In addition, we can help him to get along with friends and monitor his school life regularly.
⑦ Collaborating with counseling expert and introducing the group counceling program to the victims could be helpful.

답안 키워드

For victims
- relax and check his physical and mental states
- counseling
- full support

한국어 예상답안

① 불안한 피해학생의 마음을 우선 안정시키고, 학생의 신체적, 정신적 상태를 점검한다.
② 신변 안전보호와 비밀보장을 약속하여 대화를 유도한다. 피해학생은 대부분 보복에 대한 두려움으로 말하기를 꺼린다. 따라서 교사가 피해학생을 끝까지 지켜주려고 한다는 의지를 보여주고 피해학생에게 경찰서를 비롯한 주변에 도움을 줄 수 있는 강력한 기관이 있음을 알게 한다.
③ 피해 학생이 이야기를 시작하면, 일단 피해학생의 입장에서 생각하고 모든 이야기를 전적으로 수용한다. 피해학생의 아픔을 이해하며 상처가 아물고 학교생활에 잘 적응할 수 있도록 더욱 관심을 가지고 보살피겠다고 말한다. 피해학생은 심리적으로 위축된 상태에서 다분히 주관적인 공포감에 휩싸여 있고 부정적인 사고에 지배된다. 교사의 입장에서 피해학생을 안심시키되, 객관적인 상황판단과 합리적인 해결방안을 모색해야 한다.
④ 문제의 정도가 경미할 경우, 피해학생이 스스로 문제를 해결할 수 있도록 유도한다. 피해학생이 직접 가해학생에게 거절과 거부의 의사를 표현하고, 상대방의 사과를 당당하게 받도록 유도하고 용기를 준다.
⑤ 필요한 경우 등하교 시 다른 친구와 함께 동행하게 해준다. 피해 학생이 위축되지 않고 친구들과 잘 지낼 수 있도록 도와주며 정상적인 또래 집단 어울릴 수 있도록 유도하고 지속적으로 학교생활을 정기적으로 점검하여 폭력의 피해를 받지 않도록 보호한다.
⑥ 피해학생을 위한 집단상담 프로그램에 참여하게 한다. 전문상담교사와 협력하여 문제를 해결한다.

Q 59 학생들이 참여하고 싶은 학교 만드는 방안

You teach English at middle school, Inchon. Your school was newly appointed as a model school in your community. Your school makes an effort to make a 'good school'. Describe four concrete methods to become the school where students want to attend.

예상답안

To make the school become the place where students want to attend, academical aspects as well as personality education should be considered. First off, in terms of academical aspects, the school should provide curriculums that are interesting and real life-related to make students motivated to participate. To realize this, classroom activities should be implemented in the learner-centered way rather than the teacher-centered one since students have more responsibility and willingness to take part in the activities when they have initiative in their learning process. In addition utilizing a variety of technologies could be effective. Through this, students can be facilitated to study because they carry tons of multi-media files which can foster students' interest. Moreover, with the computer-programmed instruction, students can be given appropriate level of tasks suitable for individual proficiency level. Another alternation to raise students' participation in terms of the academic performance is utilizing various after-school programs. These programs enable students to take part in various courses beyond standard school curriculums based on their own needs or interest.

Next, teachers should consider students' individual personality at the same time. To do this, the personality education in school should be strengthened so that students can raise their sense of community and realize they have each other's backs among the students. In addition, teachers should do their best to keep the classroom circumstances neat and comfortable in which students can concentrate on their study without interruption caused by classroom environment. Based on the comfortable environment, teachers should treat each student fairly and let students know how much they concern about individual student. This can be realized through regular counseling and student guidance in democratic way given by teachers. Like this, we can make students attend to school voluntarily by providing interesting and challenging learning materials and suitable environment.

답안 키워드

academical aspects	personality education
learner-centered way	a sense of community
variety of technologies	safe and comfortable environment
various after-school programs	regular counseling and student guidance

> ⚠️ **답안작성 유의점**
>
> - **문제분석**: 말하고자 하는 주제의 영역을 정한 후에 말할 수 있도록 한다. 어느 때 학생이 학교가기 싫겠는가? 수업이 재미없고, 따분하고, 지루할 때, 그리고 학교폭력, 왕따가 횡행하고 성적이 모든 것의 판단 기준이 되어 공동체적 관계를 상실했을 때일 것이다. 즉 전인교육(학력+인성)적 측면에서 답변을 해주어야 하는 질문이다.
>
> 1. 수업이 재미있고 유익할 때 학생이 오고 싶어 한다(학력)
>   - 교사 중심의 수업이 아니라 학생중심의 수업을 하는 학교일 때 오고 싶어 한다.
>   - 공부하는 것이 자기 수준에 맞을 때 [일제식 수업-맞춤형 수업(수준별 수업)]
>   - 흥미와 관심을 느껴서 공부를 하고 싶을 때 [억지로 떠밀려서 하는 암기식 주입식 수업, 흥미를 느껴서 하는 자기 주도적 학습, 개방적이고 허용적인 분위기에서 창의성을 신장 해주는 수업]
>   - N세대에 알맞게 재미있게 가르칠 때 (칠판과 분필에 의존하는 수업- N세대에 맞는 아이시티를 활용한 다양한 수업)
>   - 끼를 살려주고 다양한 진로를 알려줄 때 (성적만 강조하는 수업 ×, 특기와 적성을 살려주는 수업, 다양한 진로를 소개하고 선택하는 수업)

- 칭찬과 격려가 있는 수업, 긍정적 예언이 있는 수업을 할 때(꾸중과 질책으로 위축되어 있는 아이들, 가정과 학교에서 듣는 부정적인 예언으로 할 수 없다는 무력감에 빠진 아이들)
2. 함께 하는 분위기, 즉 서로 존중해주고 아껴 주는 공동체적 관계가 학교에 살아 있을 때 오고 싶어 한다.
    - 마음을 터놓고 말할 수 있고 어려울 때 도와주고 항상 존중해주는 친구가 있는 학교
    - 폭력과 왕따 없는 학교=공동체의식을 심어주는 실천중심의 인성교육 가정환경과 성적, 장애 때문에 친구에게 차별 받지 않는 학교
3. 학생에게 개개인에게 관심을 보여주고 인격적으로 대해주는 보고 싶은 교사가 있을 때 오고 싶어 한다. (인성)
    - 징계와 처벌 중심의 강압적인 생활지도가 아닌 민주적이고 인격적인 생활지도가 있는 학교
    - 교사가 특정학생을 편애하거나 차별하지 않고 모든 학생을 공평 정대하게 대하는 학교
    - 교사의 온 오프라인을 통한 지속적인 상담을 잘 해주는 학급
4. 쾌적하고 청결한 환경조성으로 공부할 마음이 솟구치게 하는 학교환경이 조성되어 있을 때 오고 싶어 한다. (환경)
    - 안전사고가 없는 학교
    - 집처럼 편안함을 주면서도 집중할 수 있는 분위기가 조성된 학교
    - 다채로운 내용으로 환경정리가 잘 된 학교
5. 방과후에 다채로운 프로그램으로 학생의 욕구를 충족시켜주는 학교
    - 방과후에 질 높은 교과, 특기적성, 돌봄 프로그램을 다양하게 학교에서 운영해주어 원하는 과목을 원하는 수준으로 들을 수 있는 학교
    - 어려운 가정환경의 아이들은 이런 프로그램을 무료로 수강할 수 있게 하는 학교

Q 60 좋은 선생님이란?

If you had a good teacher and a bad teacher in your school days, tell us the reasons for saying that and their influences on you with some concrete examples.

예상답안

There are several conditions for a good teacher. First, democratic teacher who loves students and treat them equally is a good teacher. Second, being witty and open about multiple values can be another condition for a being a good teacher. Third, to have a strong sense of morality in education and insight into human quality education is also an important condition. Fourth, it is required for a respectable teacher to provide whole-person education and keep a balance between academic achievement and development students' character. To be specific, a good teacher encourages students to think creatively trying to draw out students' potential ability. Also, a good teacher aims for the best in carrying out his job of teaching. Sixth, another condition for a good teacher can be said that he empathizes students and utilizes multimedia in the class intending to maximize effectiveness in the class. Lastly, only a teacher who continuously studies his subject can be a good teacher.

답안 키워드

① Democratic teacher who loves students and treat them equally
② Being witty and open about multiple values
③ A strong sense of morality in education and insight into human quality education

④ A respectable teacher to provide whole-person education and keep a balance between academic achievement and development students' character.
⑤ A teacher who continuously studies his subject

> **⚠ 답안작성 유의점**
>
> **문제분석:** 넓게는 교육관을, 좁게는 교사관을 통틀어서 묻는 문제이다. 나쁜 선생님의 예로 방임형, 강압형 교사의 예를 들고 좋은 선생님의 예로 민주형 교사의 예를 들어주면 출제자가 원하는 답변을 할 수 있다.

- 학생을 사랑하고 민주적으로 대하는 교사
- 유머감각이 풍부하고 개방적이고 다원적인 가치를 지닌 교사
- 확고한 윤리의식을 가지고 늘 인간성 향상에 힘쓰는 교사
- 전인교육의 관점을 바탕으로 인성함양과 학력신장을 조화롭게 추구하는 교사
  - 건전한 인성의 기초 위에 창의력을 발휘하도록 이끌어주는 교사
  - 학습지도와 생활지도에 능통한 교사
  - 학생의 강점을 발견하고 키워줄줄 아는 교사
  - 수업만큼은 최고를 지향하는 교사
- 학생들의 정서를 이해하고 ICT를 자유자재로 활용할 줄 하는 교사
- 늘 연구하고 학습하는 교사

Q 61 수준별 수업의 효과적 진행방법

> There are some schools of only one class in Kyungbook province. Describe how level-differentiated lesson could be managed.

예상답안

First of all, I would organize a homogeneous group based on their proficiency level or do an instruction on individual basis. To be more specific, I would divide students based on their academic achievement and competency. I would adopt individual instruction in which I teach students considering their individual levels while I teach the whole class. Secondly, Level-differentiated class can be supported through Internet Advanced lesson as extra class. To use Internet in the class, the teacher and students can access to a cyber learning portal that provides level-differentiated learning method. With help of the portal site, students can get further or supplementary instruction if they need.

답안 키워드

① Organize a homogeneous group based on their proficiency level.
② Divide students based on their academic achievement and competency.
③ Level-differentiated class can be supported through Internet Advanced lesson.
④ Give further or supplementary instruction if they need.

한국어 예상답안

① 학급 내 능력별 동질집단을 편성하거나 개별지도 형태로 수준별 수업을 진행한다.
  - 성취, 능력 변인에 따라 수준별 분단/조를 편성하여 수업을 진행한다.
  - 개별 지도 형태로, 즉 전체학생을 지도하면서 개인적으로 수준에 맞게 지도한다.
② 인터넷을 이용하여 심화 보충학습을 실시하는 형태로 수준별 수업을 지원한다.
  - 수준별 학습을 할 수 있는 사이버 학습 포탈에 접속하여 심화 보충학습을 할 수 있다.

Q 62. 컴퓨터 게임 중독학생에 대한 대처방안과 예시

> There has been an increasing number of young people who are addicted to computer games. Your school has decided to take some actions on that matter. Discuss the measures to guide Internet game-addicted students with concrete examples.

예상답안

These days, we have too many students who are addicted to Internet game. So we have to find out the solutions for this. First, as a solution, I would suggest a regular moral education about the Internet to the students, so they can learn about adverse effect of the Internet and they also can learn how to control properly their desire to play the Internet game.

Second, school needs to provide to students something more interesting than the Internet game. Various after-school activities that would fit the students' interest could be the examples for this.

Third, the most students who are addicted to game usually don't have many friends and they are very introvert. For this problem, the teacher needs to have great consideration on them for their better relationship with their classmates, by implementing individual counselling and giving advise to them.

Fourth, it is the fundamental consideration that we have to find out the main reason of their addiction to the game. And then we can make the solutions according to the reasons. For example, we can have an interview with their parents of friends so we can find out what kind of situation make them only play the game.

Fifth, we need to let them know how to handle well between the things they have to do and the thins they want to do. For example, we can teach them that they have to do what they have to do before they play the "LOL" which is very popular game in these days.

Sixth, we need to lead them eventually to be a person who can control themselves. For this reason, letting them run a program that they can self-test their Internet addiction will be an appropriate solution.

Seventh, they usually are not good at handling their stress very well. So it is important to teach them how to deal with their stress properly by using some method such as trying to change their mind from what they have been believed in the wrong way to the one in the right way, and such a method about the way of deep breathing and stretching.

Eighth, cooperation with their parents is also an important one for their addiction problem. For this, we need to contact their parents regulary and share any information that would help.

And ninth, finally, among the solutions for the addiction, the most important one is the prevention, of course. It is hard to recover once they become addicted. So we have to give enough instruction regarding this issue.

답안 키워드

① Find out the main reason of their addiction to the game.
② Suggest a regular moral education about the Internet to the students.
③ Learn how to control properly their desire to play the Internet game.
④ Provide to students something more interesting after-school activities.
⑤ Develop students' friendship for better relationship with their classmates.
⑥ Nurture them eventually to be a person who can control themselves.
⑦ Teach them how to deal with their stress properly by using some method.
⑧ Cooperate with their parents.
⑨ Find methods of prevention and give enough instruction regarding this issue.

한국어 예상답안

1. 정기적으로 올바른 정보통신 윤리교육을 실시해야 한다. 사용법 위주로 편성되어 있는 현행 인터넷교육이 대폭 개편하여 정보통신 윤리교육을 실시할 때, 학생들은 정보화의 역기능을 정확히 이해하고 자제력을 키워갈 수 있을 것이다.
2. 학교가 인터넷 게임보다도 더 재미있는 일(운동)을 제공해줄 수 있어야 한다. 동아리 활동이나 특기적성활동 등을 활용하여 다양한 놀이문화의 장을 소개하고 건강한 취미활동을 펼칠 수 있도록 도와주어야 한다.
3. 학생들이 원만한 대인관계를 형성하도록 유도하는 것이다. 대부분 소외되거나 내성적인 학생들이 컴퓨터에 빠지는 경우가 많으므로 교사가 관심과 의도적인 교우관계 지도가 필요하다.
4. 왜 인터넷에 빠지게 되었는지 현실적인 원인(맞벌이 부부의 자녀 방임, 가까이 지내는 친구의 영향 등)을 함께 진지하게 찾아보고 해결을 모색한다.
5. 해야 할 일을 반드시 먼저 한 뒤에 적절한 시간만 인터넷을 하는 습관을 길러준다.
6. 인터넷 중독 자가진단 프로그램을 알려주어 인터넷 사용을 스스로 통제할 수 있도록 유도한다.
7. 게임에 중독된 학생을 스트레스에 취약하므로 평소 스트레스를 관리하는 법을 알려준다. 즉, 사고의 전환(인지치료), 즉 잘못된 사고(파국적 사고 must사고)를 합리적 사고로 바꾼다. 복식 호흡법(행동치료), 근육 이완법(행동치료) 등을 가르쳐 준다.
8. 가정과 연계하여 중독학생을 지도해야 한다.
9. 가장 중요한 것은 예방이다. 한번 인터넷 게임에 중독이 되면 회복하는 데는 많은 노력이 필요하다.

Q 63 인터넷 예절 교육에 들어가야 할 내용

These days, there has been an increasing problems regrading Internet use including some vicious replies or comments. If you are going to organize the education session for this matter, what would you teach the school students? Describe the contents to be included in Internet manners or Netiquette education.

예상답안

There are several elements that must be included in the Netiquette education. Firstly, sharing the students' experience of using the Internet is the one that needs to be considered. For example, students can discuss the positive and negative effects of the Internet while they do some group activities. Secondly, a teacher can ask the students to make some Netiquette rules by themselves and try to follow these when they use the Internet for a certain period. And after that period, in class conference, they can talk to each other about what they felt. In doing so, they would learn how it is good to keep the Netiquette, not harming others and themselves as well. Thirdly, a teacher can provide some cases about cyber violence, an invasion of privacy, and an illegal using of other's intellectual property right. Then the teacher can ask students to discus how to deal with these in group activity and choose one group who suggest the best solution. I do believe that these contents are the basic for the Netiquette education.

답안 키워드

① Sharing the students' experience of using the Internet.
② Asking the students to make some Netiquette by themselves and try to follow these.
③ Providing some cases about cyber violence, an invasion of privacy, and an illegal using of other's intellectual property right.
④ Asking students to discuss about how to deal with these in group activity and choose one group who suggest the best solution.

한국어 예상답안

- 인터넷의 사용 경험(순기능과 역기능) 나누기
- 네티켓을 만들어보고 적용해 보기
- 인터넷의 역기능 사례를 조사하여 인터넷의 문제점을 알아보며, 대응방안 만들어보기
- 설문조사 형태로 정보통신 윤리 의식을 조사하고 그 경과를 놓고 토론해보기
- 사이버 폭력, 개인정보오남용, 유해정보유통, 지적 재산권 침해, 사이버중독의 피해 사례 및 대응방법 익히기

Q 64 학교의 자율성 강화에 수반되는 교육적 시사점

Explain the pedagogical achievements of each school when autonomy is allowed on the school.

예상답안

First, each school can reflect its own educational ethics on the curriculum. For example, In order to emphasize people-oriented education, the school can place the physically challenged in the regular class. In this way, students can learn how to cooperate with others. Second, the school can implement various syllabi based on its students needs. For example, the school can provide career training course such as career field trip and job fair.

답안 키워드

① the school's own educational ethics
② the school's students needs

한국어 예상답안

① 다양하고 개성 있는 교육을 수행할 수 있다.
② 학교 현장 중심의 교육을 수행할 수 있다.

* 학교 자율화 조치는 획일적인 학교 운영에 자율성을 부여해 더욱 다양하고 개성 있는 교육이 가능하도록 하는 조치라고 교육부에서 주장하고 있으나 2009년 학교 자율화 추진방안은 '학교장이 입시교육을 부담 없이 하는 방안' 이라는 느낌을 지울 수 없다.

Q 65   다문화 가정의 아이들이 겪을 문제들

Describe the problems that the children from multicultural families can experience at school in terms of academic achievement and relationship between friends.

예상답안

First, language difficulty leads to under achievement because their parents can't have a good command of Korean. Another problem is that they are likely to be victims of bullying problem due to the prejudice. Lastly, they suffer from identity confusion. As a result, they have low self confidence and feel isolated.

답안 키워드

① language difficulty leads to under achievement in school
② victims of bullying problem due to the prejudice
③ low self confidence and feel isolated

한국어 예상답안

① 빈곤한 가정환경과 언어능력 부족에서 비롯된 학습부진을 겪고 있다.
② 이들은 피부색이나 언어, 혹은 출신지 때문에 편견과 차별, 그리고 왕따나 학교폭력의 대상이 되고 있다.
③ 정체불명의 외계인 같은 존재로 자신을 인식하는 등 극심한 정체성 혼란을 겪고 있다.

Q 66 자기주도 학습을 위한 선생님의 역할

Describe the teacher's guidance to let students do autonomy learning in the process of teaching and learning in four ways.

예상답안

In order to let students do autonomy learning, teachers can guide students in three ways. First of all, the teacher is not only a knowledge deliverer but should work as a guide, cooperator, and facilitator. The teacher should be a firm believer that students are the owners themselves to create their own knowledge. Secondly, the teacher should encourage student-centered learning in order to develop their autonomy. To be more specific, eliciting students' active participation in class can be carried out. Thirdly, the teacher should employ various teaching and learning strategies according to students' levels and interests. For example, the teacher can capitalize on level-differentiated classes, group work, and internet-based lessons. Lastly, the assessment system should be improved for self-directed learning. In details, criterion-referenced assessment should be adopted rather than norm-referenced one. Moreover, self-checklist can be used to help students to monitor their learning process.

답안 키워드

① not only a knowledge deliverer but a guide, cooperator, and facilitator
② encourage student-centered learning
③ employ various teaching and learning strategies
④ assessment system for self-directed learning (eg. criterion-related)

한국어 예상답안

① 교사는 지식 전달자의 역할에서 벗어나 학생중심의 교육관을 가지고 학생이 스스로 지식을 생산해내는 학습과정의 안내자, 조력자, 촉진자의 역할을 해주어야 한다.
  - 교사는 학생의 선택을 인정해 주고 발전 지향성을 지도해야 한다.
  - 교사는 학생이 스스로 문제를 해결에 접근하는 능력을 배양하도록 지도해야 한다.
  - 학습자끼리 상호작용하고 협력할 수 있는 기회를 확대해야 한다.
② 학생의 능동적 참여를 유도하는 (학생이 학습의 주도권을 쥐도록) 학생 중심의 수업을 전개해야 한다.
  - 교사는 학습동의 부여자로서 학생의 자기 학습의지를 최대한 키워줘야 한다.
③ 흥미와 수준에 적합한 다양한 교수 학습 전략을 활용해야 한다.
  - 수준별 이동수업, 소집단 편성수업, 인터넷활용수업, 협력학습, 교과통합학습, cai, nie, 문제해결학습, 상황학습, 탐구학습, 토의학습 등등을 활용한다.
④ 자기 주도적 학습능력을 신장하도록 평가방식이 개선해야 한다.
  - 평가의 의미를 서열에 두지 말고 앎의 구성 여부에 두어, 학습자 스스로 인정, 인식할 수 있도록 해주어야 한다.
  - 학생이 스스로 제기하는 문제에 주목, 학생의 인지구조나 변화양상을 평가, 학생이 제지한 해결책에 실현 가능성을 평가
  - 학습결과뿐 아니라 과정도 중시하는 평가, 학습의 다양한 측면을 학생작품 관찰 등 다양한 기법을 동원하여 평가(수행평가)
  - 재량활동, 특별활동, 방과후 교육활동을 자기 주도적 학습능력을 증진하는 방향으로 개선해야 한다.

Q 67 학원의 선행학습으로 수업 중에 집중을 못하는 학생 지도

These days, many of the students receive advanced lessons at private institute, easily to be distracted at school. Describe some of measures to guide these students.

예상답안

In order to guide the students, who received advanced lesson in the private institute, I would advice in the following three ways. To begin with, I will let the students be aware of the importance of the basic principles and notions. To be specific, I will emphasize the potential problems of advanced lessons in private institute such as discouraging their creativity and practical ability. Second, for the students who already know the lesson, I can provide more challenging tasks. For example, I will check if they properly grasped the principle by giving them the applied questions. Third, I will add the peer-teaching session into the regular class. While the advanced learners teach and explain what they know, they can not only consolidate the learnt knowledge but also can have self-satisfaction.

답안 키워드

① let the students be aware of the importance of the basic principles and notions
② emphasize the potential problems that discourage their creativity and practical ability
③ add peer-teaching session

한국어 예상답안

① 모르면서도 안다고 생각하고 수업에 집중하지 않는 경우가 많은데 원리나 개념에 대한 정확한 이해가 없는 문제풀이식 선행학습의 문제점을 일깨워주고 진지한 태도로 수업에 임하게 한다.
② 수업내용이 선행학습을 받은 학생이 이미 알고 있는 내용이라면 심화학습 과제(응용문제)를 주어 학습하게 한다.
③ 또래교수의 역할을 수행하게 하여 교학 상장의 기쁨을 맛보게 한다.

Q 68 상벌점 제도의 적용 방안

These days, reward and punishment points are more widely implemented since corporal punishment should not be applied. If you were the teacher who is in charge of the reward and punishment points, how would you implement?

예상답안

I think the first step of reward and punishment points should be students' awareness of basic courtesy by having them exposed to the model behaviors and reflecting theirs. For example, watching video clips which shows what would happen when they don't follow the rule will help students to be aware of basic courtesy. Second, teacher and student set the regulation of punishment and rewards point collaboratively. Since the rules are constructed based on their opinion, students will take responsibility for their misbehavior. Last, To make this system more practical, proper reinforcement and punishment can be carried out. For the students who get the highest point, we can award them. By doing so, it will motivate students to behave themselves. Also they can be a good model for other students. For the students who get the most penalty, teacher can send them to specialized institution like Wee center.

답안 키워드

① students' awareness of basic reward and punishment points
② set the regulation of punishment and rewards point collaboratively
③ proper reinforcement and punishment

한국어 예상답안

① 학생의 인권과 교사의 교권이 상호 존중되는 방향으로 상벌제를 규정해서 시행하여 체벌대체 효과를 제고하고 학교규칙을 준수하는 문화를 강화하겠다.
② 상벌제 시행을 통해 인권존중, 자율과 책임을 중시하는 학생 생활지도 풍토를 정착시키게 하겠다.
③ 상벌제 시행을 통해 가정, 학교, 지역사회 네트워크가 참여하고 협력하는 생활지도를 정착시키겠다.
④ 10개의 중점 지도 항목을 선정해서 생활지도의 선택과 집중을 강화하겠다.
  • 상점규정과 벌점규정은 각각 10개로 균형을 유지한다.
  • 상벌을 규정할 때는 학교 실정에 맞게 교육공동체의 의견을 유지한다.
  • 상벌제 내용을 홍보하는 활동을 강화하겠다. (상벌제 규칙 학교 홈페이지 탑재, 가정통신문 발송, 교실에 홍보물 게시, 학부모회 때 고지, 조종례와 학급자치회에서 환기)
⑤ 상점 우수 학생을 표창하겠다.
⑥ 벌점 과다 학생은 친한 친구교실에 참여시키거나 정도가 심한 경우에는 WEE center에 보내거나 전문 위탁 대안교실 프로그램 운영기관에 보내겠다.

Q 69 수업에서 영어를 하지 못하는 학생을 위한 방안

> One of your students, Sunny is afraid of speaking English. To make her speak more fluently and willingly in English, how would you guide her to speak? Present at least 3 ways to teach.

예상답안

First of all, the most important thing is to make students feel speaking in English is not difficult but comfortable and fun. Songs, chants and games are very useful in that situation. These activities become fun and comfortable, and it is very effective way to improve English in natural situation. Next thing is to adopt episode method to utilize students' experiences. By using English to make their own story, students can get motivated to improve their English skills. It contains less pressure of speaking, so this method can reduce the fear for English. And during class, teacher should not correct every single error of students, because it can increase the fear for English class. Errors don't have to be corrected unless it is disturbing the flow of communication.

답안 키워드

① songs, chants and games
② reduce the fear for English
③ no correction on errors

한국어 예상답안

① 정의적인 측면: 학생이 편하게 말할 수 있는 정의적인 분위기를 조성한다.
② 교수법적인 측면: episode method로 학생들이 자신의 이야기를 하게 한다.
③ 인지적 측면: error correction을 최소화하여 의사소통에 방해가 되지 않도록 한다.

Q 70 유학 다녀온 학생과 일반학생들의 실력차 극복

There are some students who had lived overseas a while in your class. So, there is a significant gap between students' English skills. How can you handle this situation? Describe the problems and suggest the solutions from the viewpoints of the students from overseas and the rest of the students respectively.

예상답안

In this case, I think collaboration is useful to run English class effectively. The other students except for the students from abroad can be timid and not willing to participate in the activity. And the students from abroad can be bored during the class. However, using collaborating method, students from abroad can play the role of assistant teacher, so they can participate in class with pleasure. Moreover, the other students can learn more lively and authentic language from students from abroad. As they feel that they can improve their English skills much more, they can participate during class. And for the students from abroad, teacher can offer other activities or supplies that is appropriate for their English ability.

답안 키워드

① collaboration in a mixed-level group
② play the role of assistant teacher

한국어 예상답안

① 유학 다녀온 학생
  • 수업이 지루하여 참여하기가 싫다.
  • 협동학습에서 보조교사가 되어 다른 학생을 도와줄 수 있도록 한다.
② 다른 학생들
  • 수업에 참여하기가 어렵고 정의적으로 위축되어있다.
  • 소규모 그룹 활동으로 정의적으로 편안하고 틀린 것을 말해도 놀림을 당하지 않도록 한다.

권영주

전공영어 2차
수업실연 and
면접

초판 1쇄 발행 2022년 11월 15일
개정 1쇄 발행 2023년 10월 25일
　　2쇄 발행 2024년 11월 15일
　　3쇄 발행 2025년 09월 22일

편저 권영주
발행인 공태현　**발행처** (주)법률저널
등록일자 2008년 9월 26일　**등록번호** 제15-605호
주소 151-862 서울 관악구 복은4길 50 (서림동 120-32)
대표전화 02)874-1144　**팩스** 02)876-4312
홈페이지 www.lec.co.kr
ISBN 979-11-7384-058-6 (13740)
정가 30,000원